WORKING

CAREER SUCCESS FOR THE 21st CENTURY

THIRD EDITION

Larry J. Bailey
Professor
Workforce Education and Development
Southern Illinois University
Carbondale, Illinois

Australia · Canada · Mexico · Singapore · Spain · United Kingdom · United States

Working: Career Success for the 21st Century, 3d Edition

By Larry J. Bailey

Editor-in-Chief
Jack Calhoun

Vice President/Executive Publisher
Dave Shaut

Team Leader
Karen Schmohe

Acquisitions Editor
Joseph Vocca

Project Manager
Penny Shank

Consulting Editor
Elaine Langlois

Production Manager
Tricia Matthews Boies

Production Editor
Tim Bailey

Executive Marketing Manager
Carol Volz

Channel Manager
Nancy Long

Marketing Coordinator
Linda Kuper

Art and Design Coordinator
Tippy McIntosh

Manufacturing Coordinator
Kevin Kluck

Editorial Assistant
Stephanie L. White

Production Assistant
Nancy Stamper

Cover Design
© Bek Shakirov/SIS

Compositor
Better Graphics

Printer
R.R. Donnelley & Sons, Roanoke

ISBN: 0-538-69966-3

Printed in the United States of America

2 3 4 5 6 7 08 07 06 05 04 03

For more information, contact South-Western, 5191 Natorp Boulevard, Mason, OH 45040; or find us on the World Wide Web at www.swep.com

FEATURES TO ENHANCE LEARNING

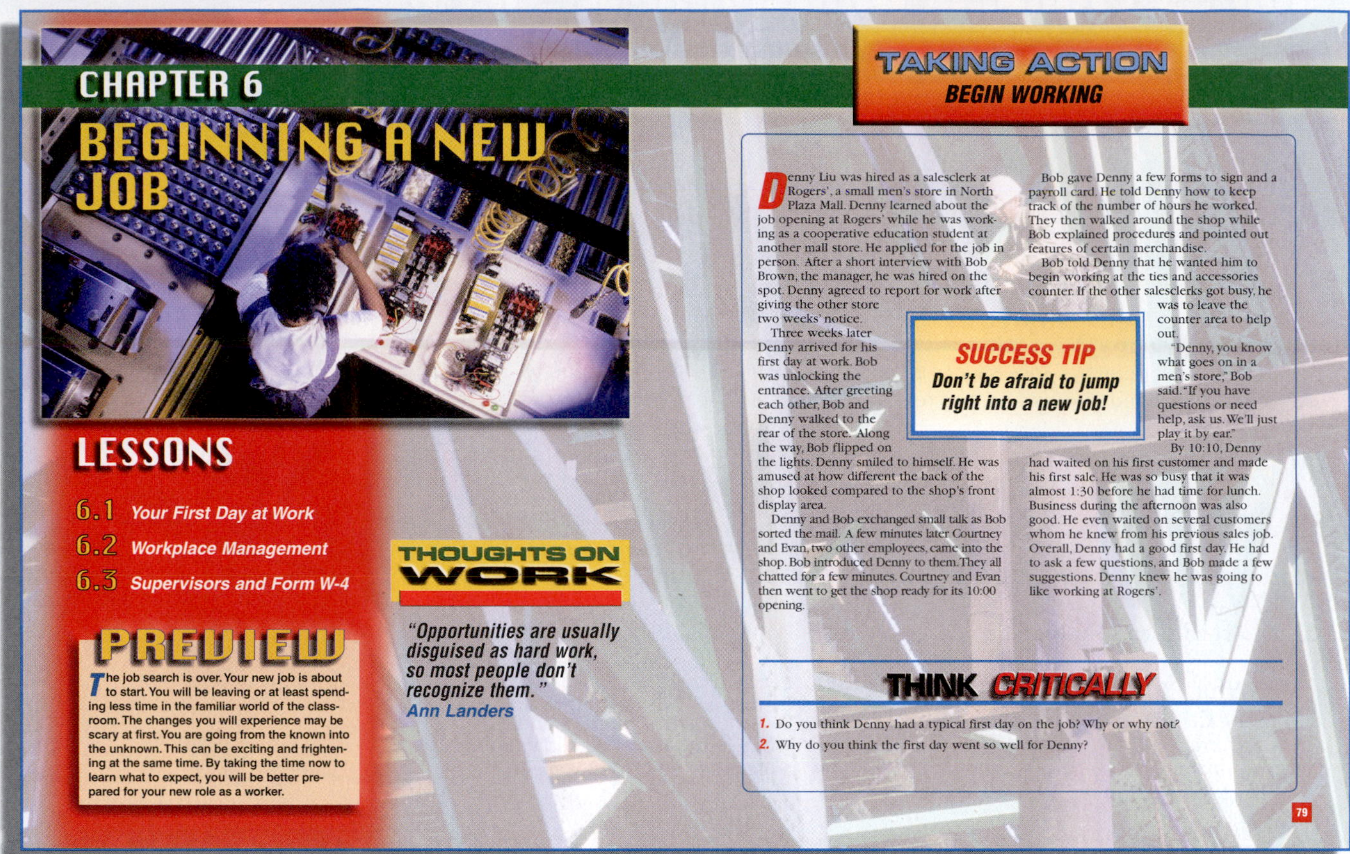

CHAPTER 6

BEGINNING A NEW JOB

LESSONS

6.1 Your First Day at Work

6.2 Workplace Management

6.3 Supervisors and Form W-4

PREVIEW

The job search is over. Your new job is about to start. You will be leaving or at least spending less time in the familiar world of the classroom. The changes you will experience may be scary at first. You are going from the known into the unknown. This can be exciting and frightening at the same time. By taking the time now to learn what to expect, you will be better prepared for your new role as a worker.

THOUGHTS ON WORK

"Opportunities are usually disguised as hard work, so most people don't recognize them."
Ann Landers

TAKING ACTION
BEGIN WORKING

Denny Liu was hired as a salesclerk at Rogers', a small men's store in North Plaza Mall. Denny learned about the job opening at Rogers' while he was working as a cooperative education student at another mall store. He applied for the job in person. After a short interview with Bob Brown, the manager, he was hired on the spot. Denny agreed to report for work after giving the other store two weeks' notice.

Three weeks later Denny arrived for his first day at work. Bob was unlocking the entrance. After greeting each other, Bob and Denny walked to the rear of the store. Along the way, Bob flipped on the lights. Denny smiled to himself. He was amused at how different the back of the shop looked compared to the shop's front display area.

Denny and Bob exchanged small talk as Bob sorted the mail. A few minutes later Courtney and Evan, two other employees, came into the shop. Bob introduced Denny to them. They all chatted for a few minutes. Courtney and Evan then went to get the shop ready for its 10:00 opening.

Bob gave Denny a few forms to sign and a payroll card. He told Denny how to keep track of the number of hours he worked. They then walked around the shop while Bob explained procedures and pointed out features of certain merchandise.

Bob told Denny that he wanted him to begin working at the ties and accessories counter. If the other salesclerks got busy, he was to leave the counter area to help out.

"Denny, you know what goes on in a men's store," Bob said. "If you have questions or need help, ask us. We'll just play it by ear."

By 10:10, Denny had waited on his first customer and made his first sale. He was so busy that it was almost 1:30 before he had time for lunch. Business during the afternoon was also good. He even waited on several customers whom he knew from his previous sales job. Overall, Denny had a good first day. He had to ask a few questions, and Bob made a few suggestions. Denny knew he was going to like working at Rogers'.

SUCCESS TIP
Don't be afraid to jump right into a new job!

THINK CRITICALLY

1. Do you think Denny had a typical first day on the job? Why or why not?
2. Why do you think the first day went so well for Denny?

79

UNIT 2 WORKING ON THE JOB

LESSON 6.2

WORKPLACE MANAGEMENT

OBJECTIVES

- DESCRIBE HOW AN ORGANIZATION CHART SHOWS THE FLOW OF AUTHORITY AND RESPONSIBILITY WITHIN AN ORGANIZATION
- LIST AREAS FOR WHICH EMPLOYERS HAVE POLICIES AND RULES

ORGANIZATIONAL STRUCTURE

During your first days on a new job, you will find out how the company is organized and what the written rules are. You will also begin to learn about the unwritten rules. Information about unwritten rules is included in Chapters 7 and 8. The company will want to know more about you, too. You will have to fill out many forms. The most common one is Form W-4. You will learn about this form later in the chapter.

Francine and Denny learned many of the same things during their first day on the job. They learned:

- How the workplace was laid out.
- Where they would be working (their workstations).
- How to keep track of hours worked.
- Where to look for posted notices such as work schedules.
- What to do if they needed help or had questions.

These are important things that all workers need to learn during their first day on the job. In the rest of this chapter, you will study other concerns of new workers.

All organizations, including companies and schools, have lines of authority and responsibility. **Authority** is the power or rank to give orders and make assignments to others. For instance, a teacher has authority in the classroom. **Responsibility** deals with the duty to follow an order or carry out a work assignment. In school, for

ETHICAL DECISIONS

Upon beginning a new job, you may know very little about a company or its management. This can happen despite your best efforts to research the company and ask thoughtful questions in a job interview. Suppose that during the orientation meeting you discover things about the company that disturb you. Perhaps the company manufactures products that are in conflict with your moral or religious beliefs. Perhaps the company officials have an attitude that is completely different from your own. You begin to wonder if this is the right job for you.

WHAT WOULD YOU DO?

82 LESSON 6.2 WORKPLACE MANAGEMENT

TAKING ACTION

Each chapter begins with a case study relevant to the chapter content. A discussion of the case study using the critical thinking questions as a starting point leads students to understand why the chapter topics are important to *them*.

DECISIONS

Making good decisions is emphasized throughout the book. Short descriptions of real-life personal and workplace situations allow students to check their decision-making skills for five types of decisions.

- Ethical: issues of right or wrong.
- Personal: should I do this or that?
- Interpersonal: relationships with others.
- Workplace: decisions on or related to the job.
- Career: planning or preparing for the future.

Your home page is the web page that appears each time you start your browser. Any page on the Web can be chosen as your home page. Many people select a web portal as a starting point for navigating the Web. Some of the more popular portals are Excite, MSN.com, Netscape, and Yahoo! Web portals provide free services and information such as current news, sports scores, weather, TV schedules, stock quotes, and search engines. At work, your employer may have the opening page of its own web site as the home page.

NOTHING BUT NET

The expected continued use of technology in almost all occupations requires familiarity with the capabilities of computers and the Internet. "Nothing But Net" provides students with basic information about navigating this vital resource.

WORKFORCE TRENDS

An awareness of trends occurring in the workforce can help students predict future employment opportunities and learn how to adapt to changing conditions. The information about how the world of work is changing is adapted from *Futurework: Trends and Challenges for Work in the 21st Century*, a U.S. Department of Labor publication.

WORKFORCE TRENDS

Since 1960, the percentage of married women in the workforce has nearly doubled. This increase is largely in response to women's rising labor market opportunities. Other factors include the need for a second income to keep up with the rising cost of living, changed attitudes about women's roles in families and society, and reduced workplace discrimination.

Suppose that you work in a medical laboratory. OSHA requires that all biological hazardous waste be weighed before it is sent to the hazardous waste management company. The limit per week that the waste management company can handle is 400 pounds. You have six containers with the following weights: 75 lb, 85 lb, 70 lb, 80 lb, 62 lb, and 60 lb. Based on the weekly limit, how many of the six containers will the waste management company take this week?

SOLUTION

You must first calculate the total weight of the six containers.

Total weight of the six containers = 75 + 85 + 70 + 80 + 62 + 60 = 432

The total weight of the six containers is more than the waste company will take. Since the weight of any of the containers will put the total weight over the limit, only five of the six containers will be taken.

MATH CONNECTION

Math is connected to success both in life and in work. Each problem checks students' knowledge of a basic math skill. The skill is reinforced by an activity in the Chapter Review.

YOU'RE A WHAT?

FARRIER

Some of the world's largest athletes rely on the work of a *farrier*. Workers in this occupation make and fit shoes for horses. Like humans, horses wear shoes for protection and comfort. At one time, farriers heated and formed rectangular steel for horseshoes by pounding it to shape over a large anvil. Now, ready-made shoes are available in a variety of sizes and materials. But knowing how to make custom shoes is still an important part of the business. Farriers trim the horses' hooves, prepare shoes, and nail those shoes to the hooves.

Farriery can be strenuous work. Farriers often lift and hold a horse's hoof for 15 minutes at a time. Most farriers are self-employed, with many working part-time while also maintaining other occupations. Farriers usually learn their craft through a combination of short-term training and apprenticeship. ■

YOU'RE A WHAT?

Unusual and, in some cases, emerging occupations point out to students the variety of employment possibilities available to them. Students can use their Internet skills to find out more about these and related unusual occupations.

- Compcierge
- Curator
- Demonstrator
- Farrier
- Food Stylist
- Forensic Scientist
- Gaffer
- Glazier
- Music Therapist
- Optician
- Pest Controller
- Phlebotomist
- Purser
- Stationary Engineer
- Technology Recycler
- Telemarketer

COMMUNICATION AT WORK

COMMUNICATING WITH BOSSES

Here are some ways to get the most out of your relationship with your boss:

Keep your boss informed about what you are doing. Make sure your boss knows how you are progressing on your assignments. If a problem arises that your supervisor should know about, provide the necessary details in a timely way.

Speak your boss's language. Find out how your boss likes to communicate with employees. Some supervisors like brief conversations. Others prefer e-mail. If your supervisor prefers talking, don't write a note.

Be considerate of your boss's time. Supervisors are busy people. If you must speak to your supervisor, arrange a time, whenever possible, that will be convenient for him or her. When speaking or writing to your boss, include only the information he or she needs to know.

COMMUNICATION AT WORK

Students need effective communication skills to find a job and to be successful throughout their working lives. A discussion of these topics can guide students to discover how their success depends on skillful communication.

- Interpersonal Relations
- Asking for Job Leads
- Illegal Interview Questions
- Creating a Positive Impression
- Communicating with Bosses
- Different Cultures
- Self-talk
- Effective Public Speaking
- Safety Warnings
- Computers
- Charts and Graphs
- Proofreading Numbers
- Getting Information
- Doing Research
- Persuasive Writing

HIGH-GROWTH OCCUPATIONS FOR THE 21st CENTURY

Electronic Semiconductor Processors

Semiconductors—also known as computer chips, microchips, or integrated chips—are the miniature but powerful brains of high-technology equipment. *Electronic semiconductor processors* are responsible for many of the steps necessary to manufacture each semiconductor that goes into a personal computer, a missile guidance system, and a host of other electronic equipment. This is the only manufacturing occupation expected to grow much faster than the average for all occupations.

Semiconductor processors manufacture semiconductors in disks about the size of dinner plates. These disks, called wafers, are thin slices of silicon on which the circuitry of the microchips is layered. Each wafer is eventually cut into dozens of individual chips.

The manufacture and cutting of wafers to create semiconductors take place in "clean rooms." Clean rooms are production areas that must be kept free of any airborne matter, because the least bit of dust can damage a semiconductor. All semiconductor processors working in clean rooms must wear special garments known as "bunny suits." Bunny suits fit over clothing to prevent lint and other particles from contaminating work sites.

Semiconductor processors must work in clean rooms because a small particle of dust can damage a semiconductor.

Operators make up the majority of the workers in clean rooms. They start and monitor the equipment that performs the various tasks during the semiconductor production sequence. They spend a great deal of time at computer terminals, monitoring the equipment. They transfer wafer carriers from one development station to the next. Once begun, production of semiconductor wafers is continuous. Operators work to the pace of the machinery that has largely automated the production process.

Technicians account for a smaller percentage of the workers in clean rooms. They troubleshoot production problems and make equipment adjustments and repairs. They also take the lead in ensuring quality control and in maintaining equipment in order to prevent the need for costly repairs.

HIGH-GROWTH OCCUPATIONS FOR THE 21ST CENTURY

Each chapter includes a description of fast-growing occupations adapted from the *Occupational Outlook Handbook*. An understanding of the duties and opportunities in these fields allows students to consider and prepare for occupations that will need workers in the future.

FOCUS ON THE WORKPLACE

HIGH-PERFORMANCE WORK ORGANIZATIONS

Historically, many kinds of work in America have been patterned after the mass production system made famous by Henry Ford in the early 1900s. In mass production, jobs are broken down into a number of simple tasks. Each worker specializes in one task, which is done over and over.

Managers do the thinking and planning for the organization. Supervisors direct the work of frontline employees. Workers under this system need only be reliable, steady, and willing to follow directions.

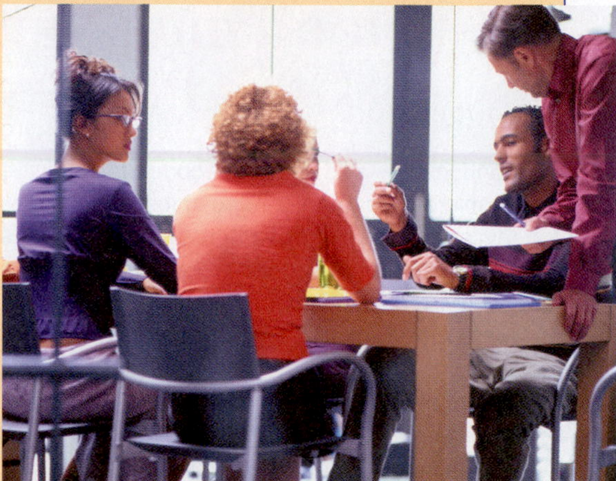

Input from frontline workers is encouraged in a high-performance work organization.

The mass production system has helped make our nation a great economic power. It has also resulted in a high standard of living for workers. This system still determines the way most factories, offices, banks, hospitals, and schools are organized.

As we begin a new century, our nation faces increasing global economic competition. To remain competitive, we must increase productivity and improve quality. The solution adopted by many companies is called a high-performance work organization.

The basic idea of a high-performance work organization is to give greater authority to frontline workers. Layers of managers disappear as teams of workers take over such tasks as quality control and production scheduling. Workers are asked to use judgment and make decisions at the point where goods and services are produced.

This type of work organization requires retraining of workers and managers. The high cost of retraining, however, is offset by gains in quality and productivity. High-performance work organizations are becoming the model for a successful future.

THINK CRITICALLY

1. Why do you think the mass production system helped make our nation a great economic power?
2. Give some examples of ways in which a high-performance work organization might help improve quality and productivity.

FOCUS ON . . .

WORK
THE WORKPLACE
THE WORKER
HEALTH AND SAFETY
SKILLS FOR LIVING

Immediately before the Chapter Review, each chapter explores an interesting topic related to the chapter content. A discussion based on the critical thinking questions can show students how the chapter is linked to a specific real-life issue.

REVIEW AND ASSESSMENT

LESSON REVIEW

Review questions at the end of each lesson check students' understanding of the key concepts discussed in the lesson. Students can find out if they are ready to move on to the next lesson or to the Chapter Review.

LESSON 6.3 REVIEW

1. How is the job of student similar to that of a paid employee?
2. What are four ways to start a good relationship with an employer? Briefly explain each.
3. What three things determine how much tax is withheld from your paycheck?

CHAPTER REVIEW

- Summarizes important concepts and principles presented in the chapter.
- Supports learning through a variety of individualized, team, and group activities.
- Provides an activity that reinforces comprehension of chapter vocabulary terms.
- Poses relevant, engaging questions that encourage students to think critically.

CHAPTER 6 REVIEW

Chapter in Brief

Lesson 6.1 *Your First Day at Work*

A. It is normal to experience some anxiety when beginning a new job. Many companies provide an orientation to help new employees get started properly. Your employer wants you to be successful on the job.

B. One person's first day at work may be quite different from another person's first day. However, most new employees do similar things and are provided with similar kinds of information.

Lesson 6.2 *Workplace Management*

A. An organization chart shows the flow of authority and responsibility within an organization. It is important to follow your company's formal and informal lines of authority and responsibility.

B. Companies have written policies and rules to help them run smoothly. You are responsible for obeying all policies and rules. Companies also have unwritten rules that you will need to learn.

Lesson 6.3 *Supervisors and Form W-4*

A. On the job, you will probably work under the direction of a supervisor. Use the supervisor for communication and direction. Accept and use the supervisor's suggestions, but don't ask for or expect special treatment.

B. Employers are required to withhold money from your paycheck for federal income tax. The amount withheld is based on information that you provide on Form W-4.

Activities

1. Some of your classmates may already have jobs. Ask these people to explain what their orientation to a new job was like. Ask them questions about their experiences on the job.
2. As a group activity, develop an organization chart for the employees in your school. At the top of the chart, start with the school district's board of education. How many levels are there? Suppose a teacher has a complaint about a board policy. With whom would he or she file a complaint? Discuss the process the teacher should follow.
3. Obtain an example of a company policy manual. You may already have one from your job, or perhaps you can borrow one from a family member or a friend. Look through the manuals in class and discuss examples of each of the seven types of policies and rules explained. Do the manuals contain types of policies and rules that are not explained in the chapter? If so, discuss the merits of these policies and rules.
4. Does your school give students a written code of conduct that oulines policies and rules? If so, discuss how it is like a company policy manual. If not, discuss possible policies or rules that could go into such a manual.
5. The supervisor at your new job expects you to assemble 15 cases every two hours. In an eight-hour shift, how many cases should you assemble?

Word Power

On a separate sheet of paper, match each definition with the correct term. All definitions will be used, and a definition will be used only once.

6. A trial period during which one's performance is being observed and evaluated
7. A mood or spirit, such as the attitude and emotion of employees
8. At work, the duty to follow an order or carry out a work assignment
9. Assigns a task or responsibility to others
10. A boss; one who gives directions and orders and oversees the work of others
11. The number of tax exemptions to which one is entitled
12. The power or rank to give orders and make assignments to others
13. To pay back money already spent
14. To be free of something, such as not having to pay taxes
15. A feeling of concern, worry, or unease
16. The legal right to be notified of a complaint against you and to state your case or point of view before a decision is made
17. A booklet given to new employees that contains an explanation of company policies and rules

a. allowances
b. anxiety
c. authority
d. delegates
e. due process
f. exempt
g. morale
h. policy manual
i. probation
j. reimburse
k. responsibility
l. supervisor

Think Critically

18. What are some of the reasons why employers want new employees to make a quick and successful transition from school to the workplace?
19. Think of an instance in your life in which your anxiety about a situation turned out to be worse than the situation itself. What might this suggest regarding anxiety toward beginning a new job?
20. Some supervisors try not to get too friendly or informal with employees whom they supervise. Do you think this is a good or bad idea? Why?
21. Under what circumstances might someone choose to specify an additional amount of withholding on line 5 of Form W-4?

90 CHAPTER 6 BEGINNING A NEW JOB

CHAPTER 6 BEGINNING A NEW JOB 91

PREFACE

Change is taking place in the United States and throughout the industrialized world. The world has become a global village in which countries compete for international standing and economic markets. Knowledge, information, and skills have become the raw materials of international commerce. Learning is the essential investment required for success in this new era. We have entered the Information Age.

In response to these needs and challenges, American education is also changing. Secondary schools across the country are reforming curricula and programs to meet increased academic requirements and higher standards. There is a clear recognition that yesterday's skills are inadequate for the world of tomorrow.

The attention being given education is not confined to basic academic skills. Some are proposing that *readiness for work* become education's fourth "R." There is a growing emphasis on integrating academic with career and technical education. Numerous business and education partnerships are being created to help young people make successful transitions from school to work. Many educational authorities and respected organizations have called for increased emphasis on workforce preparation. For example, the prestigious Committee for Economic Development has made these observations:

> When young people engage in real work, they learn lessons they are often unwilling to accept from teachers in school. Work-based learning provides conditions for learning that schools cannot easily simulate, including real deadlines, customer feedback, and problem solving with limited resources. Seeing that their work matters to others and that its quality has consequences can motivate young people not just to do an assigned job but also to rethink their commitment to school and learning.[1]
>
> More effective ties between schools and employers improve student motivation to learn, make young people more active learners, and provide experiences and tools for more informed choices about their lives.[2]

This book was written with a conscious awareness of changes that are taking place in the workplace and in the nation's schools. The author and South-Western/Thomson Learning enthusiastically support the integration of academic and work-based learning, the creation of partnerships between education and employers, and the emphasis on academic and skill standards. Further, we endorse the Learning a Living system proposed by the Secretary's Commission on Achieving Necessary Skills (SCANS), which calls for the creation of high-performance schools and high-performance workplaces. And we have used the SCANS skills as outcomes toward which the contents of this book are addressed.

Purpose and Use

This book was developed for use as a high school-level text in several types of existing and emerging work experience education and school-to-work transition programs. Descriptions of specific applications follow.

[1]Committee for Economic Development, *The Employer's Role in Linking School and Work* (New York: Committee for Economic Development, 1998), p. 22.
[2] Ibid., p. 31.

Cooperative Career and Technical Education. In cooperative education, students learn occupational skills while working part-time at a training station in their community. Students also attend classes at a local high school, including a "related" co-op class. This book is intended for use in such a class. Most related classes are one year; a few are conducted for two years. This book can be conveniently covered in one year. Sufficient topics and activities are included, however, to allow the book to be profitably used for two-year programs.

Work-study. In work-study, part-time school is also combined with a part-time job. Unlike co-op education, however, this program seeks to develop general work habits and attitudes rather than specific occupational skills. Otherwise, the program is operated very much like co-op. Work-study students enroll in a related class for which this text is ideally suited.

School-to-Work Transition. Many cities and states have developed a variety of apprenticeship, school-to-work, and youth employment programs. Some programs are privately supported and involve close collaboration between schools and employers. Others are funded under the federal Workforce Investment Act and related legislation. This book can be used as a primary text in such programs.

Working: Career Success for the 21st Century consists of 32 chapters organized into six units. The contents and objectives meet requirements for cooperative career and technical education and work-study programs in all states. The new edition has benefited from the feedback provided by many satisfied users of the second edition. Each chapter is organized, written, and produced in ways that facilitate successful teaching and learning.

Related Materials

The student textbook and instructor's wrap-around edition are the primary components of a comprehensive set of work experience education materials. A number of ancillary student and instructor materials are also provided.

The primary student ancillary is a *Student Working Papers and Exploration Package*. In Part One, more than 100 activities, problems, questions, forms, and puzzles are included to interest and challenge students. In Part Two, a "mini" *Occupational Outlook Handbook* is provided for students to explore occupational clusters and to investigate specific occupations of interest.

Teacher ancillary materials include an annotated version of the *Student Working Papers* with suggested answers for all activities in Part One. An *Instructor's Resource CD* contains chapter slide shows in the Microsoft® PowerPoint® presentations graphics program. Slides are designed to illustrate a concept or procedure or to develop a solution directly on the slide. They can be used with both the textbook and the *Student Working Papers*. The *Instructor's Resource CD* also contains pdf files for many of the instructor support materials. Thirty-two chapter tests are provided in both print and electronic formats (ExamView® Pro software). A *Lesson Plan Guide and Supplemental Activities* is available to assist teachers in planning instruction and providing students with additional practice in higher-level SCANS skills. The *Working Instructor's Resource Box* contains additional instructor support materials.

ACKNOWLEDGMENTS

Preparation of the third edition of *Working: Career Success for the 21st Century* was aided by comments and suggestions provided by the following reviewers:

Donna Blascak
William Allen High School
Allentown, Pennsylvania

Margaret Bratcher
Olympia High School
Stanford, Illinois

Mike Closner
Grandview High School
Grandview, Washington

Cheryl Conditt
Durant High School
Durant, Oklahoma

Gloria Cortez
Hillcrest High School
Dallas, Texas

Marilyn Durant
Perry High School
Massilon, Ohio

Deborah Enghauser
Educational Consultant
Centerville, Ohio

Peggy Harrier
Cincinnati State Technical College
Cincinnati, Ohio

Lynn Holliday
Rankin Vocational-Technical Center
Pearl, Mississippi

Jeselyn Jackson
Molina High School
Dallas, Texas

Ann Jordan
Great Oaks Vocational Schools
Cincinnati, Ohio

Kevin LaMountain
DeVry Institute of Technology
Phoenix, Arizona

Audrey G. Lawrence
Cooper Career Institute
Virginia Beach, Virginia

James Macke
Cincinnati State Technical College
Cincinnati, Ohio

Steve Rinard
Abilene High School
Abilene, Texas

Brian Sporleder
Bryant and Stratton College
Milwaukee, Wisconsin

Janet Tidwell
Roff High School
Roff, Oklahoma

ABOUT THE AUTHOR

Larry J. Bailey was born and raised in rural Indiana, where he learned to work as a farm laborer, carpenter, painter, factory worker, and janitor. He attended Ball State University on an academic scholarship and graduated with honors. He taught high school industrial arts prior to completing the Doctor of Education degree in Vocational and Technical Education at the University of Illinois. He held faculty research appointments at the University of Illinois and at the University of Iowa before joining Southern Illinois University in 1969, where he continues to teach and write. He is the author of six books and more than 100 other book chapters, articles, papers, and reports. He served as a member of the National Advisory Council on Career Education and the Advisory Council on Adult, Vocational, and Technical Education, State of Illinois.

CONTENTS

UNIT 1

PREPARING FOR WORK

CHAPTERS

CO-OP CAREER SPOTLIGHT

Kelli Spurgeon, *Senior Technologist*

Twenty-year-old Kelli Spurgeon, a 2001 graduate of DeVry Institute of Technology in Phoenix, Arizona, didn't go through the co-op program offered in her college. The job she had while she was a student at DeVry was just too good to give up. Kelli was the Coordinator for the co-op program in the Career Services Offices for DeVry. As Coordinator, Kelli saw firsthand how a co-op program helps students.

DeVry students, Kelli explains, "are either recent high school graduates or returning students. After three semesters at DeVry, students are eligible for the co-op program." Kelli helped students put together resumes and upload them onto the DeVry Institute web site. Employers would check the web site for prospective employees. While employers were checking students' resumes, students were checking posted jobs. Kelli would then put employer and employee together.

Students in the program work between 20 and 25 hours each week, with salaries of $8 to $12 an hour. "Some students work full-time and attend night classes," Kelli says. Employers are asked to be flexible about students' work hours. DeVry's program is also flexible with morning, evening, and night classes.

"The co-op program provides students with career-related work while still in school," Kelli says. "Students can apply their learning in the classroom to their jobs." Working with 50 to 200 students each semester, Kelli helped place Electronics Engineering Technology majors and Computer Information Systems students. Honeywell, a large technology and manufacturing company, employed many DeVry co-op students. "For $15 an hour," Kelli says, "students programmed flight simulators for Luke Air Force Base." Many of these students accepted full-time jobs at Honeywell once they graduated.

Kelli's bachelor of science degree from DeVry, which she earned in 2001 in Electronics Engineering Technology, landed her a job as a senior technologist at Sandia National Laboratories in Albuquerque, New Mexico. She may be launched on her own career in electronics engineering, but she'll always remember the students she assisted in the co-op program at DeVry. "The best part of my job," she says, "was working with the students to help them find great jobs that helped them pay for school and allowed them to apply their classroom learning."

CHAPTER 1
LEARNING ABOUT WORK

LESSONS

1.1 *Why People Work*

1.2 *Work Experience Education*

THOUGHTS ON WORK

"Work and play are words used to describe the same thing under differing conditions."
Mark Twain

PREVIEW

Most young people look forward to finishing school, leaving home, and starting out on their own. An important part of the transition from youth to young adult is getting a job. Working will enable you to establish your independence and define your own life. As a working person, you will find that other people will see and respond to you in new ways. This can be an exciting and enjoyable time of your life.

TAKING ACTION
WORK EXPERIENCE EDUCATION

Hanna is enrolled in a business occupations program. This is a type of co-op career and technical education program for students interested in secretarial, accounting, information processing, and similar occupations. In co-op career and technical education, the student learns and applies occupational skills on the job rather than only in a school shop or laboratory. Hanna has a part-time job at a firm that distributes packaging equipment. She enters data and keyboards on a computer, files, and performs other office duties.

One day the sales manager asked Hanna to sit in on a sales meeting and take notes. After the meeting, she prepared a short summary report. The manager was impressed and complimented Hanna on her ability to organize and present the material well. Afterward, the manager began to give Hanna more duties of this type.

Hanna discovered a skill and an interest of which she was not aware. She also learned that there is a demand in the business world for skilled stenographers. After graduation, Hanna will enroll in a new technical stenography program offered at a local community college. The program provides training in computer-aided transcription. This is a system in which a computer directly translates shorthand notes into English.

At the end of his junior year, Wilson, a classmate of Hanna's, had thoughts about not returning to school in the fall. He came from a large family supported only by his mother. There was little income available for extras. Wilson was discouraged with school. He did not have nice clothes or money to participate in school activities like most other students.

A friend suggested that Wilson talk to the school's work experience coordinator. With the help of the coordinator, Wilson found a work-study job at the city highway garage. A work-study program allows students to attend school part-time while working part-time. He helps clean and take care of the fleet of city-owned vehicles. While he does not want to do this type of work forever, Wilson is happy to have a paying job.

After signing up for work-study, Wilson decided to finish high school. School has become more enjoyable for him, and his grades are improving. Wilson is encouraging his younger brother and sister to enroll in a work experience program.

SUCCESS TIP

Talk to your career counselor about work experience education.

THINK CRITICALLY

1. Which benefits of work experience would be most important to you?
2. How do you think you could make use of work experience education?

LESSON 1.1

WHY PEOPLE WORK

OBJECTIVES

- *DISCUSS REASONS WHY PEOPLE WORK*
- *DEFINE THE TERMS* WORK, OCCUPATION, *AND* JOB

REASONS TO WORK

People's views about work vary greatly. It would be untrue to say that all people value and enjoy their work. For most Americans, though, work is an important part of a well-rounded life. They generally like what they do. Many studies have shown that most people would work even if they didn't have to. This view of work is not limited to adults. The interest of young people in learning about and preparing for work has never been greater.

People work for many different reasons. The reasons vary from person to person. The most common reasons for working follow.

Earn Money

The major reason why people work is to earn money. Earnings are needed to buy food, shelter, clothing, and other necessities. Beyond meeting basic needs, money is used to purchase goods and services that provide comfort, enjoyment, and security.

Social Satisfaction

People are social creatures. Working gives people a chance to be with others and to make friends. In the work environment, people can give and receive understanding and acceptance.

Positive Feelings

People get satisfaction from their work. For instance, your work may give you a sense of accomplishment. Think of how you feel when you finish a school project or a difficult job task.

Working also gives people a feeling of self-worth. Often, the feeling comes from knowing that other people will pay you for your skills.

CAREER DECISIONS

You have been working for about a year at a small nursery and garden center. You enjoy the informality, the variety of work, caring for plants, and being out-of-doors. You have learned about a job opening in the garden department of a large discount store. Your primary duties would be waiting on customers and operating the cash register. The job pays quite a bit more than you presently earn, but you do not think you would enjoy the new job as much as your present one. You cannot decide whether to give up a satisfying job for the opportunity to make more money.

WHAT WOULD YOU DO?

YOU'RE A WHAT? COMPCIERGE

Large hotels and resorts employ *concierges* to provide personal services for guests. In recent years, hotels have also begun to employ *compcierges* to provide computer and technology support services. A guest, for example, may need to remove a computer virus or may require help downloading a file from the Internet. Or, a foreign traveler may be having a problem changing printer settings to U.S. paper sizes, which are in inches rather than centimeters.

As the number of "wired" travelers increases, the need for compcierges is expected to sky-rocket. Here is how one hotel chain is meeting the need. The chain provides optional personal computers and Internet access in guest rooms. Equipment such as printers, scanners, and fax machines is provided in a supervised location convenient to all guests. A compcierge is on call as needed to help guests using hotel equipment, personal laptops, personal digital assistants (PDAs), or other equipment. ■

Prestige

Some people work because of the prestige or status they enjoy. Prestige is the admiration of society. Some occupations have more prestige than others. What occupations do you consider to have prestige?

Personal Development

Many people have a drive to improve themselves. Work can provide an opportunity to learn and grow. Work can often be a great teacher.

A sense of accomplishment is one of the greatest rewards of working.

Contributions to Health

Work can be very important for mental and physical health. This results from the work itself as well as the physical activity involved. People who are active and happy in their work tend to feel better.

Self-expression

We all have interests, abilities, and talents. Work can be a way in which we express ourselves. It does not matter what kind of work it is as long as it suits the worker and is not illegal or immoral.

WORK, OCCUPATION, AND JOB

People often use the terms *work, occupation,* and *job* interchangeably. They do have a number of similarities. In this book, however, the terms will be used in different ways.

Work

Work can be defined as activity directed toward a purpose or goal that produces something of value to oneself and/or to society. For instance, work can provide you with money and a sense of accomplishment. Work by a teacher or nurse provides benefits to society.

Another characteristic of work is that it may be paid or unpaid. If you volunteer at a local food bank or at a blood drive, it is still considered work, even though you are not paid for it.

Occupation

All occupations carry out work. An **occupation** is the name given to a group of similar tasks that a person performs for pay. For example, keyboarding, filing, maintaining records, placing phone calls, and scheduling meetings are tasks performed in the occupation of secretary. Carpenter, salesclerk, attorney, truck driver, and chef are examples of common occupations that involve groups of similar tasks.

Most occupations require specific knowledge and skills. Occupations are learned on the job or in various kinds of education and training programs. A person in an occupation can work at a number of different jobs.

Job

A **job** is a paid position at a specific place or setting. A job can be in an office, store, factory, farm, or mine. For example, a nurse can work at jobs in a doctor's office, clinic, hospital, home, school, factory, or nursing home. The relationships among work, occupation, and job are illustrated in Figure 1-1.

The typical relationship between occupation and job is that an occupation is acquired first. That is, an occupation is learned through education and training, after which a job is secured. Some jobs require no previous training. When these types of job are obtained, occupational training may follow.

Many employers offer some training for entry-level jobs, as well as more training with new equipment or new technologies. Ongoing training will help you keep your skills sharp and help you acquire new skills, making you a more valuable employee.

Most people change jobs a number of times throughout their lives. For instance, Lionel, a secretary, might leave a job at State Insurance to work at Merchants Bank. Later, he might leave Merchants Bank to work at Mercy Hospital.

Sometimes, people change both occupations and jobs. An example would be if Lionel leaves the secretarial position at Mercy Hospital to become an office manager for Suburban Realty Company.

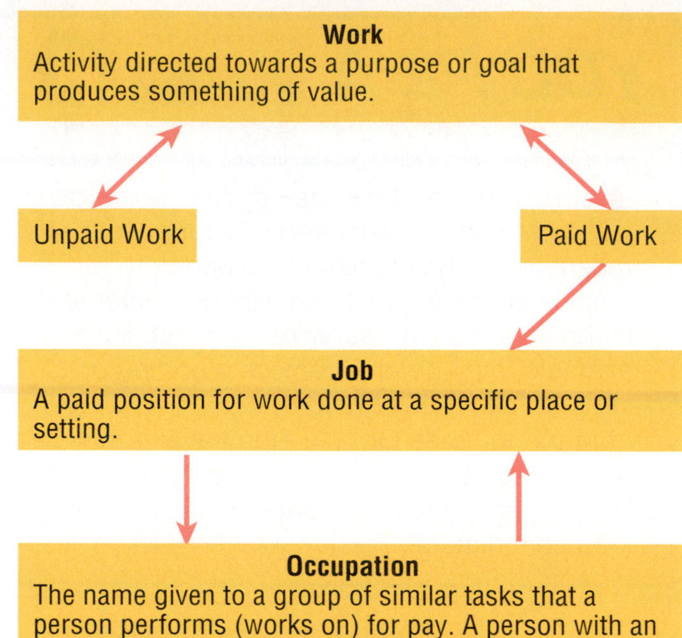

Figure 1-1 ***Can you see the relationships among work, occupation, and job?***

You should spend some time researching possible occupations and the jobs within each occupation. Suppose you are interested in an occupation in health services, but you don't like the job opportunities or don't want to complete the necessary training. The earlier you learn what you do and don't like about an occupation, the better. Now you know that you will not pursue an occupation in health services.

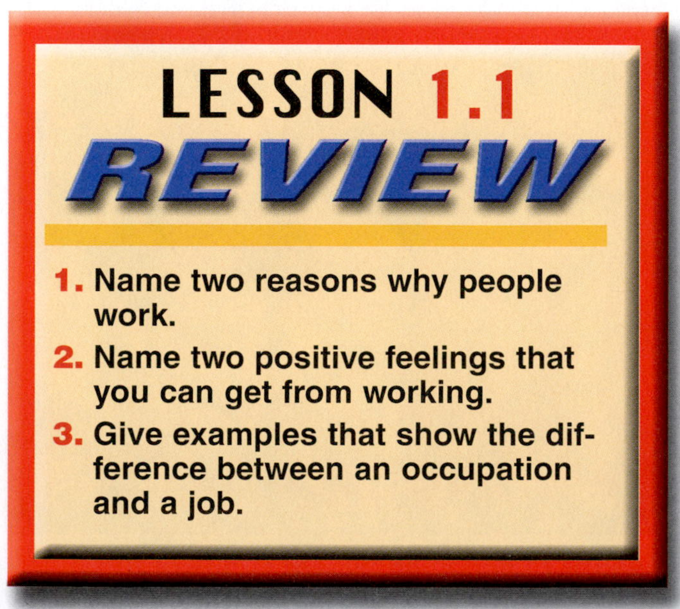

LESSON 1.1 REVIEW

1. **Name two reasons why people work.**
2. **Name two positive feelings that you can get from working.**
3. **Give examples that show the difference between an occupation and a job.**

HIGH-GROWTH OCCUPATIONS FOR THE 21st CENTURY

Advertising, Marketing, and Public Relations Managers

The objective of any firm is to market its products or services profitably. Advertising, marketing, and public relations managers direct the sale of products and services offered by their firms and the communication of information about their firms' activities.

Advertising and promotion staffs usually are small except in the largest firms. In a small firm, they may serve as a liaison between the firm and the agency to which advertising or promotional functions are contracted out. In larger firms, *advertising managers* oversee in-house account services, creative services, and media services departments. *Promotion managers* direct promotion programs combining advertising with purchase incentives to increase sales.

Public relations managers usually present ideas before clients. Do you have the presentation skills for this occupation?

Marketing managers develop the firm's detailed marketing strategy. They determine the demand for products and services offered by the firm and its competitors. They identify potential markets and develop pricing strategies to maximize the firm's share of the market while ensuring that the firm's customers are satisfied. They also monitor trends that indicate the need for new products and services and oversee product development. Marketing managers work with advertising and promotion managers to promote the firm's products and services.

Public relations managers direct publicity programs to a targeted audience. They often specialize in a specific area, such as crisis management—or in a specific industry, such as health care. Public relations managers evaluate advertising and promotion programs and serve as the eyes and ears of top management. Public relations managers may also confer with labor relations managers to produce internal company communications and with financial managers to produce company reports. They assist company executives in drafting speeches, arranging interviews, and responding to information requests.

Advertising, marketing, and public relations managers often work long hours, including evenings and weekends. Working under pressure to meet goals and deadlines is unavoidable. Substantial travel may also be involved to consult with clients and attend professional meetings.

LESSON 1.2 WORK EXPERIENCE EDUCATION

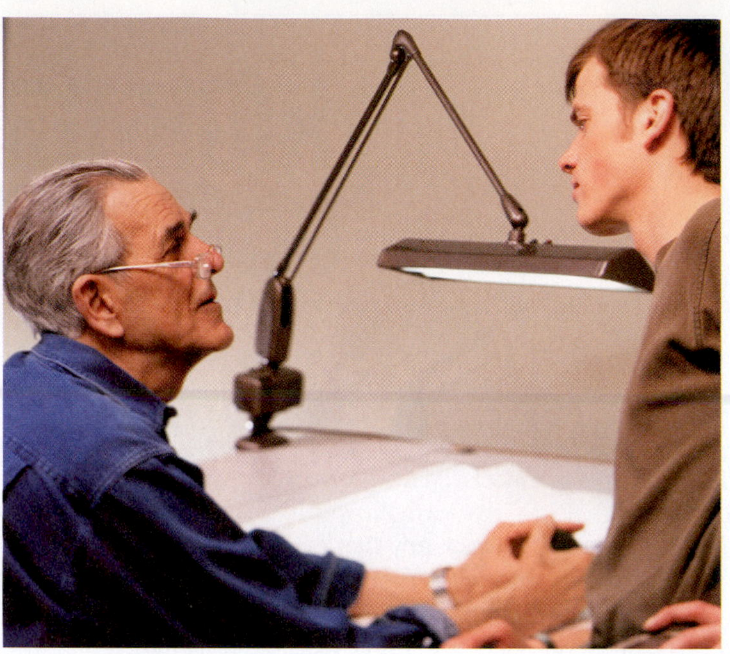

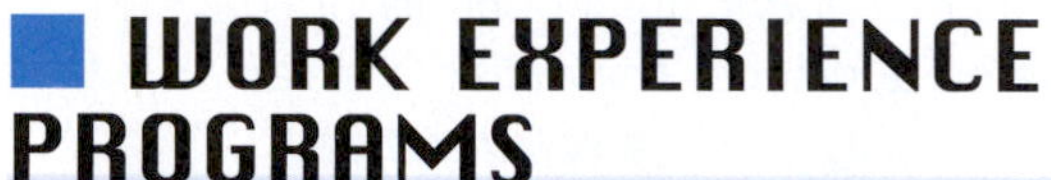

- NAME THREE TYPES OF WORK EXPERIENCE EDUCATION
- IDENTIFY THE BENEFITS OF WORK EXPERIENCE EDUCATION

WORK EXPERIENCE PROGRAMS

During the last several decades, many kinds of education programs have been developed to help young people learn about and prepare for work. Programs of this type are called **work experience education**. Their purpose is to provide opportunities for students to explore or participate in work as an extension of the regular school environment.

Unlike many countries, the United States does not have a national system of education. As a result, state and local programs like work experience education are called by many different names. Whatever it is called, a work experience program is probably one of the following.

Cooperative (co-op) Career and Technical Education

Career and technical education is a program in which students learn specific occupational skills for employment. **Occupational skills** are skills needed to perform tasks or duties of a specific occupation. One kind of career/technical education is school-based education, which is taught in classrooms, shops, and laboratories. Instruction may be provided in occupational areas such as agriculture, business, marketing, industrial-technical, and health.

Another kind of career/technical education is cooperative (co-op) career/technical education. This is a cooperative program between a secondary school or community college and a local employer. Most co-op education students attend classes at their school campus for part of the day. They spend the rest of the day working at a training site in a local business or industry. Students receive both pay and school credit for their co-op jobs.

PERSONAL DECISIONS

Your school has both school-based and co-op career/technical education. You cannot decide which one to enroll in. The advantages of the school-based program are that you know the teacher, you are familiar with the equipment, and you would be taking the course with your friends. In the co-op program, you would meet new people, earn some money, and work on more advanced equipment. Other students have told you that in co-op you will work harder and that more will be expected of you.

WHAT WOULD YOU DO?

In co-op career/technical education, the student learns and applies occupational skills on the job rather than only in a school shop or laboratory. Another part of co-op career/technical education is a related class. This is taught at the school to reinforce skills used at a job site. Students study topics such as job seeking, consumer skills, independent living, and career planning. This textbook is probably being used as part of a related class.

Co-op career/technical education follows certain guidelines and procedures. A cooperative education teacher/coordinator employed by a school system usually manages the program. The coordinator reviews and approves student applications for the program. The coordinator also approves each student's place of employment, called the **training station**.

The training station may be any type of workplace that relates to the student's career objectives. Common training stations include stores, offices, hospitals, restaurants, and auto repair shops. At the training station, the student is under the direction of a supervisor.

The cooperative education program is a three-way relationship involving the student, the employer-supervisor, and the cooperative education coordinator. Early on, all three parties sign a **training agreement** outlining the relationships and responsibilities of the parties. See the sample training agreement in Figure 1-2 on the next page. All three parties also participate in the development of a step-by-step training plan. A **training plan** describes the knowledge, attitudes, and skills to be developed by the student.

Work-study

Work-study programs, sometimes called general work experience education, are like co-op career/technical education in several ways. Both allow students to attend school part-time while working part-time. For these jobs, students receive pay and school credit. A work experience coordinator supervises each program.

Unlike co-op career/technical education, work-study is *not* a program of on-the-job training for a specific occupation. Rather, the program deals with the development of **employability skills**, the general work habits and attitudes required in all jobs. They include, for example, punctuality, dependability, and cooperation.

Many students find that the combination of school and work is more interesting than school alone. Also, the opportunity to earn money keeps some students in school who might otherwise drop out before graduation.

Exploratory Work Experience Education

Many schools provide exploratory work experience education for junior high and beginning high school students. The purpose of this type of program is to provide students with opportunities to observe work and to try out various work tasks. This is why the program is called "exploratory." Students explore various occupations in order to discover or to confirm occupational interests. Thus, the program is concerned with career guidance rather than the development of occupational or employability skills. **Career guidance** is assisting students in career planning and decision making.

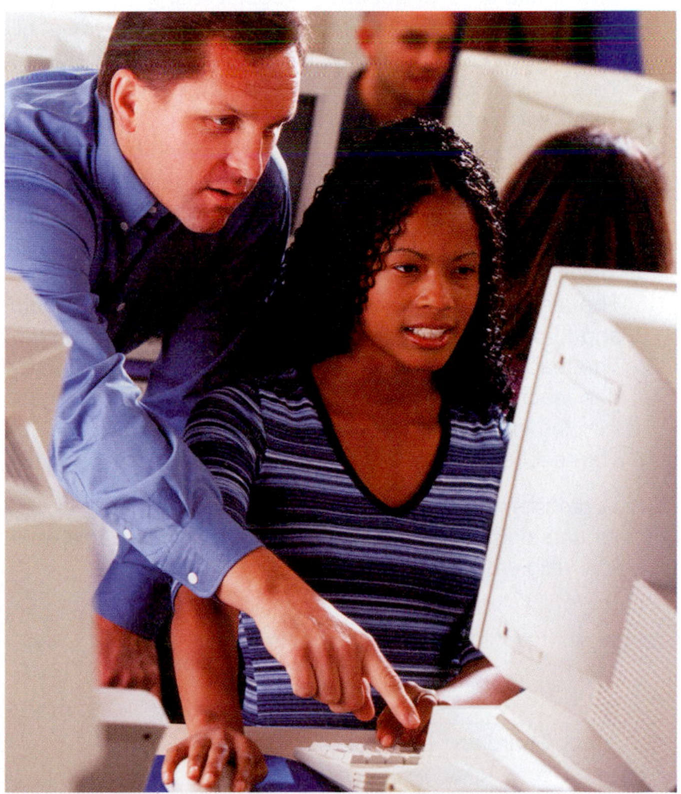

"Job shadowing" is often part of exploratory work experience. Why do you think this term is used?

TRAINING AGREEMENT

Student's Name ______________________ School ______________ Date__________

Age______ Social Security No. ______________ Job Title ______________________

Company Name ______________________ Company Address ______________________

Company Phone ______________________ Employer Identification No. ______________

Company Supervisor ______________________ Student Hours ______________________

Wages______________________ Dates Covered by Agreement______________________

Responsibilities of the Student-Learner:

1. The student-learner will keep regular attendance, both in school and on the job, and cannot work on any school day that he/she fails to attend school; he/she will notify the school and employer if unable to report.
2. The student's employment will be terminated if he/she does not remain in school.
3. The student will show honesty, punctuality, courtesy, a cooperative attitude, proper health and grooming habits, good dress, and a willingness to learn.
4. The student will consult the teacher-coordinator about any difficulties arising at the training station.
5. The student will conform to the rules and regulations of the training station.
6. The student will furnish the teacher-coordinator with all necessary information and complete all necessary reports.

Responsibilities of the Training Sponsor:

1. The training sponsor will endeavor to employ the student for at least the minimum number of hours each day and each week for the entire agreed-upon training period.
2. The training sponsor will adhere to all federal and state regulations regarding employment, child labor laws, and minimum wages and to other applicable regulations.
3. The training sponsor will ensure that the student is not allowed to remain in any one operation, job, or phase of the occupation beyond a period of time when such experiences cease to be of educational value.
4. The training sponsor will consult the teacher-coordinator about any difficulties at the training station.
5. The training sponsor will provide experiences that will contribute to the attainment of the student's career objective.
6. The training sponsor will assist in evaluating the student.
7. The training sponsor will provide time for consultation with the teacher-coordinator concerning the student.
8. The training sponsor will provide instructional material and occupational guidance for the student as needed and available.

Responsibilities of the Teacher-Coordinator:

1. The teacher-coordinator will coordinate related classroom instruction and on-the-job training to improve job performance and to better prepare the student for his/her occupational career objective.
2. The teacher-coordinator will provide the necessary related classroom instruction.
3. The teacher-coordinator will make periodic visits as necessary to the training station to observe the student and consult with the employer and training sponsor.
4. The teacher-coordinator will assist in the evaluation of the student.

This agreement may be terminated by mutual consent of the training sponsor and the teacher-coordinator.
It is understood that the parties participating in this agreement will not discriminate in employment opportunities on the basis of race, religion, sex, or national or ethnic origin.

______________________________ ______________________________

Student (Date) Training Sponsor (Date)

______________________________ ______________________________

Parent or Guardian (Date) Teacher-Coordinator (Date)

Source: Gooch, B. G. Handbook for Work-based Learning. Carbondale, IL: Southern Illinois University, 1995

Figure 1-2 Sample training agreement

COMMUNICATION AT WORK

INTERPERSONAL RELATIONS

In any workplace, you will find it easy to get along with some coworkers and difficult to get along with others. The following tips will help you work better with many different kinds of people.

Try to communicate clearly. Many disagreements can be avoided by clearly communicating what you have to say and then taking the time to make sure the other person understands.

Try to communicate politely. If you are polite to coworkers, they are more likely to treat you politely in return. Being polite fosters an atmosphere of cooperation.

Try to understand your coworker's point of view. Have you ever snapped at someone even though he or she didn't deserve it? Remember this if a coworker ever snaps at you for no apparent reason. Don't take it personally. Try to understand.

Exploratory programs may last only a few days or a few weeks. Students receive no pay for the work they do, but they usually receive school credit.

BENEFITS OF WORK EXPERIENCE

Depending on the type of program in which you are enrolled, work experience can benefit you in the following ways.

- ***You can learn occupational skills.*** You can acquire skills through on-the-job training in an actual work setting. These skills will make you more desirable to potential employers in the future. These skills may also qualify you for higher starting pay than another candidate who has not learned these skills yet.

- ***You can develop employability skills.*** Success on the job requires more than occupational skills. Work experience provides

Some students are motivated to stay in school by participating in a work-study program.

opportunities to develop the types of work habits and attitudes that employers expect. The best place to learn these habits and attitudes is in an actual workplace setting.

- ***You can establish a work record.*** It is often hard to get a job if you lack previous experience. Completing a work experience program will make it easier for you to get a job later because you can use your work experience as a reference for potential employers.
- ***You can earn while you learn.*** Earning your own money will give you a sense of accomplishment. You will be able to save money, buy things that you might not otherwise be able to afford, or both. For some students, the money they earn can be the difference between staying in school and dropping out. You may also be able to save money for future expenses, such as living on your own or getting additional training for your occupation.
- ***You can discover career interests and goals.*** Work experience can help you find out what type of career you want. You may either confirm your present interests and goals or find new ones. You may still have time in your high school career to explore other careers in a work experience setting.
- ***You can recognize the relationship between education and work.*** Work experience can provide something that may be missing at school. Education can take on new meaning as you come to recognize a greater connection between what you are learning in school and what you would do at a job.
- ***You can remain employed after graduation.*** Many students in work experience jobs are offered permanent jobs after graduation. This benefits both students and employers. If you are pleased with your job, you won't have to look for a new one. Hiring a work experience student saves the employer both interviewing and training time. Some students continue in co-op jobs while obtaining further education after high school.

WORKFORCE TRENDS

The U.S. population is becoming larger and more diverse. Over the next 50 years, the population is expected to grow by nearly 50 percent, from about 275 million in the year 2000 to an estimated 394 million in 2050. U.S. population growth is influenced by immigration and emigration rates, as well as by birth and death rates. Fully two-thirds of the projected U.S. population increase will be due to net immigration.

LESSON 1.2 REVIEW

1. Identify and briefly explain the three kinds of work experience education programs.
2. How does cooperative career and technical education differ from other forms of career and technical education?
3. Explain the role of a related class in cooperative career and technical education.
4. The term *exploratory* describes one type of work experience education. Explain why.
5. How can work experience education help you discover career interests and goals?
6. What is the benefit of establishing a work record?

FOCUS ON THE WORKPLACE

THE CHANGING WORKPLACE

When this country was founded, most people lived and worked on small, family-owned farms. The farm family raised livestock, poultry, and grain.

Computers and related technologies will continue to influence the workplace in the future.

As trading increased, small villages grew along rivers and other transportation routes. The growth of towns provided new jobs for shop owners, bankers, blacksmiths, and others. Agriculture, however, remained the base of the economy.

In the second half of the 1800s, industry in the United States expanded rapidly. Growing towns and cities needed more and more goods. Typical workers in the early 1900s had factory jobs. They produced steel, machinery, and other manufactured goods.

Growing industry and a growing population needed many kinds of business, transportation, communication, personal, and government services. In response to these demands, service industries began to expand. Typical service occupations included secretary, clerk, salesperson, and manager. In 2000, about 80 percent of all workers were employed in services.

This service economy, however, is undergoing change. A new economy is evolving based on knowledge and information. Computers are the backbone of this information society. Influencing almost all industries and occupations, computers and related technologies provide new ways of dealing with information.

With the computer have come many new occupations. These include laser nurse, computer animator, fiber-optics technician, and robotics repairer. "High-tech" industries will generate millions of new jobs into the next century. Many of you will probably work at some of these jobs.

THINK CRITICALLY

1. What do you think your family would have done for a living if you lived around the time of this country's founding?
2. How prepared are you for this "high-tech" workplace?

CHAPTER 1

Chapter in Brief

Lesson 1.1 *Why People Work*

A. For most people, work is an important part of a well-rounded life.
B. People work for many reasons, including money, social satisfaction, positive feelings, prestige, personal development, contributions to health, and self-expression. The specific reasons vary from person to person.
C. The terms *work, occupation*, and *job* have different meanings. Work is activity directed toward a goal that produces something of value. It may be paid or unpaid. An occupation is the name given to a group of similar tasks that a person performs for pay. A job is a paid position at a specific place or setting.

Lesson 1.2 *Work Experience Education*

A. Work experience programs may be called different things depending on the state and community in which you live. Generally speaking, there are three common types of work experience education: cooperative career and technical education, work-study, and exploratory work experience education.
B. Work experience programs can benefit you in a number of ways. You can learn occupational skills, develop employability skills, establish a work record, earn while you learn, discover career interests and goals, recognize the relationship between education and work, and remain employed after graduation.

Activities

1. Interview a student who has taken a cooperative career and technical education or work-study program. Ask the person what he or she thinks are the major benefits of the program. Ask also about whether the person found any disadvantages to the program. Discuss your findings in class.
2. Interview an employer who has provided a training site for a co-op or work-study student. List the ways in which the employer has benefited from the program. Prepare an oral report and present it to the class.
3. Write a paragraph about what you hope to gain from being in a work experience program. Read your statement to the class. Compare and discuss the statements of different students.
4. Examine a copy of the training agreement used by your school. Discuss the purpose and requirements of the agreement. Make sure that you ask questions about any parts that you don't understand.
5. Work is a very important part of our culture, including work-related humor. Collect cartoons about work from your local newspapers. You may be surprised at the number you find. Display them on a classroom bulletin board.

REVIEW

Word Power

On a separate sheet of paper, match each definition with the correct term. All definitions will be used, and a definition will be used only once.

6. Name given to a group of similar tasks that a person performs for pay
7. Description of knowledge, attitudes, and skills to be developed by the student participating in a work experience education program
8. Assisting students in career planning and decision making
9. Education programs designed to provide opportunities for students to explore or participate in work as an extension of the regular school environment
10. Paid position at a specific place or setting
11. Signed agreement outlining the relationships and responsibilities of the parties involved in a work experience education program
12. Work experience student's place of employment
13. Activity directed toward a purpose or goal that produces something of value to oneself and/or to society
14. General work habits and attitudes required in all jobs
15. Skills needed to perform tasks or duties of a specific occupation

a. career guidance
b. employability skills
c. job
d. occupation
e. occupational skills
f. training agreement
g. training plan
h. training station
i. work
j. work experience education

Think Critically

16. How would your future plans be changed if you suddenly won or inherited a great deal of money? Would you go to college? Would you plan on working? What type of work would you do?
17. In what ways can you influence and shape the direction of your career?
18. Are there any types of work experience programs in your school or community not mentioned in the chapter?
19. How might knowledge and skills learned in the following school subjects be applied on the job: English, mathematics, science, social studies, and foreign language?
20. In what ways might your interests and abilities be expressed in work? Cite examples of both paid and unpaid work.

CHAPTER 2

THE JOB AHEAD

LESSONS

PREVIEW

The jobs you hold during your working life represent your unique work history. One person's work history may be a movement from job to job within the same occupation. Another person's work history may include one or more changes to entirely different occupations and jobs. A third person's work history may have no orderly pattern at all. Some people are unable to establish a successful work history.

THOUGHTS ON WORK

"No man needs sympathy because he has to work. Far and away the best prize that life offers is the chance to work hard at work worth doing."

Theodore Roosevelt

TAKING ACTION
ATTITUDE IS EVERYTHING

Marcy had finished her junior year in high school and started to look for a summer job. She went to the Job Service office. Little was available for students like her. Most of the job openings were permanent positions for people 18 and over. Marcy was only 17 and could not take a permanent job.

One job was available. It was offered by someone who wanted a person to mow grass and do yard work one day a week. She took the job.

When Marcy showed up at the Porters' house, Mrs. Porter showed her what to do. For the rest of the day she mowed, raked, pruned, trimmed, and pulled weeds. The lawn and garden were beautiful and Marcy took pride in making them even more attractive. After she finished, she cleaned the mower, put away the tools, and swept the walk and driveway. Mrs. Porter thanked her and paid her.

Marcy returned a week later and did a really good job. When Mrs. Porter paid her this time, she complimented Marcy and gave her a bonus. Mrs. Porter said that it was very difficult to find people willing and able to do good work. Mrs. Porter asked Marcy if she would be interested in doing yard work for some of her neighbors.

Before long Marcy had all the jobs she was able to do. She learned that quality effort pays off. Because her work was appreciated, Marcy was able to use Mrs. Porter's name as a reference for later jobs. Mrs. Porter was a well-respected member of the community. Her recommendations helped Marcy many times in later years.

SUCCESS TIP

If you show that you are willing and able to do good work, your work will get noticed!

THINK CRITICALLY

1. What are some things that Marcy did that Mrs. Porter considered good work?
2. Why do you think Marcy had all the jobs she could do?

LESSON 2.1 WORK HISTORIES

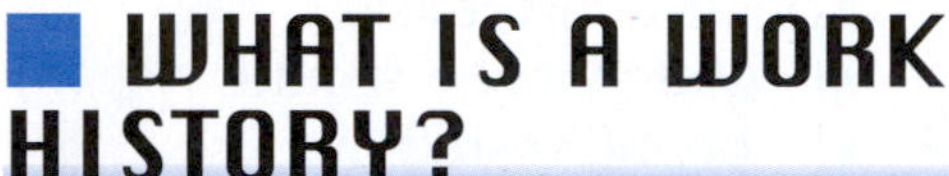

- EXPLAIN WHAT IS MEANT BY A WORK HISTORY
- DESCRIBE HOW KNOWING ABOUT WORK HISTORIES CAN AID CAREER PLANNING

WHAT IS A WORK HISTORY?

A **work history** is all of the jobs that one holds during the course of a working lifetime. The four work histories that follow illustrate how jobs can serve different purposes at different times in one's life. Jobs are often used as a way to achieve something else. One purpose may be to learn occupational skills. Another purpose may be to earn money for college. Some jobs are used to gain experience in order to **qualify**, or meet the preliminary requirements, for a better job. For most people, first jobs are only steppingstones to later ones.

SAMPLE WORK HISTORIES

Knowing about different work histories can help you think about and plan for your own career. Let's examine the work histories of four different people.

Example 1—Terry

Terry got a job in a small electronics sales and repair shop as part of a co-op program. After he graduated from high school, he took a full-time job in the electronics department of a large discount store. He often did small repair jobs for friends and neighbors during evenings and weekends.

Next, he got a job repairing televisions and installing antennas. He took this job in order to save enough money to open his own business. Terry now has a stable job as owner-manager of an electronics supply firm.

Retail sales is a great place to start working because it offers many entry-level positions.

Example 2—Marie

When Marie graduated from high school, she did not know what she wanted to do. After being out of work for several months, she found a full-time job. It was working as a salesclerk in a fashionable clothing store. From working in the store, Marie discovered that she enjoyed retail selling and had a talent for it.

After two years, she quit her job and enrolled in college to major in marketing. During college, Marie had a part-time job in a clothing store in the campus town. After she finished a marketing degree, she took a job as a sales manager for a national department store. She worked at that job for five years before staying at home for two years with young children. Marie just started working again at a job that is similar to the one she left earlier.

Example 3—Cindy

Cindy was an outstanding athlete who never worked while attending high school or college. After college, her first job turned out to be a stable one. It was as a high school teacher and coach. After six years, however, she had a desire to do something else.

A friend in the sporting goods business offered Cindy a job. She was not sure whether she would like it, but she quit her teaching job to give it a try. Somewhat to her surprise, Cindy enjoyed the challenge of the job. After a year in the job, she took another job with a large sporting goods manufacturer. She is now in charge of its school athletic sales. Cindy plans to make this a stable job.

Example 4—Rick

Rick never liked school and could not wait to get out. After high school, he got a job stocking shelves in a grocery store. He worked for a couple of months before getting into an argument with the store manager. Rick was fired.

His next job was working evenings and weekends as a service station attendant. After working at that job for about a year, Rick decided that he should learn a skill. Rick then moved to another town and got an apartment with a friend. He enrolled in a technical school to learn computer programming. He had heard this was a growing field.

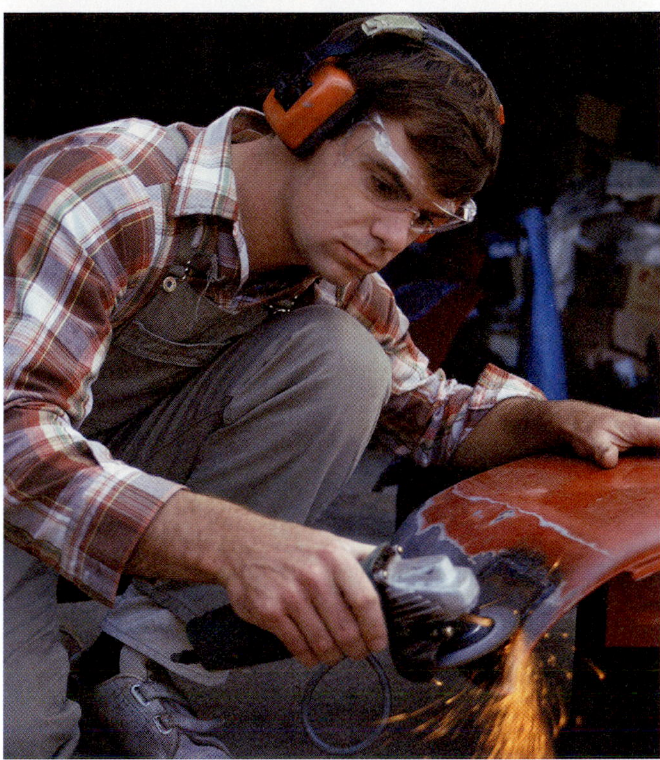

First jobs are often used to learn occupational skills.

While going to school, Rick took a part-time job at another service station. He quit school after six months because he had to study too hard. Now Rick has another job driving a delivery truck while he decides whether to join the Armed Forces or start his own business!

LESSON 2.1 REVIEW

1. **What are some reasons why people are unable to establish a successful work history?**
2. **Give an example to show how knowledge of work histories can help you think about and plan a career.**

LESSON 2.2

MOVING TOWARD A STABLE JOB

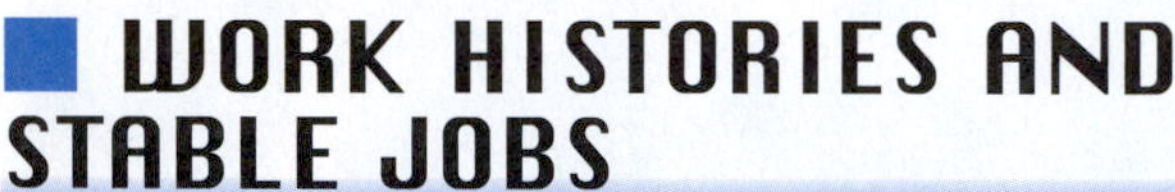

OBJECTIVES

- DISCUSS HOW DIFFERENT WORK HISTORIES CAN LEAD TO A STABLE JOB
- LIST CHARACTERISTICS OF STABLE JOBS

WORK HISTORIES AND STABLE JOBS

Different work histories can lead to a stable job. You read how Terry, Marie, and Cindy followed different paths to a stable job. One route is not necessarily better than another. Some work histories like Rick's, however, only lead to detours and dead ends.

A **stable job** is one that you consider to be permanent and that may last several years. This does not mean, however, that you stay in the job forever. Remember Cindy's example. You may have a stable job at any time in your work life. Following are additional characteristics of stable jobs. Being aware of them can help you gain greater control over your work history.

Self-direction

Gaining a stable job does not usually happen by accident. Most successful careers come from hard work and **self-direction**, which means setting goals and taking steps to get there. Part of being self-directed is developing your skills through education or training.

Once you get a job, you want to keep it. This means performing well on the job tasks you are being paid to do. It also means learning and growing on the job. Much of this involves keeping up to date with what is going on in your field.

Advancing in a job usually requires doing more than your share. To become eligible for **promotion**, or advancement to a higher-level job or position, you may also need to get more education or training. Sometimes, advancing in a career involves taking risks. A willingness to take a risk, though, often leads to greater personal and career success.

Effort Pays Off

Not enough jobs are available for everyone who wants one. This is especially true for young people. If you want to work, you may have to accept any job that you can get. It may be

> **ETHICAL DECISIONS**
>
> A fellow employee approaches you at work with some advice. "Listen," he says. "You are working too hard. Slow down a little bit. You are making the rest of us look bad. You do not want us all to be angry with you, do you?" The comments upset you. You are just trying to do the job the best way you know how. You are not trying to show anyone up. But now you wonder if you should slack off a bit.
>
> **WHAT WOULD YOU DO?**

MATH CONNECTION

Suppose you had two job offers. The first job is a short-term job, planned to last for six weeks. This job would pay $12 an hour, and you would work for 35 hours a week. The second job is a regular, long-term job, which would pay $10 an hour. You would work 40 hours a week. Which job would pay you more per week?

SOLUTION

To calculate your earnings, use this formula: Earnings per week = pay per hour × hours worked in a week

Job 1: Earnings per week = $12 × 35
= $420

Job 2: Earnings per week = $10 × 40
= $400

The first job would pay you more per week. However, this is not a stable job.

low-paying, boring, or undesirable in some other way. But a job is a job! Many adults started their careers this way.

It can be argued that there are no "bad jobs" as long as they are not illegal, immoral, or otherwise harmful. A job is a beginning. It is a way to earn money, get experience, learn skills, and prove yourself. Things can get better if you are cooperative, follow rules and directions, take an interest in what you are doing, and do your best. Employers tend to recognize and reward good work.

STABLE JOBS ADAPT TO CHANGE

The world of work is continually changing. Some industries and occupations become **obsolete**, or no longer used, as new ones are created. For example, the number of telephone operators has steadily decreased because of new electronic switching equipment. This technology, however, has created a need for new types of workers who can install and maintain such equipment. During your work life, you will probably have to adjust to great changes due to **technology**, which is the application of scientific knowledge to practical uses.

People who are more successful are generally those who anticipate and adapt to change. Eva and Mario are a good example. Eva and Mario own a typing and printing service. Most of their clients are small business owners and college students.

A few years ago, they began to get requests for desktop publishing. They had to decline the business. To meet the needs of the clients, they purchased desktop publishing software, a scanner, and a color laser printer. Mario, Eva, and the office staff took extra time to learn how to use the new software and equipment. They are glad they did. They now have more business and have been able to pay for the new equipment with the increased earnings.

Part of your preparation for a career should include planning for change. Try to develop the skills you will need in tomorrow's workplace.

LESSON 2.2 REVIEW

1. Name three reasons why a person might voluntarily leave a stable job.
2. Jobs can serve different purposes at different times in our lives. Give three examples.
3. Give an example to show how taking a risk can lead to greater success in a career.
4. How can technological change influence a career? Give one positive and one negative example.

HIGH-GROWTH OCCUPATIONS FOR THE 21st CENTURY

Computer Network Administrators and Support Specialists

The growth of the Internet, the expansion of uses for the World Wide Web, and the need for user support have stepped up the demand for information technology workers. *Database administrators* work with database management systems software and determine ways to organize and store data. They set up computer databases and test and coordinate changes to them.

Computer support specialists provide technical assistance, support, and advice to users. This group includes *technical support specialists, help desk technicians,* and *customer service representatives.* These troubleshooters answer phone calls, use automated diagnostic programs, and resolve recurrent problems. Support specialists may work within an organization or directly for a computer or software vendor as more of this type of work is outsourced, or sent outside the company.

Technicians are needed to maintain and monitor a computer network.

Other information technology workers are involved in analysis, maintenance, or design of a particular system or system part. *Network* or *computer systems administrators*, for example, design, install, and support an organization's networks, including its intranet, a private network that typically includes Internet access. They maintain network hardware and software, analyze problems, and monitor the network to ensure availability to system users. Administrators also may plan, coordinate, and implement network security measures. In some organizations, *computer security specialists* may plan, coordinate, and implement information security.

A variety of information technology occupations relate to design, development, and maintenance of web sites and servers. For example, *webmasters* are responsible for all technical aspects of a web site. This includes performance issues such as speed of access and approval of web site content. *Web developers*, also called *web designers*, are responsible for site design and creation.

The 21st century will see continued rapid growth of electronic commerce, or conducting business online. This translates into an increasing demand for information technology workers who can help organizations use technology to communicate with employees, clients, and consumers.

LESSON 2.3

THE FUTURE BEGINS NOW

OBJECTIVES

- EXPLAIN THE BENEFITS OF BUILDING A GOOD SCHOOL RECORD
- IDENTIFY WHAT YOU CAN DO TO SHAPE YOUR OWN CAREER

SCHOOL AS A WORKPLACE

Some young people regard school as something to get through so they can be free to do what they want. What is the problem with this attitude? Well, school is a workplace, too. A prospective employer will look at your school record for clues as to what kind of an employee you might be. A poor school record is hard to defend. Blaming teachers or someone else for your problems will not impress anyone.

Perhaps you have done poorly in school thus far. What can you do now? You can always work harder during what is left of your high school career. A marked improvement in your attitude and performance will be helpful later. It will show teachers and employers that you have become a more mature person.

Now is the time to change habits and attitudes that may hold you back in the workplace. If, for example, you are frequently absent or late to school, make a greater effort to go to school and

WORKFORCE TRENDS

The large number of people born between 1946 and 1964 is referred to as the "baby-boom" generation. These individuals have now reached their prime working years and constitute about 47 percent of the workforce. The youngest baby boomers will continue to participate in the workforce for many years. As this population ages, the median age of the workforce—the age that half the workers are above and half are below—will gradually rise.

WORKPLACE DECISIONS

You have been operating your own small business for several years. You make a good income and are optimistic about the future. One day a salesperson calls on you to demonstrate a new piece of manufacturing equipment. He claims that this new machine will make the current method obsolete in a few years. He also says that most businesses like yours are already planning to install the equipment. You are not so sure. The new machine is very expensive. Since your business is currently doing very well, you question whether you actually need it.

WHAT WOULD YOU DO?

to be on time. Or, if you often commit careless errors in your schoolwork, take the time to reread or recheck your work before turning it in.

SHAPING YOUR CAREER

Consider taking more courses that will strengthen your academic background. Most jobs require basic mathematics and communication skills. You may want to take more math or English. If you haven't already, how about trying a computer course? Being familiar with computers is required in most jobs. Your work experience coordinator or school counselor may have other suggestions depending on your background and needs.

In Chapter 3, you will learn how to look for a job. You may discover that a job search can be frustrating. You may end up accepting a job that is less than what you had hoped for. If so, do not get discouraged. Remember what you have learned in this chapter about the different routes to a stable, satisfying job. How you begin your career is less important than getting it started. You can then use the beginning job as a steppingstone to something better.

Different occupations require different skills. To find out what skills are needed in your chosen occupation, interview some people who have the jobs you think you would like. Ask what skills they use every day. Do they make calculations? If so, you may want to make sure you take any necessary math classes to prepare yourself. Do they have to make sales presentations to others? If so, you may want to take a course in public speaking. Do they use computers? If so, find out what programs they use and make a point of taking classes to learn these programs. Preparing yourself for your career now will help you qualify for the jobs you want.

NOTHING BUT NET

The World Wide Web, or simply the Web, is a network of millions of computers. These computers are called servers. Web servers store computer files (web pages) that contain all kinds of information, including images, sounds, and text. To access this information, you use browser software. When you key a web address such as *http://www.thomson.com*, or when you click on a link such as "Thomson Corporation," your browser requests the page represented by the address or link from the server and displays it in its proper form.

LESSON 2.3 REVIEW

1. **Why are employers usually interested in how well you have done in school?**
2. **Why is having a mature outlook important when it comes time to look for a job?**
3. **Think of an attitude you have that you need to change before you find work. What steps can you take to change it?**
4. **Name three things that you might begin to do now to influence your career.**

FOCUS ON THE WORKPLACE

COPING WITH SHIFT WORK

You may apply for or be offered a job someday that requires you to work various shifts. The demand for round-the-clock shift workers has increased significantly in the last few decades. Millions of Americans now work the night shift, which usually means working from midnight to 8 a.m. This trend is expected to continue as more businesses stay open 24 hours.

Some employees work the swing shift—4 p.m. to midnight, for example—or the night shift on a permanent basis. Others are rotated frequently from shift to shift. Time shuffling can have its price, however. The health and productivity of shift workers may suffer. An upside-down schedule disturbs the body's "inner clock." This can cause fatigue and digestive problems. Rotating shift workers also make more mistakes than workers with set shifts. For example, between midnight and dawn nurses dispense wrong medication more often and truckers have more single-vehicle accidents than do workers with set shifts.

A new breed of scientists called chronobiologists is beginning to solve some of these problems. Most problems are related to the direction and rate of shift rotation. Rotation can be clockwise, which means going to work later at each change, or counterclockwise, which means going to work earlier. Shifts may change every day or two or every several weeks. It has been found that the body adjusts better to a clockwise rotation schedule; that is, rotating from the day shift to the swing shift to the night shift. At least three weeks should elapse between shift changes. Companies trying this pattern have found major improvement in production and fewer workers' complaints about schedules.

THINK CRITICALLY

1. What are some companies in your area that might have shift work?
2. Are you surprised at the number of mistakes people make at work when they are tired? Why or why not?

CHAPTER 2

Chapter in Brief

Lesson 2.1 *Work Histories*

A. The jobs that you hold during your working life form a work history. People often have very different work histories. Knowing about work histories can help you think about and plan your own career.

B. A job can serve different purposes at different times in your life. Beginning jobs are often used to achieve something else, such as learning a skill, saving money for college, or qualifying for a better job.

Lesson 2.2 *Moving Toward a Stable Job*

A. A stable job is one that you consider to be permanent. It may last for several years. Many different routes can lead to a stable job. One route is not necessarily better than another.

B. There are other common characteristics of stable jobs. One is that most stable jobs result from hard work and self-direction. Another is that quality effort on a job usually pays off. A third characteristic is that people with successful, stable jobs are generally those who anticipate and adapt to change.

Lesson 2.3 *The Future Begins Now*

A. You can take steps now to influence the direction of your career. Work harder during what is left of your high school years.

B. Change habits and attitudes that may hold you back in the workplace. Consider taking additional courses to strengthen your academic background.

Activities

1. Ask a parent or other adult to list all the jobs he or she has held. Compare the work histories in class. What are the similarities and differences? Which types of work histories are the most common?

2. In doing Activity 1, did you note how work histories may be influenced by illnesses, accidents, economic hard times, wars, and so on? List as many factors as you can that are beyond one's control that may influence a career. Discuss your answers in class.

3. Write a list of three jobs you consider stable. Next to each, write why you think each of these jobs is stable.

4. Think about your own work habits and attitudes. Write down two or three things that need improving. We all have a few faults. Go over the list with your work experience coordinator. Discuss what you can do to improve your performance.

5. List some things you can do to help shape your future career.

REVIEW

Word Power

On a separate sheet of paper, match each definition with the correct term. All definitions will be used, and a definition will be used only once.

6. A job considered to be permanent; may last several years
7. Meet the preliminary requirements, as for a job or position
8. All of the jobs that one holds during the course of a working lifetime
9. Outdated; no longer in use
10. Setting goals and working toward them
11. Application of scientific knowledge to practical uses
12. Advancement to a higher-level job or position

a. obsolete
b. promotion
c. qualify
d. self-direction
e. stable job
f. technology
g. work history

Think Critically

13. Reread the case study about Rick's work history. Discuss why you think he has not progressed toward a stable job. What would you recommend that he do next?
14. If you are currently employed, do you think that your present job might develop into a stable job? Why or why not?
15. Do you think that hard work and quality effort pay off? Or is this just a myth that parents, teachers, and employers want you to believe?
16. Some young people not enrolled in a work experience program leave after school and go to a job. They often work from 3:30 or 4:00 in the afternoon to 10:30 or 11:00 at night. On weekends, they may put in up to 16 additional hours. Do you think that some teenagers are trying to work too much while attending high school? Share any relevant personal experiences that you may have had.
17. Several years ago, IBM Corporation began to require high school transcripts from individuals applying for entry-level jobs. This was done, in part, to send a message to students that high school performance is important. This practice has now expanded to many other companies. What is your opinion regarding this requirement?
18. Suppose you have two job offers, A and B. The jobs have different hourly wages and a different number of hours worked per week. Describe how you would determine which job pays more per week.

CHAPTER 3

LOOKING FOR A JOB

LESSONS

3.1 *Preparing to Look for a Job*

3.2 *Finding Job Leads*

PREVIEW

In this chapter and Chapters 4 and 5, you will learn how to find a job. If you do not have a job, you will be able to use the information right away. If you are working now, the material will help you in your next job search.

THOUGHTS ON WORK

"People forget how fast you did a job, but they remember how well you did it."

Howard Newton

TAKING ACTION
LOOKING FOR WORK

Jonita Johnson was anxious to start working and earning some money. She went to Mr. Sandoval, her work experience coordinator, to ask him what she needed to do to be ready to look for a job.

"First, you'll need to be very clear on what you want from a job," Mr. Sandoval said.

"I know I want to be a hair stylist eventually, but I don't have the qualifications to be a stylist now," Jonita said. "The classes I'm taking in school will get me ready for the state licensing exam. Also, I'll need to earn some money to help out at home."

"O.K. You just said two things. First, you are looking for a job in a beauty salon that is paid. Second, this position should help you gain valuable experience so you can get a good job once you pass the state licensing exam. Do you know anyone who works in a hair salon?" he asked.

"Well, one of my teachers mentioned that she knew someone who owned her own shop. She might be hiring," she replied.

"That's great!" Mr. Sandoval said. "Do you think your teacher will put in a good word for you?"

"I think so. My grades are good in her class and she likes my work."

"Write down all the information your teacher can give you about this job lead. Next, look in the newspaper for job openings. The Sunday paper usually has the most help-wanted ads. Cut out the ads that sound promising, and follow up on all the job leads," Mr. Sandoval instructed.

"I have no idea how I'm going to keep all that information straight, Mr. Sandoval," she said.

"Let me show you how job-lead cards can help."

SUCCESS TIP

Ask your friends, family, and teachers for job leads.

THINK CRITICALLY

1. What was the first step to finding a job that Mr. Sandoval discussed?
2. In your chosen field, do you know anyone who might give you a job lead?

LESSON 3.1

PREPARING TO LOOK FOR A JOB

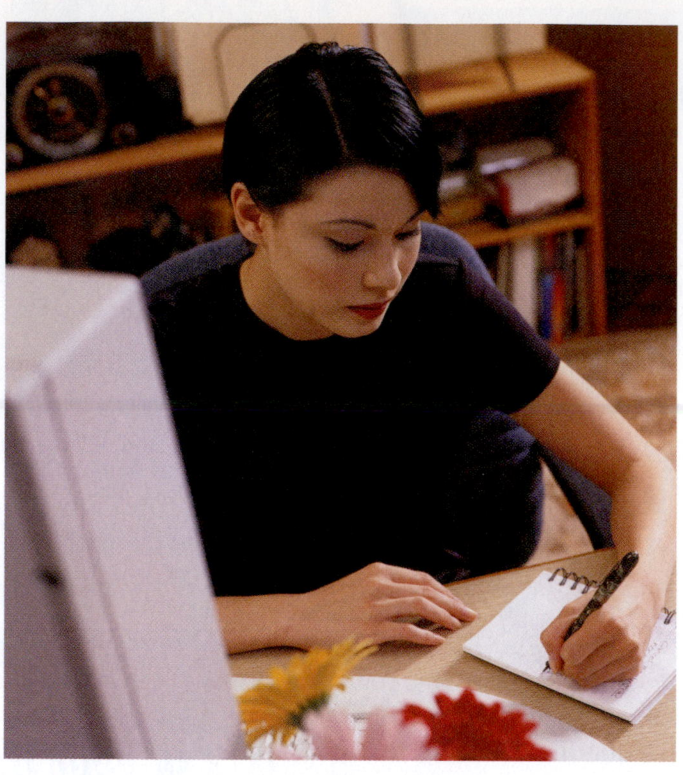

OBJECTIVES

- DESCRIBE THE IMPORTANCE OF CLARIFYING JOB GOALS BEFORE LOOKING FOR EMPLOYMENT
- EXPLAIN HOW TO GET A SOCIAL SECURITY NUMBER AND WORK PERMIT

JOB GOALS

Students enrolled in work experience education programs get jobs in several ways. In cooperative vocational education, the coordinator plays a major role. The coordinator usually "sets up" training stations in the community and interviews and selects qualified students for admission to the program. The coordinator then takes into account students' interests, aptitudes, and job goals. These are matched with suitable jobs. It is up to the student, however, to interview with the employer and get the job.

In work-study programs, a student may get a job before or after entering the program. Some students will already have a job and ask to continue it for school credit. This may be done as long as the coordinator approves the training station. Students who do not have jobs when they enroll in a work-study program will need to find one.

Thinking About Job Goals

Why do you want a job? Be prepared to answer this question. You will be hearing it often. Your work experience coordinator will certainly ask it. The coordinator wants to help you find a job that suits your interests and abilities. By getting to know you better, your coordinator can help you get a job you will enjoy. Counselors, placement officers, and others you approach for job leads will ask you about your job goals. And, of course, an interviewer will probably ask the question during a job interview.

Thinking about your job goals will help you, too. What you want out of a job will influence how and where you look for one. Since you are now enrolled in a work experience program, you have probably already done some thinking about your goals.

CAREER DECISIONS

You learn about a job opening for a part-time custodian at the shopping mall. The hours are good and the pay is decent for a beginning job. You cannot decide whether to apply. You really do not want to empty wastebaskets and mop floors. You wonder how you will feel if your friends see you working.

WHAT WOULD YOU DO?

Benefits of Work Experience

Reviewing the benefits of work experience education covered in Chapter 1 can help you clarify your job goals. If you recall, these are:

- Learning occupational skills
- Developing employability skills
- Establishing a work record
- Earning while you learn
- Discovering career interests and goals
- Recognizing the relationship between education and work
- Remaining employed after graduation

You may want to rank the benefits in order of their importance to you. Doing this can help you focus on your most important goals.

It was not difficult for Rachel to decide what she wanted out of a job. She became interested in interior design after taking courses in textiles and home furnishings and equipment. She learned about a co-op position at a large furniture store in the community that has an interior design department. She interviewed for the job and was hired. Rachel loves what she is doing. She hopes that the company will hire her permanently after she graduates. Can you name Rachel's job goals?

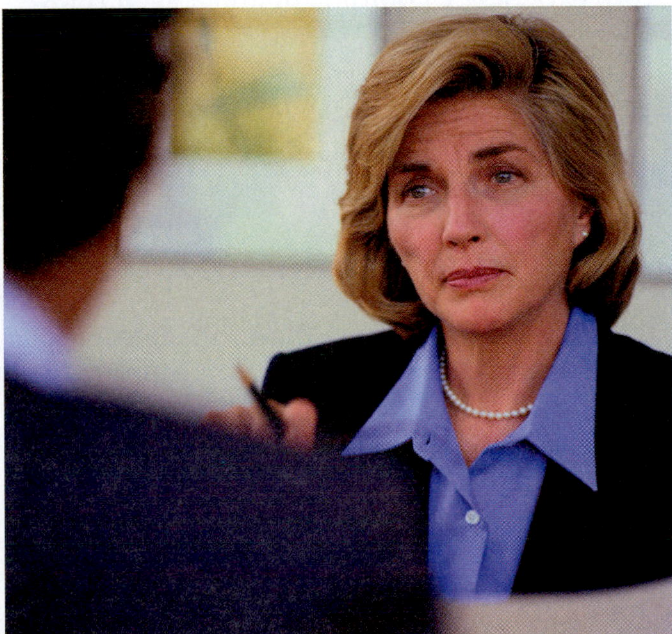

You will be asked why you want a particular job many times during your job search. Be prepared with a good answer.

WORKFORCE TRENDS

Life expectancy is projected to rise from 76 years in 1995 to 82 years in 2050. Increased life expectancy will probably have little direct effect on the composition of the workforce. However, the impacts on families, jobs, and the marketplace, such as demand for medical services, will likely be significant.

GETTING READY

Federal law requires every person regardless of age to have a Social Security number to be claimed as a dependent on Tax Form 1040. If you do not have a Social Security number, you should get one before you start a job search. You may also need to get a work permit.

Social Security Number

Social Security is a national program of social insurance. Your employer will withhold money from your paycheck for this. The money will go to the Social Security system. When you retire, you will receive income payments from Social Security. You will learn more about Social Security in Chapter 27.

In order for the government to keep a record of your earnings, you will need a Social Security number. The number will remain with you for life. No one else has the same number. An employer will ask for your number when you apply for a job or start work. Your Social Security number may have other uses, too. For example, in some states, your driver's license identification number is the same as your Social Security number.

You can apply for a number at any Social Security office. You can also download an application form from the Web at http://www.ssa.gov. You must fill out the application form and provide proof of your date of birth, identity, and U.S. citizenship. You will receive a Social Security card (see the example in Figure 3-1) about two to four weeks after you apply.

YOU'RE A WHAT? CURATOR

If you have ever visited a natural history museum or toured a historical site, you have probably viewed the work of a *curator*. Curators oversee collections in museums, zoos, aquariums, botanical gardens, nature centers, and historical sites. Most curators specialize in a particular field such as botany, art, or history. Those working in large institutions may further specialize in one area such as birds, fishes, or insects.

Curators acquire items through purchase or gifts and plan and prepare exhibits. Some write grant proposals or engage in fund-raising to support projects. Some maintain collections, others do research, and others perform administrative tasks. In small institutions, one curator may be responsible for many tasks. Computer technology and the Internet are increasingly used to catalog and organize collections and make information available to the public. ■

Figure 3-1 ***Everyone in the workforce must have a Social Security card. Be sure to apply for one if you do not have yours.***

Courtesy of Social Security Administration

Work Permit

At one time, employers were free to hire workers of any age for any type of job. It was not uncommon for young children to work long days in factories, mills, and mines.

Various federal and state laws now protect the health and safety of **minors**, or people who have not reached the full legal age. Such laws regulate working conditions and working hours of students under the age of 16 or 18. For instance, the Fair Labor Standards Act states that a person under the age of 16 may not be employed during school hours. Some states have stricter laws than others regarding child labor.

A **work permit**, however, is a form issued by school officials that gives a student legal permission to work during school hours as part of a work experience education program. A work permit restricts the number of hours worked and the types of jobs a student can perform. School officials issue work permits for students under a certain age. In some states, the age is 16. In other states, it is 18.

Besides a work permit, your state or school district may require other kinds of approval before you can work. Ask your school counselor or work experience coordinator about such rules.

LESSON 3.1 REVIEW

1. **Sarah has a part-time job. She is starting a work experience program. How can she keep her job and get school credit?**
2. **Why is it important to clarify your job goals before beginning the job search?**
3. **Why must you get a Social Security number before you start work?**

LESSON 3.2
FINDING JOB LEADS

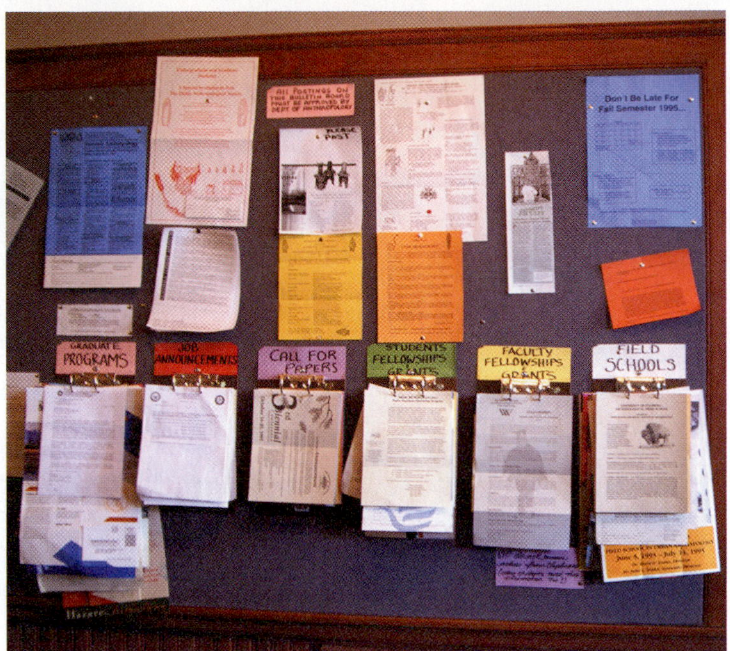

OBJECTIVES

- *IDENTIFY DIFFERENT SOURCES OF JOB LEADS*
- *ILLUSTRATE HOW TO PREPARE A JOB-LEAD CARD*

SOURCES OF JOB LEADS

It was the first day of the new school year. Sally was on the way to her work experience education class. "I wonder what job they will have for me," thought Sally.

The bell rang and students turned their attention to Mr. Amed, the teacher-coordinator. He took attendance and then began to explain about work experience education.

"A requirement of this program," he explained, "is that each of you must have a job. Some of you already have jobs. For the rest of you, your first 'job' will be to get a job. I do not have any jobs to assign."

Sally was somewhat surprised. She raised her hand to ask some questions. "Mr. Amed, I do not know where to get a job," she said. "Where do I look for jobs? And if I find one, what do I have to do to apply for it?"

"Do not worry," said Mr. Amed. "I will help you learn about sources of job leads and how to apply for a job."

If you do not have a job yet either, you will need to plan how to get one. At this point in your life, you will probably apply for an entry-level job. An **entry-level job** requires little or no experience. The following sources of job leads are those through which you are most likely to find a job.

Family and Friends

Start your job search by making a list of your relatives, neighbors, and friends. Include your working friends. They may know of job leads from their own job searches. Do not forget places where you and your family do business. You may want to have a family member review your final list.

Do not hesitate to ask family or friends for help. However, do not expect them to find a job for you. Getting a job lead is the most you should hope for. It will be up to you to pursue the lead.

> **ETHICAL DECISIONS**
>
> A schoolmate approaches you and says he heard you were looking for a job. He has a buddy who needs some people to deliver packages on weekends. The work is easy. You simply ride the bus around town and drop off packages at various places of business. The pay is $15 per hour in cash. You are told not to ask questions or to discuss the job with other people. You are concerned about taking the job because it sounds "fishy."
>
> **WHAT WOULD YOU DO?**

COMMUNICATION AT WORK

ASKING FOR JOB LEADS

By current estimates, the average American will change jobs at least seven times in his or her career. Starting or changing jobs is not easy. However, the process can be made easier if you get job leads. How can you gather job leads effectively?

Be clear about what you want. Most people want to help you, especially close friends and family members. But they can only help if they know exactly what you want. Make sure you can communicate your work history and career goals.

Don't be afraid to ask for what you want. Asking for job leads can be awkward, especially the first time. Don't get discouraged. The person you are asking probably had the same feelings you are experiencing.

Be polite and grateful for information. Have you ever heard the expression "information is power"? When you ask for job leads, you are asking someone for important information. The more polite you are, the more information you may receive, and that may help you get a good job!

In-school Sources

Three good sources of job leads may be available within your school. One is your cooperative vocational education or work experience coordinator. He or she is probably already involved in helping you. Do not sit back and wait for the coordinator to find you a job.

Most schools also have a guidance office or guidance counselor. It is common for local employers to contact counselors when looking for workers. The counselor will usually keep a list of job openings or post them on a bulletin board. Tell the counselor that you are looking for a job and ask to see any information available about job openings.

A third source is job placement offices or career centers. Interested students generally register with the office. They may receive job counseling and other services. Job counselors help to match up students with job openings and make referrals for interviews. **Referrals** are given to direct a student to employers who are hiring.

Students enrolled in postsecondary technical schools and community colleges usually have the same types of in-school assistance available as do secondary school students. In community pre-employment training projects for out-of-school youth and unemployed adults, a job placement specialist is often available.

Newspaper Classified Ads

When employers have jobs to fill, they often advertise them in the newspaper. Most newspapers have a section that includes help-wanted ads. Four common kinds of ads are shown in Figure 3-2, on the next page.

The first kind is an *open ad*. It tells about the job requirements, identifies the employer, and tells how to apply. This is the best type of ad.

The second kind is the *blind ad*. The name, address, and phone number of the employer are not shown. Employers do this to keep from being bombarded with phone calls. It also allows them to screen applications carefully. Only qualified applicants are then invited for an interview.

A *catch-type ad* is the third kind. It tends to promise good pay and downplay the qualifications needed for the job. The "catch" is that the job is usually for door-to-door salespeople or similar sales jobs.

The last kind of ad is the *agency spot ad*. Note that the ad omits the name of the employer. It is used by private employment agencies to advertise jobs available only through the agency.

PART-TIME CLERK TYPIST
Approximately 20 hours per week, including some evenings and Saturdays. Experience with keying, filing, telephone reception, and work with public desirable. Must be dependable and able to work regular hours. $7.50 per hour. Applications accepted until Tuesday, Jan. 15, 20--, at 5 p.m. to Mary Campbell, Acton Public Library, 405 W. Main, Acton, MA 01718-1416, 555-0135.

OPEN AD

CLERICAL
Local manufacturer has immediate part-time clerical position open. Involves heavy computer entry. 4 hours a day. 5 days a week. Prefer afternoons.
Write: CLERICAL
P.O. Box 75A, Union Station,
New York, NY 10112-1105

BLIND AD

EARN
$200 TO $600
Write for details.
P.O. Box 113
Sunnyvale, CA 94085-2459

CATCH-TYPE AD

Drafter
$26,000 & Up
Fee Paid
At least 2 years' experience. CAD skills required. Call us or bring in your resume to compare your experience with our company requirements.
JOLEN
EMPLOYMENT AGENCY
17 Plaza Offices, P.O. Box 531
Palestine, TX 75801-2837
555-0192

AGENCY SPOT AD

Figure 3-2 Four common types of help-wanted ads

Job Service

Every state has a system of public employment offices usually called the **Job Service**. These offices, which are located around the state, provide free services such as job counseling and training, help with resumes, and job listings. The primary purpose of the Job Service is to help workers who have lost jobs or been laid off find jobs. Services are also provided to first-time job seekers, but preference is usually given to previously employed workers.

Some offices have a youth counselor who works mainly with young people. Job Service counselors often cooperate closely with local high school work experience programs and community job training projects.

To use the Job Service, you must fill out an application. A counselor will interview you to find out your interests and qualifications. You might be asked to take an interest inventory or aptitude test. If a job is available, the counselor will arrange an interview for you.

Private Employment Agencies

These are businesses that find people jobs for a fee. The **fee** is a sum of money charged by a private employment agency for helping someone find a job, and it is paid by either the employer or the employee. If you use a private employment agency, be sure that you understand the financial arrangements *before* signing a contract or accepting an interview.

Private agencies do not generally deal with clients under 18 and those who are looking for part-time, entry-level jobs. So do not be discouraged if you are turned down by a private agency.

Direct Employer Contact

Many people find jobs by talking directly to employers. A help-wanted sign posted in a business is the oldest method of announcing a job opening. If you see such a sign, ask the employer for an application.

Employers often have unadvertised job openings. Figure 3-3 lists the 25 leading occupations for workers aged 16–24. Study this list to get an idea of the types of employers that hire a number of young workers. You might then use the Yellow Pages to make a list of companies to contact.

Another means of direct employer contact is to visit a company employment office. Go dressed as you would for an interview. Be prepared to fill out an employment application form. Check bulletin boards outside the personnel office, too. Available jobs are often listed there. Some companies also have a separate telephone number that provides prerecorded messages about openings.

OCCUPATION

1. Cashiers
2. Cooks, except short-order
3. Stock handlers and baggers
4. Waiters and waitresses
5. Janitors and cleaners
6. Secretaries
7. Laborers, except construction
8. Waiters' and waitresses' assistants
9. Sales workers, apparel
10. Receptionists
11. Child-care workers, except private household
12. Food counter, fountain, and related occupations
13. Nursing aides, orderlies, and attendants
14. Supervisors and proprietors, sales occupations
15. Child-care workers, private household
16. Truck drivers, light
17. Bank tellers
18. Construction laborers
19. Garage and service station related occupations
20. Farm workers
21. Carpenters
22. Bookkeepers and accounting and auditing clerks
23. General office clerks
24. Groundskeepers and gardeners, except farmers
25. Computer operators

***Figure 3-3* The 25 leading occupations for workers aged 16–24**

Source: Occupational Outlook Quarterly

Internet

The Internet has changed the way that most public and private institutions announce job vacancies. For example, school guidance offices and career centers often list job leads on a web page. Many newspapers, particularly those in large cities, provide online listings of job vacancies. All Job Service offices are linked through the Internet to a national database of jobs entitled "America's Job Bank." Private employment agencies typically have a web site in which their services are explained to job seekers. Finally, thousands of public and private employers list job opportunities online. Many of these also provide online job application forms and accept electronic resumes.

In addition to listing job vacancies at individual companies and institutions, the Internet has a number of sites devoted entirely or in part to jobs and job seeking. Web portals, or sites providing a wide range of services, are familiar to many Internet users. Portals like Excite, Lycos, MSN.com, and Yahoo! organize content related to dozens of popular categories, one of which is often titled "Careers," "Job Hunt," "Job Search," or something similar. Clicking on a category provides potential access to dozens of other sites. Be aware, however, that most jobs listed are for adults seeking permanent employment.

KEEPING TRACK OF JOB LEADS

"Hey, Steve," said Kevin. "I got my first job lead yesterday. I was eating lunch when I noticed the manager putting up a sign. It was for a part-time kitchen helper. So I wrote the information down."

"Great! What did the sign say?" asked Steve.

"Let me see," answered Kevin. "I have the information here someplace."

Kevin continued to search his backpack for the scrap of paper on which he took notes. Finally he said, "Darn, I must have lost it. Oh well, I will go back this weekend and get the information again."

Kevin is off to a shaky start in his search for a job. He was alert to notice the sign and to write down the information. Kevin was careless, though, in misplacing his notes. He also showed poor judgment in not going back or calling right away. When he returned on the weekend, he found the job was filled.

Preparing Job-lead Cards

Whenever you learn about a job lead, make up a job-lead card. A **job-lead card** is a card on which to record information and notes about a job lead. An example is shown in Figure 3-4. A 5- by 8-inch card works best because it gives you enough room to record information and make notes. The card has two parts.

On the "Job Lead" part (Side 1), record all important information about the job. If you have a newspaper help-wanted ad, tape it onto the card. Write down the source, date, type of position, and person to contact. Record the company name, address, phone number, and URL, if the organization has one.

Figure 3-4 Sample job-lead card

JOB LEAD
Source: *Daily Gazette*
Date: *1/20/--*
Type of Position: *Packing Clerk*
Person to Contact: *Steve*
Company Name:
Address: *Lindbergh & Olive*
Phone Number: *555-0151*
URL:

PACKING CLERKS
PART-TIME JOB OPENINGS
Please: These are not full-time jobs. We have peak business seasons in Jan., Feb., Apr., Oct. Hours will vary from 0 to 40 a week. Also may have late afternoon (3 p.m.–7 p.m.) shift available. Job requires standing & using manual dexterity while preparing and packing women's clothing, shoes, and gifts for UPS shipment. Perfect job for stay-at-home moms or dads or students. Again—not a full-time job! Near Lindbergh & Olive. No smoking. $7.30 per hour. All applicants must pass a written test.
CALL STEVE, 555-0151

ACTION TAKEN
Call Made To: *Steve (555-0151)*
Date: *1/21/--*
Contact Made With:
Date:
Results: *Asked to come in and fill out job application and take a written test.*
Date, Time, and Place of Appointment: *1/23/--, 9:30 a.m. Mid-West Packaging Inc. Use main entrance.*
Follow-up: *After test, call back (ask for Steve) on 1/28/-- for possible interview.*

On the "Action Taken" part (Side 2), record what you did to follow up the job lead. Write down the date when you contacted the employer and the name of the person with whom you talked. Also write down the results of the contact. If you get an appointment, record the date, time, and place. If you need directions, be sure to ask. Write the directions on the back of the card. Any follow-up you will do after your appointment should also be noted.

Benefits of Job-lead Cards

What are some benefits of using job-lead cards? They keep you from forgetting important information. They save you time, too. By being organized, you can get more results from the time you spend. Can you name other benefits?

Following Through

You read earlier how Kevin failed to act on a job lead. His big mistake was in not talking to the manager when he saw her posting a help-wanted sign. Had he done so, he might have gotten the job. Most employers want to fill job openings as quickly as they can.

You face stiff competition for jobs. Do not hold back. As soon as you learn about a job lead, follow through with quick action. The early applicant usually gets the job. If you do not get the job immediately, call or go back a few days later. Let the employer know that you are really interested in the job.

Motivation and persistence, so important in finding a job, are also qualities that make you a good employee. Employers recognize this. Demonstrating motivation and persistence in pursuing a job lead increases your chance of being rewarded with a job offer.

LESSON 3.2 REVIEW

1. Andrea says she would "feel funny" asking friends and family for job leads. Do you agree with her? Why or why not?
2. Your school may have three sources of job leads. Name them.
3. Name four common types of newspaper help-wanted ads.
4. What are the main differences between a public and a private employment agency?
5. Name the oldest method used to announce job openings.
6. Describe a job-lead card.
7. Why should you follow through with quick action on a job lead?

HIGH-GROWTH OCCUPATIONS FOR THE 21st CENTURY

Computer Programmers

Computer programmers write, test, and maintain the programs (software) that computers must follow to perform their functions. Programs vary widely depending upon the type of information to be accessed or generated. For example, the instructions involved in updating financial records are very different from those required by flight simulators used to train airline pilots. Although simple programs can be written in a few hours, programs that use complex math formulas may require more than a year of work. In most cases, several programmers work together as a team under a senior programmer's supervision.

Programmers write specific programs by breaking down each step into a logical series of instructions the computer can follow. They then code these instructions in a standard programming language, such as COBOL, Java, C++, or Visual Basic. Programmers usually know more than one programming language. In practice, programmers are often referred to by the language they know, such as Java programmers, or the type of function they perform, such as database programmers.

Computer programmers often are grouped into two broad types: applications programmers and systems programmers. *Applications programmers* usually focus on business, engineering, or science. They write software to handle a specific job, like tracking inventory, within an organization. They may also revise packaged software (the mass-produced software most people buy). *Systems programmers* maintain and control computer systems software, such as operating systems, networked systems, and database systems.

In software development companies, programmers may work directly with experts from various fields to create software ranging from games and educational software to programs for desktop publishing, financial planning, and spreadsheets. Much of this type of programming is in the preparation of packaged software, which constitutes one of the most rapidly growing segments of the computer services industry.

Computer programmers develop a wide variety of software—from games to accounting programs.

FOCUS ON THE WORKPLACE

TEMPORARY WORK

One of the fastest growing industries in America is the temporary services industry. Temporary services like Kelly Services and Manpower provide lists of available workers to employers who need short-term help.

Temporary workers (temps) are hired to fill in when a permanent employee quits, gets sick, or goes on vacation. Some are hired to help out when a special project requires extra people for a short time. The most common temporary jobs are for secretaries, receptionists, and bookkeepers.

Who are these temporary workers? There are five general categories.

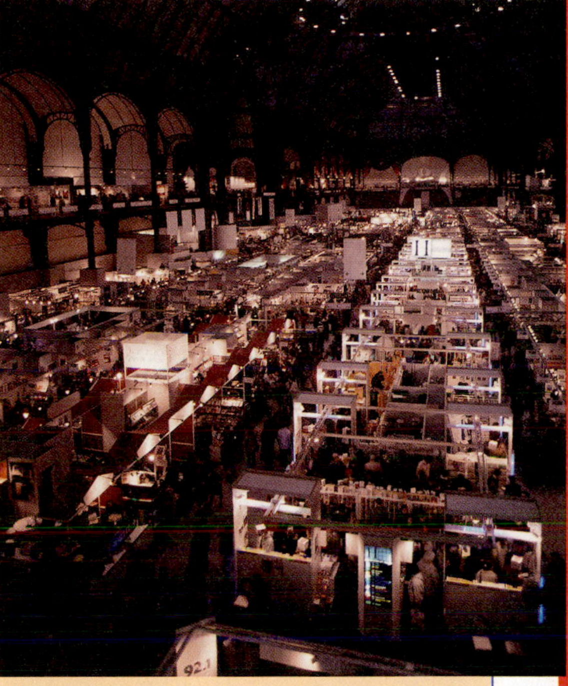

Conventions and trade shows are opportunities for many temporary jobs.

- ***Rusty Skills.*** Some people have not worked for a while and are uncertain of their abilities. "Temping" gives them a chance to brush up on their skills before looking for a permanent job.
- ***Uncertain Goals.*** Some people are not sure what type of work they want to do. Temping allows them to sample different jobs before deciding.
- ***Between Jobs.*** It can take time for new high school or college graduates to find the right position. Temping is a way to finance a job hunt so they don't have to accept the first offer.
- ***Supporting Another Occupation.*** Some people who work as writers, artists, or performers do not have permanent jobs. They do temp work to pay the bills while they pursue their preferred line of work.
- ***Extra Money.*** Students working their way through college are a major source of temps. So are retirees looking for additional income.

A temporary job may be as short as a day or as long as a year. The average length is one to two weeks. At some point in your life, a temporary job may meet your needs.

1. What are some temporary agencies in your area?
2. Explain why you would most likely try temping.

CHAPTER 3

Chapter in Brief

Lesson 3.1 *Preparing to Look for a Job*

A. What you want out of a job will influence how and where you look for it. Therefore, think about your job goals before beginning the job search. Do this by reviewing the seven benefits of work experience education.

B. Apply for a Social Security number as soon as possible. An employer will ask for your number when you apply for a job or start work. In some states, you may also need to get a work permit.

Lesson 3.2 *Finding Job Leads*

A. To be enrolled in cooperative vocational education or work-study, you must have a job. If you do not already have one, your first "job" will be to get a job.

B. The most common sources of entry-level jobs are (a) family and friends, (b) in-school sources, (c) newspaper classified ads, (d) Job Service, (e) private employment agencies, (f) direct employer contact, and (g) the Internet.

C. Whenever you learn about a job lead, make up a job-lead card. It will help you remember important information, save you time, and help you get more positive results.

D. After recording all important information about a job lead, follow through with quick action. Most employers want to fill job openings as soon as possible.

Activities

1. Find out your state's requirements on student employment during school hours. If a work permit or other type of approval is required, take the necessary steps to complete the approval process.
2. Get the help-wanted section of a Sunday newspaper that serves your geographic area. Cut out examples of the four types of ads described earlier in the chapter. Tape the examples onto a sheet of paper and label each type of ad. Then give the paper to your instructor. When you get your paper back, discuss your ads with the class.
3. Perhaps your instructor can arrange to make copies of a job-lead card. Or someone in the class might volunteer to make a sample. Duplicate enough so that each person has at least ten. Divide the printing cost among class members.
4. Use the Internet to conduct the following activities: (a) Search the classified section of a local or regional newspaper for job openings, (b) identify employers in your area having web pages and check to see if they have

REVIEW

information on employment opportunities, and (c) locate America's Job Bank on the Web at http://www.ajb.dni.us and experiment with conducting a job search using both the "Keyword" and the "Occupation" search methods.

5. The Social Security Administration has a web site entitled "YouthlinK." Locate the YouthlinK site at http://www.ssa.gov/kids and click on the "Hot Questions for Cool Teens" link. Here you will find a variety of information explaining Social Security. You can also download a Social Security application form if needed.

Word Power

On a separate sheet of paper, match each definition with the correct term. All definitions will be used, and a definition will be used only once.

6. A sum of money charged by a private employment agency for helping someone find a job
7. People who have not reached the full legal age
8. A form issued by school officials that gives a student legal permission to work during school hours as part of a work experience education program
9. A beginning job that requires little or no previous job knowledge or experience
10. Direct students to employers who are hiring
11. A state system of public employment offices that helps unemployed people find jobs
12. A card on which to record information and notes about a job lead

a. entry-level job
b. fee
c. job-lead card
d. Job Service
e. minors
f. referrals
g. work permit

Think Critically

13. What role does the teacher-coordinator play in helping students find jobs in work experience education programs?
14. Why have state and federal laws been passed restricting the hours of employment and regulating the working conditions of minors?
15. Seven major sources of job leads are discussed in this chapter. Can you think of other sources in your city or community that have not been mentioned?
16. The ease or difficulty of finding a job may be influenced by where you live, for example, whether you live in a city or rural area. What other environmental, economic, or occupational factors influence job availability?

CHAPTER 4

APPLYING FOR A JOB

LESSONS

4.1 *Data Sheets and Job Applications*

4.2 *Writing a Resume*

4.3 *Contacting Employers*

PREVIEW

Finding job leads may seem to take a long time. It does indeed take a great deal of time to contact family and friends, search the newspaper help-wanted ads, and identify other leads. Once you find a good job lead, however, things can speed up very quickly.

THOUGHTS ON WORK

"Genius is one percent inspiration and ninety-nine percent perspiration."

Thomas A. Edison

TAKING ACTION

WORK EXPERIENCE EDUCATION

Ricardo learned from his Uncle Geraldo about a bowling buddy who was expanding his hardware store. Uncle Geraldo thought his friend might be hiring some new employees and suggested Ricardo should call him.

The next day Ricardo called Mr. Tamaka at the hardware store. He explained that he was looking for a job and that his uncle had told him to call. Mr. Tamaka said that he had already received several inquiries about the job.

"However," he went on to say, "I would be happy to have you fill out a job application form. Why not stop by and see me after school tomorrow?"

"Thank you very much," said Ricardo. "I will be there at four o'clock tomorrow afternoon."

Ricardo went to see Mr. Tamaka the next day after school. He made sure that he was neatly dressed. He went with notes he had prepared about his work history. He asked for the job application and filled it out.

Donna is also on the trail of a hot job lead. She read an ad in the newspaper for a Hair Stylist/Shampoo Assistant. "Experience helpful but not necessary," the ad said. "Full training available. Send a resume to The Hair Performers, 638 North Walnut St., Muncie, IN 47308-9372."

"This sounds like what I am looking for," Donna told her family. "I'd better get a letter of application keyed and put my resume in the mail at once."

Ricardo and Donna were ready to take quick action on job leads. Ricardo already had a personal data sheet prepared to assist him in filling out a job application form. Likewise, Donna had a stack of resumes (pronounced *REZ-oo-mays*) ready and waiting. She also knew how to write a letter of application. Ricardo and Donna have learned some valuable skills needed to apply for a job. In this chapter, you will learn these skills, too.

SUCCESS TIP

Follow up on job leads quickly by having the information you need.

THINK CRITICALLY

1. What were some good steps that Ricardo took in pursuing the hardware store job?
2. Why did Donna want to get her letter of application and resume in the mail quickly?

LESSON 4.1

DATA SHEETS AND JOB APPLICATIONS

- PREPARE A PERSONAL DATA SHEET
- COMPLETE A JOB APPLICATION FORM

PERSONAL DATA SHEET

Let us say that you are in Ricardo's shoes and have to fill out a job application form tomorrow. Will you be prepared? Can you, for example, remember the name, address, and telephone number of each employer for whom you have worked? Do you know your high school class rank and grade point average (GPA)? How about **references**? Will you be prepared to list the names of individuals who are qualified to provide information about you to a potential employer?

Most employers require job seekers to fill out an application form. Some applications ask for very brief information. Others, however, may be very detailed. To be ready, you need to prepare a personal data sheet. A **personal data sheet** is a summary of personal, educational, and occupational information. You will not give it directly to an employer. You will take it with you and use it to fill out job application forms. You will also use it to prepare a resume.

A personal data sheet contains four primary types of information. A sample data sheet is shown in Figures 4-1A and 4-1B. You can add to or take out parts to meet your own needs.

A. Identification. Included in this part is personal identification information. In-school and extracurricular activities, interests, awards received, and the like are also recorded. The intent here is to provide information that explains who and what type of person you are.

B. Educational Background. Record data on your high school and any colleges, technical schools, and the like you have attended. Repeat the basic information for each school. Employers will be interested in what type of student you are.

C. Employment History. Information about all previous paid employment is included here. Start with present or most recent employment. Add employers as necessary.

PERSONAL DECISIONS

You see an ad in the newspaper for a computer operator. The job is exactly what you are looking for. However, the ad states that "prior work experience is required." You have not had any prior employment as a computer operator, but you have been operating your own computer for five years. You are confident that you can do the job. Should you ignore the stated requirement and apply for the job?

WHAT WOULD YOU DO?

PERSONAL DATA SHEET

IDENTIFICATION

Name ______________________ Soc. Sec. # ____________

Address ______________________

Telephone (   ) ______________________

E-mail Address ______________________

Hobbies/Interests ______________________

Honors/Awards/Offices ______________________

Sports/Activities ______________________

Other ______________________

EDUCATIONAL BACKGROUND

School Name and Address	Dates Attended From:	To:
High School:		
Course of Study ____________ Rank ____________		GPA ____________
Favorite Subject(s) ____________		
Other (College, Trade, Business, or Correspondence School):	From:	To:
Course of Study ____________ Rank ____________		GPA ____________
Favorite Subject(s) ____________		
Other (College, Trade, Business, or Correspondence School):	From:	To:
Course of Study ____________ Rank ____________		GPA ____________
Favorite Subject(s) ____________		

Figure 4-1A ***Follow this general outline when you prepare a personal data sheet. Use it to fill out a job application form and create a resume. (The sample data sheet continues on the next page.)***

D. References. List here the names of persons who can provide information about your personal, school, and employment background. Examples include teachers, coaches, club advisors, previous employers, and clergy. Get their permission first.

EMPLOYMENT HISTORY

(Start with present or most recent employer.)

1. Company ______________________ Telephone ( ) ______________
   Address ______________________
   Employed from Mo. _____ Yr. _____ /to Mo. _____ Yr. _____ Supervisor ____________
   Position/Title ______________________
   Last Wage __________ Reason for Leaving ______________________

2. Company ______________________ Telephone ( ) ______________
   Address ______________________
   Employed from Mo. _____ Yr. _____ /to Mo. _____ Yr. _____ Supervisor ____________
   Position/Title ______________________
   Last Wage __________ Reason for Leaving ______________________

3. Company ______________________ Telephone ( ) ______________
   Address ______________________
   Employed from Mo. _____ Yr. _____ /to Mo. _____ Yr. _____ Supervisor ____________
   Position/Title ______________________
   Last Wage __________ Reason for Leaving ______________________

REFERENCES

1. Name ______________________ Title ______________
   Address ______________________
   Relationship ______________________ Telephone ( ) ______________

2. Name ______________________ Title ______________
   Address ______________________
   Relationship ______________________ Telephone ( ) ______________

3. Name ______________________ Title ______________
   Address ______________________
   Relationship ______________________ Telephone ( ) ______________

Figure 4-1B ***Personal data sheet (continued)***

JOB APPLICATION FORM

When employers have jobs to fill, they usually ask interested people to fill out a job application form. A **job application form** is a form used by employers to collect personal, educational, and occupational information from a job applicant. The information provided on the form helps employers to sort out the best-qualified persons for the job. After screening the application forms, the employer invites a few people for an interview.

If you have done a personal data sheet, you will have taken a big step toward filling out a job application form. You will be able to copy facts and information from the data sheet directly onto the job application form. Take your personal data sheet with you each time you contact an employer or employment office.

The type of job application form used will differ from company to company. A typical form is shown in Figure 4-2 on the next page. Follow these tips in filling out a job application form.

- Before you begin to fill out the form, read it over carefully. Study the instructions so you will know what information to provide. Note which parts are "for employer use only."
- You may receive an application form through the mail or have a chance to fill it out on your own and return it later. If your keying is fair to poor, print your answers in black ink. You may want to get an erasable ballpoint pen. This will allow you to correct mistakes easily. Be as neat as possible.
- You will probably be asked to print the information. It is a good idea to print even if the form does not say to. Be sure to sign your name in those places that ask for your signature. Use your correct name, not a nickname.
- Answer all questions on the form. If a question does not apply to you, put "NA" for "not applicable." Do not leave a blank space; the employer might think you forgot to answer the question.
- Answer all questions honestly. Giving false information can catch up with you later. If you do not have the information or do not know the answer, write in "unknown."
- List the specific position or job for which you are applying. Do not write "anything" in the space. You may be willing to accept any job; however, you want to convey that you are interested in and qualified for a certain job.
- Misspelled words give a poor impression of your ability. Take a small pocket or electronic dictionary with you and use it.
- You may be asked to name the "wages or salary expected." It is best to discuss salary in a personal interview with the employer. So write "open" in the space provided.
- In the employment history part, you may be asked to give the reason for leaving a previous job. Do not put down anything that criticizes a past employer or shows that you were not an acceptable employee. Examples of appropriate reasons for leaving a job are "returned to school," left for a better job," and "job terminated."
- After you have filled out the form, check it carefully before mailing it or handing it in.

What happens after you submit the job application form? Do you wait to hear from the employer? Some employers collect job applications for a position that begins on a certain date. Other employers, who may have no jobs available at the moment, collect applications for future use. Make sure you find out what to do next. Write the information down on the job-lead card that you are using.

LESSON 4.1 REVIEW

1. What are the two main uses for a personal data sheet?
2. What kinds of people might you give as job references?
3. Why do employers use job application forms? Give an example.
4. If a question on a job application form does not apply to you, how should you answer it?

APPLICATION FOR EMPLOYMENT

(PRE-EMPLOYMENT QUESTIONNAIRE) (AN EQUAL OPPPORTUNITY EMPLOYER)

PERSONAL INFORMATION

DATE April 15, 20--

NAME Morales Ronald R.

SOCIAL SECURITY NUMBER 351-44-5751

PRESENT ADDRESS 6428 Valley Rd. Payne Ohio 45880-1482

PERMANENT ADDRESS same

PHONE NO. 419-555-0127

ARE YOU 18 YEARS OR OLDER? YES ☒ NO ☐

ARE YOU EITHER A U.S. CITIZEN OR AN ALIEN AUTHORIZED TO WORK IN THE UNITED STATES? YES ☒ NO ☐

EMPLOYMENT DESIRED

POSITION Engine and power train mechanic

DATE YOU CAN START May 1

SALARY DESIRED open

ARE YOU EMPLOYED NOW? yes

IF SO, MAY WE INQUIRE OF YOUR PRESENT EMPLOYER? yes

EVER APPLIED TO THIS COMPANY BEFORE? no

WHERE?

WHEN?

REFERRED BY Ken Jenkins

EDUCATION	NAME AND LOCATION OF SCHOOL	NO. OF YEARS ATTENDED	DID YOU GRADUATE?	SUBJECTS STUDIED
HIGH SCHOOL	Memorial High School	4	yes	vocational curriculum automotive
COLLEGE	Hillside Community College	2	yes	automotive technology
TRADE, BUSINESS, OR CORRESPONDENCE SCHOOL	NA			

FORMER EMPLOYERS (LIST BELOW LAST THREE EMPLOYERS, STARTING WITH LAST ONE FIRST.)

DATE	NAME AND ADDRESS OF EMPLOYER	PAY	POSITION	REASON FOR LEAVING
FROM June 20-- TO present	Goodman's Tire & Auto Center 219 E. Sycamore, Payne, OH 45880-1475	$12.75 hr.	service technician	currently employed
FROM June 20-- TO May 20--	Hunter's Auto Repair 2025 W. Walnut, Paulding, OH 45879-5923	$10.25 hr.	general auto repair	part-time only
FROM Aug. 20-- TO May 20--	Millcroft Service Station 436 Main St., Payne, OH 45880-1485	$7.50 hr.	auto maintenance	co-op student learner

WHICH OF THESE JOBS DID YOU LIKE THE BEST? Hunter's Auto Repair

WHAT DID YOU LIKE MOST ABOUT THIS JOB? engine diagnosis

REFERENCES (GIVE THE NAMES OF THREE PERSONS NOT RELATED TO YOU, WHOM YOU HAVE KNOWN FOR AT LEAST ONE YEAR).

NAME	ADDRESS	POSITION	YEARS ACQUAINTED
Earl Thompson	Goodman's Tire & Auto Center 219 E. Sycamore, Payne, OH 45880-1475	Service Manager	1.5
Yvonne Hunter	Hunter's Auto Repair 2025 W. Walnut, Paulding, OH 45879-5923	Owner/Manager	2.0
Leroy Hopkins	Hillside Community College 24 Given Rd., Paulding, OH 45879-5826	Automotive Instructor	2.0

Figure 4-2 ***This is a job application form that has been filled out correctly.***

LESSON 4.2
WRITING A RESUME

- UNDERSTAND THE PARTS OF A RESUME
- WRITE A RESUME

PARTS OF A RESUME

When applying in person for a job, you may be asked for a resume. A **resume** is a one-page description of a job seeker's history and qualifications for employment. You should send a resume when applying for a job by letter or fax and usually when applying by e-mail. An example of a completed resume is shown in Figure 4-3 on the next page. The resume provides the following five kinds of information.

A. Personal Information. Personal information is given at the top of the page. Your name, address, and phone number are all that is needed. If you have an e-mail address, it should probably also be included.

B. Career Goals. In the next section, give a short statement of your career goals. Be specific about the type of job you are seeking. Do not limit yourself to one particular employer, though. You want to be able to give the resume to many different employers. Examples of possible goals might be:

- ". . . to obtain training and acquire experience in retail sales."
- ". . . to gain practical work experience while saving money for college."
- ". . . to further develop my skills as a licensed practical nurse."

C. Educational Background. The third kind of information is about your education. List all high schools, colleges, technical schools, and so on. Begin with the most recent one. List any diplomas, degrees, licenses, and certificates you earned. Also mention any honors or awards you received. Name any job-related activities in which you participated. For example, Ronald Morales' performance in an engine troubleshooting contest proves he has good diagnostic and mechanical skills.

D. Work Experience. The fourth section is a summary of paid work experience. Begin with your present or most recent job. Identify each employer, the time period worked, and the type of job duties performed. Include co-op or work-study jobs here rather than in the section on educational background.

If you have limited paid work experience, it is proper to list unpaid experience, such as baby-sitting, yard work, and newspaper delivery. You can also mention volunteer work experience, such as being a junior volunteer, camp counselor, or campaign worker. If you think about it, you can probably identify many kinds of work experience that can compensate for having limited paid job experience.

E. References. The last section of the resume is a listing of references. Two or three references are satisfactory. Present and previous employers and supervisors are best.

about 1″

Ronald R. Morales

6428 Valley Road
Payne, Ohio 45880-1482
(419) 555-0127
rrmorales@buckeye.com

CAREER GOALS

My immediate objective is to obtain a job at a new car dealership as an engine and power train mechanic. My long-range goal is to become a shop supervisor or service manager. I am willing to complete additional training as required.

EDUCATIONAL BACKGROUND

June 20--: Received Associate of Applied Science Degree in Automotive Technology from Hillside Community College in Paulding, Ohio. Member of first-place team in regional engine troubleshooting competition.

July 20--: Licensed as a state auto and truck inspector (Ohio).

June 20--: Graduated from Memorial High School in Payne, Ohio. Completed two years of vocational auto and one year of cooperative vocational education. President of local Vocational Industrial Clubs of America (VICA).

about 1″ about 1″

WORK EXPERIENCE

June 20-- to present: Goodman's Tire & Auto Center, Payne, Ohio. Duties include tune-ups, general engine repair, front wheel alignment, and wheel and brake work.

June 20-- to May 20--: Hunter's Auto Repair, Paulding, Ohio. Part-time and weekend work while attending college. Performed engine diagnosis, general engine repair, tune-ups, and transmission repair.

August 20-- to May 20--: Millcroft Service Station, Payne, Ohio. Part-time cooperative vocational education student-learner. Performed routine auto maintenance and minor engine repair.

REFERENCES

Mr. Earl Thompson (Service Mgr.)
Goodman's Tire & Auto Center
219 E. Sycamore
Payne, OH 45880-1475
(419) 555-0164

Ms. Yvonne Hunter (Owner/Mgr.)
Hunter's Auto Repair
2025 W. Walnut
Paulding, OH 45879-5923
(419) 555-0192

Mr. Leroy Hopkins (Automotive Inst.)
Vocational Education Department
Hillside Community College
24 Given Rd.
Paulding, OH 45879-5826
(419) 555-0173

about 1″

Figure 4-3 ***Sample resume***

A prospective employer will probably contact the references listed to inquire about your work habits, attitudes, and skills. If you are a recent graduate, you can list instructors who are familiar with your schoolwork. A personal reference, such as a family friend, who can comment about your character may be listed as one of the references.

WRITE YOUR RESUME

If you have done a personal data sheet, you already have the basic information you will include in your resume. You will need to choose which parts of that information to use. Then you will have to arrange the information into a neat, organized format.

Your resume should be detailed enough to give an employer the information needed to judge your qualifications. It should also be brief. A busy employer wants the important facts in as few words as possible. In describing your work experience, for example, the sentence "I was responsible for analyzing the cost sheets from the production department" is too lengthy. It can be condensed into a shorter statement that provides the same information: "Analyzed production cost sheets."

The resume should have a neat, error-free, professional appearance. Try to limit the length to one page. Key the resume on the same typewriter or use the same word processing software font that you will use for your letter of application.

If you have access to a computer with word processing software, use it to prepare your resume. With word processing software, you can rearrange information easily. You can also use the spelling feature to help check your work. In addition, word processing software makes it easy to format your resume with an attractive page design.

When you have finished your resume, proofread it carefully. Ask a friend or family member to check it, too. Even if you have used the spelling feature in word processing software, you still need to read your resume over.

If you prepared your resume on a word processor and have access to a good printer, print multiple copies. Otherwise, have the copies reproduced. Use good-quality paper.

NOTHING BUT NET

Connecting to the Internet is done through a company called an Internet service provider (ISP). ISPs provide communications software if your computer doesn't have it. This software is used to establish a connection with the ISP through your modem. A modem is a device for transmitting computer data over phone lines. Most computers come with modems already installed. Once a connection with the ISP is established, you can use browser software to navigate the Web.

Most ISPs charge a monthly fee for their services. Some give you free access in exchange for viewing advertisements. Some communities also sponsor freenets that give individuals free access to the Web.

ISPs provide users with addresses so they can send and receive electronic mail. They may also provide users with server space to store a personal home page. Home pages are discussed in Chapter 8.

Save your resume file, if you used a word processor, so you can print extra copies and revise it easily in the future. If you used a typewriter, make sure you keep a copy.

LESSON 4.2 REVIEW

1. Name the five kinds of information provided in a resume.
2. What are some advantages to using word processing software to prepare a resume?

HIGH-GROWTH OCCUPATIONS FOR THE 21st CENTURY

Computer Systems Analysts, Engineers, and Scientists

The rapid spread of computers and information technology (computers, software, e-mail, the Internet, and so on) has generated a need for highly trained workers to design and develop new hardware and software systems and to incorporate new technologies. *Systems analysts* solve computer problems and help organizations meet individual computer technology needs. Systems analysts may design new systems, including both hardware and software. Most systems analysts work with a specific type of system—for example, accounting systems or scientific and engineering systems.

Systems development workers are also referred to as *systems developers* and *systems architects*. Analysts, who do more in-depth testing of products, may be referred to as *software quality assurance analysts*. In some organizations, *programmer-analysts* design and update the software that runs a computer.

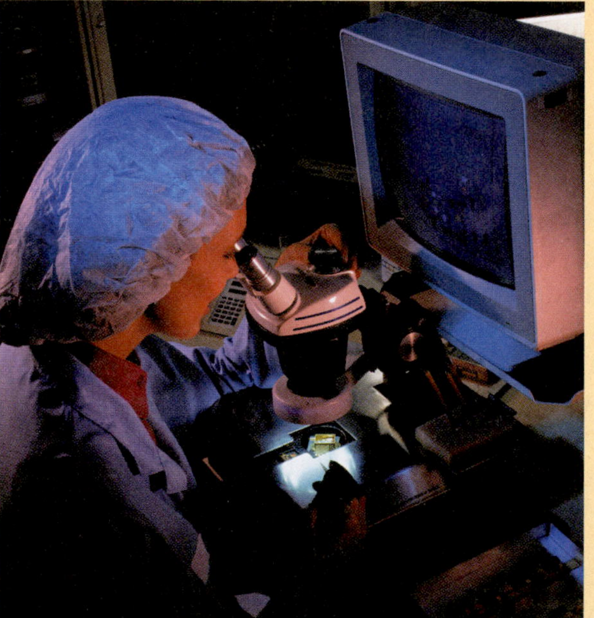

Computer hardware engineers may inspect computer chips for quality.

Many systems analysts are involved with computer networks. *Network systems and data communications analysts* design, test, and evaluate data communications systems such as local area networks (LANs), networks that span a small area; wide area networks (WANs), networks that span a large area; Internet access systems; and intranets. *Telecommunications specialists* focus on the interaction between computer and communications equipment.

Computer engineers also work with the hardware and software aspects of systems design and development. *Computer hardware engineers* usually design, develop, test, and supervise the manufacture of computer hardware, such as chips. *Software engineers* are involved in the design and development of software systems for control and automation of manufacturing, business, and management processes. Software engineers or *software developers* create and modify computer applications and utility software (software that helps computer systems run efficiently, such as file management and antivirus programs).

The title *computer scientist* is applied to a wide range of computer professionals who usually design computers and the software that runs them, develop information technologies, and develop and adapt principles for applying computers to new uses. Computer scientists perform many of the same duties as other computer professionals. But their jobs involve application of a higher level of expertise to complex problems.

LESSON 4.3 CONTACTING EMPLOYERS

- *EXPLAIN FOUR METHODS OF CONTACTING EMPLOYERS ABOUT A JOB*
- *DESCRIBE THE TWO MOST COMMON TYPES OF PRE-EMPLOYMENT TESTS*

FOUR METHODS OF CONTACTING EMPLOYERS

As you have learned, filling out a job application form is one way to apply for a job. Other methods include applying in person, by phone, by letter, and online. In all four approaches, do everything you can to present yourself and your qualifications in the best possible light.

Applying in Person

A help-wanted ad or sign will often contain the statement "apply in person." The ad or sign may give the name of a person to contact or it may say to "ask for the manager." In some cases, though, the ad only tells you the name of the company.

When you apply for a job in person, first impressions are very important. Some employers, in fact, judge an applicant's appearance, self-confidence, and social skills this way. You want to be well groomed and appropriately dressed. Introduce yourself and explain who you are. For example, you may want to say you are a high school work experience education student.

In some instances, you may have been referred by an employment agency or were encouraged to apply by a placement counselor, teacher, or other person. In such a case, also share this information. Being referred or recommended by someone known to the employer can give you an immediate edge over other applicants.

State your interest in the job advertised. If the first meeting goes well, the employer will probably ask you to fill out a job application form or leave a resume. Be prepared. Take along your personal data sheet and a copy of your resume.

Applying in person for a job usually also serves as a job interview. Most of the material in Chapter 5 on interviewing for a job will apply to this situation.

Applying by Telephone

Skillful use of the telephone is very important to a successful job search. By using the telephone, you can make many contacts in the time it takes to make one personal visit. Of course, applying

> **PERSONAL DECISIONS**
>
> One of your job-lead cards is for an opening at a business owned by your best friend's mother. You are not sure how to apply for the job. Should you call her at home or at work? Should you have your friend ask his mother for you? Should you give her a resume even though she already knows you? Should you address her as Ramona, which you normally do, or as Mrs. Cruz?
>
> **WHAT WOULD YOU DO?**

The telephone is an important tool for contacting employers.

in person will still be necessary and desirable for some job leads.

The purpose of telephoning is to convert a job lead into an appointment for a job interview. In some cases, you may be following a suggestion from a family member or friend. An opening might not exist. For other leads, you know a certain opening is available. Perhaps you are answering a help-wanted ad.

Whatever your reasons for making the call, the following guidelines should help you:

- ***Get organized before you call.*** Have your job-lead card, pen, and paper ready. Know the purpose of your call. Plan what you are going to say.
- ***Call from a quiet place.*** You do not want any background noise during the call.
- ***Speak clearly and directly into the telephone mouthpiece.*** Do not have anything in your mouth when you talk.
- ***Give your name and briefly state your business.*** Use the employer's name several times during the conversation. Make sure it is correct.
- ***Be courteous, friendly, and interested.*** Speak with a pleasant, even tone of voice. Put a "smile" in your voice, but talk naturally.
- ***Write down information quickly.*** Try not to ask the person to repeat what was said.
- ***Ask for an appointment, but do not sound pushy.*** If you get an appointment, write down the time, the place, and the interviewer's name.

Applying in Writing

Another way to act on a job lead is to write a letter of application. You might do this when acting on a suggestion from another person or responding to a newspaper help-wanted ad. A **cover letter** is a letter of application accompanied by a resume that is sent to a potential employer. The cover letter and resume may be mailed, e-mailed, or faxed.

An example of a cover letter is shown in Figure 4-4 on the next page. Such a letter should have four parts.

In the first paragraph, you should explain your reason for writing. Name the job for which you are applying. Also, tell how you learned about the job.

Use the second paragraph to briefly point out your qualifications. Give the facts, but do not brag. Employers will look carefully at this paragraph.

The third paragraph calls attention to the resume. It may also be wise to give a date when you will be available for employment.

In the last paragraph, ask for an appointment. Tell how you can be contacted. Close the letter with a courteous comment or a thank-you.

Notice that the sample letter is short and to the point. The purpose of the letter is to attract and hold the reader's interest. It should not attempt to give facts that are better stated in a resume and job interview. If you are qualified for the job, the letter and resume should make the employer want to invite you for an interview.

The form and appearance of the letter are also very important. Write several drafts of the letter until you feel it is correct. Then have a teacher or parent check it over for correct spelling and grammar.

Key the letter neatly, following a standard personal-business letter format. Use the same equipment that you used to prepare your resume: a good typewriter or a computer with word processing software and a printer that will produce clean copy. If you are using word processing software, run the spelling feature.

Proofread the letter carefully to check for errors. Ask a friend or family member to do the same. If you prepared the letter using word processing software, save the file; if not, make a paper copy. You will be able to use it in the future as a guide in writing additional letters.

2″ or center vertically

6428 Valley Rd.
Payne, OH 45880-1482
April 16, 20— **4 line returns**

Mr. Donald Young
Service Manager
Smith Auto Sales Inc.
274 Oakland St.
Payne, OH 45880-1483

Dear Mr. Young

One of your employees, Ken Jenkins, told me that you plan to hire a new mechanic in a few weeks. I would like to apply for the position.

1″ or default

My training and experience fit your job. For the last two years, I have worked at Goodman's Tire & Auto Center, primarily doing tune-ups, general engine repair, front wheel alignments, and wheel and brake work. While my present job is satisfying, I would like to work for a new car dealership where I can use my diagnostic and mechanical abilities. I hold a state inspection license and own my own tools.

1″ or default

The enclosed copy of my resume provides further details about my background. I could be available for employment following a two-week notice to my present employer.

I would be happy to meet with you for an interview at your convenience. I can be reached after 4 p.m. at 555-0127.

Sincerely **4 line returns**

Ronald Morales

Ronald Morales

Enclosure

about 1″ minimum

Figure 4-4 Sample cover letter

MATH CONNECTION

Suppose you are applying for a position that requires each candidate to be able to key an average of 30 words per minute. The last three times you tested yourself, you keyed 30, 28, and 35 words per minute. Do you fit the requirements for this position?

SOLUTION

To calculate the average words per minute, add the test rates together and divide the sum by the number of times you tested yourself.

$$\text{Average words per minute} = (30 + 28 + 35) \div 3$$
$$= 93 \div 3$$
$$= 31$$

Since your average is higher than 30 words per minute, you fit the requirements for this position.

Applying Online

Applying for a job on the Web can be done in several ways. One way is to write a cover letter, attach a resume, and send them directly to an employer by e-mail rather than standard mail. If this is done, most of the same rules for preparing a cover letter and resume are followed as explained previously.

Another type of online job application is one in which an employer provides a form to be completed and submitted electronically. Many companies have a hyperlink on the home page of their web site entitled "Employment" or a related term. When you click on this link, a new page will often open, providing some type of online application form. Figure 4-5 shows an example of an online application form.

Most forms consist of various text fields in which data are entered. For example, at the top of the form, a label may ask for "Your Name." A rectangular box called a single-line text field usually follows into which the required information is keyed. Often larger boxes called text areas are provided for multi-line text input.

After all required information has been provided, a click of the mouse transmits the form to the employer. Before submitting an online application form, however, it is a good idea to print a copy and read it carefully for spelling, grammar, and factual errors.

Another way to use the Web in a job search is to post a resume to an online database. There are numerous government agencies and private companies that provide such a service. This approach is one in which resumes are collected, organized, and made available to employers for review. Employers then initiate contact with applicants in whom they are interested.

If you have a resume already developed, it can often be e-mailed to the designated site. Or you might be asked to scan the resume and transmit an image file for inclusion in the database.

When you are planning to post a resume online, make sure the resume is formatted very simply. When a resume is transmitted electronically, word processing features such as indents, boldface, bullets, and different type sizes can cause errors, be incomplete, or disappear.

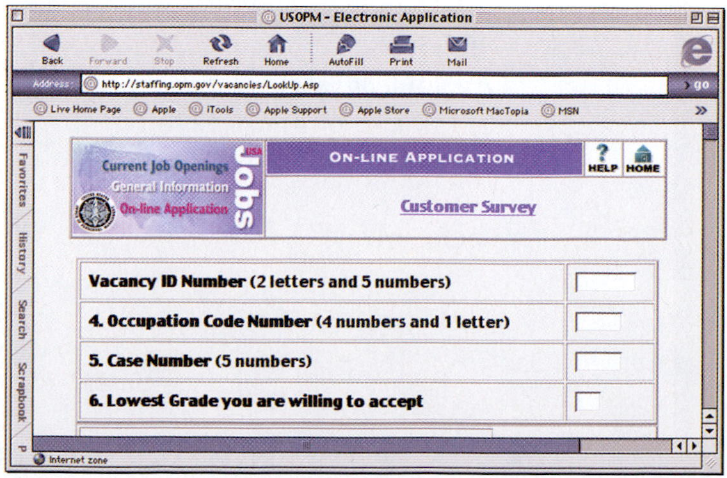

Figure 4-5 Online application

To increase the chances of your online resume being selected in a database search, you may want to replace the statement of career goals with a summary containing keywords relating to the position you want. For example, for a customer service job, your summary might say, *Strong communication and telephone skills; excellent keyboarding, computer, and Internet skills; and good organizational and interpersonal skills.*

Some agencies and companies provide resume development software online. Information is keyed into a form that the software converts into a standard resume style. As noted previously, it is very important to proofread such information carefully before submitting it to a digital database.

PRE-EMPLOYMENT TESTS

Mei-ling lives in the city that is her state's capital. A large state university is nearby. The state government and university are two of the city's major employers.

Because they hire many employees, Mei-ling applied for work at both offices. She was surprised to learn that she would have to take a test before she would be asked to interview for a job. Mei-ling found something that is very common.

To apply for almost all state and federal government jobs, applicants must take one or more pre-employment tests. A **pre-employment test** is a paper-and-pencil test or performance test administered by an employer as part of the job application process.

WORKFORCE TRENDS

The future racial and ethnic makeup of America will be considerably different than it is today. Trends show that the Caucasian share of the total population will be declining while the Hispanic share will grow faster than that of African-Americans. The Asian-American and Pacific Islander population is also expected to increase. By 2050, minorities are projected to rise from one in every four Americans to almost one in every two.

One type of pre-employment test is the **civil service test.** This test is administered to a job applicant seeking a government job. The intent of civil service testing is to promote fairness in employment. Job applicants with the highest civil service test scores are given preference in hiring.

Nongovernment (private) employers may also administer pre-employment tests. Large employers often give them as part of the job application process. For entry-level jobs with the government or private employers, the most common types of tests are general ability tests and performance tests.

General Ability Tests

A general ability test measures basic learning skills such as reading, spelling, vocabulary, and arithmetic. These written tests are similar to the types of tests that you have taken throughout your school years.

Performance Tests

In a performance test, you are asked to demonstrate skills needed for a specific occupation. Some performance tests are paper-and-pencil tests. An example would be a clerical skills test that requires you to proofread a business letter for possible errors.

Many performance tests are hands-on tests. They require you to use actual tools or machines. Suppose you are applying for a job as a data processing operator. Before being considered, you might be tested on a computer. By testing your skills now, employers avoid possible surprises later.

Taking a Test

You should not let the thought of taking a pre-employment test scare you away from a possible job. You will do better on the test if you do not spend time worrying about it.

Almost everyone experiences some test anxiety. You may be surprised to learn that mild test anxiety can be good. Studies have shown that mild stress actually improves the performance of athletes, entertainers, public speakers, and yes, test-takers. Stress can sharpen your attention, keep you alert, and give you greater energy.

Most tests don't require any advance preparation. If you haven't used your skills for a while, you may want to do some practicing before you take a performance test. The best preparation,

A performance test can be written or hands-on.

though, is probably to prepare yourself mentally and physically to take the test. Be positive. Think of the test as a chance to show what you know and can do. During the days before the test, try to exercise, relax, eat well, and get plenty of sleep.

Many tests have time limits. You will be told how much time you have. Listen carefully to the instructions you receive. If you do not understand what you are expected to do, be sure to ask questions before the test begins.

After you start the test, work steadily and carefully. Do not spend too much time on any one question. If math is required, double-check each answer. If you finish ahead of time, use the remaining time to go back and complete unanswered questions or recheck answers.

Once the test is over, do not worry about it. Employers do not expect perfection. They just want some idea of whether or not you can do the work. Do not leave until you know what the next step will be. Ask when and how you will be told the test results. Some employers will hold an interview immediately after a pre-employment test. The test may even be scored at that time. Other employers will invite applicants back after they have examined the job application and the test results. Regardless of the procedure, if your test scores are good, you probably will get a job interview.

LESSON 4.3 REVIEW

1. **Name four ways in which you can contact employers about jobs.**
2. **What is the main advantage of using the telephone in a job search?**
3. **What is the main thing you should do in the last paragraph of a letter of application?**
4. **What are the two most common types of pre-employment tests? What is the purpose of each?**
5. **If you finish a pre-employment test before the time limit is up, what should you do?**

FOCUS ON THE WORKPLACE

LIE DETECTOR AND HONESTY TESTS

If you apply for a job in which money, merchandise, or drugs are handled, you may have to take an "honesty test." One type is a polygraph, or lie detector, test. A polygraph is an electronic machine that is connected to the body of a subject. The person is asked a series of questions, while the machine records electronic impulses and other data on a graph. If the person tells a lie, the device supposedly detects slight changes in the person's breathing rate, pulse, blood pressure, or perspiration.

If a job involves handling money, you may be asked to take an honesty test.

Many experts in the field question the accuracy of polygraph tests. As a result, Congress passed a law in 1988 to restrict the use of such tests. The law prohibits polygraph tests for screening job applicants. An exception is for those seeking jobs in government, as security guards, or handling narcotics. The law also curtails the use of polygraphs for workers already on the job. Managers cannot ask employees to take the test unless there is a "reasonable suspicion" that they have committed a crime. Even then, the test is voluntary. An employee cannot be fired for refusing to take it.

To avoid the problems and cost of polygraph tests, some companies use written honesty tests. These have multiple choice or yes-no items, such as:

- Have you every stolen anything from an employer? Yes No
- Have you ever cheated in school? Yes No
- Have you ever lied to a teacher or boss? Yes No

The written test is interpreted by comparing an applicant's answers to those of persons already judged to be honest. Whether honesty tests help screen out dishonest job applicants is open to debate. But unless laws are passed restricting their use, millions of job applicants will probably be required to take these tests.

THINK CRITICALLY

1. What jobs do you think should require lie detector or honesty tests?
2. Would you apply for a job that required a lie detector or honesty test?

CHAPTER 4

Chapter in Brief

Lesson 4.1 *Data Sheets and Job Applications*

A. To aid in filling out a job application form, prepare a personal data sheet. A personal data sheet contains the types of information most often requested by employers. You will also use the personal data sheet in preparing a resume.

B. Job application forms are used by employers to help sort out qualified individuals from a pool of applicants. Follow the guidelines in this chapter to increase your chances of being selected for an interview.

Lesson 4.2 *Writing a Resume*

A. A resume is often used when applying for a job in person, by letter, or by e-mail.

B. It should be limited to one page and contain the five types of information discussed in this chapter. The resume should have a neat, error-free, professional appearance.

Lesson 4.3 *Contacting Employers*

A. You can contact an employer about a job in person, by phone, by letter, or online.

B. Applying in person usually also serves as a job interview. The purpose of phone, letter, and online contacts is to gain an interview. In all four approaches, do everything you can to present yourself and your qualifications in the best possible light.

C. Many employers administer pre-employment tests to job applicants. The most common are ability tests or performance tests. After beginning a test, work steadily and carefully.

Activities

1. Develop a personal data sheet following the model shown in Figure 4-1. Ask your instructor to look over your rough draft.
2. Using your personal data sheet, practice filling out the sample job application forms provided by your teacher.
3. Prepare a resume according to the format shown in Figure 4-3. After the resume is finished, write a sample letter of application. Turn in both to your instructor.
4. Practice role-playing in class how you would use a telephone to contact an employer for a job interview. One student can be the applicant and one the employer. Follow the guidelines on telephone use given earlier in this chapter.
5. Go to the *Occupational Outlook Quarterly* web site at http://stats.bls.gov/opub/ooq/ooqhome.htm. Find the article "Resumes, Applications, and Cover Letters" in the Summer 1999 issue ("Archives"). Use the information to develop a plain text resume.

REVIEW

6. Develop an online resume at America's Job Bank (AJB). Connect on the Web to AJB at http://www.ajb.org, read the privacy statement, sign up, and follow the instructions provided.
7. Suppose you wanted to apply for a job that required you to have an average score of 70 on four pre-employment tests. You scored 60, 72, 69, and 75 on the four tests. What is the average of the four test scores? Did you meet the requirement for the job?

Word Power

On a separate sheet of paper, match each definition with the correct term. All definitions will be used, and a definition will be used only once.

8. A form used by employers to collect personal, educational, and occupational information from a job applicant
9. A letter of application accompanied by a resume that is sent to a potential employer
10. Names of individuals listed on a personal data sheet, job application form, or resume who are qualified to provide information about the applicant.
11. A one-page description of a job seeker's history and qualifications for employment
12. A pre-employment test that is administered to a job applicant seeking a government job
13. A paper-and-pencil test or performance exercise administered by an employer as part of the job application process
14. A summary of personal, educational, and occupational information used to help fill out a job application form and to prepare a resume

a. civil service test
b. cover letter
c. job application form
d. personal data sheet
e. pre-employment test
f. references
g. resume

Think Critically

15. People sometimes make mistakes during their lifetime. These might include getting into trouble at school, getting arrested for a minor infraction, or getting fired from a job. If a question is asked about things like this on a job application, how should you respond? What if it means that your answer will keep you from getting the job?
16. If you had an option to apply for a job in person or by letter, which would you choose? Discuss the advantages of each and why you chose the option you did.
17. What do you think about the practice of requiring a lie detector test as part of the job application process? Discuss both your and the employer's point of view.

CHAPTER 5

INTERVIEWING FOR A JOB

LESSONS

PREVIEW

The interview is the best chance you have of convincing potential employers to hire you. You should prepare yourself for the interview. Practice answering questions and research the company. You must also act appropriately during the interview. Remember how important first impressions are. Finally, you must follow up to make sure that the interviewer remembers who you are and that you want the job.

THOUGHTS ON WORK

"If you do not feel yourself growing in your work and your life broadening and deepening, if your task is not a perpetual tonic to you, you have not found your place."

Orison Swett Marden

TAKING ACTION
GETTING AN INTERVIEW

Ron Morales had just gotten home from work when the telephone rang. He answered it.

"Hello, Ron Morales speaking."

"Hello, Ron, this is Donald Young at Smith Auto Sales. I have your letter of application and resume in front of me. It seems as if you would like to get out of your present job."

"No, sir, 'getting out' is not the main reason I am looking for a job," Ron replied, pleasantly but firmly. "I like my job at Goodman's, but most of our work involves doing routine repairs on older cars. I have some training and skills that I am not able to use there. I would like to work on newer cars and be able to specialize in diagnostic work."

"That is good to hear," Mr. Young said. "As you know, new car models are becoming more high-tech all the time. It is essential that technicians have the confidence and ability to do diagnostic work. This is one of the primary skills that I am seeking in hiring new technicians. I called Leroy Hopkins at Hillside Community College and he said this is one of your strong areas."

"Yes, it is. Diagnostic work is often very simple if you know how to use testing equipment."

"I agree," said Mr. Young. "If I hired you, would you have any interest in becoming a peer trainer? I think some of our less skilled technicians might benefit from having a fellow mechanic help them learn how to better use testing equipment."

"Yes, I think that I would enjoy teaching," replied Ron. "My mother is a teacher and she has always said that I have a talent for teaching."

"Ron, I would like to talk further with you and show you around our shop. Could you come in Saturday morning at 9:00?"

"Yes, I would be happy to. I will see you on Saturday at 9:00, Mr. Young. Thank you for calling."

SUCCESS TIP

Be ready to talk about what you want from a job.

THINK CRITICALLY

1. How did Ron handle the question of why he wanted a new position?
2. What do you think Ron said that made Donald Young want to interview him?

LESSON 5.1 BEFORE THE INTERVIEW

- EXPLAIN THE PURPOSE OF A JOB INTERVIEW
- NAME AND DESCRIBE THE FIVE THINGS TO DO IN PREPARATION FOR A JOB INTERVIEW

PURPOSE OF THE INTERVIEW

The **job interview** is a face-to-face meeting between you and an employer. It is generally the last and most important step in the job-seeking process. An interview for an entry-level job usually lasts about 15 to 30 minutes. You will not be invited for an interview unless the employer thinks you may be qualified for the job. The employer wants to find out in person if you have the skills for the job. Another purpose is to help the employer decide if you will be able to work well with supervisors and coworkers. Your task is to show the employer that you *are* the person for the job.

PERSONAL DECISIONS

You have an allergy to various food products. Occasionally, you unknowingly eat something that causes an allergic reaction. An unpleasant-looking skin rash appears on your face and hands. The day before a job interview you have such a reaction. You are very upset and discouraged. You don't want to go to the interview like this.

WHAT WOULD YOU DO?

An interview gives you a chance to "sell" what you can do for the employer. During the interview, an employer will judge your qualifications, appearance, and behavior. Equally important, the interview gives you a chance to **appraise**, or evaluate, the job and the company. It enables you to decide if the position meets your job goals and interests and whether this is the type of company for which you want to work.

PREPARING FOR THE INTERVIEW

Before each interview, you should take the attitude that the job you are applying for is the one you want. To present yourself in the best possible light, you will need to do several things to prepare for the interview.

Practice Your Interview Skills

You may be a little nervous when you think about going for a job interview. That is normal. To reduce your anxiety and help build your confidence, you may want to role-play some practice interviews. Something as important as a job interview deserves advance preparation. You would not go for your driver's license exam without practicing your driving skills, would you?

You may be able to set up a classroom interview situation. Arrange a desk and a couple of chairs the way you might find them in an office.

YOU'RE A WHAT? DEMONSTRATOR

Individuals who promote the sales of consumer products at grocery stores, shopping malls, trade shows, and outdoor fairs are called *demonstrators* or product promoters. Demonstrators range from part-time workers who may cook and offer samples of food products at a local grocery store to famous personalities promoting jewelry or clothing to millions of viewers on home shopping networks.

The goal of all demonstrators is to create interest in a product by demonstrating it, providing information, and answering questions. Some demonstrators, such as those on television, aim to generate sales through impulse buying. Demonstrators at a grocery store, however, concentrate more on increasing brand awareness and generating future sales by, for example, giving samples and discount coupons. ■

The instructor or a fellow student can play the role of an employer. Take turns being interviewed for a **hypothetical**, or imagined or pretended, job. Try to make "the interview" as realistic as possible.

Before you practice the interview, though, work together as a group to develop a list of questions for the interviewer to ask. These are some examples.

- I have already read your application form, but tell me something about yourself.
- Do you like school?
- What is your favorite subject? Why?
- What do you do in your spare time?
- Tell me why you applied for a job with us.
- How much do you know about the type of work we do here?
- Why do you think you would like this kind of work?
- Have you ever worked on this type of equipment before?
- Were you ever late to work in your last job?
- If I hired you, how long would you expect to stay with us?
- How much do you expect to make?
- What would you want to be doing in five years?
- When will you be available to start work?
- Do you have any questions?

As you can see from these examples, some questions can really put you on the spot if you are not prepared for them. By practicing the interview, you will become more aware of what is involved in thinking about a question and answering it out loud. It can be a valuable learning experience to discover, for example, how much you stumble and hesitate. Do not try to memorize answers, but do practice until you can respond easily. Make special efforts to rid your speech of "uhs," "you knows," and similar responses.

In addition to participating yourself, you can learn a great deal by watching others during practice interviews. Devin, for example, noticed how some individuals pause for long periods before answering a question and repeatedly change positions in their chair. He has made a mental note to try to avoid these behaviors.

Learn About the Company

Find out as much as possible about the job and the company before your interview. Start by asking people you know who might have information on the company. From personal contacts, you may learn inside information. For example, you might find out about the working conditions or the turnover rate of personnel. Further information may be available from the company itself. Ask if the company has any brochures, catalogs, annual reports, or other types of descriptive materials.

If the potential place of employment is a restaurant, retail store, or similar public place, it may be possible to get firsthand information. Visit the establishment to get a feel for the atmosphere. You can observe the type of work done and perhaps ask employees a few questions.

Next comes library or Internet research. A librarian can help you find several reference directories or web sites that tell about corporations. Some facts to look for include products or services, growth rate, and standing in the industry.

If information about the company is not available, find out something about the industry. Let's say that you are going to interview for a job in a property management firm. Find out what services these firms provide.

When you finish your research, write up a list of questions that you would like to ask about the job or the company. For example, you might ask, "Why did the job become vacant? Will any more training be required? What are the working hours? Who will my supervisor be if I get the job?"

It is generally best to avoid asking about salary or benefits in the job interview. If the information is not provided by the interviewer, you can ask after you have been offered the job.

Assemble Needed Materials

Have the materials you plan to take to the interview ready. These include the job-lead card, the personal data sheet, the resume, copies of any correspondence, a pen, paper, a list of questions you will ask, and a work permit, if needed. Also, take samples of your work if possible. Carry all the materials in a large envelope or briefcase.

See to Appearance

Your grooming and dress will influence the interviewer's final decision. Choose clothes that are appropriate for the job setting. Ron, for example, has an interview for a job as an auto mechanic. It is not necessary that he wear a coat and tie, but jeans and a T-shirt are too casual.

If you are not sure what to wear, ask your work experience coordinator or counselor for advice. Or visit the company ahead of time to see how people dress. Remember, though, you are dressing for an interview, not the job you will be doing.

Whatever clothes you decide to wear, they should be clean, pressed, and in good condition. Clothes do not have to be expensive to look neat. Do not forget to clean or shine your shoes. Avoid the heavy use of jewelry and other accessories.

Careful grooming is also very important. If you need a haircut, plan ahead to get it done. On the day of the interview, a shower or bath is a must. Wash your hair, clean your nails, and brush your teeth. Men should shave or trim beards and mustaches. No heavy-smelling colognes or aftershaves. Women should use makeup sparingly.

Check Last-minute Details

Going to an interview at the wrong place or time may seem dumb. People do it all the time, though. It will help if you write the date, time, and place of the interview on a job-lead card. Double-check the information. You may want to make a trial run so you will know where the company is located.

If more than a week goes by between the time you made the appointment and the interview, call to **confirm**, or verify, it. Here is what Elena did.

"Good morning, Solar Products Company."

"Hello, this is Elena Simon. I'm calling to confirm my appointment for 10:00 tomorrow with Ms. Han."

"Yes, Ms. Simon, she has you down."

"Good. Thank you. I'll be there tomorrow."

Plan to arrive at the interviewer's office five to ten minutes ahead of schedule. Introduce yourself and tell why you are there. Do not bring anyone with you. You do not want to give the impression that you cannot do things on your own.

LESSON 5.1 REVIEW

1. **From the interviewer's standpoint, what is the purpose of the job interview?**
2. **A job interview provides you with a chance to do two things. Name them.**
3. **Name the five things that you should do to prepare for a job interview. Why is each important?**

LESSON 5.2
DURING THE INTERVIEW

OBJECTIVES

- DESCRIBE LAST-MINUTE PREPARATIONS
- SUMMARIZE HOW ONE SHOULD ACT DURING A JOB INTERVIEW

WHILE YOU WAIT

You may have to wait a short time in an outer office or reception area. During that time, you should relax, read, or look over your list of questions. Be pleasant toward others in the reception area. Do not smoke, chew gum, or do anything distracting. The interviewer may later ask for the receptionist's opinion of you.

You may wonder what type of person the interviewer will be. Unfortunately, you have no way of knowing. If you have five job interviews, you will probably find five completely different personalities.

It is not necessary for you to like the interviewer or for the interviewer to like you. The interviewer is looking for the best person to fill a job. You are not there to be social. You are looking for a job.

Prepare yourself to deal with whatever you may find. Remain calm and do your best. If you have prepared well for the interview, you have done your homework up to this point.

EFFECTIVE COMMUNICATION

Let the interviewer set the tone and pace of the interview. Adjust yourself to the style of the interviewer. For example, if the interviewer is serious and businesslike, your style should be similar. If the interviewer is cheerful and outgoing, you may need to brighten up a little. Try to establish a **compatible** relationship, or a relationship that is pleasant or agreeable, with the interviewer.

Communication skills, which are important at every step of the job search, are more so in the job interview. Be sure to listen carefully and speak clearly. Answer each question briefly, but do not give one-word or one-line answers. If you think that the interviewer has not understood your answer or that you have not made yourself clear, try again. Stay on the topic until you are sure that the interviewer has understood your message.

Answer a question only after the interviewer is completely finished. Otherwise, you risk making a bad impression. You may also never find out the exact question or hear important information that may be added to the question.

Listening to the interviewer is as important as speaking thoughtfully and clearly. The ability to

WORKFORCE TRENDS

Deciding how far to go in school is one of the most important decisions an American worker makes. Educational attainment plays a critical role in job placement, earnings, and how long people work or are unemployed. On average, the more education individuals have, the more likely they are to seek and find jobs, earn higher wages, and retire with a pension.

COMMUNICATION AT WORK

ILLEGAL INTERVIEW QUESTIONS

There are certain questions that interviewers cannot legally ask you. These include questions about marital status, plans for children, child-care arrangements, disabilities, and health. If an interviewer asks you a question on one of these topics, how should you respond?

"Answer" a question that wasn't asked. Don't answer the question directly. Instead, give the interviewer some positive information that relates to your ability to do the job. For example, suppose an interviewer asks, "Do you have any disabilities?" You might respond, "I can assure you that there is no reason that I could not do a great job for you. Look at my work record, for example."

listen shows your attentiveness and reflects on your interest in the job. At times, you may want to ask the interviewer the meaning of a word or phrase. Do so. You must understand a question before you can answer it.

Nonverbal Communication

Body language may help or hinder communication. **Body language** is unspoken communication through physical movements, expressions, and gestures. During the interview, sit comfortably, but do not slouch. Keep your hands on your lap. Do not look at your hands or feet. Maintain good eye contact throughout the interview, but do not stare. Keep a pleasant expression on your face.

Also be aware of the interviewer's body language. Watch for nonverbal clues. If the interviewer's body language conveys something negative, think about what you are doing or saying. Then modify what needs to be changed.

Asking Questions

An interview involves two-way communications. The interviewer will ask you questions. The interviewer will also expect you to ask questions. It is wise to refer to the list of questions you made beforehand. Hold the list near your lap so you can glance at it as you talk.

Do not be in a hurry to ask questions. Wait until the interviewer invites them. A pause in the conversation once the interview is well under way may be the time for you to bring up your questions. Be careful, though, not to interrupt the interviewer. By all means, if you have not already been invited to do so, request an opportunity to ask your questions before the interview ends.

Your questions should indicate a sincere interest in the company and the job. Good questions show that you have prepared for the interview. For example, you might ask, "What opportunities are there to advance within the company?"

Use good judgment in deciding how much time to take up with questions. Try to sense whether or not the interviewer is on a tight

Asking questions is a very important part of the interview.

SOUTHWEST REALTY COMPANY APPLICANT EVALUATION

Name____________________ Interview date __________

Position applied for____________________

Criteria	Poor	Good	Excellent
1. Appearance	❑	❑	❑
2. Poise	❑	❑	❑
3. Responses	❑	❑	❑
4. Grammar and speech	❑	❑	❑
5. Background	❑	❑	❑
6. Knowledge of job requirements	❑	❑	❑
7. Interest in company	❑	❑	❑
8. Potential	❑	❑	❑

Strengths: ____________________

Weaknesses: ____________________

Based on interview, review of application, and follow-up, should an offer of employment be made? Yes ❑ No ❑

Date __________ Interviewer __________

Figure 5-1 ***Some employers use forms like this to help them rate a job candidate.***

schedule. If time seems pressing, ask only your most important questions.

Concluding the Interview

Suppose the interview is almost over. The employer has not said when a decision will be made about the job. What do you do? Ask about it. If the interviewer asks you to call back or supply more information, note it on the job-lead card.

Try to get a feeling for when the interview has run its course. The interviewer may stand or simply say right out, "Well, I think that I have enough information about you at this time." To help bring an interview to its conclusion, you can ask, "Are there any more questions I can answer?"

Many job applicants fail to ask for the job. This is a mistake. Tell the interviewer if you want the job. Say something like, "I know I can do the work, Mr. Young. I would like to have the job."

Seldom does an interviewer make a job offer or reject an applicant at the conclusion of an interview. Usually the interviewer wants to think about and compare all applicants before making a decision. In some cases, the interviewer's role is to evaluate and make recommendations only. See the bottom of Figure 5-1. The actual employment decision may be made by another person.

If you do learn that the company cannot use you, ask about other employers who may need a person with your skills. Thank the interviewer, shake hands, and leave. On the way out, thank the assistant or receptionist.

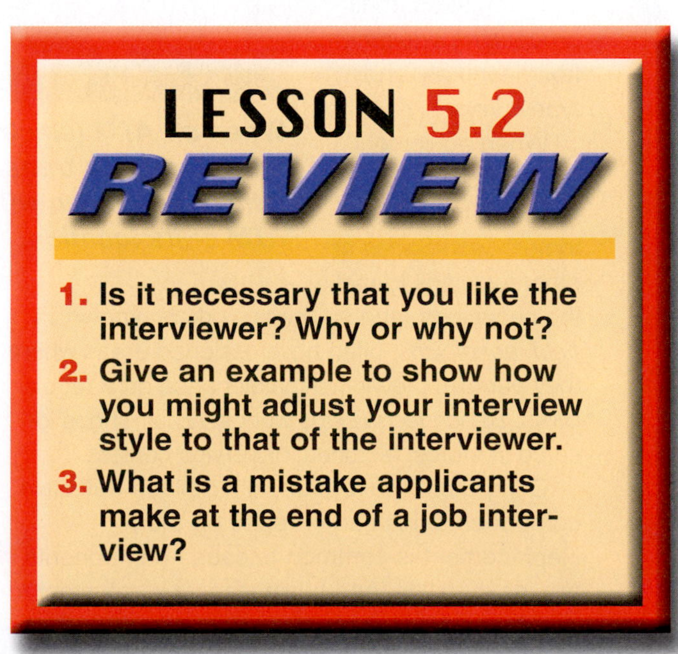

LESSON 5.2 REVIEW

1. Is it necessary that you like the interviewer? Why or why not?
2. Give an example to show how you might adjust your interview style to that of the interviewer.
3. What is a mistake applicants make at the end of a job interview?

HIGH-GROWTH OCCUPATIONS FOR THE 21st CENTURY

Data Processing Equipment Repairers

Computer and automated teller machine repairers, also known as data processing equipment repairers, install and service mainframe and personal computers; printers and other peripheral equipment; and automated teller machines (ATMs). Computer repairers primarily provide hands-on repair service. (Computer support specialists, a different occupation, provide technical assistance, in person or via telephone, to computer system users.) *Office machine repairers* work on photocopiers, cash registers, mail processing equipment, fax machines, and typewriters.

When an ATM (electronic terminal for customer banking transactions) needs repairs, a field technician will usually repair the ATM at its location.

When equipment breaks down, many repairers travel to customers' workplaces or other locations to make the necessary repairs. These workers, known as *field technicians,* often have assigned areas where they perform preventive maintenance on a regular basis. *Bench technicians* work in repair shops located in stores, factories, or service centers.

Computer repairers usually replace defective components, instead of repairing them. Replacement is common because components are inexpensive, and businesses are reluctant to shut down their computers for time-consuming repairs.

Because computers and ATMs are critical for many organizations to function efficiently, data processing repairers often work around the clock. Their schedule may include evening, weekend, and holiday shifts.

When ATMs malfunction, computer networks recognize the problem and alert repairers. Field technicians travel to the locations of ATMs and usually repair equipment by replacing defective components. Components that cannot be replaced are brought to a repair shop where bench technicians perform the necessary repairs. Field technicians also perform routine maintenance on a regular basis.

Office machine repairers usually work on machinery at the customer's workplace. Customers may also bring small equipment to a repair shop for maintenance. Common problems, such as poor copy quality, can usually be resolved by simply cleaning components. Breakdowns may also result from failure of commonly used parts, such as print heads. In such cases, the repairer usually replaces the part, instead of repairing it.

LESSON 5.3
AFTER THE INTERVIEW

- NAME AND DESCRIBE THE TWO THINGS TO DO AFTER AN INTERVIEW
- DISCUSS HOW TO RESPOND TO A JOB OFFER

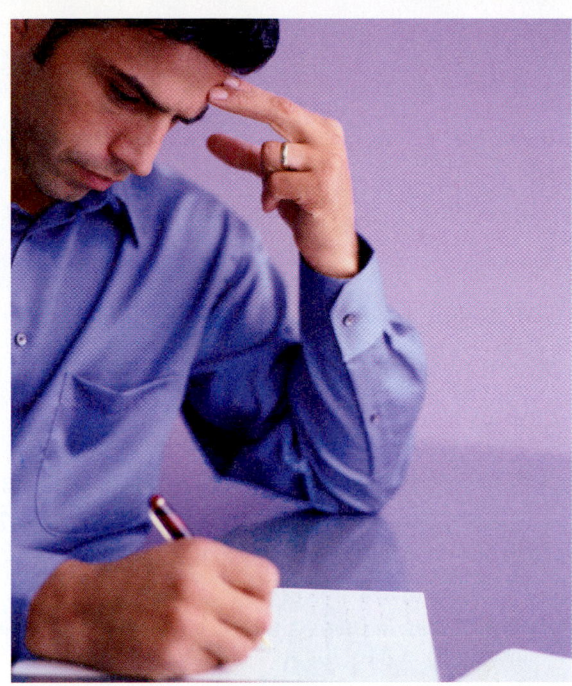

STEPS TO TAKE

You can benefit from every interview, no matter what the outcome. Take time to think about the experience as soon as possible after the interview. Review any mistakes you think you made and consider how you could have avoided them. Could you have been better prepared? Did you mention everything about yourself that the employer needs to know? Think about what you did well. Would these things help you in other interviews?

Promptly send a **follow-up letter**, or a thank-you letter, to the interviewer. Such a letter may accomplish the following things:

- It helps to build a courteous relationship.
- Having your letter keeps your name in front of the interviewer.
- Taking time to write a letter tells the interviewer of your continued interest.
- The letter allows you to reinforce key points you discussed during the interview.
- If you forgot to mention something important during the interview, you can put it in your follow-up letter.

A sample follow-up letter is shown in Figure 5-2 on the next page.

Suppose the interviewer told you that you would not be hired. Or, perhaps you are no longer interested in the job. Send a letter to thank the interviewer for considering you.

When writing a follow-up letter, refer to the guidelines for preparing a letter of application. The rules are similar for both types of letters. If someone helped arrange your interview, send a note of appreciation to him or her. This should be a simple, handwritten thank-you note.

After completing these steps, wait and try to relax. Continue to pursue other job leads in the meantime. If you have not heard from the company in a week, get in touch. You can do so sooner if the interviewer indicated that a decision would be made in less than this time.

RESPONDING TO JOB OFFERS

You may be hired or rejected during an interview. Usually, though, the employer makes a decision later. Employers like to interview several people for a job before making a choice.

CAREER DECISIONS

You have to decide between two job offers. One is a traditional job for a person of your gender. The other is a nontraditional job. You would be the only person of your gender out of eight employees.

WHAT WOULD YOU DO?

2″ or center vertically

6428 Valley Rd.
Payne, OH 45880-1482
April 16, 20—

4 line returns

Mr. Donald Young
Service Manager
Smith Auto Sales Inc.
274 Oakland St.
Payne, OH 45880-1483

Dear Mr. Young

1″ or default

1″ or default

Thank you for the interview concerning the auto mechanic position. I enjoyed meeting you and being able to tour the garage facilities.

I feel confident that I can satisfy your needs. I would very much like to have the job.

I would be happy to provide any additional information that you might require. Kindly call (419) 555-0127 with any questions.

Sincerely

4 line returns

Ronald Morales

Ronald Morales

about 1″ minimum

Figure 5-2 ***Sample follow-up letter***

A job offer is generally made by telephone. This gives the employer and the applicant a chance to discuss the details of the job offer. If the conditions of employment were not discussed earlier, ask about them before accepting. **Conditions of employment** are the specific details of a job offer, such as working hours, salary or wages, and fringe benefits. You will want to know when you start work and if there is anything special that you need to bring or be prepared to do the first day. For example, you might need to pick up a uniform. You may also receive a job offer by letter.

It is possible to be considered for a job at different places at the same time. Let's say that you have been interviewed for jobs at both Burger Barn and Chicken Shack. If Burger Barn offers you a job and you accept it, you should phone Chicken Shack and explain that you have taken another job.

What if a company offers you a job you do not want? Be polite. You never know when you may be contacting the company again. Give a brief explanation of your reasons. Regardless of your reasons, do not criticize the employer.

Not all of your interviews will result in job offers. In fact, most of them probably will not. Dealing with rejection is something we all must learn to do. Being disappointed is normal. Do not, however, react with anger toward an employer. By accepting rejection gracefully, you keep alive your chances for a future job. In all companies, employees come and go. New jobs open. If you are good enough to have been invited for an interview, then you are qualified for a job. Do not get discouraged. Whether at that company or somewhere else, a job will open up for you.

LESSON 5.3 REVIEW

1. **What five things may a follow-up letter accomplish?**
2. **You are being considered for two jobs. You receive one job offer and accept it. What should you do next?**
3. **Why is it important to accept a job rejection gracefully?**

FOCUS ON THE WORKPLACE

DRUG TESTING

During the job interview, Akira was surprised to learn that his potential employer has a drug-testing program. After the first month of employment, all workers at Allied Receiving are subject to random drug testing. The purpose of such tests is to identify employees who use illegal or illicit drugs, such as marijuana and cocaine. Not only is the use of such drugs illegal and dangerous, but the drugs have also been linked to accidents, absenteeism, and low productivity. For example, in a train crash that killed 16 passengers and injured 176 others, the engineer had been smoking marijuana.

Unpleasant as it might be, employers have the right to test applicants and employees for illegal drug use.

To identify drug users, employers often require each employee to submit a urine or hair sample for analysis. The urinalysis can detect traces of cocaine up to two days after the drug was taken. Marijuana can show up in the urine for several weeks after use. Hair analysis can detect drug use for approximately the previous 90 days.

Currently, a majority of the nation's 500 largest corporations have drug-testing programs. Testing may be required for job applicants, employed workers, or both. Some employers test workers for "cause"; for instance, if they notice a worker is not performing well. Others test randomly, without announcement and without even suspecting wrongdoing.

Even though drug testing is widely used, the practice remains controversial. Some people claim that the tests are often inaccurate. Others claim that the tests violate the prohibition on unreasonable searches in the Fourth Amendment of the United States Constitution. A number of lawsuits have been filed to stop drug testing. It will probably be many years before the courts ultimately decide on these issues.

THINK CRITICALLY

1. What jobs do you think should require candidates to be screened for drug use? Why?
2. If you were an employer, would you require drug testing of your employees? Why or why not?

CHAPTER 5

Chapter in Brief

Lesson 5.1 *Before the Interview*

A. The job interview is generally the last and most important step in the job-seeking process.

B. In preparation for an interview, you should practice your interview skills, learn about the employer, assemble needed materials, attend to appearance, and check last-minute details.

Lesson 5.2 *During the Interview*

A. During the interview, adjust yourself to the style of the interviewer. Be sure to listen carefully and speak clearly. An interview isn't just one way. Be prepared to ask the interviewer questions.

B. If you want the job, tell the interviewer near the end of the interview.

Lesson 5.3 *After the Interview*

A. After the interview, take time to think about the experience. Review any mistakes you think you made and consider how you could have avoided them. Promptly send a follow-up, or thank-you, letter to the interviewer.

B. A job offer may be made following the interview or later by phone or letter. Before accepting the offer, make sure you understand the conditions of employment. If you are rejected for a job, accept it gracefully. Don't do anything to close the door on a possible later offer or opportunity.

Activities

1. Connect to the Hoover's Online web site (http://www.hoovers.com), which provides descriptive information on more than 50,000 companies. Choose a well-known company and follow directions at the site to locate information about the company that you think would be important for a job applicant to know. You may wish to view the company web site, which you can access through a hyperlink at Hoover's Online, through a search tool such as Hotbot (http://www.hotbot.com) or, for many companies, by keying a web address with the company name in this way: http://www.companyname.com. Print the information. Later, at the direction of your instructor, summarize it. Turn in the paper to your instructor.

2. Even though they may not be listed at Hoover's Online, many small companies have web sites. Select three small companies in your area at which you might be interested in working. Use a search tool such as Google (http://www.google.com) to try to locate information about the companies. You can also use the "companyname" web address formula from Activity 1. A local Chamber of Commerce web site and online Yellow Pages are other resources. Print any information you find. Follow your instructor's directions regarding next steps.

REVIEW

3. In class, practice role-playing a job interview. Each student should have the opportunity to be interviewed. The instructor will initiate the interview with a couple of questions. Class members can then participate with additional questions.
4. If equipment is available, videotape the role-playing interview. View and discuss the tapes later. Seeing yourself on tape can often be quite informative.
5. Prepare a follow-up letter to a hypothetical job interview. Turn it in to your instructor for evaluation.

Word Power

On a separate sheet of paper, match each definition with the correct term. All definitions will be used, and a definition will be used only once.

6. Imagined or pretended
7. Pleasant or agreeable
8. A face-to-face meeting between a job seeker and a potential employer
9. To evaluate someone or something, such as a potential employer
10. To verify or make firm, such as calling to check on an appointment
11. The specific details of a job offer, such as working hours, salary or wages, and fringe benefits
12. A thank-you letter sent to an interviewer following a job interview
13. Unspoken communication through physical movements, expressions, and gestures

a. appraise
b. body language
c. compatible
d. conditions of employment
e. confirm
f. follow-up letter
g. hypothetical
h. job interview

Think Critically

14. Some class members have probably had job interviews. Those who have had interviews should describe their experiences to the class. Ask your classmates about things you would like to know regarding a job interview.
15. Despite your best planning efforts, an unexpected emergency or problem arises that prevents you from attending a job interview. How should you handle a situation like this?
16. A person with advanced education or highly marketable skills can often negotiate favorable conditions of employment following a job offer. Discuss realistically how much bargaining power a person has in applying for an entry-level job.

UNIT 2

WORKING ON THE JOB

CHAPTERS

CO-OP CAREER SPOTLIGHT

Marcos Lopez, *Public Policy Consultant*

Marcos Lopez always knew he wanted either to work with people in the public sector or to be a lawyer. He didn't know which. When he was a sophomore at Polytechnic High School in Long Beach, California, he found his answer. As a student in the co-op program, Marcos was able to learn about the two fields and to decide which best fit his goals.

Through the school's Hire-a-Youth Program, Marcos worked for three months as an intern in the Nobel Insurance Agency. He then signed on as an employee and stayed for the next three years. "A lot of the insurance laws were being written at that time," Marcos recalls. "The job at the insurance agency helped me grasp how laws affect people."

Marcos learned he belongs in the public sector. Today, at age 20, he works as a consultant for the City of Long Beach for the Department of Community Development Neighborhood Services Bureau. Marcos also attends Long Beach City College and plans to complete his studies in public policy and planning at a four-year university.

At the insurance agency, Marcos learned valuable skills that help him in his work today. "I learned administrative and management skills, people skills, and good customer service," he says. Marcos believes that the job gave him practical experience in working with people, a useful asset in his career in the public sector.

He stresses that the Hire-a-Youth program was so successful because of the standards set by the school. There were rules for the students and rules for the employers. Working hours had to be flexible, for example, so students could attend all their classes. A grade point average of at least 2.0 had to be maintained. The program's counselor regularly checked with students to see how they were doing, as well as with employers. "The counselor would ask if the job was too stressful and made sure students were handling their studies," Marcos explains. "She also contacted the employers to make sure the students were fulfilling their obligations."

While still in high school, Marcos participated in a citywide program designed to inform eighth-grade students about high school co-op opportunities. He passed along what he had learned about how the programs provide work experience and prepare students for college and careers. As a graduate of the Neighborhood Leadership Program in Long Beach, Marcos now teaches in the program. "We take people from target neighborhoods and enhance their skills to empower them to take charge of their own neighborhoods and make positive changes."

CHAPTER 6

BEGINNING A NEW JOB

LESSONS

THOUGHTS ON WORK

"Opportunities are usually disguised as hard work, so most people don't recognize them."
Ann Landers

PREVIEW

The job search is over. Your new job is about to start. You will be leaving or at least spending less time in the familiar world of the classroom. The changes you will experience may be scary at first. You are going from the known into the unknown. This can be exciting and frightening at the same time. By taking the time now to learn what to expect, you will be better prepared for your new role as a worker.

TAKING ACTION

BEGIN WORKING

Denny Liu was hired as a salesclerk at Rogers', a small men's store in North Plaza Mall. Denny learned about the job opening at Rogers' while he was working as a cooperative education student at another mall store. He applied for the job in person. After a short interview with Bob Brown, the manager, he was hired on the spot. Denny agreed to report for work after giving the other store two weeks' notice.

Three weeks later Denny arrived for his first day at work. Bob was unlocking the entrance. After greeting each other, Bob and Denny walked to the rear of the store. Along the way, Bob flipped on the lights. Denny smiled to himself. He was amused at how different the back of the shop looked compared to the shop's front display area.

Denny and Bob exchanged small talk as Bob sorted the mail. A few minutes later Courtney and Evan, two other employees, came into the shop. Bob introduced Denny to them. They all chatted for a few minutes. Courtney and Evan then went to get the shop ready for its 10:00 opening.

Bob gave Denny a few forms to sign and a payroll card. He told Denny how to keep track of the number of hours he worked. They then walked around the shop while Bob explained procedures and pointed out features of certain merchandise.

Bob told Denny that he wanted him to begin working at the ties and accessories counter. If the other salesclerks got busy, he was to leave the counter area to help out.

"Denny, you know what goes on in a men's store," Bob said. "If you have questions or need help, ask us. We'll just play it by ear."

By 10:10, Denny had waited on his first customer and made his first sale. He was so busy that it was almost 1:30 before he had time for lunch. Business during the afternoon was also good. He even waited on several customers whom he knew from his previous sales job. Overall, Denny had a good first day. He had to ask a few questions, and Bob made a few suggestions. Denny knew he was going to like working at Rogers'.

SUCCESS TIP

Don't be afraid to jump right into a new job!

THINK CRITICALLY

1. Do you think Denny had a typical first day on the job? Why or why not?
2. Why do you think the first day went so well for Denny?

LESSON 6.1
YOUR FIRST DAY AT WORK

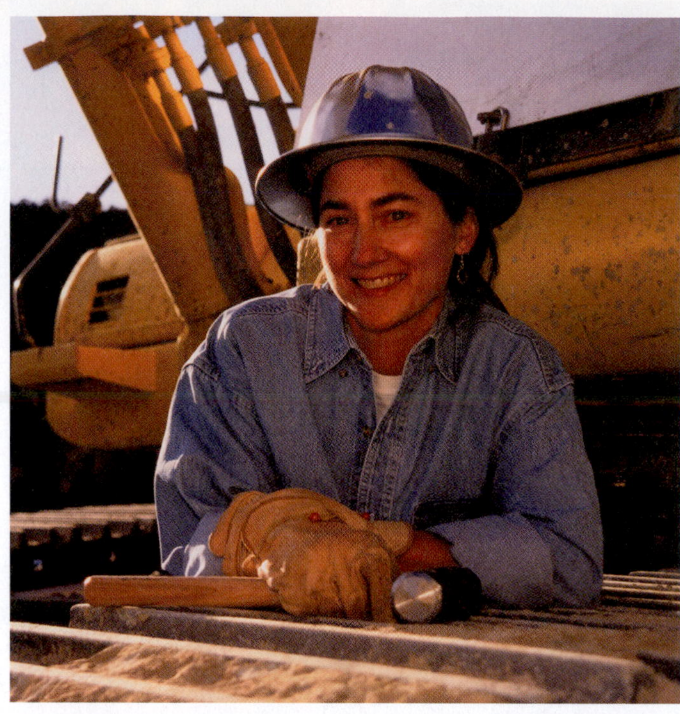

OBJECTIVES

- RECOGNIZE THAT ANXIETY TOWARD BEGINNING A NEW JOB IS NORMAL
- DESCRIBE WHAT TO EXPECT FROM AN EMPLOYER WHEN BEGINNING A NEW JOB

PRE-EMPLOYMENT ANXIETY

Anxiety is the state of feeling worried or uneasy, usually about something that may happen in the future. You may have feelings of anxiety about beginning a new job. Try to relax. Remember that the employer chose your job application from among many others. You were interviewed because the employer thought you were qualified. You were hired because the employer believed you were the best person for the job.

Starting a new job is not like wilderness training. Your employer will not expect you to endure extreme temperatures, sleep on the hard ground, and eat cold beans. Your employer probably isn't going to test you to see if you can make it. Believe it or not, your employer wants you to succeed.

Your employer more than likely understands that you are going through a stressful time. He or she understands that it will take time for you to learn the company's rules, its procedures, and any other policies.

PERSONAL DECISIONS

You have just been hired as a clerk at a grocery store. Your new supervisor tells you to report for work tomorrow at 4:00 sharp. You agree to do this and leave the store. Later, you remember that you have to take a make-up exam at school tomorrow afternoon.

WHAT WOULD YOU DO?

REPORTING FOR WORK

What you do on the first day of work depends on the company you have joined. You've already read about Denny Liu's first day on the job. Now let's look at Francine Gordon's first day.

Francine applied for a job at Northeast Electric Power Company. Two weeks later, she received a telephone call from the assistant personnel manager, who offered Francine a job as an equipment operator. Since this was the job Francine wanted, she accepted right away. Francine was told to report to work at 9:30 on Monday morning for a new employee orientation. She was also told that a parking decal for her car and a map showing the location of the meeting room would be sent to her in the mail.

Francine arrived at the plant about 9:15 on Monday. A uniformed guard at the entrance motioned for her to stop. Before Francine could say anything, the guard asked her if she was a new employee. The guard pointed out the building entrance and the lot in which she was to park.

Francine parked her car and took out her map. She was glad to have the map. The building seemed to be as long as three football fields. She entered the building and walked down the hall. She finally found the correct meeting room. There, Mr. Walsh, the assistant personnel manager, gave Francine a name tag and directed her to a seat.

At 9:35, a woman went to the front of the room. Mr. Walsh introduced her as Mrs. Ramos, the personnel manager. Mrs. Ramos welcomed the 12 new employees and introduced several staff members.

Then she gave a 15-minute slide presentation about the company. Before seeing the program, Francine had not thought much about the number of people and businesses that depended on Northeast Electric Power Company. She was already feeling proud about working for such an important company.

Mr. Walsh then took over the meeting. After answering some questions, he passed out a folder to each person. The folder contained a "Policies and Procedures Manual" and many forms. The group filled out forms and discussed the information in the folder for the rest of the day.

Some large companies, such as Northeast Electric Power Company, have a very formal employee orientation program. Because of the large number of employees that Northeast Electric Power Company hires, such a program is efficient. The company can orient several new workers at once. This kind of detailed program ensures that all employees have received the same information. Many problems can be prevented when all employees are following the same set of rules.

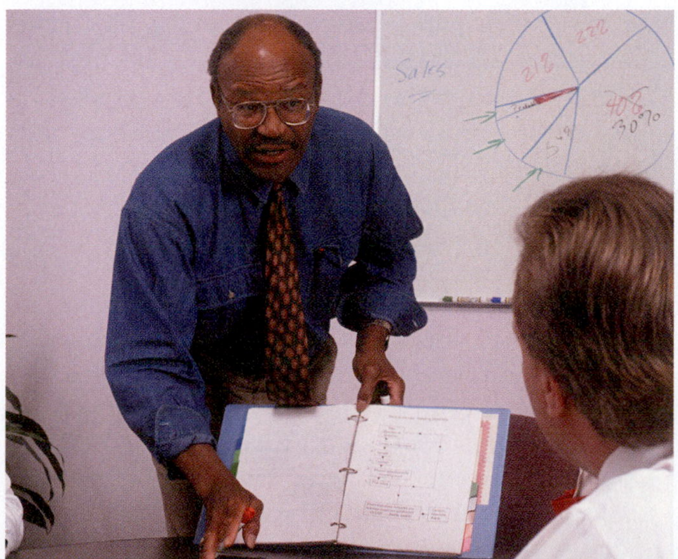

Pay particular attention to the discussion of the policy manual.

WORKFORCE TRENDS

The gap between employment rates of men and women is closing. Since 1950, the proportion of men in the labor force has declined from 86 percent to 75 percent. In contrast, the trend for women is on the rise. In 1950, one-third of women worked outside of the home. Fifty years later, 60 percent of women were in the labor force.

Now, let's contrast Francine's first day with that of Denny Liu. What a difference between Francine's and Denny's first days! Denny spent most of his first day waiting on customers. Francine, on the other hand, spent much of her first day learning about Northeast Electric Power Company. In fact, Francine didn't actually start work until two weeks later. She spent the first two weeks in class learning how to be an equipment operator.

Clearly, one person's first day at work may be quite different from another person's first day at work. However, Francine and Denny did many similar things and were provided with similar kinds of information. This was just done in different ways. Can you think of some ways that Francine's and Denny's first days were similar?

LESSON 6.1 REVIEW

1. **Name two things to remember to relieve pre-employment anxiety.**
2. **What are two reasons companies like Northeast Electric Power Company conduct employee orientation programs?**

LESSON 6.2
WORKPLACE MANAGEMENT

OBJECTIVES

- DESCRIBE HOW AN ORGANIZATION CHART SHOWS THE FLOW OF AUTHORITY AND RESPONSIBILITY WITHIN AN ORGANIZATION
- LIST AREAS FOR WHICH EMPLOYERS HAVE POLICIES AND RULES

ORGANIZATIONAL STRUCTURE

During your first days on a new job, you will find out how the company is organized and what the written rules are. You will also begin to learn about the unwritten rules. Information about unwritten rules is included in Chapters 7 and 8. The company will want to know more about you, too. You will have to fill out many forms. The most common one is Form W-4. You will learn about this form later in the chapter.

Francine and Denny learned many of the same things during their first day on the job. They learned:

- How the workplace was laid out.
- Where they would be working (their workstations).
- How to keep track of hours worked.
- Where to look for posted notices such as work schedules.
- What to do if they needed help or had questions.

These are important things that all workers need to learn during their first day on the job. In the rest of this chapter, you will study other concerns of new workers.

All organizations, including companies and schools, have lines of authority and responsibility. **Authority** is the power or rank to give orders and make assignments to others. For instance, a teacher has authority in the classroom. **Responsibility** deals with the duty to follow an order or carry out a work assignment. In school, for

> **ETHICAL DECISIONS**
>
> Upon beginning a new job, you may know very little about a company or its management. This can happen despite your best efforts to research the company and ask thoughtful questions in a job interview. Suppose that during the orientation meeting you discover things about the company that disturb you. Perhaps the company manufactures products that are in conflict with your moral or religious beliefs. Perhaps the company officials have an attitude that is completely different from your own. You begin to wonder if this is the right job for you.
>
> **WHAT WOULD YOU DO?**

example, you, as a student, are responsible for completing your assignments. The flow of authority and responsibility can be shown in an organization chart. A sample organization chart for a small kitchen equipment manufacturing company is shown in Figure 6-1.

In a typical large company, the stockholders have the ultimate authority. That is, they "own" the company. However, thousands of stockholders cannot manage a company. So, the stockholders elect a board of directors to represent them. A board of directors is normally composed of people outside the company. They meet regularly to review management, establish policy, and make recommendations.

The board hires a president to manage the company on a day-to-day basis. The president then **delegates**, or assigns, tasks to lower-ranking executives who are responsible for various company operations. In practical terms, the company president has the greatest authority and the greatest responsibility in an organization.

As you can see in the organization chart in Figure 6-1, each person or group of workers in an organization does different tasks. Note how each level in the organization is responsible to another level. Also note that some workers have more authority than other workers.

When you begin work, you will be given a job title. Where will your job fit into the overall organization? If you start out in an entry-level job, you will probably have a lot of responsibility and little or no authority. You will probably report to a supervisor who will assign work for you to do.

Answering to a supervisor or boss is called reporting to authority. You may do this in two ways. One is *formal reporting*, which is based on rank or the chain of command. For example, Figure 6-1 shows that the production workers formally report to the plant manager.

Another way of reporting to authority is *informal reporting*. This usually involves reporting to a specific person for a short time or for a certain work assignment. Suppose, for example, that you work on the accounting staff for the company shown in Figure 6-1. Your regular supervisor, the vice president for finance, assigns you to help out the sales manager on a new project. The supervisor directs you to do what the sales manager tells you. In this case, you will be informally reporting to the sales manager for a while.

It is important to follow your company's lines of authority, both formal and informal. Take time to become familiar with these by listening, watching, and asking questions.

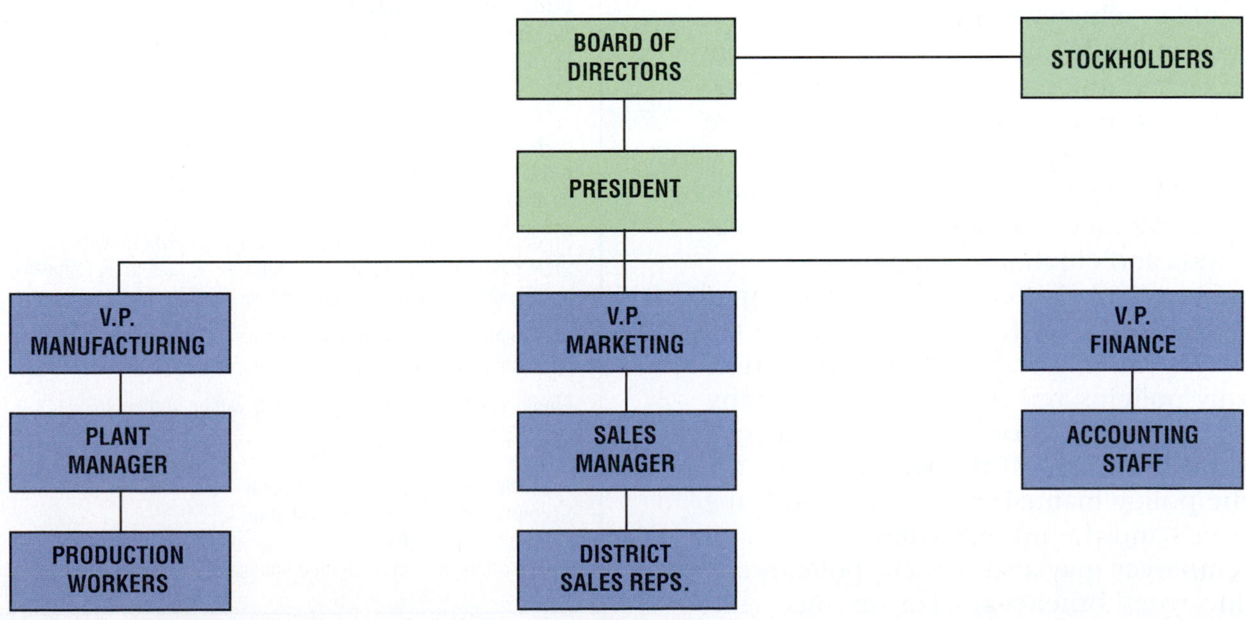

Figure 6-1 Sample organization chart

A browser is software that lets you view information and navigate the Web. The two most common browsers are Microsoft® Internet Explorer and Netscape® Navigator. Both browsers have a similar look and feel. When you are browsing through pages on the Web, it can be difficult to keep track of pages you have visited. To help you return to a page you have recently visited, the browser includes a feature called a History list. To permanently store the address of a page you frequently visit, you can use the Favorites or Bookmarks feature.

POLICIES AND RULES

Most companies have written policies and rules. These help the organization to run smoothly. Imagine, for example, what would happen to production if large numbers of workers took their vacations at the same time. Or, imagine how disruptive it would be if people came to work and left whenever they wanted.

Policies and rules also ensure that all employees receive fair and equal treatment. Some policies and rules are required by federal and state laws. Others are desirable simply to promote good morale and positive working relationships among employees. **Morale** is a mood or spirit, such as the attitude and emotion of employees.

The formal rules often appear in a company **policy manual**, which is a booklet given to new employees that contains an explanation of company policies and rules. If your company has a policy manual, you will be given a copy when you start work. If the workplace is unionized, the policy manual may contain both the employer's and the union's rules.

An employer may also present policies and rules in several other ways. For instance, rules may be explained at a formal meeting or program for new employees, as was done in Francine's orientation. In some cases, important rules appear on a sign or bulletin board in the work area or are sent as e-mail (Figure 6-2). Your supervisor or coworkers may also be useful sources of such information.

Here are some of the most common items for which employers have written policies and rules.

- ***Salaries, wages, and benefits.*** Many employers outline in writing how pay rates, benefits, and raises are decided.
- ***Attendance, absences, and punctuality.*** You must report to work on time every workday unless you have a good reason not to. If you are going to be late or absent, follow your employer's policy for reporting in. In cases of illness, you may need a medical excuse.
- ***Leave.*** Most employers provide time off, with and without pay, for various reasons. Find out your employer's policies for sick leave, vacation time, jury-duty leave, and other time off.
- ***Work schedule and records.*** You must follow company rules for hours worked, meals, breaks, and overtime work. This often means clocking in and out on time in person.

Don had a friend, Kim, clock in for him on mornings he wanted to sleep late. When the boss found out, both Don and Kim almost lost

SUBJECT: **NO-SMOKING POLICY**
DATE: Wed, 1 Aug 20-- 9:26:26-0500
FROM: "Hector Diaz" <hdiaz@stateins.net>
TO: "All Employees" <list1@stateins.net>

State Insurance has established a No-Smoking Policy aimed at protecting the health of our employees and our workplace environment.

Smoking is not permitted by any person anywhere within State's portion of the building. This rule applies to all State employees, temporary employees, visitors, and customers.

All potential new hires must be advised of this policy and must abide by it as a condition of employment.

Employees in violation of this policy will be subject to the following:

First offense:	Written reprimand
Second offense:	30 days' probation
Third offense:	Two weeks' suspension without pay
Fourth offense:	Immediate dismissal

Figure 6-2 ***Employees learn about company policies and rules in many different ways.***

their jobs. If they do this again, the employer's policy is to fire them both.

- ***Expenses and reimbursement.*** If you travel on company business or buy materials for company use, those expenses are considered company costs. The company should reimburse you for them. To **reimburse** is to pay back money that has already been spent. Company policy will explain what expenses you can be reimbursed for and how to go about getting reimbursement.
- ***Due process.*** Suppose you have a complaint about something or your boss has a complaint about you. The company may have formal procedures for solving this problem. **Due process** is the legal right to be notified of a complaint against you and to state your case or point of view before a decision is made.
- ***Probation and review.*** As a new employee, you may work for a period of time on probation. **Probation** is a trial period during which one's performance is being observed and evaluated. During this time, supervisors will carefully evaluate your work and attitude. At the end of your probation period, the employer will decide whether or not to consider you for permanent employment. Once you are a permanent employee, a supervisor will review your performance from time to time. Most employers have written policies about when and how you are to be reviewed.

Read and carefully study your company's policy manual. If you can't find rules covering these items or other items of interest, ask your supervisor about them. You are responsible for obeying all policies and rules. Not knowing the policies and rules is not a good excuse.

Not all of a company's rules are written down. You will gradually learn rules that are not in the policy manual. Some of these rules relate to appearance, work habits, attitudes, and job performance. These rules will be discussed in Chapters 7 and 8.

Victor was doing some home repairs over the weekend. He left for work Monday morning with several of his tools still lying in the garage. Later in the morning when he reached into his toolbox for a screwdriver, he remembered where it was. He had to ask another crew member to borrow one. The look on his coworker's face suggested that there is an unwritten rule about borrowing tools.

One unwritten rule that needs to be discussed here relates to how people deal with each other in day-to-day activities. In some cases, managers, supervisors, and employees are very casual. Everyone is on a first-name basis. In other cases, the workers are more formal. All workers may be addressed by last names. Ann Morales, for instance, is called Mrs. Morales, and Paul Cramer is known as Mr. Cramer.

Some organizations have a formal way of getting work done. Ways of doing things that differ from the accepted way may be frowned upon. In less formal organizations, the most important thing may be getting the work done. How the work gets done may be left to each worker. By paying attention, you will learn how your company expects you to relate to others and to get the work done.

LESSON 6.2 REVIEW

1. **Which is usually greater for beginning workers, level of authority or level of responsibility?**
2. **What is the difference between formal reporting and informal reporting?**
3. **What two purposes do written policies and rules serve in a company?**
4. **What are five ways in which a company may communicate policies and rules to employees?**
5. **What should you do if a subject of interest is not covered in the company's policy manual?**
6. **Give an example of an area that is often covered by unwritten rules.**

HIGH-GROWTH OCCUPATIONS FOR THE 21st CENTURY

Dental Assistants

Dental assistants perform a variety of patient care, office, and laboratory duties. They work at chair-side as dentists examine and treat patients. They make patients as comfortable as possible in the dental chair, prepare them for treatment, and obtain dental records. Assistants hand instruments and materials to dentists and keep patients' mouths dry and clear by using suction or other methods. Assistants sterilize and disinfect instruments and equipment and prepare tray setups for dental procedures. They also instruct patients on postoperative and general oral health care.

Dental assistants must have good manual dexterity because dentists rely on them to help with dental procedures.

Some dental assistants prepare materials for making impressions and restorations, expose radiographs, and process dental x-ray film as directed by a dentist. They may also remove sutures, apply anesthetics and cavity-preventive agents to teeth and gums, remove excess cement used in the filling process, and place rubber dams on teeth to isolate them for individual treatment.

Those with laboratory duties make casts of the teeth and mouth from impressions taken by dentists, clean and polish removable appliances, and make temporary crowns. Dental assistants with office duties schedule and confirm appointments, receive patients, keep treatment records, send bills, receive payments, and order dental supplies.

Virtually all assistants work in private dental offices. Most assistants learn their skills on the job, though some are trained in dental assisting programs offered by community colleges, trade schools, technical institutes, or the Armed Forces. Assistants must be a dentist's "third hand." Therefore, dentists look for people who are reliable, can work well with others, and have good manual dexterity.

Without further education, opportunities for advancement are limited. Some dental assistants working in the front office become office managers. Others working chair-side often go back to school to become dental hygienists.

LESSON 6.3
SUPERVISORS AND FORM W-4

- *IDENTIFY WAYS TO WORK EFFECTIVELY WITH A SUPERVISOR*
- *UNDERSTAND HOW TO FILL OUT A FORM W-4*

WORKING UNDER SUPERVISION

In the workplace, every employee is responsible to someone else. This is not unlike school. In your job as a student, you are responsible to your teachers. They, in turn, report to the principal or department head, and so on. On the job, unless you are self-employed, you will work under the direction of a **supervisor**.

Your supervisor will be responsible for training you and seeing that you learn company rules. He or she will also observe how well you perform on the job. Your success as an employee relates strongly to how well you work under supervision. Some suggestions for getting started on the right foot with your supervisor follow.

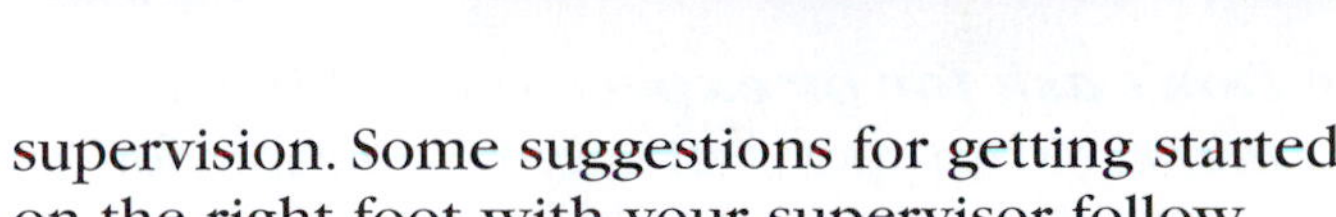

- ***Use the supervisor for communication.*** If you want to send messages to someone higher in the organization, go through your supervisor.
- ***Ask the supervisor for direction.*** Your supervisor is responsible for your work, training, and safety. Before performing tasks for the first time, go over them with the supervisor. For example, you might say, "After I get these cartons unpacked, then I should come and see you, right?" Understanding beforehand what you are to do saves everyone time. If you are ever unsure of how to do something, ask for help. Most supervisors respect people who know when to ask for help.

You have just started working in the returns department. Your supervisor says 1 out of every 36 sets of china shipped arrives with broken pieces. In a shipment of 900 sets, how many sets are likely to have broken pieces?

SOLUTION

To calculate the number of sets that will probably have broken pieces, set up the equation as fractions. Cross-multiply the numerator and denominator that are known and divide by the other denominator.

$$\frac{1}{36} = \frac{?}{900} \qquad 1 \times 900 = 900 \qquad 900 \div 36 = 25$$

In a shipment of 900 sets, you can expect 25 sets to contain damaged pieces.

Form **W-4** Department of the Treasury Internal Revenue Service

Employee's Withholding Allowance Certificate

► For Privacy Act and Paperwork Reduction Act Notice, see reverse.

OMB No. 1545-0010 **2000**

1 Type or print your first name and middle initial: John R. Last name: Nye
2 Your social security number: 315-20-4024

Home address (number and street or rural route): 1612 Fredrick St.

City or town, state, and ZIP code: Carbondale, IL 62901-1482

3 Marital Status: ☒ Single ☐ Married ☐ Married, but withhold at higher Single rate.
Note: *If married, but legally separated, or spouse is a nonresident alien, check the Single box*

4 Total number of allowances you are claiming (from line G above or from the Worksheets on back if they apply) . . . . 4 | 1

5 Additional amount, if any, you want deducted from each pay . . . . 5 | $ 0

6 I claim exemption from withholding and I certify that I meet **ALL** of the following conditions for exemption:
- Last year I had a right to a refund of **ALL** Federal income tax withheld because I had **NO** tax liability; **AND**
- This year I expect a refund of **ALL** Federal income tax withheld because I expect to have **NO** tax liability; **AND**
- This year if my income exceeds $500 and includes nonwage income, another person cannot claim me as a dependent.

If you meet all of the above conditions, enter the year effective and "EXEMPT" here . . . . . . ► 6 | 20

7 Are you a full-time student? (**Note:** *Full-time students are not automatically exempt.*) . . . . 7 ☐ Yes ☒ No

Under penalties of perjury, I certify that I am entitled to the number of withholding allowances claimed on this certificate or entitled to claim exempt status.

Employee's signature ► John R. Nye **Date ►** March 6 , 2000

8 Employer's name and address (**Employer:** Complete 8 and 10 **only if sending to IRS**) | 9 Office code (optional) | 10 Employer identification number

Figure 6-3 Your employer will ask you to fill out one of these forms. A worksheet is provided to help you figure withholding allowances.

- ***Don't ask for or expect special treatment.*** Most supervisors are responsible for many workers. All should be treated the same, so don't ask for special favors.
- ***Accept and use the supervisor's suggestions.*** Your supervisor is more experienced at the work than you. Carla thought she had a better way of doing a job task. Because she was a new worker, though, she kept quiet. Later she learned that there were good reasons, such as safety, for following standard procedures.

Your supervisor is there to direct and assist you. Be aware, however, that your supervisor has other work to do. Your goal should be to learn your job quickly and perform it well with only a minimum of supervision.

PAYROLL WITHHOLDING

Every worker must pay federal income tax. The tax system operates on a pay-as-you-go basis. This means that the employer takes income tax out of each paycheck. The amount of tax the employer withholds depends on three things:

- The amount of money you earn
- Whether you are married or not
- The number of **allowances**, or tax exemptions, you are entitled to claim. For instance, a single person is entitled to one allowance.

Your employer will keep track of how much money you earn. On Form W-4, you will provide information about your marital status and the number of allowances you are entitled to claim.

John Nye is single and only claims one allowance. His completed Form W-4 is shown in Figure 6-3. Christina Comito is a single parent with two children. She claims three allowances—one for herself and one for each child. Based on each employee's earnings, marital status, and allowances, an employer looks at a table to find how much tax to withhold.

Some people may be exempt from tax withholdings. Being **exempt** means that they do not have to pay taxes. People who earn less than a certain amount of money in a year are usually exempt. What was the amount last year that a single person with one allowance could earn before having to pay federal income tax?

LESSON 6.3 REVIEW

1. **How is the job of student similar to that of a paid employee?**
2. **What are four ways to start a good relationship with an employer? Briefly explain each.**
3. **What three things determine how much tax is withheld from your paycheck?**

FOCUS ON THE WORKPLACE

HIGH-PERFORMANCE WORK ORGANIZATIONS

Historically, many kinds of work in America have been patterned after the mass production system made famous by Henry Ford in the early 1900s. In mass production, jobs are broken down into a number of simple tasks. Each worker specializes in one task, which is done over and over.

Managers do the thinking and planning for the organization. Supervisors direct the work of frontline employees. Workers under this system need only be reliable, steady, and willing to follow directions.

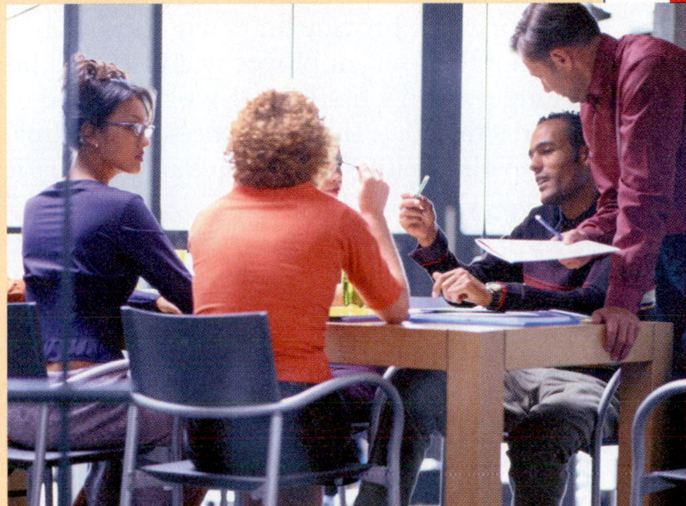

Input from frontline workers is encouraged in a high-performance work organization.

The mass production system has helped make our nation a great economic power. It has also resulted in a high standard of living for workers. This system still determines the way most factories, offices, banks, hospitals, and schools are organized.

As we begin a new century, our nation faces increasing global economic competition. To remain competitive, we must increase productivity and improve quality. The solution adopted by many companies is called a high-performance work organization.

The basic idea of a high-performance work organization is to give greater authority to frontline workers. Layers of managers disappear as teams of workers take over such tasks as quality control and production scheduling. Workers are asked to use judgment and make decisions at the point where goods and services are produced.

This type of work organization requires retraining of workers and managers. The high cost of retraining, however, is offset by gains in quality and productivity. High-performance work organizations are becoming the model for a successful future.

THINK CRITICALLY

1. Why do you think the mass production system helped make our nation a great economic power?
2. Give some examples of ways in which a high-performance work organization might help improve quality and productivity.

CHAPTER 6

Chapter in Brief

Lesson 6.1 *Your First Day at Work*

A. It is normal to experience some anxiety when beginning a new job. Many companies provide an orientation to help new employees get started properly. Your employer wants you to be successful on the job.

B. One person's first day at work may be quite different from another person's first day. However, most new employees do similar things and are provided with similar kinds of information.

Lesson 6.2 *Workplace Management*

A. An organization chart shows the flow of authority and responsibility within an organization. It is important to follow your company's formal and informal lines of authority and responsibility.

B. Companies have written policies and rules to help them run smoothly. You are responsible for obeying all policies and rules. Companies also have unwritten rules that you will need to learn.

Lesson 6.3 *Supervisors and Form W-4*

A. On the job, you will probably work under the direction of a supervisor. Use the supervisor for communication and direction. Accept and use the supervisor's suggestions, but don't ask for or expect special treatment.

B. Employers are required to withhold money from your paycheck for federal income tax. The amount withheld is based on information that you provide on Form W-4.

Activities

1. Some of your classmates may already have jobs. Ask these people to explain what their orientation to a new job was like. Ask them questions about their experiences on the job.
2. As a group activity, develop an organization chart for the employees in your school. At the top of the chart, start with the school district's board of education. How many levels are there? Suppose a teacher has a complaint about a board policy. With whom would he or she file a complaint? Discuss the process the teacher should follow.
3. Obtain an example of a company policy manual. You may already have one from your job, or perhaps you can borrow one from a family member or a friend. Look through the manuals in class and discuss examples of each of the seven types of policies and rules explained. Do the manuals contain types of policies and rules that are not explained in the chapter? If so, discuss the merits of these policies and rules.

REVIEW

4. Does your school give students a written code of conduct that oulines policies and rules? If so, discuss how it is like a company policy manual. If not, discuss possible policies or rules that could go into such a manual.
5. The supervisor at your new job expects you to assemble 15 cases every two hours. In an eight-hour shift, how many cases should you assemble?

Word Power

On a separate sheet of paper, match each definition with the correct term. All definitions will be used, and a definition will be used only once.

6. A trial period during which one's performance is being observed and evaluated
7. A mood or spirit, such as the attitude and emotion of employees
8. At work, the duty to follow an order or carry out a work assignment
9. Assigns a task or responsibility to others
10. A boss; one who gives directions and orders and oversees the work of others
11. The number of tax exemptions to which one is entitled
12. The power or rank to give orders and make assignments to others
13. To pay back money already spent
14. To be free of something, such as not having to pay taxes
15. A feeling of concern, worry, or unease
16. The legal right to be notified of a complaint against you and to state your case or point of view before a decision is made
17. A booklet given to new employees that contains an explanation of company policies and rules

a. allowances
b. anxiety
c. authority
d. delegates
e. due process
f. exempt
g. morale
h. policy manual
i. probation
j. reimburse
k. responsibility
l. supervisor

Think Critically

18. What are some of the reasons why employers want new employees to make a quick and successful transition from school to the workplace?
19. Think of an instance in your life in which your anxiety about a situation turned out to be worse than the situation itself. What might this suggest regarding anxiety toward beginning a new job?
20. Some supervisors try not to get too friendly or informal with employees whom they supervise. Do you think this is a good or bad idea? Why?
21. Under what circumstances might someone choose to specify an additional amount of withholding on line 5 of Form W-4?

CHAPTER 7

EXPECTATIONS OF EMPLOYERS

LESSONS

PREVIEW

Everyone needs time to adjust to a new job. After that, you will need to meet the same expectations as other employees. Accepting a job means you make a contract with an employer. You agree to perform certain duties in return for a certain salary or wage. Your responsibility is to do the tasks you were hired to do, in the way and at the time the employer wants them done.

THOUGHTS ON WORK

"The secret of joy in work is contained in one word—excellence. To know how to do something well is to enjoy it."

Pearl Buck

TAKING ACTION
WORK ATTITUDES

Art is an insurance agent. He also serves as secretary of the area's youth soccer association. Over the weekend, he needed to prepare a mailing for the group. So, after work on Friday, he loaded up his briefcase with supplies from the company's storeroom. He picked up a computer disk, a couple of pens, a legal pad, a ream of printer paper, a roll of tape, and a box of envelopes.

Art didn't consider taking a few office supplies to be stealing. "They won't miss this stuff," he thought. "The company made $350 million last year."

Later that week, Art heard that Janice, a coworker, was fired after her supervisor found out that she had let slip some confidential company information in an e-mail to a supplier. Art thought this was too harsh and said something to his supervisor about the firing.

"Art, giving away confidential company information is stealing," his supervisor said. "Whether it's a box of paper or a computer or a trade secret, it's all the same thing. The employee responsible can be fired, as our employment handbook states.

"Stealing is a violation of the company's trust," his employer continued. "Even if an employee who stole was kept on, that person's chances for future advancement in the company would be lessened."

Art was upset. Usually his company was very lenient with employees and gave second chances. The conversation made him worry that he might be fired if someone saw him take the supplies from the storeroom.

You have a promising future. Don't risk it by being like Art. Do not take anything owned by the company, regardless of its worth.

SUCCESS TIP
Honesty is the ONLY policy!

THINK CRITICALLY

1. Do you think that what Art did and what Janice did are the same thing?
2. If Art had been fired, do you think it would have been easy for him to find another job?

LESSON 7.1

JOB PERFORMANCE AND ATTITUDES

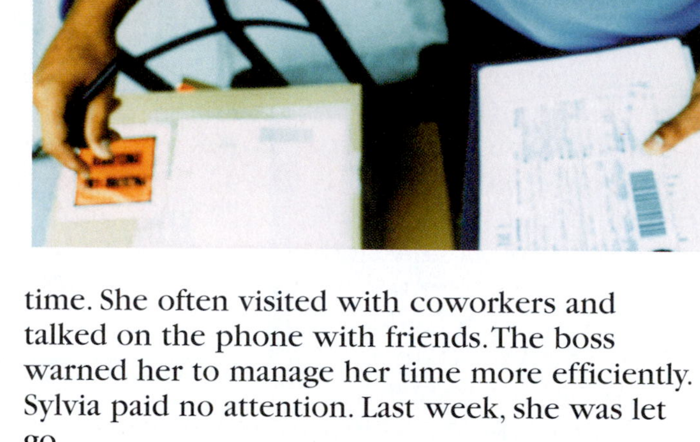

OBJECTIVES

- NAME AND DESCRIBE THE FIVE THINGS THAT EMPLOYERS EXPECT REGARDING JOB PERFORMANCE
- NAME AND DESCRIBE THE SEVEN THINGS THAT EMPLOYERS EXPECT REGARDING WORK HABITS AND ATTITUDES

EMPLOYER EXPECTATIONS

Work organizations either produce goods or provide services. Whether you are involved in producing goods or providing services, your employer will expect certain things from you.

Productivity

Employers expect employees to complete a certain amount of work. The output of a worker is known as **productivity**. Suppose Worker A does more work than Worker B. This means that Worker A is more productive.

Productivity is usually thought of in terms of goods-producing occupations such as welder, bricklayer, or factory worker. Productivity is also important in service occupations. Service-producing occupations include barber, flight attendant, salesclerk, and nurse. Whether you hammer nails or wait on tables, the employer will expect you to give a day's work for a day's pay.

Being productive means working at a steady pace during your time on the job. "Goofing off" is never okay. Sylvia learned this the hard way.

Sylvia was the sales manager of a small company. She liked her work but wasted a lot of time. She often visited with coworkers and talked on the phone with friends. The boss warned her to manage her time more efficiently. Sylvia paid no attention. Last week, she was let go.

Quality of Work

An employer expects you to do your work carefully, accurately, and thoroughly. Quality of work means how well a job is performed. Poor work quality may cancel out high productivity. For

> **WORKPLACE DECISIONS**
>
> You have been instructed to call a supplier and order replacement parts for several broken pieces of equipment. You are careful to provide all important information on quantities, part numbers, prices, and so on. After you finish, the supplier asks, "How do you want this shipped?"
>
> "Gee, the boss did not tell me," you think. There is no one else in the office to ask.
>
> **WHAT WOULD YOU DO?**

YOU'RE A WHAT? FARRIER

Some of the world's largest athletes rely on the work of a *farrier.* Workers in this occupation make and fit shoes for horses. Like humans, horses wear shoes for protection and comfort. At one time, farriers heated and formed rectangular steel for horseshoes by pounding it to shape over a large anvil. Now, ready-made shoes are available in a variety of sizes and materials. But knowing how to make custom shoes is still an important part of the business. Farriers trim the horses' hooves, prepare shoes, and nail those shoes to the hooves.

Farriery can be strenuous work. Farriers often lift and hold a horse's hoof for 15 minutes at a time. Most farriers are self-employed, with many working part-time while also maintaining other occupations. Farriers usually learn their craft through a combination of short-term training and apprenticeship. ■

example, a secretary who keys fast but makes a lot of errors is not doing the job well. Likewise, a production worker who solders many electrical components but whose soldered joints do not hold is not doing the job well.

Quality of work is very important to a company's success. Customers who receive high-quality goods or services come back for repeat business. This is why employers want their workers to do good work.

Employees who perform high-quality work take pride in their work. **Pride** is a feeling of satisfaction with what you or someone you know has accomplished or possesses.

Good Judgment

Have people ever said to you, "Use your head"? What they meant was to think about what you are doing or figure it out yourself. You cannot run to a boss every time you have a problem or must make a decision. Your employer will want you to use your judgment. **Judgment** is thinking about a problem and making the right decision.

Using good judgment is a sign of maturity that employers look for when promoting people to better jobs. If you are known as someone who makes quick decisions and has poor judgment, your time with the company may be short.

Safety Consciousness

Many jobs involve working with tools, machines, and equipment, some of which may be dangerous. For your benefit as well as that of coworkers, the employer will expect you to work safely. Part of being a safe worker is knowing how to do a job. You will have learned this through education or on-the-job training.

Your employer will expect you to perform your job in the way that you have been trained. In addition, the company will probably have safety rules that you will be expected to follow. For example, workers in certain areas of a plant may need to wear a hard hat or safety glasses.

If an accident or emergency does happen, you will be expected to follow certain steps. Let's say that a machine part gets stuck in a punch press. Your boss has told you that when this happens you should turn off the machine right away and go for help. Do what you are told. Do not try to fix the problem yourself.

Learn your company's safety rules and procedures by reading and studying printed company material. If you have any questions, be sure to ask your boss. Once you know the safety rules, practice them. Knowledge of them alone is not enough. Additional information on safety will be presented in Chapter 17.

Care of Equipment

An employer often has money tied up in expensive tools and equipment. You will be expected to take care of them and use them properly. Damaged tools and equipment cost money in two ways. First, the item must be repaired or replaced. Then, while the repairs are going on, work time is lost. Should you have questions about tools or equipment, ask them. Not doing so could cause serious problems.

Suppose you are working summers as a farm laborer. The boss asks you if you know how to drive the tractor. You say that you do. The tractor has some features that are unfamiliar to you. You decide to drive it anyhow. After a few minutes, the tractor stops dead. The mechanic says that your mistake caused several thousand dollars' worth of damage to the tractor. Even though the boss fires you, it could have been worse. In some cases, improper use of tools and equipment injures and kills workers.

Use tools and equipment as if they are your own. Think of them as if you have to pay for repairing or replacing them.

WORK HABITS AND ATTITUDES

Another type of employer expectation has to do with work habits and attitudes. These are the ways employees behave on the job. Poor work habits and a negative attitude are the main reasons most people lose their jobs. You may, for example, be a great hairstylist. You will not keep your job, though, if you cannot get along with your boss, coworkers, or clients.

Attendance and Punctuality

To avoid work delays or interruptions, employers expect workers to be on the job regularly. Let's see what happened on a construction site when a worker made a habit of "taking off."

A crew was building townhouses. Most of the workers showed up unless they had a good reason not to. Yvonne, however, frequently missed work. When she was absent, the other workers covered for her. Sometimes, though, the others were too busy with their own work to do hers, too. Yvonne's work did not get done on those days. The boss told Yvonne that if other crew members missed work as she did, the job could shut down. Yvonne got the point and changed her ways.

Punctuality is also necessary. **Punctuality** means being on time. Workplaces that are open at certain times need employees there to deal with business. An employer's profits and public image may suffer if employees are not there. Suppose a restaurant opens for business at 6:00 a.m. If some workers do not arrive until 6:30, customers will get poor service. They will eat elsewhere and tell others to do the same. Be ready to work at starting time, stay until quitting time, and take only the time set aside for lunch periods and breaks. Most workers are not paid for time they miss when they are absent or tardy.

If you must be absent or late, try to tell your supervisor as far ahead of time as possible. If you get sick one evening, for instance, notify the boss that you will miss work the next day.

1. Absent from work too frequently or for questionable reasons
2. Has to be supervised too much of the time
3. Takes no initiative when something needs to be done
4. Isn't very observant; fails to recognize errors or problems
5. Doesn't listen well
6. Arrives late or leaves early too often
7. Doesn't consider the consequences of decisions or actions
8. Too much socializing with other workers or visitors
9. Can't accept suggestions or criticism
10. Doesn't seem to care about doing a job well

Figure 7-1 ***A study of employers identified these as the ten most serious problems of young, entry-level workers (in rank order).***

Cooperation

"He or she just refuses to cooperate" is a common employer complaint about a worker. **Cooperation** means getting along with others. One aspect of cooperation is following orders. Another way of saying this is doing what you are told. Since you are likely to be a beginning worker, you will probably receive many orders.

Your job may include boring tasks, such as sweeping floors or cleaning equipment. After all, someone has to do them. If you won't, the employer will hire someone who will. Accept your assignments cheerfully, or at least willingly, and do your best. If you do, the employer will notice.

Cooperation also means being able to take criticism. When you accept wages, you agree to do the job the way the employer wants it done. The employer has a right to criticize or correct you. The employer wants you to improve your work performance. You should, too. Accept and profit from constructive criticism. Thank the employer, tell him or her you will improve, and then do so.

COMMUNICATION AT WORK

CREATING A POSITIVE IMPRESSION

To create a positive impression at work, you must do more than show up on time and do your work. Your body language, tone of voice, and willingness to work will make a difference.

Watch your body language. Some body language can put others off. Crossing your arms, scowling, glaring, sighing, and not looking someone in the eye are examples.

Have a positive tone of voice. Your tone of voice can communicate respect, a willingness to work, unhappiness, sarcasm, and so on. Make sure your tone is positive.

Show that you are willing to work. Request new assignments, complete assignments on time, and accept even dull and routine assignments with a smile.

Courtesy and cooperation go hand in hand. You can build good working relationships by being respectful, friendly, and considerate toward others. A smile or a friendly greeting tells others that you are trying to help create a positive work setting.

Interest and Enthusiasm

Employers like employees who show interest and enthusiasm toward their work. Such people are often the most productive and cooperative workers. **Interest** is a feeling of excitement and involvement. **Enthusiasm** is eagerness or a strong interest in something. Few people, of course, find everything about their job to be interesting and enjoyable. Do, however, show your enthusiasm for those parts that you like.

Your company and your coworkers also deserve your interest and enthusiasm. Keep up to date on the company's plans. Read any employee newsletter or company magazine. Try to take part in company social events and activities. You and the company will benefit.

Honesty

Employers expect honesty of their employees. **Honesty** is a refusal to lie, steal, or mislead in any way. Stealing is a serious problem in many businesses and industries. Most employees caught stealing are fired. They may face criminal charges as well.

Most stealing involves the theft of money or expensive tools and equipment. But taking office supplies and making photocopies for personal use are also forms of stealing.

Loyalty

Your employer would like you to feel a sense of loyalty to the company. **Loyalty** means believing in and being devoted to something. This means, for example, that you should not criticize the company when talking with coworkers, friends, or strangers. It is being proud of what you do and where you work.

No company, of course, is perfect. If you disagree with a company policy or action, discuss it with your supervisor.

LESSON 7.1 REVIEW

1. **How does quality of work relate to a company's success?**
2. **Name three things that an employee can do to perform a job more safely.**
3. **What should you do if you must be absent or late to work?**
4. **List four ways that an employee can be cooperative on the job.**

HIGH-GROWTH OCCUPATIONS FOR THE 21st CENTURY

Desktop Publishing Specialists

The printing process has three stages—prepress, press, and postpress (binding). Prepress workers prepare material for printing presses. They perform a variety of tasks involved with transforming text and pictures into finished pages and making printing plates of the pages. Advances in computer software and printing technology continue to change the nature of prepress work.

Desktop publishing refers to using a personal computer, in combination with text, graphics, and page layout software, to produce publication-quality documents. *Desktop publishing specialists* import word-processed files into page layout software or use a keyboard to enter text. They format this text in different sizes and styles. They also set column widths and appropriate spacing. The computer then displays and arranges the type in columns on a screen resembling a television monitor. With desktop publishing, an entire newspaper, catalog, or book page, complete with artwork, can be made up on the screen exactly as it will appear in print. The final products of a desktop publishing system are reader-ready or camera-ready documents that can then be printed or reproduced by traditional means.

Although technology has changed the printing process, workers at a print shop are still responsible for the quality of the finished product.

Preflight technicians edit the work of desktop publishing specialists and ensure the overall quality of the finished product before it is delivered to the customer. In small shops, *job printers* may be responsible for composition and page layout, reading proofs for errors and clarity, correcting mistakes, and printing.

In addition to changing the printing process, technology has also shifted employment opportunities away from traditional printing plants to advertising agencies, public relations firms, and large corporations. Many companies are turning to in-house typesetting or desktop publishing, as personal computers with elaborate graphic capabilities have become common. Corporations are finding it more profitable to print their own newsletters, reports, and other publications than to send them out to trade shops.

LESSON 7.2
RATING WORK BEHAVIOR

OBJECTIVES

- *DESCRIBE THE PURPOSES OF PERFORMANCE EVALUATION*
- *EXPLAIN THE TWO-STEP EVALUATION PROCESS*

PURPOSES OF EVALUATION

Instructors have been evaluating your work as a student for many years. On the job, your employer will also evaluate your work. A **performance evaluation** is the process of judging how well an employee is doing on the job. The employer rates your job performance, your work habits, and your attitudes.

Employee evaluation allows employers to determine how well workers are doing their jobs. Performance evaluations have several purposes.

One purpose is to decide if you deserve a pay raise and how much to give you. Employers know it is important to provide pay raises as a reward for good work.

Evaluation also helps employees become better workers. This benefits both the employee and the employer. For you, the employee, the feedback you get helps you learn and improve. You find out what your strengths and weaknesses are. For the employer, the evaluation may suggest places where you need more on-the-job training.

Finally, evaluation provides a basis for future job assignments. Let's say that an opening exists for a department supervisor. Management might review employee evaluations to see which, if any, employee could be promoted. Or, suppose your evaluation results suggest that you would do better in a different job. The employer might then transfer you to another department.

HOW YOU ARE EVALUATED

The way you will be evaluated differs from company to company. Daksha, who works for a very small company, does not often realize that her boss is evaluating her. From time to time, she and her boss discuss Daksha's work. All feedback is verbal, no forms are used, and no records are kept.

Most large firms, however, have a standard procedure for employee evaluation. The evaluations usually take place once a year, although every six months is not uncommon.

Most evaluations are done in two steps. Your boss or supervisor fills out an evaluation form. A sample form is shown in Figure 7-2 on the next page. Then you meet with the supervisor or boss. The two of you go over the form and discuss your strengths and weaknesses. The tone of this meeting should be positive and constructive, unless you are doing a really poor job.

WORKFORCE TRENDS

Over the past quarter century, wage gaps between workers with different education levels have increased. Twenty years ago, the average college graduate earned 38 percent more than the average high school graduate. Today, it is 71 percent more.

Student-Trainee Evaluation Sheet
COOPERATIVE EDUCATION PROGRAMS
Swinburn Public Schools

Reporting Month ______
Please Return By ______

Student's Name ______ Supervisor's Name ______

Training Station ______

INSTRUCTIONS: Please rate the student by circling the number on each scale below at the point that most accurately describes the student learner's progress to date. (Please feel free to make comments on the back of this paper.)

CATEGORIES	OUTSTANDING	ABOVE AVERAGE	AVERAGE	BELOW AVERAGE	UNSATISFACTORY
Personal Appearance	5	4	3	2	1
Attendance and Tardiness	5	4	3	2	1
Rate of Progress	5	4	3	2	1
Follows Directions	5	4	3	2	1
Job Judgment Decision Making	5	4	3	2	1
Attitude Toward Job	5	4	3	2	1
Ability to Get Along with People	5	4	3	2	1
Initiative (Does Things Without Being Told)	5	4	3	2	1
Safety	5	4	3	2	1
Dependability (Overall)	5	4	3	2	1

OUTSTANDING ☐ ABOVE AVERAGE ☐ AVERAGE ☐ BELOW AVERAGE ☐ UNSATISFACTORY ☐

Supervisor's Signature ______ Date ______ Letter Grade ______

Student's Signature ______

Figure 7-2 ***Sample performance evaluation form***

The discussion between you and your boss or supervisor will not be one-sided. You should have a chance to discuss what you like and dislike about your current position. This is a good time for you to discuss your future goals. Do not use the time to complain about the job or coworkers, though.

An evaluation is not just a once-a-year thing. Your boss is continually watching your job performance, work habits, and attitudes. The ratings you receive in an evaluation result from a process that goes on all the time. This is why it pays to do your best work each and every day.

If you get a negative evaluation, you will need to face up to your shortcomings. Make sure you understand what you can do to correct the problem. Your future in the company will depend on showing that you can improve your work behavior before the next evaluation. If you ignore what your boss tells you, your next evaluation could be your last.

LESSON 7.2 REVIEW

1. **For employers, what are the three purposes of employee evaluation?**
2. **Describe the two-step evaluation procedure that most companies follow.**

FOCUS ON THE WORKER

LABOR UNIONS

A labor union is a group of workers who have joined together to protect their rights. The two main types of unions are craft and industrial. A craft union is made up of skilled workers in a craft or trade, such as plumbers, musicians, or barbers. Workers in the same industry often belong to an industrial union. Perhaps you have heard of the United Auto Workers or the United Mine Workers. These are industrial unions.

Throughout its history, organized labor has fought for three main goals. These have been improvements in:

- Wages, hours, and benefits.
- Job security.
- Safe and healthy working conditions.

Unions also provide apprenticeship programs that teach work skills to young union members. Some unions have hiring halls where workers can go to find out about job openings.

This pastry chef is a union member. Does she belong to a craft union or an industrial union?

Most unions in the United States are in the Midwest and Northeast. These areas have traditionally had large construction, manufacturing, transportation, and mining industries.

An employer that has an agreement with a union is called a union shop. In a union shop, the employer can hire whomever he or she chooses. However, the employee must join the union within a certain period of time. About 20 states have so-called "right-to-work" laws that do not allow union shops. These states have open shops in which an employee does not have to join a union.

When you start a job, a coworker or supervisor may ask you to join a union. Members of the local union must vote on your membership. Usually, though, anyone who applies is accepted. You will probably pay an initiation fee to join, and you must pay regular dues. You can learn more about unions on the Internet. Many unions have web sites for news and membership information.

THINK CRITICALLY

1. Do you think labor unions are needed today? Why or why not?
2. What might be some advantages and disadvantages to being in a union?

CHAPTER 7

Chapter in Brief

Lesson 7.1 *Job Performance and Attitudes*

A. After a short period of adjustment, you will need to meet the same expectations as other employees. Your responsibility is to do the job tasks in the way and at the time the employer wants them done. Your employer will expect the following in terms of your job performance: productivity, quality of work, good judgment, safety consciousness, and care of equipment.

B. Another type of employer expectation has to do with work habits and attitudes. Your employer will expect the following: attendance, punctuality, cooperation, interest, enthusiasm, honesty, and loyalty.

Lesson 7.2 *Rating Work Behavior*

A. An employer will evaluate your job performance, your work habits, and your attitudes. Employee evaluation allows employers to determine how well workers are doing their jobs.

B. Most evaluations are done in two steps. First, your boss or supervisor will fill out an evaluation form. Next, he or she will meet with you to go over the ratings. If you get a negative evaluation, you will need to improve your performance before the next rating.

Activities

1. Work with your instructor to develop a rating sheet based on the ten items in Figure 7-1. Key the items in random order without the rankings. Key instructions that ask users to rank the items from one to ten in terms of what they see as the most serious problems of young, entry-level workers. Include space for users to add other items they consider important. Make copies of the form and ask one or more employers or supervisors to complete it. Tally the results and compare them with Figure 7-1. Discuss the results in class.
2. Assume you are an employer. What would you do or say to an employee who (a) puts the wrong kind of lubricant in a chain saw, causing it to burn up; (b) calls in sick, but on your way to lunch, you see the person playing tennis; (c) makes personal long-distance calls on company phones; (d) criticizes the company to coworkers? Think of an answer for each situation. Discuss your answers in class.
3. How much do you know about Labor Day? Go to the web site for the U.S. Department of Labor (*http://www.dol.gov*). Search for and read "The History of Labor Day." Write out answers to the following questions and turn in your paper to your instructor for evaluation. (a) When was the first Labor Day holiday celebrated? Where? (b) What is the purpose of the holiday? (c) How do you and your family or friends normally celebrate Labor Day?

REVIEW

4. Interview an employer who has provided a training site for a co-op or work-study student. List the ways in which the employer has benefited from the program. Prepare an oral report and present it to the class.

Word Power

On a separate sheet of paper, match each definition with the correct term. All definitions will be used, and a definition will be used only once.

5. A refusal to lie, steal, or mislead in any way
6. Thinking about a problem and making the right decision
7. Getting along with and working well with others
8. Being on time
9. Faithfulness; believing in and being devoted to something
10. The output of a worker; how much a worker produces on the job
11. Eagerness; a strong interest in something
12. The process of judging how well an employee is doing on the job
13. A feeling of satisfaction with what you or someone you know has accomplished or possesses
14. A feeling of excitement and involvement

a. cooperation
b. enthusiasm
c. honesty
d. interest
e. judgment
f. loyalty
g. performance evaluation
h. pride
i. productivity
j. punctuality

Think Critically

15. During the last decade or so, many U.S. manufacturers have moved their plants overseas, claiming U.S. workers are often less productive and less concerned about quality than foreign workers. Do you think this is true?
16. Some companies make employees pay for any tools or equipment they damage or lose. Do you think this practice is fair?
17. Some U.S. manufacturers, particularly in the auto industry, have begun to use "Japanese-style" management techniques. For instance, both production and management workers wear the same uniform, one with the company name on it. This is supposed to build enthusiasm and loyalty toward the company. Do you think things like this make a difference?
18. Suppose you and two other employees work as clerks at a convenience food store. One afternoon you notice that a coworker lays $2 from a customer's purchase beside the cash register. You think it is odd that he does not ring it up. When you look again, the money is gone. Over the next several days, you watch him more closely. You discover that he is stealing money. Would you say something to him, tell your boss, or keep quiet? Why?
19. As an employee, which would you rather receive: (a) a guaranteed 4 percent annual raise or (b) the possibility of a raise of between 0 and 8 percent, based on the results of an annual evaluation of your performance? Why?

CHAPTER 8

WORKER RIGHTS AND PROTECTIONS

LESSONS

THOUGHTS ON WORK

"Great works are performed not by strength, but perseverance."
Samuel Johnson

PREVIEW

In Chapter 7, you learned that an employee has certain responsibilities to an employer. An employment contract, however, isn't a one-way deal. Employers also owe certain things to their employees. Workers are entitled to fair and honest treatment regarding wages, hours, and equal pay, as well as a safe and healthful workplace.

TAKING ACTION
EMPLOYER-WORKER RELATIONS

Lordstown is a city in Ohio where a General Motors assembly plant is located. The plant was built to be the world's fastest, most fully automated auto assembly line. In 1971, the assembly line was producing 104 cars per hour. The industry average was 55 per hour.

Some GM officials thought the line could produce even more cars. They cut back workers on the line and increased the number of jobs each person had to do. The result was that many workers could not keep up with the pace. Some workers were literally riding down the line with the cars as they tried to bolt on parts.

The company took several other unpopular actions. For example, it eliminated shop rules and laid off employees. Workers complained. They filed more than 10,000 grievances. But GM officials ignored them.

Out of frustration, workers began intentionally leaving pieces off the cars. In some cases, workers inflicted costly damage to the cars. Many cars came off the line with broken windshields, missing parts, or parts piled tidily in the front seat. Some cars had torn upholstery, keys broken in the door, or other damage.

The company responded with measures that included refusing emergency breaks and increasing disciplinary layoffs. It would not add a third shift to help with the increased work.

Eventually, the workers went on strike. Between March 3 and March 24, 1972, approximately 8,000 workers participated in the strike.

After three weeks and $150 million in lost production, workers and management agreed to a settlement. Some 700 workers who had been laid off returned to their jobs. Workers who had lost their jobs in disciplinary layoffs received full back pay, and their records were cleared. The union dropped thousands of grievances and did not challenge the company's authority over production.

The episode at Lordstown marked a turning point in employer-worker relations. Manufacturers began to work with the United Auto Workers union to include workers in solving workplace problems and in making decisions about how to perform their jobs. Various groups undertook studies of the workplace. These studies resulted in programs to redesign jobs, improve working conditions, and increase workers' participation in management.

SUCCESS TIP

Understand that progress in employer-worker relations is always possible.

THINK CRITICALLY

1. Why did the GM workers go on strike?
2. How does the case of Lordstown illustrate an employer's lack of respect toward workers?

LESSON 8.1

DUTIES OF EMPLOYERS

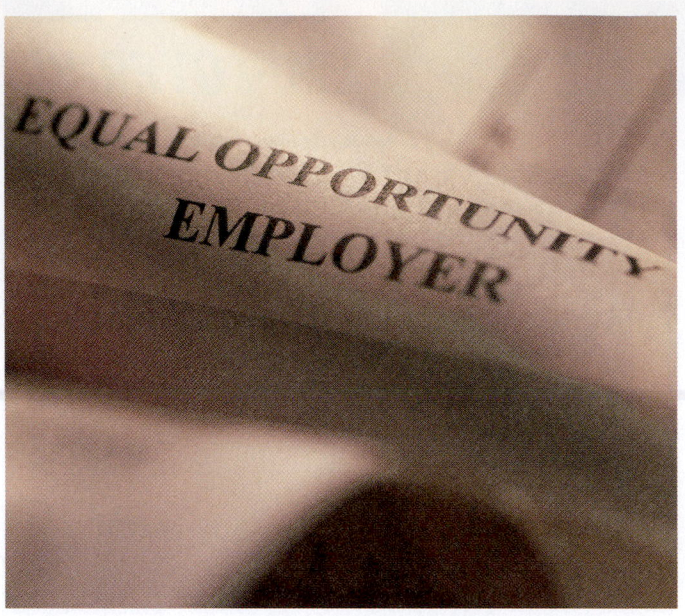

OBJECTIVES

- DESCRIBE EIGHT DUTIES OF EMPLOYERS
- DISCUSS THE VALUE OF HONESTY AND RESPECT TOWARD EMPLOYEES
- LIST THREE FAIR EMPLOYMENT PRACTICES
- EXPLAIN WORKERS' RIGHTS REGARDING PROTECTIONS AGAINST DISCRIMINATION

WHAT EMPLOYERS OWE WORKERS

Employers owe certain things to their employees. One of these, of course, is payment for their work. Other responsibilities include the following:

- ***Training and supervision.*** An employer should provide the necessary on-the-job training. Once the worker starts the job, the employer should give proper supervision and feedback. Workers need to know what to do and how well they are performing.
- ***Orientation to the workplace.*** A worker deserves information about company policies and rules. When these change, the employer should tell its workers.
- ***Honesty and respect.*** An employer owes all its workers honesty and respect.
- ***Fair employment practices.*** Laws cover child labor, work hours, and payment of wages. An employer who wants to avoid legal problems must obey such laws.
- ***Protection from discrimination.*** Laws prohibit discrimination against workers.
- ***Safe working conditions.*** Years ago, employers did not have to provide safe working conditions. Many workers paid with their lives. Employers now must follow certain health and safety standards.

The first three responsibilities in the preceding list were discussed in Chapter 6. The five remaining ones will be covered here.

HONESTY AND RESPECT

An employer who pays your salary has a right to tell you what to do as long as it is not unlawful. Most employers, however, realize that honesty and respect toward their employees are essential.

Your home page is the web page that appears each time you start your browser. Any page on the Web can be chosen as your home page. Many people select a web portal as a starting point for navigating the Web. Some of the more popular portals are Excite, MSN.com, Netscape, and Yahoo! Web portals provide free services and information such as current news, sports scores, weather, TV schedules, stock quotes, and search engines. At work, your employer may have the opening page of its own web site as the home page.

Workers are not robots. They are human beings with pride and self-worth. The historically important case study at the beginning of the chapter shows what can happen when a company forgets about the feelings of its workers.

The Lordstown story illustrates that employers cannot always force workers to do what they want them to do. The best relationship is one in which employers treat workers as they wish to be treated. Honesty and respect are the foundation for a good relationship between employers and workers.

FAIR EMPLOYMENT PRACTICES

Many state and federal laws cover **employment practices**, the manners and methods by which employers deal with their employees. A very important federal law is the Fair Labor Standards Act (FLSA). It applies to employers or companies that do business in more than one state and have annual sales above a certain amount. The FLSA covers child labor, wages and hours, and equal pay.

Child Labor

The FLSA includes laws covering workers under the age of 18. For instance, people 15 years old and younger cannot work in factories or work during school hours. Nor can those under 18 work in dangerous occupations such as mining.

Each of the 50 states also has its own child-labor laws. If both federal and state laws apply to a situation, the employer must obey the stricter standard. For instance, David is 17 and wants to work at a sawmill in his town. His state's laws would let him work there. Federal law, though, says that such jobs are too dangerous for workers under 18. David will have to wait until his next birthday to apply for a mill job.

You learned in Chapter 3 that the law is flexible to allow students to take part in work experience education programs. In most states, schools issue work permits to those between 14 and 17 years of age. This allows students to work during school hours. The program helps protect the health and welfare of minors. It regulates the types of work they may do and the hours they can work. Can you think of how a work permit benefits employers as well?

Wages and Hours

The FLSA sets standards for minimum wages and maximum hours for most workers in the United States. Many states also have laws about workers' pay. The **minimum wage** is the lowest hourly wage the law permits employers to pay workers. Remember, not all employers are covered by this law. In 1938, the national minimum wage was $.25 an hour. By September 1997, the figure had risen to $5.15 an hour.

The same law permits employers to pay a **training wage** to workers under age 20. The training wage is set at 85 percent of the minimum wage. Employers are permitted to pay this wage for the first 90 days of employment. Congress periodically raises the minimum wage. What is the current minimum wage?

The FLSA also sets the length of the **standard workweek**, which is, by law, the completion of 40 hours of work during a seven-day period. Time worked beyond 40 hours is called **overtime**. For overtime hours, employers must pay workers at a rate of $1\frac{1}{2}$ times their regular rate. The discussion of overtime pay in Chapter 10 holds special interest for us all. That material deals with how to figure overtime on a paycheck.

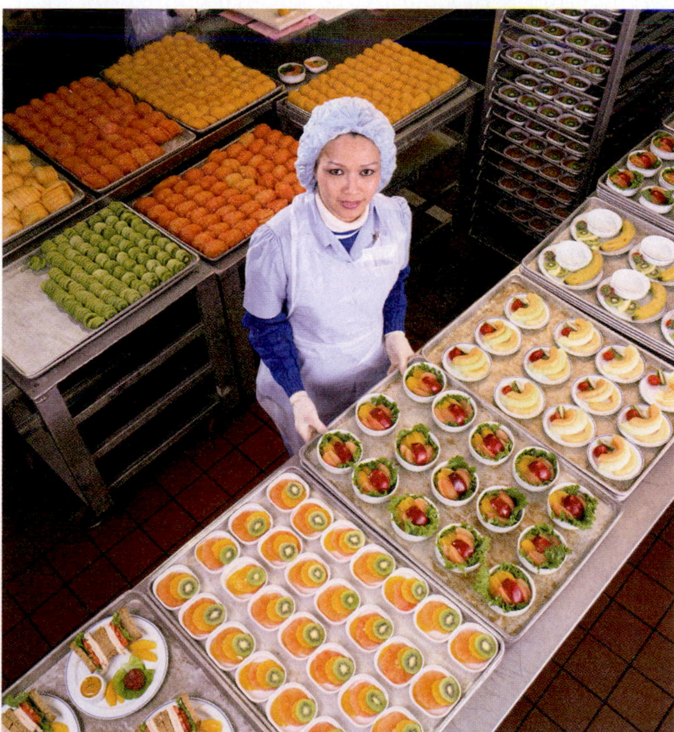

Not all businesses are covered by minimum wage laws.

ETHICAL DECISIONS

Your employer asks you to work a few extra hours on Saturday to help him catch up on an important order. Even though you have already put in 40 hours this week, you agree to do so. The next week, you eagerly open your pay envelope. You discover that you have been paid straight time for 45 hours. You call this to the boss's attention. He tells you that he does not pay overtime and that you should be glad that you have a job. You are not satisfied with his explanation.

WHAT WOULD YOU DO?

Equal Pay

John and Ruth are assistant managers for a small hotel chain. They started working for the hotel at the same time. They have equal qualifications. Ruth has learned that John makes a lot more money than she does. Ruth has tried to figure out the problem. She knows that workers sometimes receive different salaries because of shift work, skill level, seniority, and other things. Ruth has ruled out all those reasons.

The only difference that Ruth can name is that she is a woman. Ruth knows that the Equal Pay Act of 1963 outlaws different wage scales for equal work. This means that workers doing the same job must receive the same wage. What should Ruth do?

PROTECTION FROM DISCRIMINATION

As you have learned, laws protect workers from being discriminated against. **Discrimination** means favoring one person as compared to another. For example, if an employer will not hire you only because of your race, that is discrimination. Another example is being "passed over" for promotion because of your gender. So, too, is being fired from your job because you are older.

Laws cover equal treatment in such areas as hiring, promotion, and job security. They deal with the broad topics of equal employment opportunity and affirmative action.

Equal Employment Opportunity

The passage of the Civil Rights Act of 1964 gave the government a strong legal tool to prevent job discrimination. It paved the way for equal employment opportunity. Under **equal employment opportunity**, employers, unions, and

These workers receive equal pay for equal work.

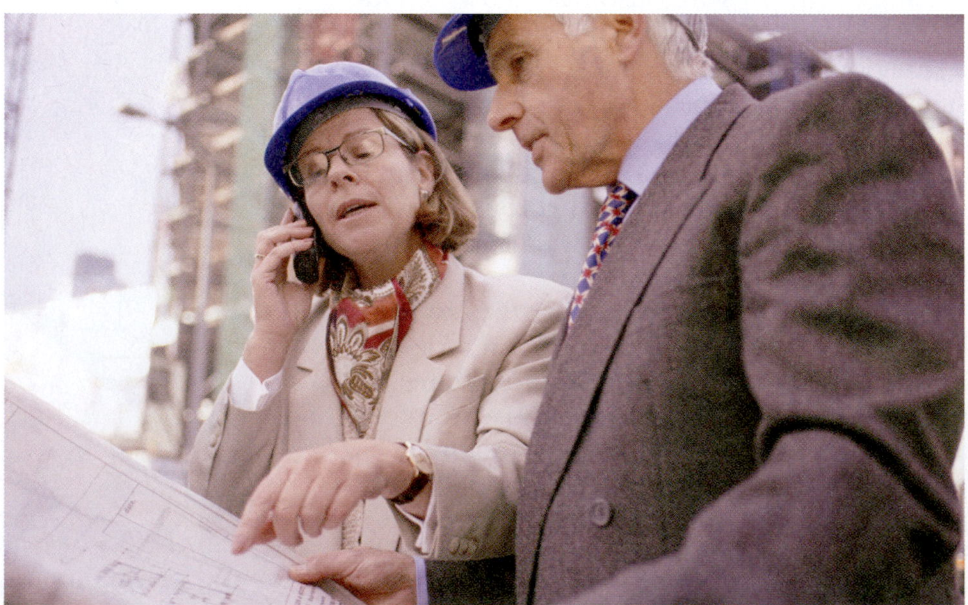

SALES

NEWSPAPER SALES REP

A national newspaper is seeking a sales representative for St. Louis/Kansas City. Responsibilities include the development of retail, vending, corporate, and college sales. Excellent salary and benefits. Car provided. Send resume and salary history to:

ARC INC.
78 W. FIFTH ST.
STE. 100
SHAKER HEIGHTS, OH 44120-5849
ATTENTION: ERIC NEANG

Equal Opportunity Employer

Figure 8-1 ***Some companies advertise that they are an "Equal Opportunity Employer."***

employment agencies cannot discriminate against people because of race, color, religion, sex, or national origin. The **Equal Employment Opportunity Commission (EEOC)** administers the Civil Rights Act and related laws.

In 1964, Warren Johnson lost his job as a landscaper. His employer had gone out of business. Warren was 56 at the time. With his experience, he figured that he would easily find a job. The first two employers to whom he applied told him he was "too old." Warren was upset. At the time, he could not legally fight the employers. Today, Warren could take action against them.

The Age Discrimination Act of 1967 was passed to prohibit discrimination against people between 40 and 70 years of age. The Rehabilitation Act of 1973 extended protection to those with physical or mental disabilities.

The most recent legislation prohibiting discrimination in employment practices is the Americans with Disabilities Act, which took effect in 1992. It gives civil rights protections to individuals with disabilities similar to those provided on the basis of race, sex, national origin, age, and religion. The EEOC also administers these laws.

Another recent employment-related law is the Family and Medical Leave Act, which took effect in August 1993. It requires employers with 50 or more workers to grant up to 12 weeks of unpaid leave a year. This allows workers to take time off to help care for a new baby or an ill family member without fear of losing their jobs.

Affirmative Action

Equal employment opportunity laws forbid job discrimination. What about those people who have been victims of past discrimination, though? For instance, many women and members of minority groups have been unjustly passed over for job promotions. This is an example of a condition that affirmative action tries to correct.

Affirmative action is a set of policies and programs designed to correct past discrimination. It is not a single federal law, although many federal regulations and laws require affirmative action in hiring and promotions. Most affirmative action programs include special efforts to hire and promote women, members of minority groups, people with disabilities, and Vietnam veterans.

LESSON 8.1 REVIEW

1. **Name three areas that the FLSA covers.**
2. **When federal and state child-labor laws conflict, which law applies? Give an example.**
3. **What is the purpose of the Equal Pay Act of 1963?**
4. **The Civil Rights Act of 1964 prohibits discrimination on what five bases? What bases were added in 1967 and 1973?**
5. **Affirmative action seeks to correct past discrimination. Give an example.**

HIGH-GROWTH OCCUPATIONS FOR THE 21st CENTURY

Electrical and Electronics Engineers

Electrical and electronics engineers are responsible for a wide range of technologies, from computer chips that process millions of instructions every second to radar systems that detect weather patterns days in advance. Electrical and electronics engineers design, develop, test, and supervise the manufacture of electrical and electronic equipment. Some of this equipment includes power-generating, controlling, and transmission devices used by electric utilities; electric motors; machinery, controls, lighting, and wiring in buildings; automobiles; and aircraft. Additional equipment includes radar and navigation systems, computer and office equipment, and broadcast and communications systems.

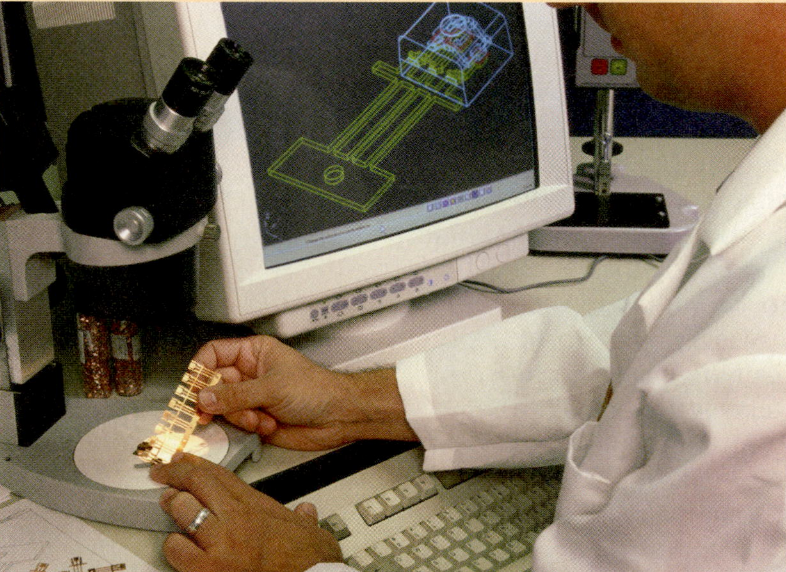

An electronics engineer may use a computer model to analyze computer chips.

Electrical and electronics engineers constitute the largest branch of engineers. They specialize in many different areas, such as power generation, transmission, and distribution; communications; computer electronics; and electrical equipment manufacturing. Some engineers specialize further in areas such as industrial robot control systems or aviation electronics. Electrical and electronics engineers design new products, write performance requirements, and develop maintenance schedules. They also test equipment, solve operating problems, and estimate the time and cost of engineering projects.

The four states with many large electronic firms (California, Texas, New York, and New Jersey) employ more than one-third of all electrical and electronics engineers. Faster-than-average job growth results from increased demand for electrical and electronic goods, including computers and communications equipment. The need for electronics manufacturers to invest heavily in research and development to remain competitive will provide many additional employment opportunities. Defense-related firms are also expected to provide many employment opportunities as aircraft and weapons systems are upgraded with improved navigation, control, guidance, and targeting systems. The fastest job growth, however, is expected to be in service industries—particularly consulting firms that provide electronic engineering expertise.

LESSON 8.2
WORKER SAFETY AND HEALTH

OBJECTIVES

- *EXPLAIN THE ROLES OF EMPLOYERS AND WORKERS REGARDING SAFETY AND HEALTH IN THE WORKPLACE*
- *IDENTIFY AGENCIES THAT DEAL WITH WORKERS' COMPLAINTS*

SAFE WORKING CONDITIONS

Have you seen workers wearing hard hats and safety glasses? Perhaps you have worn this gear yourself. Such equipment helps protect workers from injury. Years ago, many employers were often unconcerned if their employees failed to use safety equipment or otherwise acted unsafely. Some employers made employees work under unsafe or unhealthful conditions. If workers complained, they sometimes lost their jobs.

In 1971, such situations changed for the better. That year marked the beginning of the **Occupational Safety and Health Administration (OSHA)**. This government agency sets and enforces standards for safe and healthful working conditions. Examples of OSHA rules include the following:

- Each high-radiation area shall contain a sign having the radiation caution symbol and the words: CAUTION, HIGH-RADIATION AREA.
- Tools and other metal objects shall be kept away from the top of uncovered batteries.
- Exposed hot water and steam pipes shall be covered with insulating material whenever necessary to protect employees from contact with them.
- Safety shoes shall conform to certain standards.
- All workplaces shall be kept as clean as the nature of the work allows.

All employers having at least one employee must obey OSHA standards. To help employers, OSHA offers free on-site visitations. Most employers welcome suggestions that will create a better work environment. Exceptions exist, though. To discourage these, OSHA makes random inspections as well. If inspectors find hazards, the employer can be fined and the business shut down.

WORKPLACE DECISIONS

The production machine on which you work was repaired over the weekend. As you begin work on Monday morning, you notice that the safety guard has not been replaced. You immediately go to the supervisor. He tells you to go ahead and get started and he will replace the guard when he gets time. But you do not want to work on the machine unless the safety guard is in place.

WHAT WOULD YOU DO?

MATH CONNECTION

Suppose that you work in a medical laboratory. OSHA requires that all biological hazardous waste be weighed before it is sent to the hazardous waste management company. The limit per week that the waste management company can handle is 400 pounds. You have six containers with the following weights: 75 lb, 85 lb, 70 lb, 80 lb, 62 lb, and 60 lb. Based on the weekly limit, how many of the six containers will the waste management company take this week?

SOLUTION

You must first calculate the total weight of the six containers.

Total weight of the six containers = 75 + 85 + 70 + 80 + 62 + 60 = 432

The total weight of the six containers is more than the waste company will take. Since the weight of any of the containers will put the total weight over the limit, only five of the six containers will be taken.

A restaurant server in Kansas complained to her employer that it was too hot in the restaurant's kitchen area. The employer ignored her complaint. She took her complaint to OSHA. When the employer found out, he threatened her, began giving her the least desirable work, and rearranged her work schedule. The server tried to reason with the employer but finally quit because of the harassment.

The server filed a complaint with OSHA. After investigating, OSHA ordered the employer to pay the server back wages and to remove all papers about the case from her files. (Most employers keep records on each employee.) OSHA also required the employer to post a notice that advised other employees of the settlement.

Think safety every minute you are on the job.

Protecting New Workers

New employees have a much higher risk of injury than experienced workers. The Bureau of Labor Statistics (BLS) reports that about half of all work-related injuries occur during the first year of employment. Why are new workers more likely to be hurt? Studies show that new workers often do not know enough to protect themselves. One BLS study found the following:

- Of 724 workers hurt while using scaffolds, 27 percent said they had received no information on safety requirements for installing the kind of scaffold on which they were hurt.
- Of 868 workers who suffered head injuries, 71 percent said they had no instruction about hard hats.
- Of 554 workers hurt while servicing equipment, 61 percent said they were not informed about lockout procedures.

In nearly every type of injury studied by the BLS, the same story is repeated. Workers often do not receive the safety information they need. Or, if they do, they do not apply it.

What Workers Can Do

During your on-the-job training, your employer is responsible for your safety education. But you, too, play an important role. Before starting to work, be sure that you understand all necessary safety measures. If an explanation is unclear, ask

Ask about anything on the job that you do not understand. What you don't know can hurt you or your chances for advancement.

again. Practice and use what you have learned. Do not take shortcuts that could endanger your health or safety.

The following are some general safety rules. Can you think of others?

- Never use a tool or piece of equipment that lacks a safety guard or has a non-working one.
- If earplugs or other personal protective devices such as gloves or aprons are required, use them at all times.
- Do not "horse around" or play practical jokes at the workplace.
- Be especially careful when you get tired. This is when accidents are more likely to happen.
- If you work where dangerous substances are used, find out what something is before you handle it.
- Accept responsibility for your own safety on the job.

Besides taking care of their own safety and health, workers should be on the lookout for possible dangers. Employers should correct any problems that employees call to their attention. If an employer does not correct a problem, it is up to the employee to call on OSHA for help if needed. OSHA protects your right to complain to your employer, your union, and OSHA itself. It is illegal for your employer to punish you for exercising this or any other OSHA right.

AGENCIES PROVIDING SERVICES TO WORKERS

What should you do if you have a work problem dealing with fair employment practices, discrimination, or health and safety? If you are a work experience student, contact your school coordinator. He or she can help solve the problem. Apprentices and union workers can speak to the union representative. Civil service

WORKFORCE TRENDS

The increase in the proportion of women working that began after World War II has been one of the most significant social and economic trends in modern U.S. history. In 1940, 28 percent of American women were in the workforce. This rose to 40 percent in 1966, 51 percent in 1979, and 60 percent at the end of the century. Today, husbands are the sole worker in less than one-quarter of married-couple families.

Type of Complaint	Federal Agency
Child labor Wages and hours	Employment Standards Administration U.S. Department of Labor 200 Constitution Ave., NW Washington, DC 20210 http://www.dol.gov/dol/esa/
Equal pay Discrimination based on race, color, religion, sex, national origin, age, or disability	U.S. Equal Employment Opportunity Commission (EEOC) 1801 L St., NW Washington, DC 20507 http://www.eeoc.gov
Safety and health	Occupational Safety and Health Administration (OSHA) U.S. Department of Labor 200 Constitution Ave., NW Washington, DC 20210 http://www.osha.gov

Note: *Federal agencies also maintain state and local offices. Look in your telephone directory for "Government" listings.*

***Figure 8-2* These are the primary federal agencies that handle complaints regarding fair employment practices, discrimination, and health and safety.**

employees also have representatives they can turn to for help. Wherever you work, follow any procedures that appear in your company's policy manual.

If you do not have certain procedures to follow or anyone else to help you, try to work out the problem with your boss or employer. Ask for a meeting to informally discuss your complaint. Present your point of view and then listen patiently to the other person's side of the story.

If an informal meeting does not work, file a formal complaint. Write a letter to the proper company official. State your complaint clearly and briefly. Ask for an answer by a reasonable date. Be polite and businesslike in your letter. Do not make demands. Ask that the problem be solved. Keep a copy of the letter for your files.

If all your efforts to solve the problem meet dead ends, you can turn to outside help. Many federal laws and government agencies protect the rights of workers. A summary of the major types of complaints and the agencies that handle them appear in Figure 8-2 above. Ask for help at a public library if you have trouble finding the addresses or phone numbers you need.

Most employers support and respect laws and rules that protect workers. Employers may sometimes overlook a law or rule. Other times, though, an employer may violate a law on purpose. In either case, it is up to you to identify and then to report any violations you find. Learn your rights so you can be in control of your health, safety, and welfare.

LESSON 8.2 REVIEW

1. **To which employers do OSHA standards apply?**
2. **Why are new employees more likely to be hurt on the job than more experienced workers?**
3. **To protect your health and safety, what four things should you do before you start to work?**
4. **Suppose a work problem arises between you and your employer. List the steps that you should follow in trying to correct it.**

COLLECTIVE BARGAINING

Labor (workers) and management (owners/managers) both want to see a company grow and succeed. Occasionally, the two groups may disagree regarding wages, benefits, working conditions, or other matters. If the workers are union members, the two sides engage in collective bargaining to settle their differences.

Collective bargaining is an important right of union members. Because of the unequal bargaining power between an individual employee and a company, federal law permits workers to group together and negotiate common terms and conditions. The main body of law governing collective bargaining is the National Labor Relations Act.

In typical collective bargaining, union representatives present demands. Management may accept or reject the demands. It may also make a counteroffer. The two sides often negotiate for days or even weeks.

During negotiations, workers may threaten to strike if their demands are not met.

Eventually, the two sides usually agree. The agreement, called a labor contract, is put into writing. The union membership must then vote on the agreement. As a legal document, the labor contract can be enforced in a court of law. The contract usually covers a specified time period, such as three years.

After a labor contract is signed, the agreement is put into practice. A contract presents certain rules that labor and management are to follow. Sometimes, though, a complaint or grievance arises over what the rules mean or how they are carried out. For instance, a grievance might result from the firing of a worker or the violation of a safety practice.

The procedure for settling grievances is an important part of the labor contract. An employee with a grievance, along with the union representative, usually discusses the matter with the boss. Most problems are resolved at this level. If the problem is not resolved, the employee may file a complaint with a higher level of management.

THINK CRITICALLY

1. Why would a group of workers have more bargaining power with an employer than a single worker would?
2. Do you think it is important to have a procedure for settling grievances in labor contracts? Why or why not?

CHAPTER 8

Chapter in Brief

Lesson 8.1 *Duties of Employers*

A. An employer who pays your salary has a right to give you orders as long as they are not unlawful. Most employers, however, realize that honesty and respect toward their employees are essential.

B. Many state and federal laws deal with employment practices. A very important one is the Fair Labor Standards Act (FLSA). The FLSA covers child labor, wages and hours, and equal pay.

C. Laws also exist to promote equal treatment in areas such as hiring, promotion, and job security. It is illegal for employers, unions, and employment agencies to discriminate against people because of race, color, religion, sex, national origin, age, or physical or mental disabilities.

D. Affirmative action policies and programs have been established to help victims of past discrimination. These include special efforts to hire and promote women, members of minority groups, people with disabilities, and Vietnam veterans.

Lesson 8.2 *Worker Safety and Health*

A. The Occupational Safety and Health Administration (OSHA) sets and enforces standards for safe and healthful working conditions. Workers can file a complaint with OSHA if an employer refuses to correct unsafe or unhealthful working conditions.

B. New employees have a much higher risk of injury than experienced workers. These workers often do not receive the safety information they need. Or, if they do, they do not apply it. Learn and practice safety rules.

C. If you have a problem at work regarding fair employment practices, discrimination, or health and safety, try to solve it informally. If this does not work, file a formal complaint with the proper company official. If this does not solve the problem, you can turn to outside agencies for help.

Activities

1. Find some of your state's laws on two or more of these topics: child labor, minimum wage, wages and hours, and equal pay. A good beginning resource is the Department of Labor's Employment Standards Administration web site at *http://www.dol.gov/dol/esa/*. Locate additional information on your state's web site. Report your findings to the class.
2. Find out who is covered under the Americans with Disabilities Act (ADA) and what the "reasonable accommodation" requirement of the act means. The ADA home page at *http://www.usdoj.gov/crt/ada/adahom1.htm* is a good resource. Report and discuss your findings in class.

REVIEW

3. Go to the nearest OSHA office. Pick up or request booklets explaining workers' rights under OSHA. Discuss them in class. After studying them, you may want to make a bulletin board display.
4. Write an imaginary letter to an employer complaining of a work-related problem. Follow the guidelines presented in this chapter. Turn the letter in to your instructor for evaluation.
5. Suppose the weight limit in the Math Connection on page 112 was 300 lbs. To send as close to 300 lbs as possible, which containers should you send?

Word Power

On a separate sheet of paper, match each definition with the correct term. All definitions will be used, and a definition will be used only once.

6. Time worked beyond 40 hours
7. By law, the lowest hourly wage that can be paid to an employee
8. A wage rate set at 85 percent of the minimum wage that employers can pay for 90 days to workers under age 20
9. The idea, supported by law, that employers, unions, and employment agencies cannot discriminate against people because of race, color, religion, sex, or national origin
10. A set of policies and programs designed to correct past discrimination
11. By law, the completion of 40 hours of work during a seven-day period
12. The government agency that sets and enforces standards for safe and healthful working conditions
13. The manners and methods by which employers deal with their employees
14. Favoring one person as compared to another
15. The government agency that administers the Civil Rights Act of 1964 and related laws

a. affirmative action
b. discrimination
c. employment practices
d. equal employment opportunity
e. Equal Employment Opportunity Commission (EEOC)
f. minimum wage
g. Occupational Safety and Health Administration (OSHA)
h. overtime
i. standard workweek
j. training wage

Think Critically

16. Federal law and some state laws permit employers to pay a training wage for the first 90 days of employment. What is the justification for this? Do you think this is fair?
17. Affirmative action programs give special advantages to groups that were discriminated against in the past. Discuss in class the pros and cons of such programs.
18. Have you ever had a work accident or an injury on the job? If so, how might it have been prevented? Discuss your answers in class.

CHAPTER 9

HUMAN RELATIONS AT WORK

LESSONS

9.1 *Bosses, Coworkers, and Customers*

9.2 *Group Participation*

PREVIEW

At work, you will deal with many different kinds of people, including bosses, coworkers, and customers. You will probably work in groups at least some of the time. Getting along well with others, both individually and in groups, is an important work and life skill. It is a skill that you will need to learn and practice.

THOUGHTS ON WORK

"The way to get things done is not to mind who gets the credit for doing them."

Benjamin Jowett

TAKING ACTION
TWO CONVERSATIONS

Nina had a part-time job in a department store. On Friday evening, she was working in Housewares. She was reading a magazine at the counter when she became aware of a man standing in front of her, holding a clock radio.

The man said, "I bought this clock radio a couple of weeks ago. For some reason, the alarm doesn't work."

"Did you drop it or something?" asked Nina indifferently.

"No," said the man. "It just quit on its own."

Nina looked at the man skeptically. "Are you sure it's broken? Maybe you're not setting it properly."

"I can assure you that I know how to set it." The customer was getting a little angry, now.

"Did you buy it here?"

"Of course I bought it here. You can see that the box has your sales sticker on it."

"Do you have the receipt?"

It is easy to see the direction this conversation took.

Chan worked at the same department store. On Saturday, he was working in Housewares. A woman approached his register and placed a large shopping bag on the counter.

"I bought this food processor here some time ago and now it has quit working," she said.

"I'm sorry you had a problem," Chan responded. "Do you remember about when you bought it?"

"Yes," the woman replied. "It was right after Christmas. Here is the receipt."

Chan glanced at the receipt quickly. "Good. The warranty is still valid. Why don't you go pick out another one, while I write up an exchange ticket?"

After a few moments, the customer selected a food processor and walked back to the counter.

"This is the same model and price, but it's a different color," she said.

"Is that color okay?" Chan asked.

"Yes, I actually like it better."

"Well," Chan said, "that worked out nicely, didn't it? Will you please sign this form, while I put it in a bag for you? You shouldn't have any trouble with this one. Come back and see us."

SUCCESS TIP

For most businesses, customers are the reason you are there, so treat them well!

THINK CRITICALLY

1. Compare the service that the two salesclerks gave their customers. List some things that Nina said and did wrong and Chan said and did right.
2. What are some ways that employees can give good service to customers?

LESSON 9.1

BOSSES, COWORKERS, AND CUSTOMERS

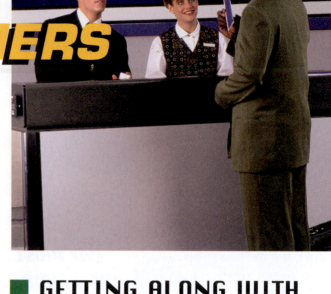

- EXPLAIN THE IMPORTANCE OF HUMAN RELATIONS TO SUCCESS ON THE JOB
- DISCUSS WAYS TO GET ALONG WITH BOSSES AND COWORKERS
- IDENTIFY THREE REASONS WHY CUSTOMERS PATRONIZE A PARTICULAR BUSINESS

HUMAN RELATIONS

You deal with people every day of your life. You may talk, joke, plan, study, argue, and so on. Some of these dealings are more important than others. For instance, you go into a store to buy a quart of milk. Chances are that your conversation with the clerk will not influence life much. On the other hand, a talk with your boss, coworkers, or teacher just might. Your dealings with others influence your happiness and success. They also may affect others. Ask Carlos.

Guy was supposed to pick up his friend Carlos on the way to school. Guy got up late and, in his hurry to get to school, forgot Carlos. So an unhappy Carlos had to walk two miles to school. He got to school late, missed a test, and had to go to detention after school. Guy's mistake caused problems for Carlos.

Some human relations are pleasant. Others are very difficult. **Human relations** are interactions among people. Unless we become hermits, we cannot get away from other people. So we need to develop human relations skills. This is especially true for workers. It is a fact that many fired workers lose their jobs because they cannot get along with others.

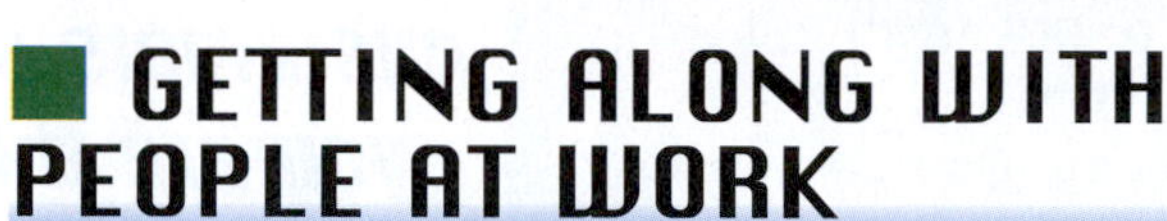

GETTING ALONG WITH PEOPLE AT WORK

Suppose you and another student with whom you do not get along very well find yourselves in the same English class. Chances are that you will not need to work closely with the other student. On the job, though, you may have to work closely all week with someone whom you really do not like. In such cases, you will both need to put personal feelings aside.

WORKFORCE TRENDS

Since 1960, the percentage of married women in the workforce has nearly doubled. This increase is largely in response to women's rising labor market opportunities. Other factors include the need for a second income to keep up with the rising cost of living, changed attitudes about women's roles in families and society, and reduced workplace discrimination.

COMMUNICATION AT WORK

COMMUNICATING WITH BOSSES

Here are some ways to get the most out of your relationship with your boss:

Keep your boss informed about what you are doing. Make sure your boss knows how you are progressing on your assignments. If a problem arises that your supervisor should know about, provide the necessary details in a timely way.

Speak your boss's language. Find out how your boss likes to communicate with employees. Some supervisors like brief conversations. Others prefer e-mail. If your supervisor prefers talking, don't write a note.

Be considerate of your boss's time. Supervisors are busy people. If you must speak to your supervisor, arrange a time, whenever possible, that will be convenient for him or her. When speaking or writing to your boss, include only the information he or she needs to know.

At work we have to deal with all kinds of people. These include bosses, coworkers, and customers. We may like some people more than others. Even so, we must try to get along with everyone. Understanding our bosses, coworkers, and customers can make this task easier.

Most employees have a boss. The boss may be the company's owner, a crew chief, a foreman, or a department head. Whoever your boss is, you will need to form a working relationship with him or her. Working effectively with supervisors was discussed in Chapters 6 and 7.

Good employees try to understand the boss's position. Being a boss is never easy. For instance, how would you feel if you had to fire someone? Bosses sometimes must do this. They must always provide workers with instructions and helpful criticism. Good bosses act in the interest of the company, not out of friendship.

Sometimes, workers and bosses become friends. Even so, this should not influence their work behavior. The company should still come first. If you and your boss are not friends, that is fine. You can still have a good relationship. Some bosses make it a policy not to be friends with people they supervise.

Strong friendships depend on interpersonal attraction. **Interpersonal attraction** is a tendency to be drawn to another person, often because of similar characteristics and preferences. Think about it. Why do people become your friends? Well, they are probably somewhat like you. We enjoy being with people who are like us in at least some ways. We choose such people for friends, and they choose us. At work, though, interpersonal attraction is not as important. What is important is doing your share of the work and following rules.

As a new worker, you can be sure that your coworkers will be watching you. They will expect you to do your share of the work. Your coworkers probably will not mind helping you from time to time. They will expect you to do the same when they need help. But your coworkers will not put up with doing their work and yours, too—at least, not for long.

Following the rules is important. Rules make sure that employees in similar jobs receive equal treatment. If you ignore the rules, you are indicating that you are different or better than the other workers. Your coworkers will not like your ignoring the same rules that they are expected to follow.

Sometimes, being different has its place at work. **Seniority** refers to the length of time someone has worked for a company. Workers with the most seniority have the most privileges. Respecting seniority rules will help you get along with coworkers.

In January, Tina requested a week's vacation in June. Mrs. Suriel, the boss, came to talk to her. She said that Sven, who had the same job title as

Tina, wanted the same week off. Mrs. Suriel told Tina she could not do without both of them that week. Since Sven had been there two years longer than Tina, he would get to take that week. Tina thanked Mrs. Suriel for telling her. She then started to think about choosing another week.

In a work setting, territorial rights may develop. **Territorial rights** are unwritten rules concerning respect for the property and territory of others. Some workers come to feel that they control a certain office, area, or sales territory. When you are on their turf, they expect you to behave as they wish. An example might be that you are not supposed to use someone's tools without asking permission first. Be alert for such things. Try to respect others' territorial rights.

Doing your share of the work and following the rules lead to good feelings among coworkers. Other ways to maintain good relationships with coworkers include the following:

- ***Appearance.*** Maintain good personal hygiene and grooming. Do not underdress or overdress.
- ***Courtesy.*** Be pleasant, friendly, and courteous. Do not force relationships with coworkers. In time, some may become your friends.
- ***Attitude.*** Be positive. Do not complain about your job. Clint sometimes gets tired of being a "go-fer" for others. He doesn't let it discourage him, though. Clint is glad to have a job and looks forward to a promotion soon.
- ***Interest.*** Show interest in the job. Pay attention to what coworkers are doing and show them you feel their interests are important.
- ***Loyalty.*** Do not criticize the company or gossip about bosses or coworkers. Those you talk to will wonder what you are saying about them!
- ***Tolerance.*** Try to tolerate the opinions, habits, and behaviors of coworkers. Being different is all right. Marta, for instance, is a vegetarian. She sometimes eats bean, cucumber, and alfalfa sandwiches. From her, some coworkers have learned more about good eating habits.
- ***Maturity.*** Be agreeable and avoid arguments. If conflicts arise, talk them out.
- ***Dependability.*** Always do what you say you will do. Quinn agreed to work overtime on Saturday afternoons. Last Saturday would have been a great sailing day. Quinn went to work because he had given his word. He would have preferred to have gone to the bay.

Always be pleasant, friendly, and courteous to your coworkers.

- ***Openness.*** Be open to suggestions and change. Ask coworkers for advice. Offer to help them.
- ***Ethics.*** Do not try to get ahead at the expense of others. Yolanda is the department's most creative layout artist. She lets her work speak for itself. Yolanda never criticizes the other artists' work to make herself look better.

GETTING AND KEEPING CUSTOMERS

The purpose of a business is to make a profit. Some businesses sell goods, such as clothing, hardware, or autos. Others sell services, such as insurance, haircuts, or dry cleaning. A business sells its goods or services to customers.

Not all customers are called by that name. An accountant may speak of clients, and a nurse, of patients. **Clients** are the business customers of a professional worker. **Patients** are persons under treatment or care by a medical practitioner. What about users of library services? In a sense, they are customers, even though they do not pay for their service directly. They are **patrons**, customers of certain service-producing businesses or institutions.

Relationships between employees and customers are important to the success of a business. Let's look at some reasons why a customer deals with a certain business and how employees can encourage customers to return.

One reason customers patronize a business is they like the product or service provided. To

INTERPERSONAL DECISIONS

You have been cutting and styling Mrs. Laird's hair for about six months. You are beginning to dread her coming into the shop. You like Mrs. Laird, but her young son is a terror. You wish she would not bring him along. He is loud and obnoxious and disturbs the other customers. He always wants something from his mother and cries when he does not get his way. You do not want to make Mrs. Laird angry, but something has to be done about the boy.

WHAT WOULD YOU DO?

patronize means that you trade with or give your business to a certain individual or company. Leigh, for instance, goes to Stegels' because she likes their almond ice cream. Rafael has his hair cut at Rich's because he likes Rich's work. Customers who patronize a business have certain wants or needs. A competent worker who treats customers well encourages business.

Darcy is a landscaper for Sunrise Nursery. Last month, Mr. Clements, a client, said he wanted more flowers and shrubs around his house. He did not have anything special in mind. Darcy said she would think about it and call him. She did so and then made an appointment with Mr. Clements. Darcy brought design sketches, catalogs, and a price estimate. She had everything Mr. Clements would need to make a decision. Darcy's efforts paid off. She got that job and other new customers in the neighborhood.

Businesses that provide services after a sale also encourage customers. The services may include things such as product repair, refunds, or quick processing of a claim. At the beginning of this chapter, you read about two salesclerks, Nina and Chan, who were asked to exchange a product. The very different service the two provided probably determined whether their customers would return to the store for repeat business or would never shop there again.

A third reason customers return to a business is **goodwill**—acts of kindness, consideration, or assistance. These are the little things about a business. Examples include reputation, honesty, and attitude toward customers. Employees promote goodwill in many ways.

- Shaheen calls as many customers as possible by name. She also knows which ones like to be called by their first names and which by their last.
- Ingmar knows that people often come into the store just to look around. He makes them feel welcome and then stays back until they ask for or seem to need help.
- Many adults come into Monique's store to buy toys or gifts for their children or young friends. They appreciate it when she offers suggestions about items that children like.
- Some customers at the ice cream shop where Cleveland works have trouble deciding on a flavor. He offers them free samples.
- Jillian remembers when she was in college and didn't have much money. Her restaurant is the most popular one near campus. Why? Heaping plates of good food, of course.

LESSON 9.1 REVIEW

1. **Why are many workers fired?**
2. **How important is it for you to be friends with the boss?**
3. **Name two ways to start out on the right foot with coworkers.**
4. **How should you relate to a coworker whose opinions, habits, or behaviors are different from yours?**
5. **What should you do if a coworker offers advice or suggestions?**
6. **What are three reasons why customers deal with a certain business?**

HIGH-GROWTH OCCUPATIONS FOR THE 21st CENTURY

Electronic Semiconductor Processors

Semiconductors—also known as computer chips, microchips, or integrated chips—are the miniature but powerful brains of high-technology equipment. *Electronic semiconductor processors* are responsible for many of the steps necessary to manufacture each semiconductor that goes into a personal computer, a missile guidance system, and a host of other electronic equipment. This is the only manufacturing occupation expected to grow much faster than the average for all occupations.

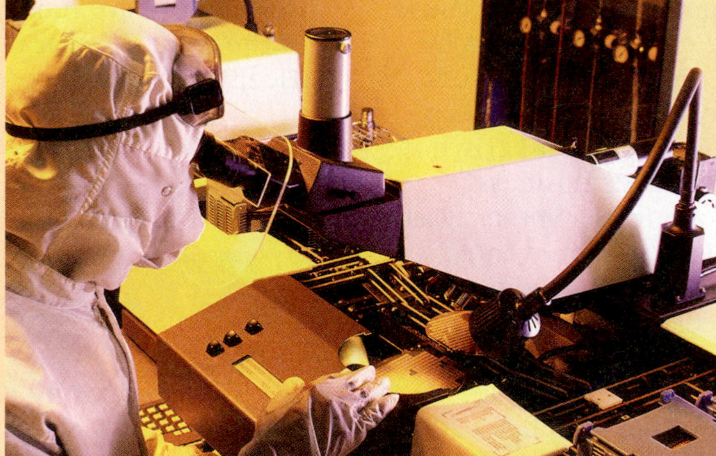

Semiconductor processors must work in clean rooms because a small particle of dust can damage a semiconductor.

Semiconductor processors manufacture semiconductors in disks about the size of dinner plates. These disks, called wafers, are thin slices of silicon on which the circuitry of the microchips is layered. Each wafer is eventually cut into dozens of individual chips.

The manufacture and cutting of wafers to create semiconductors take place in "clean rooms." Clean rooms are production areas that must be kept free of any airborne matter, because the least bit of dust can damage a semiconductor. All semiconductor processors working in clean rooms must wear special garments known as "bunny suits." Bunny suits fit over clothing to prevent lint and other particles from contaminating work sites.

Operators make up the majority of the workers in clean rooms. They start and monitor the equipment that performs the various tasks during the semiconductor production sequence. They spend a great deal of time at computer terminals, monitoring the equipment. They transfer wafer carriers from one development station to the next. Once begun, production of semiconductor wafers is continuous. Operators work to the pace of the machinery that has largely automated the production process.

Technicians account for a smaller percentage of the workers in clean rooms. They troubleshoot production problems and make equipment adjustments and repairs. They also take the lead in ensuring quality control and in maintaining equipment in order to prevent the need for costly repairs.

LESSON 9.2
GROUP PARTICIPATION

OBJECTIVES

- ***UNDERSTAND WHY EMPLOYEES ARE ASKED TO WORK IN TASK GROUPS***
- ***DISCUSS WAYS TO PARTICIPATE EFFECTIVELY IN A TASK GROUP***

PURPOSES OF TASK GROUPS

Most people, at least some of the time, work in groups. These are called task groups or work groups. A **task group** is a work group formed to accomplish a particular objective. Groups are often formed to brainstorm a new product, discuss quality control problems, or plan a new sales strategy. There is a trend in business and industry to use more and different types of task groups. But do groups really perform better than individuals?

Groups are generally superior to most individuals at many but not all tasks. A school newspaper, for example, benefits by having different people write columns on events, club activities, sports, and the like. It would be hard for one person to write about all these things. For tasks requiring a lot of effort, groups are faster than individuals. An example is building a house.

WORKING IN TASK GROUPS

The following guidelines will help you work effectively in a group:

- ***Show your readiness to help the group.*** A group depends on the willingness of each member to accomplish its work. Do your share of the work on a regular basis, and volunteer your efforts from time to time for special group projects.
- ***Accept the role the group gives you.*** Groups have leaders and followers. Followers are often in greater demand. Pitch in and do whatever the group needs, whether it is recording minutes, stuffing envelopes, or cleaning up after a meeting.
- ***Carry out your role as best you can.*** Sports teams often have role players who go into the game to do certain things. Can you think of examples? Role players make a

PERSONAL DECISIONS

You enjoy being in the club and are always eager to help out. In fact, you probably do more than anyone else. It is getting to the point that whenever something needs to be done, club members look to you. You have been asked a number of times recently to substitute for someone who has other plans. Some members seem to be taking advantage of your willingness to always pitch in.

WHAT WOULD YOU DO?

YOU'RE A WHAT? FOOD STYLIST

We have all seen food ads and illustrations in newspapers, magazines, and cookbooks. Movies and TV programs show people preparing or eating food. *Food stylists* prepare food for the camera. They make food appear attractive with props, substitutions, and cosmetic shortcuts. Food stylists might put grill marks on hot dogs with a soldering iron or puff up a pastry with mashed potatoes.

Food stylists need a knowledge of food and cooking techniques and an ability to be creative. Although some large corporations hire stylists for their test kitchens, nearly all stylists are self-employed. Earnings are usually based on daily pay rates. A cookbook might take months to finish. But many jobs last only one day. ■

valuable contribution to a team or a group. Do your job well. The group and you will both benefit.

- ***Share your views.*** Do not hold back on a good idea or suggestion. Your solution may be perfect. Offer your feelings and opinions, even if they differ from what others think. Groups sometimes make poor decisions or choices. If you believe this is the case, say so.
- ***Do not dominate meetings.*** Someone who talks too much irritates other members. Do not overpower others, even though you may have the right answers or the best ideas.
- ***Accept group decisions.*** Offer your views during a discussion. But do not argue once the group makes a decision.
- ***Encourage other members.*** Doing your best on a job will encourage others to do so, too. A kind word from time to time always helps. Remember to pass out compliments and congratulations for a job well done.
- ***Think of solutions, not past problems.*** Suppose you have a fight with a family member. Dwelling on the problem will not help. Thinking of how to solve it will. The same is true in task groups. Focus on finding solutions to problems.
- ***Be proud of group success.*** Completing a hard task is very satisfying. Should success come, enjoy it with fellow group members.

Getting along well with others is an important work and life skill. As a skill, it must be learned and practiced.

Try to make every meeting worthwhile.

LESSON 9.2 REVIEW

1. Why is it important to know how to work in groups?
2. Groups are generally superior to most individuals at many tasks. Give an example.
3. What should you do if a task leader assigns you a job to do?
4. When is the best time to provide an opinion on a group decision?

FOCUS ON THE WORKER

RELATING TO WORKAHOLICS

Workaholics often spend long hours at the office.

At some point in your career, you may work for or with a workaholic or become one yourself. Understanding and getting along with workaholics is a special case in human relations.

Workaholics are people who are addicted to their work. In her book *Workaholics*, Marilyn Machlowitz provides two examples of workaholics. An elderly attorney sat at his desk working while his office building was on fire. He ignored the fire and sirens until he was forcibly removed by firefighters. A pregnant publicist felt labor pains. She rushed to her doctor's office. When she found out that delivery was still hours away, she went back to work.

Workaholics exist in every occupation. It is not necessary to be employed to be one. Many homemakers are workaholics. As a group, workaholics are surprisingly happy. They are doing what they love. They cannot seem to get enough of it. If they are in the right job, they can be extremely productive.

There is another side to the workaholic at work. According to Machlowitz, workaholics may be among the world's worst workers. They suffer few ills themselves. But they often wind up doing damage to their companies. They frequently create a pressure-cooker atmosphere. They demand a great deal. They expect everyone to be as dedicated to work as they are.

Workaholics often have difficulty delegating work to others. They tend to be critical of coworkers. Even their high energy level causes problems. Workaholics may try to do everything themselves.

As you see, it can be difficult to work with a workaholic. The truth is, says Machlowitz, that workaholics are better suited to be business owners than employees. They just do not do well in a business organization working with or managing people.

THINK CRITICALLY

1. Do you think you may be a workaholic? Why or why not?
2. Would you want to work for a workaholic? With a workaholic?

CHAPTER 9

Chapter in Brief

Lesson 9.1 *Bosses, Coworkers, and Customers*

A. Human relations are very important to job success. Many fired workers lose their jobs because they cannot get along with others.

B. Bosses act in the interest of the company. They do not act out of friendship. Workers and bosses sometimes become friends. It is more important, though, to learn to work effectively with the boss than to become friends.

C. Doing your share of the work and following the rules lead to good feelings among coworkers. Other ways of maintaining good relationships with coworkers include appearance, courtesy, attitude, interest, loyalty, tolerance, maturity, dependability, openness, and ethics.

D. Relationships between employees and customers are important to the success of a business. Customers deal with a certain business for several reasons. One is that customers like the product or service provided. A second reason is the types of follow-up services provided. A third is the goodwill provided.

Lesson 9.2 *Group Participation*

A. Most people work in groups from time to time. Do the following to be an effective group member: Show your readiness to help the group, accept the role the group gives you, carry out your role as best you can, share your views, do not dominate meetings, accept group decisions, encourage other members, think of solutions, not past problems, and be proud of group success.

B. Relating effectively to others is a skill. As a skill, it must be learned and practiced.

Activities

1. Identify a human relations problem that you have had with another student or a coworker. What was the nature of the problem? Based on what you have learned in this chapter, how could you have helped avoid the problem? Share your answers in class.
2. This chapter gave several reasons why customers deal with certain businesses. Think about your favorite businesses. Can you add any reasons to those the text gives? As a class, list the reasons on the board.
3. Invite an employer who uses task groups to speak. Ask the person to talk about how to get along in task groups. Prepare a list of questions beforehand.

REVIEW

Word Power

On a separate sheet of paper, match each definition with the correct term. All definitions will be used, and a definition will be used only once.

4. A work group formed to accomplish a particular objective
5. Interactions among people
6. The length of time someone has worked for a company
7. The business customers of a professional worker
8. Unwritten rules concerning respect for the property and territory of others
9. Persons under treatment or care by a medical practitioner
10. Customers of certain service-producing businesses or institutions
11. Acts of kindness, consideration, or assistance
12. To trade with or give one's business to a certain individual or company
13. A tendency to be drawn to another person, often because of similar characteristics and preferences

a. clients
b. goodwill
c. human relations
d. interpersonal attraction
e. patients
f. patronize
g. patrons
h. seniority
i. task group
j. territorial rights

Think Critically

14. Human relations skills are also important for bosses. What does it take beyond being a good coworker to be an effective boss?
15. Many people see themselves as getting along well with others. Yet you have read that many fired workers lose their jobs because they cannot get along with others. What are some causes of "bad attitudes" and conflicts among people at work?
16. Even though people work in groups, they still like to maintain their individuality. What are some of the ways that people express their individuality on the job?
17. Certain occupations like police officers, nurses, and attorneys deal with people who are often emotionally upset. What types of special human relations skills do these people need? What other occupations require these skills?

CHAPTER 10

EARNINGS AND JOB ADVANCEMENT

LESSONS

PREVIEW

In this chapter, you will learn about how your earnings are figured and about different types of payroll deductions. You will also learn about pay raises, promotions, and what is involved in changing jobs.

THOUGHTS ON WORK

"Opportunity is missed by most people because it is dressed in overalls and looks like work."
Thomas Edison

TAKING ACTION

PAY RAISES

Alice worked in the claims department of an insurance company for more than three years. Eight other people worked in the same department. Alice was clearly the best worker. One of her coworkers said that Alice always did the work of two people.

All workers in the department got regular pay raises. Alice had always gotten the same raise as everyone else. This year, however, Alice believed that things would be different. She had received an exceptionally good evaluation. The company had also had a very profitable year.

Alice was looking forward eagerly to receiving a generous raise. She already had plans for what she would do with the extra money. When her raise came through, however, Alice found that she had gotten the same amount as the other workers.

Alice was upset. She knew that her boss could have gotten her a higher raise. She made an appointment to discuss her raise with Ms. Lorch, her boss.

Alice asked Ms. Lorch why she kept getting the same average raise as everyone else even though she did more work. Ms. Lorch agreed that Alice was the most valuable employee in the department. But she explained that if she gave Alice a higher raise, it would create bad feelings within the department.

That was enough for Alice. She started looking for another job. It did not take her long to find one either. She then resigned from the insurance company.

A few months later, Alice was having lunch with a friend, one of her former coworkers. The woman told Alice that things had not been going well in the claims department since Alice had left. Alice's replacement could not do the amount of work that Alice could. The new person also made a lot of errors, something that Alice seldom did. Just that day, the friend had heard Ms. Lorch say that she wished she had Alice back.

SUCCESS TIP

You might not want to stay where there is no reason to do well.

THINK CRITICALLY

1. Why was Alice unhappy that she received the same raise as her coworkers?
2. Why do you think it didn't take Alice very long to find another job?

LESSON 10.1

YOUR JOB EARNINGS AND PAYCHECK

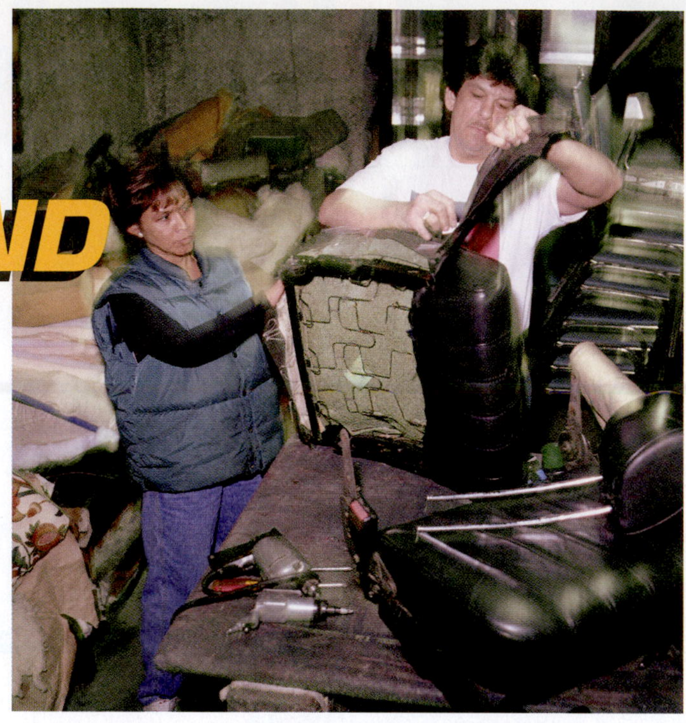

- IDENTIFY AND DESCRIBE DIFFERENT FORMS OF COMPENSATION
- DESCRIBE HOW A PAYCHECK IS FIGURED
- STATE THREE GUIDELINES REGARDING WORKING FOR A PAY RAISE

YOUR JOB EARNINGS

When you get paid, you will receive a paycheck and an attached statement of earnings. Some people cash or deposit their paycheck and throw away the pay statement. This is not a good idea. You may have lost money because of an error. Or too much money may have been withheld for certain deductions.

The amount of your paycheck depends on how you are paid and on the deductions taken out. How do you know if your paycheck is accurate? Read on.

The total amount of income and benefits you receive for your job is your **compensation**. Employees are compensated in many ways.

- ***Wages.*** Most workers receive a set hourly wage. To arrive at the amount of pay, an employer multiplies the hourly wage by the number of hours worked. For example, if Sean receives \$7.20 an hour and he works a 40-hour week, his weekly wages are \$288.00 (\$7.20 × 40). Most hourly workers are paid weekly.
- ***Overtime.*** For working more than 40 hours a week, most hourly workers get **overtime pay**. The overtime wage is usually 1½ times the normal hourly wage. Let's say that Sean worked 45 hours one week. He would receive \$7.20 an hour for the first 40 hours and \$10.80 an hour (\$7.20 × 1.5) for the 5 extra hours. His weekly wages would be \$342.00 (\$288.00 + \$54.00).
- ***Salary.*** Some workers receive a salary instead of an hourly wage. Salaried workers are paid a set sum of money per week, month, or year, instead of by the hour. Teachers' salaries are

ETHICAL DECISIONS

Each payday you carefully go over your check. Several times, you have found mistakes in which you were underpaid. The boss always apologizes and makes the correction. This payday, however, you discover you have been overpaid by \$20. You share this information with a coworker. He tells you to forget it, since you have probably been cheated out of more than \$20 by the company. You have been thinking about this all weekend.

WHAT WOULD YOU DO?

usually a certain amount for nine or ten months. Some salaried workers are paid weekly. Others receive checks every other week. Some people must really plan ahead! They get paid only once a month.

Salaried workers may put in more than 40 hours a week. Even so, they usually do not receive any extra pay. Do you think this is fair?

- ***Piece rate.*** In this method, the worker is paid for the amount of work performed. A sewing machine operator, for example, might be paid $.80 for each piece of goods completed. If 112 such pieces were done in one day, the worker would get $89.60 (112 × $.80) for that day.
- ***Commissions.*** Most sales workers receive all or part of their pay through commissions. A commission is an amount the worker receives for making a sale. Real estate agents and insurance brokers are some workers who receive commissions. Can you name others?

  Most commissions are a certain percentage of the total sale. Rita Yang, for example, is a real estate agent. She gets a 2 percent commission on each house she sells. Last week, Rita sold a house for $146,000. This meant a $2,920 commission ($146,000 × 0.02). She does not do that every day, though.
- ***Tips.*** Some workers receive a minimum hourly wage and earn the rest of their compensation from tips. Examples include restaurant servers, porters, and cab drivers. Can you think of any others? A tip or gratuity is an amount of money given in return for a favor or service. *Tips* is an acronym for the phrase "to insure prompt service."
- ***Bonuses.*** A bonus is extra money a company gives workers as a gift or a reward for good work. Most bonuses come from employers that are willing to share some of the company profits. Auto manufacturing companies, for example, often distribute annual profit-sharing amounts of several thousand dollars to each worker.
- ***Fringe benefits.*** Fringe benefits are indirect forms of compensation. That is, they are given instead of cash. Do you or members of your family get company-paid insurance? How about paid holidays, vacations, and sick days?

Tips are often a large part of the pay for service workers.

These are the most common fringe benefits. If you do not get fringe benefits, don't be discouraged. Most entry-level and part-time jobs offer few fringe benefits. Chances are you will get some later.

YOUR PAYCHECK

When you get your first check, look it over carefully. Make sure that your name is spelled right and your address and Social Security number are correct.

Your first paycheck may surprise you. Most new workers don't take home the pay they expect. Why is this so? You are right if you said that the employer has taken money out for certain reasons. Let's go back and see how the employer figures your earnings.

The amount of salary or wages that you earn during a certain time period is your **gross pay**. For example, if you work 20 hours a week at $6.80 an hour, your gross pay is $136.00 (20 × $6.80). From this amount, deductions are made for taxes, retirement, and so on. **Deductions** are certain amounts that are withheld from the paycheck of an employee. After

PERIOD FROM 02/18 TO 02/24 20 --					
NAME					
20	REG. HR. @	6	80	136	00
	OT. HR. @				
TOTAL EARNINGS ➔				136	00
F.I.C.A.		10	40		
WITHHOLDING U.S. INCOME TAX		5	00		
STATE INCOME TAX		7	20		
TOTAL DEDUCTIONS ➔				22	60
NET PAY				113	40

***Figure 10-1** Always examine your paycheck and statement. Ask your supervisor about any item on them you do not understand.*

these deductions are subtracted from your gross pay, you are left with **net pay** or take-home pay.

A pay statement or **statement of earnings** attached to your paycheck shows your gross pay, deductions, and net pay. A sample pay statement for a person paid weekly is shown in Figure 10-2.

Payroll deductions are of many types. The employer must take out, or withhold, some of them. Other deductions, though, depend on what you request the employer to withhold. Some common types of payroll deductions are the following:

- ***Income taxes.*** Your employer must withhold federal income tax from your earnings and send it to the federal government. When you start your job, you will need to fill out a Form W-4. This was covered in Chapter 6. Based on your answers on the form and what you earn, the employer figures the amount of federal tax to withhold each payday. Depending on where you live, the employer may withhold state and local taxes, too.
- ***FICA.*** The acronym FICA stands for Federal Insurance Contributions Act. The FICA tax is better known as the Social Security tax. Most jobs in the United States are part of the federal Social Security program. Both you and your employer pay into this fund. Social Security is

***Figure 10-2** Sample statement of earnings*

FIRST TRUST CORPORATION
2 COMPUTER DR. TROY, NY 12179-5483
Pay Statement

Co. Code	Department	File No.	Clock No./ID	Name	Pay Period	Pay Date
5XQ	301712	35637	05502	Roberts, Esther	Ending 01/24/--	01/22/--

Hours/Units	Rate		Earnings		Type	Deduction		Type	Deduction		Type
40	632	80	632	80	REG B	3	68	DENTAL	23	73	HEALTH

	Gross		Fed. With. Tax		Social Security		State With. Tax		City With. Tax		Sui./Dis.		Net Pay
This Pay	632	80	83	00	48	41	21	08				84	452.06
YTD	1,898	40	249	00	145	23	63	24			2	52	

MATH CONNECTION

Juan earns \$320 a week in salary plus a 5% commission on his total sales. He is paid once a month. This month his sales amounted to \$30,000. His deductions for the month are as follows:

Federal income tax, \$367.00
FICA, \$212.67
U.S. Savings Bonds, \$100.00

What is Juan's gross pay for the month? What is his net pay?

SOLUTION

Juan's gross pay is the sum of his salary and his commission.

$$\text{Gross pay} = \text{Salary} + \text{Commission}$$
$$= (\$320 \times 4) + (\$30{,}000 \times 0.05)$$
$$= \$1{,}280 + \$1{,}500$$
$$= \$2{,}780$$

Juan's net pay is the difference between his gross pay and his deductions.

$$\text{Net pay} = \text{Gross pay} - \text{Deductions}$$
$$= \$2{,}780.00 - (\$367.00 + \$212.67 + \$100.00)$$
$$= \$2{,}780.00 - \$679.67$$
$$= \$2{,}100.33$$

discussed further in Chapter 27. Notice in Figure 10-2 that the employer withheld \$48.41 during this pay period for Social Security from Esther Roberts's paycheck.

- ***Insurance.*** Many employers offer group life and health insurance programs to full-time employees. Employers often pay all or part of the insurance cost. If you must pay, the employer may withhold the premium from your paycheck. Esther Roberts's employer contributes 70 percent toward health insurance and provides free life insurance. Esther pays \$23.73 per week for health insurance, \$3.68 for dental insurance, and \$.84 for supplemental income and disability coverage.
- ***Union dues.*** Most union members can pay their dues through payroll deductions.
- ***Charity.*** Many workers donate to charity through payroll deductions. A common example of a charity is United Way.
- ***Savings.*** Do you find it hard to save? If so, see if your employer can withhold money for savings. For instance, the employer may be willing to deduct money for a savings account or U.S. Savings Bonds.

When you start a job, the employer should explain your deductions to you. If no one does, ask. After all, the deductions are your money.

NOTHING BUT NET

http://www.nasa.gov

Each web page has a unique address called the Uniform Resource Locator (URL). The first part, *http://*, stands for hypertext transfer protocol. This is the language that computers on the Web use to communicate with each other. The second part of the URL, *www.nasa.gov*, is known as the domain name. This is the name of the server to which you are connected. The *gov* part of the domain name indicates that the site is part of the federal government. Other commonly used extensions include *com* for business, *edu* for educational institutions, *mil* for military, *org* for nonprofit organizations, and *net* for networks.

PAY RAISES

Pay raises benefit both employees and their employers. The idea of a pay raise may be an incentive for you to do a good job. An **incentive** is a potential reward to work toward. After getting a raise, you may feel better about your job. This, in turn, may make you continue to

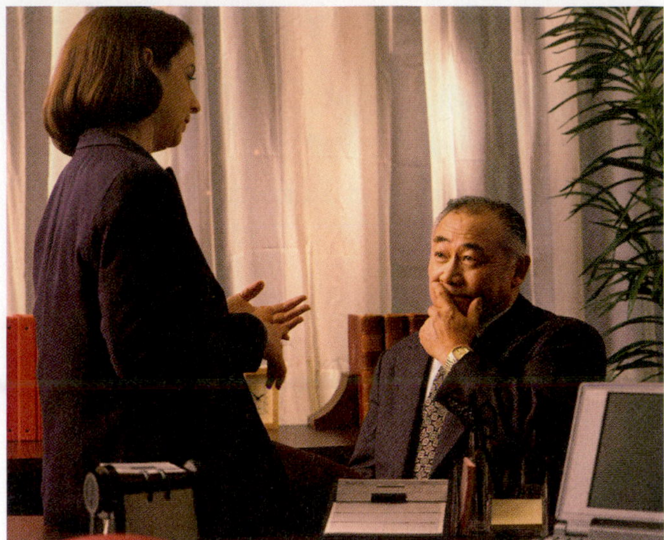

Good workers who do not get raises may go elsewhere.

improve your work. Improved work makes employees more valuable to the company.

Most companies want to keep good employees, so they give them raises. Good workers who do not get raises may go elsewhere, like Alice in the example at the beginning of the chapter.

In many jobs, employees receive automatic raises every 6 months, 12 months, and so on. An **automatic raise** is a regular pay raise received by all employees. All employees may get the same dollar amount or the same percentage amount. In some cases, the amount of the raise depends on the type of job. Production employees may get higher raises than office workers, for instance.

Some employers give merit raises instead of, or in addition to, automatic raises. A **merit raise** is based on the amount and quality of an employee's work. Most of these employers use a performance evaluation to determine merit raises.

Not all employers have a set policy on pay raises. In such cases, it may be up to the employer to decide when an employee deserves a raise. Or the employee may be expected to ask for a raise. This type of situation is common in small businesses.

Suppose you decide to ask for a raise. If you are a new employee, do not expect one until after you have learned the job and shown you can do it well. You must earn a raise. Some workers want a raise because they are not making as much money as they would like. An employer will not be impressed by a worker who asks for a raise to buy a DVD, for instance.

Before you speak to your boss about a raise, plan what you will say. Think about what you have done well. Make a list of specific examples.

Ask for a raise when the company is doing well and the boss has had a good week. Do not ask for a raise during a time when you should be working. Ask for an appointment to discuss a raise during break, at lunch, or after work.

When asking for a pay raise, tell the boss why you deserve one. Steve, for example, pointed out to his boss that sales had increased 18 percent since he had started working in the department.

Ask your boss what workers must do to get a pay raise. If you have done all those things, tell the boss. Be clear. Talk about exactly what you have done. If the boss says there is no rule for granting raises, present your case.

When asking for a raise, show confidence and respect. If you are turned down, do not argue with the decision. Just say that you will keep working hard and hope that you get a raise later. If you feel strongly that you deserve a raise, you may want to follow Alice's example.

LESSON 10.1 REVIEW

1. The amount of your paycheck depends on what two things?
2. Why is it important to check your pay statement often?
3. List and briefly explain each form of compensation.
4. What type of workers receive all or part of their pay through commissions?
5. Which payroll deductions are employers generally required to make? Which ones are optional for you?
6. What is the FICA tax?

HIGH-GROWTH OCCUPATIONS FOR THE 21st CENTURY

Engineering, Natural Science, and Computer System Managers

These managers use advanced technical knowledge of engineering, science, and computer and information systems to oversee a variety of activities. They determine scientific and technical goals within broad outlines provided by top management. Engineering, natural science, and computer system managers make detailed plans for the accomplishment of these goals.

To perform effectively, they must possess knowledge of administrative procedures, such as budgeting, hiring, and supervision. In addition, these managers use communication skills extensively. They spend a great deal of time coordinating the activities of their unit with the activities of other units or organizations.

Engineering managers supervise people who design and develop machinery, products, systems, and processes or direct and coordinate production, operations, quality assurance, testing, or maintenance in industrial plants. Many are plant engineers, who direct and coordinate the design, installation, operation, and maintenance of equipment and machinery in industrial plants. Others manage research and development teams that produce new products and processes or improve existing ones.

Natural science managers oversee the work of life and physical scientists, including agricultural scientists, chemists, biologists, geologists, medical scientists, and physicists. These managers direct research and development projects and coordinate activities such as testing, quality control, and production. They may work on basic research projects or on commercial activities. Natural science managers sometimes conduct their own research in addition to managing the work of others.

The research work of chemists is directed by natural science managers.

Computer and information systems managers direct the work of systems analysts, computer programmers, and others in computer-related occupations. These managers plan and coordinate activities such as the installation and upgrading of hardware and software, programming, systems design, the development of computer networks, and the implementation of Internet and intranet sites. They analyze the computer and information needs of their organization and determine personnel and equipment requirements. They also assign and review the work of subordinates and purchase necessary equipment.

LESSON 10.2 JOB CHANGES

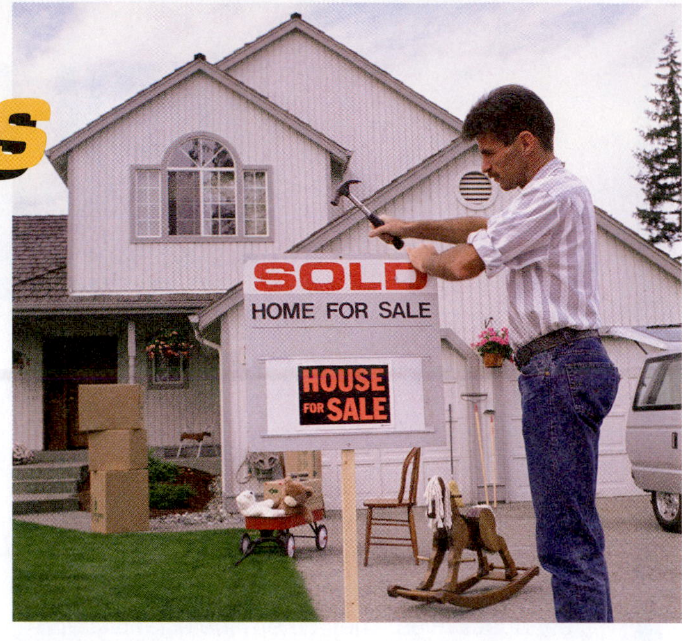

- IDENTIFY THE MOST COMMON REASONS FOR CHANGING JOBS
- EXPLAIN WHAT TO DO WHEN VOLUNTARILY LEAVING A JOB

REASONS FOR JOB CHANGES

Most people start working in a low-paying, entry-level job. An entry-level job is a good way to earn money and gain valuable experience. Usually, though, an entry-level job is not one that you want to keep forever. You may want to advance within the company or move to a better job in another company.

Job Promotions

A **promotion** is advancement to a higher-level job within a company. The new position usually brings a new title, more money, and more responsibility. Some promotions also bring the chance to supervise others. Opportunities for promotion differ among occupations and industries. For example, most workers in skilled trades have less chance for promotion than do sales representatives. Large businesses offer more chances for promotion than do small ones.

Promotion opportunities occur for two reasons: a new position is created within the company or a vacancy occurs because someone was promoted or left the company. How can you put yourself in line for a promotion? You can begin during the job interview. Ask, "What are my chances for advancement if I perform well?" Suppose you work where you can advance. Do the best work you can every day. Employers notice workers who do their jobs well and get along with others.

Even if you are a good employee, remember that promotions take time. Employers want to watch you over a period of time. Even when an employer thinks you are ready, an opening may not yet exist. Or a worker who has the same job as you may have more seniority. If so, the person with seniority will probably get promoted first.

While many people want promotions, not all of us want to be the boss or have a better job. A higher-level job is not for everyone.

CAREER DECISIONS

You have been working at a farm implement dealership since your senior year in high school. You like the job and the people who work there. The business, however, is barely making enough profit to stay alive. You have only had one small raise in three years. You have been laid off for a couple of months each winter. The prospects for additional raises or promotions do not look good. You understand the dealer's financial problems, but you have your future to think about.

WHAT WOULD YOU DO?

When the job of office manager opened up, Seymour's coworkers encouraged him to apply. He was the most experienced accounting clerk in the company, got along with everyone, and knew the business well. He applied for the job and got it.

Seymour soon found out that being an office manager was different than he had thought. He had to assign work, manage the office budget, make on-the-spot decisions, and do many other things. To get everything done, he began to come to work earlier and stay later. Once he started giving orders, Seymour sensed tension between himself and the other employees. His most painful moment was when his boss ordered him to fire one of the clerk-typists.

Seymour is not alone. All businesses have people like him. They are great workers but are not suited to be supervisors. No matter what your job, try to work toward something you will like. For many workers, that is the job they have now.

Other Reasons

Years ago, most people stayed on a job for most of their working lives. Things have changed since then. While some people stay on the same job, most of us do not. The most common reasons for changing jobs are as follows:

- ***Lack of opportunity with present employer.*** You may be in a dead-end job that offers little chance for pay raises and promotions.
- ***Better opportunity elsewhere.*** Perhaps you like the job you have but another company offers you an even better job. Often such a change involves a pay raise.
- ***Dislike for present occupation or job.*** Not everything looks as good up close as it did from afar. Perhaps you thought you would really enjoy your present occupation. After doing it for a while, though, you see that it's just not what you want to do for the rest of your life. You may want to train for another occupation. Or you may like your occupation (what you do) but dislike your job (where you work). If so, changing jobs is probably the answer.
- ***Change in personal or family situation.*** You may need to quit a job because of such things as illness or a move to a new area.
- ***Loss of job.*** Perhaps your company's business slows down and lays you off. Maybe the employer even goes out of business. These things are not your fault. Being fired probably is, though. Either way, you are out of a job.

WORKFORCE TRENDS

The U.S. Bureau of Labor Statistics predicts that, during 1996–2006, almost 40 percent of workers entering the workforce will be members of minority groups. People of color, women, and immigrants will make up nearly 70 percent of new workers.

Being Fired

Being fired is much different than leaving a job on your own. Some employers may ask you to leave but give you the chance to resign. Resigning will make it easier to find another job. If you are fired or must resign, try to turn disaster into a learning experience. Never make the same mistake twice.

- Phyllis was fired but was not sure why. It would have been easy for her to never go back. Instead, she made an appointment with her former boss to find out why she was fired. After learning about some of her poor work habits, she decided to improve on her next job.
- Theo was let go because he did not have the skills for the job. He decided to start classes at the community college.
- Sharlene lost her job because of too many absences. She did not think the boss would fire her. When the boss did, Sharlene was shocked. She will do her best to see it will not happen again.
- Ed was told that he had a bad attitude. It was true. He could not get along with the boss, coworkers, or customers. Ed talked with a good friend who helped him understand what he was doing wrong. Ed now sees that he was carrying a chip on his shoulder.

If you have made mistakes like Phyllis, Theo, Sharlene, or Ed, admit them. Do not lie to yourself or blame someone else. The best approach,

2″ or center vertically

893 N. Rigeway St.
Statesboro, GA 30458-1347
August 8, 20— 4 line returns

Ralph W. Wilson, Manager
Hoags Drugs, Inc.
416 Webster Dr.
Statesboro, GA 30459-3820

side margins 1″ or default

Dear Mr. Wilson

This is to inform you that I have decided to resign from my present position and return to college. I plan to continue working through August 30. I would be happy to do whatever I can to help train a replacement.

Hoags is a fine company with many wonderful employees. I have enjoyed my job and have learned a great deal from you and the rest of the shipping department crew. Thank you very much for the opportunity to have worked here.

Sincerely 4 line returns

James R. Long

James R. Long

about 1″ minimum

Figure 10-3 ***Sample letter of resignation***

though, is not to do things that result in getting fired. Use what you have learned in this and earlier chapters to be a more effective worker.

LEAVING A JOB

No matter what the reason that you are changing jobs, plan the change carefully if you can. Do not make a quick decision. Some workers get angry and quit. Later, most of these people regret what they did.

Earlier in the chapter, you read about Alice being turned down for a raise. It would have been a mistake for her to quit on the spot. Instead, she made sure she had a new job first. Another mistake would have been to say, "If you don't give me a raise, I'm going to quit." What do you think would have happened then?

Once you have decided to leave, find out if the company has rules about quitting a job. If so, follow them. If not, give your employer at least two weeks' notice. Tell your boss before you mention it to your coworkers.

Follow up your verbal notice with a written letter of resignation, (Figure 10-3). A **letter of resignation** is a letter written by an employee notifying an employer of the intent to quit a job. Such a letter should contain the following points: (a) the fact that you are leaving, (b) a date when you plan to leave, (c) the reason you are leaving, (d) an offer to help train your replacement, and (e) a thank-you for the chance to work there.

Once you have told your employer you are leaving, do not let up. Do your job as best you can through the last day. Do not criticize your boss or brag to your coworkers about your new job. Your employer will watch and evaluate you through your last day. Your boss's good opinion may be valuable to you in seeking future jobs. Therefore, try to leave on good terms with your employer.

LESSON 10.2 REVIEW

1. **Name two reasons why promotion opportunities occur.**
2. **Is promotion for everyone? Why or why not?**
3. **List five common reasons for changing jobs.**
4. **Why is it best to leave a job on good terms with your employer?**

FOCUS ON THE WORKPLACE

EMPLOYER-SPONSORED CHILD-CARE ASSISTANCE

Growing numbers of working mothers, dual-earner families, and single-earner families have greatly increased the need for child care. Close to 20 million young children now spend part of their day being cared for by other people. Child-care assistance has become the hot new fringe benefit.

An increasing proportion of private companies and public employers provide on-site child care. Many other employers provide referral services to help employees find out about child-care options in their community.

Businesses that cannot provide child care sometimes offer dependent-care-assistance plans. These plans allow parents to set aside a certain amount, often several thousand dollars, in tax-free income each year to help pay for child care.

The major reason that companies offer child-care assistance is to attract and hold good employees. For instance, one department head turned down a job across town that offered a large salary increase. She put it this way: "I spend the lunch hour with my six-month-old son. They couldn't put a price tag on having my child within a few minutes of me."

Employer-sponsored child-care assistance has increased in response to growing numbers of working mothers, dual-earner families, and single-earner familes.

Child-care assistance is expensive, and few companies pay 100 percent of the costs. Usually, employees contribute a portion that amounts to about one-third to one-half of the cost of private, community child care.

Experts predict that more employers will offer child-care assistance in the future. The future is also likely to bring more workplace options, such as flextime, job sharing, and telecommuting. Such options can help working parents maintain a balanced family life.

THINK CRITICALLY

1. How important would having child care on-site at your workplace be to you if you had children?
2. What are some concerns that parents might have about child care?

CHAPTER 10

Chapter in Brief

Lesson 10.1 *Your Job Earnings and Paycheck*

A. The amount of your paycheck depends on how you are paid and on the deductions taken out. Employees are compensated in many ways. These include wages, salary, piece rate, commissions, tips, bonuses, and fringe benefits.

B. The total amount of salary or wages that you earn is your gross pay. From this, certain deductions are made. After deductions are subtracted from the gross pay, you are left with net pay. The most common types of payroll deductions are income taxes, FICA, and miscellaneous deductions such as insurance, union dues, charity, and savings.

C. Pay raises benefit both employees and employers. Some workers receive automatic raises every so often. Merit raises may be given instead of, or in addition to, automatic raises. Not all employers have a set policy on pay raises.

Lesson 10.2 *Job Changes*

A. A promotion is advancement to a higher-level job within a company. Opportunities for promotion differ among occupations, industries, and employers. Earning a promotion usually takes time and is based on outstanding performance.

B. Most people do not stay on the same job all their lives. There are many different reasons for changing jobs.

C. Some people are fired or given a chance to resign. If this happens to you, try to learn from the experience.

D. No matter what the reason for a job change, try to plan it carefully. Follow company guidelines for resigning and leaving a job. Try to leave on good terms with your employer.

Activities

1. Suppose that you earn $7.20 an hour. One week, you work 48 hours. You are paid the normal rate for the first 40 hours and time and a half for overtime. What is your gross pay for the week?

2. Let's say that you are going to leave your job for a better one. Write a sample letter of resignation. Hand it in to your teacher for evaluation.

3. Role-play a conversation you might have with your supervisor to ask for a raise. Plan out what you are going to say beforehand.

4. Nat earns a salary of $280 a week plus a 5% commission on his total sales. This month his sales amounted to $26,000. His deductions are as follows:

- Federal income tax, $294.00
- State tax, $52.44
- FICA, $185.13
- Credit union, $65.00
- Charity, $35.00

Based on these figures, what is Nat's gross pay for the month? How much are his total deductions? What is his net pay?

Word Power

On a separate sheet of paper, match each definition with the correct term. All definitions will be used, and a definition will be used only once.

5. Certain amounts that are withheld from the paycheck of an employee
6. A letter written by an employee notifying an employer of the intent to quit a job
7. The amount on a paycheck; the take-home pay of an employee after deductions are subtracted from gross pay
8. A regular pay raise received by all employees
9. A pay statement; the attachment to a paycheck that shows your gross pay, deductions, and net pay
10. A potential reward to work toward
11. Advancement to a higher-level job within a company
12. The total amount of income and benefits received for a job
13. The wage received for working more than 40 hours a week, usually $1^1/_2$ times the normal hourly wage
14. A pay raise based on the amount and quality of an employee's work
15. The amount of salary or wages earned during a certain time period, before deductions are withheld

a. automatic raise
b. compensation
c. deductions
d. gross pay
e. incentive
f. letter of resignation
g. merit raise
h. net pay
i. overtime pay
j. promotion
k. statement of earnings

Think Critically

16. If you were a salesperson, would you rather be paid a salary or a straight commission? Discuss the advantages and disadvantages of each.
17. In recent years, workers in a number of industries have been forced to take pay cuts and give up benefits in order to save their jobs. Would you be willing to take a pay cut to keep a job?
18. Do you think that you would like to be a supervisor? Why or why not?
19. The decision to change jobs and move elsewhere is often complicated for married couples in which both people work. Discuss how you might feel about giving up a good job in order to move with your spouse.

CHAPTER 11

APPEARANCE ON THE JOB

LESSONS

PREVIEW

At work, you will be expected to maintain a good personal appearance. Your appearance influences how other people see you and will greatly affect your job success. A good personal appearance means keeping yourself clean, healthy, neat, and attractive. It also means dressing properly. This chapter provides some guidelines for hygiene, grooming, and dressing for work.

THOUGHTS ON WORK

"There's no labor a man can do that's undignified—if he does it right."
Bill Cosby

TAKING ACTION

APPEARANCE AT WORK

Janet was enjoying her new job at the warehouse for a large supermarket chain. She was earning good wages, and she liked the work she had to do. Janet was learning some new skills, and she found her coworkers easy to get along with.

Janet had been on her job for only ten days when Mr. Bedrava, the boss, called her into his office. After asking her to sit down, Mr. Bedrava seated himself behind his desk.

"Janet," Mr. Bedrava said, "your appearance and grooming impressed me a lot when I interviewed you for this job. In fact, that is one of the reasons I hired you.

"But since you started work," Mr. Bedrava continued, "your looks have changed. Some of your coworkers have complained about body odor, too. I am disappointed. I do not want our customers to think that your appearance is an indication of how we do business."

Mr. Bedrava stood up. "Please think about cleaning up your act. I hope we will not have to talk about this again."

This straight talk embarrassed Janet. "Gee, I am sorry," she said. "I did not think it mattered that much how warehouse workers looked.

"I understand what you are saying, though," Janet continued. "Many people do see me in this job. Thanks for giving me another chance."

As Janet left Mr. Bedrava's office, she decided that from then on she would take better care of her personal appearance.

Like Mr. Bedrava, most employers and bosses take note of their employees' appearance. In fact, many performance evaluations have a section on appearance. No matter what your job, your employer will expect you to groom and dress properly.

SUCCESS TIP

Pay attention to personal hygiene and appearance at work.

THINK CRITICALLY

1. Why was Mr. Bedrava so concerned about Janet's poor hygiene and grooming?
2. What are some steps that Janet should take immediately to improve her appearance at work?

LESSON 11.1
GROOMING AND APPEARANCE

OBJECTIVES

- EXPLAIN WHY GOOD HYGIENE AND GROOMING ARE IMPORTANT ON THE JOB
- LIST FIVE RULES FOR GOOD GROOMING AND APPEARANCE

APPEARANCE MATTERS

An appropriate appearance on the job begins with **personal hygiene**, keeping one's body clean and healthy. In most jobs, being clean is not enough. It is also necessary to be neat and attractive, or to use good **grooming**. Rules for personal hygiene apply to everyone. What is considered to be attractive or good grooming varies from person to person and job to job. For instance, a hairstyle that looks good on one person may not suit another. What is considered to be proper makeup in one job setting may be inappropriate in another.

TIPS FOR GROOMING AND APPEARANCE

Some of the following tips may apply to you and your job situation. Others may not.

Hairstyling

For most jobs, hair should be neat, trimmed, and not too faddish. Beyond this, how you wear your hair is up to you. Whatever style you choose, hair should be neatly combed or brushed.

A hairstylist can help you choose a style that goes well with your features and hair type. When deciding on a hairstyle, be sure to think about how much care it will need.

Shaving

A grooming choice for men is whether to be clean-shaven or to grow a mustache or beard. Going to work with a growth of stubble is not a good choice. Should you decide to grow facial hair, start during a vacation. If you do grow a mustache or beard, shave your neck and the uncovered parts of the face. Weekly trims are in order, too.

> **PERSONAL DECISIONS**
>
> **You have always wanted long, polished nails. One Saturday you go to a salon for artificial nails. You think they are gorgeous. At work on Monday, things are not so good. The longer nails interfere with your keyboarding. Your work has slowed and you are making more mistakes. The supervisor notices and suggests you have the nails trimmed. "I cannot," you think. "I paid a lot of money for these nails."**
>
> **WHAT WOULD YOU DO?**

Deodorants and Antiperspirants

Even after bathing, underarm perspiration odor can develop quickly. Many people use a deodorant for odor or an antiperspirant for wetness. Choose whatever fits your needs.

Wendy, a realtor, has always perspired heavily. Moving to Texas made her problem worse. Deodorant was no longer enough. Perspiration stains on her clothing embarrassed Wendy, especially when she was with clients. Antiperspirants reduced her perspiration and embarrassment.

Skin Care and Cosmetics

Your skin may need care beyond daily bathing. The most common problem is dry skin. In colder climates, heated homes and low humidity cause skin to become dry and itchy. In such cases, moisturize your skin often with lotion. Hands may need special attention. Abused hands get rough and sore and look bad. To help heal them, use hand lotion often. This applies to both men and women.

Many women choose to use cosmetics or beauty aids to improve their appearance. If you do, don't overdo them. Too much makeup can dry out the skin and cause irritation. Cosmetic counters in large department stores often have people who can advise you on cosmetic use.

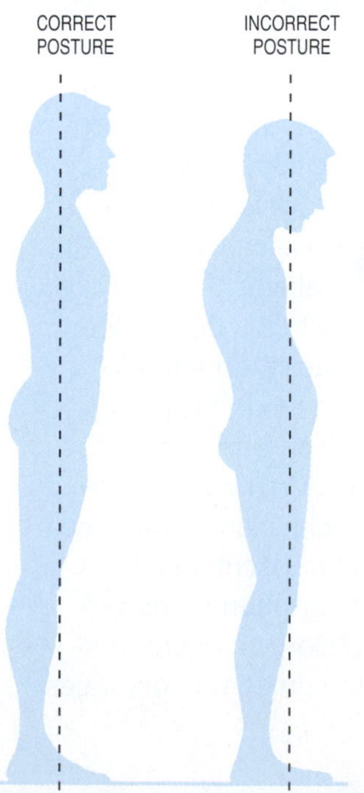

Figure 11-1 ***Make an effort to demonstrate good posture.***

WORKFORCE TRENDS

The Americans with Disabilities Act and labor shortages have increased job opportunities for people with disabilities. New technology is making it easier for employers to accommodate these workers and for them to do their jobs better. Studies have shown that workers with disabilities rank as well as or better than their peers in job performance, attendance, and safety.

Posture

Matthew is always clean and well groomed. His poor posture, however, ruins his appearance. **Posture** is the way you stand, walk, and sit. People with poor posture have a stooping head and shoulders and a belly that sticks out. They look lazy and lacking in self-confidence. This may be untrue, but poor posture sends out the wrong message.

A person with good posture appears poised and self-confident. Good posture, like good grooming, is necessary to make a good impression on the job. It also makes you feel better and helps fight fatigue. Figure 11.1 shows the difference between correct and incorrect posture.

LESSON 11.1 REVIEW

1. **For most jobs, what is the basic rule about hairstyles?**
2. **Suppose Kyle, a surveyor, wants to grow a beard. When should he start?**
3. **What is the purpose of a deodorant? An antiperspirant?**
4. **How does good posture help you to make a good impression on the job?**

HIGH-GROWTH OCCUPATIONS FOR THE 21st CENTURY

Health Information Technicians

Every time medical personnel treat a patient, they make a record of what they observe and how the patient is treated medically. This record includes information the patient provides concerning symptoms and medical history. The results of examinations, reports of x-rays and laboratory tests, diagnoses, and treatment plans are also included. *Health information technicians* organize these records and evaluate them for completeness and accuracy.

Health information technicians, also called *medical record technicians*, begin to assemble patients' health information by making sure their initial medical charts are complete. They ensure all forms are completed, properly identified, and signed and all necessary information is in the computer. They may talk to physicians or others to clarify diagnoses or get more information. Health information technicians need a strong clinical background to analyze medical records.

A health information technician organizes patient medical records and makes sure the records are accurate and complete.

Technicians assign a code to each diagnosis and procedure. They consult classification manuals and rely, also, on their knowledge of disease processes. Technicians then use a software program to assign the patient to one of several hundred "diagnosis-related groups," or DRGs. The DRG determines the amount the medical facility will be reimbursed if the patient is covered by Medicare (a federal health insurance program) or other insurance programs using the DRG system. Technicians also use computer programs to tabulate and analyze data to help improve patient care or control costs, for use in legal actions, or in response to surveys.

Health information technician is one of the few health occupations in which there is little or no physical contact with patients. Duties vary with the size of the facility. In large to medium facilities, technicians may specialize in one aspect of health information, such as Medicare coding. Some technicians supervise health information clerks and transcribers. A health information administrator often manages the department. In small facilities, an accredited health information technician sometimes manages the department.

LESSON 11.2

DRESSING FOR THE JOB

OBJECTIVES

- UNDERSTAND THE IMPORTANCE OF DRESSING APPROPRIATELY AT WORK
- SUMMARIZE GUIDELINES ON DRESSING FOR THE JOB

DRESS FOR SUCCESS

Clothes are important to your overall appearance on the job. Some jobs require a uniform. If yours does, make sure the uniform you wear is always clean and pressed.

If your job does not require a uniform, deciding how to dress will be more difficult. On most jobs, however, the employer expects workers to dress in a certain way. A bank teller, for instance, is supposed to look professional. For a man, this usually means a suit or nice slacks and jacket, with a dress shirt and tie. For a woman, professional dress includes a suit, a dress, or a nice skirt or slacks with a blouse or sweater. If in doubt, notice what the other employees wear. If you have any questions, ask your boss.

CLOTHING GUIDELINES

Here are several rules that will help you choose clothes for work and care for them properly.

- ***Wear what fits your job.*** Think about your job. Will you get dirty and greasy? Will you need protection from sun, wind, rain, or cold? Will you be handling food? Buy clothing that is well suited for the work you will do.
- ***Wear what looks good on you.*** Within the expectations or requirements for the job, wear clothes that look good on you. Do not try to dress like someone else. Choose clothes that match your physical features and personality.

CAREER DECISIONS

You just started a co-op job at a large savings and loan association. You are aware of how important it is to look good on the job. Everyone at work dresses so nicely. But you only have a couple of decent outfits. You do not have the money for new clothes. You feel very self-conscious at work. You know you look more like a student than an employee. You are thinking about looking for a new job where you could wear a uniform or more casual clothes.

WHAT WOULD YOU DO?

COMMUNICATION AT WORK

DIFFERENT CULTURES

You know that appearance is very important in American culture. How often do people draw conclusions about others based on things like length or style of hair, grooming, fitness, and style or quality of clothes?

At work, you are likely to come in contact with people whose personal appearance is very different from what you are used to. Suppose you have a transportation job. One of the drivers might be a Sikh American man who wears a turban. Some of your customers might be Asian Indian women who sometimes wear saris.

Do not draw conclusions about people whose culture you don't understand. Keep an open mind. Show people from other cultures the same courtesy and respect you do everyone else. Make an effort to learn about different cultures by talking to people and reading about cultures at a library or on the Web.

- ***Plan your wardrobe carefully.*** You will probably not be able to buy your entire **wardrobe** (your clothing) all at once. So build around a number of basic items. For instance, a pair of gray slacks will go with many different shirts, blouses, or sweaters. You can wear a navy blazer formally or informally.

  Fad clothes may be fun off the job. But unless such clothes are required on your job, do not wear them to work.
- ***Learn how to coordinate clothes.*** Teach yourself to mix and match your clothes. For instance, do not wear a plaid shirt or blouse with different plaid slacks. Libraries have magazines and books that can help you learn about fashion. A variety of web sites have fashion suggestions and shopping guidelines.
- ***Choose quality, well-made clothing.*** The most expensive clothes are not always the best quality. Nor are clothes with a popular name or label always the best. Compare clothes and prices in many different stores before you decide to buy. After all, you will live with your choices for a long time.
- ***Take proper care of your clothes.*** Think about clothing care before you buy. Easy-care fabrics are more practical than ones that require frequent ironing or dry cleaning. Do not go to work in dirty clothes or clothes that look as if you slept in them. To prevent heavy wrinkling, hang up or fold clothes properly. Iron wrinkled clothes. Clothes have attached tags that tell how to care for them. Follow the instructions carefully.

Michele's clothes are well chosen and fit her nicely. She is careless, however, in taking care of them. Her winter coats have been missing buttons for two years. Today, she wore a dress that has a ripped arm seam. In spite of her nice clothes, Michele often looks sloppy. Her coworkers joke about her appearance.

The way you look influences how other people see you and will greatly affect your job success. Everyone can look good. Remember that a winning appearance depends more on knowledge and effort than it does on physical beauty.

LESSON 11.2 REVIEW

1. If you aren't sure about how to dress on the job, what two things might you do?
2. List six basic rules for clothing choice, wear, and care.

FOCUS ON HEALTH AND SAFETY

SUN PROTECTION

Jobs requiring outdoor work pose a special skin care problem. Long-term exposure to the sun will cause your skin to become wrinkled and leathery. Premature aging of the skin is not the main problem, though. Dermatologists believe that continued exposure to the sun leads to skin cancer. The process can be likened to filling up a bottle with liquid. Each day's sun gets added to a lifetime's worth of exposure. After enough exposure, skin cancer may result.

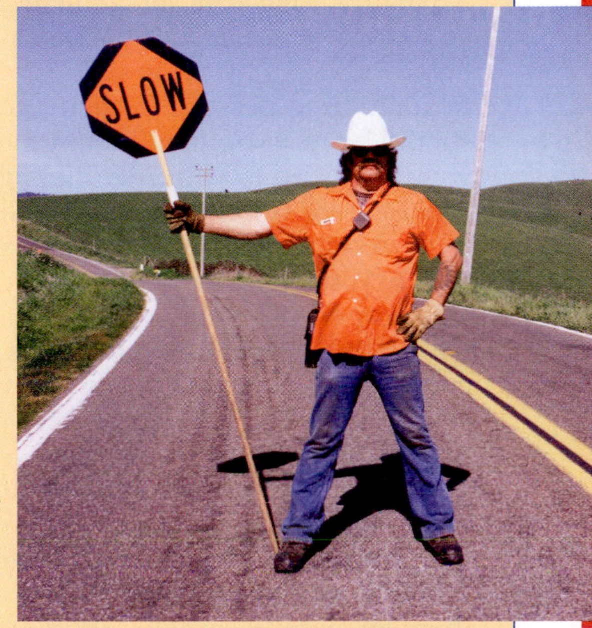

Each day's sun gets added to a lifetime's worth of exposure.

Skin cancer is the most common type of cancer in the United States. More than one million Americans develop skin cancer every year. And the numbers continue to grow annually. There are two primary reasons for the increase in skin cancer. One is that children and teens are tanning younger and spending more time in the sun than ever before. Another reason is damage to the earth's ozone layer that blocks the sun's harmful rays. As a result, individuals are exposed to increased levels of ultraviolet radiation.

What should you do if you have to work in the sun for long periods of time? The best protection is to keep the skin covered. Wear a hat, long-sleeved shirt, and long pants. Another solution is to apply special lotions and creams called **sunscreens** to your skin. Sunscreens are rated according to a numerical "sun protection factor" (SPF). A lotion with an SPF of 2, for example, allows you to stay in the sun two times longer than you could without any protection. Many dermatologists, however, recommend nothing less than an SPF of 15, especially on the face. Sunscreens are not just for weekends on the beach. They should be used each day that you are outside exposed to the sun.

THINK CRITICALLY

1. A recent survey by the American Academy of Dermatology found that only 15 percent of Americans wear sunscreen whenever they go outside, only 14 percent wear it year-round, and more than a quarter don't usually wear sunscreen. Why do you think this is so?
2. What are the possible dangers of too much sun exposure? How can you prevent overexposure?

CHAPTER 11

Chapter in Brief

Lesson 11.1 *Grooming and Appearance*

A. No matter what your job, remember your employer will expect you to groom and dress properly. What is considered to be a good appearance, however, varies from job to job.

B. In addition to personal hygiene, grooming is important on the job. Hair should be neat, trimmed, and not too faddish. Beyond this, how you wear your hair is up to you. A grooming decision for men is whether to be clean-shaven or to grow a mustache or beard. To control underarm odor, use a deodorant; for wetness, use an antiperspirant. Your skin may need care beyond daily bathing. Women should use cosmetics and other beauty aids properly.

C. Posture is the way you stand, walk, and sit. Good posture, like good grooming, is necessary if you want to make a good impression on the job.

Lesson 11.2 *Dressing for the Job*

A. Clothes are important to your overall appearance on the job. If in doubt, notice what other employees wear or ask your boss.

B. The following rules will help you choose clothes for work and care for them properly: Wear what fits your job. Wear what looks good on you. Plan your wardrobe carefully. Learn how to coordinate clothes. Choose quality, well-made clothing. Take proper care of your clothes.

Activities

1. Invite a hairstylist to class to discuss hair care and hairstyling as they relate to appearance on the job.
2. Invite a clothing store representative to class to discuss how to make the most of a basic wardrobe.
3. Prepare a bulletin board that shows proper dress and appearance for different occupations. Each person in the class should contribute something from a magazine or other source. Try to show occupations for which students in the class are preparing.
4. Lands' End, the clothing retailer, has a web site at which you can build a 3-D model of yourself to try on various clothing combinations. Log on to *http://www.landsend.com*, click on "My Model" or "My Virtual Model," follow instructions to build the model, and then experiment with trying on clothes. The Lands' End site offers other interactive features that can help you choose clothing for work. Try one of these other features.

REVIEW

5. Sunscreens are rated by SPF numbers. The numbers correspond to the degree of protection provided. Prepare a chart or poster explaining the numbering system.

Word Power

On a separate sheet of paper, match each definition with the correct term. All definitions will be used, and a definition will be used only once.

6. The position of a person's body while standing, walking, or sitting
7. Maintaining a neat, attractive appearance
8. Wearing apparel; one's clothing
9. Special lotions or creams used to protect the skin from the sun's ultraviolet rays
10. Keeping one's body clean and healthy

a. grooming
b. personal hygiene
c. posture
d. sunscreens
e. wardrobe

Think Critically

11. What are your feelings toward someone who has poor personal hygiene or an inappropriate appearance? Pretend that you have a friend or coworker with such a problem. Discuss your feelings and how you might go about telling the person.
12. Good appearance varies from job to job. Discuss some examples. Give examples that illustrate both different grooming practices and different types of dress.
13. Some companies have what are called "casual Friday" dress days. Most students probably work for such a company or know a family member or friend who does. Discuss advantages and disadvantages of this practice.
14. Hairstyles, use of beauty aids, and clothing styles often differ from one region of the country to another. Perhaps you have lived or traveled in regions different from where you live now. Discuss some of these differences.
15. Many companies have dress codes for their employees. Dress codes can extend to hairstyles and even to accessories. Sometimes employees feel that a dress code violates their privacy or is discriminatory. For example, a major airline was sued recently over its dress code. A male employee challenged the company's policy of allowing women to wear earrings and ponytails, but not men. The employee lost the case. Do you think companies should be allowed to set dress codes? Are there instances in which it might make sense for an employer to make exceptions to its dress code for individual employees?

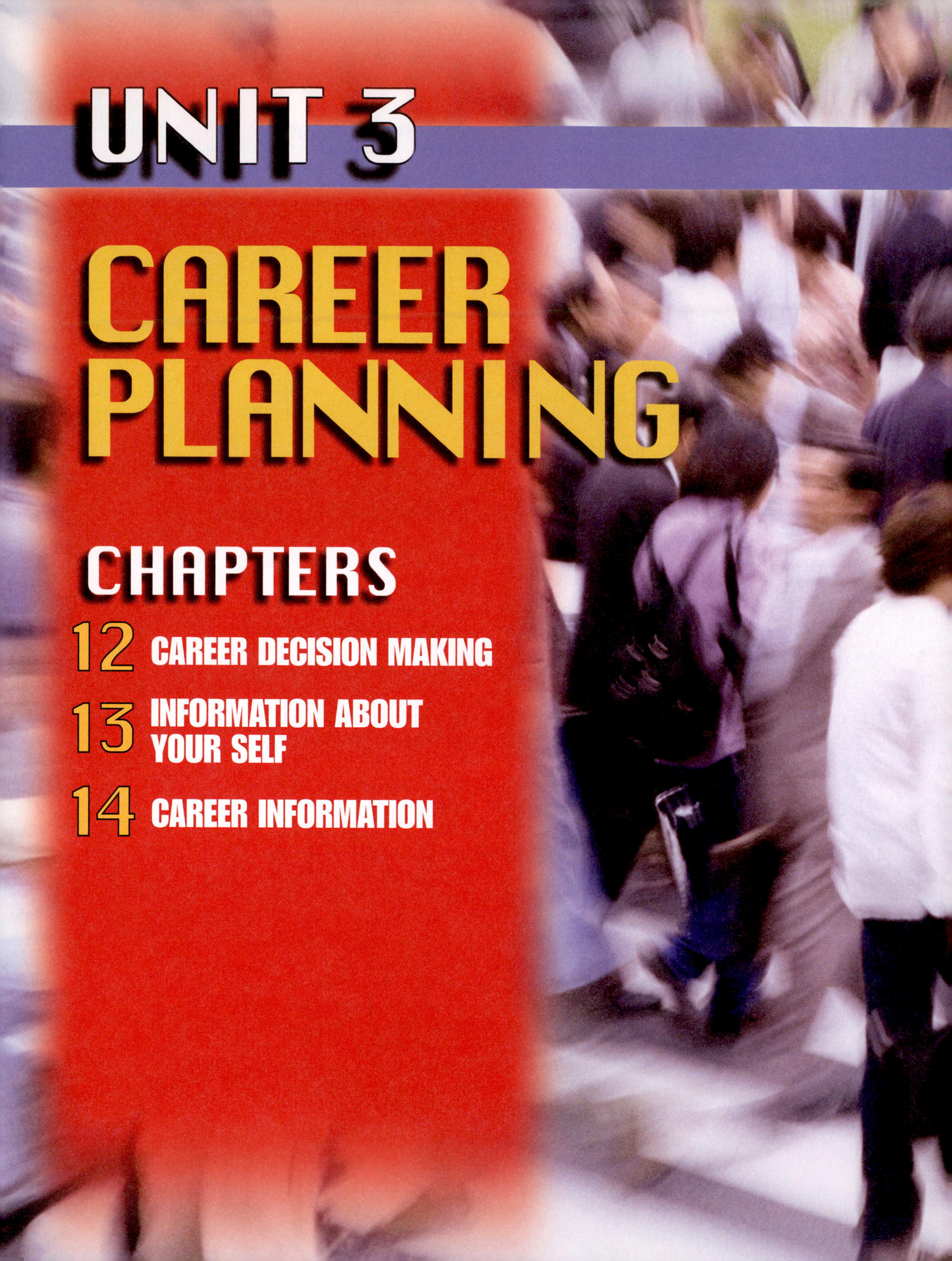

UNIT 3

CAREER PLANNING

CHAPTERS

CO-OP CAREER SPOTLIGHT

Pearlena Warren, *Medical Assistant*

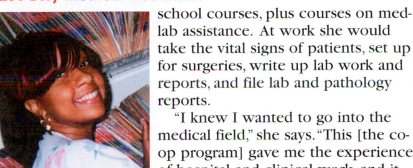

When 18-year-old Pearlena Warren was in second grade, she witnessed two first-grade girls fighting. "One girl was kicking the other girl, who was crying and saying she was hurt. I hate to see kids hurt or sick." Pearlena says. She decided then, at age 7, that she would someday be a pediatrician. This is a challenging career goal for anyone, but especially for a child from a low-income family in Detroit's inner city.

When Pearlena was ready to attend high school, she chose Crockett Career and Technical Center. After reading about the school's med-lab assistant program, she enrolled in it during her senior year. Pearlena reasoned that the program was a way to earn money while going to school and to learn skills that would take her closer to her goal of being a pediatrician.

Pearlena took four classes in the mornings and worked in the afternoons at Detroit Receiving Hospital as a medical assistant. In the evenings, she spent long hours at the library studying to maintain her 3.0 GPA. She took the usual high school courses, plus courses on med-lab assistance. At work she would take the vital signs of patients, set up for surgeries, write up lab work and reports, and file lab and pathology reports.

"I knew I wanted to go into the medical field," she says. "This [the co-op program] gave me the experience of hospital and clinical work, and it gave me experience with people." While continuing to work as a medical assistant, Pearlena pursued her goal of being a pediatrician by entering Wayne State University in the fall of 2001. As an experienced medical assistant, she had a step up on other freshmen in her class.

When people around her say that medical school is too long or too hard and she will never make it, Pearlena thinks of her determination to help children. She also recalls how her mother has had to struggle. "I want to be able to take care of her," Pearlena says. She offers other students this advice: "Focus on your goal and don't let anything get in the way."

CHAPTER 12

CAREER DECISION MAKING

LESSONS

12.1 *The Decision-making Process*

12.2 *Individuals and Decision Making*

PREVIEW

You make many decisions every day. Some are more important than others. A simple five-step process can help you make better decisions. When you are making an important decision, be thorough and weigh all the information. Accept responsibility for what happens to you.

THOUGHTS ON WORK

"Hard work spotlights the character of people: some turn up their sleeves, some turn up their noses, and some don't turn up at all."

Sam Ewing

TAKING ACTION

MAKING DECISIONS

During the past year, Terrance has worked part-time at a local clothing store as part of a cooperative career and technical education program. Since the store is rather small, Terrance has had the opportunity to do different kinds of work there. As a result, he has learned many new skills.

Of course, Terrance sells merchandise. He is adept at operating the cash register and rarely makes an error. In addition, Terrance has become knowledgeable about the different kinds of clothes the store sells. When a customer asks for recommendations, he can always provide them. Terrance is also good at helping people make purchasing decisions. Quite a few customers prefer to deal with Terrance when they shop at the store.

Terrance prices merchandise as well as selling it. From time to time, he also helps with payroll records and tax reports. He has spent some time learning how to use the payroll software.

SUCCESS TIP

Take opportunities to learn new skills when they become available to you.

Terrance has even had the chance to prepare advertising. He has written copy for newspaper and radio ads as well as flyers. His window display for an Easter sales promotion brought many compliments from customers and coworkers. Terrance's most interesting experience to date was going with the store manager, Mrs. Enrico, on a buying trip to New York City.

Terrance has found that he likes his job very much. In fact, he would like to work in some area related to business after graduation.

On the way back from the buying trip, Mrs. Enrico offered Terrance a full-time job after graduation. "You are one of the best workers I've ever had," she told him. "You have a promising future with our store."

Terrance had not intended to stay at the store. He had planned to go away to college. He cannot decide whether to accept the offer of a full-time job or go to college.

THINK CRITICALLY

1. What do you think Terrance should do?
2. How should Terrance go about making his decision?

LESSON 12.1

THE DECISION-MAKING PROCESS

- LIST AND SUMMARIZE EACH STEP IN THE DECISION-MAKING PROCESS
- UNDERSTAND HOW TO USE THE DECISION-MAKING PROCESS IN MAKING AN OCCUPATIONAL CHOICE

A FIVE-STEP PROCESS

Decision making involves choosing between two or more **alternatives** or options. Some people make no effort to identify the choices available to them. But choosing not to decide is also a choice. Most everyday decisions, such as "What shall I wear today?" are made without much thought. But decisions like the one facing Terrance are not as easy to make. He needs to follow a systematic decision-making process that will help him organize important information and make the decision that is best for him.

A simple five-step decision-making process is shown in Figure 12-1 and explained in the following paragraphs. The same steps are followed whether you are making a decision about a career, choosing a college, or buying a used car. The more important the decision, the more time and effort should be devoted to it.

Defining the Problem

The term **problem** here refers to a question in need of a solution. The decision-making process begins when you become aware of a problem and see the need to make a decision. Perhaps the problem is broad and long-range, such as "What are my goals in life?" Maybe it is an intermediate-range problem, such as "For what occupation do I want to prepare?" A problem like "How can I earn some money to pay for Saturday's date?" is an immediate one.

Terrance has partially solved the long-range problem of setting goals in life by determining that he would like to work in some area related to business after graduation. He still must solve the more immediate problem of whether to continue working at the clothing store. After

CAREER DECISIONS

You are attending a two-year technical institute, majoring in automotive technology. After two semesters you decide to change your major to machine tool technology. The counselor says you can make the change, but you will have to take overload hours and attend an extra semester. You are anxious to finish school and begin work. You cannot decide whether the additional time and effort will be worthwhile.

WHAT WOULD YOU DO?

Step 1: Define the Problem.
Become aware of a problem and see the need to make a decision.

↓

Step 2: Gather Information.
Obtain information about the problem.

↓

Step 3: Evaluate the Information.
Organize the information into categories. Identify the pros and cons of each possible choice. Eliminate any unacceptable choices.

↓

Step 4: Make a Choice.
Select the alternative that leads to the most desirable result and has the highest possibility of success.

↓

Step 5: Take Action.
Put your choice into action and commit yourself to making the decision work.

Figure 12-1 ***Learning this five-step process can help you to plan your career better.***

making a choice, he may have to decide on future educational plans.

Gathering Information

Once the problem is known, gather the necessary information. You cannot make a good decision without it. How do you know how much information is enough? You don't. The amount of information you gather and the time you spend gathering it should be related to how important the decision is. In other words, the more important the decision, the more information is needed.

To help decide whether to continue working at the clothing store, Terrance made an appointment with Mrs. Enrico. He explained that he liked retail sales and his job at the clothing store. He also explained that he wanted to go to college. Mrs. Enrico was very understanding and encouraging. She told Terrance what he could expect over the next several years in terms of responsibilities and salary at the store. She also gave Terrance the choice of working at the store part-time.

Evaluating the Information

In this step, you organize the information you have gathered into categories. You then identify the pros and cons of each possible choice and eliminate any unacceptable choices. A rating scale or checklist may be of help as you do this.

After talking to Mrs. Enrico, Terrance wrote down the three choices he had:

1. Work full-time at the store and not go to college
2. Quit the job at the store and go away to college
3. Go to the nearby community college part-time and work at the store part-time

For each alternative, Terrance wrote down advantages and disadvantages. For instance, if he chose the first alternative, Terrance would have a full-time salary. He could probably buy the car he had been wanting. On the other hand, he might want to change jobs someday. In that case, a degree would be a strong advantage. He also reviewed the alternatives with his parents to see if they could add any information.

Making a Choice

At this point, you choose one of your alternatives. Making a choice is often difficult because rather than choosing between desirable and undesirable alternatives, you must choose from among several desirable alternatives. Look for

WORKFORCE TRENDS

The proportion of working mothers with children under six has risen faster than the proportion of all working women. Women are more likely to return to work after having children if they were firmly established in the workforce before childbirth. Mothers are also more likely to return if they have spousal support, provide a substantial proportion of household income, work part-time, have telecommuting options, can avoid overtime hours, and have supervisor and coworker support.

the alternative that leads to the most desirable result and has the highest possibility of success.

It was finally time for Terrance to choose. He decided on Choice 3—working part-time and going to college part-time. By working, he could pay for his education without having to borrow money. A community college would also be cheaper than a four-year school, since he could live at home. And who knows? Maybe he will want to transfer to a four-year college in two years.

Taking Action

At this point, you begin to carry out the alternative you chose in Step 4. Suppose that you have weighed alternatives and decided to seek a job in a distant city. The best thing to do before you leave home is to find a job in the new place. Or at least try to identify several promising job leads.

Taking action also involves committing yourself to making the decision work. If you are moving to a new city, for example, it might be a while before you find a job there. It would be easy to give up. Stick with your job search, but make sure your expectations are realistic.

Having made his choice, Terrance informed his parents and Mrs. Enrico. They all agreed with Terrance's decision and thought that he was wise to have made it. Terrance felt good about having put the decision behind him. Now it was time for him to start deciding what courses to take in school.

OCCUPATIONAL DECISION MAKING

Let's see how the decision-making process might be used in making an occupational choice. As each step is explained, refer occasionally to Figure 12-2. The first step is defining the problem. In this case, the question is, "Which occupation should I choose?"

In Step 2, you collect information. In choosing an occupation, you must gather information about your own (self) characteristics and about occupations. The three major types of self-information are interests (things you like to do), aptitudes (things you are good at), and work values (attitudes and beliefs about the importance

Step 1: Define the Problem.
Which occupation should I choose?

↓

Step 2: Gather Information.
- Identify interests and aptitudes.
- Develop a list of occupational alternatives based on self-information.
- Collect occupational information.

↓

Step 3: Evaluate the Information.
- Organize the information.
- Compare and evaluate occupational information.
- Evaluate your own feelings and attitudes.
- Eliminate unacceptable occupational alternatives.

↓

Step 4: Make a Choice.
Based on your work values and career goals, choose the occupation that seems best to you now.

↓

Step 5: Take Action.
Begin a job search or enroll in an appropriate education program that will prepare you for the occupation.

Figure 12-2 ***This is how the decision-making process is applied to making an occupational choice.***

of work activities). You will learn more about self-information in Chapter 13. You will use the information you have gathered about your interests and aptitudes to develop a preliminary list of occupational alternatives. You will then explore each occupation on the list. In Chapter 14, you will learn how to do an occupational search.

In the third step, you organize the information and identify the pros and cons of each possible choice. A form like the one shown in Figure 12-3 is helpful at this point. You consider the information carefully and eliminate those occupations that are unacceptable for one reason or another.

By the fourth step, you have only a few alternatives left. Each of the choices seems equally desirable. You may be happy with any one of the choices. What you try to do, though, is choose the one alternative that seems best at this time. There is no guarantee that your choice will

CHECKLIST FOR EVALUATING POSSIBLE OCCUPATIONAL ALTERNATIVES

Name of occupation______________________________

	Yes	No	Not Sure
1. The work involved in this occupation is the type of work I'd like to do.			
2. I believe I have the ability to do well in this occupation.			
3. This occupation involves doing work that is important to me.			
4. The typical working conditions for this occupation are acceptable to me.			
5. I'm willing to complete the necessary education or training requirements to qualify for this occupation.			
6. I have the educational background to be admitted to any required education or training program.			
7. The future employment outlook for this occupation is good.			
8. I would be satisfied with the amount of earnings that is typical for this occupation.			
9. There are other related occupations in which I could work after learning this occupation.			
10. I believe I have enough information about this occupation to make a decision.			

On a scale of 1 (low) to 10 (high), I'd give this occupation a final ranking of_____.

Figure 12-3 ***Using a checklist like this one can help you evaluate alternatives.***

work out. You must choose based upon your best judgment. Considering your work values may be helpful in this step.

Once you have made a decision, you are ready to put your choice into action. Starting a cooperative education program is an example of taking action. Perhaps you are not sure what type of educational program will meet your needs. If this is the case, you should start the decision-making process again. This time the problem is, "What type of educational program should I choose?"

During any of the five steps, you may wish to seek help from a counselor, teacher, parent, or other adult. Talking about goals and alternatives often helps people make decisions. The final decision, though, will be yours.

LESSON 12.1 REVIEW

1. **When is a systematic decision-making process best used?**
2. **Name and briefly explain each step in the decision-making process.**
3. **In choosing an occupation, you collect two types of information in Step 2. Name them.**

HIGH-GROWTH OCCUPATIONS FOR THE 21st CENTURY

Home Health and Personal Care Aides

Home health and personal care aides help elderly, disabled, and ill persons live in their own homes instead of a health facility. Most work with elderly or disabled clients who need more care than family or friends can provide. Some home health and personal care aides work with families in which a parent is incapacitated and small children need care. Others help discharged hospital patients who have relatively short-term needs.

In general, *home health aides* provide health-related services, such as administering oral medications under physicians' orders or the direction of a nurse. In contrast, *personal care aides* provide mainly housekeeping and routine personal care services.

Because of the assistance provided by home health aides, elderly people are able to stay in their own homes.

Most home health and personal care aides provide some housekeeping services, as well as personal care. They clean clients' houses, do laundry, and change bed linens. Some aides plan meals, shop for food, and cook. Home health and personal care aides may also help clients move from bed, bathe, dress, and groom. Some accompany clients outside the home, serving as guides, companions, and aides.

Home health and personal care aides also provide instruction and psychological support. Home health aides may check pulse, temperature, and respiration; help with simple exercises; and assist with medication routines. Occasionally, they change dressings, use special equipment such as a hydraulic lift, give massages and alcohol rubs, or assist with braces and artificial limbs.

In home care agencies, it is usually a registered nurse, physical therapist, or social worker that assigns duties and supervises home health and personal care aides. Aides keep records of services performed and of clients' condition and progress. They report changes in a client's condition to the supervisor or case manager. Home health and personal care aides also participate in case reviews, consulting with the team caring for the client.

LESSON 12.2
INDIVIDUALS AND DECISION MAKING

OBJECTIVES

- IDENTIFY AND DESCRIBE DIFFERENT DECISION-MAKING STYLES
- DISCUSS THE NEED TO ACCEPT RESPONSIBILITY FOR CAREER PLANNING
- EXPLAIN THREE FACTORS THAT CAN INFLUENCE DECISION MAKING

DECISION-MAKING STYLES

The decision-making process is a tool. How well you use this tool depends largely on your style of decision making and your willingness to accept responsibility and take action.

In watching a baseball game, you will notice that players have different batting styles. For example, one batter will move quickly into the batter's box, crowd the plate, and swing at the first ball that comes near the strike zone. Another batter will delay stepping into the box, stand deep in the box, step out of the batter's box if the pitcher is too slow, and not swing until the pitch is exactly right.

People also have different **decision-making styles**, or typical ways of making decisions. These styles are gained over a long period of time. Seven styles of decision making are most common.

- ***The agonizer.*** These people collect information and spend a lot of time evaluating it. In fact, they spend so much time doing this that they end up not knowing what to do! They get overwhelmed with all the data.
- ***The mystic.*** Have you heard someone say a decision was made because it "felt right"? Such a decision is based on **intuition**, a feeling or hunch. Some people make most of their choices this way.
- ***The fatalist.*** These people do not believe that they have much control over their choices. So, they do not spend much time gathering information.

CAREER DECISIONS

You plan to go to a business school next year. You have already applied and been accepted. Now, you are using a decision-making process to choose a program of study. You have collected information and given the problem a great deal of thought. The difficulty is that you like two programs (specializations) equally well.

WHAT WOULD YOU DO?

MATH CONNECTION

Suppose you are deciding between two jobs that will pay exactly the same. One factor you are considering is the cost of commuting. One job is at a company that is 15 miles away. The second is at a company that is 5 miles away. If gasoline is $1.75 a gallon, and your car gets 20 miles to a gallon, how much extra money per week would you have if you took the second job?

SOLUTION

(1) Multiply the number of miles you would drive by two to determine how far you would drive each day. (2) Multiply this number by the number of workdays per week. (3) Divide the product by the number of miles to a gallon your car gets. (4) Multiply the dividend by the cost per gallon of gas. (5) Subtract the cost of gas for the second job from the cost of gas for the first.

Weekly cost of gas (Job 1):		Weekly cost of gas (Job 2):	
	(1) $15 \times 2 = 30$		(1) $5 \times 2 = 10$
	(2) $30 \times 5 = 150$		(2) $10 \times 5 = 50$
	(3) $150/20 = 7.5$		(3) $50/20 = 2.5$
	(4) $7.5 \times \$1.75 = \$13.13$		(4) $2.5 \times \$1.75 = \$4.38$

Amount of extra money you would have if you took the second job $= \$13.13 - \$4.38$
$= \$8.75$

You would have $8.75 extra per week if you took the second job.

Leon is an education major. His parents insist that he live at home and attend the local university. They will pay his tuition and expenses if he does this. However, the school's education department is weak. State University, 200 miles away, has a strong department. Leon, an excellent student, would like to go there. But he is convinced he has no choice.

- ***The evader.*** John is a junior in high school. He has taken a general program of study because he has made no career decision. He hopes that if he delays long enough, the problem will go away. In its worst form, this style of decision making is known as "the ostrich style." Ostriches stick their heads in the sand. John is behaving like an ostrich. He hasn't made any career decision at all.
- ***The plunger.*** These people eagerly make decisions. In fact, they are usually too eager to do so. The plunger frequently chooses the first alternative that comes to mind.
- ***The submissive.*** "What do you want me to do?" Sound familiar? Such people always want someone else to make a decision for them. If no one will make the decision for them, submissives will make it themselves based on what they think someone else would want them to do.
- ***The planner.*** These people are likely to use a good decision-making strategy. They are thorough and weigh all the information. Such people seek to maintain a balance between facts and emotions. Is this your decision-making style?

Being a planner can have several benefits. For instance, it can increase your chances of being satisfied with your decision. By collecting information about a number of alternatives and carefully weighing the facts, you increase the chances of choosing what is best for you.

In addition, being a planner will provide you with more choices. A skilled decision maker usually develops many alternatives from which to choose. Having several alternatives gives you more freedom than if you had only one or two. Planning will help you gain greater control over your life.

YOU'RE A WHAT? FORENSIC SCIENTIST

Blood splatters, spent shell casings, and forged signatures are the nuts and bolts of forensic science. *Forensic scientists* study the evidence collected at a crime scene. Police detectives use the evidence in their investigation. And prosecuting attorneys use the evidence to present the case in court.

Whenever a crime is committed, police try to collect evidence that might provide clues to solving the case. The evidence, such as blood or fiber samples, is then turned over to forensic scientists for analysis. They use a variety of scientific methods and complex instruments to study and analyze the evidence. Forensic scientists prepare reports explaining their analysis and describe the methods used to support their conclusions. Finally, they may testify in court as expert witnesses on the evidence.

TAKING CHARGE OF YOUR LIFE

The benefits of successful decision making are achieved only if the process is used. And that depends on your willingness to accept responsibility for making decisions and for taking action to carry them out.

Part of becoming a mature person is accepting responsibility for what happens to you. This does not mean that luck, natural ability, family advantages, or discrimination do not play a part. It is clear that they do. For instance, George W. Bush's being elected President of the United States was certainly helped by the wealth and name he inherited from his family. The success of Ted Williams at baseball was influenced by his nearly perfect eyesight.

On the other hand, it is possible to identify many examples of famous or successful people who did not have such advantages or who had only average ability. Success and happiness depend largely on the choices you make.

Too many people blame someone or something for what happens to them. For example, in conversations about grades, students often say things like, "Mr. Anderson gave me a D in English." In truth, teachers do not give grades at all. Teachers simply assign grades to students' work. If you receive an A, you earned it. The same is true if you receive a D.

OTHER INFLUENCES ON DECISION MAKING

We have discussed how information, decision-making style, and willingness to accept responsibility all influence decision making. Now, let's discuss three more factors related to decision making. These are previous decisions, environment and experiences, and real-world restrictions.

A major feature of the Web is hypertext capability. Hypertext enables a user to jump from one page to another on the Web without keying the URL. For example, in a web site concerning the federal government, the word "Congress" might be highlighted. Clicking on this word would bring information about Congress to the screen. Hyperlink text is sometimes underscored or in a different color. Photos, buttons, and other images can also be used as hyperlinks. Such images typically have a colored border to provide the reader with a visual clue. The cursor usually changes to a hand when it passes over a hypertext link.

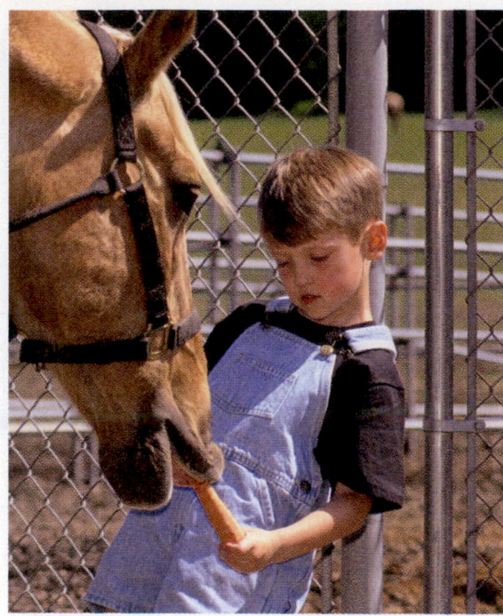

How might this boy's later career choices be influenced by his early association with animals?

Previous Decisions

One decision may influence later ones. To illustrate, let's consider Dee Dee, a tenth-grade student who is deciding what courses to take next year. She picks a health occupations course. By making this decision, Dee Dee will begin to move toward a health career and away from other fields such as business and food service. Her decision isn't final, though. Dee Dee may change direction later—even as an adult. Important choices that influence later career decisions include selecting school courses and college majors, gaining work experience, marrying, and joining the military.

Environment and Experiences

Your **environment** is your surroundings. It includes your family, neighborhood, friends, school, church, and the like. Your **experiences** are what you do and what happens to you in your environment. Environmental and experience factors may strongly influence your choices.

Luis, for example, decided to become a veterinary assistant. His decision was heavily influenced by three environmental and experience factors. He grew up on a farm where he developed a love for animals. He worked part-time at his uncle's animal hospital and enjoyed that experience. And he lived near a college that offers the only veterinary assistant's program in the state.

Real-world Restrictions

There are a number of **reality factors** over which we have little control that often influence decisions. These can be persons, events, or situations. Sam would like to be a musician, but the reality is that he would have trouble supporting himself. So he chooses another occupation and plays for parties on weekends. Someday he may be able to work as a musician full-time.

Often what appear to be real-world restrictions are not. For instance, Sarah didn't think she would have enough money to attend a certain school. She was happy when the school gave her the scholarship she applied for. That, and a student loan, will help get her through the program.

Other reality factors include age, experience, qualifications, abilities, physical characteristics, and so on. In making career decisions, everyone faces real-world restrictions. When you face such a situation, either try harder or choose another alternative.

LESSON 12.2 REVIEW

1. Match these characteristics with decision-making styles: (a) delaying a career decision, (b) overwhelmed with all the data, (c) choosing the first alternative that comes to mind.
2. Which is the best decision-making style to use?
3. Being a planner can have several benefits. Name three.
4. Explain what is meant by "accepting responsibility for what happens to you."
5. Give an example of how previous decisions may influence later ones.
6. Name three reality factors that can limit career decisions.

FOCUS ON THE WORKER

ENVY IN THE WORKPLACE

This chapter has stressed that success and happiness depend on your own efforts. This does not mean, however, that other people cannot help or hinder you. In her book, *The Snow White Syndrome*, Betsy Cohen points out that envy is often a by-product of success. Envy is dissatisfaction or dislike at the success or good fortune of another. In the fairy tale, Snow White's beauty led the Wicked Queen to try to kill her.

Unfortunately, envy exists in the workplace. The more successful you are, the more envy you are likely to arouse. In the workplace, an envious person can hurt you. This is because your success often depends on others' cooperation. If someone is envious, he or she can make you look bad. Here are some ways that envy is expressed:

- "Forgetting" instructions or deadlines
- Gossiping or lying behind your back
- Being continually late, stubborn, or resistant
- Clever put-downs
- Excessive compliments and flattery
- Outright destruction of your work

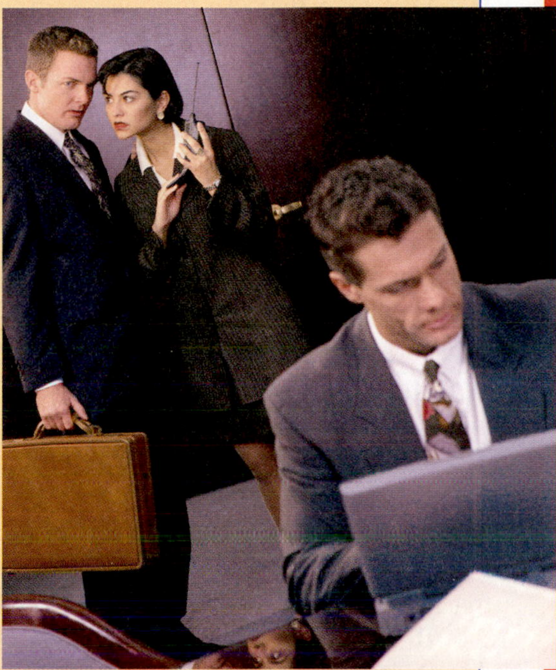

Successful people must be prepared to face the envy of others.

Envious people act to control you. They want to bring you back to their level. To avoid being a victim of envy, learn to recognize it. Try to develop a tolerance for it. Do not make it worse by flaunting your strengths. Be considerate toward coworkers. Build on other people's achievements. Remember that envy reflects what other people may see, not the real you.

If you are ambitious and aspire to be successful, be prepared to face envy. It exists in many workplaces. If you achieve success, someone is probably going to be envious.

THINK CRITICALLY

1. Think of a time when you or someone you know was envious of another person. How did you or the person you know act toward this person?
2. Look at the list of ways that envy is expressed. List strategies for dealing with three of them.

CHAPTER 12

Chapter in Brief

Lesson 12.1 *The Decision-making Process*

A. Decision making involves choosing between two or more alternatives. The more important the decision, the more time and effort should be devoted to it. Decision making involves the following five steps: (1) defining the problem, (2) gathering information, (3) evaluating the information, (4) making a choice, and (5) taking action.

B. In an occupational decision, Step 2 involves collecting information about personal characteristics and occupational alternatives. During any of the five steps, you may wish to seek help from a counselor, teacher, parent, or other adult.

Lesson 12.2 *Individuals and Decision Making*

A. How well you use the decision-making process depends on your style of decision making and your willingness to accept responsibility and take action. Seven styles of decision making are most common: the agonizer, the mystic, the fatalist, the evader, the plunger, the submissive, and the planner. The planner is the preferred style.

B. Being a planner can have several benefits. It can increase your chances of being satisfied with your decision. It can provide you with more choices. It will help you gain greater control over your life.

C. A very important part of growing up is accepting responsibility for what happens to you. Your success and happiness will depend largely on the choices you make. Too many people blame someone or something for what happens to them.

D. Three other factors also influence decision making. These are previous decisions, environment and experiences, and real-world restrictions.

Activities

1. You have probably used a problem-solving method in one of your science or math classes. Compare the problem-solving method with the decision-making process. How are they similar and different? Discuss your answers in class.
2. Find out which decision-making style is most common in your class. Be honest and write on a piece of scrap paper which of the seven styles you use (no names on papers). Summarize results on the board and discuss the outcome in class.
3. Groups as well as individuals can use the decision-making process. As a class, apply the decision-making method to a real or hypothetical situation. For example, what type of computer would be best for use in the class?

REVIEW

4. Suppose you are considering job offers from two companies. The pay is the same; however, one company is 10 miles from your home and the other is 20 miles. If gasoline is $1.60 a gallon, and your car gets 25 miles to a gallon, how much more money would you have each week if you took the first job?

Word Power

On a separate sheet of paper, match each definition with the correct term. All definitions will be used, and a definition will be used only once.

5. A question in need of a solution or an answer
6. What you do and what happens to you in your environment
7. Persons, events, or situations over which we have little control that often influence decisions, such as the high cost of going to an Ivy League college
8. A feeling or hunch
9. One's surroundings, including neighborhood, family, friends, and the like
10. The process of choosing between two or more alternatives or options
11. Typical ways in which people make decisions
12. Options to choose from in making a decision

a. alternatives
b. decision making
c. decision-making styles
d. environment
e. experiences
f. intuition
g. problem
h. reality factors

Think Critically

13. Identify and discuss a variety of situations in which a systematic decision-making process should be used.
14. How is an occupational decision different from a job decision? You may want to review Figure 1-1 on page 6 before answering.
15. Decisions are influenced by previous decisions made and not made. Identify and discuss some of the important decisions you have made and not made. How did they turn out? Might the outcome have been different had you used a systematic decision-making process?
16. Do you believe that you have the power to influence the direction of your life and career?
17. We tend to think of reality factors as negative things, such as not having enough money or lacking qualifications. Can you think of positive reality factors that also limit or restrict choices?

CHAPTER 13

INFORMATION ABOUT YOUR SELF

LESSONS

PREVIEW

If you are in your teens, you can look forward to 40 or more years of working. That is a long time—especially if you work at an occupation that you dislike. Wouldn't you rather have an occupation that you enjoy doing, that you are good at, and that involves work that is important to you?

This chapter will show you how to gather information about your self that can help you make a satisfying occupational decision.

THOUGHTS ON WORK

"Success in business requires training and discipline and hard work. But if you're not frightened by these things, the opportunities are just as great today as they ever were."

David Rockefeller

TAKING ACTION
CHOOSING AN OCCUPATION

Like everybody else in her class, Carrie is trying to decide what she should do after high school. She is getting plenty of advice.

"You're a talented athlete," Mr. Keenan, her track coach, tells her. "I think you should consider a career as a physical education instructor."

"You have good business skills, and you like working on your own," says Sensei Wolfe, Carrie's karate instructor. "Why don't you try going into business for yourself?"

"My advice is to choose an occupation that will always be needed," says her Uncle Joe. "Be a nurse, Carrie. You will never have a hard time finding a job as a nurse."

Carrie has always assumed that she would go to college, and her grades are certainly good enough. She has followed her guidance counselor's advice about taking a variety of courses. This term, Carrie is getting a great deal of pleasure out of the volunteer projects she does for her Community Service class.

Carrie has also followed her counselor's advice about participating in extracurricular activities. In addition to track and karate, she has worked in the backstage crew for many school plays. Carrie volunteers at the zoo and can be counted on to help in any school fundraising project.

For the past two years, Carrie has worked part-time at her karate school. She team-teaches beginning and intermediate youth classes and works in the school store.

"What I don't know," says Carrie to her friend Emerson, "is how to put all this together. There are different things I like to do, and there are different things I'm good at. I think my Uncle Joe is right that it's important to choose a stable occupation. What kind of occupation can I find that will let me do what I like? And what if I make the wrong choice?"

SUCCESS TIP

Before choosing an occupation, look at what you like, what you are good at, and what is important to you.

THINK CRITICALLY

1. What advice can you give Carrie on how to begin choosing an occupation?
2. Think of adults you know who are in the workforce. Do their jobs seem to be a good match for their interests and aptitudes?

LESSON 13.1

GETTING SELF-INFORMATION

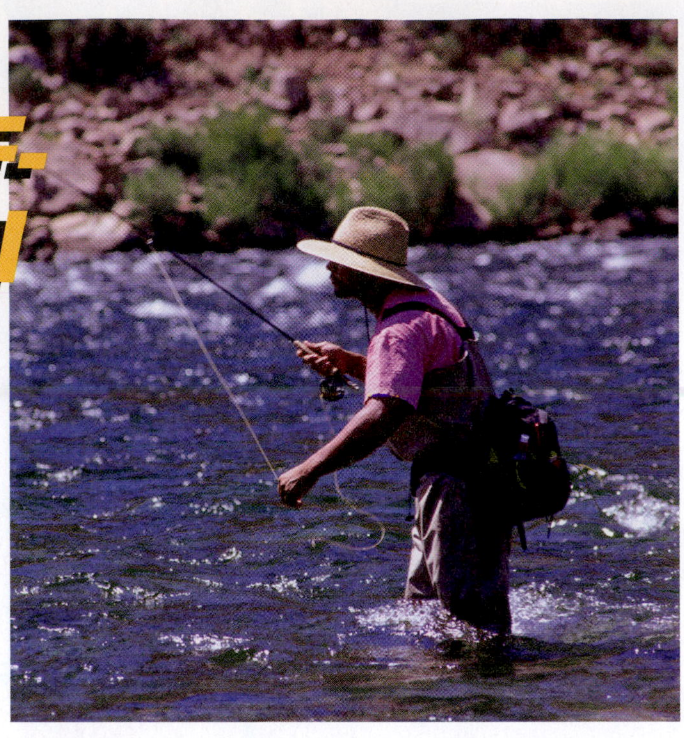

OBJECTIVES

- *DISCUSS HOW SELF-INFORMATION CAN HELP YOU MAKE MORE SATISFYING OCCUPATIONAL DECISIONS*
- *DESCRIBE THE THREE TYPES OF SELF-INFORMATION AND HOW THEY ARE MEASURED*

LEARNING ABOUT YOUR SELF

Before you select an occupation, you should first answer the question, "Who am I?" This means that you should learn more about your **self**. Your self includes your physical characteristics, your behavior, how you think, and many other things. Self is the sum of everything you are. Knowledge about your self is called **self-information**. This information can help you make a more satisfying occupational decision.

In this chapter, you will learn about three types of self-information. By learning more about what you like to do (**interests**), what you are good at doing (**aptitudes**), and what is important to you about the work you do (**work values**), you will make better choices about what you want to be.

TYPES OF SELF-INFORMATION

When making an occupational decision, you should have information about your interests, aptitudes, and work values.

Interests

We all make choices based on likes and dislikes. We choose different types of food, music, clothes, hobbies, and so on because we enjoy one thing more than another. For instance, if you enjoy Chinese food, you may choose to go to Chinese restaurants when eating out. If you dislike Greek food, you probably won't go to many Greek restaurants. William, for instance, enjoys hunting, fishing, camping, and hiking. His interests relate to outdoor activities.

Your interests can lead to occupations that might suit you. William's outdoors interests

WORKFORCE TRENDS

The proportion of single-parent families has more than doubled over the last 30 years, up from 11 percent in 1970 to 27 percent of family households with children today. Single parents who work not only face the challenge of raising children without the assistance of another parent in the home, but usually must do so with much less income than a two-parent family.

suggest that he might do well in occupations such as forester, game warden, or recreation worker.

Debbie likes working with her personal computer. She enjoys creating computer graphics and designing web pages. Debbie is also experimenting with a program that will play music on the computer. For what kinds of occupations do you think Debbie might be suited?

By thinking about your likes and dislikes, you are taking the first step toward learning about your self. Do you prefer indoor or outdoor activities? Would you rather work alone or with people? Do you like to work with tools and machines or data and figures? Do you enjoy music or art?

School courses and activities can offer clues to occupations that might be of interest. What school subjects do you like best? Think about school activities, such as clubs, plays, concerts, and fundraising events. Don't forget about hobbies. What do activities and hobbies reveal about your interests?

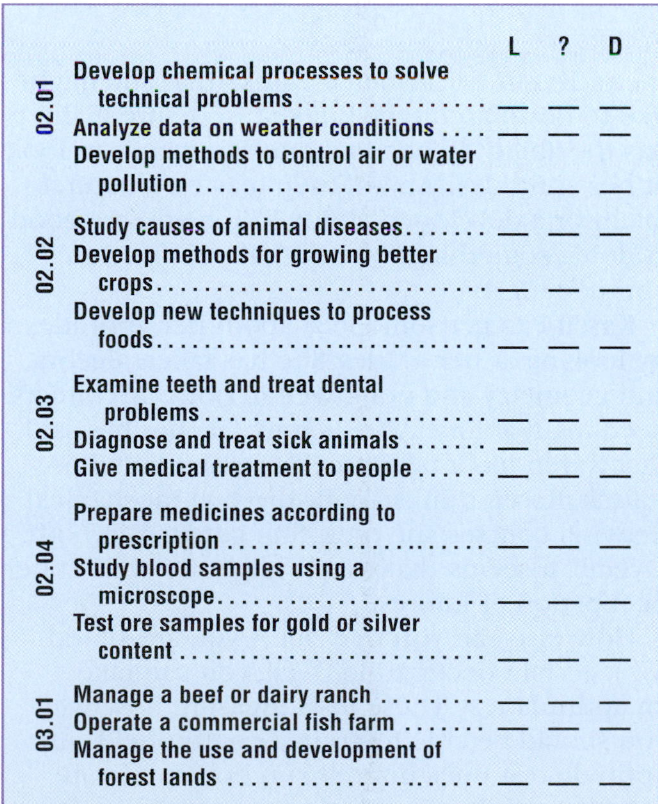

		L	?	D
02.01	Develop chemical processes to solve technical problems	___	___	___
	Analyze data on weather conditions	___	___	___
	Develop methods to control air or water pollution	___	___	___
02.02	Study causes of animal diseases	___	___	___
	Develop methods for growing better crops	___	___	___
	Develop new techniques to process foods	___	___	___
02.03	Examine teeth and treat dental problems	___	___	___
	Diagnose and treat sick animals	___	___	___
	Give medical treatment to people	___	___	___
02.04	Prepare medicines according to prescription	___	___	___
	Study blood samples using a microscope	___	___	___
	Test ore samples for gold or silver content	___	___	___
03.01	Manage a beef or dairy ranch	___	___	___
	Operate a commercial fish farm	___	___	___
	Manage the use and development of forest lands	___	___	___

Figure 13-1 ***Here are sample items from the Interest Checklist.***

Source: U.S. Employment Service

Your interests may include hiking or other outdoor activities.

Vera, for example, belongs to the Journalism Club and works on the yearbook and school newspaper. English has always been her favorite subject. All Vera's interests point in the direction of a career in the communications field.

In addition to thinking about your interests, you might want to complete an occupational interest inventory. Figure 13-1 shows several statements taken from the *Interest Checklist* of the U.S. Employment Service. As you can see, this inventory contains a list of work activities. For each activity, you indicate whether you like it, dislike it, or don't know. Most interest inventories use a similar approach.

An interest inventory is not a test. There are no right or wrong answers. However, responses to the items need to be carefully interpreted. Assistance from a teacher or counselor is usually required.

Chances are that your answers will form a pattern. Let's see how the *Interest Checklist* can help you identify occupational interests. Go back to Figure 13-1. You will see that the statements of work activities are listed in groups of three. To the left of each group is a four-digit number. This number corresponds to one of 66 work groups found in a government publication called the *Guide for Occupational Exploration (GOE)*. Copies are in many school libraries.

Let's say that you marked L ("like") for the three work activities in Work Group 02.04. Work

COMMUNICATION AT WORK

SELF-TALK

From high school basketball players to Olympic gymnasts, many athletes are taught to use positive self-talk to help themselves succeed. *I can make this free throw. I can see myself doing every step of my routine perfectly.* Self-talk is the running commentary that we keep up all the time inside our heads. It is how we explain to ourselves what happens around us and what we do.

Suppose you fail an important math test. Do you say to yourself, "I'm no good at math. What difference does it make, anyway?" Or do you say, "I know I can do this. I should have studied longer Saturday. I'll go talk to the math teacher and find out what I can do to bring up my grade."

Research has shown that positive self-talk can do more than help people win at sports. It can help them ward off illness, reduce stress, and cope with medical problems. Positive self-talk can help you manage yourself at work. It can also help you become what you want to be.

Ralph was a camera operator for a public television station. After a while, he decided that he wanted to become an airline pilot. Ralph was not sure that he could do this. When he encountered something difficult in his training, Ralph would talk himself through it beforehand in his head. He would also visualize himself having done it successfully. These techniques helped give Ralph confidence that he could achieve his goals.

Group 02.04 is called "Laboratory Technology." This means that you have shown an interest in work activities relating to laboratory technology.

Once you identify your interests, you can relate them to occupations by using one of several common occupational resources. The *Interest Checklist*, for instance, is keyed to the *GOE*. The *GOE* explains each work group and lists occupations in that group. Occupations in the laboratory technology group include, for example, medical technologist, food tester, seed analyst, and film laboratory technician.

The results of an interest inventory do not mean that the occupations that are suggested are the only ones for you. They simply represent alternatives that you should investigate. Learn more about these occupations and others as well. And learn more about your self. Don't base your occupational choice solely on the results of an interest inventory.

Aptitudes

Are there occupations in which you are interested, but you wonder if you would do well in them? Karen, for instance, thinks that she might like to be an architect. But she isn't sure if she has the ability to become one. She needs to look at her aptitudes. An aptitude may be a natural talent or a developed ability. When you are good at doing something, we say that you have an aptitude for it.

Karen can get some idea about her aptitudes by looking at her grades. She has taken algebra and geometry and done well in both. Architects need math ability. Also, her art teacher has said that Karen has a talent for designing and illustrating. Karen thinks about the two mechanical drawing courses she took. She got an A in both. Overall, it seems that Karen might do well in her occupation of interest.

How else can you find out if you are suited for a certain occupation? Well, you can take an aptitude test. These tests measure how well you should be able to do in a certain field. An aptitude test does not tell you how well you actually will do or are doing. Scores on an aptitude test give you an idea of how well you might do. The six most common aptitudes covered by such tests are as follows:

- Verbal aptitude—using words well
- Numerical aptitude—doing math quickly and accurately
- Clerical speed and accuracy—picking out letters or words quickly and arranging number and letter combinations in order
- Manual dexterity—moving the hands easily and skillfully
- Mechanical reasoning—understanding mechanical principles, how things work, and how tools are used
- Spatial visualization—forming mental pictures of the shape, size, and position of objects

The types of questions included in an aptitude test vary widely depending on the aptitude being measured. Several different examples are shown in Figure 13-2. Each question has only one correct answer.

A separate score is given for each aptitude that is being tested. The scores are often reported as percentile ranks. For example, Joe received a percentile rank of 85 on mechanical reasoning. This means that Joe scored better than 85 percent of the people who took the test.

Your teacher or counselor will help you interpret your aptitude test results. After you speak with him or her, the rest will be up to you.

Work Values

Values are attitudes and beliefs about things we think are important in life. For instance, Americans believe strongly in the right of free speech. This is a basic democratic value that we think is important.

Values that relate to work and career are called work values. These are feelings about the importance or worth of an activity or occupation. Suppose you would like to have an occupation in which you could help other people. Helping others would be a work value for you. You would want this value to be part of or expressed by the work you do.

Work values can also be thought of as needs that we try to meet in our work. For example, Fred gave up a good job with a large insurance company to start his own business. He did so because he wanted to make his own decisions. For Fred, the need for independence was not being met in his former job.

What are some work values? The following are several examples:

- Altruism—helping other people
- Creativity—inventing things, designing products, or developing new ideas
- Achievement—having feelings of accomplishment from doing a job well

1. Which two words have the same meaning?
   (a) open (b) happy (c) glad (d) green
2. Which two words have the opposite meaning?
   (a) old (b) dry (c) cold (d) young
3. Add (+) the two numbers below and then select the correct answer (a, b, c, or d).
   766 / 11
   (a) 677 (b) 755 (c) 777 (d) 6561
4. Julie works 8 hours a day, 40 hours a week. She earns $8.40 an hour. How much does she earn each week?
   (a) $240.00 (b) $267.60 (c) $303.60 (d) $336.00
5. At the left is a drawing of a flat piece of metal. Which object at the right can be made from this piece of metal?

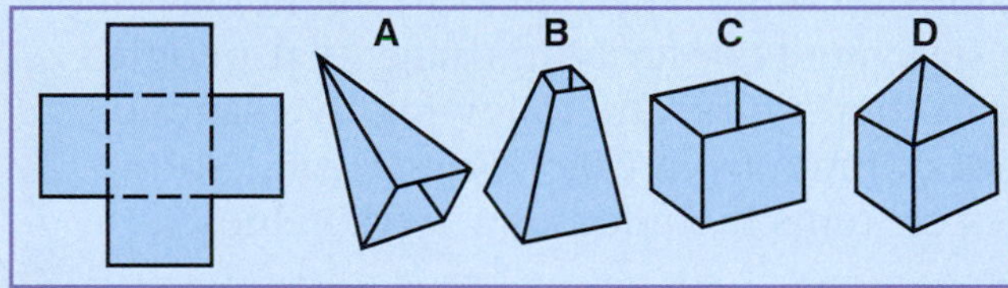

Which pairs of names are the same (S) and which are different (D)?

6. W. W. Jason . . . W. W. Jason
7. Johnson & Johnson . . . Johnson & Johnsen
8. Harold Jones Co. . . . Harold Jones and Co.

For questions 9 through 12, find the lettered figure that is exactly like the numbered figure.

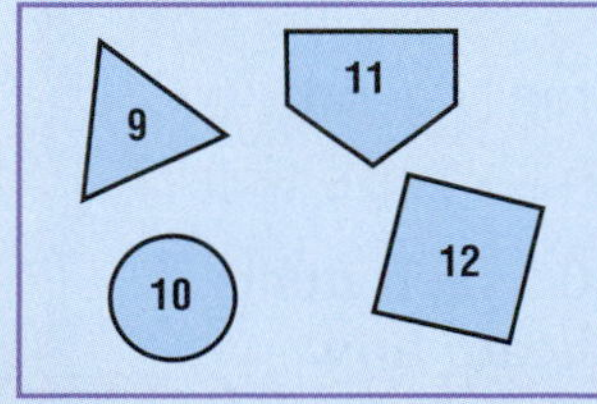

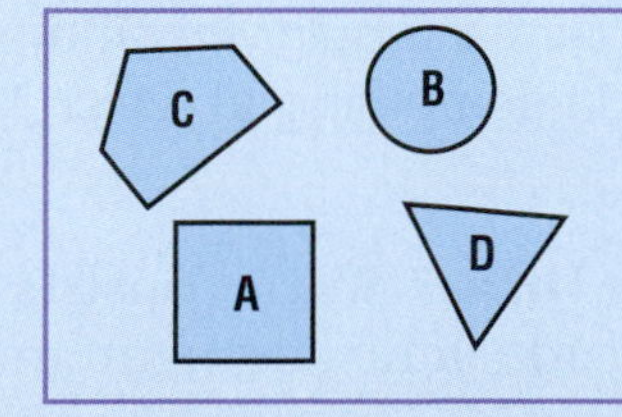

Figure 13-2 ***Here are sample aptitude test questions.***

Source: "Doing Your Best on Aptitude Tests," GPO

GAFFER

There are dozens of behind-the-scenes occupations involved in the production of films, videos, and TV programs. One important occupation is the *gaffer*, who is the set's chief lighting technician. The gaffer supervises a crew of *juicers* (electricians) and *grips* (equipment handlers) in setting up the lights and hooking them to a power source.

Gaffers lay out the lighting plan, figure out which lighting units will work best, and coordinate getting the lights where they're needed. Color temperature meters are then used to balance and fine-tune the lighting. Often, the gaffer uses colored, filtered, or indirect lighting to create some type of special effect, such as a romantic restaurant scene.

- Independence—being able to work in your own way
- Prestige—wanting to be looked up to
- Financial success—earning enough to buy the things you want
- Security—having a steady job even in hard times
- Surroundings—being in a pleasant work environment
- Variety—having the opportunity to do many types of tasks

You can identify your work values by taking a work values measure. Such measures generally include statements describing things that people look for in their work. The following five sample statements, drawn from *The Values Scale*,[1] show the types of items included in a work values measure.

It is now or will in the future be important for me to:

5. help people with problems.
8. discover, develop, or design new things.
23. know that my efforts will show.
42. have a regular income.
65. do something at which I am really good.

The Values Scale consists of 106 such items. You read each statement and indicate how important it is according to a four-point rating scale: (1) little or no importance, (2) some importance, (3) important, or (4) very important. Interpretation of this measure is very simple. For instance, Questions 23 and 65 in the example relate to the "Achievement" work value. Let's say that you assigned a rating of 4 to Questions 23 and 65. This means that work that gives you a feeling of achievement is very important. Most occupations, of course, involve several kinds of work values.

Unlike interest inventories and aptitude tests, the results of a work values measure are not as easily related to specific occupations. This is

[1]Super, Donald E. and Nevill, Dorothy D. *The Values Scale*. Palo Alto, CA: Consulting Psychologists Press, 1985.

CAREER DECISIONS

In going over the results of a work values measure with the counselor, you learn that your highest-rated values are financial success, independence, and prestige. It is true. You would like to be wealthy and independent and have people look up to you.

"Big deal," you think. "Now all I have to do is go out and find someone who will give me an important job and pay me a lot of money. That is a joke. Work values measures are a waste of time. I will probably end up working in the mines like the rest of my family."

WHAT WOULD YOU DO?

Floral designers are likely to have creativity as a work value.

because work values come from feelings that are more personal. As a result, work values scores are not as useful in helping to identify which occupations to explore.

A work values measure is better used in Step 4 of the decision-making process than in Step 2 (refer back to Figure 12-2 on page 160). You will recall that Step 4 is the one in which you make a choice from among a small number of desirable occupational alternatives. Knowledge of work values can help you make final career choices that will lead to your future goals.

Earl took a work values measure. The results suggested that altruism, security, and surroundings are important to him. These results tend to confirm his interest in becoming a technology education teacher. Norma found out that creativity and variety are the most important values for her. She is leaning toward becoming a floral designer or interior designer.

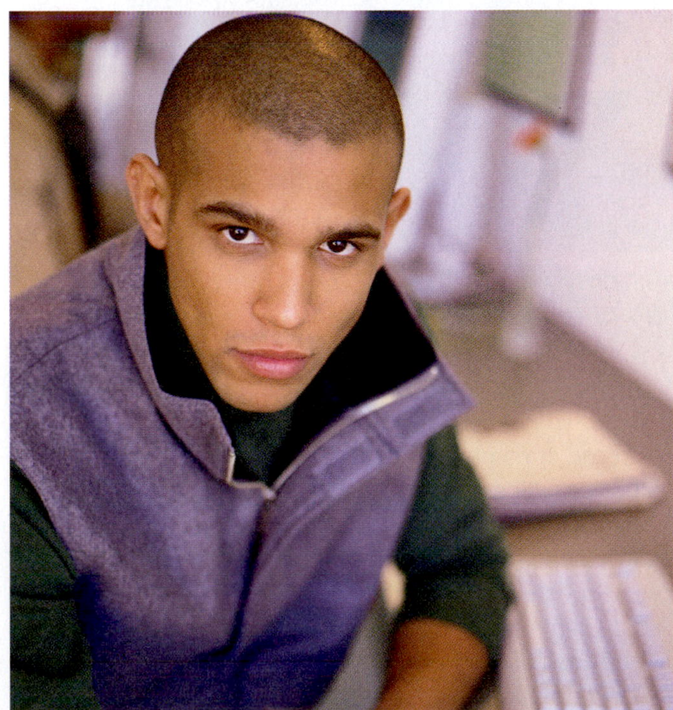

An interest in computers may lead to a satisfying occupation.

LESSON 13.1 REVIEW

1. What question should you ask yourself before choosing an occupation?
2. There are three types of self-information used in career decision making. Name them.
3. What can participation in school activities reveal about your self?
4. Why is it incorrect to call an interest inventory a test?
5. Without taking an aptitude test, how can you find out about your aptitudes?
6. If you are good at diagnosing and repairing auto engines, what two aptitudes do you have?
7. Name three suitable occupations for a person who values independence.
8. At what point in the career decision-making process is knowledge of work values important? Explain.

HIGH-GROWTH OCCUPATIONS FOR THE 21st CENTURY

Human Service Workers and Assistants

Human service workers and assistants is a generic term for people with various titles, including *social service assistant, case management aide, social work assistant, community support worker, alcohol* or *drug abuse counselor, mental health aide, community outreach worker, life skill counselor,* and *gerontology aide.*

Human service workers and assistants provide direct and indirect client services. They assess clients' needs, establish their eligibility for benefits and services, and help clients obtain them. They also provide emotional support. These workers monitor and keep case records on clients and report progress to supervisors and case managers.

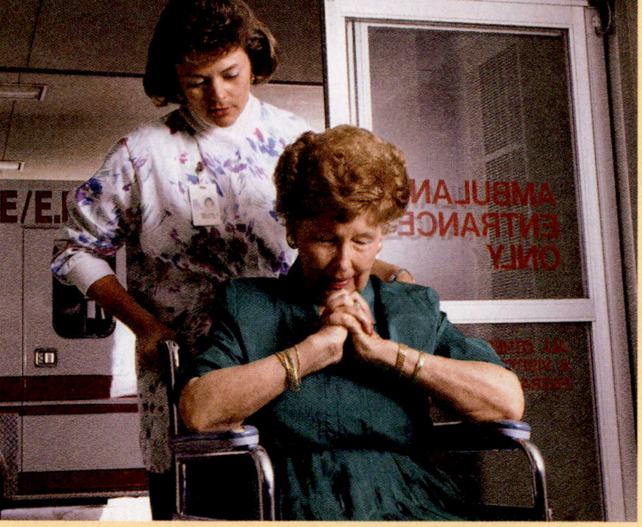

Transportation of clients is only one of the many services provided by human service workers and assistants.

In addition, human service workers and assistants arrange for transportation or transport clients themselves. They may accompany clients to group meal sites, adult day-care centers, or doctors' offices. These workers may telephone or visit clients' homes to make sure services are being received or to help resolve disagreements. They also may help clients complete insurance or medical forms, as well as applications for financial assistance.

Human service workers and assistants play a variety of roles in a community. They may organize and lead group activities, assist clients in need of counseling, or administer a food bank or emergency fuel program. In halfway houses, group homes, and government-supported housing programs, they assist adults who need supervision with personal hygiene and daily living skills. They review clients' records, monitor medication, talk with family members, and confer with caregivers to gain insight into clients' backgrounds and needs. These workers also help clients become involved in community recreation programs and in other activities.

In psychiatric hospitals, rehabilitation programs, and outpatient clinics, human service workers and assistants work with professional care providers to help clients master everyday living skills. They also teach clients to communicate more effectively and to get along better with others.

LESSON 13.2
WORKING WITH SELF-INFORMATION

OBJECTIVES

- *EXPLAIN HOW INTERESTS, APTITUDES, AND WORK VALUES MAY BE SIMILAR OR DIFFERENT*
- *ILLUSTRATE HOW INTERESTS, APTITUDES, AND WORK VALUES MAY BE EXPRESSED OUTSIDE OF ONE'S JOB*

RELATIONSHIPS AMONG FACTORS

Interests, aptitudes, and work values relate to each other. Sometimes they agree and sometimes they conflict. For some people, interests, aptitudes, and work values may all point to the same choice.

Robert, for example, wants to be a fashion designer. He has been interested in fashion design ever since he was a child. He has the aptitude, having already won several ribbons and awards in design competitions. Fashion design is usually done in pleasant surroundings, which is important for Robert.

For other people, though, interests, aptitudes, and work values may seem to point in different directions. This is not unusual. Nor is it something to worry about.

Jean, for example, has a high aptitude for mechanical reasoning and manual dexterity. But mechanical principles and using tools and machines don't interest her. She really wants to do some type of work that is mentally challenging and involves working with people.

Suppose your self-information conflicts. Choose based on the interest, aptitude, or work value that means the most to you. Then, try out your choice and see how it works. If you are not satisfied, look for something else. Your first occupational choice does not have to be a permanent one. You can learn from your decisions.

CAREER DECISIONS

You have always been interested in electronic gadgets. You enjoy taking things apart to find out how they work. The two electronics courses you took were your favorite courses.

This year, you are working as a co-op student at Apollo TV and Electronics. Most of your time is spent as a "go-fer" helping to install home entertainment centers and satellite dishes. Occasionally, you get to do a minor repair job like cleaning the heads on a VCR or soldering a loose connection on a stereo receiver. The job is nothing like you thought it would be. You are beginning to wonder if you made the wrong occupational decision.

WHAT WOULD YOU DO?

Each decision you make will provide you with information that will help you make better decisions in the future.

SELF AND OTHER LIFE ROLES

An occupation can be a very important part of your life. However, it is only one part of a total **lifestyle**, or way in which a person lives. People have other **life roles**, or parts of their lives, in addition to being workers. Some examples of life roles are citizen, spouse, parent, and student.

Many people lead happy and productive lives even though their jobs do not satisfy all of their interests, aptitudes, and work values. People pursue hobbies, sports, and leisure activities. Many people also participate in clubs, church, and the like. Let's take a look at some examples.

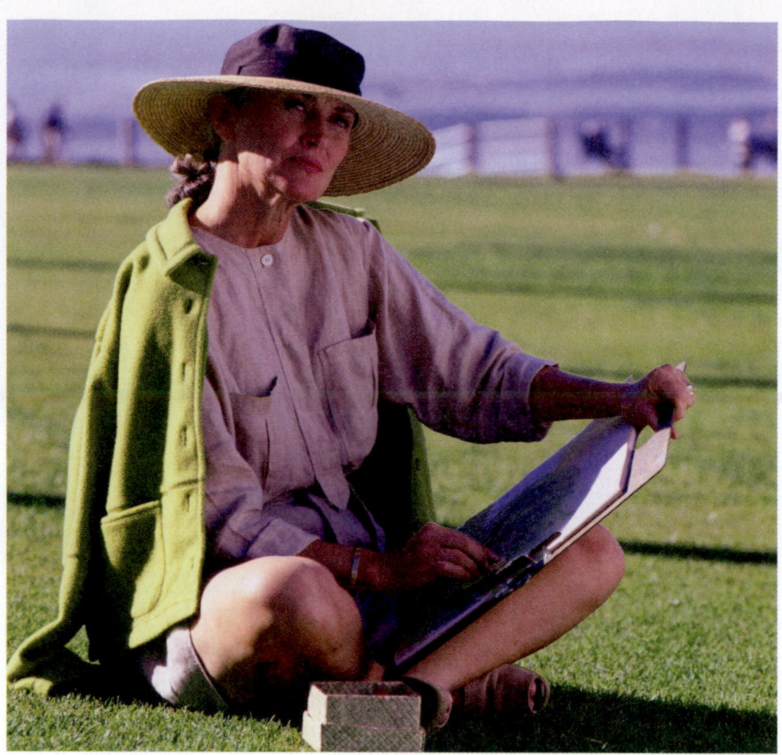

A hobby can provide an outlet for expressing your self.

Michelle is a human resources officer of a large company and really enjoys her work. She also is a very talented artist. Michelle manages to set aside about ten hours each week to work on her painting. By continuing to paint, Michelle can satisfy her strong need for creative expression.

Gregorio works as a heavy equipment operator. His work is okay, but his first love is old cars. He has a 1964 Ford Mustang that he has been restoring for about six years. He found the car rusting away in a junkyard. For Gregorio, working on his Mustang is a satisfying hobby and a major source of enjoyment.

Rosalyn is pharmaceutical sales representative and a former college softball player. She is successful in her work, but she misses being involved in softball. To satisfy her interests, Rosalyn coaches a little league softball team. She is a good coach and teacher of softball. Her young players respect her for taking the time to help them. They are not aware, however, that Rosalyn gets more enjoyment out of it than they do.

Andy is an operating room technician. He helps during surgery. His job involves a great deal of stress and anxiety. Andy sometimes wishes that the job was less demanding. To help deal with the stress, he sings in his church choir. Singing allows Andy to satisfy interests and abilities that he doesn't use on his job.

All of these people have found ways to express themselves outside of their jobs. You may be fortunate enough to work at an occupation that uses all your interests, aptitudes, and work values. If not, many outside activities can provide you with outlets for expressing your self.

LESSON 13.2 REVIEW

1. **What should you do if your interests, aptitudes, and work values point in different directions?**
2. **Why do people often pursue hobbies and other activities very different from what they do in their jobs?**

FOCUS ON THE WORKER

MID-CAREER CHANGE

Information about your self can help you make more satisfying occupational decisions. For young people, interests and aptitudes tend to be the more meaningful types of self-information. For adults, however, work values are usually the most important factor. It is estimated that millions of U.S. workers age 25 and over voluntarily change occupations every year. A primary reason is to pursue work values not being met in their current occupations.

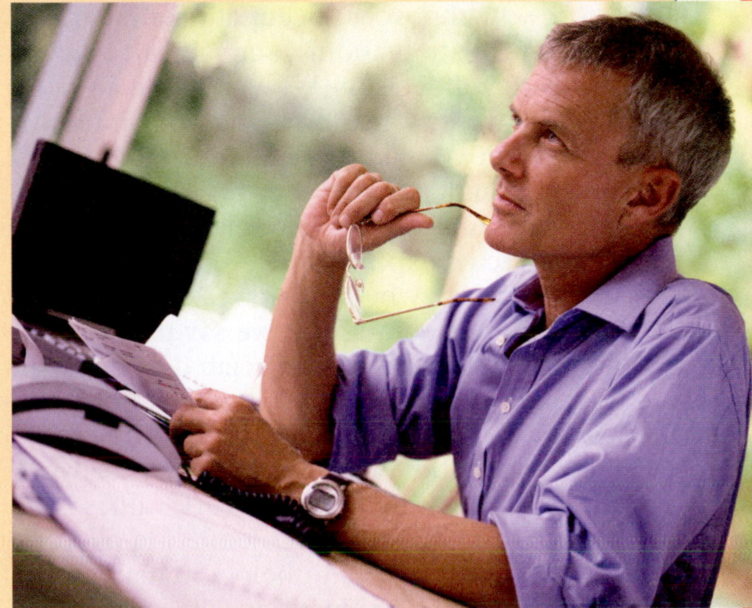

More and more people change educational and occupational goals throughout their lifetimes.

Earl, for example, was an engineer for a large manufacturing company. After 15 years, he had climbed the corporate ladder to become a manager. But he found he was working harder and enjoying it less. So, at age 37 he left the company to become a community college instructor. He hoped to gain more freedom in his work and spend more time with his family.

Arlene and her husband, Joe, owned and managed an automotive parts business for ten years. She had always been fascinated by the stock market. At age 40, she decided to leave the family business to train as a stockbroker. She now says it was the best move she ever made.

Mid-career changes are usually brought on by the desire for greater earnings, achievement, or happiness or simply the realization that one is not suited for a certain occupation. Usually they result from a combination of age, unhappiness, and a feeling of being trapped in an occupation.

Changing occupations, however, is not something to be taken lightly. It involves considerable risk. It can lead to a sharp drop in income and lots of insecurity and anxiety. Mid-career decisions are usually successful if they are well planned and based on good self-information.

THINK CRITICALLY

1. Why would a person want to change careers after many years?
2. What are some considerations when making a decision to change careers?

CHAPTER 13

Chapter in Brief

Lesson 13.1 *Getting Self-information*

A. Before you choose an occupation, first answer the question, "Who am I?" Such information about your self can help you make a more satisfying occupational decision. When making an occupational decision, you should have information about your interests, aptitudes, and work values.

B. Things that you like to do are called interests. You can identify your interests by thinking about your likes and dislikes or by taking an interest inventory. Interests can be related to occupations that you may wish to investigate or explore.

C. An aptitude may be a natural talent or a developed ability. When you are good at doing something, we say that you have an aptitude for it. Like interests, aptitudes can be related to occupations. You can identify your aptitudes by looking at your grades or by taking an aptitude test.

D. Work values are your feelings about the importance or worth of an activity or occupation. You can identify your work values by taking a work values measure. Knowledge of work values is not as useful as knowledge of interests and aptitudes in identifying occupations to explore. But you can use your work values to help you make a final choice from among a number of desirable occupational alternatives.

Lesson 13.2 *Working with Self-information*

A. Interests, aptitudes, and work values sometimes all agree. When this happens, decision making is not difficult. In other cases, interests, aptitudes, and work values conflict. This is not unusual, nor is it something to worry about. If the information conflicts, base your choice on the interest, aptitude, or work value that means the most to you. Then, try out your choice and see how it works.

B. You may be fortunate enough to work at a job that uses all your interests, aptitudes, and work values. If not, outside activities (such as hobbies, sports, clubs, and church) can provide you with a variety of outlets for expressing your self.

Activities

1. Make an appointment with your guidance counselor to review your student records. Find out if you have taken any type of interest, aptitude, or work values inventory or test. If you have, ask the counselor to interpret the results for you.
2. To what extent are your interests, aptitudes, and work values being met in your work experience job? Rate the job in the terms of your overall satisfaction on a scale of 1 (low) to 10 (high). What are you doing or can you do to

REVIEW

express interests, aptitudes, and work values not being met in your job? Discuss your answers in class.

3. Perhaps your teacher or counselor can arrange to have you take an interest inventory, aptitude test, or work values measure. One approach is readily available online at the Internet Career Connection. Visit http://www.iccweb.com and click on "interest inventory" to complete the measure.

Word Power

On a separate sheet of paper, match each definition with the correct term. All definitions will be used, and a definition will be used only once.

4. Knowledge about your self, particularly in relation to career decision making
5. The way in which a person lives
6. Things that one is good at doing; natural talents or developed abilities
7. The various parts of one's life, such as citizen, parent, spouse, and worker
8. Attitudes and beliefs about the importance of various work activities
9. The sum of everything one is, including physical characteristics, behavior, how one thinks, and many other things
10. Things that one likes to do

a. aptitudes
b. interests
c. life roles
d. lifestyle
e. self
f. self-information
g. work values

Think Critically

11. This chapter has explained self-information in relation to occupational decision making. Discuss how self-information may also be used to assist in making educational decisions.
12. As you mature, new interests develop and old ones are left behind. Think of examples of how your interests have changed from the time when you were younger. What does this suggest in terms of your occupational interests?
13. Self-information can help you identify occupations that you might wish to have. Discuss why it is important to investigate and explore these occupations prior to making a final decision.
14. A recent Gallup poll found that, while nearly 90 percent of employed adults age 18 and over are generally satisfied with their jobs, 77 percent enjoy the time that they spend away from work more than the time that they spend working. Do these findings contradict one another? Can you draw any conclusions from them?

CHAPTER 14

CAREER INFORMATION

LESSONS

THOUGHTS ON WORK

"Confidence is the most important single factor in this game [golf], and no matter how great your natural talent, there is only one way to obtain and sustain it—work."
Jack Nicklaus

PREVIEW

You may already have a good idea of what occupation you will pursue. Maybe you are interested in more than one occupation. Or you might have no idea of where to get occupational information. In this chapter, you will learn about occupations, how they are classified, and how you can use this information to research occupations that interest you.

TAKING ACTION
INVESTIGATING OCCUPATIONS

The school guidance counselor gave Mel an interest inventory since Mel was uncertain which occupations would best suit him. The results suggested several occupations that Mel might like. These were electrician, aircraft mechanic, refrigeration mechanic, and tool and die maker.

These indeed are occupations that appeal to Mel, but he does not know very much about them. He wonders, for example, what workers in these occupations actually do. He has many other questions as well. What are the job skills necessary to succeed in each of these occupations? If he doesn't have the skills, where could he get training? How much education or training would he need? How much more school or night school would he need to get a good job? Do the occupations have a good outlook for the future? How much money do people in such occupations earn? Would he need to join a union?

To answer his questions, Mel needs to collect information about these occupations. Learning how to use resources on occupational information is an important part of career decision making. The school guidance counselor had a number of resources to help Mel answer these and other questions. After researching the occupations on his interest inventory, Mel has a much better idea of what it would be like to work in each of them.

Based on his research, Mel chooses the occupation of electrician. Mel has learned that job opportunities for skilled electricians are anticipated to be very good and that the income he can expect to earn is more than he hoped. After graduating from vocational school, he plans to take a job with a large company and complete an apprenticeship program. Perhaps one day he will have his own business.

SUCCESS TIP

Take the time to research possible occupations.

THINK CRITICALLY

1. What questions do you have about occupations that you are considering?
2. What kind of information about these occupations would you need to make an informed decision?

LESSON 14.1
THE WORLD OF WORK

OBJECTIVES

- EXPLAIN HOW OCCUPATIONS AND INDUSTRIES ARE GROUPED
- DESCRIBE TRENDS IN THE GROWTH OF GOODS AND SERVICE INDUSTRIES
- DESCRIBE EMPLOYMENT TRENDS IN OCCUPATIONS

OCCUPATIONS AND INDUSTRIES

By the year 2008, it is estimated that 161 million people will be employed in the United States labor force. People work in hundreds of different types of offices, stores, factories, mines, farms, and other workplaces. Workers are employed in thousands of different occupations. This network of occupations and workplaces (industries) is often called the **world of work**.

Because of the large number of occupations and industries, special grouping systems are used to make it easier to collect and publish information about the world of work. A group is a collection of two or more things that are alike in some way. For example, fruits, vegetables, and grains are groups of food. Groups are sometimes called categories, classifications, families, or clusters.

About a dozen different systems are used to classify information about the world of work. The two most important classification systems are occupational and industrial.

Classifying Occupations

The U.S. Department of Commerce has developed a grouping system called the **Standard Occupational Classification (SOC)** system. The SOC classifies occupations based on the type of work performed. For instance, the Mechanics, Installers, and Repairers division includes workers who maintain and repair various kinds of machines and equipment. These include motor vehicles, appliances, communication equipment, electrical and electronic equipment, and related equipment and machines.

The SOC consists of the divisions shown in Figure 14-1. These divisions form the basis for the ***Occupational Outlook Handbook* (*OOH*)**. The *OOH* is a reference source produced by the federal government that provides occupational information and data. It is an excellent resource for occupational information. You will learn more about the *OOH* later in this chapter.

Classifying Industries

Another important grouping system is the **Standard Industrial Classification (SIC)**. The SIC basically describes where people work. It is a grouping of different workplaces according to the type of product produced or service provided. The Manufacturing division, for instance, includes industries that use machines or chemical processes to change materials or substances into new products.

In the SIC system, all places of employment are called **industries**. In other words, hospitals,

OCCUPATIONAL GROUPS	SAMPLE OCCUPATIONS
1. Managerial and Management-related Occupations	accountants, bank officers, health inspectors, purchasing agents, school administrators, insurance underwriters
2. Engineers, Surveyors, and Architects	architects, drafters, surveyors, engineers, cartographers
3. Natural, Computer, and Mathematical Scientists	computer systems analysts, chemists, geologists, meteorologists, statisticians
4. Lawyers, Social Scientists, Social Workers, and Religious Workers	psychologists, social workers, ministers, lawyers, economists
5. Teachers, Librarians, and Counselors	elementary teachers, secondary teachers, professors, librarians, counselors
6. Health Diagnosing and Treating Practitioners	chiropractors, dentists, optometrists, physicians, veterinarians
7. Registered Nurses, Pharmacists, Dietitians, Therapists, and Physician Assistants	dietitians, pharmacists, registered nurses, speech pathologists, physical therapists
8. Health Technologists and Technicians	dental hygienists, surgical technicians, health record technicians, licensed practical nurses, radiologic technologists
9. Writers, Artists, and Entertainers	radio and TV announcers, photographers, dancers, musicians
10. Technologists and Technicians, Except Health	air traffic controllers, legal assistants, broadcast technicians, electronics technicians, computer programmers
11. Marketing and Sales Occupations	cashiers, insurance agents, real estate brokers, travel agents, securities sales workers
12. Administrative Support Occupations, Including Clerical	bank tellers, bookkeepers, secretaries, telephone operators, postal clerks
13. Service Occupations	firefighters, correction officers, chefs, barbers, flight attendants
14. Agricultural, Forestry, Fishing, and Related Occupations	farmers, ranchers, animal caretakers, timbercutters, gardeners
15. Mechanics, Installers, and Repairers	automotive mechanics, appliance repairers, millwrights, office machine repairers, TV service technicians
16. Construction Trades and Extractive Occupations	carpenters, bricklayers, electricians, coal miners, rotary drill operators
17. Production Occupations	meatcutters, typesetters, dental laboratory technicians, machine tool operators, welders
18. Transportation and Material Moving Occupations	pilots, truck drivers, construction machinery operators, oil pumpers, locomotive engineers
19. Handlers, Equipment Cleaners, Helpers, and Laborers	construction laborers, dock hands, garbage collectors, parking attendants, vehicle cleaners
20. Job Opportunities in the Armed Forces	officers, sonar operators, missile engineers, troop leaders, ship captains, navigators, demolition experts, and thousands of occupations with the same title as in the civilian sector

NOTE: The SOC actually consists of 22 divisions, but only these 20 are used in the *Occupational Outlook Handbook*. A revised SOC having 23 divisions will be incorporated into the 2004–05 edition of the *OOH*.

Figure 14-1 ***This is the primary way the federal government classifies occupations.***

schools, grocery stores, restaurants, banks, and hundreds of other types of workplaces are industries. The SIC system is divided into the two broad sectors and ten major divisions shown in Figure 14-2 on the next page.

It is important to understand the SOC and SIC systems. This is because the government collects and reports information about occupations and industries this way. The following sections provide illustrations of how the SOC and SIC are used.

Tomorrow's Jobs

To project future job trends, the Bureau of Labor Statistics analyzes population patterns, economic and social change, and technology. By

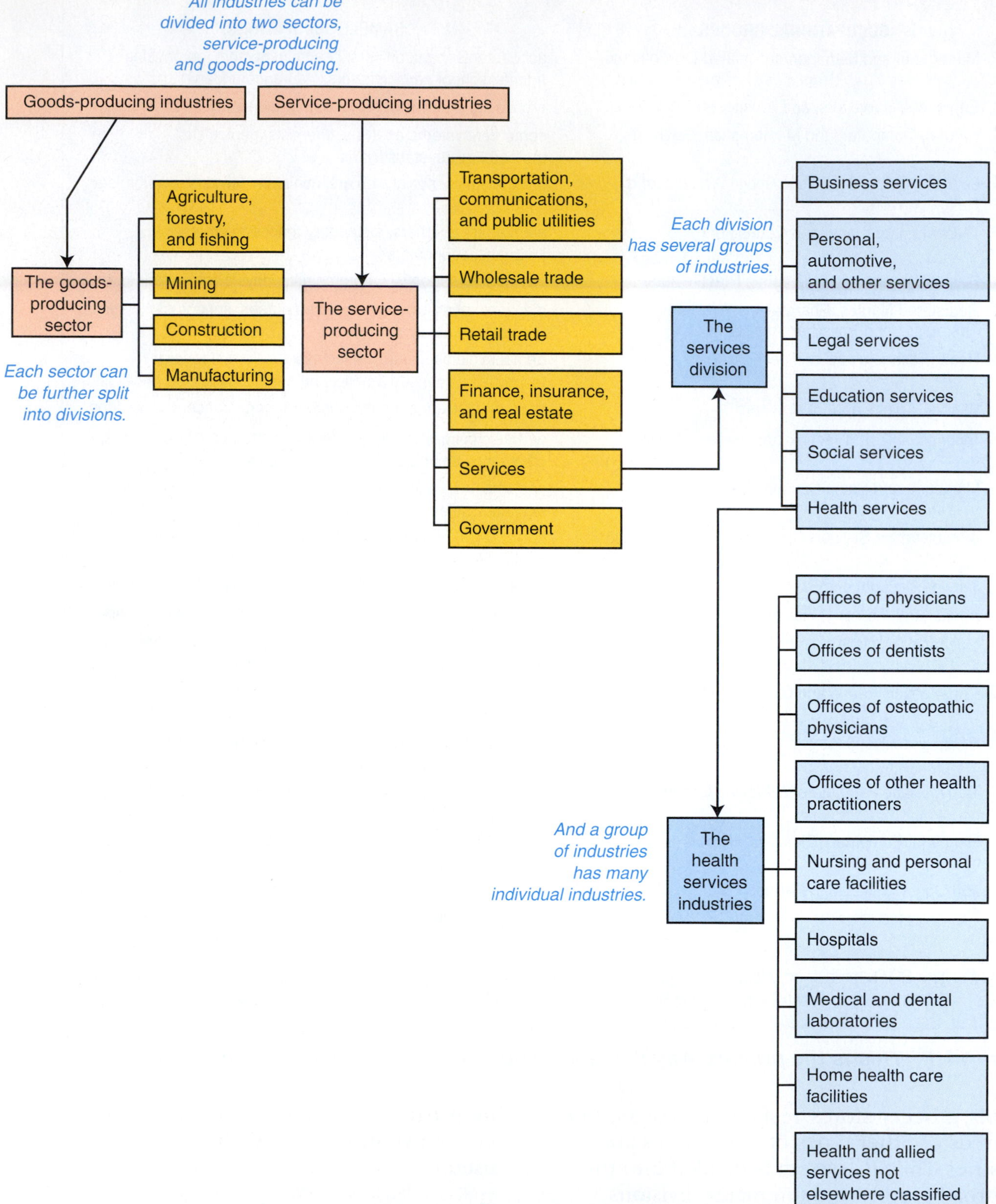

Figure 14-2 Industries are classified by sector, division, group, and industry in the SIC system. Note: Between now and 2005, the SIC will be undergoing transition into a new North American Industrial Classification System (NAICS).

their nature, job projections are only educated guesses. But such projections can help you know about future opportunities in industries and occupations of interest. After all, you may not want to train for an occupation that will be in little demand.

EMPLOYMENT TRENDS IN INDUSTRIES

Since about 1960, employment in service-producing industries has been increasing at a faster rate than employment in goods-producing industries. **Service-producing industries** are those companies and businesses that produce or provide some type of personal or business service, such as transportation, finance, insurance, and trade. **Goods-producing industries** are those companies and businesses, such as manufacturing, construction, mining, and agriculture, which produce some type of product. Nearly eight of every ten jobs are in service industries, such as health care, trade, education, repair and maintenance, transportation, banking, and insurance.

Rising incomes, higher living standards, and an aging population have helped contribute to the rapid growth of service industries. The result has been greater demand for health care, entertainment, and business and financial services. People with higher incomes may spend heavily on eating out, personal fitness, recreation, and the like. The large group of "baby boomers" (76 million) born between 1946 and 1964 are also using more health services. In addition, the growth of cities and suburbs has brought a need for more local government services.

Through the year 2008, employment is expected to increase faster in service-producing industries than in goods-producing ones. In fact, service-producing industries are expected to account for approximately 19.1 of the 19.5 million new wage and salary jobs to be generated over the 1998–2008 period.

Within industries, growth will vary widely (see Figure 14-3). Growth will be the greatest in the Services group, which includes business, personal, legal, education, social, and health services. In the goods-producing sector, Construction and Agriculture, Forestry, and Fishing are the only divisions that will grow.

Sandra is interested in a job in the manufacturing industry. She was discouraged to read that jobs in this industry will probably decline in the future. Upon further reading, however, she found that some specific industries in the group (such as the electronic, drug, and aerospace manufacturing industries) may actually grow.

Percentage change in employment, 1998–2008

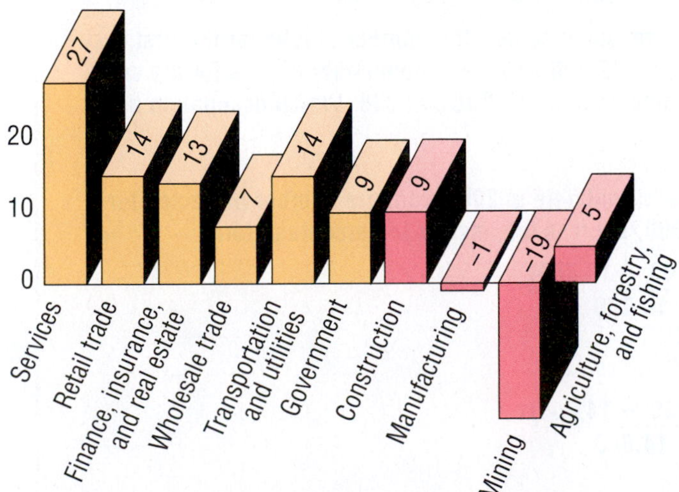

***Figure 14-3* Some industries will grow more rapidly than others.**

Source: Bureau of Labor Statistics

EMPLOYMENT TRENDS IN OCCUPATIONS

Future employment among occupational groups, like that within industries, will vary greatly. The fastest growth will be in professional and technical occupations. Growth will also vary within a specific occupational group. Therefore, it may be better to examine the outlook for specific occupations than for various occupational divisions.

Information about projected trends is useful in several ways. It might, for instance, suggest to a person planning a career that he or she select an occupation for which future employment is expected to grow. On the other hand, it might suggest to a worker in a declining occupation that he or she consider retraining for a different one.

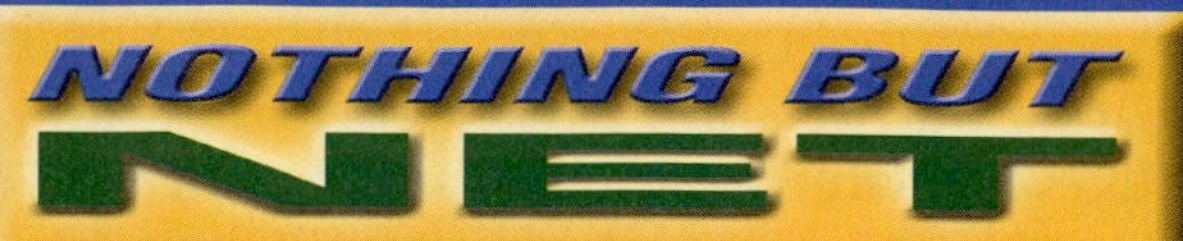

Getting online and surfing favorite sites can be enjoyable. Often, however, you may want to locate specific information for a school or work assignment or for personal use. To find specific information, use a search engine such as AltaVista, Google, or HotBot. A search engine uses keywords that you provide to search millions of web pages worldwide. It then compiles a listing of related web pages. You simply click on a hyperlink to retrieve a page. For better search results, use specific keywords, such as "Mexican pizza recipes" rather than simply "pizza."

To obtain a complete picture of occupational trends, you will need to know two things. One is the rate of growth (percent) of an occupation. The other is the numerical increase of workers. The relationship between rate of growth and size of change for two occupations is shown in Figure 14-4.

From the chart, you can see that between 1998 and 2008 the rate of growth for desktop publishing specialists will increase by 73 percent. Yet, the number of new jobs for desktop publishing specialists between 1998 and 2008 will only be about 19,000. On the other hand, the growth rate for cashiers will increase only about 17 percent. But the actual number of new jobs for cashiers between 1998 and 2008 will be about 556,000. Study the chart in Figure 14-4 until you understand the difference.

Figure 14-5 on page 192 shows the occupations that are projected to have the fastest growth rate between 1998 and 2008. Of the 20 occupations growing fastest, 8 are health-related and another 8 are computer-related. Overall, Figure 14-5 shows that the fastest-growing occupations will be those requiring a college degree or some type of technical training. Why do you

MATH CONNECTION

You are considering two occupations. According to a local job resource center, the number of jobs for the first occupation in your area was 10,700 in 2000, and it is projected to be 12,400 by 2008. The number of jobs for the second occupation in your area was 14,600 in 2000, and it is projected to be 17,200 by 2008. Which occupation has the greatest percentage increase projected for jobs?

SOLUTION

To calculate a percentage increase, subtract the number of jobs available in 2000 from the number projected for 2008. Next, divide the difference by the number of jobs in 2000. Express the answer in percentage form.

$$\text{Projected percentage increase (Occupation 1)} = \frac{(12{,}400 - 10{,}700)}{10{,}700} = 0.159 = 15.9\%$$

$$\text{Projected percentage increase (Occupation 2)} = \frac{(17{,}200 - 14{,}600)}{14{,}600} = 0.178 = 17.8\%$$

The second occupation has a greater percentage increase projected for jobs.

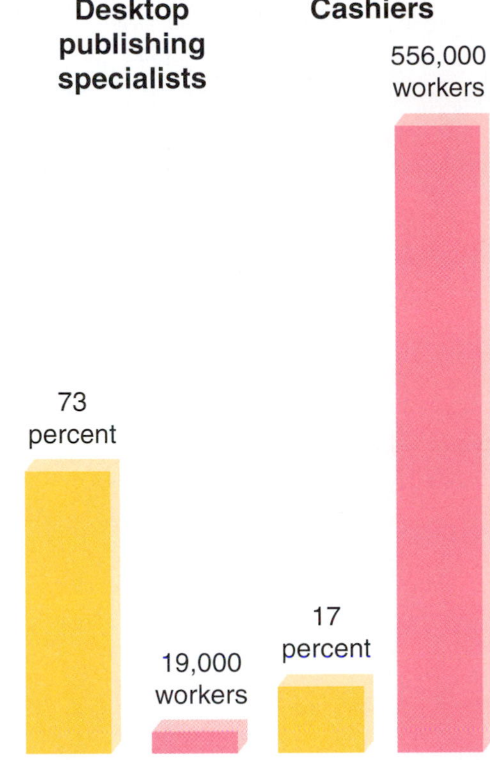

Figure 14-4 ***Even though an occupation is expected to grow rapidly, it may provide fewer openings than a slower-growing but larger occupation.***
Source: Bureau of Labor Statistics

The number of new jobs for cashiers is expected to increase.

think that most of the occupations are in the health and computer fields?

In Figure 14-6 on page 193, the occupations shown are projected to have the greatest actual growth in number of jobs during the period 1998 to 2008. These 20 occupations are expected to add about 8 million jobs, 39 percent of all projected growth.

Another important fact is that most new jobs shown in Figure 14-6 require on-the-job training or skills learned through vocational and technical education. Only 4 of the 20 occupations shown normally require a bachelor's degree or higher.

LESSON 14.1 REVIEW

1. **Why are classification systems used to organize information about work?**
2. **In the SOC system, how are occupations grouped? In the SIC system, how are industries grouped?**
3. **What types of industries are projected to grow the fastest? Explain why.**
4. **How can projections about future occupational trends help people in career decision making?**
5. **To understand future occupational trends, you must know two types of information. Name them.**
6. **What characteristics do the fastest-growing occupations shown in Figure 14-5 have in common?**
7. **How many of the occupations shown in Figure 14-6 require a bachelor's degree or higher?**

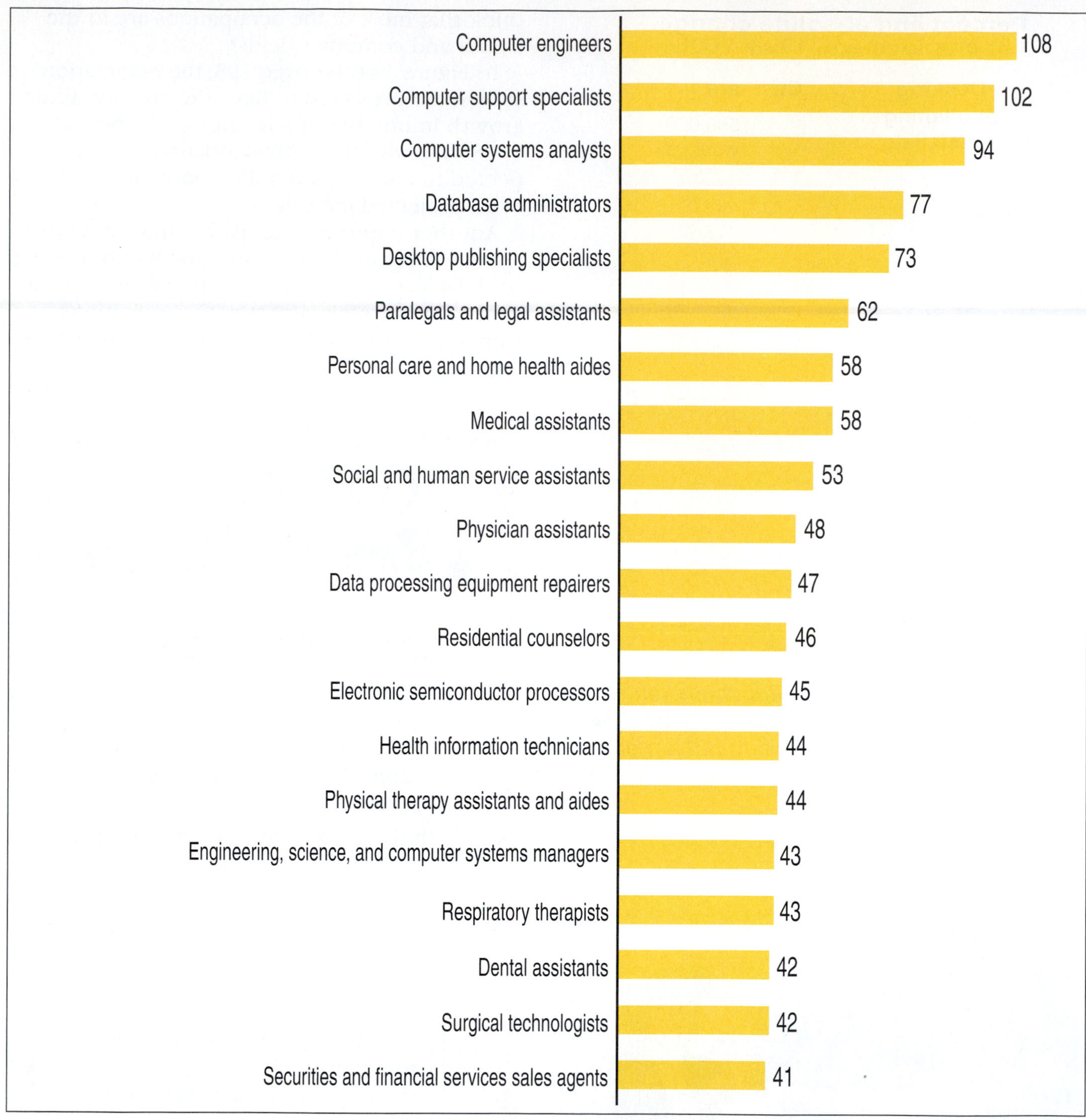

Figure 14-5 ***The 20 fastest-growing occupations, projected for 1998–2008 by percent increase***

Source: Occupational Outlook Quarterly

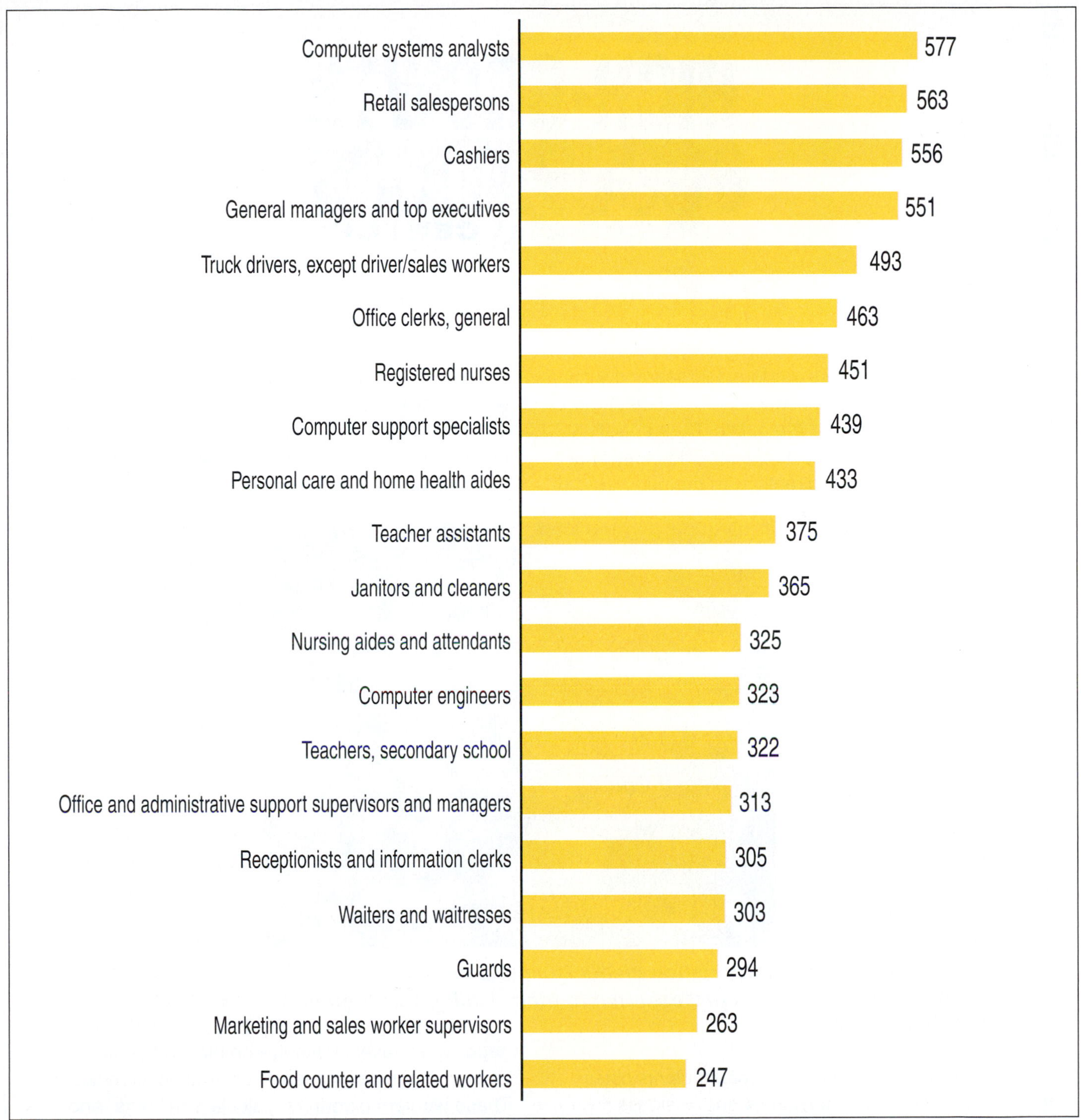

Figure 14-6 ***These occupations will have the largest numerical increases, projected for 1998–2008. Numbers shown are in thousands.***
Source: Occupational Outlook Quarterly

HIGH-GROWTH OCCUPATIONS FOR THE 21st CENTURY

Information Clerks

Information clerks are found in nearly every industry in the nation, gathering data and providing information to the public. Their specific duties vary as widely as the job titles they hold. Because they deal directly with the public, a professional appearance and pleasant personality are imperative for most information clerks.

Hotel, motel, and *resort desk clerks* register arriving guests, assign rooms, and check guests out at the end of their stay. They also keep records of room assignments and other registration information on computers. When guests check out, these clerks prepare and explain the charges, as well as process payments.

Interviewing and *new account clerks* obtain information from individuals and business representatives who are opening bank accounts, gaining admission to medical facilities, participating in consumer surveys, and completing various other forms. By mail, by phone, or in person, these workers solicit and verify information, create files, and perform related tasks.

Receptionists answer phones, route calls, greet visitors, respond to inquiries from the public, and provide information about the organization. These workers are often the first representatives of an organization a visitor encounters. As a result, they need to be courteous, professional, and helpful.

Reservation and *transportation ticket agents* and *travel clerks* assist the public in making travel plans and reservations and purchasing tickets for a variety of transportation services. Most reservation agents work for large hotel chains or airlines, helping people plan trips and make reservations. Transportation ticket agents work in airports and train and bus stations selling tickets, assigning seats to passengers, and checking baggage. Most travel clerks are employed by membership organizations, such as automobile clubs. These workers plan trips, calculate mileage, and offer travel suggestions for club members.

Information clerks in hotels must be pleasant and professional in their dealings with guests.

Although their day-to-day duties vary widely, most information clerks greet customers, guests, or other visitors. Many also answer telephones and either obtain information from or provide information to the public. Most information clerks use multiline telephones, fax machines, and personal computers.

LESSON 14.2

EXPLORING OCCUPATIONS

OBJECTIVES

- *USE THE* OCCUPATIONAL OUTLOOK HANDBOOK *TO CONDUCT AN OCCUPATIONAL SEARCH*
- *LIST OTHER SOURCES OF CAREER INFORMATION*

USING THE *OOH*

With the information you now have about your self and employment trends, you are ready to start an **occupational search**. In this type of search, you collect information about an occupation of interest using one or more printed resources or databases. There are many helpful resources. One of the best and easiest to use is the *Occupational Outlook Handbook* (*OOH*).

Why is it useful to know how to use the *OOH*? Well, the *OOH* is available in more guidance offices and public libraries nationwide than any other occupational resource. It is also found on the Web at http://www.bls.gov/oco/. And since the *OOH* is revised every two years, the information included is up-to-date.

The occupations included in the *OOH* are primarily in growing fields. Most require some education or training beyond high school.

The *OOH* describes about 250 occupations in detail. These occupations constitute approximately 87 percent of the labor force. An **occupational description** tells you what the work in an occupation is like—the tasks involved, the working conditions, the earnings, and so on. The *OOH* descriptions are organized into the same eight categories, which makes comparing occupations easier:

1. Nature of the work
2. Working conditions
3. Employment
4. Training, other qualifications, and advancement
5. Job outlook
6. Earnings
7. Related occupations
8. Sources of additional information

A less detailed listing of about 70 additional occupations is provided in the appendix of the print *OOH*. In the online *OOH,* these listings can be found with the rest of the occupational descriptions. These occupations represent an additional 4 percent of the labor force. About 9 percent of occupations are not covered in the *OOH*.

Let's say you are following the five-step decision-making process explained in Chapter 12. In Step 2, you used self-information to identify a list of occupations that might suit you. Now it is time to do an occupational search to learn more about each of your choices. In doing a search, you will find it helpful to use a form like the one shown in Figure 14-7 on the next two pages. That way you can organize information from each of the occupational descriptions. Your instructor will provide you with copies of the form.

OCCUPATIONAL SEARCH FORM

TITLE OF THE OCCUPATION ______________________________

NATURE OF THE WORK

List five major tasks that workers in this occupation perform.

1. ______________________________
   ____
2. ______________________________
   ____
3. ______________________________
   ____
4. ______________________________
   ____
5. ______________________________
   ____

WORKING CONDITIONS

Write down the normal working hours, if they are listed. ______________________________

____

Describe the typical working conditions. ______________________________

____

____

Are there any unpleasant or dangerous aspects to this occupation? ______________________________

____

EMPLOYMENT

Number of jobs in the occupation ______________ Year provided __________

In what types of industries or locations do people in this occupation work? ______________

____

TRAINING, OTHER QUALIFICATIONS, AND ADVANCEMENT

What is the preferred or required level of education or training? ______________

____

List any licensure or certification requirements. ______________________________

____

Figure 14-7 This form allows you to summarize information from the eight parts of the typical OOH occupational description.

List any special abilities or qualifications recommended or required.____________________

____

What opportunities are there for advancement?____________________________

JOB OUTLOOK

Check the statement in each column below that best describes the future outlook for this occupation.

Change in Employment

___ Faster than average growth

___ Average growth

___ Slower than average growth

___ Little change

___ Decline

Opportunities and Competition

___ Very good to excellent opportunities

___ Good opportunities

___ May face competition

___ Keen competition

EARNINGS

Write down the average yearly starting salary, if available. ____________________

Range of average yearly earnings______________Year provided ______________

RELATED OCCUPATIONS

List the titles of related occupations.

1. ______________________________
2. ______________________________
3. ______________________________
4. ______________________________
5. ______________________________
6. ______________________________
7. ______________________________
8. ______________________________

SOURCES OF ADDITIONAL INFORMATION

List names and addresses of places where further information may be obtained.

____

____

____

____

____

____

Source of information: *Occupational Outlook Handbook* 20___/20___ Edition, pages ______

____

Figure 14-7 ***Continued***

Now get a copy of the most recent edition of the *OOH* or go to the web site given above. At the top of the form, write the name of the occupation that interests you. If you are using the print *OOH,* turn to the Index of occupations near the end. This will give you page numbers for where your chosen occupation is discussed. In the online *OOH,* you can find the occupation through the search feature or the A–Z Index. If you do not get good results in seaching for the singular form of an occupation (for example, *cabinetmaker*), search for the plural form (*cabinetmakers*).

As you read the occupational description, fill out the search form. Feel free to make notes on the form or add other information that you think is important. Repeat this process for as many occupations as you want to research.

After you have finished collecting information, compare and evaluate it. For help in doing this, refer back to Figure 12-3, "Checklist for Evaluating Possible Occupational Alternatives."

OTHER SOURCES OF CAREER INFORMATION

Many publishing companies and other organizations produce resources for occupational exploration and decision making. Your teacher or career counselor may introduce you to such materials, or you may find them on your own. The section on "Sources of Career Information" in the online *OOH* at http://stats.bls.gov/oco/oco2002.htm is a good place to start.

WORKFORCE TRENDS

You have read that most job growth since 1960 has been in the service sector. One force driving this growth has been a shift in household tasks from busy household members to service workers. Family members do some, other work is bought from third parties (day-care workers, housekeepers, take-out restaurants, accountants, and the like), and some is simply left undone.

PERSONAL DECISIONS

You have identified three occupations that you want to learn more about. You get an *Occupational Outlook Handbook* and look up the first occupation. You copy down important facts and data for later study. You follow the same procedure for the second occupation. For the third occupation, however, no information is available in the *OOH*.

WHAT WOULD YOU DO?

The greatest change in the use of occupational information is the development of electronic databases available on CD-ROM and the Internet. Many high schools, community and junior colleges, career centers, and state Job Service offices have access to such resources. Most of you have used or will be using a computer or other electronic tool at some point in your decision making.

It does not matter whether you use a book or a computer to find occupational information. The important thing is that you find it. A thorough occupational search will open up many possible choices to you. From these, you can make your decision. Good decisions, like the one you are trying to make, result from using complete, up-to-date information.

LESSON 14.2 REVIEW

1. **Why is it useful to know how to use the *OOH*?**
2. **Most occupational descriptions in the *OOH* contain eight kinds of information. Name them.**
3. **Does the *OOH* contain information on all occupations? Explain.**

FOCUS ON WORK

MILITARY OCCUPATIONS

The largest employer in the country is the military services (Army, Navy, Air Force, Marine Corps, and Coast Guard). In 2000, more than 1.2 million individuals were on active duty in the Armed Forces. About 1 million of these people were enlisted personnel; the remainder were officers.

The major occupational groups in the military are similar to those in the civilian sector. More than 75 percent of military occupational specialties have civilian counterparts. Nearly 25 percent of enlisted persons are involved with electrical, electronic, mechanical, and related equipment. This reflects the highly technical and mechanical nature of the military. Officers (about 15 percent of all military personnel) are concentrated in administration, medical specialties, and directing combat activities.

Aviation continues to be a large part of the U.S. Armed Forces.

Military life is more disciplined and structured than civilian life. There are dress and grooming requirements. Certain formalities, such as saluting officers and obeying military laws and regulations, must be followed.

Hours and working conditions vary. Most military personnel usually work 8 hours a day, 5 or 5½ days a week. Some assignments, however, require night and weekend work or being on call at all hours. All may require travel and periodic relocation.

Each year, the Armed Forces hire more than 365,000 new enlisted and officer personnel. So, opportunities (technical and nontechnical) are usually plentiful. The five services offer more than 300 schools and 10,000 courses of instruction. A section on "Job Opportunities in the Armed Forces" may be found in the *Occupational Outlook Handbook*. A separate resource called the *Military Career Guide* is also available in print form and on the Web at http://www.militarycareers.com/.

THINK CRITICALLY

1. Are there some military jobs that appeal to you? If so, what are they?
2. How do civilian occupations differ from those in the military?

CHAPTER 14

Chapter in Brief

Lesson 14.1 *The World of Work*

A. The network of occupations and industries is called the world of work. Because of the number of different occupations and industries, grouping systems are used to organize information about the world of work. The two most important grouping systems are the Standard Occupational Classification (SOC) and the Standard Industrial Classification (SIC).

B. The SOC classifies occupations according to the type of work performed. The SOC divisions are used as the basis for the *Occupational Outlook Handbook*. The SIC describes where people work. In the SIC system, all places of employment are called industries.

C. About eight out of every ten jobs are in service industries. Through the year 2008, employment is expected to increase faster in service-producing industries than in goods-producing ones. Services are supposed to account for almost all new jobs between now and 2008.

D. To understand occupational trends, it is necessary to look at both rate of growth and numerical increase of workers. The fastest-growing occupations are computer- and health-related. But a large proportion of occupations having the greatest increase in number of jobs includes retail sales, clerical, personal service, and food counter and related workers.

Lesson 14.2 *Exploring Occupations*

A. The *Occupational Outlook Handbook* is a very important resource that you need to learn how to use. The *OOH* contains detailed occupational descriptions for about 250 occupations. These constitute approximately 87 percent of the labor force.

B. Follow the recommended procedure for occupational searches.

Activities

1. Use an *OOH* and copies of Figure 14-7 to conduct an occupational search. Your instructor can arrange to have the form duplicated. Follow the steps described in this chapter.
2. With the help of your teacher or counselor, identify a person who works in your occupation of interest. Make arrangements to interview the person to find out his or her feelings about the occupation. If possible, also arrange to visit his or her place of employment. Before the interview, work with classmates to develop an interview form. Going over the information that you have already collected on the occupational search form may help you identify questions you want to ask. After the interview, report to the class on what you have learned. Discuss whether the interview confirmed or changed your interest in the occupation.

REVIEW

3. Invite your school guidance counselor to class. Ask the counselor to describe and demonstrate any additional career information resources in your school's guidance office, library, or career center.
4. The numbers in parentheses just below the title of most occupations listed in the *OOH* refer to the "O*NET" classification used by state employment service offices. In the online *OOH,* these numbers appear at the bottom of an occupational description. To learn more about O*NET, go to the web site http://www.doleta.gov/programs/onet/. Discuss your findings in class.

Word Power

On a separate sheet of paper, match each definition with the correct term. All definitions will be used, and a definition will be used only once.

5. Those companies and businesses that produce or provide some type of personal or business service, such as transportation, finance, insurance, and trade
6. Those companies and businesses, such as manufacturing, construction, mining, and agriculture, which produce some type of product
7. An informal phrase used to describe the network of occupations and industries that exists within the American economic system
8. Information about a specific occupation that explains what the work is like—the tasks involved, the working conditions, the earnings, and so on
9. A system of grouping occupations based on the type of work performed
10. The process of collecting information about an occupation of interest using one or more printed resources or databases
11. A reference source produced by the federal government that provides occupational information and data
12. A system of grouping industries according to the type of product produced or service provided
13. In the SIC system, places of employment, such as factories and hospitals

a. goods-producing industries
b. industries
c. occupational description
d. *Occupational Outlook Handbook (OOH)*
e. occupational search
f. service-producing industries
g. Standard Industrial Classification (SIC)
h. Standard Occupational Classification (SOC)
i. world of work

Think Critically

14. If you are really interested in a particular occupation, how concerned should you be about its future job outlook?
15. To make a good occupational decision, you should consider several types of information (nature of the work, working conditions, job outlook, earnings, and so on). However, there are very few perfect occupations. Most occupational decisions involve a compromise among various factors. Provide examples and discuss how occupational decision making involves compromise.

UNIT 4

SUCCESS SKILLS

CHAPTERS

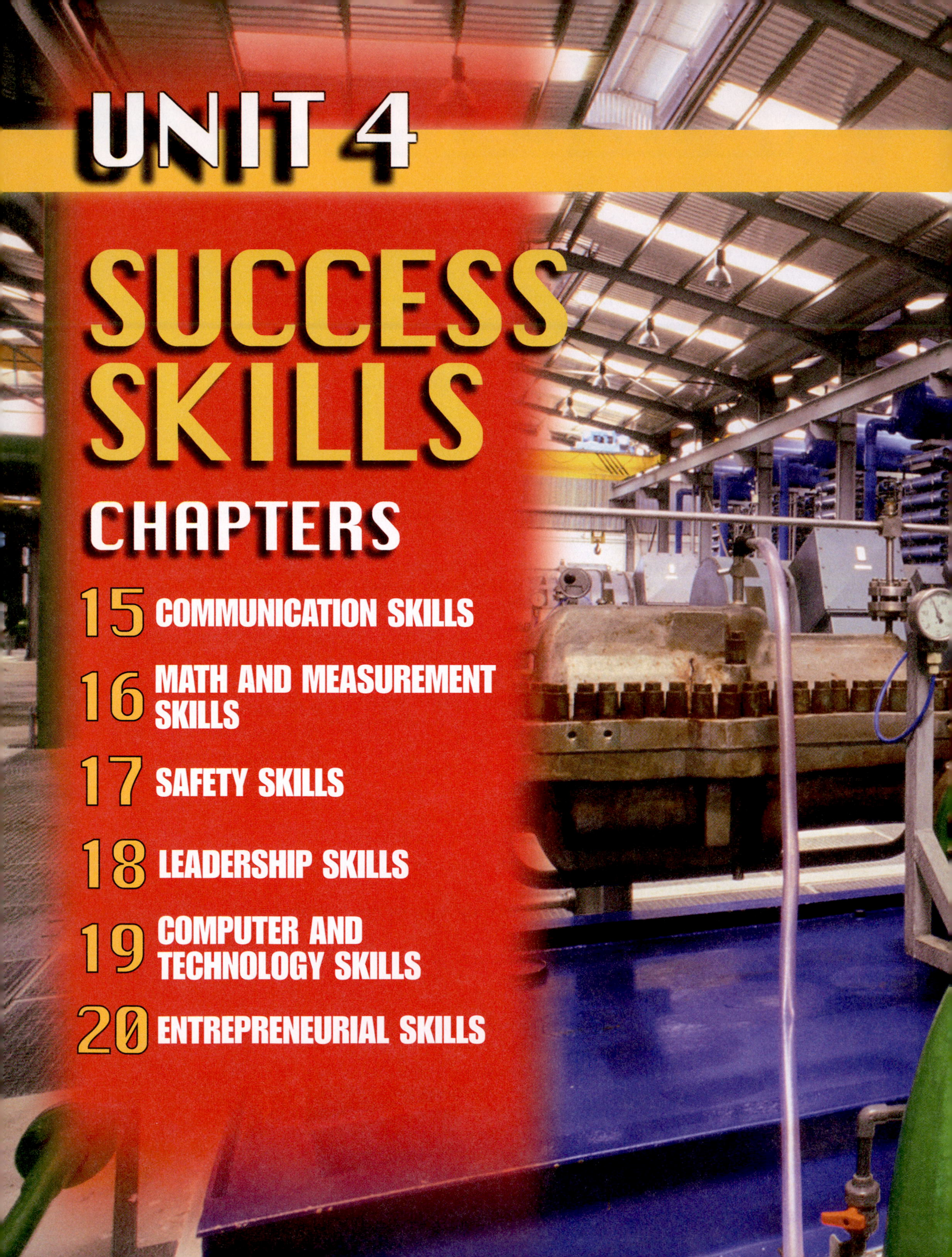

CO-OP CAREER SPOTLIGHT

Josh Trochelman, *Chef*

In his junior year of high school, Josh Trochelman entered the Greene County Career Center with the goal of becoming a chef. The career center, which is in Xenia, Ohio, works with the local high school to provide co-op educational opportunities for students.

After two years at Beavercreek High School, students may opt to spend their last two years at the career center. "The career center is like taking college courses in high school to prepare you for the real world," Josh says. "We had to take regular high school courses, but they all had to do with our chosen careers." In math classes, for example, Josh learned about weights and measurements, useful knowledge for a culinary arts major.

Freshmen and sophomores from the high school visit the career center. They try out different classes to find out what they like and what careers might interest them. "You get to see what you want to do before signing up for classes," Josh explains.

In their junior year, their first year at the career center, culinary arts students have regular classes during the first and fifth through seventh periods. The second, third, and fourth periods are lab classes in which student chefs-in-the-making operate the school's restaurant. Like each student in the culinary arts program, Josh worked in all areas of the restaurant. He learned, for example, how to properly set up a table and serve a meal, how hot the water should be for washing dishes, and how to plan and prepare meals. "It's real-world experience," he says of the restaurant lab that serves students, teachers, and visitors to the school.

In their second year, students have classes all morning and lab in the afternoon for the first couple of months. Then lab alternates with their work schedules. One of the requirements of the program is that students work at least 15 hours each week at their jobs. Josh worked as a prep cook at Wellington Grille, an upscale restaurant in Beavercreek, where he hopes to return one day as a chef.

In 2001, Josh was a freshman at Sinclair Community College in Dayton, Ohio, where he was majoring in culinary arts. He planned to transfer in the fall of 2002, with a $9,000 scholarship, to Sullivan University in Louisville, Kentucky, to complete an associate degree in culinary arts.

I'd recommend the career center," Josh says. "It's a way to get real-life experience while still in school."

CHAPTER 15

COMMUNICATION SKILLS

LESSONS

PREVIEW

According to *Effective Business Communication*, typical workers spend about 70 percent of their workday hours communicating. About 45 percent of communication time is spent listening; 30 percent, speaking; 16 percent, reading; and 9 percent, writing. In the following material, we will examine these four skills.

THOUGHTS ON WORK

"All labor that uplifts humanity has dignity and importance and should be undertaken with painstaking excellence."

Martin Luther King, Jr.

TAKING ACTION
COMMUNICATING AT WORK

Joan was excited about her first day of work as a clerk at a car dealership. Marion, who was training her, took time to show her how the phones were to be answered. "Good morning (or afternoon). Championship Cars, Joan speaking. How may I help you?"

Next, Marion showed Joan the list of do's and don'ts for answering customer questions and transferring calls. The list was ten pages long! Marion said that it was very important for Joan to read the list carefully and to learn how to answer customer calls as quickly as possible. Joan would need to be very professional on the phone. "After all," Marion told her, "first impressions of a business tend to stay with customers."

Marion advised Joan that the best way to handle customer calls was to listen carefully. "Customers usually tell you what they need. If they don't, then ask a few questions and listen again."

Later, Marion showed Joan how to use the office e-mail software. She explained that the different departments within the dealership frequently used e-mail to communicate with each other. Joan was pleased to notice that the software included a spelling checker. She always liked to check her spelling before she sent out anything written.

Finally, Marion showed Joan how to use the fax machine. Marion instructed Joan to use her computer to prepare and print out faxes. Handwritten faxes were not acceptable at the dealership.

A few weeks later, Marion stopped by Joan's desk one day to talk to her. "I just wanted to let you know that the quality of your work is being noticed," she said. Marion continued, "You are friendly and professional with customers, and your e-mails and faxes are clear and error-free. Keep up the good work!"

SUCCESS TIP

Just about every profession will require you to use different types of communication.

THINK CRITICALLY

1. For which tasks does Joan use her communication skills?
2. Why is it important to have good communication skills at work?

LESSON 15.1
LISTENING AND SPEAKING

OBJECTIVES

- STATE GUIDELINES FOR GOOD LISTENING
- DISCUSS RULES FOR EFFECTIVE SPEAKING

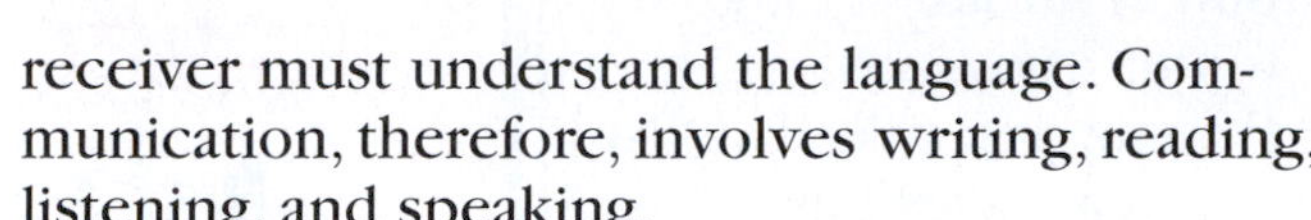

LISTENING

To be successful on the job, you need three types of skills: (a) occupational skills, (b) employability skills, and (c) basic academic skills. Occupational skills are the technical or manual abilities unique to a certain occupation. People learn these skills through career and technical education or other types of education and training programs. Certain skills, such as honesty, good grooming, and a positive attitude, are required in all jobs. These are employability skills. You read about employability skills in Chapters 7, 9, and 11.

Workers need basic academic skills, too. Joyce learned this during her first week as a stockhandler at Meadows Garden Center. She thought that all she would have to do was care for the plants—she was mistaken. Mrs. Wilkinson, Joyce's boss, often had to correct her grammar, spelling, and math. Mrs. Wilkinson told Joyce that workers need many kinds of skills. Knowing how to do the work itself isn't enough. Many employers feel as Mrs. Wilkinson does.

This chapter deals with communication skills, one set of academic skills. **Communication** involves sending information, ideas, or feelings from one person to another. This is done through language. Language may be spoken or written. Before communication can take place, a receiver must understand the language. Communication, therefore, involves writing, reading, listening, and speaking.

Communication links the working world. Listening may be its weakest link. It has been said that poor listening costs employers billions of dollars every year.

Poor listening takes many forms. For instance, the boss told Murray to include price lists with the report he was about to mail out to the district sales managers. Murray was not listening carefully and sent out just the report. A couple of days later, the phones started ringing. The agents wondered where their price lists were. Murray knew he had goofed. He sent out a second mailing right away. By not following directions, Murray cost the company time and money. Common causes of poor listening include distractions, prejudging, overstimulation, and partial listening.

Distractions

Have you ever thought of something else while someone was talking? It's often hard *not* to do this. Most of us talk at a rate of about 125 words per minute. The average mind can handle about 600 to 800 words per minute. This means that there is a gap between the rate at which people are able to speak and the rate at which listeners are capable of thinking. Therefore, the mind tends to wander.

YOU'RE A WHAT? GLAZIER

One of the construction trades, *glaziers* select, cut, install, replace, and remove all types of glass. In commercial construction, glaziers are involved in the installation of storefront windows for supermarkets, banks, auto dealerships, and similar establishments. Glass panels are also used for doors, office dividers, and skylights. In high-rise construction, cranes and hoists with suction cups are used to lift and place heavy glass window panels.

In residential jobs, much of the glazier's work is replacing broken windows, doors, and mirrors. Some glaziers work in plants that manufacture windows or furniture. Others work in retail glass shops that cut and sell new mirrors and glass for tabletops, replace broken glass in picture frames, and the like. Glaziers have to work carefully to avoid cuts and other injuries and the expense of accidentally breaking glass during installation. ■

A distraction is something that diverts your attention. For instance, suppose you are talking to the boss and someone turns on a noisy machine. Perhaps the workplace lighting flickers on and off. Your mind might wander to the distraction. Other common distractions are telephone calls, changes in temperature, and new smells. What kinds of problems could being distracted cause later?

Prejudging

Sometimes listeners try to outguess the speaker. This is called prejudging. Here is an example. Mrs. Krause asked to meet with the salesclerks before the store opened. Carla began to feel nervous. She thought that Mrs. Krause was going to criticize her for something she had done. She started to think what her answer would be. But Mrs. Krause just wanted to review check-approval policies. Carla had prejudged what Mrs. Krause was going to say. As it turned out, Mrs. Krause complimented Carla. She was the only one who was doing that task correctly!

Overstimulation

Another cause of poor listening is overstimulation. A listener becomes too eager to respond to the speaker, as shown in the following example. Mr. Costa was demonstrating to Lee and the other apprentices how to adjust an air compressor and spray gun. He said that enamel requires a higher air pressure than lacquer. He misspoke—lacquer requires higher air pressure.

Lee caught the error and couldn't wait to correct him. But Lee was so eager to point out the mistake that she didn't pay attention to the rest of the demonstration.

Partial Listening

Partial listening can take several forms, including fragmented listening and pretend listening. Fragmented listening is when the listener listens only for certain things. For example, Harold works as a graphic artist for a large department store. Twice a year, the store manager talks to all employees about company goals. The only time Harold pays attention is when the manager says something about the art department.

Pretend listening is when the listener either doesn't care what is going on or is waiting for a turn to talk. Margo is a maintenance worker for the same company as Harold. She thinks it is a waste of time for maintenance workers to attend the manager's presentation. Though she pretends to listen, she thinks about everything but company plans and goals. By not concentrating on the message being delivered, Harold and Margo miss very important information.

The following are a number of guidelines for good listening. Rate yourself in terms of how good a listener you are. You should:

- Have a questioning attitude. Good listeners want to understand what is being said.
- Concentrate on what is being said. Listening requires effort and active participation.

COMMUNICATION AT WORK

EFFECTIVE PUBLIC SPEAKING

For some individuals, giving presentations to coworkers or speeches to community groups is part of their job. For others, it is something they have to do on occasion—for example, explaining how to use some new equipment or reporting on the progress that has been made on a project. Here are some guidelines for effective public speaking.

Know your subject. If you are not already familiar with your subject, research it at a library or on the Web. You can also talk to people who are knowledgeable about your topic.

Organize what you have to say. Outline the main points to be covered. Write them down on note cards.

Practice your speech beforehand. Make sure it is not too short or too long. Practice looking at your audience and speaking loudly enough so that everyone will hear you.

Give the speech with confidence and enthusiasm. As *Communicating for Success* says, remember, your audience is made up of people. You have years of experience in talking to people.

- Eliminate distractions by turning off noisy machines, closing doors, moving closer to the speaker, and so on.
- Use your eyes as well as your ears and mind. Observe the facial expressions and body language of the speaker. These are often as important as what is said.
- Listen between the lines for what the speaker doesn't say. The Coldwell Company's president told workers that someone had bought the company. Though he didn't say so, it sounded as if the plant might be relocated.
- Get all the facts before evaluating or reacting to them.
- Write down important things before you forget them.
- Ask questions if you do not understand something.

SPEAKING

Effective speaking requires correct pronunciation, clear enunciation, use of standard English, and good grammar. Each of these will be summarized. Sections on telephone skills and voice mail are also included.

Correct Pronunciation

Pronunciation is the way in which words are spoken. Most words have several syllables. For instance, the word *advertisement* has four syllables: ad-ver-tise-ment. Correct pronunciation means saying the proper sound for each syllable and accenting the right syllable. Thus, the word *advertisement* may be pronounced as "ad-vur'-tiz-ment," with the accent on the second syllable. Also, notice that the third syllable is pronounced as "tiz" rather than "tise."

What does effective speaking require?

Clear Enunciation

Enunciation refers to how distinctly or clearly one speaks. Many people, for instance, don't clearly enunciate contractions such as *we're*. That is, they say "weer" instead of "we're." How do you say *we're*?

Poor enunciation and bad pronunciation often go together. As a result, words like *are* and *our* often sound alike. The same is true for *fire* and *far*. Say these two pairs of words out loud to find out how clearly you enunciate.

Use of Standard English

American English takes many forms. One is the informal slang that many teenagers use. Can you give some examples? It's fun to speak like this with friends. Informal slang is nonstandard English. So is poor grammar. **Standard English** is the usual form of language used by the majority of Americans. Most employers will expect you to use standard English on the job.

Good Grammar

Since grade school, you have studied grammar in language arts and English classes. A language's **grammar** is a set of rules about correct speaking and writing. All languages have dozens of rules.

Grammar rules are pretty easy to understand. Even so, many people continue to say things like "they ain't here" instead of "they aren't here." Can you think of reasons why people break so many grammar rules when they speak?

Why should you use good grammar? Well, your getting and keeping a job may depend on it! How you speak makes an impression on an employer. Suppose you are interviewing people for a job. Two applicants have strong job skills. One says things such as "I done it" and "I couldn't find it nowhere." The other person speaks correctly. Whom would you hire? Poor grammar may cause an employer to doubt your ability. It can also turn away customers.

Telephone Skills

In Chapter 4, you learned how to use the telephone as part of a job search. Proper use of the telephone is also required on the job. An employee represents the company in a business transaction. An employee's time also costs the business money. Therefore, an effective speaker conducts telephone conversations with courtesy and efficiency.

Handle phone calls politely and efficiently.

When answering a business call, you should observe these guidelines:

- Answer in a pleasant, helpful tone of voice. Identify the company at once. For example, you might say, "Hello, Edwards and Company" or "Edwards and Company, may I help you?"
- Listen attentively as the caller gives the reason for calling. Be prepared to record a phone message. If you take a message, record complete information: the date, the time, the caller's name and number, the nature of the call, and any follow-up action required.
- Route the call to the person best able to meet the caller's need. An appropriate response would be, "Thank you, I'll transfer you to Mr. Weber, our sales manager."
- If the caller wants to talk to a specific person, you might ask, "May I tell her who is calling?"
- Often, the desired person will not be able to accept the call. In this case, your response might be, "I'm sorry, Mrs. Knight is away from her desk. May I ask her to return your call?"
- Always fulfill your promise to the caller. Pass on the message, track down the correct information, return the call yourself, or do whatever else is required.

- Pleasantly conclude all calls; for example, "Thank you for calling."

Similar courtesies should be used when placing a business call. Follow these rules:

- Before placing a call, have your purpose clearly in mind. Write down the points you want to make. Have any necessary reference material at hand.
- If you are placing an order, complete a written order form beforehand.
- Identify yourself at once and state your reason for calling. For example, you might say, "Hello, this is Arnold Swartz at Midwest Publishers. I'm calling to inquire if our order is ready to be picked up."
- If necessary, name the person or department you are trying to reach. After identifying yourself, say something like, "I would like to speak with Mr. Sullivan in the service department."
- Your call should be direct and businesslike. But don't forget to talk in a warm and friendly tone.

Voice Mail

When you place a call, you probably often hear a message like this: "Hello, this is Graham Bell. I am away from my desk for a short time. Please leave a message following the beep." Many businesses use computerized telephone answering systems known as voice mail. These systems can direct calls to a specific individual or extension and also allow callers to leave messages.

Voice mail is best used to communicate a short message. You might use it, for example, to inform a customer that an order is ready or to request that a client return your call. Many of the telephone skills explained in the previous section should also be applied in using voice mail.

Messages left on a voice mail system should be brief, clear, and complete. Follow these guidelines:

- Greet the recipient and identify yourself and your company. State your telephone number, even if you are not asking that the call be returned. For example, you might say, "Hello, Mrs. Pate. This is Julian Curtis at Cyberworks. My number is 555-0129."
- Provide a brief message, such as "I'm calling to confirm our meeting on Thursday afternoon at 3 p.m."
- Invite the listener to contact you if necessary. Say, for example, "If you have questions prior to the meeting, please give me a call."
- Conclude the call in such a way that the recipient will know you have completed the message. Say, for example, "I am looking forward to meeting you tomorrow."

Recording an outgoing message involves different rules. If you are recording a message on your home answering machine, it can be personal and informal. This is an example: "Hi, this is Jenny. I can't talk right now. Leave a message after the beep and I will call you back."

A message recorded for the voice mail system at work should be more businesslike. A workplace message may also be changed frequently to reflect your appointment and travel schedules. Here's an example: "Hello, this is Jenny McCormack. I will be traveling most of the day on Tuesday, October 17, but will be checking voice mail messages frequently. Please leave a message and I will return your call promptly."

LESSON 15.1 REVIEW

1. **Which type of communication skill is used most by the average worker? Which type is used least?**
2. **What three types of skills are needed to succeed on the job?**
3. **Name and provide an example of each of the four common causes of poor listening.**
4. **What does having a "questioning attitude" when listening mean?**
5. **What are the four things required to be an effective speaker?**

HIGH-GROWTH OCCUPATIONS FOR THE 21st CENTURY

Management Analysts

Management analysts, often referred to as *management consultants*, analyze and propose ways to improve an organization's structure, efficiency, or profits. For example, a small company that needs help managing inventories and expenses may employ a consultant who is knowledgeable regarding just-in-time inventory—keeping just a small amount of inventory on hand and ordering more as needed.

Management analysis firms range in size from a single practitioner to large organizations employing thousands of consultants. Some analysts and consultants specialize in a specific industry, while others specialize by type of business function, such as human resources or information systems. In all cases, analysts and consultants collect, review, and analyze information in order to make recommendations to management.

Management analysts are usually hired to help a company solve a specific problem.

Organizations use consultants for a variety of reasons. Some lack the internal resources to handle a project, while others need a consultant's expertise to determine what resources will be required and what problems may be encountered if they pursue a particular opportunity. To retain a consultant, a company first requests proposals from a number of qualified consulting firms. These proposals include the estimated cost and scope of the project, staffing requirements, references from previous clients, and a completion deadline. The company then selects the best proposal.

After obtaining a contract, management analysts first define the nature and extent of the problem. During this phase, they analyze relevant data, which may include annual revenues, employment, or expenditures, and interview managers and employees while observing their operations. The analysts then develop solutions to the problem. In the course of preparing their recommendations, analysts take into account the nature of the organization, the relationship it has with others in that industry, and its internal organization and culture.

Once they have decided on a course of action, consultants report their findings and recommendations. Suggestions are usually submitted in writing, but oral presentations are also common. For some projects, management analysts are retained to help implement their suggestions.

LESSON 15.2
READING AND WRITING

- IDENTIFY WAYS TO IMPROVE READING SKILLS
- CORRECTLY USE DIFFERENT FORMS OF WRITTEN BUSINESS COMMUNICATION

READING

Like listening, reading is a way to receive information. Both require concentration and understanding. More so than listening, however, reading requires recognizing words before you can understand their meaning. Look at Figure 15-1. The first line is in Spanish, the second is in shorthand, and the third is in English. You may understand only the third line. Some of you may understand only lines 1 and 3, and so on. Language is like a code. Unless you can recognize and attach meaning to it, you can't understand it.

Let's see if you can recognize and understand these English words: *glabella*, *larrikin*, *neap*, and *scrieve*. Are any of them familiar to you? Probably not. The words might as well be written in Italian (unless, of course, you know that language). This points out the importance of vocabulary. Your **vocabulary** is the total of all the words you know. You cannot understand what you read unless you know the meaning of the words used.

Improve Your Vocabulary

Your vocabulary already consists of thousands of words. Keep adding new words to your vocabulary. Don't just pass over words that you don't know. As you find new words, look up their meanings in a dictionary. Small electronic dictionaries are very convenient. After you learn a word, use it in your speaking and writing. Vocabulary building is a lifelong task.

Practice Reading

Because reading is a skill, people can improve it through practice. Reading newspapers and magazines is a good way to practice. So, too, is reading material in your field. You will improve your reading and learn at the same time.

Of course, you must read some things that are not interesting to you. On your own time, though, follow your interests, hobbies, and so

PERSONAL DECISIONS

You recognize that you should probably read more books. On a number of occasions, you have checked books out of the library. Each time you begin a book eager to read it. However, it is not long before you lose interest and put it aside. You feel guilty about not sticking with a book until it is finished.

WHAT WOULD YOU DO?

1. ¿Sabes el nombre de la profesora?
(question in Spanish)

2.  [shorthand]
(question in shorthand)

3. Do you know the teacher's name?
(question in English)

Figure 15-1 ***These three lines mean the same thing in different languages.***

on. If you don't want to spend money, check out materials from a public library, or take advantage of the many newspaper and magazine sites on the Web. A good web site to explore is *http://trfn.clpgh.org* (choose the "News" link).

WRITING

Most workers spend less time writing than listening, speaking, or reading. Even so, writing is probably the most important form of business communication. This is because good business practices require that permanent records be kept of all business operations, transactions, and agreements. Denny learned this the hard way.

Denny was asked to answer the phone while the boss went out. He took two calls and left messages on her desk. A few moments after she returned, Denny saw the boss approaching.

"Who are these messages from?" she said. "I can't read them."

What could Denny say?

Written communication takes place within a company and between organizations. Internal communication takes the form of notes, business forms, and memorandums. External communication mainly takes the form of business letters. Increasingly, electronic mail is being used for both internal and external communication.

Notes and Business Forms

A note is the most informal type of written business communication. Many notes are short, handwritten messages. Electronic fax messages (Figure 15-2) are common examples. A wide variety of preprinted notes are used in business to record phone messages, route information, send directions, and so on.

Business forms are another type of written communication. Businesses often use preprinted forms to record business operations. Here are some examples of common business forms:

- Petty cash form
- Sales call report
- Purchase order
- Quotation form
- Job work order
- Stock requisition
- Packing list
- Receiving form
- Production form
- Invoice

Notes and business forms are usually simple to complete. However, they need to be readable and accurate. For a message to be readable, write or key it neatly. Spell words correctly. If you aren't sure about the spelling of a word, check a dictionary. Always check messages for possible errors before transmitting them.

ABC FAX

American Boating Corporation
One Riverside Plaza, Sandusky, OH 44870-1218
Public Affairs Department FAX 419/555-0167

No. of pages (including this page) 1

To: Sam Davis

Company: STU 419-555-0190

From: Ted Bortz 419/555- 0165

If copy is unreadable, call Gina Fox at 419/555-0166.

MESSAGE

Finally able to put my hands on all 3 slides you asked to use. You should have them very soon.

Figure 15-2 ***Messages on fax forms are often handwritten.***

Always check over written messages for possible errors before transmitting them.

If you are using software to compose a message, run the spelling and grammar checkers before sending it. Then proofread the message for errors the spelling and grammar checkers may have missed (for example, if you keyed *hat* instead of *that*).

Memorandums

Within companies, memorandums are the main form of written communication. Memorandums are also called memos. Memos carry messages upward, downward, and across departmental lines. For instance, a stock clerk may write a memo to a boss. The boss may respond with a memo to the department. Or the boss may send a memo to someone in another department.

Most memos deal with daily business matters. They are usually brief. Their tone tends to be rather informal. Memos are used to communicate four types of information:

- Instructions or explanations
- Announcements and reports
- Requests for information, action, or reaction
- Answers to requests

A company may provide preprinted forms or software templates for memos, or memos may be keyed on plain paper. A typical memo with its major parts labeled is shown in Figure 15-3 on page 216. What type(s) of information does this memo communicate?

Little introductory information is necessary in a memo. But the first paragraph is often used to explain the purpose of the memo. A memo is usually limited to one main topic. Headings, underlining, or capitalization of words can be used to call attention to key points.

Business Letters

Why are business letters so common when it is so easy to place phone calls? Phone calls aren't permanent records. Business letters are. In many cases, someone follows up a phone call with a business letter.

The average worker is more likely to write notes and memos on the job than business letters. Even so, it is still important to know how to write a good business letter. You saw in earlier chapters, for example, several cases where people wrote personal-business letters during a job search. A good business letter should:

- Communicate a clear message.
- Convey a professional, businesslike tone.
- Be well organized.
- Use correct grammar, spelling, and punctuation.
- Have an attractive appearance.

PERSONAL DECISIONS

You come home from school grumbling about the grade you received on a written assignment. The teacher always marks off for misspelled words regardless of how good the paper is otherwise. You tell your sister Amy that you do not think it is fair.

"If I were you, I would not worry about it," says Amy. "You do not have to be concerned about spelling when you get out of school. At work, we use word processing software that automatically identifies and then corrects any spelling errors."

WHAT WOULD YOU DO?

A sample letter with its major parts labeled is shown in Figure 15-4 on page 217. The letter uses block style. In block style, all lines (except the printed letterhead) begin at the left margin.

An alternative to block style is modified block style. In this style, the return address (if not in the letterhead), date, complimentary close, and writer's name and title begin near the center of the page. Paragraphs may be blocked, or the first line may be indented one-half inch.

The letter in Figure 15-4 uses open punctuation, which means there is no punctuation after the salutation or complimentary close. An alternative is mixed punctuation. Mixed punctuation means using a colon after the salutation and a comma after the complimentary close.

When writing a business letter, make a draft copy first. Then, rewrite the letter as necessary. Before sending it, read the letter carefully for errors. As a final step, make a copy for your records. If you are using word processing software, do spelling and grammar checks before proofreading the letter, and save an electronic copy.

Electronic Mail

Due to the rapid growth of the Internet, electronic mail (e-mail) is becoming the preferred form of personal and business communication. E-mail is convenient and inexpensive. It allows a user to electronically send, receive, and store messages 24 hours a day. Messages can be easily organized and stored in electronic files for future reference. A major advantage of e-mail is that multiple copies of a message can be transmitted as easily and inexpensively as a single copy.

To use e-mail, you need an e-mail account and software to compose and transmit a message. Naturally, the intended receiver of your message must also have an e-mail account and address. An e-mail message looks somewhat like a business memo, as shown in Figure 15-5 on page 218.

E-mails are generally brief and informal and are used for many of the same purposes as traditional memos. Even though most companies are sending a greater proportion of business communication by e-mail, traditional business letters are still used for more formal correspondence.

WORKFORCE TRENDS

About 16 percent of employed men and 12 percent of employed women belong to unions. Over the last century, union membership has followed the rise and fall of American industries. As the share of manufacturing jobs declined, so did the percentage of workers who belonged to unions. But the 1990s saw an increase in union-organizing drives, especially in industries such as health care and state and local government, where future growth is expected.

E-mail messages should follow many of the same guidelines previously discussed for business notes, memos, and letters. Because of the nature of electronic communication, however, writers need to be aware of certain additional guidelines. These guidelines are summarized in Figure 15-5.

LESSON 15.2 REVIEW

1. In what ways are listening and reading the same?
2. List two ways to improve reading skills.
3. Why is writing probably the most important form of business communication?
4. Memos are used to communicate four types of information. Name them.
5. What four steps should be followed in writing a business letter?

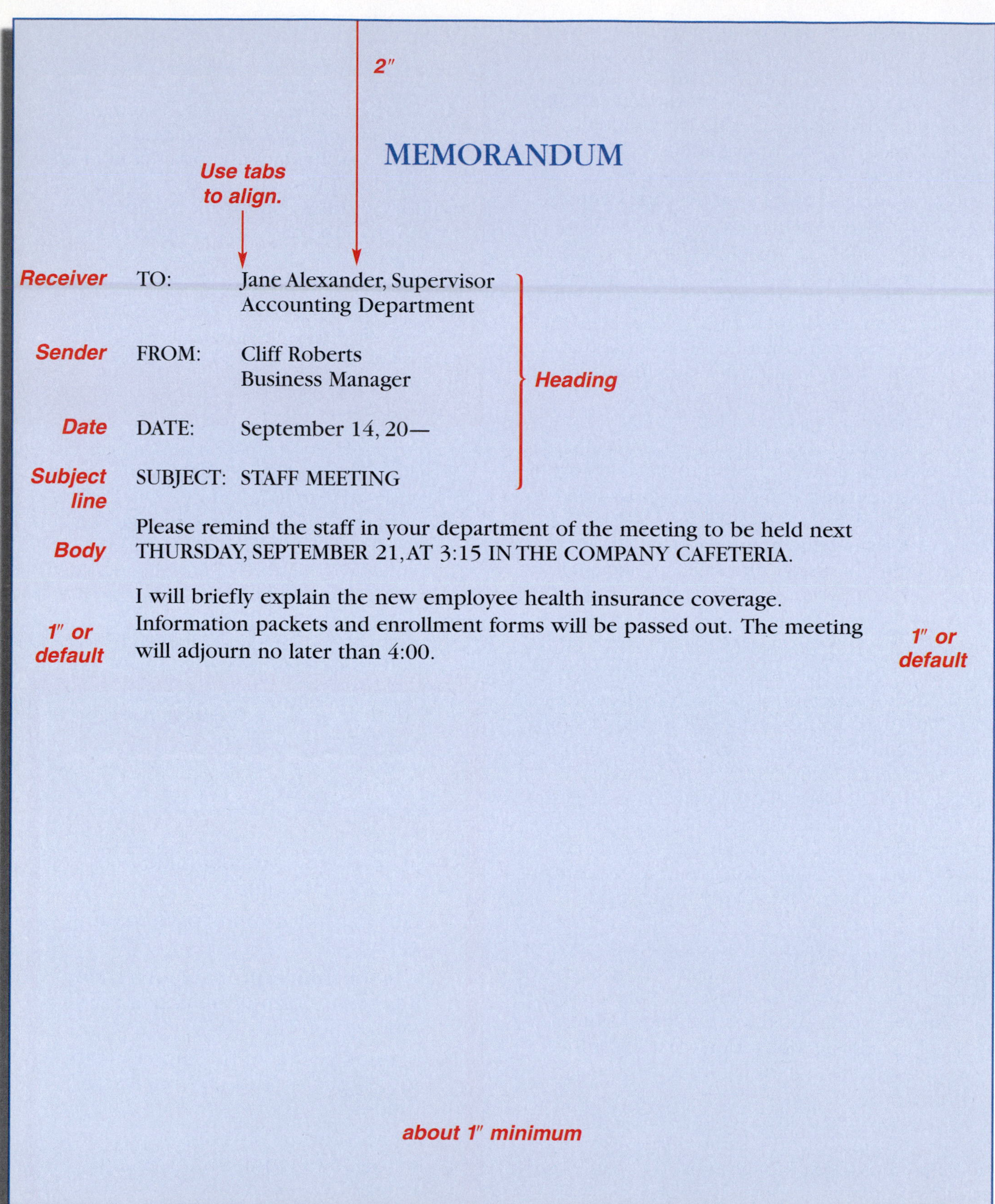

MEMORANDUM

TO: Jane Alexander, Supervisor
Accounting Department

FROM: Cliff Roberts
Business Manager

DATE: September 14, 20—

SUBJECT: STAFF MEETING

Please remind the staff in your department of the meeting to be held next THURSDAY, SEPTEMBER 21, AT 3:15 IN THE COMPANY CAFETERIA.

I will briefly explain the new employee health insurance coverage. Information packets and enrollment forms will be passed out. The meeting will adjourn no later than 4:00.

Figure 15-3 The main parts of a typical interoffice memo

2″ or center vertically

Northern University
2134 Central Avenue
Albany, NY 12201-4396
(518) 555-0100

Date August 29, 20— 4 line returns

Letter address
Cooperative Education Student
Central High School
1900 W. Main St.
Muncie, IN 47302-1416

Salutation Dear Student

1″ or default | 1″ or default

Body

Business letters should be keyed on good-quality, white, standard-size (8-1/2- by 11-inch) paper. They should be single-spaced. Double spacing should be used between paragraphs, before and after the salutation, and before the complimentary close. Four line returns should be used between the date and the letter address. Four line returns should also be used between the complimentary close and the keyed writer's name to provide space for the writer's signature.

Center letters vertically or set a top margin of 2 inches. If you use your word processor's center page feature, insert two line returns below the last keyed line to put the letter in reading position. Set side margins at 1 inch or use the default settings for your word processor. The bottom margin should be at least 1 inch.

Most businesses have letterheads that include their address. If your employer does not, key the business's address (the return address) before the date, as in the letter on page 55.

Preparing a letter correctly and keying it neatly help make a favorable impression on the reader. A proper business letter shows evidence of a sincere and serious interest in the subject being conveyed. Use a business letter for all of your important written communication.

Complimentary close Sincerely 4 line returns

John J. Burns

Writer John J. Burns
Writer's title Professor

about 1″ minimum

Figure 15-4 The main parts of a business letter

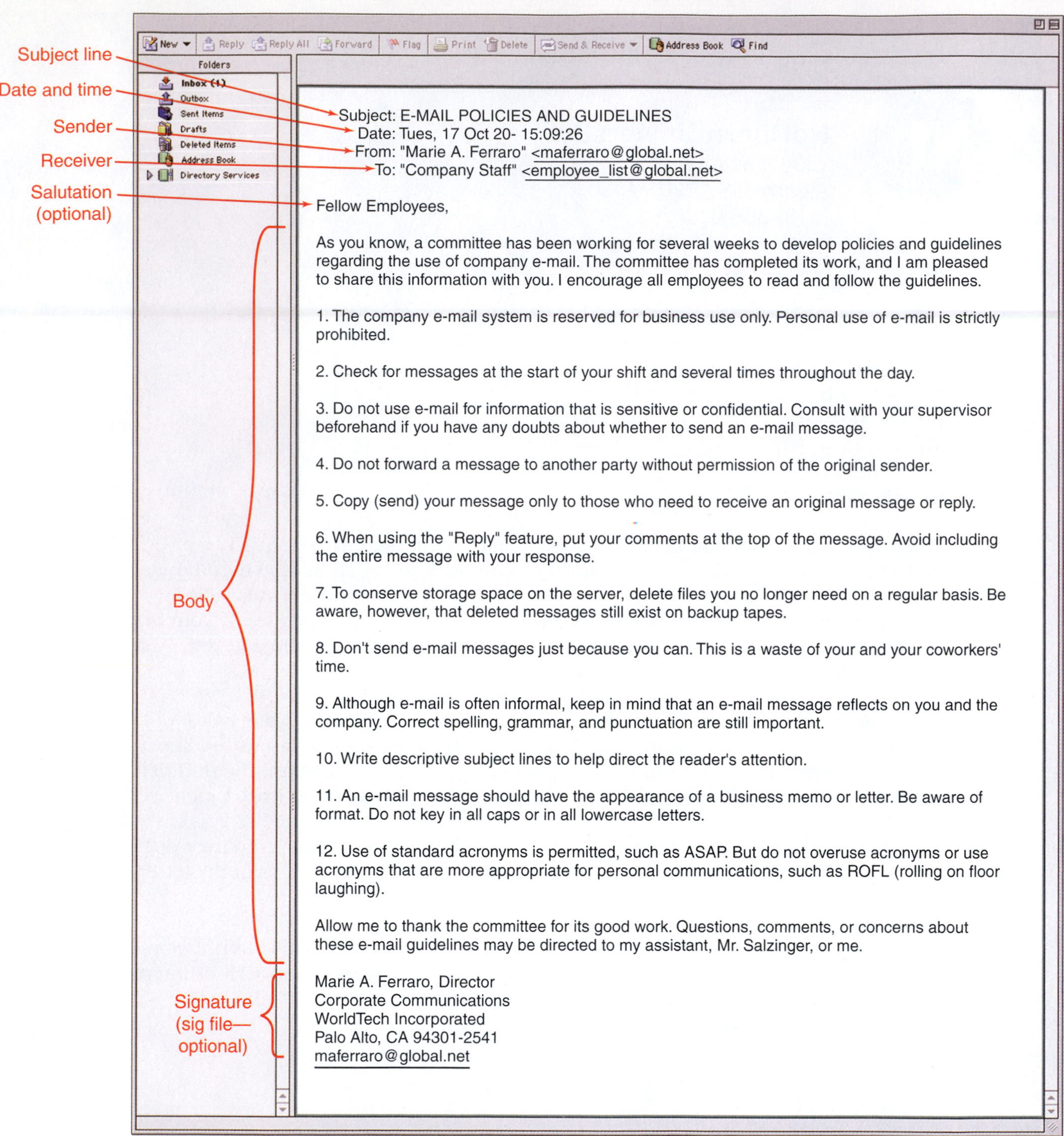

Subject: E-MAIL POLICIES AND GUIDELINES
Date: Tues, 17 Oct 20- 15:09:26
From: "Marie A. Ferraro" <maferraro@global.net>
To: "Company Staff" <employee_list@global.net>

Fellow Employees,

As you know, a committee has been working for several weeks to develop policies and guidelines regarding the use of company e-mail. The committee has completed its work, and I am pleased to share this information with you. I encourage all employees to read and follow the guidelines.

1. The company e-mail system is reserved for business use only. Personal use of e-mail is strictly prohibited.

2. Check for messages at the start of your shift and several times throughout the day.

3. Do not use e-mail for information that is sensitive or confidential. Consult with your supervisor beforehand if you have any doubts about whether to send an e-mail message.

4. Do not forward a message to another party without permission of the original sender.

5. Copy (send) your message only to those who need to receive an original message or reply.

6. When using the "Reply" feature, put your comments at the top of the message. Avoid including the entire message with your response.

7. To conserve storage space on the server, delete files you no longer need on a regular basis. Be aware, however, that deleted messages still exist on backup tapes.

8. Don't send e-mail messages just because you can. This is a waste of your and your coworkers' time.

9. Although e-mail is often informal, keep in mind that an e-mail message reflects on you and the company. Correct spelling, grammar, and punctuation are still important.

10. Write descriptive subject lines to help direct the reader's attention.

11. An e-mail message should have the appearance of a business memo or letter. Be aware of format. Do not key in all caps or in all lowercase letters.

12. Use of standard acronyms is permitted, such as ASAP. But do not overuse acronyms or use acronyms that are more appropriate for personal communications, such as ROFL (rolling on floor laughing).

Allow me to thank the committee for its good work. Questions, comments, or concerns about these e-mail guidelines may be directed to my assistant, Mr. Salzinger, or me.

Marie A. Ferraro, Director
Corporate Communications
WorldTech Incorporated
Palo Alto, CA 94301-2541
maferraro@global.net

Figure 15-5 ***The main parts of an e-mail message***

FOCUS ON THE WORKPLACE

ELIMINATING GOBBLEDYGOOK

The term *gobbledygook* was coined years ago by a Texas congressman. He had been reading government reports full of bloated, empty words. Gobbledygook, then, refers to wordy, vague, unclear language. This language disorder (also called *double-speak*) is found in education, government, science, and all other fields. Here are some examples:

- *Articulate*—talk to one another
- *Vertical insertion*—invasion by paratroopers
- *Social-expression product*—greeting card
- *Protein spill*—vomit
- *Guest-relations facility*—restroom
- *Atmospheric deposition of anthropogenically derived acidic substances*—acid rain

Why did this auto dealer use the word* pre-owned *instead of* used *to describe the cars for sale?

Gobbledygook seems to be used for several reasons. Sometimes, people want to make common things seem more important. So an elevator operator becomes a *vertical-transportation-corps member*. A toothpick becomes a *wooden interdental stimulator*.

Jargon is sometimes used to hide the truth. In one medical report, the term *therapeutic misadventure* was used to refer to an operation that killed the patient. An airline's report referred to a plane crash as the *involuntary conversion of a 727*.

Gobbledygook should never be used. It lowers the value of language. It makes words and ideas more difficult to understand. Clear, simple speaking and writing are always the best approach. Word pollution, like other forms of pollution, needs to be cleaned up.

THINK CRITICALLY

1. Can you provide other examples of vague, unclear, or misleading language?
2. Why do you think people use gobbledygook?

CHAPTER 15

Chapter in Brief

Lesson 15.1 *Listening and Speaking*

A. In addition to occupational and employability skills, basic academic skills are required for job success.

B. Communication links the working world. Listening may be its weakest link. Common causes of poor listening include distractions, prejudging, overstimulation, and partial listening.

C. Effective speaking requires correct pronunciation, clear enunciation, use of standard English, and good grammar. An important application of effective speech is use of the telephone.

Lesson 15.2 *Reading and Writing*

A. Reading requires recognizing words before you can understand their meanings. Therefore, effective readers need a large vocabulary. Because reading is a skill, it can be improved through practice.

B. Writing is probably the most important form of business communication. It is good business to keep records of what goes on. Internal communication (communication within a company) takes the form of notes, business forms, memorandums, and e-mail. External communication (communication between organizations) mainly takes the form of business letters, although e-mail is increasingly being used.

Activities

1. During your school years, you have probably taken several achievement tests. Make an appointment with a school counselor to review your performance in language and communication skills tests. If you have done average or better on such tests, you probably have the basic communication skills for most entry-level jobs. If your skills are below average, ask the counselor for suggestions on how to improve your skills.
2. Keep a list for one day of slang words and phrases that you hear classmates and other people using. The next day, share the list with the class. Discuss what words and phrases of standard English could be substituted for them.
3. Try to learn a new vocabulary word each day. There are several web sites that can help you, one of which is "Daily Buzzword" at ***http://www.wordcentral.com/***. Visit it and begin to increase your vocabulary.
4. Assume that you are in charge of organizing the annual company picnic. Write a pretend memo to company employees. The memo should provide all important details about the picnic. Hand the memo in to your teacher for evaluation.

REVIEW

5. List several of your hobbies or recreational interests. Go to the library and find out what books are available on these subjects. Choose a book and read it. Make a short oral report to the class.
6. Give a five-minute speech to the class concerning some aspect of your job that you know well. Select a subject that you can explain in five minutes. Follow the guidelines in "Communication at Work" on page 208. Afterward, discuss the strengths and weaknesses of each speech.

Word Power

On a separate sheet of paper, match each definition with the correct term. All definitions will be used, and a definition will be used only once.

7. The usual form of language used by the majority of Americans
8. A set of rules about correct speaking and writing
9. The total of all the words known by an individual
10. How distinctly or clearly one speaks
11. Sending information, ideas, or feelings from one person to another
12. The way in which words are spoken

a. communication
b. enunciation
c. grammar
d. pronunciation
e. standard English
f. vocabulary

Think Critically

13. Computers, robots, and other forms of technology are changing many types of occupations and businesses. How is business communication changing as a result of new technology?
14. There are geographic differences in the way people use language. You may have lived or traveled in areas different from where you now live. Discuss some of the interesting and colorful words and phrases that people use in different parts of the country.
15. An acronym is a word formed from the first or other letters in several words. An example is ASAP (as soon as possible). Identify and discuss some of the acronyms that are used in personal and business communication.
16. If someone were to open and read a letter you had written, that would be a violation of the law and of your privacy. The same cannot be said of e-mail. Contrary to what many people believe, the e-mail that you write at work is not private. Employers can read e-mail that their employees have written. People have, in fact, been fired for including in e-mail sensitive or unethical information. Do you think employers should be allowed to read employee e-mail? Why or why not?

CHAPTER 16

MATH AND MEASUREMENT SKILLS

LESSONS

PREVIEW

Like communication skills, math is also important on the job. Some occupations use math more than others. A carpenter, for instance, uses math more than an aerobics instructor. Math is taught from early grade school through high school. We assume here that you have already learned basic math and measurement skills. This material does not seek to introduce new math content. Rather, it shows how basic math and measurement skills are used in the workplace.

THOUGHTS ON WORK

"Nobody ever lost his shirt when his sleeves were rolled up."
Erik Hoffer

TAKING ACTION

MATH SKILLS ADD UP

Jim was looking for a job in the retail industry. He wasn't great at math, but he thought that the skills he had would enable him to get a good job. He had also worked previously at a video rental store. Jim went to a music store at a nearby mall and filled out an application.

The manager, Mr. Rodriguez, called Jim to schedule an interview. On the day of the interview, Jim made sure he was neatly dressed, and he had prepared answers to the usual interview questions. Jim showed up for the interview on time and politely greeted the store manager.

Mr. Rodriguez interviewed Jim and gave him an overview of the entry-level position available. After a brief tour of the store, Mr. Rodriguez handed Jim a sheet of paper. It was a math test with ten problems. The problems had to do with totaling purchases and figuring discounts and sales tax.

"When you are ringing up sales, the cash register will total purchases and compute discounts and sales tax for you," the manager said, "but I am looking for employees who can think on their feet and make these computations on paper or in their heads. Sometimes you will need to do this."

Mr. Rodriguez continued, "You are a strong candidate for the position, but you must get at least eight of the ten questions correct on this test. You have 15 minutes." Mr. Rodriguez then left the room.

Jim was scared. He wanted the job. He had no idea that math skills would be so important. At first, his mind went blank. Then, he carefully read each question. He had an easy time with the questions about adding sums and figuring sales tax, but the discount questions were tougher. He finished the test with two minutes to spare and checked his answers.

The store manager returned and reviewed Jim's test. Jim had gotten nine of the ten problems correct. "Congratulations," said Mr. Rodriguez, extending his hand. "When can you start?"

SUCCESS TIP

You can profit from strong math skills at work!

THINK CRITICALLY

1. Why do you think math skills are important in retail sales?
2. What are some other occupations that require math skills?

LESSON 16.1
BASIC MATH

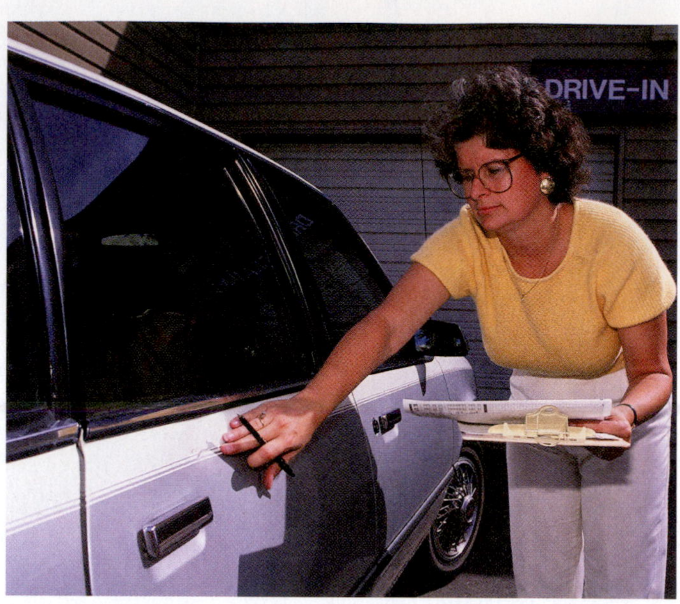

- IDENTIFY OCCUPATIONS REQUIRING MATH AND MEASUREMENT SKILLS
- APPLY MATH SKILLS TO COMPUTATION OF TOTAL PURCHASE AMOUNT, TRADE DISCOUNT, CASH DISCOUNT, MARKUP, SALES TAX, AND MARKDOWN

WHO USES MATH?

This lesson explains some common uses of arithmetic at work. Sometimes these uses are called "business math." Many occupations require business math skills. These include retail occupations such as cashier, store manager, and buyer, as well as other occupations such as bank teller, office assistant, truck owner-operator, claim representative, and ticket agent. What business math skills do you use in your job?

The next part of the chapter deals with basic measurement. This is sometimes called "vocational math" or "shop math." Many workers need to use measurement on their jobs. Such occupations include nurse, dental technician, carpenter, drafter, machinist, and sheet metal worker. How much measurement is done on your job?

In later chapters of the book, you will apply math skills again. You will figure interest and taxes, compare prices, and use so-called consumer math in other ways.

COMMON USES OF ARITHMETIC

The following examples show some common ways in which arithmetic is used on the job. They are total purchase amount, trade discount, cash discount, markup, sales tax, and markdown.

Total Purchase Amount

Most of your purchases involve single items. For instance, you buy a pair of running shoes for $54.95. The total amount of your purchase is easy to figure: 1 × $54.95 = $54.95. In most states, you must add sales tax, too.

Businesses, however, often buy large numbers of the same item. A sporting goods store, for example, might buy dozens of pairs of running shoes. To find the total amount of the purchase, multiply the number of items by the price of one item (the unit price).

WORKPLACE DECISIONS

In observing your boss, you are surprised at the amount of math that she uses. She seems to constantly be analyzing sales data and entering numbers into a calculator. You would like to be able to move up in the company or perhaps own a small store of your own someday. However, math has always been your weakest subject. You wonder whether you would be able to perform the math part of the business.

WHAT WOULD YOU DO?

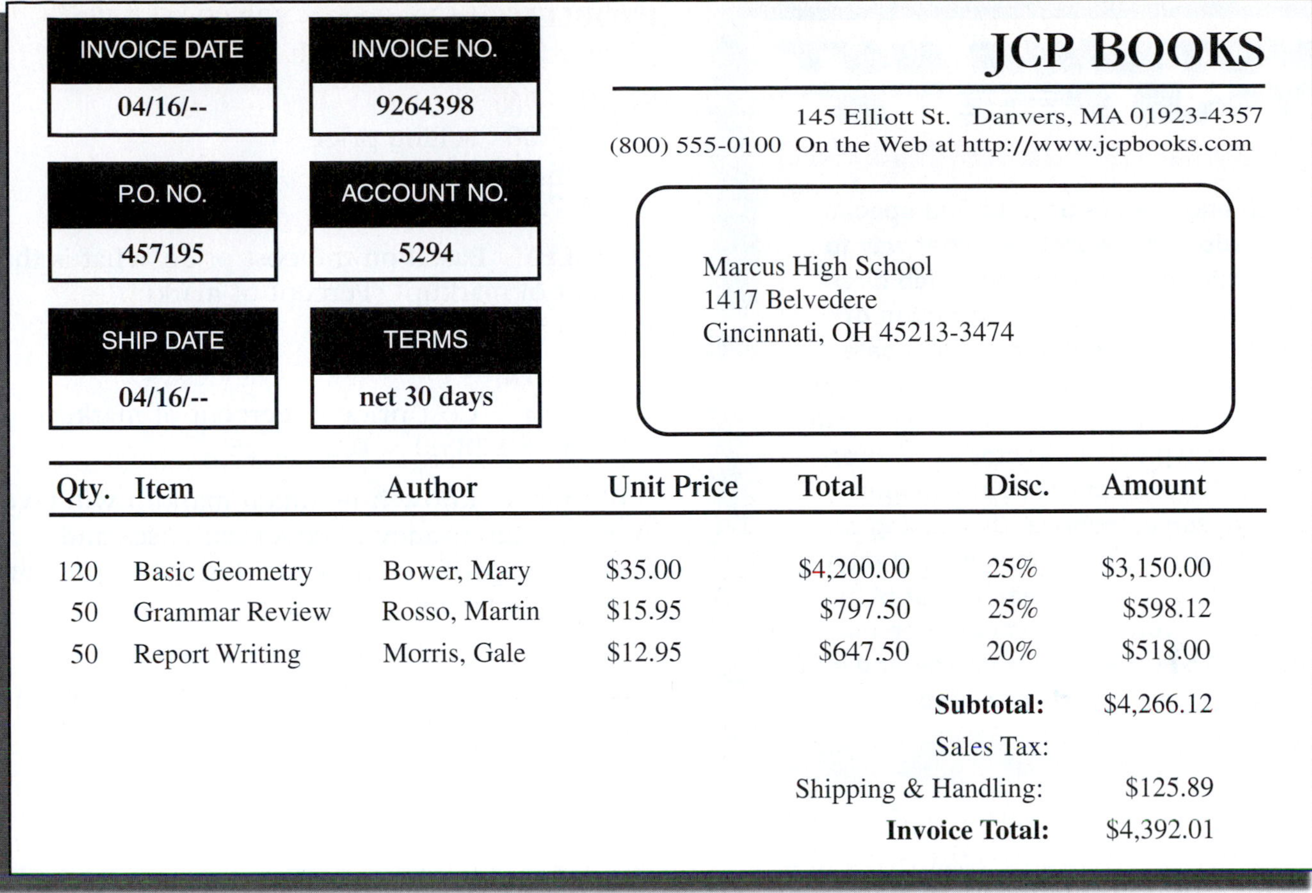

INVOICE DATE	INVOICE NO.
04/16/--	9264398

P.O. NO.	ACCOUNT NO.
457195	5294

SHIP DATE	TERMS
04/16/--	net 30 days

JCP BOOKS

145 Elliott St. Danvers, MA 01923-4357
(800) 555-0100 On the Web at http://www.jcpbooks.com

Marcus High School
1417 Belvedere
Cincinnati, OH 45213-3474

Qty.	Item	Author	Unit Price	Total	Disc.	Amount
120	Basic Geometry	Bower, Mary	$35.00	$4,200.00	25%	$3,150.00
50	Grammar Review	Rosso, Martin	$15.95	$797.50	25%	$598.12
50	Report Writing	Morris, Gale	$12.95	$647.50	20%	$518.00
					Subtotal:	$4,266.12
					Sales Tax:	
					Shipping & Handling:	$125.89
					Invoice Total:	$4,392.01

Figure 16-1 ***A common use of math in business is to fill out invoices.***

PROBLEM: Figure the total amount of a purchase of 24 pairs of shoes at $42.95 each, 15 pairs of socks at $1.85 each, and 3 dozen packages of shoelaces at $0.89 each.

SOLUTION: Quantity × Unit price = Amount

Shoes:	24 × $42.95 =	$1,030.80
Socks:	15 × $ 1.85 =	27.75
Laces:	36 × $ 0.89 =	+ 32.04
Total amount		$1,090.59

This skill is important for people who prepare invoices. An **invoice** is a bill for goods. An example of an invoice is shown in Figure 16-1.

Trade Discount

A **trade discount** is a deduction from the catalog (list or suggested retail) price of an item. Trade discounts are usually given to retailers to enable them to sell merchandise at a greater profit. In some cases, buyers get special discounts when ordering large quantities of something. The trade discount is a percentage of the list or selling price.

PROBLEM: An office desk is listed in a catalog at $680. Business customers can buy the desk at a trade discount of 30%. How much will a business have to pay for the desk? (What the business pays is the net purchase price.)

SOLUTION: 30% = 0.30

$680.00
× 0.30
$204.00 Discount

$680.00
− 204.00
$476.00 Net purchase price

Cash Discount

Every sale between a business buyer and seller involves **terms**. The terms state the time limit within which the buyer must pay. A common term of sale is "net due in 30 days." This means that the buyer has 30 days in which to pay the bill. After 30 days, the buyer must pay the price plus interest. Note the terms shown in Figure 16-1.

NOTHING BUT NET

Search engines are used to find specific information on the Web. Another way to locate information is to use a web directory. A web directory is a collection of hyperlinks organized into subject categories. A directory is much like the table of contents for a book. All of the well-known web portals provide directories of information. For example, Yahoo! has more than a dozen categories. By clicking on "Entertainment," then "Music," and then "Downloads," you will reach a list of hyperlinks where you can download free music files. Visit a portal of your choice and surf through the directories provided.

To encourage prompt payment, the seller may offer a cash discount. A **cash discount** is a reduction in price, often of several percent, offered to a buyer to encourage early payment on an account. A cash discount benefits both the buyer and the seller. The buyer saves money, while the seller has a paid account.

PROBLEM: An invoice for $510 has terms of net due in 30 days with a 3% discount given for payment within 10 days. What is the sale price if the buyer pays within 10 days?

SOLUTION: 3% = 0.03

$510.00	
× 0.03	
$ 15.30	Discount

$510.00	
− 15.30	
$494.70	Net amount of payment

Markup

A retailer buys goods from a supplier to resell. Remember the running shoes? The price the store paid is called the "cost price." To make money, the retailer then added an amount (the **markup**) to the cost price. (Selling price = Cost price + Markup)

PROBLEM: An item costs $28.00; its selling price is $35.00. How much is the markup?

SOLUTION:

$35.00	Selling price
− 28.00	Cost price
$ 7.00	Markup

PROBLEM: Based on the cost price, what is the percent of markup? (Percent of markup = Markup ÷ Cost price)

SOLUTION:

Markup ÷ Cost price = Percent of markup
$7.00 ÷ $28.00 = 0.25 or 25%

Businesses know how much markup will give them enough money to cover expenses and make a fair profit, so they add the markup to an item before trying to sell it.

PROBLEM: A radio costs $42.00 and will be sold at a markup of 30% of the cost price. What is the selling price?

SOLUTION:

$42.00	Cost price
× 0.30	Markup
$12.60	

$42.00	Cost price
+ 12.60	Markup
$54.60	Selling price

Businesses mark up merchandise to cover their expenses and make a profit.

Sales Tax

Most states and cities have sales tax on goods and services. Sales taxes usually range between 1 and 7 percent. The sales tax is added on to the purchase price of goods and services. Why is no sales tax shown on the invoice in Figure 16-1?

PROBLEM: Someone buys a sweater for $38.00 and a pair of slacks for $46.00. A 5% sales tax is added to the purchase price. What is the total amount of the purchase?

SOLUTION:

$38.00		
+ 46.00		
$84.00	Purchase price	
+ 4.20	($84.00 × 0.05)	Sales tax
$88.20	Total amount	

Markdown

Most retail stores have periodic sales to move slow-selling merchandise, clear out end-of-season goods, or attract customers to the store. A reduction in the selling price of a product is called a **markdown**. The markdown is usually expressed as a percent.

PROBLEM: A merchant is having a sale on all summer swimwear at 40% off (markdown). What is the sale price of a swimsuit that was originally priced at $55.00?

Most retail stores have periodic sales.

WORKFORCE TRENDS

Union members overall earn nearly one-third more than nonunion workers. Unionized Hispanics make 54 percent more than their nonunion counterparts; African-American workers, 45 percent more. Higher benefits, lower workplace inequality, lower workforce instability, and greater job security are additional advantages of union workers.

SOLUTION:

$55.00	Original price
× 0.40	Markdown
$22.00	

$55.00	Original price
− 22.00	Markdown
$33.00	Sale price

LESSON 16.1 REVIEW

1. Calculating total purchase amount, trade discount, markup, sales tax, etc., is often called "business math." Why?
2. How does a cash discount benefit a buyer? A seller?
3. A company is billed $1,850 with a cash discount of 5% offered for payment within ten days. How much could it save?
4. What is the difference between cost price and selling price?
5. What is the selling price of a dress that costs $60 and is marked up 40%? If the dress is later put on sale at a markdown of 25%, what is the new selling price of the dress?

HIGH-GROWTH OCCUPATIONS FOR THE 21st CENTURY

Medical Assistants

Medical assistants perform routine administrative and clinical tasks to keep the offices and clinics of physicians, podiatrists, chiropractors, and optometrists running smoothly. In small practices, medical assistants usually handle both administrative and clinical duties and report directly to an office manager, physician, or other health practitioner. Those in large practices tend to specialize in a particular area under the supervision of department administrators.

Physicians depend on medical assistants to perform many administrative and clinical tasks.

Medical assistants perform many administrative duties. They answer telephones, greet patients, update and file patient medical records, fill out insurance forms, handle correspondence, schedule appointments, arrange for hospital admission and laboratory services, and handle billing and bookkeeping.

Clinical duties vary according to state law and include taking medical histories, recording vital signs, explaining treatment procedures to patients, preparing patients for examination, and assisting the physician during the examination. Medical assistants collect and prepare laboratory specimens or perform basic laboratory tests on the premises, dispose of contaminated supplies, and sterilize medical instruments. They instruct patients about medication and special diets, prepare and administer medications as directed by a physician, authorize drug refills as directed, telephone prescriptions to a pharmacy, draw blood, prepare patients for x-rays, take electrocardiograms, remove sutures, and change dressings.

Medical assistants may also arrange examining room instruments and equipment, purchase and maintain supplies and equipment, and keep waiting and examining rooms neat and clean.

Assistants who specialize have additional duties. *Podiatric medical assistants* make castings of feet, expose and develop x-rays, and assist podiatrists in surgery. *Ophthalmic medical assistants* help ophthalmologists provide medical eye care. They administer diagnostic tests, measure and record vision, and test the functioning of eyes and eye muscles. They also show patients how to use eye dressings, protective shields, and safety glasses and how to insert, remove, and care for contact lenses.

LESSON 16.2
BASIC MEASUREMENT

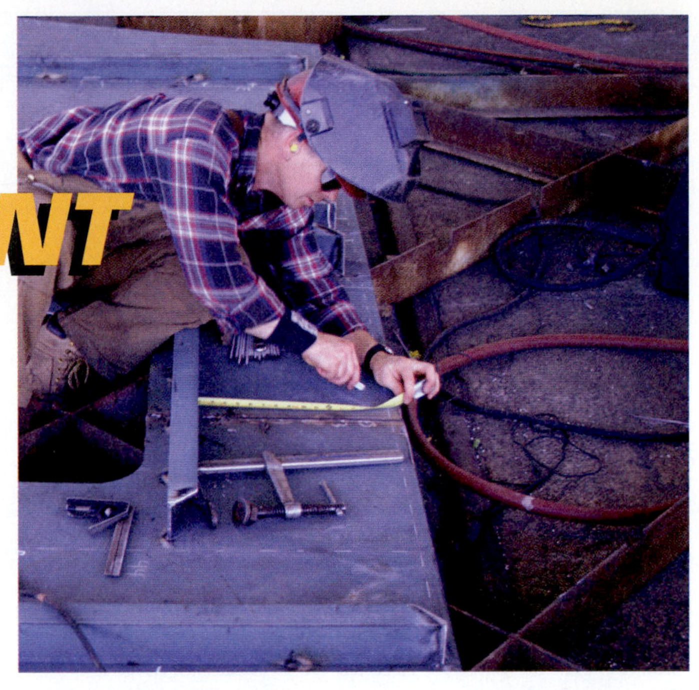

- CALCULATE SURFACE MEASURES AND VOLUME MEASURES
- CONVERT MEASURES FROM ONE UNIT TO ANOTHER

SURFACE AND VOLUME MEASURES

Measurement is the act of determining the dimensions, quantity, or degree of something. The object can be volume, area, distance, temperature, time, energy, or weight. Measurement answers the question "How much?" It does so in a uniform and standardized way. This means, for example, that all inches are the same length. As you learned in Lesson 16.1, many workers use basic measurement skills on their jobs.

Surface Measurement

Being able to calculate the surface measures of areas and perimeters is necessary on many jobs. Construction workers, for example, must figure perimeter and area measures in order to know how much concrete, lumber, and other materials to order. Workers in the printing industry must figure perimeters and areas to cut specific sizes of paper stock.

The **perimeter** of an object is the distance around it. Perimeter is measured in standard linear units, including miles, feet, inches, kilometers, meters, centimeters, and millimeters. You find the perimeter by adding together the lengths of the outer edges of the figure for most shapes. For circles and some irregular figures, you will need to use simple formulas.

A rectangle is a four-sided object having a right angle (90 degrees) at each corner. The page you are reading is a rectangle. Most walls and floors are rectangles. Even a square is a rectangle. Some common rectangles are shown in Figure 16-2 on the next page.

Rectangles have two pairs of sides. Each pair is equal in length. To find the perimeter, you add together the lengths of all sides. Suppose you are building a fence to enclose a dog kennel. Using the measurements shown in Figure 16-2, you add the length of the two 20-foot sides

> **WORKPLACE DECISIONS**
>
> You have just finished preparing the site for pouring a concrete patio. You overhear the boss saying that the job will probably require about 10 yards of concrete. That does not sound right to you, so you make a quick calculation. You come up with 12 yards. You want to tell the boss he is wrong, but you are not sure how he will react.
>
> **WHAT WOULD YOU DO?**

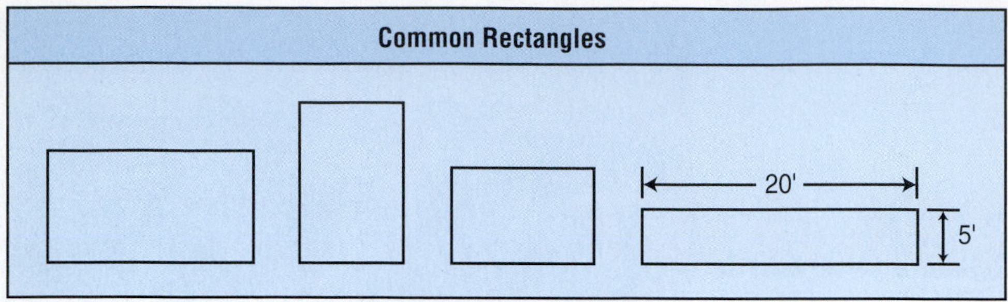

Figure 16-2 ***The rectangle is a familiar geometric shape.***

together with the length of the two 5-foot sides to find that the perimeter is 50. Thus, you need 50 feet of fencing to build the kennel. If all sides were of equal length, you could have found the perimeter by multiplying the length of one side by four.

The perimeter of a circle is called the **circumference**. To find the circumference, you must know the diameter or the radius of a circle. A circle with a radius of 8 inches and a diameter of 16 inches is shown in Figure 16-3.

To determine the circumference, you must use a formula. The formula is as follows:

Circumference = 3.14 × diameter
or $C = 3.14 \times D$
(Note: The 3.14 does not change.)

Let's say that you are going to form and install an exhaust duct in a woodworking shop. Using the dimensions shown in Figure 16-3, how wide of a piece of sheet metal will you need to roll it into a cylinder that is 16 inches in diameter?

Step 1: Set up the equation.
$C = 3.14 \times D$

Step 2: Place values into the formula and multiply.
$C = 3.14 \times 16$ inches
$C = 50.24$ inches

You will need a piece of sheet metal 50.24 inches wide plus a little extra for the seam.

The same process in reverse will help you to determine the diameter or radius of a circle, if you know the circumference. To find the diameter, you divide the circumference by 3.14. For example, a circle with a circumference of 35 feet has a diameter of 11.15 feet ($D = 35 \div 3.14$).

The **area** is the number of square units of space on the surface of a figure enclosed by the perimeter. Area calculation uses several simple formulas, each of which is suited to a certain geometric shape. Areas are given in units of square measure such as square feet, square inches, or square meters.

For rectangles, the formula for determining area is as follows:

Area = length × width
or $A = l \times w$

For example, the area of a rectangular room that is 8 feet long and 12 feet wide is 96 square feet ($8 \times 12 = 96$). If the room were square with each side being 12 feet, then the area would be 144 square feet ($12 \times 12 = 144$).

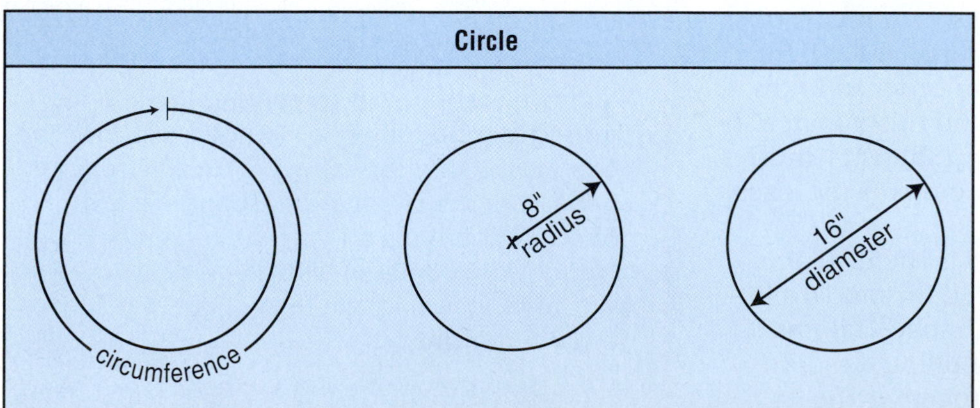

Figure 16-3 ***The main dimensions of a circle are circumference, radius, and diameter.***

To find the area of a circle, you again use a formula that contains the constant 3.14, as well as the value of the radius. The formula is written as follows:

Area (A) = $3.14 \times r^2$

The r^2 means the radius is squared. In other words, you multiply the radius of the circle by itself before multiplying it by 3.14. The symbol for squaring is a 2 that is placed slightly above and following the number to be squared. For example, suppose a circle has a radius of 4. The square of the radius (r^2) would be 4×4, or 16.

Suppose you are going to pour a round concrete pad for a storage tank. To determine how much concrete is needed, you first must figure the area. The radius of the pad is 8 feet. You would work the problem in the following steps:

Step 1: Set up the equation.
$A = 3.14 \times r^2$

Step 2: Place values into the formula and multiply.
$A = 3.14 \times 8^2$
$A = 3.14 \times 64$
$A = 200.96$ square feet

Before ordering the concrete, you would need to calculate the volume of concrete needed. This is explained in the next section.

Volume Measurement

Like perimeters and areas, volume measures are often used on the job. Volume is the amount of space an object takes up. It can be expressed in units of cubic measure such as cubic inches, cubic yards, and cubic feet. It can also be given in units such as gallons, quarts, ounces, and bushels.

To determine the volume of a figure that contains all right angles, such as a rectangular figure or cube, the formula is as follows:

Volume = length × width × height
or $V = l \times w \times h$

So, for example, to find the volume of a rectangular box that is 4 feet long, 2 feet wide, and 1 foot high, you multiply $4 \times 2 \times 1$, which equals 8 cubic feet.

If the dimensions are in different units, they will have to be converted to the same unit of measurement before multiplying. Let's say that you are going to lay a 6-inch gravel base in a ditch before installing a sewer pipe. The ditch is 30 inches wide and 150 feet long.

To pour concrete for an aqueduct, you would need to make both surface and volume measures.

Step 1: Set up the equation.
$V = l \times w \times h$

Step 2: Place values into the formula.
$V = 150$ feet × 30 inches × 6 inches

Step 3: Convert all measures to the same units. In this case, use feet.
$V = 150$ feet × 2.5 feet × 0.5 foot

Step 4: Multiply.
$V = 187.5$ cubic feet

You would need 187.5 cubic feet of gravel. However, since gravel is usually sold by the cubic yard, you would need to divide 187.5 by 27 (1 cubic yard contains 27 cubic feet). How many yards of gravel would you need?

SYSTEMS OF MEASURE

To be effective on the job, you should be able to work with the basic units of measure in the conventional (or English) and metric systems. You should be familiar with procedures for

Suppose you work for the government. Your supervisor has told you to order 4,000 cubic meters of concrete for a building job. In stores, concrete is sold by the cubic yard. To order the correct amount, you need to convert cubic meters to cubic yards. How many cubic yards should you order?

SOLUTION

To calculate the number of cubic yards in 4,000 cubic meters, multiply 4,000 cubic meters by the conversion equivalent of 1.31 cubic yards per cubic meter (see the conversion chart in Figure 16-6 on page 234).

$$4{,}000 \times 1.31 = 5{,}240 \text{ cubic yards}$$

You should order 5,240 cubic yards of concrete.

converting measures from one unit to another within the same system. You also need to be able to convert measures from the conventional system to the metric system and vice versa.

You are probably most familiar with the conventional system of measure. It is the one used most often in the United States. Some conventional units of measure and their relationship to each other are shown in Figure 16-4.

Within the same unit or type of conventional measure, conversion to equivalent measures usually involves division or multiplication. For example, to find the number of cubic feet required to hold 20 gallons of water, you would divide the 20 gallons by the conversion equivalent of 7.5 gallons per cubic foot:

$$20 \div 7.5 = 2.67 \text{ cubic feet}$$

To find the number of square feet in 20 square yards, multiply 20 square yards by the conversion equivalent of 9 square feet per yard:

$$20 \times 9 = 180 \text{ square feet}$$

Most of the world, except for the United States, uses the metric system of measure. However, Congress passed a trade bill in 1988 that required all federal agencies to convert to the metric system by 1992.

This means, for example, that if the Justice Department wants to buy paper, it must be measured in centimeters, not inches. If the Department of Defense wants to buy gasoline, it must do so in liters, not gallons.

This law will not force private companies to convert to the metric system. It seems likely, however, that it will encourage them to do so.

Linear Units
1 foot = 12 inches
1 yard = 3 feet or 36 inches
1 mile = 5,280 feet or 1,760 yards

Weight Units
1 pound = 16 ounces
2,000 pounds = 1 ton
1 pint = 1 pound

Area Units
1 square foot = 144 square inches
1 square yard = 9 square feet
1 square mile = 3,097,600 square yards

Time Units
1 minute = 60 seconds
1 hour = 60 minutes
1 day = 24 hours

Volume Units
1 gallon = 231 cubic inches
1 cubic foot = 7.5 gallons
1 cubic foot (water) = 62.5 pounds
1 gallon (water) = 8.3 pounds
1 bushel (struck) = 2,150.4 cubic inches
1 bushel (heaped) = 2,747.7 cubic inches
1 cubic foot = 1,728 cubic inches
1 cubic yard = 27 cubic feet

***Figure 16-4* These are conventional units of measure.**

Linear Units	Area Units
1 millimeter = 0.001 meter	1 square centimeter = 100 square millimeters
1 centimeter = 0.01 meter	1 square meter = 10,000 square centimeters
1 decimeter = 0.1 meter	1 square kilometer = 1,000,000 square meters
1 meter = 1,000 millimeters, 100 centimeters, 10 decimeters	
1 kilometer = 1,000 meters	**Volume Units**
	1 milliliter = 1 cubic centimeter
Weight Units	1 milliliter = 0.001 liter
1 milligram = 0.001 gram	1 centiliter = 0.01 liter
1 centigram = 0.01 gram	1 deciliter = 0.1 liter
1 decigram = 0.1 gram	1 liter = 1,000 milliliters, 100 centiliters, 10 deciliters
1 gram = 1,000 milligrams, 100 centigrams, 10 decigrams	1 kiloliter = 1,000 liters
1 kilogram = 1,000 grams	

Figure 16-5 ***These are metric units of measure.***

Some occupations and industries use the metric system a lot. The fields of medicine, engineering, and science are examples. Metric units of measure are shown in Figure 16-5.

Conversions between and across units of measure in the metric system are in whole numbers and are divisible by 10. This is a major advantage over the conventional system of measure. For example, a centimeter is 10 millimeters and 20 cubic centimeters is equal to 20 milliliters. To find the number of meters in 86.2 kilometers, simply multiply by 1,000:

$$86.2 \text{ kilometers} \times 1{,}000 = 86{,}200 \text{ meters}$$

There will be times on the job when you will work with both conventional and metric units of measure. It often becomes necessary to convert measurements from one system to another. To do so, you can use the conversion chart shown in Figure 16-6 on the next page.

Let's say that you want to express 30 square feet (ft^2) in terms of square meters (m^2). Since 1 square foot is about 0.09 square meter, you must multiply the number of square feet by 0.09:

$$30 \text{ ft}^2 \times 0.09 = 2.7 \text{ m}^2$$

The conversion chart is very useful for making quick and easy conversions from metric to conventional and from conventional to metric. However, keep in mind that the converted values are only approximate. If greater accuracy is needed, consult a table that has the conversion values listed to three decimal points.

A number of sites on the Web provide calculators that can be used to automatically make conversions from metric to conventional and from conventional to metric. One such location is *http://www.worldwidemetric.com/metcal.htm*. Go to this site, and try some conversions.

LESSON 16.2 REVIEW

1. **Why are uniform and standardized measures necessary in business and industry?**
2. **How many 4- by 8-foot sheets of plywood are needed to cover a 16- by 32-foot roof?**
3. **How many cubic feet of storage space is contained in a warehouse that is 40 yards long and 15 yards wide and that has 12-foot ceilings?**
4. **Which system of measure is used by most countries in the world?**
5. **The temperature is 78 degrees Fahrenheit. How many degrees Celsius is this?**

FROM METRIC TO CONVENTIONAL

Symbol	When You Know	Multiply by	To Find	Symbol
		LENGTH		
mm	millimeters	0.04	inches	in
cm	centimeters	0.39	inches	in
m	meters	3.28	feet	ft
m	meters	1.09	yards	yd
km	kilometers	0.62	miles	mi
		AREA		
cm^2	square centimeters	0.16	square inches	in^2
m^2	square meters	1.2	square yards	yd^2
km^2	square kilometers	0.39	square miles	mi^2
ha	hectares (10,000 m^2)	2.47	acres	
		MASS (weight)		
g	grams	0.04	ounces	oz
kg	kilograms	2.2	pounds	lb
t	tonnes (1,000 kg)	1.1	short tons	
		VOLUME		
ml	milliliters	0.03	fluid ounces	fl oz
l	liters	2.11	pints	pt
l	liters	1.06	quarts	qt
l	liters	0.26	gallons	gal
m^3	cubic meters	35.31	cubic feet	ft^3
m^3	cubic meters	1.31	cubic yards	yd^3
		TEMPERATURE (exact)		
°C	Celsius temperature	9/5 (then add 32)	Fahrenheit temperature	°F

FROM CONVENTIONAL TO METRIC

Symbol	When You Know	Multiply by	To Find	Symbol
		LENGTH		
in	inches	2.54	centimeters	cm
ft	feet	30.48	centimeters	cm
yd	yards	0.91	meters	m
mi	miles	1.61	kilometers	km
		AREA		
in^2	square inches	6.45	square centimeters	cm^2
ft^2	square feet	0.09	square meters	m^2
yd^2	square yards	0.84	square meters	m^2
mi^2	square miles	2.59	square kilometers	km^2
	acres	0.41	hectares	ha
		MASS (weight)		
oz	ounces	28.35	grams	g
lb	pounds	0.45	kilograms	kg
	short tons (2,000 lb)	0.9	tonnes	t
		VOLUME		
tsp	teaspoons	4.93	milliliters	ml
Tbsp	tablespoons	14.79	milliliters	ml
fl oz	fluid ounces	29.57	milliliters	ml
c	cups	0.24	liters	l
pt	pints	0.47	liters	l
qt	quarts	0.95	liters	l
gal	gallons	3.79	liters	l
ft^3	cubic feet	0.03	cubic meters	m^3
yd^3	cubic yards	0.77	cubic meters	m^3
		TEMPERATURE (exact)		
°F	Fahrenheit temperature	5/9 (after subtracting 32)	Celsius temperature	°C

Figure 16-6 ***These are approximate conversion charts.***

FOCUS ON WORK

CALCULATOR REVIEW

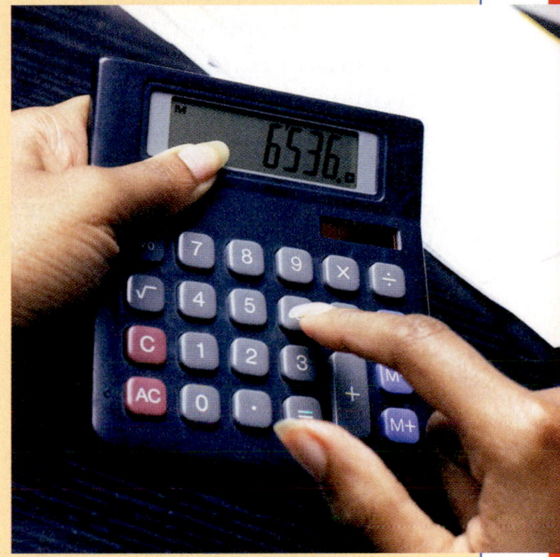

A calculator is used for many workplace tasks.

The calculator is an essential tool in the workplace. Let's review its operation. A calculator has number buttons and command buttons. The arrangement of the buttons and which command buttons are included will vary among different models.

Push **CE** if you make a mistake in your last entry.

Push **C** if you make a mistake and want to redo the problem.

Turn on the calculator. To add 34 and 57, push **3 4 + 5 7 =**. The answer appears on the screen: **91**.

Subtraction (64 − 8 =), multiplication (27 × 6 =), and division (135 ÷ 7 =) are done in a similar manner. Simply enter the first number in the calculation; press **−**, **×**, or **÷**; enter the second number; and press **=**.

The calculator has no commas and no dollar signs. To add $3,618 and $4,192, push **3 6 1 8 + 4 1 9 2 =**. The screen shows this total: **7810**. When you write the total, include the dollar sign and comma: $7,810.

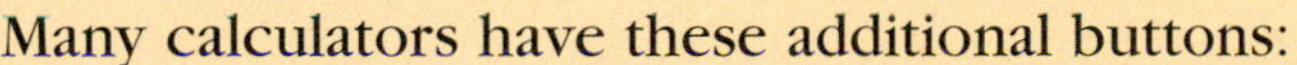

Many calculators have these additional buttons:

- The **MR** button reads or displays the memory number.
- The **MC** button clears the memory to zero.
- The **M+** button enters or adds to the memory number.
- The **M−** button subtracts from the memory number.

Placing a number in memory is useful for figuring sales tax, markup, and markdown. (The steps on your calculator may vary slightly. Read the directions.) If you want to add a sales tax of 3.5%, push **3 . 5 M+**. To calculate the tax on $54.95, push **5 4 . 9 5 × MR %**. The answer is **1.92325** or $1.92.

If the tax increases from 3.5% to 4.0%, the actual increase is 0.5%. To increase the tax by that amount, push **. 5 M+**. To decrease the tax by 1.25%, push **1 . 2 5 M−**. Push **C** to clear the memory when you have finished.

THINK CRITICALLY

1. For what tasks at work could or do you use a calculator?
2. Calculators, computers, cash registers, and other machines automatically perform many math calculations on the job. This being the case, how important is it that you be able to do math by hand?

CHAPTER 16

Chapter in Brief

Lesson 16.1 *Basic Math*

A. Basic math and measurement skills are used by many workers.

B. One group of math skills is often called "business math." Business math involves being able to figure total purchase amount, trade discount, cash discount, markup, sales tax, and markdown.

Lesson 16.2 *Basic Measurement*

A. Basic measurement skills ("vocational math" or "shop math") involve being able to perform surface measurement (perimeter and area) and volume measurement.

B. Most countries, except for the United States, use the metric system of measure. Even so, some occupational fields use the metric system a lot.

C. You should be familiar with how to convert measures from one unit to another in the same system. You also need to be able to convert measures from the conventional system to the metric system and vice versa.

Activities

1. List all the ways you use math and measurement skills in your co-op or work experience job. Compare your list with other students' lists. What skills does the class find are the most common?

2. For the classroom in which you are meeting, perform the necessary measurements and calculations to answer the following questions:

a. What is the perimeter of the classroom?
b. How much area of floor space is contained within the classroom?
c. How much area of wall space is taken up by window and door openings?
d. How much volume is contained within the classroom?
e. Identify a circular-shaped object in the classroom, such as a wastebasket. What is the circumference of it?

3. Identify as many occupations as possible that might make the types of calculations performed in Activity 2.

4. How many kilometers do you travel to work? What is the average distance for the entire class? You may wish to use a metric calculator on the Web like the one at *http://www.worldwidemetric.com/metcal.htm*.

5. To find the average of a set of numbers, you can add them on a calculator and divide by the number of items in the set. Here is an example:

$(140 + 145 + 146 + 149 + 144 + 146) \div 6 = 145$

The average is 145. Another way to find the average is to pick a "benchmark" number less than or equal to the smallest number. In the preceding example, 140 would be the benchmark. Now, add the difference between

REVIEW

each number and the benchmark. Then find the average of the difference: (0 + 5 + 6 + 9 + 4 + 6) ÷ 6 = 5. The average of the difference is 5. Add this to the benchmark and you get 145. This shortcut can save you considerable time. Often, you can add the numbers in your head without using a calculator. Using benchmarks, find the averages of the following numbers: (a) Prices of $200, $220, $210, $215, and $230 (b) Lengths of 47, 46, 51, 45, 52, 46, and 49 inches (c) Temperatures of 80, 72, 75, 74, 73, 77, 81, and 76 degrees Fahrenheit.

6. Suppose you have a cookbook from England. You want to make something that requires 65 milliliters of milk. How many fluid ounces is this?

Word Power

On a separate sheet of paper, match each definition with the correct term. All definitions will be used, and a definition will be used only once.

7. The distance around the outside of an object
8. A bill for goods
9. An amount added by a retailer to the cost price of goods that allows it to cover expenses and make a fair profit
10. A reduction in price, often of several percent, offered to a buyer to encourage early payment on an account
11. A deduction from the catalog (list or suggested retail) price of an item
12. The number of square units of space on the surface of a figure enclosed by the perimeter
13. The act of determining the dimensions, quantity, or degree of something
14. The perimeter of a circle
15. That part of an invoice or other sales agreement that states the time limit within which a buyer must pay for merchandise received from a seller
16. A reduction in the selling price of a product

a. area
b. cash discount
c. circumference
d. invoice
e. markdown
f. markup
g. measurement
h. perimeter
i. terms
j. trade discount

Think Critically

17. Should the United States convert to the metric system? Discuss the advantages and disadvantages.
18. In "rough carpentry" work, measurements within 1/4 inch are considered accurate. Other jobs, such as installing cabinets, require more accurate measurement. Discuss and give examples of how standards of accuracy in measurement vary among different occupations.
19. How much is the sales tax in your state? What types of goods and services does it cover? If your state does not have sales tax, discuss these questions for a neighboring state.

CHAPTER 17

SAFETY SKILLS

LESSONS

PREVIEW

Many activities involve some risk of injury. This chapter describes the nature of accidents and discusses steps to take in avoiding accidents. It describes federal agencies and private organizations that are devoted to public safety. It also introduces the three E's of safety.

THOUGHTS ON WORK

"I never did anything by accident, nor did any of my inventions come by accident; they came by work."

Thomas A. Edison

TAKING ACTION

SAFETY FIRST

Jorge picked Anna up at her parents' house to take her out to dinner. Jorge opened the passenger door of his car politely for Anna and asked that she put on her seat belt.

As they drove to the restaurant, Jorge and Anna passed a group of teenagers they knew from school in a convertible. There were about eight people in the convertible, and it didn't look as though anyone had a seat belt on. As the car came to a stop sign, everyone got out and changed seats except the driver. The teenagers laughed as they jumped back in the car and sped away.

At the restaurant, Jorge and Anna enjoyed a nice, quiet meal. They noticed that one of the servers kept overloading his tray with dirty dishes that he was taking back to the kitchen. At one point, the server stumbled and nearly dropped the tray. Luckily, he recovered his balance and did not fall.

Jorge and Anna decided to go for a stroll at a nearby park along the ocean. It was a beautiful night and they walked for a while. There were a number of boaters enjoying the night air as well. Anna pointed out a speedboat that had a group of people on it. They were all drinking and no one was wearing a life preserver. Two of the men began trying to push each other off the boat. Jorge and Anna watched as a Coast Guard vessel approached the speedboat, arrested the operator, and towed the boat away.

Later, when he was driving Anna home, Jorge heard sirens behind him. He looked in his rearview mirror and saw an ambulance coming. He immediately slowed down, put on his turn signal, and pulled over to let the ambulance go past him.

SUCCESS TIP

Safety is important everywhere you go.

THINK CRITICALLY

1. How many unsafe behaviors and conditions can you find in this story?
2. What are some things you do that aren't safe?

LESSON 17.1

ACCIDENTS AND PERSONAL SAFETY

OBJECTIVES

- *DESCRIBE THE NATURE OF ACCIDENTS ACCORDING TO TYPE AND CLASS*
- *DISCUSS RULES FOR PERSONAL SAFETY*
- *EXPLAIN WHAT TO DO IN A FLOOD, TORNADO, HURRICANE, AND EARTHQUAKE*

ACCIDENTS

Safety experts define an **accident** as an unplanned event often resulting in personal injury, property damage, or both. Accidents rank fifth behind heart disease, cancer, stroke, and chronic pulmonary disease as a cause of death among the general public. For teenagers and young adults, however, accidents are the leading cause of death.

Even though accidents are unexpected, this does not mean that they occur by chance. Almost all accidents can be prevented by eliminating unsafe behavior and conditions and by following basic safety rules. In this chapter, you will learn more about accidents and what you can do to prevent them. Statistical data reported in this chapter are from *Injury Facts* 2000 Edition by the National Safety Council.

In a typical year, accidents kill more than 97,000 Americans, and about 21 million more suffer disabling injuries. A **disabling injury** is one causing death, permanent disability, or any degree of temporary total disability beyond the day of the accident. Accidents and injuries are estimated to cost the nation about $470 billion annually. There is no way to calculate the cost in human lives. Data on accidents are reported by type and class.

Type refers to the cause of the accident. The leading causes of accidental death in the United States are shown in Figures 17-1 and 17-2. For people under age 75, motor vehicles lead as a cause of accidental death. For people between the ages of 15 and 24, about 76 percent of accidental deaths are caused by motor vehicles. Of these deaths, about 70 percent are of males.

WORKPLACE DECISIONS

It is your turn to work the Saturday evening shift. Normally, you do not mind working until 9:00 p.m. Tonight, though, you badly want to see the game. If you hurry, you may be able to see the last half.

At quitting time, you quickly clean up. It only takes you a few minutes to wipe off the tables, clean the counter, and empty the trash. By 9:15, you are on your way.

As you are heading through the door to the gym, you suddenly stop. Did you remember to lock the door before you left work? You think so, but you are not sure.

WHAT WOULD YOU DO?

Types of Accidents	Number of Deaths
Motor vehicle	41,300
Falls	17,100
Poisoning	11,000
Drowning	4,000
Suffocation/Choking	3,200
Fires	3,100
Firearms	700
All other types	16,500
Total	96,900

Figure 17-1 ***Major causes of accidental death in the United States***

Courtesy of National Safety Council, Injury Facts 2000 Edition.

The second highest cause of accidental death overall is falls. But for persons ages 15 to 24, it is drowning. For young adults ages 25–44, poisoning (mostly from drugs) is second only to motor vehicle accidents as the leading cause of accidental deaths. For people over age 75, falls are the leading cause of accidental death, followed by motor vehicle accidents.

Class refers to where the accident occurs. More accidents take place in and on motor vehicles than in any other class. Home accidents are second, followed by accidents in public places. Accidents at work trail far behind. Over the last 50 years, the death rate for all four classes of accidents has declined steadily.

RULES FOR PERSONAL SAFETY

Safety is freedom from harm or the danger of harm. The word *safety* also refers to the precautions taken to prevent accidents. In this section, you will examine some of the things to do and avoid in order to prevent accidents at home, at school, on the job, and elsewhere.

In the Home

You probably consider your home a safe place. But about 30 percent of all accidental deaths and about one-third of all disabling injuries occur in and around the home. This translates into one death every 18 minutes and one disabling injury every 5 seconds. In addition, millions of people suffer minor (but painful) cuts, burns, and bruises.

Good housekeeping is one of the most important safety defenses. Keep everything in its proper place. Do not leave shoes, toys, books, or other objects on the floor and stairs where someone could trip over them. Put kitchen knives, other utensils, tools, and household cleaners away immediately after you use them.

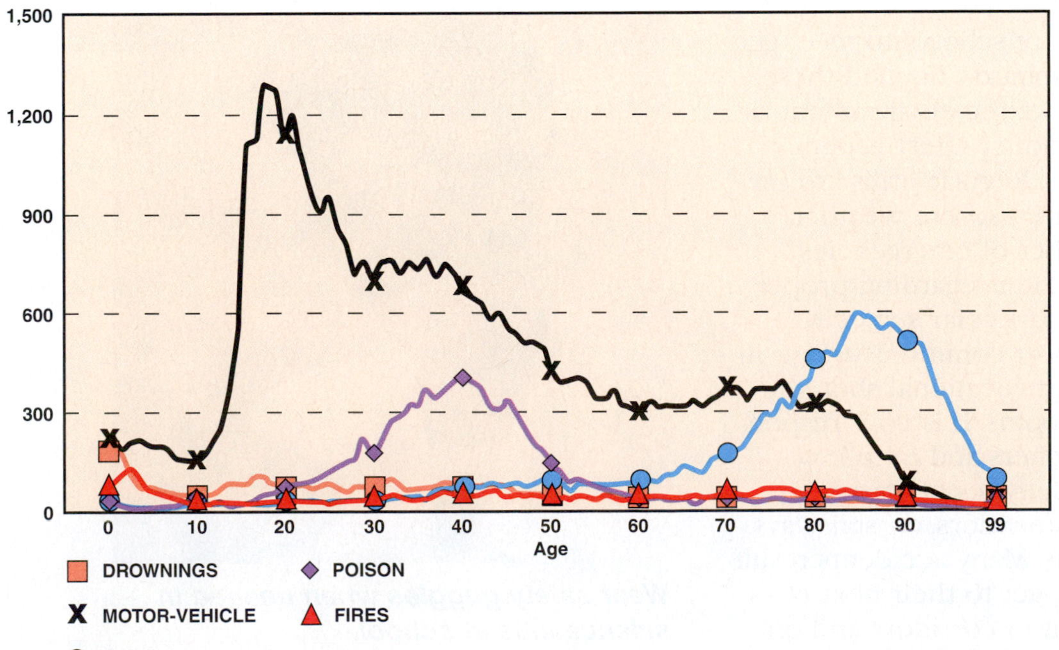

Figure 17-2 ***Leading causes of accidental death by age***

Courtesy of National Safety Council, Injury Facts 2000 Edition.

In many homes, the kitchen is the busiest and most dangerous room. Climbing and reaching cause many accidents. Use a ladder or a firm chair to reach objects in high places. Store appliances and other heavy objects on low shelves. Turn pot handles toward the back of the range to avoid burns and scalds. To prevent cuts, keep kitchen knives in a rack, not loose in a drawer. Kitchens often have types of floor coverings that can become very slick when wet. Immediately wipe up water, grease, or anything else spilled on the floor.

Falls are also one of the worst dangers in the bathroom. Install nonslip strips in the tub or shower and provide handrails to prevent falls while bathing.

Water is an excellent conductor of electricity. So, dry your hands thoroughly before using a hair dryer, razor, or other electrical appliance. A plugged-in radio or other appliance could electrocute you if it falls into water. To **electrocute** is to cause death by electric shock. Unless radios, televisions, and stereos are battery-operated, keep them out of the bathroom.

In the yard, lawn mowers are the cause of many injuries. Wear a shirt, pants, and heavy work shoes when operating a mower. Be alert to anything lying on the ground that might be thrown by running over it. Wear safety goggles when using string-type weed cutters.

At School

State and local laws require schools to meet certain health and safety standards. Beyond these, school officials try to make the environment as safe as possible. They conduct safety programs for students and teachers. Regular drills are carried out to prepare for fires, severe weather, earthquakes, or other types of emergencies. Teachers provide instruction regarding proper safety practices in their particular subjects.

Accidents in school most commonly occur in gyms, on athletic fields, in vocational shops, in science labs, and in art rooms. It is your responsibility to work with teachers and to follow their instructions in these types of classes. Accidents also occur in corridors, on stairways, and in regular classrooms. Many accidents result from students rushing to get to their next class or home. Stay to the right in corridors and on stairs. Do not run, crowd, or shove. In classrooms, keep your feet out of the aisles. Do not throw pens, pencils, or paper clips, which can cause serious eye injuries.

On the Job

Workplace safety has improved greatly over the years. In 1939, about 15,500 workers in the United States lost their lives on the job. Sixty years later, the workforce was more than three times as large, but the accidental death total was reduced by two-thirds. Still, about 5,100 workers were killed and about 3.8 million disabling injuries occurred in 1999 at work. Your safety responsibilities as an employee are as follows:

- ***Learn and obey rules.*** Supervisors and experienced workers have learned best how to do the job. Listen, observe, and follow their instructions. Always obey rules and regulations for shop or office safety practices.
- ***Consult procedures.*** If you do not know how to do something, stop and consult the procedures manual or rules. Or ask your supervisor or experienced coworkers.
- ***Watch for hazards.*** Many companies depend on employee assistance in identifying safety hazards and in changing safety procedures. Think about what you are doing. As you observe safety hazards or have ideas for improvements, make them known.

Wear safety goggles when needed in science labs at school.

COMMUNICATION AT WORK

SAFETY WARNINGS

At work, safety warnings appear on everything from cleansers to metal stamping machines. But do people read them? You might be surprised to learn that even doctors do not always read safety warnings. In 2000, the Food and Drug Administration proposed changing how prescription drug warnings were written because some doctors were not reading them. As a result, they were unaware of how side effects of drugs could harm certain patients. In fact, 7 of the 11 drugs taken off the market for safety problems from 1997 to 2000 were banned partly because they were being prescribed to the wrong patients despite label warnings.

Warnings are the last resort of manufacturers to ensure that people use their products safely. If a product cannot be designed so as to be completely safe, and if safeguards to prevent its misuse cannot be built in, then warnings must be provided. To be safe at work, always read warnings thoroughly before using a product and be sure you understand them.

- ***Report accidents and injuries.*** Accident reports are one of the best means of identifying safety hazards that need to be corrected. Participate in accident and injury reporting and investigation. Insurance benefits to the injured person sometimes depend on this.
- ***Become involved.*** Encourage other workers to act and work safely. Try to set a good example. Volunteer to participate in the shop, department, or company safety committee.
- ***Perform as trained.*** This is your most important responsibility regarding safety. Use the correct tools to perform your tasks. Allow enough time to finish a task safely. Avoid distractions. Follow operating procedures for using equipment and perform tasks according to training specifications. Do not operate machinery or drive under the influence of alcohol, drugs, or certain medications. Be neat and practice good housekeeping.

In Recreation

Many types of outdoor recreation have some element of hazard. The major causes of accidents are inexperience, overconfidence, and fatigue. General rules for safe recreation include keeping physically fit, learning the basic skills of the particular activity, selecting a safe area, using proper equipment and dress, avoiding overexertion, and never taking chances. Some activities present special problems.

Drowning is the fourth major cause of fatal accidents. Anyone who goes in, on, or near the water should learn how to swim. Two important rules to follow are never to swim alone and always to be aware of your limitations.

Boating accidents have become an increasing problem. The chief causes of boating accidents are speeding, poor judgment, and recklessness. Operator fault is a factor in half the boating

Know how to swim and use proper equipment for water sports.

casualties. Boaters should know the safety limitations of their craft and never exceed the safe speed. The U.S. Coast Guard establishes and enforces boating regulations. A boat operator should learn to follow such regulations.

Rifles, pistols, and shotguns are deadly weapons. Never point a gun at anyone. Guns should be unloaded before cleaning or storing. All firearms should be kept in a locked case or cabinet. Ammunition should be stored away from the firearms in a locked container.

On the Road

Today's automobiles and roads are built to be safer than ever before. More people are using seat belts. As a result, the death rate has dropped in relation to the number of miles driven. The current rate of less than 1.5 deaths per 100 million miles of travel compares with the rate of about 7 deaths in 1950. But the actual number of accidents keeps rising. This is due to the fact that there are more drivers and more autos on the road every year.

The causes of traffic accidents are difficult to determine. A number of things contribute to every accident. Improper driving is involved in more than 60 percent of all accidents. This includes speeding, failure to yield the right-of-way, following too closely, and driving left of the center line. Alcohol is a factor in about 40 percent of fatal accidents. Unsafe vehicles are a factor in at least 10 percent of accidents.

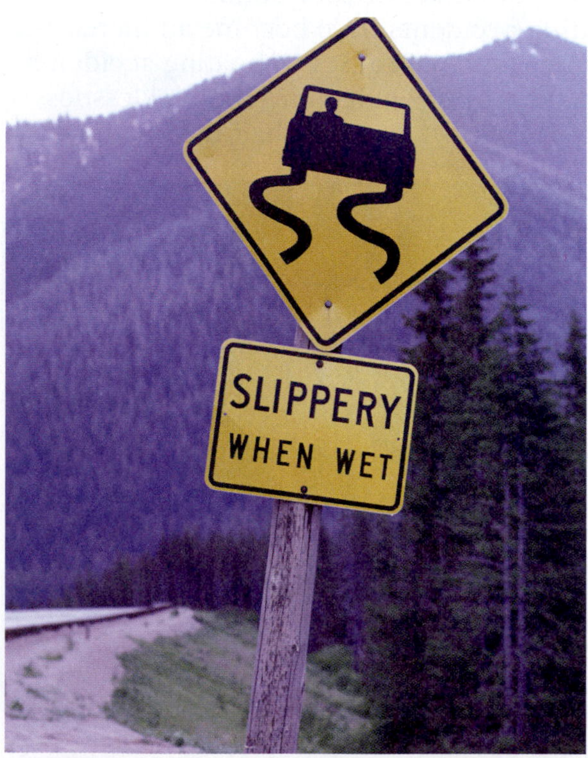

Adjust your speed to weather conditions.

WORKFORCE TRENDS

A recent study found that productivity in unionized firms with high-performance workplaces is about 10 percent higher than in comparable nonunion firms. Most union shops have adopted programs in which up to half the workers meet regularly to discuss workplace issues. When unionized firms allow production workers to share in the firms' profits, productivity reaches rates 20 percent higher than in nonunion firms.

Pamela cannot wait for classes to begin next semester. She will be enrolled in driver education. She looks forward to learning how to drive and being able to use the family car. She is wise to take driver education. It is one of the most valuable tools in traffic safety. People who have taken driver education have fewer accidents.

You can help prevent auto accidents and injuries by following commonsense rules. Use seat belts every time you drive. Obey the speed limit. Adjust your speed to traffic and weather conditions. Be a courteous driver. Stay a safe distance behind other vehicles and signal when you plan to turn or change lanes. Never drive under the influence of drugs or alcohol. Keep your car in good running order.

NATURAL DISASTERS

Many accidents and deaths result from natural disasters. A **natural disaster** is an uncontrollable event in nature that destroys life or property. Such tragedies often strike suddenly. Natural disasters differ from many other types of accidents in that they are not preventable. You can lessen the risks, however, if you know what to do during a flood, tornado,

Location	Type	Date	Number of Deaths
Galveston, TX	tidal wave	September 1900	6,000
Johnstown, PA	flood	May 1889	2,209
Florida	hurricane	September 1928	1,833
Ohio and Indiana	flood	March 1913	732
New England	hurricane	September 1938	657
Illinois	tornado	March 1925	606
Louisiana	hurricane	September 1915	500
San Francisco, CA	earthquake	April 1906	452
St. Francis, CA	flood (dam burst)	March 1928	450
Florida	hurricane	September 1935	409

Figure 17-3 ***The ten largest U.S. natural disasters in terms of fatalities. Why have there been fewer deaths in recent years?*** *Courtesy of National Safety Council.*

hurricane, or earthquake. Some safety rules apply to all natural disasters.

Flood conditions typically build up over hours and days. Leave a flood area as soon as a warning is announced. Do not be caught in a low-lying area. After returning from a flood, have electrical wiring and appliances checked before using them. Boil drinking water until health officials say that the water supply is safe.

Tornadoes occur most frequently in late spring and early summer. Be alert to threatening weather during these periods. If you hear a warning or see a tornado coming, go to a basement or inside room without windows. If you cannot move to another room, get under a heavy table or lie flat on the floor. If you are in a car, do not try to outrun the tornado. Get out of the car and lie in a ditch.

Hurricane forecasting has improved tremendously in recent years. Weather bureaus work closely with local radio and television stations to broadcast information about hurricanes and other weather-related problems. After learning of a hurricane warning, keep your radio or television on for further information. Follow the instructions of local officials. After the storm, avoid loose electrical power lines and report them immediately to the power company.

Earthquakes are the most sudden natural disaster. In an earthquake, you must react within seconds to the danger. If you are indoors, take cover under a table or desk. If you are outside, move away from buildings or other structures where you might be struck by falling objects. If you are in a car, stop immediately in a safe area and stay in the car.

LESSON 17.1 REVIEW

1. What is the leading cause of accidental death among teenagers and young adults?
2. What is the leading type (cause) of accidental death in the United States? Where (class) do most accidents occur?
3. Give three examples of how good housekeeping helps prevent home accidents.
4. What is the most important thing you can do on the job regarding safety?
5. Name the major causes of outdoor recreation accidents.
6. The number of accidents and deaths on the road has increased despite safer autos and roads. Why?
7. What types of improper driving practices cause auto accidents?
8. How do natural disasters differ from other types of accidents?

HIGH-GROWTH OCCUPATIONS FOR THE 21st CENTURY

Medical and Health Services Managers

The term *health services manager* describes individuals who plan, direct, coordinate, and supervise the delivery of health care. Future managers must be prepared to deal with integrated health care delivery systems, restructuring of work, technological innovations, and an increased focus on preventive care. They will be called upon to optimize efficiency in health care facilities and the quality of the health care provided. Increasingly, health services managers are expected to improve efficiency of services ranging, for example, from inpatient care to outpatient follow-up care.

Optimizing the efficient operation of health care facilities is the responsibility of health services managers.

Large facilities usually have several assistant administrators to handle daily decisions. They may direct activities in areas such as nursing, surgery, therapy, or medical records. Or they may direct activities in non-health areas such as finance, housekeeping, human resources, and information management. In smaller facilities, top administrators handle more of the daily operations. For example, many nursing home administrators manage personnel, finance, facility operations, and admissions.

Clinical managers have more specific responsibilities than generalists and have training and/or experience in a specific clinical area. For example, directors of physical therapy are experienced physical therapists. These managers establish and implement policies, objectives, and procedures for their departments; evaluate personnel; develop reports and budgets; and coordinate activities with other managers.

In group practices, managers work closely with physicians. A small group of 10 or 15 physicians might employ one administrator to oversee personnel matters, billing and collection, budgeting, planning, equipment outlays, and patient flow. A large practice of 40 or 50 physicians may have a chief administrator and several assistants, each responsible for different areas.

Health services managers in health maintenance organizations (HMOs) and other managed care settings perform functions similar to those in large group practices, except their staffs may be larger. In addition, they may do more work in the areas of community outreach and preventive care than managers of a group practice.

LESSON 17.2
PUBLIC SAFETY

OBJECTIVES

- NAME EXAMPLES OF GOVERNMENT AGENCIES AND PRIVATE ORGANIZATIONS THAT PROMOTE PUBLIC SAFETY
- STATE THE THREE E'S OF SAFETY

ORGANIZATIONS THAT PROMOTE SAFETY

Safety is everyone's business. The roles of employers and workers regarding safety and health in the workplace were explained in Chapter 8. In this chapter, you have learned more about the individual's safety responsibilities. In the following section, you will learn what government agencies and private organizations do to promote public safety.

Public safety refers to all efforts by federal, state, and local governments to protect persons and property. These include legislation, such as traffic ordinances and building codes, and regulatory activities, such as control of air pollution. Police and fire protection services are devoted to public safety. School and public transportation systems also play important safety roles. For instance, if you have flown in a commercial airliner, you know that the flight attendants provide safety instruction before each departure.

Government Agencies

Many agencies of the United States government are devoted to safety. The following are several examples. The Consumer Product Safety Commission protects consumers from unsafe household goods. The National Transportation Safety Board works to ensure the safety of all types of transportation. The Federal Aviation Administration creates and enforces air safety regulations. Safety in motor vehicles is the responsibility of the National Highway Traffic Safety Administration.

In Chapter 8, you learned how the Occupational Safety and Health Administration works to reduce hazardous job conditions. Most state, county, and city governments also have departments concerned with safety and health.

> **PERSONAL DECISIONS**
>
> You had a great time at the picnic. The weather was good and the food was delicious. You enjoyed seeing your old friends. It is now time to hop in the car for the long drive home.
>
> About halfway back to the city, the sky starts to darken. The wind begins to blow, and you see lightning in the distance. After a few more miles, the first drops of rain hit the windshield. The rain is soon coming down in torrents. It is only 4:30, but it is so dark that you have to turn on the headlights. The windshield wipers are going full speed. Even so, you can barely see the center line. You wonder what would happen if you had to stop suddenly. You would like to pull off the highway, but you are not very familiar with the road.
>
> **WHAT WOULD YOU DO?**

YOU'RE A WHAT? MUSIC THERAPIST

Most of us enjoy listening to music, and some of us play or perform music. But a *music therapist* uses music to help treat emotional, physical, or psychological conditions. Music can help individuals listen to each other, pay attention to each other, and work together. Aggressive children, for example, can learn to channel hostility by beating a drum. As members of a class band, they become interactive where they otherwise would not be.

A musical instrument can be a way to build connections between a therapist and a client. Through directed play with an instrument, for example, a child or other individual can have fun, develop an interest, and be successful. A child begins to realize, "If I can do this, maybe I can do other things." This becomes a starting point from which to build other skills and behaviors. ■

Private Organizations

A number of nonprofit, private organizations engage in activities to promote personal and public safety. The following are the most common. The National Safety Council collects and distributes information on every aspect of accident prevention. It publishes *Safety & Health* magazine and other periodicals; issues pamphlets, bulletins, and posters; and aids in developing community safety programs. The American Red Cross conducts instruction in first aid and water safety. It also issues safety information. Underwriters Laboratories tests and certifies electrical appliances, automobile and boat safety equipment, and burglar and fire alarms.

Figure 17-4 ***A UL seal on a product or component means that it has been checked for safety from fire, electric shock, and other hazards.***

Courtesy of Underwriters Laboratories.

THE THREE E'S OF SAFETY

The three E's of safety are engineering, education, and enforcement. Proper *engineering* of buildings, highways, machines, and appliances eliminates many accident hazards. Through *education*, people can be made aware of accident problems and ways to prevent them. *Enforcement* of safety rules prevents many accidents. The three E's of safety require expenditures of time and money. But these expenditures are small compared with the savings in human suffering, compensation costs, medical expenses, and lost time.

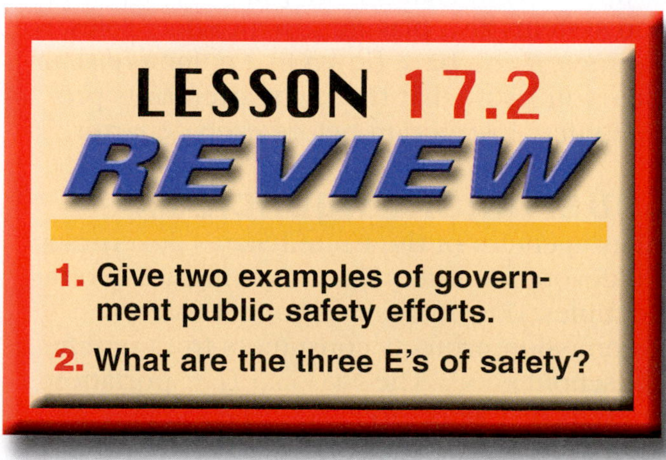

LESSON 17.2 REVIEW

1. Give two examples of government public safety efforts.
2. What are the three E's of safety?

FOCUS ON HEALTH AND SAFETY

SAFETY-BELT USE SAVES LIVES

This is what can happen if you do not buckle up when you drive.

The United States is the only industrialized nation in the world that does not require its citizens to buckle up. Even though there is no federal law, most states have passed their own safety-belt laws. The first state law took effect in New York in December 1984. By the end of the century, 49 states plus the District of Columbia had such legislation (the exception being New Hampshire). All 50 states and D.C. have mandatory child safety seat laws.

The simple reasons behind safety-belt laws are that they save lives and help prevent serious injury. Lap/shoulder belts reduce the risk of fatal injury to front seat passenger car occupants by 45 percent and by 60 percent for light truck occupants. The majority of the more than 2 million disabling traffic injuries suffered each year could be reduced to scratches, cuts, and bruises by buckling up. Most of the millions of minor traffic injuries could be avoided altogether.

Traffic deaths and injuries cost more than $180 billion a year in lost wages, medical expenses, insurance costs, and property damage. These costs could be cut sharply through safety-belt use.

When air bags are used with safety belts, fatalities are reduced by an additional 11 percent. Beginning in September 1997, all new passenger cars were required to have driver and passenger air bags. In 1998, the same requirement went into effect for light trucks.

THINK CRITICALLY

1. Discuss a traffic accident that you were involved in or know about. Were the people wearing seat belts?
2. Why do you think the United States is the only industrialized country in the world that does not have a national safety-belt law?

CHAPTER 17

Chapter in Brief

Lesson 17.1 *Accidents and Personal Safety*

A. An accident is an unplanned event. Accidents are the leading cause of death for teenagers and young adults. Almost all accidents can be prevented by eliminating unsafe behavior and conditions and by following basic safety rules.

B. Accidents are reported by type and class. The leading type (cause) of accidental death is motor vehicles. More accidents take place in and on motor vehicles than in any other class (location).

C. Safety refers to the precautions you take to prevent accidents. Know and practice rules for personal safety in the home, at school, on the job, in recreation, and on the road.

D. Natural disasters often strike suddenly. You can lessen the risks if you know what to do during a flood, tornado, hurricane, or earthquake. Some safety rules apply to all natural disasters.

Lesson 17.2 *Public Safety*

A. Safety is everyone's business. Individuals and employers are responsible for personal safety. Many federal government agencies and a number of private organizations are devoted to public and personal safety.

B. The three E's of safety are engineering, education, and enforcement. The costs of safety are small compared with the savings in human suffering, compensation costs, medical expenses, and lost time.

Activities

1. The instructor will divide the class into small groups. Each group should prepare a bulletin board display on workplace safety. The display should be changed periodically until each group has completed its assignment.
2. Assume you are at a party and some of the people have been drinking. The driver of your car has had too much to drink, but he insists on driving home. Do you allow him to do so? Do you ride with him? Role-play this situation with one person as the driver and the rest of the class as people at the party.
3. Have you heard of Students Against Driving Drunk (SADD)? Perhaps you have a chapter in your school or community. Invite a representative of SADD to the class to explain about the organization. Your class might take the lead in getting a chapter started in your school if you do not already have one. Visit the web site *http://www.saddonline.com/* for more information.
4. Assume that a cook trainee badly cut her hand in the kitchen. She had to be taken to the emergency room for stitches. Try to estimate the total cost of this accident. Include lost wages of the injured person and the driver, medical bills, lost productivity, and anything else you can think of.

REVIEW

5. Many government agencies and private organizations work in the field of personal and public safety. Select one of the following organizations. Read about it in an encyclopedia, on the Web, or in another source and prepare a short, written report.

- National Transportation Safety Board
- Federal Aviation Administration
- National Highway Traffic Safety Administration
- Consumer Product Safety Commission
- Occupational Safety and Health Administration
- United States Fire Administration
- Nuclear Regulatory Commission
- U.S. Coast Guard
- Federal Railroad Administration
- U.S. Forest Service
- Mine Safety and Health Administration
- National Bureau of Standards
- National Safety Council
- American Red Cross
- National Fire Protection Association
- Underwriters Laboratories
- Association for the Advancement of Automotive Medicine
- Insurance Institute for Highway Safety
- American Industrial Hygiene Association
- American Society of Safety Engineers

Word Power

On a separate sheet of paper, match each definition with the correct term. All definitions will be used, and a definition will be used only once.

6. An injury causing death, permanent disability, or any degree of temporary total disability beyond the day of the accident
7. Freedom from harm or the danger of harm
8. An unplanned event often resulting in personal injury, property damage, or both
9. All efforts by federal, state, and local governments to protect persons and property
10. An uncontrollable event in nature that destroys life or property
11. To cause death by electric shock

a. accident
b. disabling injury
c. electrocute
d. natural disaster
e. public safety
f. safety

Think Critically

12. You probably were not aware of the large number of safety agencies and organizations shown in the list at the top of this page. Why do you think so many different groups are working to improve personal and public safety?
13. Discuss all of the things your employer does to promote safety. Name as many things as you can. All class members should contribute. Your instructor may ask you to bring in copies of safety manuals or other printed material provided by the employer.
14. Think of an accident you had at home, at school, at work, or during a recreational activity. What was the cause? Discuss how the accident might have been avoided.

CHAPTER 18

LEADERSHIP SKILLS

LESSONS

PREVIEW

When you hear the word *leadership*, what comes to mind? Many people think of a particular person, such as a high government official, a sports figure, a person of wealth, or a prominent celebrity. This view equates leadership with status, wealth, office, and celebrity. But are all such people leaders? Of course not. In this chapter, a different view of leadership is provided.

THOUGHTS ON WORK

"Good work habits help develop an internal toughness and a self-confident attitude that will sustain you through every adversity and temporary discouragement."

Paul J. Fleyer

TAKING ACTION
LEADERSHIP OPPORTUNITIES

Tyrell and some friends in his business classes were wondering if there was a way that they could learn more about business and meet other students. They had heard about various national student organizations that they might join. They didn't know which group would be the right one. There weren't any organizations currently at their school.

Tyrell was talking about this with one of his business teachers, Mrs. Munoz. She asked if Tyrell was interested in forming a chapter of one of the national organizations at the school. If so, she said that it would take a lot of work. She volunteered to be an advisor or sponsor. She also gave Tyrell the names of some national organizations and information about each one.

Tyrell showed this information to his friends who were also interested in forming a chapter. They discussed the pros and cons of the various groups. At the end of the discussion, they had narrowed their choices to two organizations.

Mrs. Munoz suggested that Tyrell and his friends contact nearby chapters of the two groups to set up a meeting with representatives. She also suggested having a set of questions ready.

The students followed Mrs. Munoz's advice. Tyrell telephoned the local chapters and arranged for several members to meet with him and his friends. The representatives were friendly and informative. They provided an overview of the local chapters' activities and discussed the benefits of membership. Tyrell and the other students had many questions, which the members readily answered.

After the meetings, Tyrell and his friends voted on which organization to join. Tyrell went to tell Mrs. Munoz about their choice. Mrs. Munoz said that she would contact the national organization to find out how to set up a new chapter. She also recommended to Tyrell that he run for president of the chapter.

SUCCESS TIP

Step into a leadership role when you are needed.

THINK CRITICALLY

1. Why would a student want to join a national student organization?
2. Why would Mrs. Munoz recommend to Tyrell that he run for president of the chapter?

LESSON 18.1
ORGANIZATIONAL LEADERSHIP

OBJECTIVES

- *DEFINE* LEADERSHIP
- *LIST SIX TYPES OF LEADERSHIP SKILLS*
- *EXPLAIN THE PURPOSES OF A CAREER AND TECHNICAL STUDENT ORGANIZATION*
- *IDENTIFY CAREER AND TECHNICAL STUDENT ORGANIZATIONS*

WHAT IS LEADERSHIP?

Dozens of books have been written on the subject of leadership. One book notes the existence of more than 350 definitions of leadership. We focus here on only one part of leadership—that is, leadership within an organization.

Organizations are oriented toward achieving certain goals. An insurance company, for example, exists to sell insurance, meet the needs of its customers, and make a profit. This goal orientation is important for our definition of leadership. **Leadership** is the process of influencing people in order to accomplish the goals of the organization.

LEADERSHIP SKILLS

A number of writers have described the characteristics of effective leaders. John Zenger, president of a leadership training firm, identified six types of leadership skills. They are summarized in the following paragraphs.[1] These six types of skills represent actions and behaviors that most leaders seem to share. As you read about them, however, keep in mind that a given leader might not be strong in all of them. Also, be aware that leaders may exhibit these characteristics in different ways.

Leaders Are Good Communicators

Leaders enjoy communicating and use every opportunity to convey their message. A leader's message often has to be repeated again and again. Leaders are effective in large meetings or in one-on-one discussions. Some rely on written or other forms of communication. For instance, they may use models or drawings to get a point across. Leaders view information as something to be shared, not hoarded. They use interaction with others to gather and present information.

> **PERSONAL DECISIONS**
>
> Several friends approach you saying that they would like to nominate you for office in a career and technical student organization. You are pleased that they respect your ability. If you were elected, it would mean extra work and responsibility. You are not sure that you have the time or could do the job.
>
> **WHAT WOULD YOU DO?**

[1]Zenger, J. H. "Leadership: Management's Better Half," *Training*, December 1985, pp. 44–53.

A leader is not always the person in charge of a meeting or an organization. You can often identify the leader of a group by the way he or she communicates: Who is most persuasive? Who speaks with knowledge and authority? Who is able to express what others have been trying to say? To whom do others really listen? Who talks last on the subject?

Not all leaders are naturally gifted communicators. President Abraham Lincoln and Mahatma Gandhi, who led the Indian nationalist movement against British rule, were basically shy people. Deep beliefs about their missions drove them into the limelight. Lincoln and Gandhi gained the skill of communicating through self-discipline. They never shied away from communicating their visions and beliefs.

Leaders Develop Committed Followers

The best leaders recognize that they cannot do everything themselves. Leaders involve others. They ask for advice, information, and solutions to problems and provide positive feedback. They help make the people in the organization feel responsible for what happens.

By involving people, leaders encourage them to be self-reliant and to practice self-management. An example of this is the use of task groups, which was discussed in Chapter 9. Leaders understand the power of groups and what groups can accomplish. They meet frequently with their groups to encourage them and create a strong team spirit.

Leaders recognize that people are more productive if you help them to advance. Leaders share credit with their associates. Good work is praised and rewarded. Leaders foster and thrive on the success of others.

Leaders Set High Standards

Leaders are not satisfied with "average" and do not tolerate poor workmanship or shoddy performance. They challenge people to stretch and reach new heights. They set high standards and expect high-quality performance. At the same time, however, leaders tolerate honest mistakes.

Edwin Land, founder of Polaroid, said, "The first thing you naturally do is teach the person to feel that the undertaking is manifestly important and nearly impossible. . . . That draws out the kind of drives that make people strong." The leader's style *pulls* rather than *pushes* people.

Leaders Are Role Models

Many individuals earn a position of leadership because of their prior skills and successes. Leaders should represent the values of the units they lead. A captain of an athletic team is frequently the star player. A district sales manager is often a super salesperson.

Leaders know that people copy their behavior. If they work harder, the group will pick up the pace. If they slow down, the group pace slackens. Leaders send a clear signal by their own behavior. A few years ago when a major automobile manufacturer was facing a financial crisis, every employee was aware that the company CEO cut his own salary to $1 per year.

Contrast this example with that of another executive whose company faced a similar financial crisis. He called the employees together to inform them of layoffs and budget cuts. After the presentation, he flew in a private jet to a fancy resort for a weekend of golf. Workers resented his behavior. The company's financial problems grew worse as a result of low employee morale and reduced productivity. The executive was later fired.

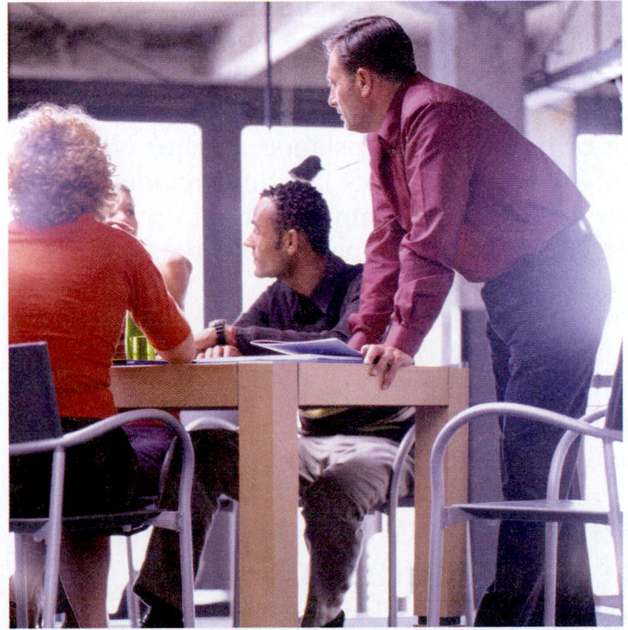

Leaders understand the power of groups and what groups can accomplish.

NOTHING BUT NET

Multimedia capabilities are a major reason why the Web is so widely used and enjoyed. Multimedia refers to any combination of text, images, sounds, video, and animation to communicate a message. Most multimedia files are stored on servers that users can access to read, listen to, or view the files. For example, when you click on a hypertext link, you might retrieve a current news story with photos. Streaming multimedia lets you hear or view continuous sound or video, such as a live concert or a sporting event. Multimedia applications on the Web are expected to increase in the future as faster Internet connections become available.

Leaders Search Out Key Issues and Problems

Leaders are good at uncovering and solving difficult problems. They want to know as much as possible about the matter. They ask tough questions, such as these: How did this happen? How long has this been going on? What is being done to correct this? Who is responsible for it?

Leaders know how to focus attention on an issue or problem. For instance, a major chemical company requires every lost-time accident to be reported to the company president on a daily basis. This has helped make the entire company more safety-conscious.

The president of a large computer chip manufacturer wanted to turn around the performance of a particular division. So he moved his desk next to the division's general manager. This was a clear signal that improvement was expected.

Leaders Are Involved in External Relations

Leaders do not stay chained to their desks. Leaders represent the organization and serve as links to the outside world. They get involved with outside groups. They participate in professional or trade associations. They are in frequent contact with other businesses and other leaders. They get involved in community activities and service organizations.

Summary

Only a few people will lead nations. Many more will lead companies, departments, or small groups. Some people start with better-developed abilities than others. But the skills described here can be learned by everyone. The next section introduces a type of organization that can help you develop leadership skills.

CAREER AND TECHNICAL STUDENT ORGANIZATIONS

Career and technical student organizations (CTSOs) are nonprofit, national organizations with state and local chapters. They are supported primarily by student-paid dues. Each organization is linked with an occupational area, such as business, home economics, or health occupations. These organizations function as an integral part of career and technical education.

Specific goals and objectives vary from one organization to another. But all have similar overall purposes: to develop leadership skills and good citizenship. The organizations provide students with opportunities to function as junior members of the trade or profession. Students apply skills learned in the classroom and interact with others in the occupational area. They develop a respect for the occupation and its **code of ethics** (rules for professional practice and behavior). Other outcomes include providing service, developing decision-making skills, and building confidence.

The national organization generally produces written guidelines for teacher/advisors, student handbooks, and promotional materials. In addition, the organization may sponsor national conferences, leadership development workshops, competitions, and award programs.

CTSO PROFILES

There are several different CTSOs. A brief profile of each CTSO follows.

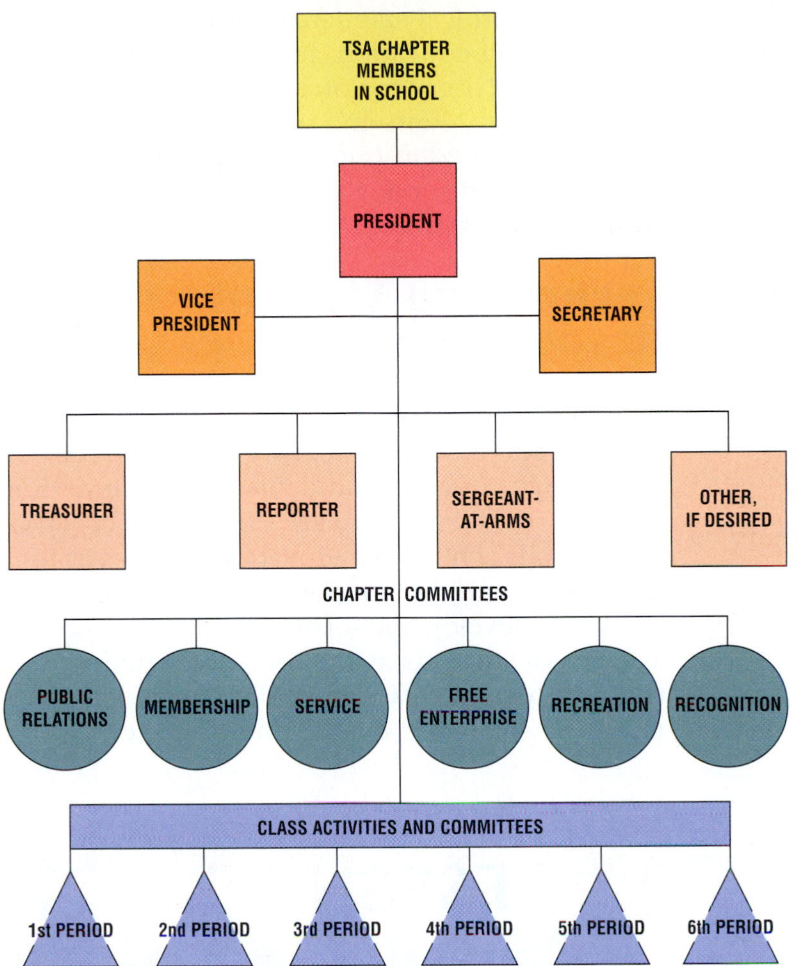

Figure 18-1 ***This chart shows how a local student organization might be structured.***
Courtesy of Technology Student Association.

Business Professionals of America (BPA)

This organization changed its name from the Office Education Association to reflect the fact that business education is incorporating new and expanding areas, such as middle management and entrepreneurship. The BPA is for students enrolled in business and office education programs at the secondary and postsecondary levels. Its mission is to help prepare a world-class workforce through development of leadership, citizenship, academic, and technological skills.

Distributive Education Clubs of America (DECA)

DECA is an organization for future leaders in marketing, merchandising, and management. One purpose of the organization is to contribute to occupational competence in distributive education. It also promotes understanding of and appreciation for the responsibilities of citizenship in a free enterprise system. Memberships in the following divisions are available: high school, two-year postsecondary, college, alumni, and professional.

Future Business Leaders of America-Phi Beta Lambda, Inc. (FBLA-PBL)

FBLA-PBL seeks to bring business and education together in a positive working relationship. The association has several divisions. The purposes of FBLA (high school students) and FBLA Middle Level (junior high, middle, and intermediate school students) are to develop vocational and career-supportive competencies and to promote civic and personal responsibilities. PBL is for postsecondary students. Its purpose is to provide opportunities for junior college and college students to develop competencies for business and office occupations or business teacher education.

National FFA Organization

First known as the Future Farmers of America (FFA), this group was founded in 1928 to make instruction more interesting and practical by combining work experience, competitive livestock judging, and agricultural leadership development activities with classroom instruction. It is part of the high school vocational agriculture/agribusiness instruction program that prepares students for careers in agriculture. The National FFA Organization encourages entrepreneurship, positive work attitudes, and responsible citizenship.

Family, Career and Community Leaders of America (FCCLA)

FCCLA is for young men and women in family and consumer sciences education in public and private schools through Grade 12. It focuses on a variety of youth concerns, including teen pregnancy, parenting, family relationships, substance abuse, peer pressure, environment, nutrition and fitness, teen violence, and career exploration. Involvement in FCCLA offers members the opportunity to expand their leadership potential and develop skills for life.

Health Occupations Students of America (HOSA)

The health care system needs workers who are technically skilled, people-oriented, and capable of providing leadership as members of a team. HOSA enhances the delivery of quality health care and promotes health care careers. Activities focus on leadership, social skills, community service, career preparation, and fund-raising. HOSA is for secondary, postsecondary, and adult students in health occupations programs.

National Young Farmer Educational Association (NYFEA)

NYFEA educates agricultural leaders and helps recruit people into agricultural careers. This group emphasizes leadership training, business skill development, and community service. Activities such as contests and community service projects allow individuals to apply what they have learned. Membership and activities are open to all interested people.

National Postsecondary Agricultural Student Organization (PAS)

PAS promotes individual growth, leadership, and strong personal ethics for students who are pursuing agricultural careers. PAS is available to students in approved postsecondary institutions offering associate degrees or vocational diplomas and/or certificates.

SkillsUSA-VICA

SkillsUSA-VICA prepares America's high-performance workers. This group promotes leadership, teamwork, citizenship, and character development. It builds and reinforces self-confidence, work attitudes, and communications skills. SkillsUSA-VICA emphasizes total quality at work, high ethical standards, superior work skills, lifelong education, and pride in the dignity of work. The organization serves high school and college students and professional members who are enrolled in training programs in technical, skilled, and service occupations, including health occupations.

Technology Student Association (TSA)

Once known as the American Industrial Arts Student Association, TSA is the only student organization devoted exclusively to the needs of technology education students. The organization is open to students who are enrolled in or have completed technology education courses at the elementary, middle, and high school levels. Activities develop the leadership and personal abilities of students as they relate to the industrial and technical world. TSA helps students make informed and meaningful career choices.

LESSON 18.1 REVIEW

1. Organizations are oriented toward achieving certain goals. Name an organization (other than the examples in the book) and list two of its goals.
2. In what way is information viewed by a leader?
3. How do leaders involve other members of the organization?
4. Give an example of how a leader can serve as a role model.
5. What are the general purposes of a career and technical student organization?
6. What types of activities are conducted by career and technical student organizations?

HIGH-GROWTH OCCUPATIONS FOR THE 21st CENTURY

Nursing and Psychiatric Aides

Nursing and *psychiatric aides* help care for physically or mentally ill, injured, disabled, or infirm individuals confined to hospitals, nursing or residential care facilities, and mental health settings. Nursing aides, also known as *nursing assistants*, *geriatric aides*, and *hospital attendants*, perform routine tasks under the supervision of nursing and medical staff. They answer patients' call bells, deliver messages, serve meals, make beds, and help patients eat, dress, and bathe. Aides may also provide skin care to patients; check temperature, pulse, respiration, and blood pressure; and help patients get in and out of bed and walk. They may escort patients to operating and examining rooms, keep patients' rooms neat, set up equipment, or store and move supplies. Aides observe patients' conditions and report any changes to the medical staff.

In nursing homes, nursing aides interact with elderly residents in positive ways.

Aides employed in nursing homes are often the principal caregivers, having more contact with residents than other members of the staff. Since some residents stay in a nursing home for months or years, aides develop ongoing relationships with them and interact with them in a positive, caring way.

Psychiatric aides are also known as *mental health assistants* and *psychiatric nursing assistants*. They care for mentally impaired or emotionally disturbed individuals. They work under a team that may include psychiatrists, psychologists, psychiatric nurses, social workers, and therapists. In addition to helping patients dress, bathe, groom, and eat, psychiatric aides socialize with them and lead them in educational and recreational activities. Psychiatric aides may play games such as cards with patients, watch television with them, or participate in group activities such as sports or field trips. They observe patients and report any physical or behavioral signs that might be important for the professional staff to know. They also accompany patients to and from wards for examination and treatment.

LESSON 18.2
PARLIAMENTARY PROCEDURE

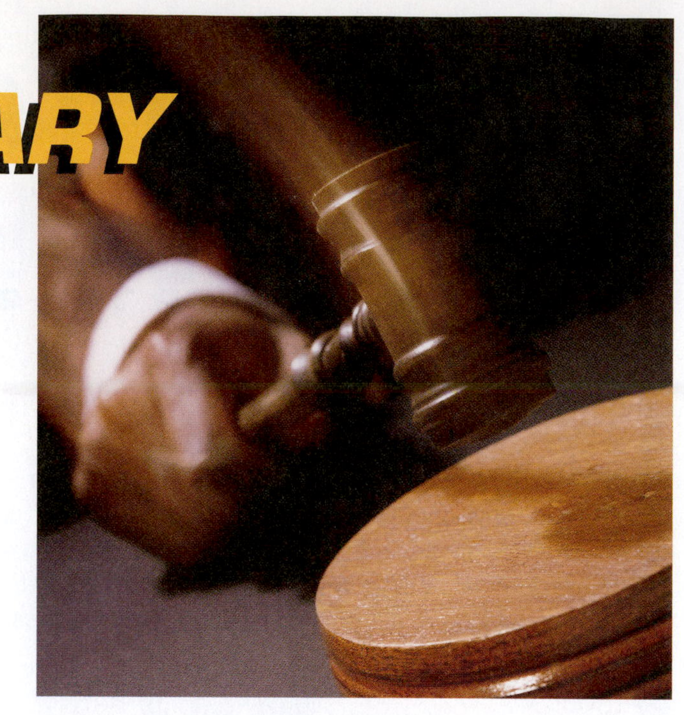

OBJECTIVES

- *DEMONSTRATE KNOWLEDGE OF HOW GROUPS THAT FOLLOW PARLIAMENTARY PROCEDURE ARE ORGANIZED*
- *EXPLAIN WHAT HAPPENS IN A MEETING UNDER PARLIAMENTARY PROCEDURE*

BASIC PRINCIPLES

Parliamentary procedure is a way to conduct a meeting in a fair and orderly manner. It is called parliamentary because it comes from the rules and customs of the British Parliament. The United States Congress and other lawmaking bodies follow parliamentary procedure. The rules are used in simpler form by business and professional groups, school organizations, and social clubs. The basic principles of parliamentary procedure are majority rule, protection of the minority, and the orderly consideration of one subject at a time.

Bylaws

An organization operating according to parliamentary procedure adopts a set of bylaws. The **bylaws** define the basic characteristics of the organization and describe how it will operate. They explain qualifications for membership and procedures for selection of members. The bylaws state the duties of officers and how they will be elected. They also explain how committees will be formed and what their functions will be. All members of an organization should be provided with a copy of the bylaws.

Officers and Committees

An organization usually elects a president (or chair), a vice president, a secretary, and a treasurer. Some groups also elect a sergeant-at-arms or other officers. The president presides at meetings and supervises the work of other officers and committees. The vice president assists the president and chairs meetings when the president is absent. The secretary notifies members of meetings, keeps the minutes, and takes care of all correspondence and committee reports. The treasurer keeps a record of income and expenses and prepares the financial reports. The sergeant-at-arms maintains order during meetings.

WORKFORCE TRENDS

American workers are healthier and more productive than ever. Young workers are better protected against workplace injuries. These gains benefit not only workers and their families but also employers. Employers can focus resources on increasing their competitive positions, rather than paying workers' compensation for preventable injuries and illnesses.

MATH CONNECTION

Suppose your career and technical student organization is voting on an amendment to change the bylaws. For the motion to be approved, two-thirds of those present must vote in favor of it. The 25 members at today's meeting just took a vote on a motion, and 20 voted for it. Should the motion be approved?

SOLUTION

Convert two-thirds to a percentage by dividing 2 by 3. Then calculate the percentage of those who voted in favor of the motion by dividing the number who voted for it by the number present.

$2/3 = 2 \div 3 = 0.67 = 67\%$

Percentage of members who voted for the motion: $20 \div 25 = 0.8 = 80\%$

Since 80% is larger than 67%, the motion should be approved.

Most organizations elect officers once a year. This is often done at the first meeting of the new year. A member may nominate a fellow member. Usually, after two or more people have been nominated, the voting takes place by secret ballot. The person receiving the majority vote is the elected officer. A **majority** is a vote of at least one more than half of the people who vote. If no candidate receives a majority, balloting is continued until one receives a majority.

Certain duties of an organization are handled by committees. Most organizations have two types of committees. One type, the standing committee, deals with regular and continuing matters, such as membership and finance. A second type, the special committee, is formed whenever it is necessary to work on a specific matter. Examples might be to plan a social event or to revise the bylaws. Special committees break up when their task is done. Committees are either appointed or elected according to the bylaws.

HOLDING A MEETING

Most organizations require that a quorum be present before a meeting may begin. A **quorum** is a majority of the total membership. An organization's bylaws usually provide for an **order of business**. This is the standard series of steps followed in a meeting. A typical order of business is shown in Figure 18-2 on page 262. A meeting actually proceeds according to a list of items to be taken care of at that particular meeting, which is called an **agenda**. A typical agenda for a career and technical student organization is shown in Figure 18-3 on page 263.

An important part of any meeting is making, discussing, and disposing of motions. A **motion** is a brief statement of a proposed action. There are four types of motions:

- ***Main motions*** are the tools used to introduce new business.
- ***Secondary motions*** provide ways of modifying or disposing of main motions.
- ***Incidental motions*** arise out of business being conducted.
- ***Privileged motions*** deal with the welfare of the group, rather than any specific proposal.

The most common motions are summarized in Figure 18-4, on page 264. The motions are listed in order of **precedence**, or rank of priority.

ETHICAL DECISIONS

Your career and technical student organization has had a successful year fund-raising. You are meeting to discuss how to spend the chapter's money. A motion is on the floor to authorize spending it for a party. There is a lot of support for the motion. You would enjoy a party, but you think it is an inappropriate way to use the money. You are not sure if you should speak against the motion.

WHAT WOULD YOU DO?

PARTS OF A CHAPTER MEETING

It is customary for every group to adopt a standard order of business for the meeting. When the organization's by-laws do not provide for or require a specific order, the following is in order.

1. **Call to Order**
   "Will the meeting please come to order."
2. **Roll Call**
   "Will the secretary please call the roll."
3. **Reading and Approval of Minutes**
   "Will the secretary please read the minutes of the last meeting." The minutes are read and the chair asks:

   "Are there any corrections to the minutes?" The chair pauses to hear any corrections offered, if there are none, the chair says, "There being no corrections, the minutes will stand approved as read."

   If there are corrections, the chair recognizes the correction(s) and asks, "Are there further corrections to the minutes?" If there are none, the chair states, "There being no further corrections, the minutes will stand approved as corrected."
4. **Adoption of Agenda**
   This step is provided to insure that (1) all persons are aware of what has been proposed for discussion at the meeting; (2) that all persons are given the opportunity to have whatever matter(s) they feel is (are) important to the organization placed on the agenda for discussion; and (3) to provide a limit to and order for the matters to be discussed at the meeting.

   To achieve this, the presiding officer states, "The following items are proposed for discussion at this meeting." After reading the list of proposed agenda items, the presiding officer asks, "Are there other matters that should be discussed at this meeting?" If there are additional matters requiring discussion, the chair places them in their proper positions on the agenda.

   The chair, after insuring that all pertinent matters will come before the meeting, reads the entire agenda and states, "There being no other matters that should come before this meeting, the agenda for this meeting will stand as read."
5. **Report of Officers and Standing Committees**
   Officers, boards, or standing committees should be called upon to report in the order in which they are mentioned in the constitution or by-laws of the organization.
6. **Report of Special Committees**
7. **Unfinished Business**
   "We have now come to unfinished business. Our agenda lists the following matters as unfinished business." The chair reads from the agenda and states, "We will hear these matters in the order in which they have been mentioned."
8. **New Business**
   "We have now come to new business. Our agenda lists the following matters as new business . . ." The chair reads from the agenda and states, "We will hear them in the order in which they were mentioned."
9. **Program**
   Programs such as exhibitions, demonstrations, etc., which are incidental to the business meeting, will be scheduled for presentation at this time.
10. **Adjournment**
    Unqualified form:

    Proposer moves for adjournment; motion is seconded; chair calls for a vote; action depends upon majority vote. The motion cannot be discussed.

    Qualified form:

    Proposer moves for adjournment within a definite time or adjournment to meet again at a specified time; motion is seconded; the chair calls for discussion; a vote is taken; action depends upon majority vote; can allow for legal continuation of the meeting.

Figure 18-2 ***Typical parts of a chapter meeting***

Courtesy of Technology Student Association.

PLANNING AND CONDUCTING A MEETING

Planning and conducting a meeting are two tasks that every member should be able to perform correctly and with ease. To do this, certain knowledge and skills should become part of your repertoire.

The President, with assistance from the chapter officers, should meet prior to the time of the regularly scheduled meeting to plan the agenda. Minutes from the previous meeting should be examined so that any unfinished business can be noted for discussion at the upcoming meeting.

The agenda is a list of those activities to be engaged in and those items of business to be brought before the membership for discussion at the next meeting. A standard order of business is used when preparing an agenda. You should be aware of and apply the order of business in the planning and conducting of all meetings. A typical chapter agenda is shown below.

SCHOOL CHAPTER AGENDA

DATE September 16, 20--

TIME 1:30 p.m.

PLACE Mills Godwin High School

I. **CALL TO ORDER**

II. **OPENING CEREMONY**(Roll call, introduction of visitors)
- Visitors: Mr. Joseph Long, Miss Laura East

III. **READING OF MINUTES**

IV. **OFFICER AND STANDING COMMITTEE REPORTS**
- Treasurer's Report
- Enterprising/Finance Committee to report on fund-raising activities

V. **SPECIAL COMMITTEE REPORTS** (none)

VI. **UNFINISHED BUSINESS**
- Halloween Dance to be held October 30–Selection of band

VII. **NEW BUSINESS**
- The purchase of TSA blazers for chapter offices

VIII. **ANNOUNCEMENTS**
- Members who have not turned in their money for the trip to Washington, D.C. must do so today.
- The Executive Committee will meet on September 25 in the Technology Education Lab at 12:00 noon. Bring your lunch with you. Beverages will be served.

IX. **PROGRAM**
- Miss Laura East, from the State TSA office, will speak on the Virginia TSA Annual Conference to be held in May.

X. **CLOSING CEREMONY**

***Figure 18-3* A typical chapter agenda**

Courtesy of Technology Student Association.

Action	Statement
Privileged Motions	
Adjourn the meeting	"I move that we adjourn."
Recess the meeting	"I move we recess until . . ."
Secondary Motions	
Postpone consideration of a matter without voting on it	"I move we table the motion."
End debate	"I move the previous question."
Have a matter studied further	"I move we refer this matter to a committee."
Amend a motion	"I move that this motion be amended by . . ."
Main Motions	
Introduce business	"I move that . . ."
Resume consideration of a previously tabled motion	"I move we take from the table . . ."
Reconsider a matter already disposed of	"I move we reconsider our action relative to . . ."
Incidental Motions	
Raise a question about parliamentary procedure	"Point of order."
Withdraw a motion	"I ask permission to withdraw the motion."
Seek information about the matter at hand	"Point of information."

Figure 18-4 **Common motions listed in order of their priority**

When the group is considering a main motion, secondary motion, or privileged motion, no motion listed below it may be introduced. Any motion listed above it, however, may be introduced. Incidental motions have no precedence. They must be decided or disposed of before returning to the business under consideration. Each motion must be disposed of in some way before another item of business can be taken up.

Different rules apply to a motion regarding whether it needs to be seconded, whether the motion is debatable, whether it can be amended, and so on. (To second a motion is to state your support for it, so that discussion or voting may begin.) An organization often has a **parliamentarian** who advises the presiding officer (chair) on matters of procedure. Even though motions differ, the general procedure is the same.

To make a motion, a member obtains the floor by rising and addressing the chair. The chair recognizes the member by announcing his or her name. The motion is stated. Usually, it must be seconded by another member. After this, the chair restates the motion for the benefit of all members. It is then open to debate (discussion).

Debate continues until all members who wish to speak have had an opportunity. Members then vote on the motion. Those in favor of the motion say "Aye"; those against the motion say "No." If the majority of members vote to accept the motion, it is approved.

Parliamentary procedure does not have to be mysterious and complicated. However, it is something that takes time to learn. One of the best ways to learn it is to join and participate in a career and technical student organization.

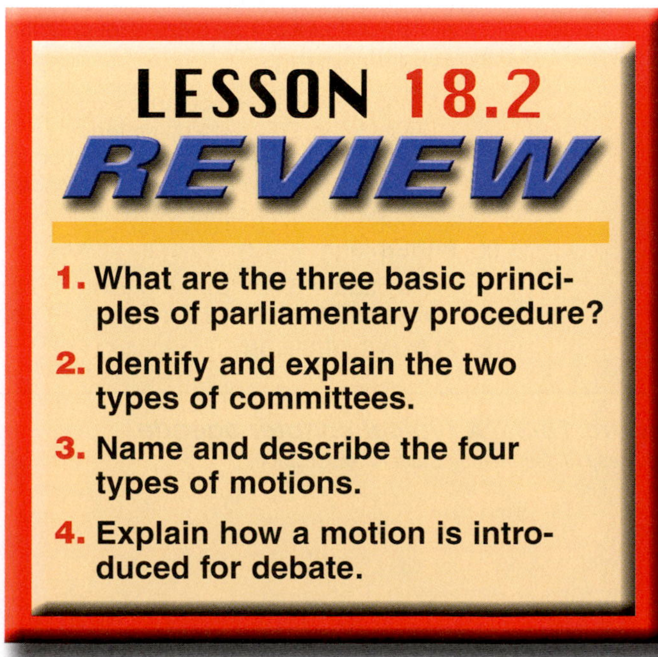

LESSON 18.2 REVIEW

1. What are the three basic principles of parliamentary procedure?
2. Identify and explain the two types of committees.
3. Name and describe the four types of motions.
4. Explain how a motion is introduced for debate.

FOCUS ON THE WORKER

TRADE AND PROFESSIONAL ASSOCIATIONS

Trade and professional associations are an important part of our economic, social, and working lives. A trade association seeks to advance common business interests of members. Some trade associations cover a business function, such as manufacturing, distribution, or retailing. For instance, several retail stores may form a trade association. Others are based on the types of goods or services produced. Peanut farmers, service station operators, or restaurant owners, for example, may form an association.

A professional association is made up of people with a common occupational background.

The most important goal of a trade association is more income from its product or service. Activities of trade associations may include advertising, sponsoring research on new products, and promoting high standards for products, services, or members. To get its message out, a group may produce pamphlets or sponsor tours. It may also publish a magazine for members and hold yearly conventions. For some trade associations, lobbying for favorable laws (trying to persuade public officials to support them) is a major activity. To pay for these activities, trade associations collect dues from members.

A professional association is made up of people with a common occupational background such as teacher, pilot, secretary, or chef. Members often need to have an academic degree, license, or certificate to join an association. Professional associations inform members about new developments and issues. They publish journals and hold meetings and conventions. Some associations have student memberships. If a professional association related to your occupation is available, join it. Most individual associations maintain web sites that are easily located using a standard Internet search engine.

THINK CRITICALLY

1. What are some advantages of joining a trade or professional association besides those mentioned above?
2. Is lobbying a good idea? Why or why not?

CHAPTER 18

Chapter in Brief

Lesson 18.1 *Organizational Leadership*

A. Leadership is the process of influencing people in order to accomplish the goals of the organization. John Zenger identifies six types of leadership skills: Leaders are good communicators, develop committed followers, set high standards, are role models, search out key issues and problems, and are involved in external relations.

B. Leadership skills can be learned by everyone.

C. Career and technical student organizations (CTSOs) are an integral part of career and technical education. Students in CTSOs function as junior members of a trade or profession, applying skills learned in the classroom and interacting with others in an occupational area.

Lesson 18.2 *Parliamentary Procedure*

A. Parliamentary procedure is a way to conduct a meeting in a fair and orderly manner. The basic principles of parliamentary procedure are majority rule, protection of the minority, and the orderly consideration of one subject at a time.

B. Bylaws define the basic characteristics of the organization and describe how it will operate. An organization usually elects a president, vice president, secretary, and treasurer. Certain duties of an organization are handled by standing and special committees.

C. An important part of any meeting is making, discussing, and disposing of motions. There are four types of motions: main, secondary, incidental, and privileged. Each motion must be disposed of in some way before another item of business can be taken up.

Activities

1. Identify a famous person who has been referred to as a leader. Rate her or him in relation to each of the six types of leadership skills. Use a scale of high, average, and low. What is the overall rating? Considering how leadership is described in this chapter, could the person be called a leader?
2. Find out the types of career and technical student organizations in your school. For each, list the qualifications for membership and invite a representative to talk to the class. Select an organization of interest and join it.
3. If your school does not have a CTSO in your occupational area, find an organization that interests you and determine how to start a chapter by writing to the national office or visiting its web site.
4. Practice parliamentary procedure by role-playing a meeting. Elect a president, vice president, and secretary. The officers develop an agenda, which the secretary prepares and distributes. Conduct a meeting according to the agenda. Focus on making, discussing, and disposing of sample motions.

REVIEW

5. Suppose a member of your CTSO moves to end a debate. Two-thirds of those present must vote in favor of this motion for it to be approved. If 20 people are present, and 12 people vote for the motion, should it be approved?

Word Power

On a separate sheet of paper, match each definition with the correct term. All definitions will be used, and a definition will be used only once.

6. The process of influencing people in order to accomplish the goals of the organization
7. A standard series of steps followed in a meeting
8. In parliamentary procedure, the order of priority among the four types of motions used in a meeting
9. Printed information that defines the basic characteristics of an organization and describes how it will operate
10. Nonprofit, national organizations with state and local chapters that exist to develop leadership skills and good citizenship among members
11. A brief statement of a proposed action by a participant in a meeting
12. A list of items to be taken care of at a particular meeting, by which the meeting proceeds
13. A vote of at least one more than half of the people who vote
14. The formal rules used to conduct a meeting in a fair and orderly manner
15. A majority of the total membership of an organization
16. A group member who advises the chair on correct parliamentary procedure
17. Rules for professional practice and behavior

a. agenda
b. bylaws
c. career and technical student organizations (CTSOs)
d. code of ethics
e. leadership
f. majority
g. motion
h. order of business
i. parliamentarian
j. parliamentary procedure
k. precedence
l. quorum

Think Critically

18. A characteristic of leaders is the ability to develop committed followers. There have been instances throughout history in which individuals have gained committed followers for illegal or immoral purposes. Think of some historic or present examples. Should such people be called leaders?
19. A person may be named head of an organization or be elected to an office without being a leader. Discuss some of the things, other than leadership, that allow people to rise in an organization.
20. Strong leaders may be scattered throughout an organization. Identify and discuss as many examples as you can.
21. You have probably been in meetings that dragged on without anything being accomplished. Discuss how parliamentary procedure might prevent this.
22. It has been said that "If you want to manage somebody, manage yourself." Discuss the meaning of this statement.

CHAPTER 19

COMPUTER AND TECHNOLOGY SKILLS

LESSONS

19.1 *How Computers Work*

19.2 *Computer Hardware and Software*

19.3 *The Internet and the Future of Computers*

PREVIEW

Computers are found in many workplaces. There are few jobs that do not require some computer skills, and new jobs involving computers are created every day. The better you understand computers and how they can help you do your job, the more valuable you will be as an employee.

THOUGHTS ON WORK

"If your work is becoming uninteresting, so are you. Work is an inanimate thing and can be made lively and interesting only by injecting yourself into it. Your job is only as big as you are."

George C. Hubbs

TAKING ACTION

COMPUTERS ARE EVERYWHERE

My-thuh wakes up on a typical morning and gets ready for work. Every morning she checks her e-mail. Her friends like to stay in touch using e-mail. My-thuh responds to a few e-mails and then remembers that she has to get gas that morning.

At the local gas station, My-thuh can use her credit card at the pump to pay for her purchase. My-thuh likes this because it saves her time. Since she pays her credit card bill in full every month, using her credit card does not cost My-thuh any extra money.

At work, My-thuh says hello to a few coworkers on the way to her cubicle. She works as a customer service representative for a major department store chain. My-thuh must log on to the computerized phone system to begin to take calls. The phone system keeps track of how many phone calls she takes, how long each call is, and when she logs off the system for a break.

My-thuh takes calls from salesclerks who are trying to open store credit accounts for customers. Customers usually want to have their credit applications processed in minutes. To do this, My-thuh takes the customer's credit information and enters it into her computer. A computer program accesses the customer's credit information. If the customer's information fits the acceptable credit guidelines, the application is approved. If not, the application may take longer to process or may be rejected.

My-thuh also logs credit application acceptances, rejections, and delays for further processing into a computer database. Her supervisor uses this database to track the results of credit requests.

At the end of the day, My-thuh stops at a local grocery store to pick up some groceries. She has a store card that gives her a discount at the checkout. She knows that when she uses her card, a computer is recording information about her buying habits, but that is fine with her. My-thuh receives coupons in the mail from the grocery store chain for products she regularly buys.

SUCCESS TIP

Learn how to use computers at work, school, and home.

THINK CRITICALLY

1. How would My-thuh's day be different without computers?
2. How do you use computers at work, school, or home?

LESSON 19.1
HOW COMPUTERS WORK

- *EXPLAIN THE IMPORTANCE OF KEYBOARDING SKILLS*
- *SUMMARIZE HOW A COMPUTER WORKS*

KEYBOARDING SKILLS

The previous four chapters dealt with knowledge and skills that have always been important on the job. To those we must now add what is called computer literacy. **Computer literacy** is a general knowledge of what computers are, how they work, and for what they can be used. Chances are that your future work will involve some contact with computers.

Wayne graduated from high school without learning much about computers. He lost out on several good jobs after interviewers learned that he could not use a computer. Wayne got the message and signed up for a computer course.

Wayne got a job in the parts department of a plumbing supply business. In this job, he uses a computer more often than a pen. He orders parts, does billings, keeps inventory, and does dozens of other tasks on the computer. He wonders what it must have been like in the parts department before the computers arrived.

A **computer** is an electronic tool. Like other tools, it helps people do various kinds of work. It can do simple arithmetic and can solve complex mathematical problems. With an optical device, it can read a printed page and write (display) text and graphics on a screen. If it has a voice synthesizer, it can even "talk." It can direct equipment to do tasks. Unlike people, a computer can work 24 hours a day without getting tired. It runs on little electricity and seldom breaks down. It can

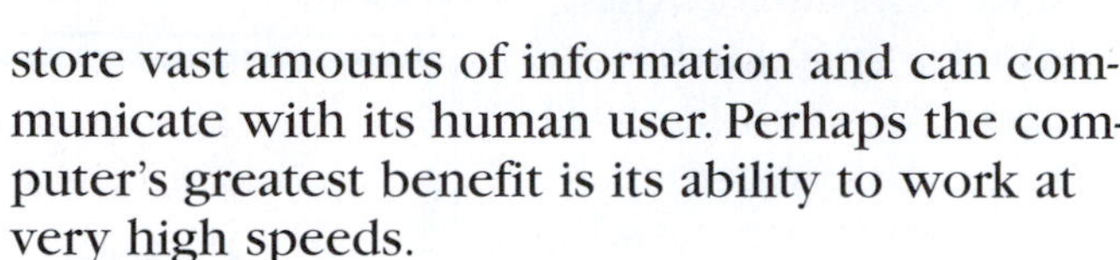

store vast amounts of information and can communicate with its human user. Perhaps the computer's greatest benefit is its ability to work at very high speeds.

Like Wayne, you will probably need to learn keyboarding skills if you have not already. **Keyboarding skills** means the ability to type and to give commands to a computer using a keyboard.

The arrangement of letters and numbers on the keyboard is the same as for a typewriter. Keyboard operation varies a little depending on the type of computer and the software. Still, for all keyboards, the basic commands and procedures are similar. No matter what type of business or industry you work in, you will benefit by knowing how to use a computer keyboard.

UNDERSTANDING COMPUTERS

In very simple terms, the computer works in three steps: (a) it receives instructions, (b) it does tasks according to these instructions, and (c) it shares the results:

Input → Processing → Output

The computer solves problems much as people do. For instance, let's compare how you and the computer would add $20 + 43$.

Input

You receive information by either reading or hearing the numbers. The computer receives information in the form of electronic signals.

Processing

You draw upon your knowledge of arithmetic in your memory. You bring together the data (20, 43) and the method (addition) and come up with the answer.

The computer draws upon a program stored in its memory. A **program** consists of instructions on how to solve a certain problem or do a certain task. Bringing the data from input and the instructions from memory, the computer adds the numbers.

Output

You report the result (63) by writing down the answer or saying it out loud. The computer changes the result from electronic language to human language. It presents the result in print, sound, or another form.

Now let's go beyond this simple explanation. To do this, we will need to relabel the second step and divide it into three parts. The input-processing-output sequence now appears as follows:

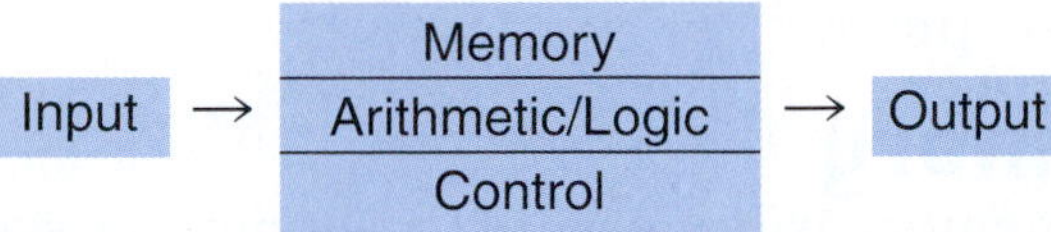

Here we have the workings of a modern computer system: (a) input, (b) memory, (c) arithmetic and logic, (d) control, and (e) output.

Input

Input devices let users enter information and change it into electronic signals the computer can use. The most common input device is a keyboard. Another frequently used device is a mouse. Some other input devices are modems, light pens, touchpads, scanners, and magnetic tapes and disks (such as hard disks, 3.5-inch floppies, and Zip disks). A **modem** is an electronic device for transmitting computer data over standard telephone lines or fiberoptic cable.

Three kinds of input are fed into the computer. One is programs. The others are data (text

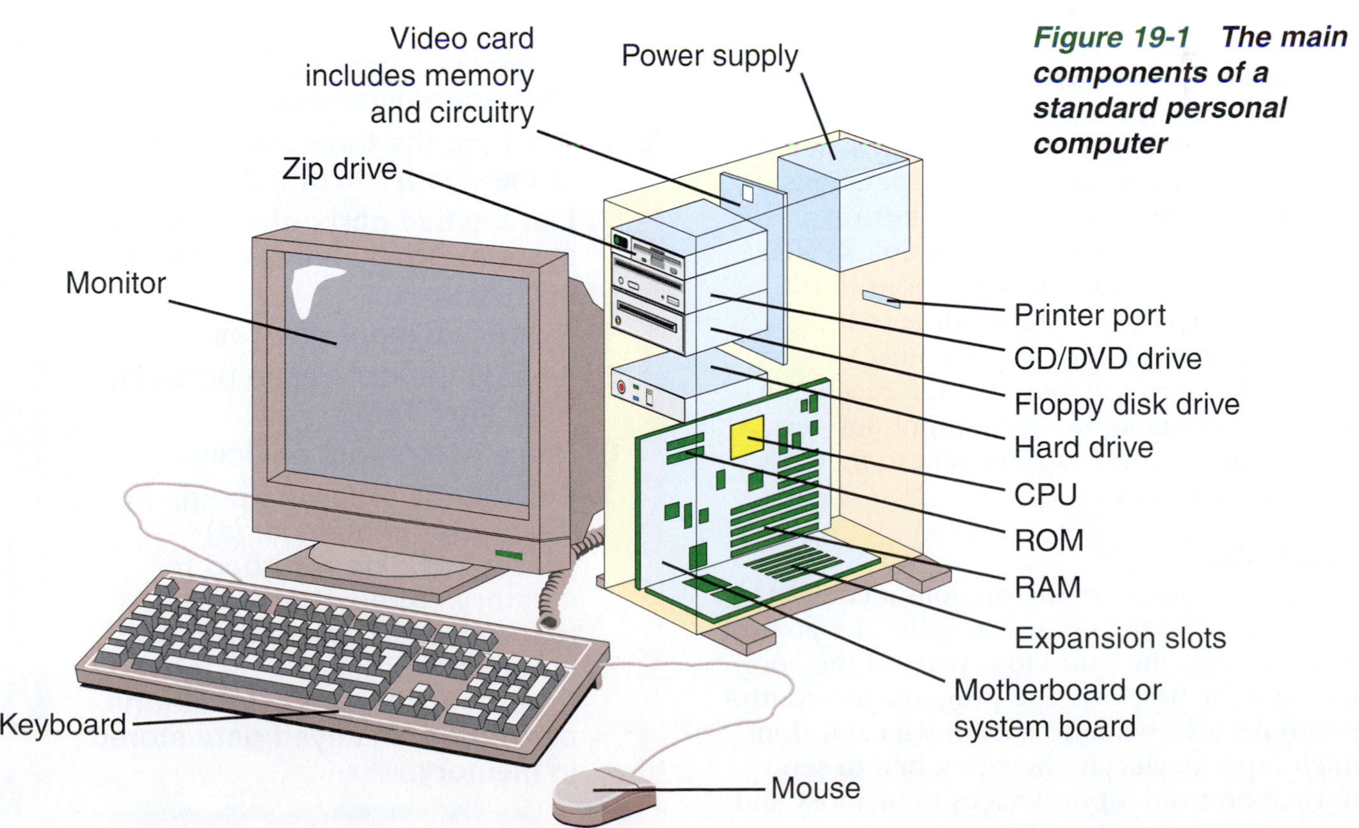

Figure 19-1 The main components of a standard personal computer

and numbers) and commands entered by the user. Input is sometimes sent to memory and sometimes to the arithmetic and logic section of the computer.

Memory

The memory is the part of the computer system that records and stores data and programs. These data and programs stay in memory until other parts of the computer need them.

The memory has several parts. One important part is ROM, which stands for *read-only memory*. The manufacturer pre-programs the ROM, which is permanent. The ROM tells the computer to do different things, depending on the uses of the computer.

Another important part is working memory. It is called RAM (*random-access memory*). This part stores programs currently being used and data being processed. When the computer is turned off, it erases everything in RAM.

Programs and files that are permanently stored on the computer are on the hard disk. They are loaded from here into RAM when they are needed. The hard disk is often considered a storage device rather than part of memory.

Arithmetic and Logic

The arithmetic and logic section (ALU) is the heart of the computer. It does the actual processing. As you might guess from the name, the ALU does this by means of math operations.

The ALU adds, subtracts, multiplies, divides, and compares numbers. To do complex calculations, it combines the four operations into a number of steps as a program directs. It does these tasks in millionths of a second.

The arithmetic and logic section receives its input from memory and from input devices. After processing, the data are sent to memory or to an output device.

Control

Part of the program of instructions a computer receives goes to the control section. The control section directs the other four parts of the computer system. Based on the program, the control section decides when to accept data and from which input device. It chooses when to send information from input devices to memory and when to send it to the arithmetic and logic section. The control section decides when to call up a program and data from storage. And it decides when the computer's work should go to an output device.

Output

Output devices change data from electronic language into forms that people can understand. Most output is displayed, printed, or stored.

Output may appear on the computer monitor or be printed. Sometimes it is stored on magnetic disks or tapes. The same devices frequently serve both input and output functions.

Some computer systems transmit output as spoken words or music. Output can also consist of instructions that tell machines such as robots to do certain kinds of work.

LESSON 19.1 REVIEW

1. **Name two characteristics of a computer keyboard.**
2. **What are the three major steps in the operation of a computer?**
3. **List the five parts of a computer system. Briefly tell what each part does.**
4. **Name five input devices.**
5. **What is the difference between ROM and RAM?**
6. **Name two output devices.**
7. **Rewrite the following steps in the proper sequence: (a) processed data returned to memory, (b) numbers keyed, (c) processed data shown on monitor, (d) stored data moved for processing, (e) calculations performed, (f) keyed data stored in memory.**

LESSON 19.2

COMPUTER HARDWARE AND SOFTWARE

OBJECTIVES

- *IDENTIFY TYPES OF COMPUTERS AND COMPUTER HARDWARE*
- *NAME AND DESCRIBE THE TWO TYPES OF COMPUTER SOFTWARE AND SIX TYPES OF APPLICATION SOFTWARE*

COMPUTER HARDWARE

A computer consists of several interconnected pieces of equipment. The physical equipment that makes up a computer is called **hardware**. The most important piece of hardware is the central processing unit (CPU), which does the actual processing or computing. In fact, the term *computer* is sometimes used just for the CPU, while the term *computer system* is used for the computer and its input and output devices. A typical home or small business computer system is shown on the next page.

A computer system usually has several input and output devices. These devices are called **peripherals** because they are located outside of the CPU. The keyboard, mouse, and monitor are common peripherals. So are printers, scanners, microphones, and speakers. Peripherals, of course, are computer hardware.

Computers vary greatly in size, speed, storage capacity, and cost. The most familiar computer is the personal computer, or simply PC. The standard PC is a general-purpose computer designed for home and office use. A PC system can sit easily on a desktop and can run a wide variety of software applications. Smaller portable PCs are called notebooks. Even smaller handheld computers are available. These include personal digital assistants, or PDAs, and various types of wireless devices that serve multiple uses as phones, pagers, and Internet appliances.

For personal computers, the CPU is contained on a single tiny silicon chip. This is called a **microprocessor**. Microprocessors can be considered the smallest computers. They are built for specific purposes, such as controlling fuel usage in an automobile engine. Millions of microprocessors are used every year in telephones,

PERSONAL DECISIONS

You are very interested in computers. You have subscribed to a computer magazine to learn more about them. You are saving money to buy a PC. But the more you read, the more confusing it gets. There are so many different brand names and models from which to choose. When you do get close to making a decision, you read that a more powerful and cheaper model will be out soon. Should you buy or continue to wait?

WHAT WOULD YOU DO?

A typical PC system consists of a keyboard, CPU, monitor, and printer.

microwave ovens, DVDs, fax machines, and hundreds of other products.

Very powerful desktop computers, which are slightly larger than the standard PC, are called workstations. They combine the ease of use of a PC with the power and functions of larger computers. Workstations are used primarily for scientific and engineering work and office automation.

Minicomputers and mainframe computers are the midsize and large systems used in business, industry, and government. Multiple terminals (keyboard and monitor combinations) allow hundreds, or even thousands, of people to use one of these computers at the same time. Regardless of size, all computers have similar features and components.

COMPUTER SOFTWARE

Computer **software** is the instructions that tell the computer what to do. *Software* and *programs* mean the same thing. There are two main types of software. One is system software, which manages what happens inside the computer. The other is application software. These are the programs used to perform certain tasks, such as word processing.

System Software

A computer must have a program before it can do anything. Most computers are sold with operating system software installed. When you first "boot up" the computer, system software is loaded into the computer's main memory. Once booted, the computer is ready to receive the commands required to begin an application.

For early operating systems, the user had to key commands, which were sometimes quite lengthy. Today, most popular system software uses what is called a **graphical user interface (GUI)**. The majority of PCs use the Microsoft® Windows® operating system, which has a GUI. GUIs use menus and small pictures called **icons**. Instead of keying a command, you can use a mouse to choose it from a menu or double-click on an icon (click twice).

Application Software

The widespread use and acceptance of computers in the workplace are due to their ability to accomplish useful tasks. This is done through application software. Six common types of application software are described below.

- ***Word processing.*** One of the most common uses of PCs is for word processing. Word processing software, like Corel® WordPerfect® and Microsoft® Word, lets you create (key) documents such as letters, memos, and reports. This software provides many helpful features for editing and formatting documents. Like other application files, word-processed files can be printed, stored electronically, and recalled for future use.
- ***Spreadsheet.*** The financial records kept by accountants and bookkeepers are called spreadsheets. Almost any problem in which data are put into rows and columns and used in calculations can be prepared with spreadsheet software. It is used for budgeting, sales forecasting, income projection, and investment analysis. As new data are added, calculations can be redone automatically. Spreadsheet software can also be used to produce graphs, charts, and reports.
- ***Database management.*** Magazine publishers, insurance companies, airlines, manufacturers, and many other businesses maintain large

YOU'RE A WHAT? OPTICIAN

Opticians fit eyeglasses and contact lenses, following prescriptions written by optometrists or ophthalmologists. They begin by examining prescriptions to determine lens specifications. Eye and facial measurements are taken. Opticians recommend eyeglass frames and lenses based upon the customer's occupation, habits, and facial features. They assist customers in trying on different frame styles until a suitable choice is made.

Once the lenses and frames have been determined, the optician prepares appropriate work orders. Ophthalmic laboratory technicians follow the work orders to grind lenses and insert them in a frame. For contact lenses, work orders are usually sent directly to lens manufacturers. When the glasses or contact lenses are received, the optician helps to fit the eyewear and provides the customer with information regarding use and care. ■

files of customer and inventory data. Your public library probably has its card catalog stored in a computer. This is done with database management software. Such software is used to organize, store, and retrieve information.

- ***Personal information management.*** Personal information management software helps users organize their information. Features may include e-mail, a calendar, an address book, and a task or assignment list.
- ***Presentations.*** Electronic presentation software is used to create slide shows to accompany oral presentations. With this software, you can create slides that include text, graphics, sound, and even animation and video.
- ***Communications.*** Transferring data from one computer to another is done with communications software. Traditionally, this software was used primarily for e-mail and to search electronic databases on the Internet. Today, web browsers such as Microsoft Internet Explorer and Netscape Navigator are commonly used for these tasks. Using the Internet for communications and other purposes is discussed in more detail in the next lesson.
- ***Software suites.*** Many types of application software are commonly known as stand-alone programs. This means that they work by themselves. A user, however, often needs to switch between applications and use material from one application in another (for example, to create a bar chart from the statistical data in a spreadsheet for use in a presentation). To make this easier, integrated software suites have been developed. One popular suite includes word processing, spreadsheet, personal information management, and electronic presentation software. Integrated software has many advantages for home, office, and small business users.

LESSON 19.2 REVIEW

1. What three components make up a computer system?
2. Name and define the two types of computer software.
3. Identify the type of application software used for each of the following tasks: (a) storing inventory data, (b) writing a business report, (c) transferring data to another computer, (d) creating a slide show, and (e) preparing a budget.

HIGH-GROWTH OCCUPATIONS FOR THE 21st CENTURY

Office and Administrative Support Supervisors and Managers

All organizations need timely and effective office and administrative support to operate efficiently. *Office and administrative support supervisors and managers* coordinate this support. Planning the work of staff and supervising them are key functions of this job. After allocating work assignments, supervisors oversee the work to ensure that it is on schedule and meets quality standards. When overseeing long-term projects, the supervisor may meet regularly with staff members to discuss their progress.

Office and administrative support supervisors and managers also evaluate the performance of workers. If a worker has done a good job, the supervisor records this information in the employee's personnel file and may recommend a promotion or other award. If a worker is performing poorly, the supervisor discusses the problem with the employee and how to improve performance. The supervisor might send the employee to a training course or arrange personal counseling. If the situation does not improve, the supervisor may recommend a transfer, demotion, or dismissal.

Clerical workers are supervised and evaluated by office and administrative support supervisors and managers.

These supervisors and managers interview and evaluate prospective clerical employees. When new workers arrive on the job, supervisors provide an orientation to acquaint them with the organization and its operating routines. They also help train new employees in organization and office procedures. When new office equipment or updated computer software is introduced, supervisors train experienced employees to use it efficiently. Or they may arrange for special outside training for their employees.

Office and administrative support supervisors and managers often act as liaisons between the clerical staff and the professional, technical, and managerial staff. This may involve implementing new company policies or restructuring the workflow in their departments. They must also keep superiors informed of their progress and of any potential problems. Supervisors may have to resolve interpersonal conflicts among the staff. In organizations covered by union contracts, office and administrative support supervisors and managers must know the provisions of labor-management agreements and run their departments according to these agreements.

LESSON 19.3

THE INTERNET AND THE FUTURE OF COMPUTERS

OBJECTIVES

- EXPLAIN HOW THE INTERNET WORKS
- DISCUSS THE POSSIBLE FUTURE IMPACT OF COMPUTERS

THE INTERNET

The Internet has the potential to be one of the most significant technological developments of all time. It is already influencing the ways in which we learn, work, communicate, spend leisure time, conduct business, and engage in many other aspects of our personal and professional lives.

When two or more computers are linked together by cable or wireless means, this is called a **network**. Networks enable computers to share software, data files, and printers and other equipment. For example, a high school might have dozens of computers connected in what is called a local area network (LAN). The **Internet** is an "*inter*connected *net*work of networks" that links millions of smaller computer networks worldwide.

A Brief History

The Internet originated in the late 1960s through a project funded by the U.S. Defense Department. The purpose was to link government research facilities and other agencies in a network to share computer resources and data. The ARPANet, as it was called, was intended to serve only a few thousand scientists and computer specialists.

Throughout the 1970s, the ARPANet grew steadily. Other countries began to join the network, and other networks came into existence. In the early 1980s, the National Science Foundation began to create a national "backbone" network for supercomputers called the NSFNET. By the end of the decade, the Defense

> **WORKPLACE DECISIONS**
>
> You work for your grandparents in a small, family-owned business. After taking a computer course in school, you have become aware of what computers can do. You see a number of ways that a computer could be used in the business. You suggest to your grandfather that he buy a computer.
>
> "Son, we do not have the money for an expensive computer," he says. "Besides, the old-fashioned way has been working just fine for years." You are disappointed, but you still believe that a computer would be a wise investment.
>
> **WHAT WOULD YOU DO?**

COMMUNICATION AT WORK

COMPUTERS

Just 20 years ago, it was hard for people to imagine that computers would have anything to do with communicating at work. If you had to send a business letter, you wrote it out in longhand and then keyed it on a typewriter. You had to be careful because mistakes weren't easy to fix. You painted them out with thick, white correction fluid or typed over them using paper squares that left a chalky dust on the page.

Now we can use word processing software to create the perfect letter. It offers us different designs and even checks the spelling. We have desktop publishing software to produce flyers and newsletters as attractive as if they came from a print shop. We have communications software and the Internet, which make possible e-mail, videoconferencing, instant messaging, and chat.

In a short time, technology has created many new ways to communicate at work. Yet the fact that we can do more, more quickly, should be a caution to us. It is easy, in our haste, to say the wrong thing in an e-mail. With videoconferencing, people are sometimes more casual about preparing for a meeting than before. Taking care and time in our communication at work, both orally and in writing, is just as important as it always has been—perhaps even more so.

Department had shut down its network and moved over to the more advanced NSFNET. The collection of networks soon became known simply as the Internet.

Despite its growth, the Internet was difficult to use and was limited to communicating data and text-based information. This began to change in the early 1990s with development of the **World Wide Web**. The Web is a network within the Internet that provides sounds, pictures, and moving images in addition to text. The introduction of the Web helped make the Internet popular and easier to use.

The arrival of browser software in 1993 further simplified use of the Internet and began an era of explosive growth. A **browser** is a type of software used to locate and display information on the Web. Even though the Web represents only part of the Internet, most people now use the terms *Internet*, *Net*, and *Web* interchangeably.

How the Internet Works

To access the Internet, you instruct your communications software (which comes with most computers) to connect with an Internet service provider, or ISP. An ISP is an organization like America Online that provides Internet access, usually for a fee. To connect, you generally key a password and perhaps a local telephone access number and click on "Connect."

Most users connect to an ISP via a modem. In the future, users will have a variety of higher-speed network and wireless alternatives by which to access the Internet.

To navigate the Web and view pages, users need a browser, like Microsoft Internet Explorer or Netscape Navigator. Most computers come with browser software. It can also be downloaded free from the manufacturer's web site.

Once a user is connected to the Internet, the user's computer can interact with other computers using what is called a "client/server model." The resources of the Internet, such as information and e-mail services, are stored on host computers called servers. Your computer, called the client, requests the desired information from the server. Client and server software interact to deliver and display information in the appropriate format. This is done simply and automatically because of the development of the World Wide Web and the use of web browsers.

Web Basics

Typically, when you connect to an ISP, your browser is launched and displays your home page. A home page is the starting point from which to begin navigating or "surfing" the Web. The home page might be the opening page of your school's or employer's web site or of a popular web portal such as America Online or Yahoo! It might also be a personal page.

The Web is made up of various sites, each of which has an electronic address called a Uniform Resource Locator (URL). An example of a URL is http://www.swep.com, the address for the web site of the publisher of this book. To visit a specific web site, you key the URL into the appropriate box in your browser window. The box might be labeled "Location," "Address," or something similar (see Figure 19-2).

Another way to go to a web site is to click on a hyperlink. Hyperlinks enable a user to jump from one page to another on the Web without keying the URL. A hyperlink can be text that is underscored or in a different color or a graphic. The hyperlink is one feature that makes the Web so popular and easy to use.

The most common uses of the Internet are as follows:

- ***Communication.*** Probably the most popular use of the Internet is e-mail. Billions of e-mail messages are sent and received each day. Two additional forms of communication are increasingly being used on the Internet. One is telephony, which refers to using a computer to place and receive telephone calls. The other is videoconferencing, which allows a user to have face-to-face conversations with other people on a network.
- ***Research.*** The Internet can be regarded as a huge library that stores millions of files of information. Students, scientists, teachers, and other professionals use the Internet to access databases and share information. The average citizen uses the Internet to collect a variety of information, including airline schedules, consumer product reviews, medical information, recipes, stock quotes, tax forms, travel maps, and weather forecasts.
- ***News and entertainment.*** For many individuals, the Internet is becoming the preferred source of news. Many newspapers, magazines, and television networks maintain web pages. On the Web, information can be updated continually throughout a 24-hour news cycle. The Web is also used to play interactive games, download videos, and view concerts live. As audio and video technologies improve and wireless devices become more common, using the Web for news and entertainment is bound to increase.
- ***Consuming goods and services.*** To purchase a product, we have traditionally shopped at a local store or used a mail-order catalog. To pay an electricity bill, we have

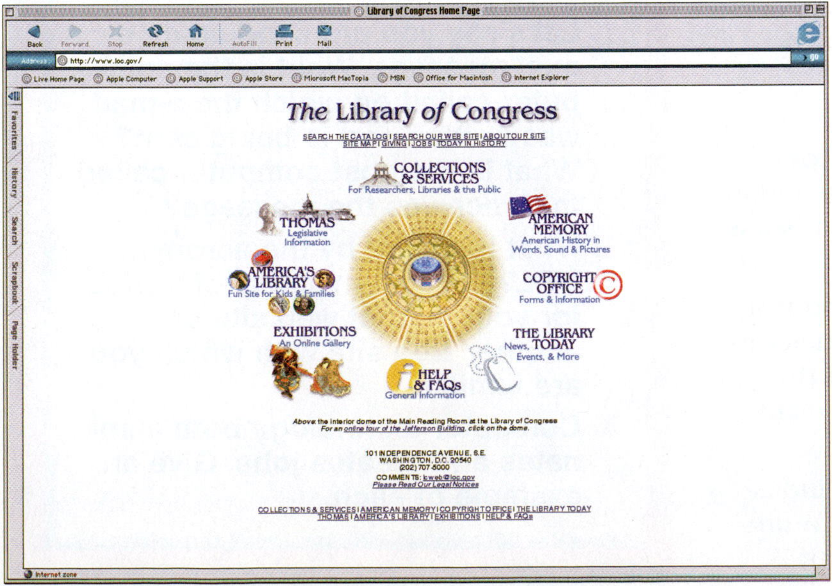

Figure 19-2 The Library of Congress web site

written a check and mailed it to the utility company. Now, we are likely to use the Internet for shopping, purchasing, and even paying bills, with online banking. Almost everything you can buy in your community can be purchased through the Internet.

Internet Issues

The development and increasing use of the Internet has brought with it a number of problems and issues. Not all of the information on the Web is accurate and appropriate. Some is intentionally misleading, hateful, or violent or presents adult content. Controlling access to inappropriate materials is an ongoing concern for parents and schools. Internet security and fraud are also serious issues.

THE FUTURE OF COMPUTERS

The rapid development of computer technology should continue in the future. Computers will get smaller, more powerful, and less expensive. At the same time, they will become easier to use. Programming will be simpler. Technology for giving spoken commands to computers will continue to improve. All of these changes will have a great impact on the workplace. Predicting the future is risky. However, the following changes seem likely:

- The number of occupations that require computer literacy and keyboarding skills will continue to increase. Eventually, most occupations will involve computer use.
- Employment in areas involving computers and robots will increase dramatically. Computer technology will create many new industries and occupations. Try to guess what some of these might be.
- The use of industrial robots will expand from the assembly line to all phases of manufacturing. In the totally automated factory of the future, robots will replace humans for many tasks.
- The automation of offices and service industries will increase. In the office of the future, most communication will be carried out electronically. Electronic storage and transmission of information may finally lead to the "paperless office" predicted since the 1970s.
- Major shifts in job patterns will occur. Computers and robots may eliminate millions of jobs.
- Technology can also create jobs. Many experts believe that, in the long run, technology will produce more jobs than it takes away.
- Workers losing their jobs to automation will need to be retrained. To keep up with new technology, all workers will need continuing education and training.

You live in an exciting time. Not since the Industrial Revolution has the workplace undergone such changes. Some people call the modern era of electronics "the second industrial revolution." The computer is leading this revolution.

How much do you know about computers, and how much do you use them? If your knowledge and experience are limited, think about taking a course or getting a friend to teach you keyboarding skills. Not being able to use a computer could hold you back from getting or advancing in a job.

LESSON 19.3 REVIEW

1. **Let's say you are sending an e-mail message. What is the computer called on which the e-mail was written and is being sent? What is the host computer called that receives the message?**
2. **What is meant by the acronym *URL*? Give an example of a URL for your school web site or another web site with which you are familiar.**
3. **Computer technology both eliminates and creates jobs. Give an example of each.**

FOCUS ON HEALTH AND SAFETY

REPETITIVE MOTION INJURY

We usually associate on-the-job injuries with occupations like police officer, coal miner, and farmer. One of the fastest-growing types of occupational injuries, however, is found among people who work with computers. It is called repetitive motion injury (RMI).

This disorder can arise when a person must repeat movements of the hands, fingers, or arms many times a day, day after day. Keyboarding is highly repetitive. Computer users are more likely to develop RMI if they use incorrect keyboarding techniques, particularly not keeping the wrists straight. When a wrist is repeatedly flexed and extended, its tendons may become irritated and swell. The swelling presses on nerves, causing tingling and numbness in the fingers and hand. Pain may also occur in the arm, elbow, or shoulder.

RMI can often be avoided by setting up a workstation properly and using good keyboarding techniques.

RMI can often be avoided by setting up a computer workstation for maximum comfort and efficiency, using good keyboarding techniques, and taking frequent breaks. Here are some suggestions:

- Adjust chair height so thighs are horizontal and feet are flat on the floor. Sit back with your back and neck erect. Upper arms should be perpendicular to the floor and relaxed.
- Forearms should be parallel to the slant of the keyboard. Keep wrists straight and do not rest them on any surface.
- Adjust the computer screen height so that the top is at or just below eye level.
- Keep your fingers curved and upright. Strike each key lightly using the fingertip.
- Grasp the mouse loosely. Keep your fingers, hands, arms, and shoulders relaxed.
- Take a 15-minute break for every hour of intensive keying.

Working long hours at a keyboard does not necessarily mean that one will develop RMI. This disorder, like most on-the-job injuries, can be prevented.

THINK CRITICALLY

1. Think about your work, school, and personal activities. Should you be concerned about RMI?
2. What, if any, changes should you make to the way you use a computer to reduce your chances of developing RMI?

CHAPTER 19

Chapter in Brief

Lesson 19.1 *How Computers Work*

A. Computer literacy is a general knowledge of what computers are, how they work, and for what they can be used. A computer is an electronic tool. It helps people do various kinds of work.

B. Computer keyboards are similar in terms of basic commands and procedures. You will benefit by knowing how to use a computer keyboard.

C. The computer works in three steps: it receives instructions, it does tasks according to these instructions, and it shares the results. This is called the input-processing-output sequence. Processing can be divided into three parts: memory, arithmetic and logic, and control.

Lesson 19.2 *Computer Hardware and Software*

A. A computer system consists of the CPU and several interconnected pieces of hardware called peripherals. Computer systems vary greatly in size, speed, storage capacity, and cost.

B. There are two main types of computer software. System software manages what happens inside the computer. Application software is used to perform certain tasks, such as word processing.

Lesson 19.3 *The Internet and the Future of Computers*

A. The Internet is a "network of networks" that links millions of smaller computer networks around the world. The World Wide Web is the part of the Internet that provides sound, pictures, and moving images in addition to text. The Web is most commonly used for communication, research, news and entertainment, and consuming goods and services.

B. The rapid development of computer technology should continue in the future. The number of occupations that require computer literacy and keyboarding skills will increase. If your knowledge and experience of computers are limited, think about learning to use computers.

Activities

1. Identify as many ways as you can that computers are being used in your school. Do not limit your answers to just instruction.
2. Choose an occupation in which you are interested. Find out how workers in that occupation use computers. Present your findings in an oral report to the class.
3. Look in the Yellow Pages of your phone book to find out the number and types of different computer businesses in your area. Also, examine the classified section of your Sunday newspaper. How many job ads can you find for computer-related occupations? Discuss your findings in class.

REVIEW

4. Identify as many sources as possible in your school or community regarding how you might learn or improve your computer skills.
5. Do you have a favorite web site? List three web sites that you visit regularly. Combine your list with those of your classmates to compare interests.

Word Power

On a separate sheet of paper, match each definition with the correct term. All definitions will be used. One definition will be used twice (there are two terms that mean the same thing).

6. An electronic device for transmitting computer data over standard telephone lines or fiberoptic cable
7. Instructions on how to solve a certain problem or do a certain task; the instructions that tell a computer what to do
8. Small pictures that users can double-click on to give commands to software to perform specific functions
9. A network within the Internet that provides sounds, pictures, and moving images in addition to text
10. A general knowledge of what computers are, how they work, and for what they can be used
11. The ability to type and to give commands to a computer using a keyboard
12. An electronic tool that can store and process data and can direct the work of other tools
13. Pieces of computer equipment attached to the main computer unit, such as the keyboard, mouse, and monitor
14. The physical equipment that makes up a computer
15. Software used to locate and display information on the Web
16. A feature of modern operating system software that provides icons and menus from which the user can select commands, typically with a mouse
17. An "interconnected network of networks"
18. Two or more computers linked together by cable or wireless means
19. A CPU contained on a single chip

a. browser
b. computer
c. computer literacy
d. graphical user interface (GUI)
e. hardware
f. icons
g. Internet
h. keyboarding skills
i. microprocessor
j. modem
k. network
l. peripherals
m. program
n. software
o. World Wide Web

Think Critically

20. Critics say that computers put too many people out of work. They believe that someday computers will take over most of what workers now do. Do you agree? Discuss in class the human costs and benefits of computers.
21. People are often reluctant to use new technology. Why do you think this is so? How might you change the attitude of someone who feels this way?
22. In what types of occupations do computers have the greatest potential use? The least potential use? Explain your answers.

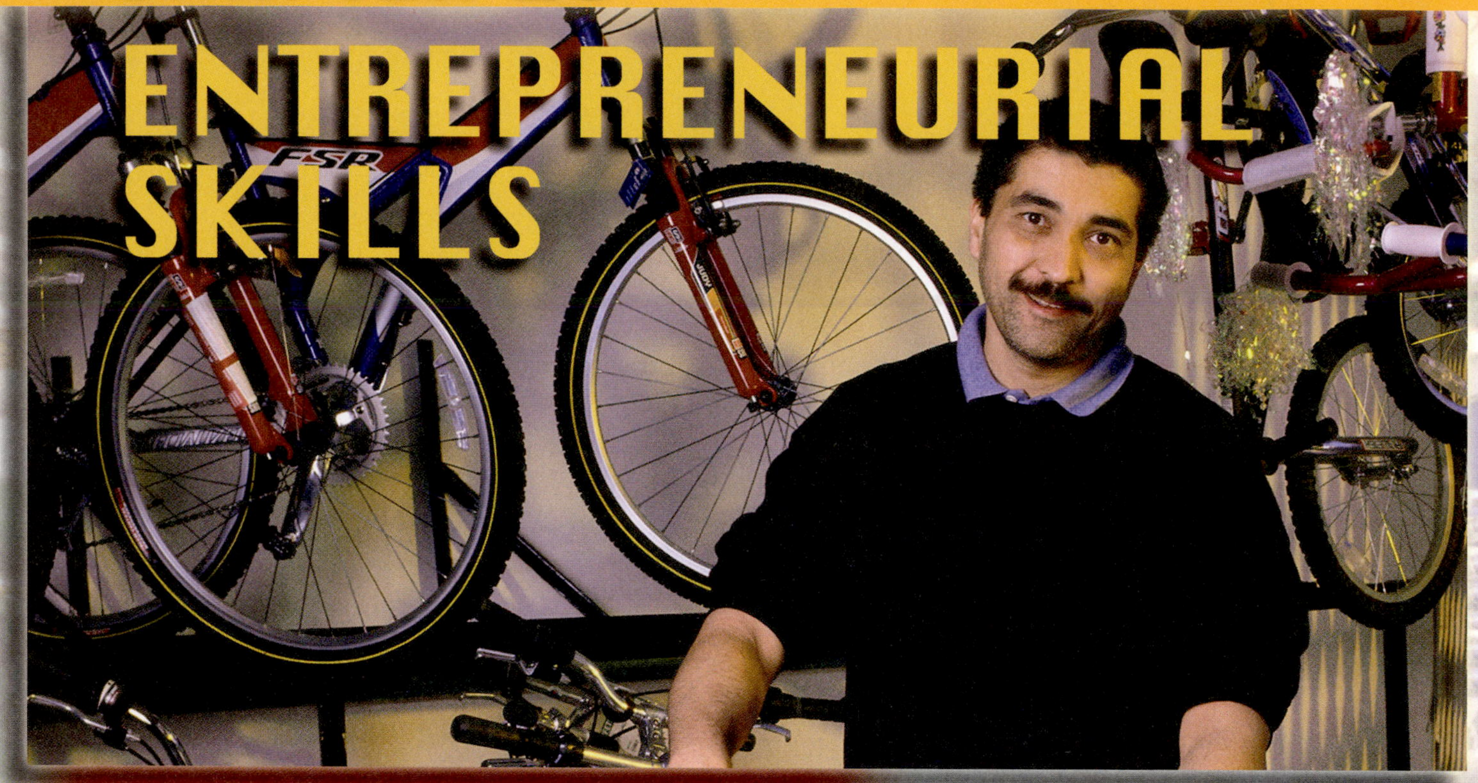

CHAPTER 20

ENTREPRENEURIAL SKILLS

LESSONS

PREVIEW

It has often been said that small businesses are the backbone of the American economy. In fact, small businesses employ more total workers than large companies. What kind of people start a small business? What does it take to succeed on your own? In this chapter, you will learn about small businesses and find answers to these questions.

THOUGHTS ON WORK

"Work relieves us from three great evils: boredom, vice, and want."
French Proverb

TAKING ACTION
A BUSINESS DECISION

Janice works as an assistant in a beauty salon. She washes clients' hair, schedules appointments, launders smocks and towels, and stocks supplies. Janice is in cosmetology school. She is studying to become a hair stylist.

The owner of the salon, Julie, is a good businessperson. The salon has a solid base of loyal customers. Julie has three skillful stylists working for her, whom she treats very well. She takes them to workshops to learn the latest styles and techniques. The salon is always neat and attractive and stocks a good array of products.

One of Janice's friends from school, Petra, wants to start her own salon after graduation. Petra already has a dozen steady customers from among her friends, family, and neighbors. She wants Janice to go into business with her. "Wouldn't you like to work for yourself instead of somebody else?" she asks.

"I don't see how I could afford to do that, just out of school," Janice replies.

"We could obtain a loan to get started. My cousin owns a building in North Park. He runs a catering business out of the back and is willing to rent the front to me. You know what a good neighborhood that is. Before you know it, we'd have more clients than we could handle. Think about it."

Janice has always wanted her own business. That is one reason she chose to be a hair stylist. But wouldn't it be better to work in an established salon for a while, learn more, and build up a base of customers? She is also concerned about taking on a loan just out of school. She decides to talk to Julie about it.

Julie confirms Janice's ideas about getting experience and building a customer base. "You should think carefully, too, before going into business with someone. You need to be sure that you can work together and that you have the same goals for the business.

"Operating your own business is a big job," Julie adds. "It takes more than just a good opportunity to get a business started and make it run smoothly." They talk about a typical day at the salon and all the responsibilities that Julie has. Janice didn't realize how many hours Julie works and how many different tasks she does at the salon.

"Think about it," Petra repeats.

> **SUCCESS TIP**
> **People starting their own business see opportunities and often take risks to pursue them.**

THINK CRITICALLY

1. What are some things that Janice needs to consider in making her decision?
2. What ideas do you have for a small business?

LESSON 20.1
SELF-EMPLOYMENT

OBJECTIVES

- NAME CONTRIBUTIONS THAT SMALL BUSINESS MAKES TO OUR SOCIETY
- DISCUSS ADVANTAGES AND DISADVANTAGES OF SELF-EMPLOYMENT
- OUTLINE WHAT IT IS LIKE TO OWN AND OPERATE A SMALL BUSINESS

NATURE OF SMALL BUSINESS

As a cooperative education or work experience student, you are working in a business owned or managed by someone else. In the future, you may continue to work as an employee for another person, or you may decide to become an entrepreneur. An **entrepreneur** is someone who runs his or her own business. The person is **self-employed**.

Small businesses are found in agriculture, construction, sales, services, and every other type of industry. They are located throughout the country. Many are in big cities, but a large number are in small towns. Small businesses are as scattered and different as the people who own them.

Importance of Small Business

Small business makes many important contributions to our society. One contribution is the creation of new jobs. As new businesses begin and expand, they hire new workers. The majority of all new jobs are provided by businesses employing fewer than 20 people.

Another contribution is that small businesses often recycle old buildings. It is not unusual, for example, to find a restaurant or a dry cleaning business housed in what used to be a service station. Can you think of examples in your town or neighborhood?

A third contribution is that small business provides opportunities for women and minorities to get started in business. About 39 percent of all self-employed people are females, and 19 percent are minorities. The percentage for both groups is increasing steadily each year.

The most important contribution of small business comes from new inventions, products,

WORKPLACE DECISIONS

The company you work for is losing business to foreign competition. The owner says he cannot compete if he has to continue paying high labor costs. He is looking for a buyer. If he cannot sell the business, he is going to shut it down.

A group of employees has been meeting to help find a solution. One option being considered is for the employees to buy the company and run it themselves. This has been done successfully in a few businesses.

WHAT WOULD YOU DO?

and services. Many of the great success stories of American business have been the result of people who had a new idea or a better way of doing things.

Form of Organization

A business can be organized as a proprietorship, partnership, or corporation.

- ***Proprietorship.*** This is the simplest and most common form. A **proprietorship** is a business owned by one person, who receives all the profits. The owner may have employees.
- ***Partnership.*** A **partnership** is a business that has two or more co-owners. Partnerships often come about because proprietors need additional money or want help running a business. Owners in a partnership share in the company's management and profits.
- ***Corporation.*** A **corporation** is very different from the other two forms of business. In return for a fee paid to the state, a corporation receives a **charter**, a legal document that gives the corporation permission to conduct certain business activities. The owners of a corporation are called **stockholders**. They have become owners by purchasing stock or shares of ownership in the company. The stockholders elect a **board of directors**. The board makes major decisions about the company, such as hiring the company president.

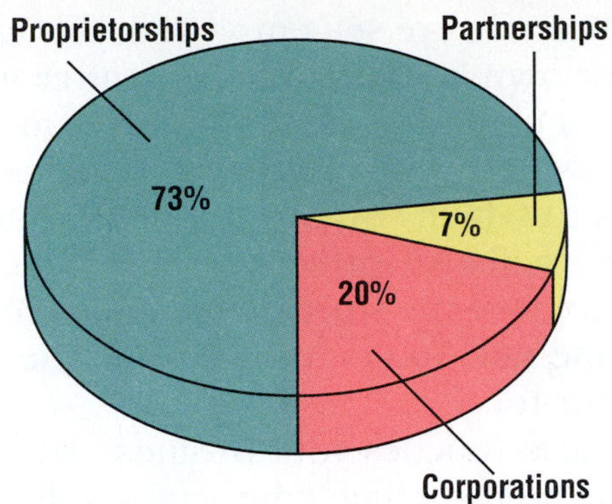

Figure 20-1 ***Proprietorships make up about 73 percent of all small businesses.***

ADVANTAGES AND DISADVANTAGES OF SELF-EMPLOYMENT

Being self-employed is different from working for someone else. Before starting a business, you should consider the advantages and disadvantages of working for yourself. We asked some entrepreneurs about the benefits of self-employment. Here is what they told us:

"I never liked working for other people. I like to try new things. That can be a problem when you are an employee. In my business, I can take full advantage of new ideas that appeal to me."

"Being self-employed, I can make my decisions quickly. I used to work for a large corporation in which decision making was very slow."

"I enjoy having a flexible schedule. Last week, my wife took two vacation days. I arranged my schedule so we could go camping."

"In the shop where I worked, I did only one task. Now I can work on a project from beginning to end. I can use *all* my skills. And I am working toward goals that are important to me."

"I am proud to be a business owner. Four years ago, we opened this small supermarket. We now have three, which will belong to our kids someday."

"When you work for yourself, no one can fire you!"

All work situations have negative points. Self-employment is no exception:

"In the beginning, the appliance-repair business brought in little money. But we still had to pay rent and other expenses."

"I am a freelance graphic artist. My income varies a lot. It is either feast or famine, it seems."

"We are store owners in a one-industry town. As soon as the plant started layoffs, we were affected. And it wasn't our fault! If this keeps on, we may have to close. We could lose the money we have put into the business. And we could lose our house and other property, too. We are hoping for the best."

"Being self-employed is high-pressure. All the decisions are my responsibility. If I make a major mistake, all of us around here could be out of work."

"I often put in 60- or 70-hour weeks."

Even when you are self-employed, you will not be your own boss entirely. No matter what business you choose, you must satisfy your customers, as well as your **creditors** (persons or companies to which you owe money). Your competitors will also influence what you do. For instance, suppose the store down the street has a two-for-one sale. You may have to do the same at your store, too.

The law also touches your business. Health authorities and insurance companies will expect you to meet certain standards and to follow certain regulations. You will have to abide by wage and hour laws and keep proper tax and business records as well.

No one person can represent the experiences of all entrepreneurs. The following case study, however, will give you a good idea of the advantages and disadvantages of self-employment. The workday of Ann Kirsten shows many of the freedoms, uncertainties, and responsibilities shared by small business owners.

Ann spends most of the morning working in her office.

SELF-EMPLOYMENT CASE STUDY

As an entrepreneur, Ann Kirsten does many types of work tasks. In a large business, each work task would probably be done by a single person. As you read this piece, which has been reprinted and slightly adapted from the *Occupational Outlook Quarterly*, keep in mind the variety of things that Ann has to be able to do.

The day begins. On a typical workday, Ann Kirsten arrives at Country Gifts 'n' Crafts, her small gift and card shop, at about 10 a.m. Stepping inside, she takes a sharp owner's look around the store, which holds a miscellaneous assortment of wares: crystal salad bowls, candles, neckties, placemats, scented soap, and toys are among the many items in stock.

The store opens at 11 a.m. and Ann hurries to make sure everything is in order. She sets out a pitcher of orange juice and a tray of muffins—a bonus for early customers—and checks to see that the store's shelves are well stocked and tidy. Spotting a few gaps, she tells the two full-time salesclerks who have just arrived to shelve supplies of candleholders and cards. She also instructs the employees to unpack a recently arrived carton of stainless steel serving bowls, tag them with the prices she has determined, and display them near the crystal salad bowls.

Answering the mail. Satisfied that everything is in order, Ann takes the morning mail upstairs to a small room filled with so many cardboard boxes that it looks more like a stockroom than an executive office. Settling down at her desk, she opens the mail, taking special note of new merchandise catalogs, bills, and a customer check that has been returned by the bank because of insufficient funds. She pays a few bills, answers some letters, and files the rest into appropriate piles for future action.

Ann spends the rest of the morning in her office filling out several government forms required of self-employed persons. She is interrupted by a telephone call from a supplier who regrets that Ann's last order will be delayed for three weeks. A **supplier** is a person or agency that distributes goods to **retailers**, businesses like Ann's that sell directly to consumers. Annoyed, but unable to do anything about the shipment date, Ann shrugs off the incident.

Unexpected caller. A few minutes later, a sales representative unexpectedly walks in and tries to sell Ann a new line of paper placemats and napkins. Ann generally buys her merchandise from wholesale houses in New York City, which she visits about six times a year.

Wholesale houses are businesses that sell to retailers rather than to consumers. Occasionally Ann does buy from a visiting salesperson. Today she declines, however, believing that her current line of paper table items is adequate. Ann takes her time about making this decision, since her income hinges on her ability to make sound judgments about what her customers will buy. If she invests in an item that does not sell, she loses money.

Waiting on customers. At 1 p.m., Ann goes back downstairs to relieve her clerks during their lunch hours. Before starting the store 7 years ago, Ann enjoyed a 15-year career in public relations. She likes working with people and enjoys waiting on and talking to customers.

The clerks return and Ann grabs a quick lunch before running a business errand at the post office. She then takes time out for a haircut. Inasmuch as she is her own boss, Ann can take time off whenever she wants. Generally, however, she is reluctant to spend too much time away from the store, since there is always so much work to be done.

Bookkeeping, too! Back at the office, Ann goes over the books with her accountant, who keeps track of income and outgo and evaluates the store's performance. Looking at recent sales income and expenses, Ann briefly remembers the days when she worked for other people. Back then, she regularly collected a paycheck from which her employers had withheld money for state and federal income taxes. Her share of payments for Social Security benefits, a health insurance plan, and other programs that assured her income during retirement or periods of sickness had also been deducted. And like most employers, the organizations for which she worked had paid part of the cost of these benefits.

Looking over the books, Ann is happy to see a good rate of profit. If the store's income had not met expenses for the last several months, she would have had to make up the difference out of her own savings. This rarely occurs nowadays, but like many new businesses, the store lost money during its first several months.

Ann recalls, too, how she had to borrow money to start the business and persuade a lender that she could succeed. Then there had been the years of meeting payments on the borrowed money as well as interest for its use. These payments had to be made regularly, for a merchant is helpless without a good credit rating. As she looks back, Ann is gratified to see that it has all paid off.

End of a long day. Ann finishes conferring with her accountant at 6 p.m. and then goes downstairs to help wait on customers until the shop closes at 7. Several boxes of merchandise have arrived, and Ann stays for an hour after closing to unpack and shelve a few items. She generally puts in at least a nine-hour workday—not counting "time off" when she reads magazines to keep up with buying trends or thinks about new ideas for the store—and works six days a week.

Every once in a while, Ann remembers the days when she was salaried and worked a 40-hour, Monday-through-Friday week. She strongly believes, however, that the present freedom and challenge of being her own boss and the knowledge that her efforts are paying off in money that goes into her own pocket more than make up for the long hours and other disadvantages.

LESSON 20.1 REVIEW

1. **Why isn't there such a thing as a typical small business?**
2. **Name four important contributions that small business makes to our society.**
3. **Briefly explain the three forms of business organization.**
4. **Give four advantages and four disadvantages of self-employment.**
5. **Ann Kirsten performs many different types of work tasks, such as supervising employees and ordering merchandise. Name five more work tasks she performs.**

HIGH-GROWTH OCCUPATIONS FOR THE 21st CENTURY

Paralegals

Lawyers are responsible for the legal work they perform. But they often delegate many legal tasks to *paralegals*, also known as *legal assistants*. One of a paralegal's most important tasks is helping lawyers prepare for closings, hearings, trials, and corporate meetings. Paralegals investigate the facts of cases and ensure all relevant information is considered. They also identify laws, judicial decisions, legal articles, and other materials that are relevant to assigned cases. After they analyze and organize the information, paralegals may prepare written reports that attorneys can use in determining how cases should be handled. Should attorneys decide to file lawsuits on behalf of clients, paralegals may help prepare and assist attorneys during trials. Paralegals also organize and track files of case documents and make them available to attorneys.

Paralegals perform research for lawyers and may help prepare and assist attorneys during trials.

Paralegals are found in all types of organizations, but most are employed by law firms, corporate legal departments, and various levels of government. In these organizations, they may work in all areas of the law, including litigation, personal injury, corporate law, criminal law, employee benefits, intellectual property, labor law, and real estate.

Paralegals who work for law firms sometimes work overtime when they are under pressure to meet deadlines. Such commitment, however, is often rewarded with bonuses and extra time off. A small number of paralegals own their own businesses and work as freelance legal assistants to attorneys or corporate legal departments.

A growing number of paralegals use computers in their work. Computer software packages and the Internet are used to search legal literature in computer databases and on CD-ROMs. In litigation involving many supporting documents, paralegals may use computer databases to retrieve, organize, and index various materials. Imaging software allows paralegals to scan documents directly into a database. Billing programs help them track hours billed to clients. Computer software packages are also used to perform tax computations and explore possible tax strategies for clients.

LESSON 20.2
SMALL BUSINESS AND YOU

- IDENTIFY INGREDIENTS NECESSARY FOR A SUCCESSFUL BUSINESS
- EVALUATE YOUR OWN SELF-EMPLOYMENT TRAITS
- DESCRIBE FACTORS TO CONSIDER IN CHOOSING A BUSINESS

INGREDIENTS FOR SUCCESS

A successful business requires more than just interest and a desire to make money. Studies of businesses and conversations with business owners suggest that three things are necessary for a successful business: the right personality, know-how, and money.

Personality

Not everyone has the right personality for self-employment. Success in business is not based on wishful thinking. If you want to be your own boss, you need to be honest about your strengths and weaknesses. The traits needed by a self-employed person are as follows:

- Ability to take action when needed
- Ability to lead others
- Being dependable and trustworthy
- Being a good organizer
- Ability to work hard
- Ability to make good decisions
- Having a positive attitude
- Being honest and open
- Ability to accomplish goals
- Desire to succeed
- Willingness to take risks

Know-how

Self-employed people need some knowledge in various areas of business. These include finance, economics, management, marketing, accounting, and commercial law. Business know-how is usually learned through coursework and on-the-job training. Before starting out on their own, most entrepreneurs have experience working in others' businesses.

CAREER DECISIONS

You are a very good auto mechanic and take pride in your work. You can diagnose difficult problems that other mechanics often cannot solve. Customers also know your work is good. Many of them specifically request that you work on their cars. This irritates some of your coworkers.

Recently, several customers have remarked that you are too good a mechanic to work for someone else. They say you ought to consider starting your own business.

WHAT WOULD YOU DO?

MATH CONNECTION

You are thinking about starting a business that makes and sells widgets. Your fixed monthly expenses (loan payment, rent, utilities, salaries, etc.) would be $6,300. It would cost you $4 to make and ship each widget. You plan to sell the widgets for $5.20 each. How many widgets would you have to sell per month to break even (for your income to equal your expenses)?

SOLUTION

To determine how many widgets you would have to sell per month to break even, first determine your markup on each widget (your net earnings).

Retail price − Cost = Net earnings
$5.20 − $4.00 = $1.20

Then, divide your fixed monthly expenses by your net earnings per widget.

Fixed monthly expenses ÷ Net earnings = Number of widgets
$6,300 ÷ $1.20 = 5,250

You would have to sell 5,250 widgets per month to break even.

Pat King started his own restaurant last year. He had worked for many years as a manager for a national chain before making his decision. Even after starting their business, many owners continue to expand their knowledge. They study on their own and enroll in management training programs and workshops. A helpful organization for entrepreneurs is the Small Business Administration (SBA).

The SBA is an agency of the federal government. Its purpose is to encourage, assist, and protect the interests of small business. The SBA produces and distributes low-cost management assistance publications and conducts management workshops and courses. The agency also makes loans to small businesses. A public librarian can help you find the location of the nearest SBA office. Or you can visit the SBA web site at *http://www.sba.gov/*.

Before starting a business in a trade, technical, or professional occupation, it is necessary to learn the required skills. For example, Kerry and Jill got training in electronics, worked for someone else, and then started their own electronics repair business.

Another way to get business know-how is to buy a franchise. A **franchise** is a contract with a company to sell its goods and services within a certain area. Some well-known franchises are H&R Block, Domino's Pizza, Subway, Midas, and Mail Boxes Etc. Franchise fees range from several thousand to several hundred thousand dollars.

Money

The third key to successful self-employment is money. An entrepreneur must have enough capital (money) to start a business. Often this

NOTHING BUT NET

Most users connect to the Internet through standard telephone lines using a modem. This is a simple and relatively inexpensive technology that works well for e-mail and viewing text pages and simple graphics. But for viewing and downloading multimedia files and watching streaming video, high-speed access called broadband is preferred. The two most common types of broadband are cable and DSL (Digital Subscriber Line). Broadband connections are 50 or more times faster than standard dial-up connections. But broadband is also more expensive and is not available in all geographic locations.

money can be borrowed from banks and other lending institutions. Business owners must pay rent, utilities, and other operating expenses. Equipment and supplies must be purchased. Retailers must be able to buy a large enough supply of merchandise to attract and hold customers. Employees must be paid. And, of course, there must be enough left over for the owner's salary.

The cost of going into business depends on the type of business, the location, the size, and other factors. Often, the business that can be started with a small amount of money is also the business with the least potential for profit. On the other hand, businesses with good profit potential are out of the reach of most people because of the money required to begin.

Most small businesses start out slowly. It takes time for a new business to establish a reputation and build up a base of loyal customers. The Small Business Administration says it takes four to six months for some businesses to be self-supporting. Others take even longer. Unfortunately, some businesses never succeed and must close.

ARE YOU THE TYPE?

To succeed in business, you must honestly evaluate your strengths and weaknesses. You will be your most important employee. If you recognize that you are weak in a certain area, you may be able to improve yourself or find a partner or hire an employee to help you. The exercise in Figure 20-2 will help you discover if you have the traits needed for self-employment.

How did you do? Count up the number of "Yes" answers. If most of your answers are "Yes," you may have what it takes to run your own business. Review your answers again. Make sure you did not answer "Yes" because of wishful thinking.

If you have several "No" or "Not Sure" answers, you should probably not risk your money and time starting a business. You should recognize, however, that you can take steps to improve yourself and increase your chances of success.

ENTREPRENEUR RATING SCALE

	Yes	Not Sure	No
1. I am a self-starter. I get things done.			
2. I like people. I can get along with just about anybody.			
3. I am a leader. I can get most people to go along when I start something.			
4. I like to take charge of things and see them through.			
5. I like to have a plan before I start. I'm usually the one to get things lined up when our group wants to do something.			
6. I like working hard for something I want.			
7. I can make up my mind in a hurry if I want to.			
8. People can trust me. I do what I say.			
9. If I make up my mind to do something, I'll see it through.			
10. I am always careful to write things down and to keep good records.			

Figure 20-2 ***Complete this exercise to see if you have the traits to be a successful entrepreneur. (Do not write in this book.)***

Source: Starting and Managing a Small Business of Your Own, Small Business Administration

WORKFORCE TRENDS

Workers in small businesses experience a disproportionate number of workplace fatalities. Although companies with 10 or fewer employees account for only about 15 percent of employees, 32 percent of all work-related fatalities reported in 1998 occurred in small businesses. At the end of the 20th century, the risk of fatality in businesses with 10 or fewer employees was four to five times that in businesses with 100 or more employees.

CHOOSING A BUSINESS

If you are serious about going into business, you must first identify the business you want to be in. You need to be clear about the kind of business even though you may not know exactly which one. For example, you may be sure you want to go into retailing but not know what sort of store to open. Or you may decide that some other business is better than the one you originally considered. The time to change your mind is before you start a business, not after.

You might also begin by writing out a summary of your background and experience. Include what you have learned on jobs, in school, and from hobbies that relate to your business interests. Then write down what you would like to do. Try to match up what you have done with what you would like to do. If you do not like the business you choose, your lack of interest will probably lead to failure.

The more experience and training you have, the better your chances of success. So pick a field you know a lot about. The best way to learn about a business is through actual experience. Seek a job working for somebody else in the business you are considering. Try to pick a well-managed, successful company. Once hired, gather as much management know-how as you can.

Education will help, too. While there may be no educational requirements for starting your own business, the more schooling you have, the better equipped you should be. For example, in most businesses, you must know how to figure interest and discounts, keep simple and accurate records, and take care of correspondence. How might you learn these skills in school?

Get all the facts you can about the kind of business you want to start. Find out what the appropriate trade association is, what it publishes, and what help it offers. Visit similar businesses for a firsthand idea of how they operate.

Read magazines, newspapers, and newsletters on the subject. Collect as much information as possible from other sources, even the competition. Talk with the local Chamber of Commerce, local business groups, banks, and the like.

Try to determine if potential customers need or want the type of business in which you are interested. Do not take anything for granted. Even if certain products and services meet certain needs, people may want something different.

The business you are thinking about should be in tune with the trends of the time. Choose a field in which growth is expected. You will need to study and seek advice from people who are in a position to know. Successful business owners are those who can make accurate predictions about the future.

LESSON 20.2 REVIEW

1. **Name the three main ingredients necessary for self-employment.**
2. **What is the SBA? What does it do?**
3. **Why are the first six months often crucial in getting a new business started?**
4. **Are you the type of person who might be a successful entrepreneur? Why or why not?**
5. **Why is having a trade or a technical skill a good first step in becoming an entrepreneur?**

FOCUS ON THE WORKPLACE

THE GROWTH OF SMALL BUSINESS

The first settlers in this country arrived from Europe. They came seeking freedom to live, speak, work, and worship. Many Colonial Americans chose business as a way of life. These early businesspeople were some of the first to speak out against British rule. Paul Revere, for example, was a silversmith before he became a revolutionary. Almost everyone who signed the Declaration of Independence was a businessperson or professional of some kind. For these individuals, the ideal of "life, liberty, and the pursuit of happiness" included the freedom to be one's own boss.

For about a century after the American Revolution, small businesspeople and farmers provided most of the country's goods and services. Thousands of hardworking men and women realized the American dream. They helped to lay the foundation for the Industrial Revolution of the late 1800s.

Machines invented during the Industrial Revolution led to the building of great factories. Gradually, more people went to work in cotton mills, steel mills, auto assembly plants, and other manufacturing industries.

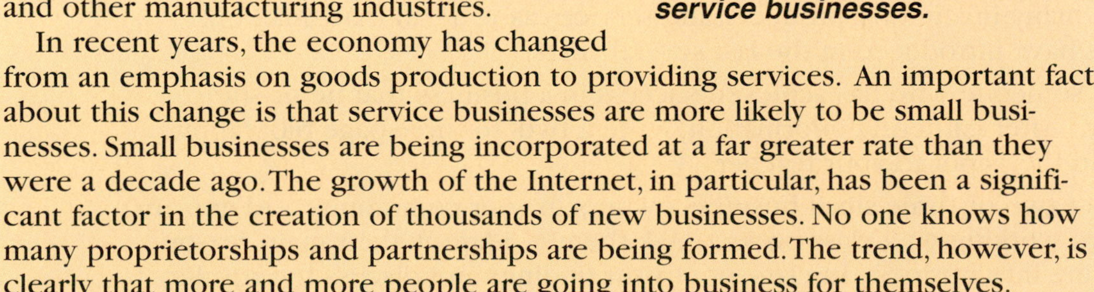

The growth of small businesses is partly due to the increase in service businesses.

In recent years, the economy has changed from an emphasis on goods production to providing services. An important fact about this change is that service businesses are more likely to be small businesses. Small businesses are being incorporated at a far greater rate than they were a decade ago. The growth of the Internet, in particular, has been a significant factor in the creation of thousands of new businesses. No one knows how many proprietorships and partnerships are being formed. The trend, however, is clearly that more and more people are going into business for themselves.

THINK CRITICALLY

1. Why would people come to America to build small businesses?
2. How has the economy changed in recent years? What does this mean for entrepreneurs?

CHAPTER 20

Chapter in Brief

Lesson 20.1 *Self-employment*

A. Small businesses are found in every type of industry. They make many important contributions to our society. Small business creates new jobs, recycles old buildings, provides opportunities for women and minorities, and originates many inventions, products, and services. A business can be organized as a proprietorship, partnership, or corporation.

B. Self-employment has many advantages and disadvantages.

Lesson 20.2 *Small Business and You*

A. Being a successful businessperson requires the right personality, know-how, and money. Before considering starting a business, you should honestly evaluate your strengths and weaknesses. Not everyone is suited to owning his or her own business.

B. If you are serious about going into business, pick a field you know a lot about. The more experience and training you have, the better your chances of success. Find out all you can about the kind of business you want to start. Try to determine whether potential customers need or want the type of business in which you are interested. Choose a field in which growth is expected. Successful business owners are those who can make accurate predictions about the future.

Activities

1. You learned earlier that the most important contribution of small business is new inventions, products, and services. With your classmates, try to identify as many inventions, products, and services as you can that small businesses have introduced in the last several years.
2. Select someone who has achieved success in a business that he or she started. After gathering information, write a two- to three-page biography. Turn in the paper to your teacher.
3. Contact two or three small business owners in your community and explain you are working on a class project. Ask them to identify their main reason for going into business. In class, pool your findings and discuss the results.
4. Search the Web or check the reference section of a local public library for franchise directories. A good source is the *Franchise Opportunities Handbook* published by the U.S. Government Printing Office. Select a franchise in which you are interested. Write to the franchiser, asking for a franchise package for prospective owners. This information may also be available on the franchiser's web site. Report your findings to the class.
5. Your instructor will give you three copies of the "Entrepreneur Rating Scale" in Figure 20-2. Complete one copy yourself. Give one to a parent or family

REVIEW

member and one to your supervisor at work and ask them to rate you. Compare the ratings and discuss the results with your teacher.

6. You are thinking about buying a franchise to sell sunglasses. Your fixed monthly expenses would be $4,500. The sunglasses cost you $6 a pair. You plan to sell them for $15 a pair. How many pairs of sunglasses would you have to sell per month to break even?

Word Power

On a separate sheet of paper, match each definition with the correct term. All definitions will be used, and a definition will be used only once.

7. Persons or companies to which money is due
8. A form of business organization in which two or more persons co-own the business
9. Businesses that sell directly to consumers
10. A legal document giving a corporation permission to conduct certain business activities
11. A person or agency that distributes goods to retailers
12. Not working for someone else; owning and operating one's own business
13. A form of business organization in which one person owns the business
14. A contract with a company to sell its goods and services within a certain area
15. Individuals elected by stockholders to make major decisions about a company
16. Someone who runs his or her own business
17. The owners of a corporation; individuals who purchase stock or shares of ownership in a company
18. A form of business organization in which stockholders own the business
19. Businesses that sell to retailers rather than to consumers; see also *supplier*

a. board of directors
b. charter
c. corporation
d. creditors
e. entrepreneur
f. franchise
g. partnership
h. proprietorship
i. retailers
j. self-employed
k. stockholders
l. supplier
m. wholesale houses

Think Critically

20. New businesses are often started because they provide something better or different. Name and discuss products and services that you are dissatisfied with that could possibly lead to the creation of a new business.
21. Think about recent trends and how society is changing. Discuss the types of businesses that are likely to be successful five years from now. Provide reasons for your predictions.
22. During the last several decades, dozens of young computer, software, and Internet whizzes became millionaires while still in their teens. How were they able to accomplish so much at such a young age?

UNIT 5

MANAGING YOUR MONEY

CHAPTERS

CO-OP CAREER SPOTLIGHT

Andrea Gusty, *Journalist*

In Southwest Alaska, in a rural village accessible only by air or river, 18-year-old Andrea Gusty became a local celebrity and radio personality while still a student at Aniak High School and its Vocational Technical Center. In the village of Aniak, where Andrea lives, there are no radio or television stations. There is not even a newspaper. The closest radio station is more than 100 miles away. So how did this high school student from a remote Alaskan village manage to become a radio correspondent? She attributes her success to hard work and her school's co-op program.

When she was a sophomore, Andrea's radio broadcasting teacher, Mike Lane, helped her attend the Alaska Native Youth Media Institute, a summer program for Alaska Native and Native American students interested in media careers. Andrea spent two summers at the institute, which led to her first job as a correspondent: covering the Kuskokwim 300 Sled Dog Race, a 300-mile event. She also covered the First Annual Sobriety Fest. In a two-part series, Andrea interviewed band members and speakers and reported on the fun and fiddle dance. During an election for a state representative, Andrea provided live coverage for Bethel, Alaska, radio station KYUK. For KNBA, an Anchorage station, Andrea broadcast a weekly program during the holiday season on Slavic, a Russian Orthodox Christmas celebration. As a result of her Christmas broadcast, KNBA sent her to Minneapolis to speak as a panelist at a weeklong seminar of the National Alliance for Media Arts and Culture, a nonprofit association that promotes film, video, audio, and online/multimedia arts.

An honor student with a 3.86 GPA, Andrea played varsity basketball and volleyball, attended classes full-time, worked as a radio correspondent, and worked at the local phone company part-time in a co-op job. Andrea would attend class for the first hour, work during the second- and third-hour classes, and then return to school for the fourth- through seventh-hour classes.

As a receptionist at the local phone company, Andrea says that she learned a lot about communications. She adds, "Bob Colliver, the president of Bush-Tell, Inc., tries to employ honor students to help them pay for college." Andrea's work at Bush-Tell, coupled with her journalism classes at school, helped her prepare to enter the Medill School of Journalism at Northwestern University in Illinois, where she began her freshman year in the fall of 2001. Andrea plans on becoming a journalist.

CHAPTER 21

OUR ECONOMIC WORLD

LESSONS

21.1 *Principles of Economics*

21.2 *The American Free Enterprise System*

PREVIEW

The 140 million people employed in the workforce produce trillions of dollars' worth of goods and services a year. This activity occurs without the government telling people where to work or what to produce.

Our system works well because people are free to make economic decisions and improve their financial condition. We have responsibilities as both consumers and producers. In this chapter, you will learn about the American economic system and your part in it.

THOUGHTS ON WORK

"The man who does not work for the love of work but only for money is not likely to make money nor find much fun in life."

Charles M. Schwab

TAKING ACTION
ECONOMIC CHOICES

Jean is very excited. She just got her first job. The only problem is that she will have to buy a car to drive to work. Jean will have to get a used car, since she cannot afford a new one.

Jean gets on the Internet to find out what to look for in buying a used car. Then she spends some time looking for different makes and models within her budget. She is even able to use the Internet to find several cars that interest her at two local dealers.

Jean visits the two dealers, as well as a third in the area. She looks at the cars she found on the Internet and at some other cars, too. Two of the dealers have similar cars that Jean would like. One car is priced higher than the other. Jean goes back and forth between the two dealers and is able to negotiate a price that is $250 less than the cost of the lowest-priced car.

Jean needs some new clothes for her job. She drives to a nearby mall and spends a few hours shopping. Some of the stores are having sales. By going to several different stores, Jean is able to find plenty of suitable clothes within her budget. The name-brand coat she wants for the fall is too expensive, however. Jean really likes the coat, so she decides to put it on layaway and pay for it a little at a time.

Jean is class treasurer, so she stays after school on Monday to attend a meeting. The class officers have to decide whether to spend class dues on a picnic at the beach or a trip to an amusement park. Jean thinks the beach would be more fun for everybody, so that's what she votes for, and that's what wins.

That evening, Jean watches the local news. There is a proposal to allow a second cable company to operate in the county. Those county council members who favor the proposal argue that this would bring cable prices down and improve the quality of service. Jean hopes the proposal passes. She thinks her family pays too much for cable TV, and the cable service doesn't carry some of the channels she would like.

SUCCESS TIP

In a free enterprise system, you can make many choices.

THINK CRITICALLY

1. What are some examples of choices in this case study?
2. How might a second cable company bring prices down and improve service?

LESSON 21.1
PRINCIPLES OF ECONOMICS

OBJECTIVES

- LIST THE FOUR FACTORS OF PRODUCTION
- EXPLAIN THE CIRCULAR FLOW OF ECONOMIC ACTIVITY
- ILLUSTRATE HOW SUPPLY AND DEMAND INFLUENCE MARKET PRICES
- NAME TWO TYPES OF ECONOMIC SYSTEMS

FACTORS OF PRODUCTION

Economics is the study of how goods and services are produced, distributed, and used. Economics is also concerned with how people and governments choose what they buy from among the many things they want. You probably do not have much trouble spending your paycheck. The hard part involves making choices from among the many things you need and want. Federal, state, and local governments have the same types of choices to make. Making choices is the most important economic issue with which individuals and governments must deal.

The city of Centerville, for example, would like to build a new swimming pool at the city park. However, there is not enough money left in the budget after the city pays employees' salaries and bills. These expenses include street maintenance, garbage collection, and snow removal. A city, like an individual or family, has only so much money to spend.

Meeting the needs of people and nations from what is available leads to the economic activity called production. **Production** is the making of goods available for human needs and wants. Production takes place when a farmer grows corn, a nurse cares for patients, or a barber cuts hair. In one way or another, all production involves the following four resources, or factors:

- ***Natural resources.*** Materials provided by nature are important to production. Soil, water, mineral deposits, and forests are all examples of a nation's resources. Human beings do not create them.
- ***Labor.*** Labor includes all of the people employed in the workforce. Both the skills of the workforce and the amount of labor help to determine the amount of production.
- ***Capital.*** Most people think of capital as money. To the economist, however, capital (sometimes called capital goods) is any person-made means of production. Tools, machines, and factories are examples of capital goods. Capital used skillfully can greatly increase productivity.
- ***Management.*** Management refers to the people who organize and direct the other three factors. Entrepreneurs, whom we discussed in Chapter 20, make up a large part of this resource. Managers assume the risk of operating a business. The need for good organization and management applies to both single-person businesses and large corporations.

THE CIRCULAR FLOW OF ECONOMIC ACTIVITY

Several kinds of economic activities help people satisfy their needs and wants. Production is one such activity. A second kind of economic activity is **consumption**. This is the process of using goods and services that have been produced. Buying a pair of shoes, drinking juice, and going to a movie are all different kinds of consumption. All of us are consumers.

There is a close relationship between consumers and producers. This is called the circular flow of economic activity. The circular flow is illustrated in Figure 21-1. Here is how it works. Suppose that you work in business or industry. The inside bottom arrow in the figure shows that you give your services (your labor and skills) to a producer who employs you. The business or industry (producer) pays you a salary or wages for your work, as indicated by the outside bottom arrow. You also receive goods and services from producers, as the inside top arrow shows. For these goods and services, you pay money to producers, as indicated by the outside top arrow.

SUPPLY AND DEMAND

Whenever goods and services are bought and sold, a **market** is created. A market may be a neighborhood grocery store or an international grain market. Buyers and sellers may meet in person, or they may conduct their business by telephone, mail, satellite transmission, or the Internet.

In a free economy, market prices rise and fall according to supply and demand. **Supply** is the amount of goods or services available for sale. **Demand** is the willingness of consumers to spend money for goods and services. When demand is greater than supply, the seller will often raise the price of a product or service. This encourages the producer to provide a greater supply. Eventually, the supply begins to catch up with the demand. If the supply becomes greater than the demand, the seller may lower the price to help get rid of the

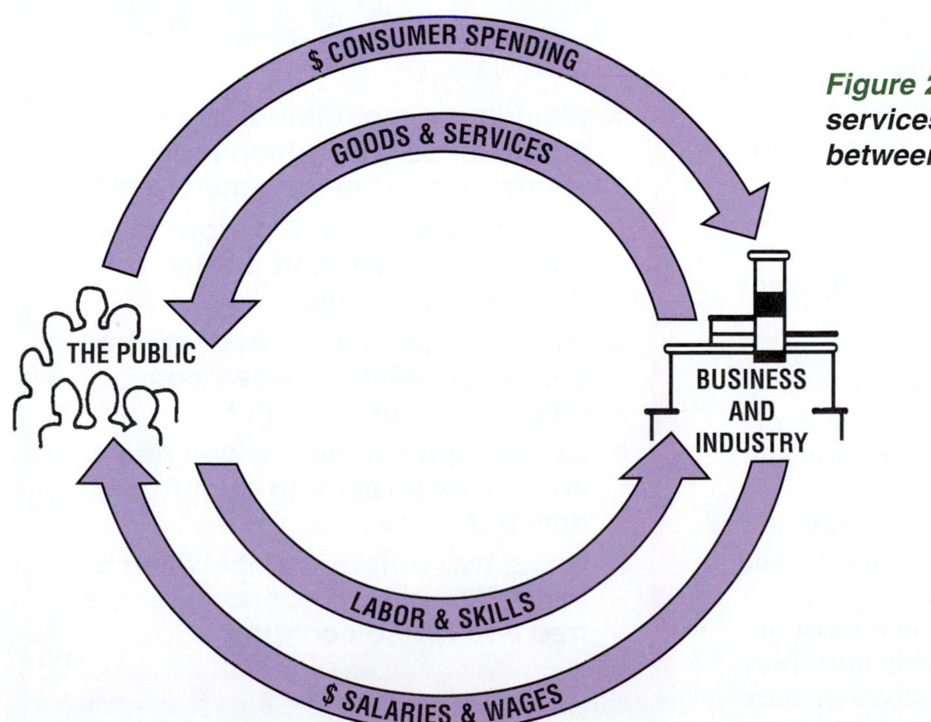

Figure 21-1 ***A circular flow of goods, services, and money takes place between consumers and producers.***

WORKFORCE TRENDS

Roughly 50,000 workers die every year from occupational diseases. Fatalities from occupational diseases are frequently overlooked because they tend to occur long after workers are exposed to harmful chemical or physical agents. Shipyard jobs with exposure to asbestos during World War II, for example, were associated with numerous cases of lung cancer from the 1960s through the 1980s.

excess supply. Can you provide an example of such a product or service?

In a market, competition helps to keep prices down. **Competition** refers to the efforts of sellers to win potential customers. Suppose there is only one seller for a product or service. Prices will be high. Consumers have no real choice. But if there are many sellers, each competes with the others. Shoppers benefit from the lower prices that result.

ECONOMIC SYSTEMS

Countries do not solve their basic economic problems in the same ways. There are different economic systems. One major type is the centrally planned economy. Under this system, the people have no voice in economic decision making. A central authority (government) owns all resources and sets wages. The group in power also controls all production and distribution. For example, the central government decides how much production should be devoted to consumer goods, such as automobiles and washing machines.

A second major type of economic system is free enterprise. In such an economy, people and industries can do more or less as they please. Private individuals and industries own most of the resources and control production and distribution. People can work for themselves or they can sell their labor to someone else for a salary or wages. Consumers can buy and sell as they choose. Such buying and selling creates markets in which supply and demand influence prices.

In actual practice, neither of these economies is ever found in pure form. Historically, the former Soviet Union leaned heavily toward a centrally planned economy. In the late 1980s, however, the Soviet Union and other Communist nations of Eastern Europe began to relax government control of the economy. Private ownership of farms and factories began to be allowed.

The United States leans heavily toward a free enterprise economy. The government, however, owns many resources and runs various industries. It also controls prices for some items and regulates the manufacture and sale of certain products, such as drugs. Both the United States and the countries of the former Soviet Union, then, are what economists call mixed economies.

LESSON 21.1 REVIEW

1. **What is the most important economic issue with which individuals and governments must deal?**
2. **All production involves four factors. Name them and briefly describe each one.**
3. **What phrase is used to describe the relationship between consumers and producers?**
4. **Explain how market prices rise and fall as a result of supply and demand.**
5. **Name two differences between a centrally planned economy and a free enterprise economy.**

HIGH-GROWTH OCCUPATIONS
FOR THE 21st CENTURY

Physical Therapist Assistants and Aides

Physical therapist assistants and aides perform parts of physical therapy procedures and related tasks selected and delegated by a supervising physical therapist. About two-thirds of the jobs held by physical therapist assistants and aides are in hospitals or offices of physical therapists. Others work in nursing and personal care facilities, outpatient rehabilitation centers, offices and clinics of physicians, and home health agencies.

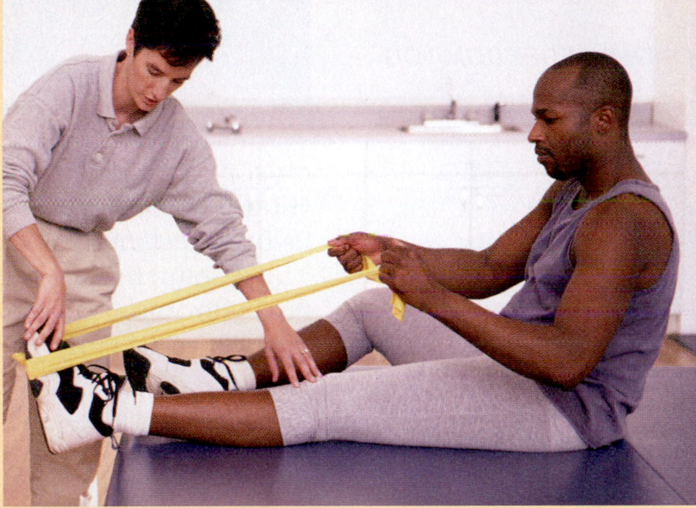

The treatment procedures performed by physical therapist assistants help people recover from injuries or diseases.

These workers assist physical therapists in providing services that help improve mobility, relieve pain, and prevent or limit permanent physical disabilities of patients suffering from injuries or diseases. Patients include accident victims and individuals with disabling conditions, such as lower back pain, arthritis, heart disease, fractures, head injuries, and cerebral palsy.

Physical therapist assistants perform a variety of tasks. Treatment procedures delegated to these workers, under the direction of therapists, involve exercises, massages, electrical stimulation, paraffin baths, hot and cold packs, traction, and ultrasound. Physical therapist assistants record the patient's responses to treatment and report to the physical therapist the outcome of each treatment.

Physical therapist aides help make therapy sessions productive, under the direct supervision of a physical therapist or physical therapist assistant. They are usually responsible for keeping the treatment area clean and organized and preparing for each patient's therapy. When patients need assistance moving to or from a treatment area, aides push them in a wheelchair or provide them with a shoulder to lean on. Because they are not licensed, aides perform a more limited range of tasks than physical therapist assistants do.

The duties of aides include some clerical tasks, such as ordering supplies, answering the phone, and filling out insurance forms and other paperwork. The extent to which an aide or an assistant performs clerical tasks depends on the size and location of the facility.

LESSON 21.2

THE AMERICAN FREE ENTERPRISE SYSTEM

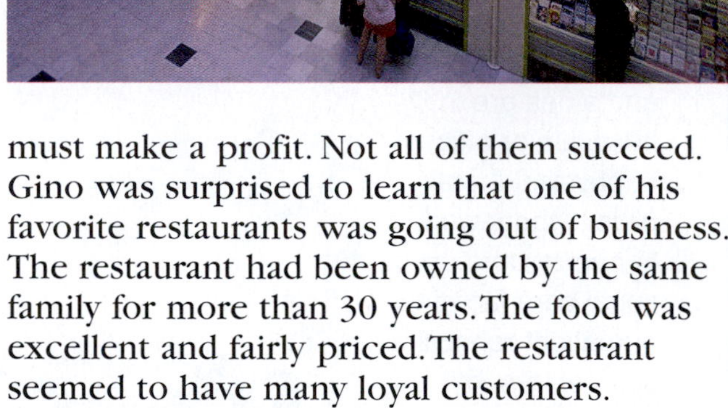

- SUMMARIZE CHARACTERISTICS OF THE AMERICAN FREE ENTERPRISE SYSTEM
- NAME THREE THINGS REQUIRED FOR ECONOMIC GROWTH
- DISCUSS TYPES OF ECONOMIC FREEDOM YOU ENJOY

CHARACTERISTICS OF FREE ENTERPRISE

The United States is said to have a free enterprise economy, even though it does not exist in a pure form. For the most part, the American economy runs by itself without government interference. People and industries make most of their own economic decisions. Let's look more closely at this system.

Private Ownership

Suppose you go to a busy part of your town or city. You stop for an oil change at a shop owned by a friend. He says your car will be ready in half an hour. Since it is time for lunch, you go next door to a cafe to eat. The auto service shop and the cafe are two examples of private ownership. They are owned and operated by individuals who have risked their own money to make a profit. For the most part, people can set up any legal kind of business they wish.

Profit Motive

Business owners want to make as much money as possible. To at least stay in operation, businesses must make a profit. Not all of them succeed. Gino was surprised to learn that one of his favorite restaurants was going out of business. The restaurant had been owned by the same family for more than 30 years. The food was excellent and fairly priced. The restaurant seemed to have many loyal customers.

PERSONAL DECISIONS

A new brand of athletic shoes has just been introduced. These shoes are "hot." Merchants can hardly keep them in stock. You go to the store to buy some. You love the shoes but are shocked by the price. They are about $30 more than what you usually pay. You would have to charge them since you do not have enough cash. Your mom suggests that you wait a few months until the price comes down. You doubt that they will be any cheaper later on.

WHAT WOULD YOU DO?

COMMUNICATION AT WORK

CHARTS AND GRAPHS

Economic information is often presented in charts and graphs. We see them in newspapers, magazines, and TV news broadcasts. Economists and people in business use charts and graphs to present information in a way that is easy to understand. Being able to read and use charts and graphs is a valuable workplace skill. There are three common types:

- A pie chart is a circle divided into wedge-shaped parts. Pie charts are useful for showing the size of each part in relation to the whole. A pie chart is often used to represent a budget. Each wedge represents part of the budget. You can see a pie chart on page 287.
- Bar graphs are useful for comparing items. A bar graph might be used to compare the amount of surplus (extra money) in the federal budget over several years. There would be one bar for each year. The bars would be different heights, depending on how much money each represented. You will find several examples of bar graphs in Chapter 14.
- Line graphs are also useful for making comparisons. They generally show trends or change. A line graph might show how much the federal government has spent over the past ten years. Amounts of money would be on the vertical axis. Years would be on the horizontal axis. Points would be plotted on the graph for the amount of money spent each year. These points would be connected with lines. Page 241 shows a line graph.

Since Gino wanted to own a restaurant, he checked into buying it. In examining the financial records of the business, Gino discovered why it was being sold. Mr. Colletti, the owner, may have known how to prepare good food, but his knowledge of running a business was sadly outdated.

Gino figured that the costs of operation were about 20 percent higher than they should have been. He concluded that by using good business practices, such as wholesale buying, quantity purchasing, and control of overhead, he could make a good profit. What's more, he could do it without sacrificing quality or service.

Competition

Jenny wanted to buy a certain brand and style of shoes. Each store that carried the shoes wanted a different price. What did Jenny do? She bought from the store where she would get the most for her money. If one company had a monopoly on the shoe business, Jenny would not have had a choice. A **monopoly** is exclusive control over the supply of a product or service. Every pair of shoes in all the stores would have been the same price.

Free enterprise needs competition. It forces producers to be efficient and encourages a wide variety of goods and services. Competition is so important to the American economy that the government has passed laws to forbid or regulate monopolies.

If one company had a monopoly on shoes, prices would be the same everywhere.

YOU'RE A WHAT? PEST CONTROLLER

Unwanted creatures such as ants, mice, roaches, and termites infest buildings and households. *Pest controllers* locate, identify, destroy, and repel pests. They use their knowledge of pests' lifestyles and habits, along with an arsenal of techniques. The most common method of pest control is pesticide application.

Pest controllers also use traps, baits, and poisonous gases to control pests. They advise clients on sanitation practices and use of physical barriers to manage pests. Because of health and environmental risks associated with pesticide use, state and federal laws require pest controllers to be certified through training and examination. Since pests are a bigger problem in warm climates, about half of all pest controllers work in the Sunbelt states.

Freedom of Choice

You have already read that people having certain resources can start a business. They are not the only ones who have choices. Consumers and workers do too.

Consumer choices influence the types of goods and services produced. For instance, if consumers stop buying a certain product, it will probably disappear from store shelves. Buyers also help determine the prices of goods. Marketers will price as highly as they think the market will bear. If they are wrong, prices will fall. Prices also go down if there is heavy competition.

A similar situation exists with workers. They seek to be paid as much as possible. In a free enterprise economy, they are able to work for whomever they choose. And people who want to change jobs can do so.

Profit and competition help control this system. Some say that in free enterprise, markets are self-regulated. This means that supply and demand help set prices for goods and wages for workers.

ECONOMIC GROWTH

The United States economy has grown steadily throughout the years. In order for this growth to continue, several things must occur. First, a portion of the nation's resources must be used to produce capital goods, such as tools, machines, and factories. Second, individuals and businesses must use a portion of their income for savings and investments. Third, the nation must use a portion of its resources for education and training. These influences on economic growth will now be illustrated.

You have read about the four factors of production. As you will recall, these are natural resources, labor, capital, and management. Companies use these factors to provide capital goods and consumer goods and services. A country cannot grow if it uses all of its resources to produce consumer goods and services. These do not produce anything of further value. Think about it. Once you buy them, a pair of jeans loses value. Capital goods, on the other hand, create future economic worth. Suppose a trucking company puts money into new rigs and loading docks. Workers use the docks over and over to load goods onto trucks. These, in turn, carry cargo to distant markets.

When buying new capital goods, businesses often borrow money. For example, Mrs. Luna decides to add on to her flower shop. She does not have all the funds she needs. The bank gives her a loan. Where does First City Bank get this money? It comes from deposits from people like you. When the savings rate is high, banks have more money to lend to businesses. The economy can grow.

Capital goods produce value. So do workers and managers. Offering further training to employees benefits a business. Skilled workers and managers contribute to future production and growth. Many employers pay for this education.

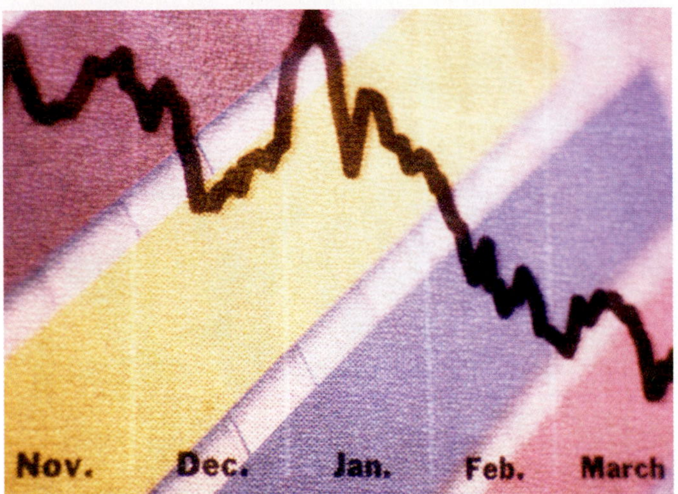

Line graphs are often used to show economic changes over time.

Patterns of Economic Growth

A free enterprise economy goes through various cycles. Tracing these shifts is like following the path of a roller coaster. A period of expanding economic growth is known as **prosperity**. During these good times, unemployment is low. Workers receive steady pay raises because companies make high profits. Since so many people are working, they buy many consumer items. This leads to increasing production. The supply of goods meets the demand, so prices stay down.

A downturn in the economy is called a **recession**. Let's see what can happen. Suppose there is a strong national feeling that the economy will turn bad. While concerned consumers save more of their incomes, goods pile up on shelves. Companies make production cutbacks, which lead to worker layoffs. Young people seeking their first jobs cannot find work. People then have less money to spend, so they buy even fewer goods.

If a recession gets worse, a depression can result. A **depression** is a severe recession marked by stagnant business activity. In this situation, very large numbers of people become unemployed. Consumers purchase only what they really need. Business failures increase. Production drops further and even more workers lose their jobs.

Major fluctuations in economic growth have occurred for decades. Yet there is much disagreement (even among economists) regarding causes and solutions. Many heated national debates result from disagreement among politicians and others over inflation, recession, and unemployment.

Inflation

A serious and frequent problem of our economic system is **inflation**. This is when prices of goods and services rise sharply. A *slight* upward trend in prices is very typical of free enterprise and is not very serious. Wages usually increase along with prices. When prices go up much faster than wages, though, money loses some of its value. Let's see how this can happen.

Workers at The Jiffy Company do not think their wages are keeping up with the cost of living. Through their union, employees bargain for pay increases. To cover the raises, the company increases the prices of its products. Consumers buying a Jiffy food processor, for example, will now pay more for it. If there are price increases throughout the economy, Jiffy's workers will continue to seek higher wages.

PERSONAL DECISIONS

Business has been great at the shop where you work. You received a raise and are working a good deal of overtime. You are using the extra money to buy clothes and other things you have always wanted. One day at break, you show a coworker a picture of the new watch you put on layaway. "It is neat," he says. "But if I were you, I would not spend all of my paycheck. Good times will not last forever."

"I thought business was good," you say.

"It is," he responds. "This is the way it always is before things slow down and we get laid off."

You have not thought about that. You wonder if you should go ahead and buy the expensive watch.

WHAT WOULD YOU DO?

What causes inflation? There is no single, easy answer. However, economists generally agree that the following factors contribute to inflation:

- Excessive consumer demand
- Government spending and deficits (A **deficit** is how much has been spent over budget or over what has been taken in.)
- Increased energy costs
- Decreased productivity
- Government regulations
- Fear of future inflation

Even though the causes are complex, inflation can be curbed. During the 1990s, for example, the annual inflation rate averaged only 3 percent. But during the 1980s, it was 5.6 percent; and in the 1970s, it was 7.1 percent. The highest annual inflation rate during the last three decades was in 1980, when the inflation rate reached 13.5 percent. All segments of society, including government, business, labor, and consumers, must work together to ensure such high rates do not return.

ECONOMIC FREEDOM

You have learned that in a free enterprise system, individuals make most of the economic decisions. Another way of saying this is that people in a market economy enjoy economic freedom. Economic freedom consists of the following rights:

- The right to choose an occupation
- The right to change occupations or jobs
- The right to engage in business and to make a profit
- The right to spend money as one chooses
- The right to offer our goods or services at prices we decide
- The right to reject prices on goods or services we may want to buy
- The right to use property and wealth to produce income
- The right to succeed, limited only by one's ambition and ability

Economic freedom is not available to everyone in the world. Like other freedoms, people often take economic freedom for granted. Economic freedom can be lost or weakened if individuals, businesses, and governments fail to act as responsible consumers and producers.

The right to choose an occupation is one of the economic freedoms we enjoy.

LESSON 21.2 REVIEW

1. List the four characteristics of free enterprise discussed in the lesson.
2. Why is it important for individuals and businesses to save and invest money?
3. Why is it important for companies to invest in training for workers and managers?
4. The economic growth of a free market economy goes through cycles like the path of a roller coaster. Give an example.
5. List six factors that economists generally agree contribute to inflation.

FOCUS ON SKILLS FOR LIVING

COUNTERFEIT GOODS UNDERCUT THE ECONOMY

Few customers are aware that they may be buying counterfeit goods. Hundreds of fake products have flooded the market. These include jewelry, jeans, handbags, auto parts, toys, electronic appliances, perfumes, and even prescription medicines.

The economic toll is staggering. Counterfeit goods cut into company profits, reduce taxes paid, and cost jobs. Health and safety are also major concerns. Imagine driving around with fake brake shoes on your car! The death of a helicopter pilot was linked to the failure of a fake rotor assembly part. Many people are taking drugs and using health care products that contain ineffective or wrong ingredients.

A U.S. Customs Canine Enforcement Team inspects arriving international mail.

Source: U.S. Customs/Photo by James Tourtellote

Here is an example of how fake products are produced and distributed. A dishonest importer signs up a foreign manufacturer to make a shoddy oil filter. The manufacturer produces the filters. They are packaged into large crates generically labeled "oil filters" to pass U.S. Customs. The importer receives the filters and packs them in boxes printed with a real brand name. They are sold to a legitimate wholesaler as overstock (extra stock that is not needed). The wholesaler, who is unaware they are fake, sells the filters to reputable retail outlets. Consumers then come along and buy the phony filters at gas stations, auto dealers, chain stores, and the like.

There are a number of things you can do to protect yourself. Be wary when looking for hard-to-get toys and other fad items. When shopping for a product having a high-status trademark, read labels carefully and pay close attention to workmanship. Look for sloppy printing, misspelled words, and altered logos on packages. Do not buy a product when the packaging is missing or not up to standard. Buy only at reputable places of business. If you do happen to get taken, you will be more likely to get a refund.

THINK CRITICALLY

1. Some people knowingly buy counterfeit products. Why would they do this?
2. What are some effects that counterfeit products have on the economy?

CHAPTER 21

Chapter in Brief

Lesson 21.1 *Principles of Economics*

A. Economics is the study of how goods and services are produced, distributed, and used. It is also concerned with how people and governments choose what they buy from among the many things they want.

B. Meeting the needs of people and nations from what is available leads to the economic activity called production. All production involves four resources: natural resources, labor, capital, and management. Consumption is the process of using goods and services that have been produced. The circular flow of economic activity links consumers and producers.

C. Whenever goods and services are bought and sold, a market is created. In a market, competition helps to keep prices down.

D. In a centrally planned economy, the government owns all resources and controls production and distribution. In a free enterprise economy, private individuals and industries own most of the resources and control production and distribution.

Lesson 21.2 *The American Free Enterprise System*

A. The American free enterprise system has four main characteristics: private ownership, profit motive, competition, and freedom of choice. The system runs largely by itself without government interference.

B. For economic growth to continue, (1) a portion of the nation's resources must be used to produce capital goods, (2) individuals and businesses must use a portion of their income for savings and investments, and (3) the nation must use a portion of its resources for education and training.

C. A free enterprise economy goes through cycles. A period of expanding economic growth is known as prosperity. A downturn in the economy is called a recession. A very serious recession can lead to a depression.

D. Inflation is when prices of goods and services rise sharply. These factors are thought to contribute to inflation: excessive consumer demand, government spending and deficits, increased energy costs, decreased productivity, government regulations, and fear of future inflation.

E. Economic freedom is not available to everyone in the world. It can be lost or weakened if individuals, businesses, and governments fail to act as responsible consumers and producers.

Activities

1. As a class, try to identify someone in your community who once lived in a country with a centrally planned economy. Invite the person to class to share personal experiences. Prepare questions beforehand.
2. As a class, identify the countries that maintain centrally planned economies. Then divide into small groups corresponding to the number of countries.

REVIEW

Each group should collect information about the country and the current status of its economy and present a report to the class.

3. You often hear news reports about the gross domestic product (GDP). What is it? How is it figured? How is it used as a measure of economic growth? Use encyclopedias or other resources to answer these questions.
4. As a class, invite people who lived through it to speak about the Great Depression, which occurred during the 1930s. Prepare questions ahead of time.

Word Power

On a separate sheet of paper, match each definition with the correct term. All definitions will be used, and a definition will be used only once.

5. A downturn in the economy
6. The process of using goods and services that have been produced
7. A sharp increase in the costs of goods and services
8. The willingness of consumers to spend money for goods and services
9. The amount of goods or services available for sale
10. The efforts of sellers to win potential customers
11. Exclusive control of the supply of a product or service
12. A severe recession marked by stagnant business activity
13. The making of goods available for human needs and wants
14. How much has been spent over budget or over what has been taken in
15. A period of expanding economic growth
16. An area of economic activity created whenever goods and services are bought and sold
17. The study of how goods and services are produced, distributed, and used

a. competition
b. consumption
c. deficit
d. demand
e. depression
f. economics
g. inflation
h. market
i. monopoly
j. production
k. prosperity
l. recession
m. supply

Think Critically

18. In the early 1980s, large automakers lost billions of dollars. Thousands of autoworkers lost their jobs. Yet the price of new cars continued to rise. This seems to contradict what we have learned about the law of supply and demand. Discuss this situation in class.
19. Discuss how the following individuals might contribute to inflation: (a) a union leader negotiating a labor contract, (b) a merchant setting prices for goods, (c) a factory worker assembling car parts, (d) a consumer shopping for a DVD player, and (e) an elected official preparing a new budget.
20. What are some of the things the government often does during periods of recession to help stimulate the economy and relieve unemployment?

CHAPTER 22

THE CONSUMER IN THE MARKETPLACE

LESSONS

22.1 *You as a Consumer*

22.2 *Advertising and the Consumer*

22.3 *Consumer Rights and Responsibilities*

PREVIEW

As a buyer, you will make decisions all your life. Today, you may choose between two brands of shampoo. In a few years, you may need to make more important choices, such as which house to buy. Making a mistake then could be very costly. By learning wise consumer skills now, you might save yourself problems later.

THOUGHTS ON WORK

"Take the best that exists and make it better. When it does not exist, design it. Accept nothing nearly right or good enough."
Sir Frederick Henry Royce

TAKING ACTION
CONSUMER CHOICES

Mike goes to evening school and works part-time. Even though his job pays well, Mike never seems to have any money. In fact, he lives from paycheck to paycheck. Let's take a moment to see where Mike's money goes.

Mike cashes a paycheck for $120 every Friday. On the way home, he likes to treat himself to dinner at his favorite restaurant. It costs him $10 for his meal. When he gets to his house, he gives his parents $15 for room and board.

Mike likes to go out with his buddies on Friday nights. They usually go bowling or to the mall or a movie. This Friday, they go to the mall. They stop at a music store. His friends want to buy a CD by one of their favorite artists that just came out. The CD costs $18.99. On an impulse, Mike gets it, too. With tax, his purchase comes to about $20.

Mike has to put gas in his car on Monday. Filling his car costs $17. He eats lunch out every day. It costs him $6 on Monday, about what he usually pays. On Tuesday, he and some coworkers go out to lunch to celebrate someone's birthday. Mike's share of the bill is $10.

That evening, Mike's dad shows him the telephone bill. Mike pays for calls he makes to his girlfriend, Janine, who is going to college out of town. He gives his dad $18 for his long-distance calls.

Are you keeping track? It is Tuesday, and Mike has just $24 left. Janine is coming home on Thursday for a long weekend, and he wants to take her out to a movie that night. Mike decides to skip lunch on Wednesday and Thursday to save his money for movie tickets. This is something he does often.

When Mike is driving home on Wednesday, his front right tire blows out. Mike has known that he should replace the tire for some time, but he could never seem to find the money. Since Mike doesn't have any savings, he has to borrow $65 from his parents to pay for a new tire. Mike can't believe his luck. The insurance and loan payments for his car are coming up, too. When will he ever be able to get ahead?

SUCCESS TIP

Being a wise consumer begins with making good choices.

THINK CRITICALLY

1. What are some poor choices that Mike makes?
2. What are some ways that Mike could save money?

LESSON 22.1

YOU AS A CONSUMER

OBJECTIVES

- GIVE EXAMPLES OF GOODS AND SERVICES THAT ARE CONSUMED
- NAME AND DESCRIBE THE THREE STAGES INVOLVED IN CONSUMING GOODS AND SERVICES

GOODS AND SERVICES

A market is created whenever two or more parties come together to buy and sell. At one time, a typical market was a clearing along the river. There were few items to buy and few choices available.

Now, a market may be a department store, service station, grocery store, movie theater, or barbershop. All markets operate basically the same way. That is, sellers wish to attract buyers and then make a profit on a sale. Buyers, on the other hand, look for good quality at a low price.

A **consumer** is someone who buys or uses goods and services. **Goods** are articles that are produced or manufactured. Some goods, such as food, are used up almost immediately. Other goods, such as tools, last for many years. A house is also a type of good. If properly built and maintained, a house may last for a long time.

Services differ from goods. Services involve the payment of money to people and businesses for work performed. Having a suit dry-cleaned and getting a haircut are personal services. We pay fees to doctors, dentists, and lawyers in exchange for their knowledge and skills. Buying life insurance or obtaining a credit card involves the use of business services. Many common services that we use are for maintenance and repair work, such as having an automobile tuned up or a television fixed. Entertainment and recreation are also types of services that we often purchase.

Money buys food, clothing, and other necessities. We also buy goods and services that we want but may not need. Designer jeans and a concert ticket are examples of things we may want. People often use the term *need* when they really mean *want*. To say that you need a new pair of designer jeans is probably not true. You may want the jeans, but you do not actually need them. Needs are necessities; wants are luxuries.

WHAT IS CONSUMING?

Being a consumer is more than simply paying money for something. Consuming involves three stages—choosing, buying, and using.

Making Choices

Buying always involves making choices. You have to eat in order to stay alive, so that really is not a choice. However, you do have to make decisions about what you eat. Do you eat a balanced diet or only pizza and soft drinks? Do you prepare meals at home? Or, like Mike, do you eat in restaurants or skip meals to have money for movie tickets?

Sometimes, you have to choose between two similar products or services. Suppose you are going to buy a pair of shoes. The two pairs you

MATH CONNECTION

You are grocery shopping and need to get dry cat food. You can buy a $4^1/_2$-lb bag for $4.19 or an 18-oz box for $1.49. Which is the better buy?

SOLUTION

Convert one of the weights so both are in the same units. Then divide the price by the weight.

Since there are 16 ounces in a pound, $4^1/_2$ lbs = 72 oz.

$4.19 ÷ 72 = $.06 per ounce

$1.49 ÷ 18 = $.08 per ounce

The $4^1/_2$-lb bag is the better buy.

like vary in price and quality. How do you decide which pair to buy?

Some choices involve different kinds of products or services. Let's say you would like to have a hair permanent and a sweater. But you only have enough money for one of these. Which will you decide to buy?

Another type of choice is whether to spend your money or save it. This may be the most difficult choice of all. If you save some of your money, it will mean doing without some things that you would like to have now.

Buying Wisely

This stage begins once you have decided to buy. Knowledge and planning are very important to wise buying. There are several ways to learn about different products and services. You can talk with friends and family, attend special classes, do research on the Web, and read consumer magazines. *Consumer Reports* is perhaps the best-known consumer magazine. It rates various products in terms of price, quality, and other factors. Knowing which products are rated highly can save you shopping time as well as money. There are still other things you can do to be a good shopper.

Bill Martin is a wise consumer. Let's see how he saves money on food and clothing. First of all, Bill never shops for food when he is hungry. He knows that when he is hungry he tends to buy food on impulse.

To avoid exceeding his food budget, Bill plans what he will buy. He writes everything on a list and follows it. Bill knows the grocery stores in his town run sales on weekends, so he shops then when possible. He buys generic products when he can, because the quality is good and the prices are lower. **Generic products** state only the common name of the product on the label ("grape juice"). **Brand-name products** have a unique name given to them by the manufacturer ("Welch's Purple 100% Grape Juice").

Large sizes of cereal and canned food are often good buys. Bill chooses the large size when he is sure that he will use up the product. If some of the food is wasted, a large size isn't a bargain. Last week, Bill saw some dented cans in a bin. He passed the bin without buying because the food might have been spoiled. Spoiled food, no matter how cheap, is no bargain.

PERSONAL DECISIONS

You live in the city where you work and share an apartment with several friends. You all pool grocery money and take turns shopping and cooking. You are more thrifty than your roommates. You often buy store brands and generic products rather than more expensive brand-name foods. One day, as you are unloading groceries, one of your roommates comes into the kitchen.

"What is this stuff?" she bellows. "I am not eating this generic junk! We can afford to buy some decent food."

WHAT WOULD YOU DO?

Recently, Bill went to a department store to look for a new shirt. He found four he liked but rejected two right away. The care label on one said, "dry-clean only." Over several years, dry cleaning can be expensive. The other rejected shirt was 100 percent cotton and would need to be ironed. Of the two remaining shirts, one was better-made than the other.

However, before buying the better-made shirt, Bill decided to do some comparison shopping. **Comparison shopping** means finding out the cost of a product or service at several different places before making a decision to buy. Bill first checked prices in a mail-order catalog. They were slightly cheaper than the store's, but he would have to wait for the shirt to be delivered and pay postage. Then Bill saw a discount store's ad for shirts. When Bill reached the store, a clerk was putting shirts on a shelf. Two of them were exactly what Bill wanted. The labels showed they were brand-name shirts. Best of all, the shirts were on sale for 25 percent off.

Buying wisely also involves the careful use of credit. Some businesses sell products or services for less when you pay cash. If you charge a purchase, it is important to know how much more you will pay. Usually, if you pay within a certain amount of time, the credit is free. If you do not pay right away, though, credit may be expensive.

Examine clothing carefully before buying.

Using Goods and Services Properly

Wise consuming does not end after you bring a product home. If a product is ruined because of carelessness, you have wasted money. Treat products as if you want them to last forever. Suppose you just bought a new hair dryer. Save the receipt in case you have to return the product. Read the instructions carefully *before* trying it.

Once you are sure the item works, check the packaging for the warranty card. A **warranty** is a guarantee or promise that a product is free from defects. Fill out the card, make a photocopy for your records, and send it in right away.

Always use products according to the directions. If you misuse a product, *you* are responsible for any damage. Manufacturers will not honor warranties on misused products.

Being a wise consumer of services is also important. For example, the price of an oil change may vary by $10 or more depending on where you have a car serviced. Watch for advertising by automobile dealers, discount stores, service stations, and tire and appliance service centers. Such businesses frequently lower the price on oil changes simply to increase business and get you into their shop. If you want to save the most money, buy the oil and filter at a discount store and change the oil yourself.

LESSON 22.1 REVIEW

1. How are the goals of a buyer and a seller different?
2. What is a need? A want?
3. The process of consuming has three stages. Name and briefly describe them.
4. Give three reasons why Bill Martin is a wise consumer.
5. Why should you use and care for a product properly?

LESSON 22.2

ADVERTISING AND THE CONSUMER

- *EXPLAIN ADVANTAGES AND DISADVANTAGES OF ADVERTISING*
- *IDENTIFY DIFFERENT ADVERTISING TECHNIQUES*
- *DESCRIBE SALES TRAPS TO AVOID*

ROLE OF ADVERTISING

Sellers of goods and services use advertising to attract potential buyers. **Advertising** is any type of public notice or message intended to aid in the sale of a product or service. It is all around us. It is in newspapers and magazines. Ads also appear on television, buses, signs, billboards, and the Web. Do you receive advertising in the mail? This form is called **direct-mail advertising**.

Advertising is very important for both sellers and consumers. From a business point of view, the purpose of advertising is to aid in selling goods and services. For consumers, advertising provides information about goods and services for sale.

What are some ways that advertising helps you, the consumer? Well, suppose you see two newspaper ads for A-1 tents. One store's price is cheaper than the other's. Without leaving your home, you can decide where to buy the tent at the better price. This way, you do not have to go from store to store to check prices. You save time and money.

The next day, you hear a radio spot in which the announcer talks about a bargain tune-up at Smith's Garage. A while later, you see an ad in the window of Pope's Auto. On the same tune-up, Pope's offers a better price than Smith's. Again, by comparing advertising, you are able to save money.

Do you complain about ads on radio and television? Without advertising, many of your favorite programs would go off the air. This is because most of the costs of producing these programs are paid for by advertising. Newspapers, magazines, and web sites are also operated with money made through advertising. As you can see, without advertising our world would be quite different than it is now.

Advertising also has disadvantages. Consumers pay for it. The cost of advertising often ranges from 0 to 5 percent of the selling price of a product or service. So \$.50 of a \$10 price tag could be advertising costs.

Advertising can be expensive in yet other ways. It can convince us to buy things we may not actually need. Jason knows this—now.

Jason had been saving his hard-earned money for a used motorcycle. He already had \$300. Last

NOTHING BUT NET

Most high schools sponsor a variety of cocurricular clubs that students can join to share their interests. Thousands of discussion groups have been created on the Web for similar reasons. For example, people who are interested in country music can create a mailing list and use e-mail to communicate among themselves. Subscribing is free and easy to do. Once your name is on the list, you will begin to receive copies of e-mail messages submitted by members. You can read and contribute messages as you wish.

Another common setup is to post messages at a web site. Anyone can go to the site, read messages, and post a reply or start a new discussion.

winter, he kept seeing ads for leather coats. Jason already had a nice coat, but many of his friends had leather ones. Jason thought they looked great.

On the way to the bank one day, Jason was passing a clothing store. On an impulse, he went in. He entered with $300 and left with a leather coat and a few dollars. After several weeks, Jason was sorry he had not saved the money. He had to start saving for a motorcycle all over again.

ADVERTISING TECHNIQUES

To get us to remember their products or services, advertisers use means such as pictures, slogans, and jingles (catchy tunes and slogans). In fact, we may often use a brand name to refer to a whole class of products. For example, how many times have you heard "Scotch tape" instead of "cellophane tape"? How about Kleenex tissues, Xerox copies, and Levi's jeans? Can you think of other examples?

Once people are familiar with a product's name, they may buy the product. But advertisers do not take chances. To achieve their aims, advertisers use proven methods, such as the following:

- ***Endorsements.*** Famous people present the advertising message. For example, a well-known athlete may tell you she uses a Whammo tennis racquet. If the racquet is good enough for her, it should suit you. Right? That is what the advertiser wants you to think.
- ***Familiarity.*** You hear a jingle over and over. The advertiser wants you to become familiar with a product and remember it.
- ***Association.*** This approach often is seen during the holiday season. Here is an example. A horse-drawn sleigh passes through a beautiful, snow-covered landscape. This pleasant scene is then associated with the product being advertised.
- ***Goodwill.*** Some advertisers work hard to create a good public image. They may provide health tips, donate money to worthwhile causes, or engage in other activities. A major fast-food restaurant chain, for example, paid for the swimming and diving facility used at a recent Olympic Games.
- ***Successful living.*** This approach appeals to people's desire for success, wealth, status, or beauty. For instance, one manufacturer of men's shoes uses the phrase "Shades of the Sophisticated Man" in its advertisements. The message is that you will be more sophisticated if you wear the shoes.
- ***Emotional appeal.*** Many ads contain messages related to happiness, friendship, and other pleasant emotions. "Buy a diamond for someone you love" is an example of a type of theme that frequently appears.
- ***Economic appeal.*** Messages about spending, saving, and making money are featured in many ads. An example is, "No money down. No payments until after the holidays!"
- ***Conformity.*** This approach encourages you to buy something because others have it. You may hear, "Our product is used by millions of satisfied customers." An example of a slightly different approach is, "By using this camera, you, too, can be an expert photographer."

- ***Scare tactics.*** We all want to avoid situations that are dangerous, embarrassing, or otherwise unpleasant. Who wouldn't want to prevent an auto accident? Sure-Grip tires will keep you from having one. This advertiser wants you to think you may have an accident if you do not use the product.
- ***Intellectual appeal.*** Many products claim to help you become more informed or better educated. Or they appeal to your intelligence. Perhaps the following sounds familiar: "Smart people have found this dishwashing soap to be the better product."
- ***Health and comfort.*** This approach is used in ads for products such as aspirin, skin creams, and vitamins. The ads tell you how the product will improve your health or make you feel better.

SALES TRAPS

There is nothing wrong with advertising as long as it is honest. If you dislike an ad's message, you can choose not to buy. Problems occur when advertising is misleading. Be alert to the following deceptive (misleading) practices:

- ***False pricing.*** When consumers see an item that has been marked down, they naturally believe it is a bargain. Sale prices are usually lower than regular prices. However, some merchants raise the regular price *before* marking an item down. Let's say that the suggested price for a watch is $80. The seller changes the price tag to read "$120." The watch is then "marked down" to $80. A consumer buys the watch, believing that $40 has been saved. The truth is that the watch was bought at the regular price.
- ***Bait and switch.*** This occurs when an ad offers a product or service that is not available. For example, a meat and cheese shop advertises a cut of meat at a bargain price. When you get to the store, you find out that the meat has all been sold (or maybe they had none to begin with). The ad was used as bait to get you to the store. The clerk then tries to sell you a more expensive cut (the switch).
- ***Referral sales plans.*** A few sellers of services and expensive products use this technique. How does it work? Suppose someone contacts you about siding for your house. You are offered a "special introductory deal" on new siding. The seller explains that, although you will pay full price for the siding, you will receive a bonus of $200 for each new purchaser you refer. You then discover that it is very difficult to find customers for the company. (Its bad reputation is probably known. The seller may even have left town.) Most consumers are never able to earn their bonus money.

Sylvan's Department Store

RAINCHECK

ITEM ______

MODEL/SIZE ______

REGULAR PRICE ______ SALE PRICE ______

AD DATE ______ STORE NO. ______ QUANTITY ______

NAME ______

ADDRESS ______

CITY ______ STATE ______ ZIP ______

TELEPHONE ______

AUTHORIZED SIGNATURE ______

***Figure 22-1** Merchants who sell out of an advertised product sometimes give rainchecks. What does a raincheck mean?*

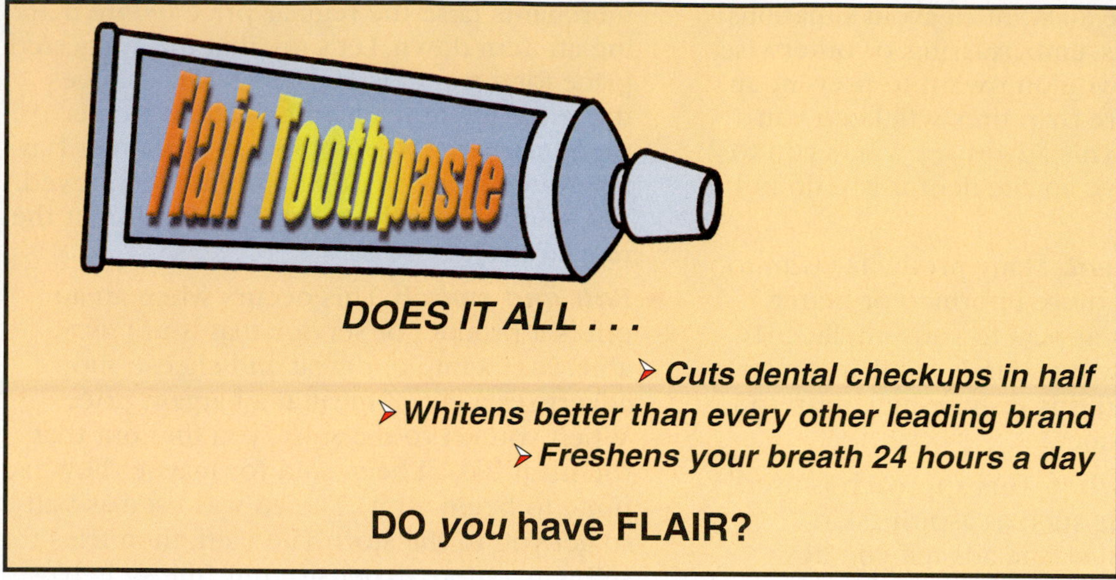

Figure 22-2 ***What advertising techniques and misleading practice are used in this advertisement?***

- ***Unclear, untrue, and overstated claims.*** Some products are advertised as being "improved" or "lasting 50 percent longer." Look carefully at such ads. Are the advertisers keeping facts from you? Do they tell you *how* a product has been improved? If so, does what they say make sense? If a product is said to last longer, ask yourself, "Longer than what?" Your question might not have an answer.

  Other ads use descriptions like "stain-resistant" or "never needs ironing." Such descriptions may have several meanings. For example, a coat that is "stain-resistant" cannot be expected to resist *all* stains.

  A **guarantee** is a pledge that something is exactly as stated or advertised. Ads that say a product is guaranteed are often unclear and untrue. If you are told a product is guaranteed, make sure the guarantee is in writing. Another problem phrase is "lasts a lifetime." Few products do. If a product claim seems too good to be true, it probably is not true.

- ***Clever sales tactics.*** Salespeople use various techniques to get you to buy. Some use high-pressure or fast-talking approaches. Others flatter you or are very friendly because they want to make it difficult for you to say no. Sometimes, a salesperson who is having trouble getting you to buy will turn you over to a second salesperson. A favorite sales trick is to say, "The price is going up tomorrow." A similar line is, "This is the last item available."

LESSON 22.2 REVIEW

1. Advertising has advantages and disadvantages for consumers. Name two of each.
2. Identify the advertising technique used in each of the following ads: (a) a famous person speaks for the product, (b) a company provides athletic uniforms with its name on them, (c) a company explains how its product will make you more attractive, (d) you are told how a certain service will save you money, (e) an accident or other dangerous situation is shown.
3. What is meant by "bait and switch"? Give an example.

HIGH-GROWTH OCCUPATIONS FOR THE 21st CENTURY

Physician Assistants

Physician assistants (PAs) provide health care services with supervision by physicians. They should not be confused with medical assistants, who perform routine clinical and clerical tasks. PAs are formally trained to provide diagnostic, therapeutic, and preventive health care services, as delegated by a physician.

Working as members of the health care team, PAs take medical histories, examine patients, order and interpret laboratory tests and x-rays, and make diagnoses. They also treat minor injuries by suturing, splinting, and applying casts. PAs record progress notes, instruct and counsel patients, and order or carry out therapy. In 46 states and the District of Columbia, physician assistants may prescribe medications. PAs may also have managerial duties. Some order medical and laboratory supplies and equipment and may supervise technicians and assistants.

Physician assistants always work with the supervision of a physician. However, PAs may provide care in rural or inner-city clinics where a physician is present for only one or two days each week, conferring with the supervising physician and other medical professionals as needed or required by law. PAs may also make house calls or go to hospitals and nursing homes to check on patients and report back to the physician.

Physician assistants are qualified to interpret x-rays and make diagnoses.

Many PAs work in primary care areas such as general internal medicine, pediatrics, and family medicine. Others work in specialty areas, such as general and thoracic surgery, emergency medicine, orthopedics, and geriatrics. PAs specializing in surgery provide preoperative and postoperative care and may work as first or second assistants during major surgery.

Employment of PAs is expected to grow much faster than the average for all occupations. This is because PAs are cost-effective and productive members of the health care team. Physician assistants can help relieve physicians of many routine duties and procedures.

LESSON 22.3

CONSUMER RIGHTS AND RESPONSIBILITIES

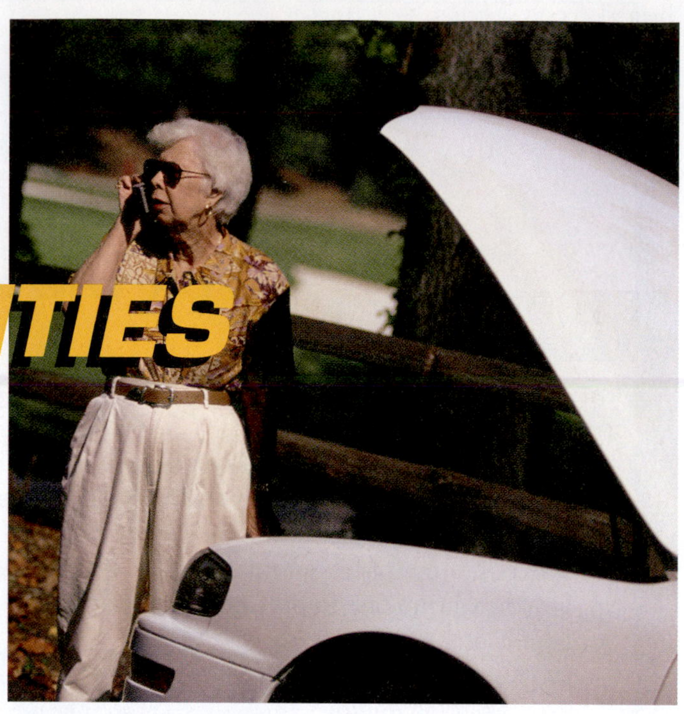

OBJECTIVES

- DISCUSS TYPES OF CONSUMER RIGHTS
- DESCRIBE RESPONSIBILITIES OF CONSUMERS
- SUMMARIZE STEPS TO TAKE IN DEALING WITH CONSUMER PROBLEMS

CONSUMER RIGHTS

Consumers have not always had rights. Until the last century, there were few laws to protect buyers. If consumers bought defective products, it was their problem. Since they had no legal responsibility, producers often paid little attention to safety and quality. After many consumers were harmed by unsafe products and faulty merchandise, the public began to demand tougher standards.

Laws now require manufacturers to make safety their concern. Consumers have a right to expect that what they buy is safe. Laws also protect consumers who buy faulty merchandise. After an item is sold, the producer must stand behind it. Consumer rights regarding credit, interest rates, insurance, housing, and so on, are discussed in this unit and the next.

Cathy bought a Cookbetter microwave. After she had used it for several months, she read a recall notice in the newspaper. A **recall** is a public request by a manufacturer for the return of a product that may be defective or contaminated. Many people had reported problems with the microwave. It had even caused several fires. When Cathy took the microwave back to the seller, she got a new one.

Laws protect buyers in another way. Free enterprise works best when consumers have choices. In the past, it was easy for a single company to control an industry, such as oil. The company could charge whatever it wanted and consumers had to pay. This is known as a monopoly. You learned about monopolies in Chapter 21. Today, strong federal laws regulate monopolistic practices.

Until the 1960s, there wasn't much information available about products and services. People often bought according to what they had

PERSONAL DECISIONS

You see an advertisement in the paper for an item you have wanted. You stick the ad in your pocket and head for the store. You find the item and take it to the checkout counter. The clerk rings it up at the regular price. You point out the item is on sale. The clerk brushes off your comment and says that the ad in the paper is in error.

WHAT WOULD YOU DO?

heard from advertisers and friends. Now the government and many private associations and businesses provide a wide variety of consumer information and services. Smart shoppers take advantage of their right to obtain consumer information.

CONSUMER RESPONSIBILITIES

Along with consumer rights come responsibilities. First of all, you owe it to yourself to learn how to choose, buy, and use goods and services. This chapter has given you some tips on wise consuming. In upcoming chapters, you will read more about smart shopping. Your study of consumerism will not end here, though. Such learning is a lifelong process.

Assertiveness

To protect yourself and other consumers, you have a responsibility to speak out. Be **assertive**. This means being firm and positive in stating one's position or point of view. If you think a business has not behaved properly, speak politely but firmly to a salesperson. Whenever you are not satisfied with the salesperson's response, see the manager.

Should you continue to receive poor products and services, take your business elsewhere. Buying goods and services is somewhat like casting a vote. Through the things that you buy or do not buy, you vote for or against a business.

State your position firmly and positively when you receive unsatisfactory service.

Honesty

You expect businesses to be fair and honest with you at all times. As a responsible consumer, you should also be fair and honest. You may not realize it, but all consumers pay a penalty for a few dishonest people. When a person steals from a department store, for example, the store may suffer a temporary loss. However, to make up for this loss and others, the store will raise its prices.

CONSUMER COMPLAINTS

Most of the time, you will be satisfied with goods and services you purchase. Sometimes, however, you may be disappointed. Here is a list of the most common consumer problems.

- Difficulties in getting a product repaired or replaced as promised in the warranty
- Misleading advertising, labeling, or packaging
- Defective products; for example, a cell phone may malfunction the first time you use it
- Being overcharged for a product or service
- Poor service or work of bad quality
- Goods that were ordered and paid for but never received
- Errors in computerized billing

Suppose you have such a problem. How will you resolve it?

Before Complaining

If you wish to make a **complaint**, or express your dissatisfaction with a product or service, do not write a nasty letter or hire a lawyer. In fact, you should never write a nasty letter to a business! Review the whole situation and try to resolve it in the simplest manner possible.

- ***Save everything.*** Keep track of all paperwork related to what you buy. This includes copies of order forms, receipts, and warranties. It is difficult to settle a complaint without proof of purchase.

WORKFORCE TRENDS

One million workers suffer violent assaults on the job each year. In a recent year, the total included 615,000 simple assaults, 264,000 aggravated assaults, 79,000 robberies, and more than 51,000 rapes and sexual assaults. Robberies and other crimes are a primary motive for workplace homicide, accounting for 79 percent of the approximately 1,000 violent workplace deaths that take place yearly.

- ***Think it through.*** You may have a faded blouse or broken tool, but who is at fault? The reason the blouse faded was because you washed it in hot water instead of cold. The tool broke because you used it improperly. You should not expect the seller or manufacturer to replace such a product.

  Many products do not work properly because people fail to follow instructions. This is often true for electrical appliances. If a product does not do what it should, reread the instructions. Look at the product again. Ask a friend or family member to do the same. Then return the item or call a service technician.

- ***Give the seller a chance.*** If you know there is a problem and you are not at fault, take the product back to where you bought it. Make sure you have the receipt and anything else you might need. Be prepared to explain the problem. Think over what you want the merchant to do. For example, do you want a replacement, a refund, or a repair?

  Ask to see someone who can handle your problem. Many larger stores have a complaint or customer service department. Explain your case to the person in charge. Do not be either too timid or too aggressive. Usually, if you are fair and reasonable, the other person will be also. You may be surprised at how quickly the problem is resolved. Sellers do not want to lose customers.

Making a Formal Complaint

If the seller cannot or will not help you, complain to the manufacturer. Get the name and address from the seller, the product, the Web, or a librarian. When you do not have the name of a person to write to, address the letter to the customer service department. A sample letter appears in Figure 22-3 on page 327. The Better Business Bureau says a complaint letter should contain the following information:

- ***What you bought.*** Describe the product. Does the item have a size and color? Is there a serial number?
- ***Where you bought it.*** Give the complete address of the seller.
- ***When you bought it.*** The date of purchase is important.
- ***How you paid for it.*** Specify how you paid for the item. Did you use cash, a check, a credit card, or a money order? Attach copies of necessary papers. Never send originals. Paperwork may include receipts, cancelled checks, and sales contracts.
- ***What the problem is.*** Let the facts speak for themselves.
- ***What you want.*** Do you want a refund? Would you like the item repaired? Be clear.

Make a copy of the letter for yourself. You should receive a response within two or three weeks. If you do not, contact your local Better Business Bureau or consumer rights group for help.

LESSON 22.3 REVIEW

1. **What are your rights and responsibilities as a consumer? Name two of each.**
2. **How is buying a product or service similar to casting a vote?**
3. **What should you do before writing a formal letter of complaint?**
4. **What six points should be included in a complaint letter?**

436 Lincoln Rd.
Monroe, MI 48162-3459
June 12, 20—

Mr. Gerald Morris
Customer Service Manager
Barkley Tackle Company
1003 Seventh St.
Eau Claire, WI 54701-2845

Dear Mr. Morris:

On June 7, 20—, I purchased a 5′6″ Barkley casting rod (Model No. 96) at Lunker Sporting Goods Store at 49 Washington Way in Monroe, Michigan. The selling price was $49.95, which I paid in cash. A photocopy of the receipt is attached.

Several days later, I used the rod for the first time. As I tried to make a routine cast, the rod tip snapped off. I had only used the rod for about an hour.

I took the rod back to the store and explained what had happened. I was told by Mr. Robert Stark, the store manager, that the rod was not guaranteed. I insisted I had used it only once, but he said there was nothing he could do.

I'm very sorry that the rod broke, but I do not believe that I was at fault. I have always used Barkley fishing products without any previous problems. This letter is to request that you provide me with a replacement rod or a refund. I'm sure you will agree that this problem should not have happened.

Sincerely yours,

Brad Corder

Brad Corder

Attachment

Figure 22-3 ***A sample letter of complaint***

FOCUS ON SKILLS FOR LIVING

BUYING A USED CAR

Check everything from price to tires when you buy a used car. Then relax and enjoy it!

For most of us, car ownership begins with buying a used car. In fact, used car sales far outnumber new car sales. Many people simply cannot afford a new car. Others, though, actually prefer a used car to a new one. They say that used cars are a much better value for the money.

The majority of used cars are bought from private owners, new car dealers, used car dealers, and auto rental companies. Each source has advantages and disadvantages. A good car at a fair price may be found through any of the four sources. New car dealers, however, are probably the best overall source.

New car dealers sell used autos that have been traded in for new ones. They usually keep only the newer and better cars on their lots. Cars are usually reconditioned and offered with some type of warranty. The dealer wants you to be satisfied and come back later to buy a new car. However, used car prices at a new car dealership are usually higher than elsewhere. This is because of the greater cost of doing business.

Once you have located a car that interests you, make a careful inspection. You do not have to be an expert on cars to spot major problems. Look for body damage and signs of rust. Look under the car for holes in the exhaust system and for evidence of fluids leaking from the engine, radiator, transmission, or brakes. Drive the car and listen for noises, rattles, and vibrations. Note anything about which you feel suspicious or uncomfortable. Not all problems are serious. But find out what things will need to be fixed or replaced if you decide to buy.

A careful examination of a used car and a test drive should help you eliminate unacceptable cars. Before agreeing to buy, however, take several more steps:

- ***Get an idea of the price for the year and model car that you are considering.*** Check the *Official Used Car Guide* published by the National Automobile Dealers Association (NADA). The NADA guide can be found at most credit unions, banks, and public libraries. The same information can be found on the Web at http://www2.nadaguides.com/.

- ***Confirm the mileage.*** The law requires that the seller provide the buyer with a signed statement indicating the current mileage. Anyone who illegally tampers with an odometer or fails to provide the required disclosure statement may be sued.
- ***Take the car to a mechanic for an inspection.*** You should not rely solely on your judgment about a car. Hidden problems in the engine, transmission, or rear axle are of the most concern because these are costly to repair.
- ***Contact the previous owner.*** Federal law requires dealers to have this information. Most reputable dealers will give you the name and phone number of this person. Call the person and explain that you are thinking about buying his or her car. You may be surprised at how cooperative and honest this person can be.

HELPFUL WEB SITES FOR USED CAR BUYERS

General

- Kelley Blue Book
  http://www.kbb.com
- Edmunds.com
  http://www.edmunds.com

Insurance

- SmartMoney.com
  http://www.smartmoney.com
- insure.com
  http://www.insure.com

Loan Calculator

Kiplinger.com
http://www.kiplinger.com/tools/
(Choose "How much will my monthly car payments be?")

- ***Check out the warranty.*** The Federal Trade Commission requires sellers of used cars (except private owners) to place a large "Buyers Guide" window sticker on each car. The guide makes clear what type of warranty is provided with the car. Many consumer experts say not to buy a used car as is. Get a warranty, even if it is just for 30 days. A warranty provides important financial and legal protection.

Now you are ready to finalize the deal. Most buyers and salespeople expect to haggle a little over the price. However, do not expect the salesperson to lower the price much. Nor should you expect the seller to do a lot of free repairs as part of the deal. The margin of profit on a used car is fairly low.

Dealers try to make it easy for you to buy a car by providing financing. However, their rates will often be higher than you can find elsewhere. Do not be afraid to tell the salesperson that you will get your own financing. To hold the car, you may be required to leave a small deposit.

Once you pay for the car, it is yours. You will then need to arrange for insurance, license plates, and a new title. After that, you can sit behind the wheel, buckle up, and take your car for a cruise. Drive carefully.

THINK CRITICALLY

1. Would you want to buy a used car? Why or why not?
2. What steps would you take to buy a used car?

CHAPTER 22

Chapter in Brief

Lesson 22.1 *You as a Consumer*

A. A consumer is someone who buys or uses goods and services. Goods are articles that are produced or manufactured. Services involve the payment of money to people and businesses for work performed.

B. Being a consumer is more than simply paying money for something. Consuming involves three stages: choosing, buying, and using.

Lesson 22.2 *Advertising and the Consumer*

A. For the seller, advertising aids in selling goods and services. For the consumer, it provides information about goods and services for sale.

B. Sellers use various advertising techniques to accomplish their purpose.

C. There is nothing wrong with advertising as long as it is honest. Problems occur when advertising is misleading. Be alert to deceptive practices.

Lesson 22.3 *Consumer Rights and Responsibilities*

A. Consumers are protected by laws on safety, faulty merchandise, and competition in the marketplace. Government and private associations and businesses provide a variety of consumer information and services.

B. Along with consumer rights come responsibilities. Learn how to choose, buy, and use goods and services. Speak out regarding poor products and services. Be fair and honest in your business dealings.

C. Sometimes, you may have a complaint about a product or service. Try to resolve the problem in the simplest manner possible. Make a formal complaint if simpler approaches do not work. Be businesslike in your efforts.

Activities

1. Prepare a list of five different grocery items. Visit at least three stores and record the price of each item. What were your findings? Which store is the most expensive? The least expensive? Which stores carry generic brands? Were those items priced lower than brand-name products?
2. Find examples of the advertising techniques discussed in this chapter (endorsements, familiarity, and so on). Pool your ads with those found by your classmates. Choose the best ads for a bulletin board display.
3. Conduct an election for your class's or school's favorite television commercial. Nominate candidates. Prepare an election ballot and circulate copies to classmates. Count the ballots and declare a winner. Send a letter to the winning company explaining what the class has done.
4. Think of a problem you have had with a product or service. Write a sample complaint letter to the manufacturer. Follow the guidelines provided in this chapter. Turn in the letter to your teacher.

REVIEW

5. As a class activity, develop a list of things to look for in buying a used car. Include things to examine visually and through a test drive.
6. You can buy two 8-oz packages of cheese for $3 or a 24-oz package for $3.99. Which is the better buy? Why?

Word Power

On a separate sheet of paper, match each definition with the correct term. All definitions will be used, and a definition will be used only once.

7. Someone who buys or uses goods and services
8. Articles that are produced or manufactured
9. Work performed by individuals and businesses for others
10. Goods given a unique name by the manufacturer
11. Advertising sent to potential customers through the mail
12. Any type of public notice or message intended to aid in the sale of a product or service
13. A guarantee or promise that a product is free from defects
14. An expression of dissatisfaction with a product or service
15. Firm and positive in stating one's position or point of view
16. A public request by a manufacturer for the return of a product that may be defective or contaminated
17. A pledge that something is exactly as stated or advertised
18. Goods that state only the common name of the product on the label
19. The process of finding out the cost of a product or service at several different places before making a decision to buy

a. advertising
b. assertive
c. brand-name products
d. comparison shopping
e. complaint
f. consumer
g. direct-mail advertising
h. generic products
i. goods
j. guarantee
k. recall
l. services
m. warranty

Think Critically

20. Think of a major purchase you made recently. Did you do comparison shopping? If so, explain how you went about it. If not, explain why not.
21. Until recently doctors and lawyers have been prohibited from advertising. It is still a controversial issue. What is your opinion on this practice?
22. Have you ever ruined a new product by failing to read or follow instructions? If so, discuss your experiences in class.
23. What does it mean to say that buying a certain thing is "false economy"? Discuss examples of consumer practices that illustrate false economy.
24. Have you ever been cheated by a dishonest seller or misleading advertising? If so, discuss your experiences in class.
25. You or other members of the class have probably bought used cars. Share your experiences and discuss the following questions: Where was the car bought? Was a fair price paid? Were any hidden problems discovered after the sale? Was the car covered by a warranty? You can probably think of additional questions.

CHAPTER 23

BANKING AND CREDIT

LESSONS

23.1 *Financial Institutions*

23.2 *Checking Accounts*

23.3 *Credit and Its Use*

PREVIEW

As you grow older, your use of money will probably change. Rather than pay cash for all of your purchases, you will find that it is often more convenient to write a check. Sometimes you may want to use credit. The credit may be in the form of a loan or a charge purchase. Knowing how to use checking, credit, and other financial services is an important life skill for everyone.

THOUGHTS ON WORK

"I think we have to appreciate that we're alive for only a limited period of time, and we'll spend most of our lives working. That being the case, I believe one of the most important priorities is to do whatever we do as well as we can."
Victor Kiam

TAKING ACTION
GIVE YOURSELF CREDIT

Nancy has had her first job for about two months. She lives with her parents. Whenever she has a bill or owes her parents money, she pays in cash.

Now Nancy is considering moving out on her own. Her friend Aurora has asked her if she would like to share an apartment. Nancy went with Aurora this morning to look at the apartment and liked it very much. After showing them around, Mr. Bellamy, the leasing agent, gave each of them a rental application. Nancy and Aurora thanked Mr. Bellamy and said that they would get back to him.

As Nancy reads the application at home, she realizes that the leasing company wants a lot of financial information about her. It wants to know where she is employed, if she has any debts, where she does her banking, and if she owns any assets. It also wants her permission to run a credit report.

Because Nancy always cashes her paychecks and pays with cash, she knows she won't have a credit history with anyone other than her parents. She also does not have a checking account. Nancy wonders if these things are going to get in the way of getting the apartment. She calls Mr. Bellamy to ask him.

Mr. Bellamy is surprised to discover that Nancy has no credit history and no checking account. But he proposes a solution.

"You might be able to pay your rent in cash to your roommate, and she can write the rent check to us," he says. "Also, you can have just your roommate's name on the rental agreement if you are worried about your application being rejected."

Nancy explains Mr. Bellamy's suggestion to her parents. They both tell her that it is not a good idea. "If you are planning to rent this apartment with Aurora, both your names should be on the rental agreement," her mother says.

Her father agrees. "Having your name on the agreement gives you important rights as a tenant."

"I guess it's time for me to get a checking account and start to establish a credit history," says Nancy. "Where do you think I should apply for a credit card?"

SUCCESS TIP

Checking accounts and credit can make your life easier, if you manage them well.

THINK CRITICALLY

1. How could a checking account help Nancy?
2. Why is it important to establish a credit history?

LESSON 23.1
FINANCIAL INSTITUTIONS

- NAME AND DESCRIBE THE FOUR MAJOR TYPES OF FINANCIAL INSTITUTIONS
- DISCUSS HOW ELECTRONIC BANKING MAY CHANGE MONEY MANAGEMENT

TYPES OF INSTITUTIONS AND SERVICES

A bank used to be the place to go to save money, borrow money, or open a checking account. Today, four major types of financial institutions provide these services and others.

Commercial Banks

Commercial banks may also be known as bank and trust companies or community banks. Commercial banks are the most common type of financial institution. They are **full-service banks**, banks that offer customers a full range of financial conveniences and services. These include checking and savings accounts, loans, safety deposit boxes, credit cards, drive-up windows, money orders, traveler's checks, and **automated teller machines**, or **ATMs**. An ATM is an electronic terminal in which customers can insert a plastic card to withdraw cash, make deposits, or transfer funds to another account. Commercial banks offer still other conveniences and services for borrowers and savers.

Mutual Savings Banks

Mutual savings banks began early in the 19th century in order to serve ordinary people that commercial banks often overlooked. In theory, a mutual savings bank is owned by its depositors. However, a board of trustees directs the bank's operations and acts on behalf of the depositors. Any profits that are earned are distributed to depositors as interest. There are only about 18 states that charter mutual savings banks. Most are in the Northeast.

Such banks generally provide the same services as commercial banks. In addition, they offer some of the services of a savings and loan association. One of the main attractions of mutual savings banks is that they often pay a slightly higher rate of interest than commercial banks. Since the mid-1980s, many of these banks have become what are known as stock savings banks. Such banks are operated by a board of directors elected by shareholders. Profits are distributed to stockholders as cash dividends.

WORKFORCE TRENDS

At one time, classified ads for employment were divided into "men wanted" and "women wanted." It was unusual to see women or members of minority groups as television news anchors. Far fewer women or minority group members were in jobs as supervisors, firefighters, police officers, doctors, and college professors. Since the passage of the Civil Rights Act of 1964, minorities and women have made significant economic progress.

Each Depositor Insured to $100,000

FDIC

FEDERAL DEPOSIT INSURANCE CORPORATION

Your savings federally insured to $100,000

NCUA

National Credit Union Administration, a U. S. Government Agency

Figure 23-1 ***Look for these seals at your bank or credit union. The FDIC insures deposits in banks. The NCUA insures savings deposits in credit unions.***

a. *Courtesy of Federal Deposit Insurance Corporation.* b. *Courtesy of National Credit Union Administration.*

Savings and Loan Associations

Other names for these institutions are building and loan associations, cooperative banks, savings associations, and homestead associations. They were started in the early 1800s by groups of people who pooled their savings so that each person, in turn, could borrow enough money to build a house. Savings and loan associations are now in all states. They provide more home mortgage business (loans to buy homes) than all other lenders combined.

Credit Unions

Credit unions (CUs) are nonprofit savings and loan cooperative associations. They are made up of people who have something in common. This could be a place of employment, a union membership, or the like. For example, all employees of a particular school district might form a credit union. Members govern credit unions. They only accept savings from and make loans to people who belong to the credit union. At the end of the year, a well-run credit union often has a surplus to distribute to its members.

Credit unions provide savings accounts, consumer loans, and financial counseling. A convenient feature of CUs is that members can often make deposits and loan payments through payroll deductions.

Changes in Financial Institutions

During the last several decades, many banking laws have been changed to allow financial institutions to be more competitive. Now financial institutions can pay higher rates of interest than before. Another result of the changes is that the four major types of financial institutions have begun to offer similar services.

YOU'RE A WHAT? PHLEBOTOMIST

The detection, diagnosis, and treatment of disease often depend on a variety of medical laboratory tests. *Phlebotomists*, who draw blood samples for analysis, play an important role in this process. A number of medical personnel draw blood as part of their overall duties. But, for phlebotomists, this is their primary duty. Most of them are employed by hospitals and large clinics.

The skill of a phlebotomist consists of using a rather large needle to draw blood from a vein in a patient's arm with as little pain as possible. The ability to calm patients is often as important as the ability to draw the blood. In addition to being skilled and efficient, the phlebotomist must follow standard safety practices. Failure to do so can result in accidentally transmitting serious viruses like hepatitis and HIV. ■

Financial institutions now actively compete for business. This is good news for the consumer. It means, however, that consumers should shop around and compare services, charges, and rates of interest.

The experience of Teresa Romero is a good case in point. When Teresa learned that her bank was raising the service charge on checking accounts, she began to ask about charges and services elsewhere. She discovered that she was eligible to join the credit union where her mother worked. Teresa received no-cost checking and was paid monthly interest on her checking account balance.

ATMs can be very convenient.

ELECTRONIC BANKING

In the future, electronic banking may change the way you manage money. **Electronic banking** is a broad term used to describe various types of electronic fund transfers (EFTs). There are five common types of EFT services:

- ***Automated teller machines (ATMs).*** These 24-hour electronic terminals permit you to bank at your convenience. You simply insert your EFT card in the machine and enter your personal identification number (PIN). You can then withdraw cash, make deposits, or transfer funds between accounts.
- ***Telephone banking systems.*** These systems permit you to telephone your bank and instruct it to pay certain bills or transfer funds between accounts. Transactions are conducted via voice mail menus and Touch-Tone commands.
- ***Computer banking systems.*** Banking through the Internet is becoming very popular. Individuals can pay bills, transfer funds, check account balances, and generally manage their accounts completely online.
- ***Direct deposits or withdrawals.*** You can arrange for sums of money that you receive on a regular basis, such as a paycheck, to be deposited automatically into your checking account. You can also have regular bills, such as rent payments and insurance premiums, paid in the same way, by automatic withdrawals from your account.
- ***Point-of-sale transfers.*** These transfers let you pay for retail purchases with your EFT or debit card. A **debit card** is a plastic card used to immediately transfer funds for a purchase from a bank account to a seller. This is similar to using a credit card, except that the money for the purchase is immediately transferred.

Electronic banking can be very convenient. A possible disadvantage, however, is that your EFT card and PIN are used for all transactions. If they should be lost or stolen, you must immediately notify your bank. You also need to carefully examine receipts and monthly statements for errors. When you open an EFT account, your bank will provide you with written information on your rights and responsibilities.

LESSON 23.1 REVIEW

1. There are four major types of financial institutions. Name and briefly describe them.
2. Name and briefly describe the five types of EFT services.

LESSON 23.2
CHECKING ACCOUNTS

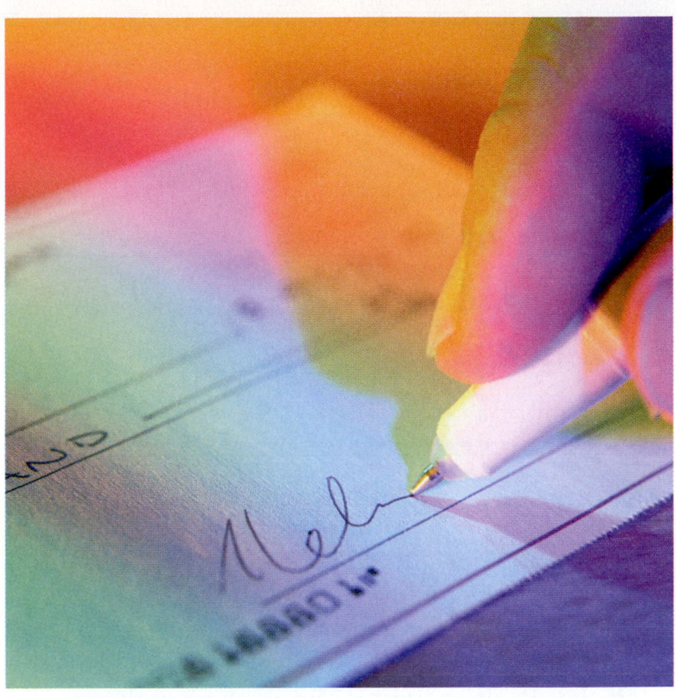

- DESCRIBE TYPES OF CHECKING ACCOUNTS AND HOW TO OPEN AN ACCOUNT
- ILLUSTRATE HOW TO WRITE AND ENDORSE A CHECK, MAINTAIN A CHECK REGISTER, MAKE A DEPOSIT, AND RECONCILE A BANK STATEMENT

UNDERSTANDING CHECKING ACCOUNTS

Checking accounts are one of the most commonly used banking services. Checking accounts have two main advantages: safety and convenience. Checks provide a safe and convenient way to pay bills. It is unsafe to carry large amounts of cash. Also, keeping large amounts of money at home is unwise. Michael found this out.

Michael never thought he needed a checking account. He liked to go to the bank on Friday evenings and cash his paycheck. He then paid for all of his purchases in cash. The cash he did not carry with him was kept in a tennis ball can that was stored on the hall closet shelf. No one would ever think of looking there for money, Michael thought.

Michael returned from a movie late Friday night to discover that his apartment had been burglarized. His television and DVD player were the only things that he noticed were missing. As he sat down on the couch to think about what to do, Michael remembered his money. He went to the hall closet. As he opened the closet door, an empty tennis ball can rolled off the shelf.

Michael had insurance to cover the cost of replacing the television and DVD player. But he was heartsick to lose the money he needed to live on for the rest of the month. Needless to say, Michael opened a checking account the next time he got paid.

Checks can be used as freely as cash. They are safer than cash, however, because only the person to whom a check is made out can get the money. A second advantage of checks is that they make it easier to keep good financial records. A canceled check (a check that has been paid and returned to you for your records) is legal proof of payment. Be sure to save your canceled checks.

Without the use of checks, our economic system could not function. Individuals and businesses write billions of checks each year. A very elaborate national system allows millions of checks to be processed daily. Let's see how the system works.

Assume that you take your car in for repairs and the bill comes to $65. Rather than pay the mechanic in cash, you write a check. That is, you write instructions to your bank, the American National Bank, to deduct $65 from your account and pay it to Joe's Garage. Joe then takes your check to his bank, Mid-America Bank, and deposits it in his account.

Mid-America Bank does not collect payment directly from the American National Bank. It would be ridiculous for a bank to pay separately

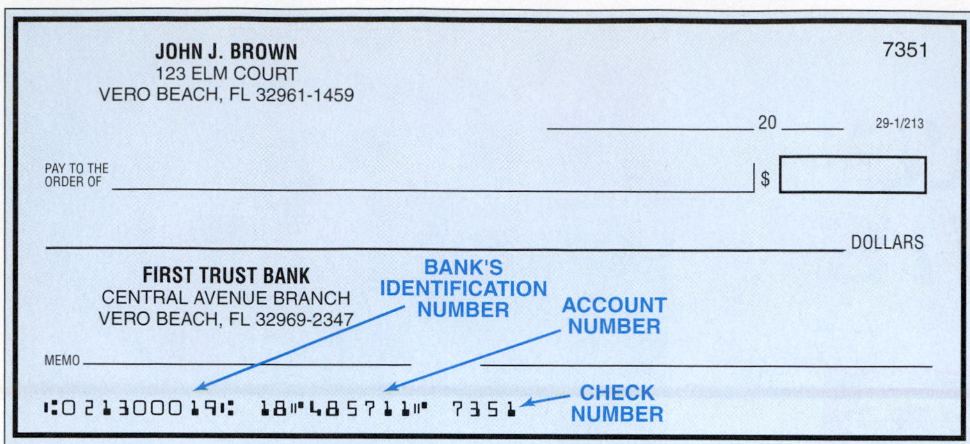

JOHN J. BROWN
123 ELM COURT
VERO BEACH, FL 32961-1459
7351
20
29-1/213
PAY TO THE ORDER OF
$
DOLLARS
FIRST TRUST BANK
CENTRAL AVENUE BRANCH
VERO BEACH, FL 32969-2347
BANK'S IDENTIFICATION NUMBER
ACCOUNT NUMBER
MEMO
CHECK NUMBER

Figure 23-2 ***The coded numbers at the bottom of a check are read by a computer. This speeds up check processing considerably.***

for every check written by a customer and receive separate payment for every check credited to a customer's account. Instead, a bank sends all of its checks to a centralized clearinghouse. The checks are added up at the clearinghouse each day. Each individual bank then makes or receives just one daily payment to or from its fellow banks.

After the check has cleared (has been authorized and credited to Joe's account), it is returned to the American National Bank. This bank subtracts $65 from your account. The check is stamped "paid" and will be returned to you along with other canceled checks.

Types of Checking Accounts

Banks usually offer a variety of checking accounts. The names given to these accounts may vary from bank to bank. However, the two basic types of checking accounts are regular and special. A regular account, often called a minimum balance account, requires that the customer maintain a certain minimum balance. As long as the minimum balance is in the account, there is no extra charge. If the balance drops below the minimum amount, however, the customer will have to pay a service charge.

A second basic type of checking account is the special account, often called a cost-per-check account. With this type of account, you pay a flat monthly service charge plus a small amount for each check you write. Special accounts are for people who only write a few checks each month. A young person opening his or her first checking account should carefully consider this type of account.

Another type of checking account is an interest-bearing account called a **negotiable order of withdrawal (NOW) account**. These accounts were first offered at savings and loan associations and are now available at many commercial and savings banks as well. A withdrawal order is just like a check, except that it is written against a savings account rather than a checking account. Your money earns interest up to the day the order clears. However, most NOW accounts require that you maintain a balance of at least several hundred dollars.

Most credit unions offer a type of checking account called a **share draft account**. It is very similar to a NOW account. You write drafts (checks) against a credit union savings account. Your money earns interest until the draft clears. Many share draft accounts have no monthly service charges at all. However, for the account to earn interest, the credit union often requires a minimum balance of $500 to $750.

If abused, a checking account can become very expensive. For example, if you overdraw your account, or write a check for more than you have in it (an **overdraft**), the check will be returned. Your bank will charge you a fee for every check like this that "bounces." If you write a check to someone and decide to stop payment on it, or order your bank not to pay it, the bank will usually charge you for this as well. As you are shopping around for a place to open a checking account, request an information sheet that describes all of the institution's services and charges.

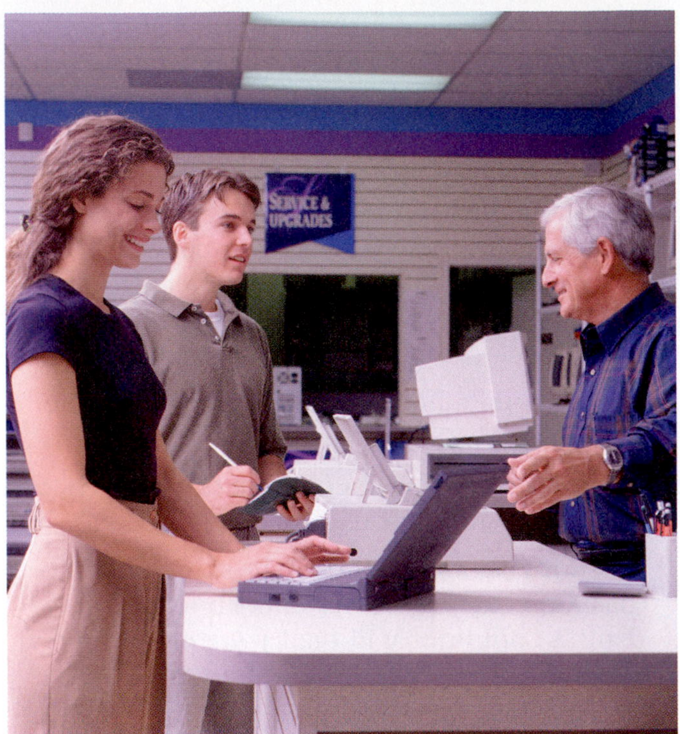

Both a bank and a retail business will charge a fee for a check that bounces.

Opening a Checking Account

Once you have decided on a bank and checking account, opening an account is very simple. You need only fill out a form known as a **signature card**. The signature card asks for your name, address, phone number, Social Security number, and similar data. At the end of the card, there is a place for your signature. The signature that you put on the card should be your legal name, not a nickname.

MANAGING A CHECKING ACCOUNT

Maintaining an accurate, up-to-date checkbook requires knowledge and practice of a few important rules. Here are some steps and guidelines to follow.

Writing a Check

A blank check requires five kinds of information. One additional kind is optional. Each of these will now be discussed. Refer to Figure 23-3 as you read about each part.

- ***Date.*** Record the date on the check. This will help you keep accurate records. Never date a check ahead of time (**postdating**) because you do not have enough money in your account. If the party to whom you wrote the check cashes it, you might overdraw the account.
- ***Payee.*** The person or institution that you write the check to is the **payee**. It is proper to ask individuals how they would like the check made out. On their bills, many businesses indicate how to write the check. If the name is a long one, it is acceptable to abbreviate. However, use common abbreviations, such as "Inc.," "Co.," and "Assoc."
- ***Numerical amount.*** You record the amount of the check in two places. At the end of the line where you fill in the name of the payee, you write the amount of the check in dollars and cents; for example, "10.50." If the check is

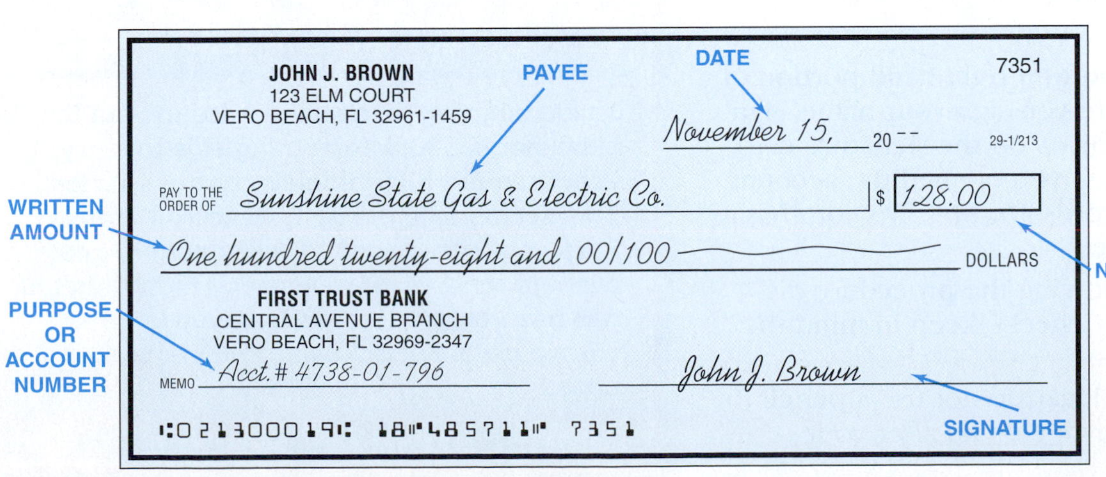

Figure 23-3 A correctly written check

for under a dollar, put a zero in front of the decimal point and insert the word *cents* ("0.85 cents"). To keep someone from altering the check easily, place the figures close to the dollar sign.

- ***Written amount.*** On the long line near the middle of the check, you will see the word *Dollars*. Here you write out the same amount that you wrote in numerals earlier. Use this form: "Ten and 50/100" or "Fifty-three and 00/100." If the amount is less than one dollar, write in "Only eight-five cents" and draw a line through the word *Dollars*. If there is any blank space left after you have written in the amount, draw a wavy line between the written amount and the word *Dollars*. Otherwise, someone could alter the check.

  If there is ever a difference between the numerical amount and the written amount of a check, the written amount is the legal one. Generally, however, a bank will contact the writer before it will accept a check with differing amounts.
- ***Purpose or account number.*** In the lower left-hand portion of a check, there is a space labeled "For" or "Memo." This space does not have to be filled out, but it is always a good idea to do so. This is where you indicate the purpose of the check; for example, "auto tune-up" or "birthday gift." When you pay bills, some companies may ask you to write a policy or account number on the check. Next to "Memo" or "For," you would write "Acct. #4738-01-796" if that were your number. Routinely filling in this line can help you later as you review a budget or prepare an income tax return.
- ***Signature.*** The bottom right-hand portion of the check is where you sign your name. Sign it exactly as it appears on the signature card you filled out when you opened the account. Do not use the words *Mr.*, *Mrs.*, *Ms.*, or *Miss* as part of a signature.

In addition to following the procedure discussed for filling out checks, keep in mind the following guidelines:

- Even though it is legal, do not use a pencil to write a check. Anyone could alter your check.
- You can write a check to yourself and cash it. Simply write "Cash" as the payee and present it to the bank. Some banks might also ask you to sign the back of the check.
- If you make an error on a check, do not correct it. Instead, write "VOID" across the face of the check and file it with your canceled checks. Then make out a new check. Remember to write "VOID" in your check register, too. Check registers are discussed below.
- Do not sign a blank check and let someone else fill in the amount.
- Do not leave your checkbook or blank checks in a place where someone can take them.
- Do not give a blank check to someone who has forgotten his or her checkbook. The bank's computer will read *your* electronic number and subtract the money from your account.

Keeping a Check Register

After you open an account, you will receive a supply of imprinted checks and a **check register**. The register is where you keep a record of checks written, deposits made, and other transactions. One checkbook style has a stub attached to each check. Another uses a two-part form (a carbon copy behind each check) that provides customers with a record of the transaction (Figure 23-4). The most popular means of

PERSONAL DECISIONS

You like having a checking account, but the checkbook is just something else to carry. You often put it in the glove box of your car. This seems safe enough, since you always keep your car locked. After shopping one evening, you return to your car to find that it has been burglarized. Your stereo is gone, and so is your checkbook. You are very upset.

WHAT WOULD YOU DO?

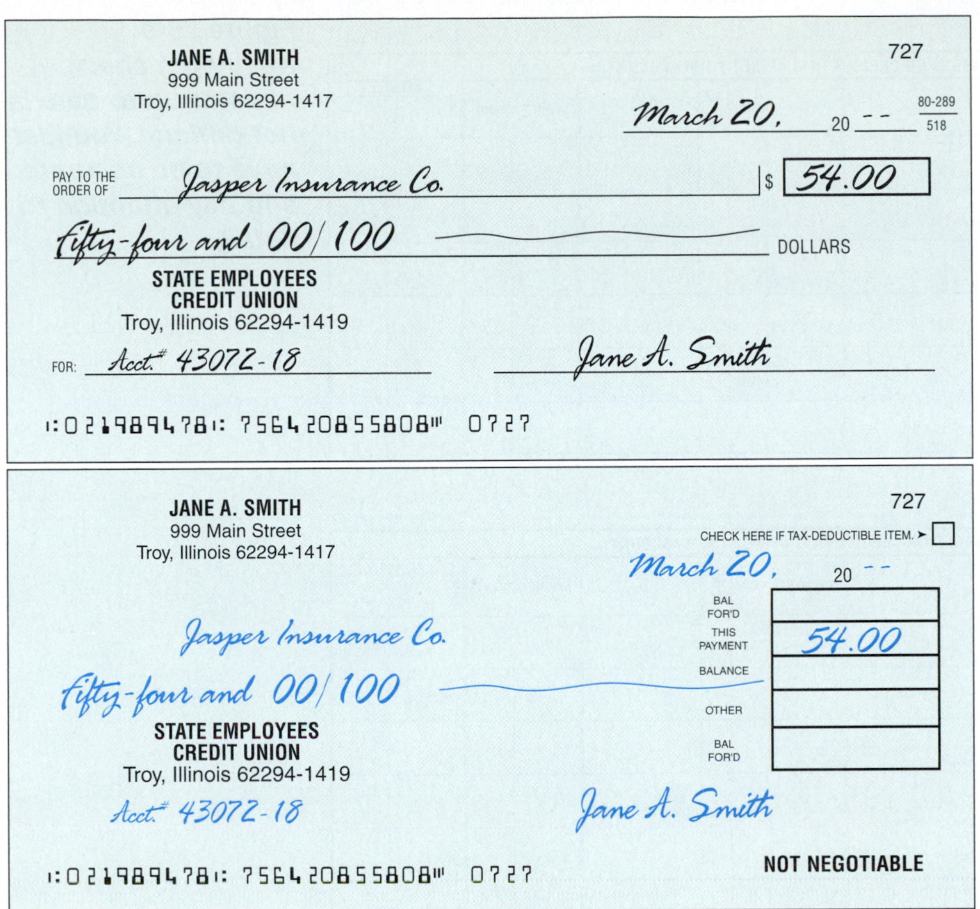

JANE A. SMITH
999 Main Street
Troy, Illinois 62294-1417

727

March 20, 20 --

80-289
518

PAY TO THE ORDER OF Jasper Insurance Co. $ 54.00

Fifty-four and 00/100 DOLLARS

STATE EMPLOYEES CREDIT UNION
Troy, Illinois 62294-1419

FOR: Acct.# 43072-18

Jane A. Smith

021989478 7564 20855808 0727

JANE A. SMITH
999 Main Street
Troy, Illinois 62294-1417

727

CHECK HERE IF TAX-DEDUCTIBLE ITEM.

March 20, 20 --

BAL FOR'D	
THIS PAYMENT	54.00
BALANCE	
OTHER	
BAL FOR'D	

Jasper Insurance Co.

Fifty-four and 00/100

STATE EMPLOYEES CREDIT UNION
Troy, Illinois 62294-1419

Acct.# 43072-18

Jane A. Smith

NOT NEGOTIABLE

021989478 7564 20855808 0727

***Figure 23-4** Some banks and credit unions use a two-part form that provides customers with a record of the transaction.*

recording checks is to use the type of check register shown in the photo on this page.

A common mistake people make in maintaining a checking account is not recording checks in the register. This often happens when someone is in a hurry. Get in the habit of filling out the check register *at the time you write a check*. If you don't, you won't know the correct balance and might overdraw the account.

Overdrawing a checking account can be very embarrassing. One day Jackie got a phone call from her friend Barbara who worked at The Clothes Rack. Barbara called about a check that Jackie had written to buy a new outfit. The bank had returned the check to the store because of insufficient funds. Jackie felt humiliated.

In looking over her check register, Jackie found that she had not recorded a check written to the gas company. It was near the end of the month when she wrote a $53.46 check to The Clothes Rack. There was only $46.20 in her account and the check bounced. Jackie immediately took another check to Barbara.

Figure 23-5 on page 342 shows two common ways to maintain a check register. Study each part of the illustration. Both ways work well; so choose the one that you prefer. The column next to the "payment/debit" column may be used to

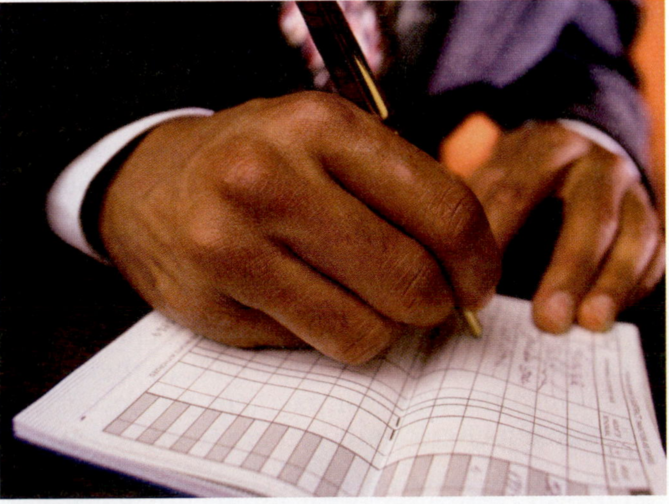

Fill out the check register at the time you write a check.

ONE-LINE ENTRY

RECORD ALL CHARGES OR CREDITS THAT AFFECT YOUR ACCOUNT.

NUMBER	DATE	DESCRIPTION OF TRANSACTION	PAYMENT/DEBIT (-)	✓ T	FEE (IF ANY) (-)	DEPOSIT/CREDIT (+)	BALANCE
							$ 282 34
7341	3/25	Cash	$ 150 00		$	$ 255 67	388 01
7342	3/25	Sunshine State Telephone	25 00				363 01
7343	3/27	Unico Life Ins.	8 70				354 31
7344	3/27	FBB Ins.	5 78				348 53
7345	3/27	Payson Cable	19 75				328 78
7346	3/27	State Bank	400 00			305 67	234 45
7347	4/1	Mishiki Credit Corp.	257 62			485 45	462 28
7348	4/1	Feldspar Motel	68 00				394 28
7349	4/1	Buy-All Supermarket	36 11				358 17
7350	4/3	Kitchen and Bath Co.	90 91				267 26

TWO-LINE ENTRY

RECORD ALL CHARGES OR CREDITS THAT AFFECT YOUR ACCOUNT.

NUMBER	DATE	DESCRIPTION OF TRANSACTION	PAYMENT/DEBIT (-)	✓ T	FEE (IF ANY) (-)	DEPOSIT/CREDIT (+)	BALANCE
							$ 282 34
7341	3/25	Cash	$ 150 00		$	$	150 00
		Car repair					132 34
Deposit	3/25	Deposit check				255 67	255 67
							388 01
7342	3/25	Sunshine State Telephone	25 00				25 00
		Telephone bill					363 01
7343	3/27	Unico Life Ins.	8 70				8 70
		Insurance					354 31
7344	3/27	FBB Ins.	5 78				5 78
		Insurance					348 53
7345	3/27	Payson Cable	19 75				19 75
		Cable bill					328 78

Figure 23-5
Keeping a check register up to date is not difficult. You just have to be accurate and pay attention to detail.

check off items when you balance a statement. Or, if you prefer, you can indicate in this column which items are tax-deductible (T).

Endorsing a Check

Suppose a friend writes you a check. What do you do with it? You take it to your bank and endorse it there. An **endorsement** is your signature, sometimes with a brief message, on the back/left side of a check. You must endorse a check before you can cash or deposit it. There are three common types of endorsements: blank, restrictive, and full (Figure 23-6).

- A blank endorsement is simply your written signature. Once you have signed a check, it can be treated as cash. Anyone can then present it to the bank for payment. So, never endorse a check until you are ready to cash it.
- A restrictive endorsement is a message and a signature that restrict the use of the check. The most common restrictive endorsement is "For deposit only," followed by a signature. This is usually used when you wish to send a check by mail to a bank for deposit. With this message, the check can't be used for any other purpose.
- A full endorsement is used when you want to pay someone else with a check that is made out to you. This is done by writing "Pay to the order of," writing the person's name, and then signing your name. This endorsement transfers the right of payment from you to a new payee.

Endorse a check exactly as it is made out. Do this even if your name is written improperly or misspelled. When there is an error, you endorse the check first as is, followed by the correct way. For example, suppose a check to Sharon Robbins is made out incorrectly to "Sharon Robins." She would endorse it first as "Sharon Robins" and then as "Sharon Robbins."

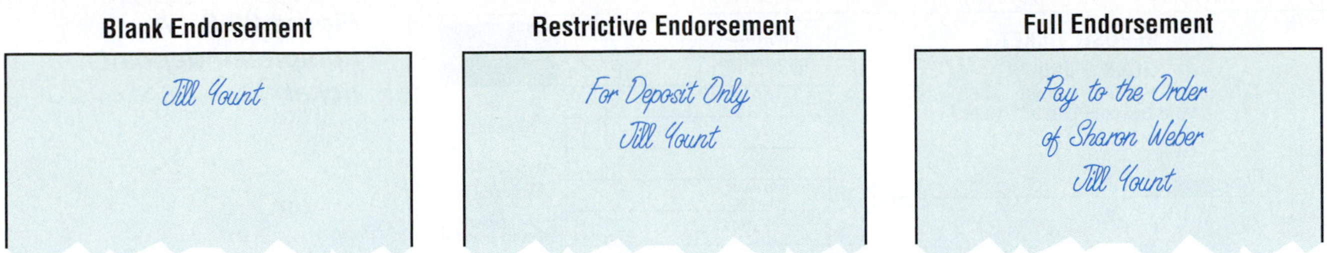

Blank Endorsement
Jill Yount
Restrictive Endorsement
For Deposit Only
Jill Yount
Full Endorsement
Pay to the Order
of Sharon Weber
Jill Yount

Figure 23-6 **Different forms of endorsements are used for different purposes.**

Similarly, a check written to Skip Turner would be endorsed as "Skip Turner," followed by "James A. Turner."

Federal law guarantees customers of financial institutions timely access to money they deposit. The law also requires customers to use uniform standards to endorse checks. Figure 23-7 summarizes these rules. If you fail to follow the rules for endorsing checks, you will still get your money. But it could take longer.

Making a Deposit

The process of putting money into a checking account is known as making a deposit. To do this, you fill out the preprinted **deposit ticket** that comes with your supply of checks. A deposit ticket is used to deposit any combination of currency, coins, and checks. You can receive a portion of the deposit in cash, if you wish. Figure 23-8 on page 344 shows a completed deposit ticket.

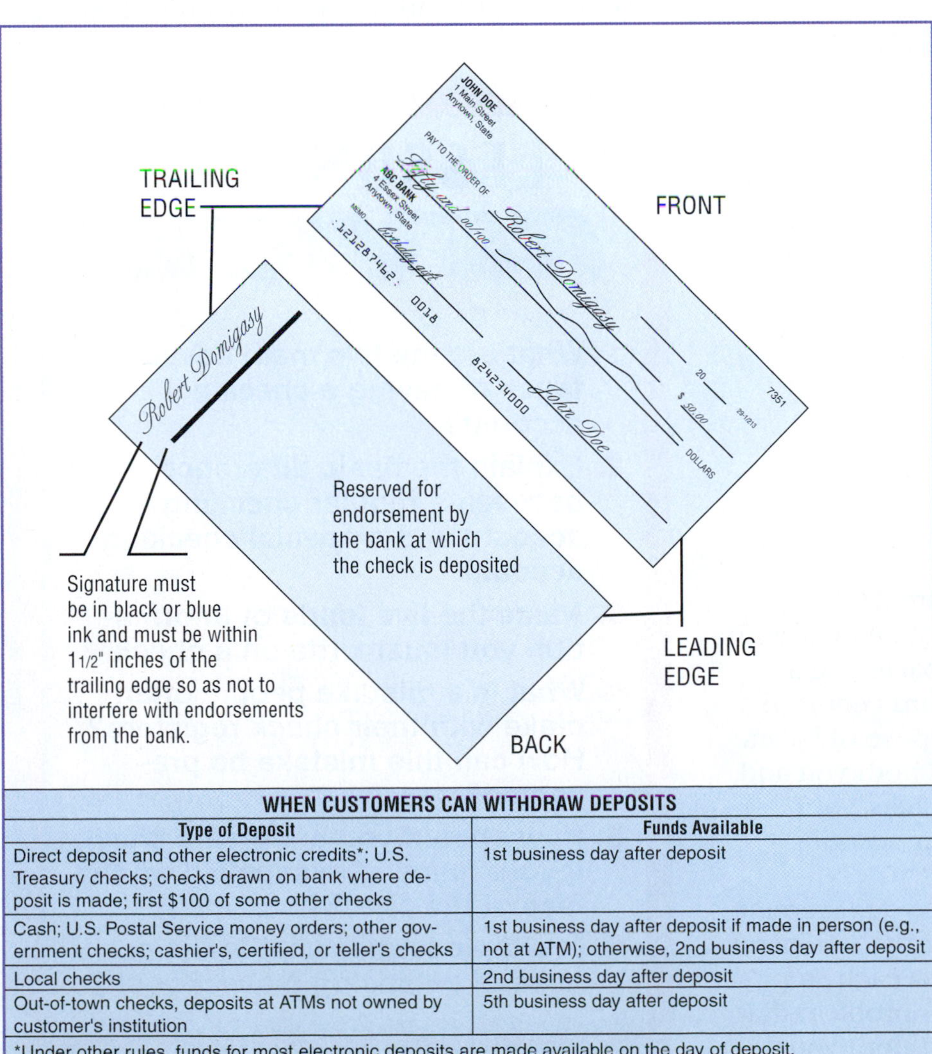

TRAILING EDGE

Reserved for endorsement by the bank at which the check is deposited
Signature must be in black or blue ink and must be within 1 1/2" inches of the trailing edge so as not to interfere with endorsements from the bank.
LEADING EDGE

WHEN CUSTOMERS CAN WITHDRAW DEPOSITS

Type of Deposit	Funds Available
Direct deposit and other electronic credits*; U.S. Treasury checks; checks drawn on bank where deposit is made; first $100 of some other checks	1st business day after deposit
Cash; U.S. Postal Service money orders; other government checks; cashier's, certified, or teller's checks	1st business day after deposit if made in person (e.g., not at ATM); otherwise, 2nd business day after deposit
Local checks	2nd business day after deposit
Out-of-town checks, deposits at ATMs not owned by customer's institution	5th business day after deposit

*Under other rules, funds for most electronic deposits are made available on the day of deposit.

Figure 23-7 **Rules for endorsing checks and withdrawing deposits**

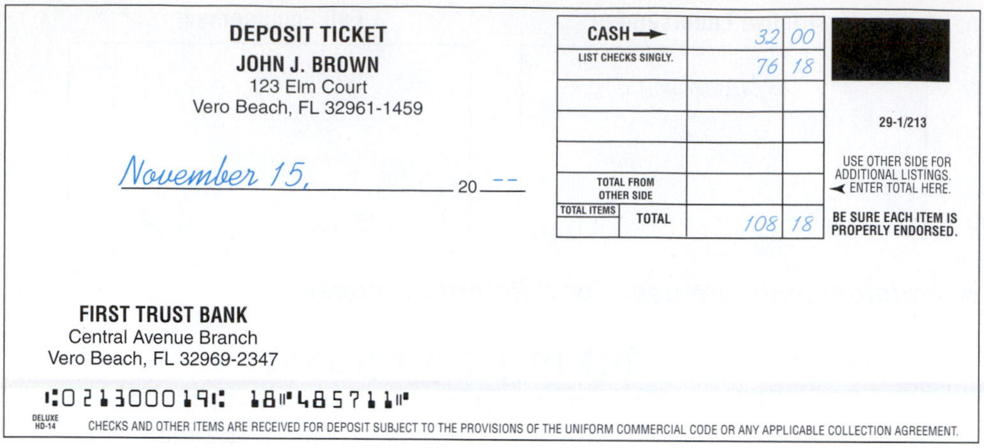

DEPOSIT TICKET				
JOHN J. BROWN 123 Elm Court Vero Beach, FL 32961-1459	CASH →	32	00	
	LIST CHECKS SINGLY.	76	18	
November 15, 20--				29-1/213
				USE OTHER SIDE FOR ADDITIONAL LISTINGS. ENTER TOTAL HERE.
	TOTAL FROM OTHER SIDE			
	TOTAL ITEMS / TOTAL	108	18	BE SURE EACH ITEM IS PROPERLY ENDORSED.
FIRST TRUST BANK Central Avenue Branch Vero Beach, FL 32969-2347				

⑆0213000191⑆ 181⑈485711⑈

DELUXE HD-14 CHECKS AND OTHER ITEMS ARE RECEIVED FOR DEPOSIT SUBJECT TO THE PROVISIONS OF THE UNIFORM COMMERCIAL CODE OR ANY APPLICABLE COLLECTION AGREEMENT.

Figure 23-8 ***A completed deposit ticket***

When you make a deposit, the bank will return to you a receipt showing the amount of the deposit. Check this to make sure it agrees with the amount you wrote on the deposit ticket. Record the deposit right away in your check register.

Balancing a Statement

Once a month, the bank will send you a packet that includes a **statement of account** and the canceled checks that you wrote. Canceled checks are not returned if you have the type of checks shown in Figure 23-4. The statement is a summary of all your transactions for a given period. It includes the following:

- The amount of each check and the date the bank received it
- The deposits you made
- Any service charges
- Any interest earned
- Beginning and ending balances

Study the example shown in Figure 23-9.

The process of comparing the statement with your check register is known as balancing a checkbook. In some cases, the word **reconciling** may be used instead. The purpose of balancing a checkbook is to ensure that both you and your bank have recorded your checks, your deposits, and other activity in your account accurately.

Instructions on how to balance your account are usually printed on the back of the statement (Figure 23-10 on page 346). Follow each step exactly as described. If you have a problem that you cannot figure out, do not wait until you receive the next statement. Rather, call or go to the bank right away and ask someone to help you.

After you have balanced your checkbook, make any necessary changes in the register. For example, you may need to record amounts for service charges, interest, or an overdraft fee.

LESSON 23.2 REVIEW

1. **What are the two main advantages of having a checking account?**
2. **Explain the basic difference between a regular checking account and a special checking account.**
3. **Name the five kinds of information you must write on a check.**
4. **What is a mistake people often make with their check registers? How can this mistake be prevented?**
5. **How should you endorse a check if your name is misspelled on the face of the check?**
6. **In simple terms, what is the purpose of balancing a checkbook?**

PAGE 1 OF 1

FIRST TRUST BANK
Central Avenue Branch
Vero Beach, FL 32969-2347

JOHN J. BROWN
123 Elm Court
Vero Beach, FL 32961-1459

002 613 CY

13435711
6134357116

STATEMENT OF YOUR ACCOUNT(S) FOR PERIOD 11-15-XX THROUGH 12-13-XX

SUMMARY OF REGULAR ACCOUNT # 18 485711

BALANCE LAST STATEMENT	502.10
DEPOSITS AND OTHER ADDITIONS	1910.78
CHECKS AND OTHER SUBTRACTIONS	1306.12
BALANCE THIS STATEMENT	1106.76

TAXPAYER ID NUMBER **123 45 6789**

DATE	TYPE OF TRANSACTION	CHECKS	SUBTRACTIONS	ADDITIONS	BALANCE
11-15	BEGINNING BALANCE				502.10
11-18	DEPOSIT			405.24	907.34
11-22	CHECKS POSTED (3)	67.20			840.14
11-23	DEPOSIT			650.15	
11-23	CHECKS POSTED (1)	17.75			1472.54
11-25	CHECKS POSTED (4)	519.45			953.09
11-28	CHECKS POSTED (1)	44.00			909.09
11-29	CHECKS POSTED (3)	47.20			861.89
11-30	DEPOSIT			305.24	
11-30	CHECKS POSTED (1)	50.00			1117.13
12-05	CHECKS POSTED (3)	363.27			753.86
12-06	CHECKS POSTED (1)	149.69			604.17
12-07	DEPOSIT			305.24	909.41
12-08	CHECKS POSTED (1)	4.00			905.41
12-09	CHECKS POSTED (1)	43.56			861.85
12-12	DEPOSIT			244.91	1106.76

CHECKS POSTED (• INDICATES SEQUENCE BREAK)

CHECK	AMOUNT	DATE	CHECK	AMOUNT	DATE	CHECK	AMOUNT	DATE
7242	50.00	11–30	7249	21.20	11–29	7255	16.00	11–29
7243	44.00	11–28	7250	8.70	11–25	7256	10.00	11–29
7244	17.75	11–23	7251	47.20	11–22	7257	13.27	12–05
7245	10.00	11–22	7252	10.00	11–22	7258	43.56	12–09
7246	400.00	11–25	7253	17.66	11–25	7259	300.00	12–05
7247	50.00	12–05	7254	93.09	11–25	7260	149.69	12–06
7248	4.00	12–08						

***Figure 23-9** Every month your bank will send you a bank statement. This is a summary of all your transactions during that time period.*

It's Easy to Balance Your Account. Follow the instructions and use the reconcilement form below.
Reconcilement Instructions:

- Check off each paid check on your checkbook stub register.
- Be sure that all **checks posted** and **other subtractions** shown on your checking account have been subtracted from your checkbook balance and that all **deposits** and **other additions** have been added.
- List and total under "Checks Outstanding" all checks not paid by the bank during this statement period.
- Fill in the ending balance shown on this statement.
- Add the deposits made after the close of this period.
- Deduct the checks still outstanding.
- The result should be the same as the balance remaining in your checkbook.

Checks Outstanding						Reconcilement Form	
Check No. or Date	Amount	Check No. or Date	Amount	Check No. or Date	Amount		
	$	Total Forwarded	$	Total Forwarded	$	Balance as of this statement, shown on front	$
						Add deposits not yet shown on front.	
						Total	$
						Subtract total checks outstanding.	$
Total or Carry Forward		Total or Carry Forward		**Total**	**$**	**This result should agree with your checkbook balance.**	$

Please examine at once.
Your account will be considered correct if no report is received by our auditors in 14 days, except that matters involving your line of credit or electronic transfer(s) must be reported within 60 days.

Figure 23-10 ***You can keep your account balanced if you follow this step-by-step procedure.***

HIGH-GROWTH OCCUPATIONS FOR THE 21st CENTURY

Police Officers

People depend on *police officers* to protect their lives and property. Law enforcement officers perform these duties in a variety of ways, depending on the size and type of organization. In most jurisdictions, they are expected to exercise authority when necessary, whether on or off duty.

About 65 percent of state and local law enforcement officers are uniformed personnel, who regularly patrol and respond to calls for service. Police officers who work in small communities and rural areas have general law enforcement duties. They may direct traffic at the scene of a fire, investigate a burglary, or give first aid to an accident victim. In large police departments, officers usually are assigned to a specific type of duty, such as foot patrol.

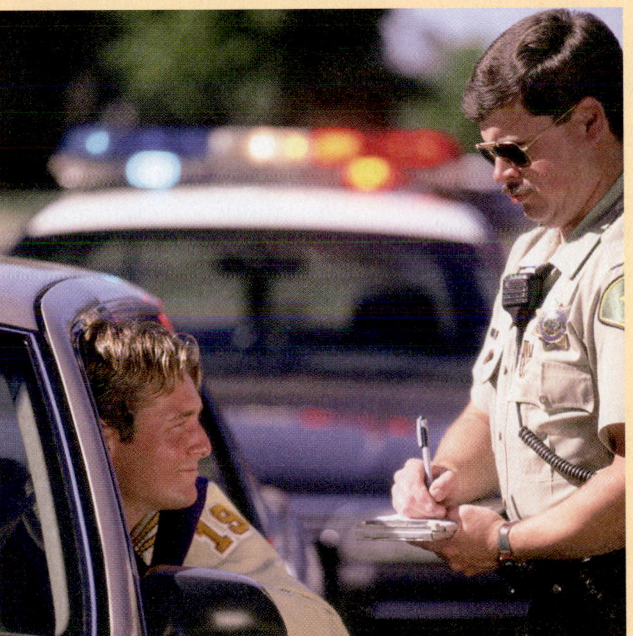

Duties of police officers vary from resolving problems in the community to apprehending criminals to enforcing traffic laws.

Police agencies are usually organized into geographic districts, with uniformed officers assigned to patrol a specific area, such as part of the business district or outlying residential neighborhoods. Officers may work alone, but in large agencies they often patrol with a partner. While on patrol, officers attempt to become thoroughly familiar with their patrol area and remain alert for anything unusual. Suspicious circumstances and hazards to public safety are investigated or noted, and officers are dispatched on individual calls for assistance within their district. During their shift, they may identify, pursue, and arrest suspected criminals, resolve problems within the community, and enforce traffic laws.

Some police officers specialize in such diverse fields as chemical and microscopic analysis, training and firearms instruction, or handwriting and fingerprint identification. Others work with special units such as horseback, bicycle, motorcycle, or harbor patrol; canine corps; or special weapons and tactics (SWAT). About 10 percent of local and special law enforcement officers perform jail-related duties, and about 4 percent work in courts. Regardless of job duties or location, police officers at all levels must write reports and maintain meticulous records that will be needed if they testify in court.

LESSON 23.3

CREDIT AND ITS USE

OBJECTIVES

- NAME AND DESCRIBE THE TWO BASIC TYPES OF CREDIT
- CALCULATE THE COST OF CREDIT

TYPES OF CREDIT

Credit refers to the receipt of money, goods, or services in exchange for a promise to pay. People may get credit in the form of loans. This form is called loan credit. Sales credit is also available. With this type of credit, consumers can delay their payments for goods and services.

Loan Credit

Loan credit involves money borrowed in order to buy something. Most of these loans are for major expenses. A borrower may not have cash on hand to pay for a house, car, or college education. The buyer usually gets a loan at one place and spends the cash in another. For example, you may secure a loan from a credit union. You will then use the money to buy a car at a local dealership.

Buyers generally pay back loan credit in equal installments over a fixed time period. In the case of an auto loan, for example, you might pay installments of $180 per month for 48 months.

Sales Credit

When using loan credit, you borrow money. Sales credit, however, allows you to purchase goods and services directly and delay paying until later. There are three main types of sales credit: open charge accounts, revolving charge accounts, and installment accounts.

Many businesses provide open charge accounts to customers with good credit ratings. Don Marshall has a charge account at Polk's Department Store. One day, he decides to charge two sweaters there. After telling the clerk he is making a charge purchase, Don presents his charge plate. He signs a receipt and takes home his purchase. The bill arrives a few weeks later.

The revolving charge is probably the most common form of consumer sales credit. Most revolving charge accounts are credit card

PERSONAL DECISIONS

You are excited about buying your first car. You got a good deal and the finance rate is reasonable. The last step is to sign the installment sale contract. In going over the contract, you discover that the amount financed includes charges for "credit life and disability insurance" and "extended warranty." You ask the salesperson about these items. He says that they are optional but that most people buy them. They only add a few dollars to the monthly payment. You are not sure whether you need them.

WHAT WOULD YOU DO?

COMMUNICATION AT WORK

PROOFREADING NUMBERS

In managing your own money and at work, you will sometimes have to check numbers. Here are some tips that will help you do a good job and not make mistakes.

- Set aside some time to proofread when you are fresh and not in a hurry.
- If you have a rough copy and a finished copy, read one against the other, using two envelopes or pieces of paper to guide you line by line. Then read the finished copy straight through.
- Read numbers aloud. For long lists of numbers, you may want to read with a partner.
- Try reading numbers in groups. For example, the telephone number 513-555-0116 can be read in three parts: *five-one-three*, *five-five-five*, *zero-one-one-six*.
- Double-check all calculations. For example, when you are adding numbers, add them once from top to bottom and then again from bottom to top.

accounts offered by chain stores, oil companies, and banks. Bankcards have names such as Visa and MasterCard. With them, you can charge many goods and services, such as restaurant meals, airline tickets, and auto repairs.

Like Don, credit card customers receive a monthly statement of all transactions. Don paid his entire bill. He could also have made a minimum payment or could have sent some other amount. But had he done that, he would have paid a finance charge. Finance charges will be discussed in the next section.

Installment accounts are the third major type of sales credit. People may use them to buy

You can use a credit card to make many different kinds of purchases.

items such as furniture and home appliances that exceed the credit line of revolving charge accounts (the amount of credit available). Stores that do not honor credit cards may offer installment plans.

The customer usually makes a small down payment. An installment contract detailing payment terms for the balance is signed. It typically calls for fixed monthly payments and a finance charge. Installments are paid over several months or years. Finance charges are often higher than those for revolving accounts.

THE COST OF CREDIT

The cost of credit varies from lender to lender. Fortunately, the law requires lenders to tell you in writing before you sign an agreement how much the charges will be. To understand the agreement, you will need to know the terms *finance charge* and *annual percentage* rate.

The **finance charge** is the total dollar amount you pay for using credit. It includes interest, service charges, insurance premiums, and other fees. For example, borrowing $100 for a year might cost you $15 in interest and $2 in service charges. The finance charge will be $17.

The **annual percentage rate (APR)** is the percentage cost of credit on a yearly basis.

	APR	Length of Loan	Monthly Payment	Total Finance Charge	Total Cost
Creditor A	14%	3 years	$205.07	$1,382.52	**$7,382.52**
Creditor B	14%	4 years	**$163.96**	$1,870.08	$7,870.08
Creditor C	**15%**	4 years	$166.98	$2,015.04	$8,015.04

Figure 23-11 ***The cost of credit varies according to the APR and the length of the loan.***

Suppose you borrow $200 for one year and pay a finance charge of $20. If you keep the entire $200 for 12 months and then pay it back in one lump sum, you are paying an APR of 10 percent. However, if you repay the $200 and finance charge in 12 equal monthly installments (a total of $220), you do not really get to use the $200 for the whole year. In fact, you get to use less and less of the $200 each month. The $20 charge for credit amounts to an APR of 18 percent.

The APR is your key to comparing credit costs regardless of the amount of credit or the repayment period. All lenders, such as banks, stores, and credit card companies, must state the cost of their credit in terms of both the finance charge and the APR. The law says you must be aware of this information before signing a credit contract.

To actually compare credit costs, you must take into account the APR and length of the loan. Let's assume you are buying a used car for $7,500. You pay $1,500 down and borrow $6,000. The relationship among three different credit arrangements is shown in Figure 23-11.

The loan with the lowest total cost is that offered by Creditor A. If you are looking for a lower monthly payment, you can get that by choosing Creditor B and paying the loan back in four years instead of three. However, the lower monthly payment will add $487.56 to the total finance charge. The 15 percent APR of the loan offered by Creditor C would add another $144.96 to the finance charge.

Other terms, such as the size of the down payment, will also make a difference in the cost of credit. Be sure to consider all aspects of a loan before making a choice.

Credit card users should be aware of the cost of credit.

LESSON 23.3 REVIEW

1. **Name and briefly explain the two basic types of credit.**
2. **What are the three main types of sales credit?**
3. **What does the finance charge include?**
4. **What is the practical purpose of the APR?**
5. **Let's say you bought a new car, paying $2,000 down and $178.60 a month for three years. What was the total cost of the car?**

FOCUS ON SKILLS FOR LIVING

YOUR CREDIT HISTORY

When you apply for credit, the potential lender will usually request a credit report on you from a credit bureau. A credit bureau is a private organization that provides information to businesses regarding the credit history of customers. Your credit file contains four major types of information:

- Personal information, such as name, address, previous addresses, marital status, and number of dependents
- Information about your salary, your spouse's salary, and other income
- The status of your current accounts, what kinds of loans you now have, and whether you pay your bills in full and on time
- Any court judgments or liens against you. A lien is a charge against your property for failure to pay a debt. Accounts turned over to a collection agency are also noted.

People who use credit cards or who have bank loans should find out if the information in their credit bureau files is correct.

The credit bureau only compiles information and provides it to the merchant or potential lender. That person judges how creditworthy you are.

Federal law gives you the right to know what information is in your file. If you are refused credit on the basis of a credit report, the merchant must give you the name and address of the bureau. You are entitled to a free credit report from the bureau. If you disagree with information in the file, the bureau must reinvestigate and remove information that cannot be verified.

Even if you are not turned down for credit, you should look at your credit file from time to time. A local bank or merchant can tell you the name of the credit bureau nearest you. Write or call the bureau to ask how to obtain a credit report. You can also obtain credit reports on the Internet. Although some services on the Internet offer free credit reports, in most cases you will be charged a fee. You can ask to have errors corrected, outdated information removed, and missing information added to the file.

THINK CRITICALLY

1. Why would a merchant or potential lender want the information that a credit file provides?
2. Why is it a good idea to look at your credit file from time to time?

CHAPTER 23

Chapter in Brief

Lesson 23.1 *Financial Institutions*

A. There are four major types of financial institutions: commercial banks, mutual savings banks, savings and loan associations, and credit unions.
B. Increased competition among financial institutions helps consumers.

Lesson 23.2 *Checking Accounts*

A. Checking accounts are one of the most commonly used banking services. They are safe and convenient.
B. When writing a check, include a date, payee, numerical amount, written amount, purpose or account number (optional), and signature.
C. The check register is where you keep a record of checks written, deposits made, and other transactions.
D. An endorsement is a signature, sometimes with a brief message, needed to cash, deposit, or transfer ownership of a check.
E. Your bank will send you a monthly statement of account. Comparing it with your check register is known as balancing a checkbook.

Lesson 23.3 *Credit and Its Use*

A. Credit refers to the receipt of money, goods, or services in exchange for a promise to pay.
B. The finance charge is the total dollar amount you pay for using credit. The annual percentage rate (APR) is the percentage cost of credit on a yearly basis. The APR is your key to comparing credit costs.

Activities

1. As a class, count the financial institutions in your community, suburb, or region of the city. Classify each according to the four types of institutions discussed in this chapter. Which is the most common type?
2. A group of students should visit at least three financial institutions to learn about the types of checking accounts. Which type best meets your needs in terms of cost and convenience? Discuss your answers in class.
3. Ask an adult to let you do these tasks for him or her: write a check, record a transaction in a check register, and make a deposit to a checking account.
4. The instructor will provide a sample statement of account and check register. Follow the procedure in Figure 23-10 to reconcile the statement.
5. Get a credit card application and read it carefully. Is an annual fee required? What is the APR? How is the finance charge figured? What is the credit limit? What is the minimum monthly payment required?
6. Compare interest rates being charged for consumer loans at several different types of financial institutions in your area. Which offers the best rates?

REVIEW

Word Power

On a separate sheet of paper, match each definition with the correct term. All definitions will be used, and a definition will be used only once.

7. The process of comparing a bank statement with one's personal check register to verify accuracy
8. The total dollar amount paid for the use of credit
9. A check written for more than is in an account
10. The percentage cost of credit on a yearly basis
11. A plastic card used in electronic banking to immediately transfer funds for a purchase from a bank account
12. A summary of all transactions completed in a checking account for a given time period
13. Various types of electronic fund transfers
14. The receipt of money, goods, or services in exchange for a promise to pay
15. Placing a date on a check that is ahead of the current date
16. A form that is completed to open a checking account
17. Banks offering many financial conveniences and services
18. The person or institution to which a check is written
19. Electronic terminals in which customers can insert a plastic card to withdraw cash, make deposits, or transfer funds
20. An interest-bearing checking account in which a draft (check) is written against a credit union savings account
21. An interest-bearing checking account in which a withdrawal order (check) is written against a savings account
22. A booklet or forms for keeping a record of checking account transactions
23. A signature, sometimes with a brief message, on the back/left side of a check needed to cash, deposit, or transfer ownership of it
24. A preprinted form used to make a deposit in a checking account

a. annual percentage rate (APR)
b. automated teller machines (ATMs)
c. check register
d. credit
e. debit card
f. deposit ticket
g. electronic banking
h. endorsement
i. finance charge
j. full-service banks
k. negotiable order of withdrawal (NOW) account
l. overdraft
m. payee
n. postdating
o. reconciling
p. share draft account
q. signature card
r. statement of account

Think Critically

25. Discuss advantages and disadvantages of electronic banking.
26. Some futurists are saying that we are headed for a "checkless" or "moneyless" society. Do you think that time will ever come?
27. Many people buy merchandise from catalogs or the Internet. Which of the following methods of payment are the safest and offer the greatest consumer protection: money order, check, or credit card? Why?
28. A young person often must have a parent or other adult co-sign a credit application. What does this mean? Do you think the requirement is fair?

CHAPTER 24

BUDGETING, SAVING, AND INVESTING MONEY

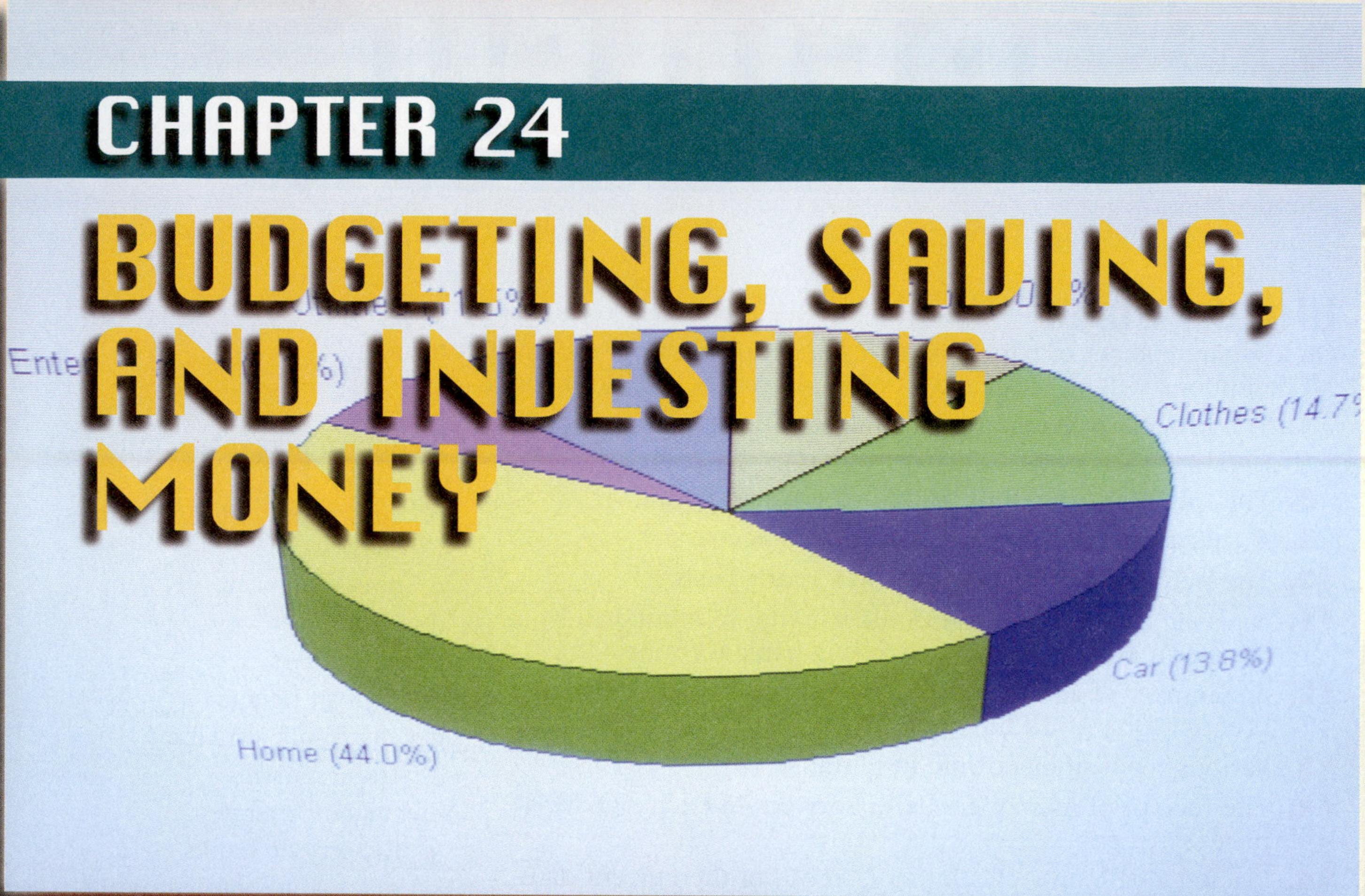

LESSONS

24.1 *Budgeting Money*

24.2 *Saving Money*

24.3 *Investing Money*

PREVIEW

People often refer to someone's financial status with terms like *rich, middle-class*, and *poor*. Financial well-being, of course, is related to how much money you earn. The way you spend money, however, is also important. Many people who earn average incomes live comfortably and securely. Wise money management depends on knowledge and skill in budgeting, saving, and perhaps investing money.

THOUGHTS ON WORK

"Don't be afraid to give your best to what seemingly are small jobs. Every time you conquer one it makes you that much stronger. If you do the little jobs well, the big ones tend to take care of themselves."

Dale Carnegie

TAKING ACTION

SAVING FOR YOUR FUTURE

Anna is frustrated. Even though she has a well-paying job, she cannot seem to make ends meet. At the end of the month, she has very little left over after all her bills are paid. She doesn't know where all her money has gone.

To make matters worse, her parents and relatives keep advising Anna to save and invest for her future. She should save, they say, so that if an unexpected expense comes up, such as a car repair, she won't have to go into debt to cover the expense. She should invest to secure a comfortable retirement. Relatives have told Anna that she might need as much as $1 million saved for retirement by the time she is 65!

"That's great in theory," Anna thinks. "I don't disagree. I just don't know how to save and invest when I can barely get by."

Anna has tried to limit her spending by not going to restaurants very often and not going to the mall to buy things for her new apartment. This strategy seems to be helping. It is still not enough.

Add to Anna's troubles that her car is not doing well. She will have to pay for expensive repairs or she will have to buy a new car within a year. She cannot get to work without her car.

SUCCESS TIP

Find out how to save and invest early.

Anna has not had a vacation in two years. One day, she would like to buy a small house and fix it up herself. She also has a number of charities to which she would like to contribute. All of these things take money. Anna wonders how anyone can afford to get ahead.

Luckily Anna has a cousin, Jose, who seems to understand saving and investing. Even though Jose earns less than Anna, he has been saving and investing for three years. Anna decides to ask him for advice.

THINK CRITICALLY

1. Why do you think Anna has trouble with saving?
2. What are some reasons that Anna might want to start a savings plan?

LESSON 24.1
BUDGETING MONEY

OBJECTIVES

- IDENTIFY YOUR OWN PERSONAL INCOME AND SPENDING PATTERNS
- NAME AND DESCRIBE THE FOUR STEPS INVOLVED IN DEVELOPING AND USING A BUDGET

INCOME AND SPENDING PATTERNS

A good first step in learning how to manage money is to find out where your money is coming from and where it is going. You will do this by maintaining a record of **income** (money coming in) and **expenditures** (money that is spent). A simple form for tracking income and expenditures is shown in Figure 24-1. You can use a form to cover a week or any time period you choose.

To fill out a form like this one, begin by inserting the total amount of cash you have on hand at the beginning of the week. Don't include savings. Then, start keeping detailed records of all income and expenditures. For income, include take-home pay as well as tips and any money you receive from gifts or allowances. List all expenditures, regardless of how small.

At the end of the week, total up all income and expenditures. How much money is left at week's end? It should equal initial cash on hand plus or minus income and expenditures. Say your initial cash on hand is $75. You spend $50, and your aunt sends you $15 as a birthday gift. The end-of-week cash balance would be $40.

Once you have kept your records for a few weeks, figure your average income and expenditures. Add up all the income for the period and divide by the number of weeks covered. Do the same for expenditures. Keeping a record of income and expenditures over a period of time can help you understand your financial condition and spending habits. The data in Figure 24-1 show, for example, that the pattern of expenditures cannot continue much longer. You can then use this information to set up a budget for yourself.

DEVELOPING AND USING A BUDGET

A **budget** is a plan for managing income and expenditures. Such a spending plan will help you get the most benefit from your earnings. The four steps involved in developing a budget are as follows:

1. Establishing goals
2. Estimating income and expenditures
3. Setting up the budget
4. Following and revising the budget

The process is similar for everyone—individuals and families, young people and adults.

Establishing Goals

Goals should be set before you work out the details of your budget. Identify what you need and want. As you decide on goals, discuss them

RECORD OF INCOME AND EXPENDITURES

Week *Feb. 4-10* 20 --

Cash on hand *$50.80*

Date	Item	Income	Expenditure
4	Allowance & lunch money	$30.00	
4	School lunch ticket		$10.50
5	Gas in car		$24.00
6	Babysitting	$42.00	
7	Basketball game		$4.25
	Snack afterward		$6.00
8	Movie w/friends		$8.50
	Pizza afterward		$6.00
9	Shopping (new music CD)		$16.75
10	Personal care items		$12.00

End-of-week cash balance *$34.80* Totals *$72.00* *$88.00*

Figure 24-1 ***Records like these help determine patterns of income and expenditures for individuals, families, and businesses.***

with your family. If the budget is for a family, all family members should participate. Goals should be kept realistic in relation to present and expected future income.

To focus on your goals, list them according to time periods. Be as specific as possible. Bear in mind that there are short-range, medium-range, and long-range goals.

Naturally, goals change along with situations. For example, if you are single and live at home, your goals are probably different than they will be when you leave home. If you marry, your goals will change again, as they will if you have children. With two people working, the family goals may be different than they would be if only one were working, and so on.

Once you have decided on your goals, write them down, as in Figure 24-2 on page 358. Save your list. You will need to refer to it as you plan the budget.

Estimating Income and Expenditures

Once you have decided on goals, estimate your income and expenditures. A budget may cover any convenient budget period. Most people like to plan a budget around how often they get paid, such as weekly, bimonthly, or monthly.

PERSONAL (OR FAMILY) GOALS

Goals for this year: ____________

____

____

Goals for the next five years: ____________

____

____

Long-term goals: ____________

____

____

Figure 24-2 ***Write out your financial goals so you will know what you are working toward.***

If you have kept records of income and expenditures for a four- to six-week period, you should be able to arrive at fairly close estimates. If the budget is for a family, records of income and expenditures should be kept over a three- to six-month period. Figure out your average income per budget period. Now review. Did you include all regular income, such as wages, salary, and tips? How about variable income, such as bonuses, gifts, interest, and dividends?

PERSONAL DECISIONS

You have done your best to develop and follow a budget. You are careful to stick to budget estimates, but every month there is an unexpected expense. It never seems to be the same type of expenditure. One month it is a car repair; the next month, a medical bill; another month, an increase in insurance; and so on. You are very frustrated and about ready to "trash-can" the budget.

WHAT WOULD YOU DO?

Individuals whose income varies may have special difficulty making estimates. Examples include seasonal workers, salespeople on commission, farmers, and other self-employed people. In these cases, it is usually better to base the budget estimates slightly below the average income. It is always easier to spend extra money than it is to come up with cash to cover a shortage.

Ann is a sales representative who earns most of her income from commissions. The more she sells, the more she earns. During the last six months, her income has been about 30 percent above normal. Business has been so good that she traded her car in on a new one. She can make payments with the extra commissions she is earning.

She got a call today from one of her best clients. "Hello, Ann, this is Cliff at Dramon Corporation. I'm afraid I'll have to cancel that big order you wrote up for me last week. My field representatives are telling me that business is slowing down. We could be moving into a recession."

What if an economic slowdown is on the way? Ann's future commissions will probably fall. Ann now wishes she had not gone in debt for the new car.

Regarding expenditures, your previous records should help you identify the major categories of items. Next, review the list to make sure you have not left out a seasonal expenditure or some other item that does not show up in your records. A checkbook register together with bills and receipts can help you remember such information.

As you review your record of expenditures, decide whether to continue your present spending pattern or to make changes. If you are satisfied with how you have saved your money, allow similar amounts in your budget estimates. Suppose your records point out poor buying habits or overspending. In that case, you must decide to make changes.

Setting Up the Budget

Now that you have established your financial goals and have estimated income and expenditures, you are ready to set up your spending plan. The sample budget form shown in Figure 24-3 consists of three main parts.

HOUSEHOLD BUDGET FORM

Month *Jan.* 20 --   Estimated Income $ *1,706*

Expenditure	Estimate	Actual	Difference (+ or −)
Savings			
Emergency reserve	$42	$42	0
Goals	$60	$36	+$24
Regular Expenses			
Rent or mortgage payment	$360	$360	0
Utilities	$200	$235	−$35
Insurance	$120	$120	0
Auto payment	0	0	0
Credit or loan payments	$96	$96	0
Other ( )			
Variable Expenses			
Food and beverages	$420	$415	+$5
Clothing	$60	$92	−$32
Transportation	$120	$114	+$6
Household	$48	$48	0
Medical care	$36	$28	+$8
Entertainment	$72	$82	−$10
Gifts and contributions	$36	$30	+$6
Taxes	$36	$36	0
Other ( )			
TOTALS	$1,706	$1,734	−$28

Figure 24-3 ***Using a budget form like this can improve the quality of your life and help you meet future goals successfully.***

The first part of the budget is for savings. **Savings** is cash set aside in a bank account to be used for financial emergencies and goals. It is important to set aside this money as soon as you are paid. If you wait until the end of the budget period, there may be nothing left for savings.

You should save a regular amount of income for use in an emergency. For a family, the amount should equal *at least* one month's total income. Once you have reached your figure to set aside for emergencies, start shifting money to savings goals and investments.

The next two parts of the budget include regular and variable expenditures.

Regular Expenditures

Regular expenditures, sometimes called fixed expenditures, are those essential monthly payments that are usually the same amount each month. Here is a list of common regular expenditures. Your regular expenditures may be slightly different.

- ***Rent or mortgage payment.*** This fixed expenditure covers your basic housing needs. Renters pay their landlord. Buyers of a property make payments to the lender that granted the mortgage. A mortgage payment usually includes property taxes and insurance.
- ***Utilities.*** These include services such as electricity, telephone, gas, and water. Even though these amounts vary, you should list them as regular expenses because they are essential monthly payments. Suppose you have trouble deciding how much to budget for utilities? Check with the utility companies. Many of them have a plan whereby you can pay a fixed amount each month based on your average utility usage.
- ***Insurance.*** Include here all insurance premiums not covered by payroll withholding and mortgage payments. Life and auto insurance are two common examples.
- ***Auto payment.*** You may not have an auto loan. However, many people do, and they make monthly installment payments on it.
- ***Credit or loan payments.*** These may include payments on charge accounts or student loans, for example. Not everyone has credit or loan payments.

Variable Expenditures

Variable expenditures are day-to-day living expenses. They may change depending on the time of year, spending habits, and so on.

- ***Food and beverages.*** This category includes food and beverages purchased for home use as well as essential meals eaten away from home, such as school lunches. Optional purchases, such as a snack after the game, should be listed under "Entertainment."
- ***Clothing.*** Include here the cost of buying and maintaining your clothes. Be sure to consider expenditures for repairs, alterations, dry cleaning, and laundry.
- ***Transportation.*** Include here the cost of using public transportation. If you own a vehicle, be sure to consider expenditures for gas, oil, repairs, tolls, and license plates.

You can often save money by pumping your own gas.

- ***Household.*** This includes the cost of buying and maintaining furniture and appliances. Furniture payments could instead be included in "Credit or loan payments." If you rent, the property owners may or may not provide furniture. Everyone must buy cleaning supplies. Homeowners may have extra expenses, such as paint and lawn care products.
- ***Medical care.*** You can plan ahead for some of your medical care. For example, you know if you have to take regular medication or have periodic checkups. Try to set aside some money for variable medical and dental expenses not covered by insurance.
- ***Entertainment.*** This category includes vacations, hobbies, concert tickets, sporting events, and the like. If you have children, babysitting might be an entertainment expense.
- ***Gifts and contributions.*** Besides gifts, be sure to consider contributions to charity, political parties, special causes, and the like.
- ***Taxes.*** Include here amounts for taxes not withheld from your paycheck or included in a mortgage payment. Keep in mind that it is often necessary to pay extra income taxes at the end of the year.

These items are the expenditures that most families have. You should feel free to add or subtract items as necessary and arrange them in the way that works best for you. Once you have developed a list of expenditures for your budget, enter on the budget form a dollar amount for each item. The total of all items in the "Estimate" column should equal the amount entered for "Estimated Income."

Following and Revising the Budget

Following a budget involves the **allocation**, or distribution, of income to the various items in the budget. It also involves keeping accurate records of expenditures.

One way to allocate income is to deposit all or most of it in a checking account and then to write checks for items as necessary. Another common method is to cash your paycheck, divide the cash according to budget categories, and place it in separate envelopes labeled with your main budget headings. You can then take money out of the envelopes as needed.

A good choice is probably a combination of the two methods. Place most of your paycheck in a checking account. Write checks for larger and regular expenses. Keep the remaining cash on hand for smaller purchases. Regardless of which method you use, refer to your budget often. Otherwise, your spending plan is useless.

Keeping accurate records is an important part of maintaining a budget. If paid by check, major expenditures are easy to keep track of. Be sure to write everything in your check register. Small cash purchases can be another matter. Because you make so many of them, it is tempting to ignore them. Failure to note these items makes your budget useless.

To account for cash purchases, use a form like the one shown in Figure 24-1. If it does not meet your needs, modify it or develop a new one. Another approach is to get an expandable manila file, label each pocket with a main budget heading, and file receipts in it. To jot down items for which you do not have a receipt, keep a notepad and pen near the file. All family members who spend money should get in the habit of saving and filing receipts.

At the end of the budget period, go over your receipts and records. Enter the information in the column labeled "Actual" using the budget form in Figure 24-3. Write in the total amount spent for each line item in the budget. A **line item** is a single entry, or budgeted item. In the next column, record the difference between the "Estimate" and the "Actual" amounts. For example, if you estimated $120 for transportation but only spent $114, write in "+$6." However, suppose you spent $135. In that case, you would put down "−$15."

After you have filled in all the information, add up the totals for the "Actual" and "Difference" columns. Now you must face up to reality. How does your spending compare to your estimates? If the figures are similar, you should be proud of yourself. If not, try to find the problem. Perhaps your estimates were not accurate or realistic. Or maybe the estimates were good, but you had trouble sticking to them. If there is a problem with the estimates, revise them. If the problem is with you, resolve to do a better job next time.

Do not expect to have a perfect budget the first time you set one up. A budget is something you must keep working and reworking. Even after you arrive at a budget that is right for you, you will need to change it from time to time.

LESSON 24.1 REVIEW

1. What two factors influence financial well-being?
2. Why should you keep a record of income and expenditures?
3. What four steps are involved in developing a budget?
4. Name two situations that might cause goals to change.
5. Why is it important to set aside money for savings as soon as you are paid?
6. Explain how to allocate income to budgeted items.
7. Name two reasons why actual expenditures might be quite different from budget estimates.

LESSON 24.2
SAVING MONEY

- DISCUSS THE IMPORTANCE OF SETTING ASIDE A PORTION OF INCOME FOR SAVINGS
- NAME AND DESCRIBE THE TWO BASIC TYPES OF SAVINGS ACCOUNTS
- COMPUTE INTEREST RATE RETURNS ON SAVINGS

WHY SAVE?

If all of your paycheck goes for bills, you are working for someone else! Ask Ralph. On the first of the month when he gets paid, Ralph writes checks for all of his monthly payments. Checks go for rent, a car payment, utilities, and various credit card accounts. After putting aside amounts for groceries and insurance, Ralph has little left. He keeps his fingers crossed every month. Ralph knows that an illness or emergency would be a financial disaster.

One weekend at a family gathering, Ralph was talking about his financial situation with his Uncle John. Uncle John, a banker, listened patiently until Ralph had finished. Then he said, "Ralph, you must learn to *pay yourself first*." What Uncle John meant was that Ralph should reward himself for working. He should take a portion "off the top" of his paycheck and put it into savings.

There are two reasons to set aside cash for savings. First, you will have some funds available to meet a financial emergency. Suppose Ralph follows his uncle's advice and opens a savings account. Then, should his old car suddenly break down, Ralph won't have to worry about how he will pay for repairs. Second, a savings account allows you to achieve financial goals. Ralph, for example, may want to save for new stereo components.

In Chapter 23, you read about the four types of financial institutions that offer checking accounts. Those institutions—commercial banks, mutual savings banks, savings and loan associations, and credit unions—accept savings deposits as well. It is not necessary to have both

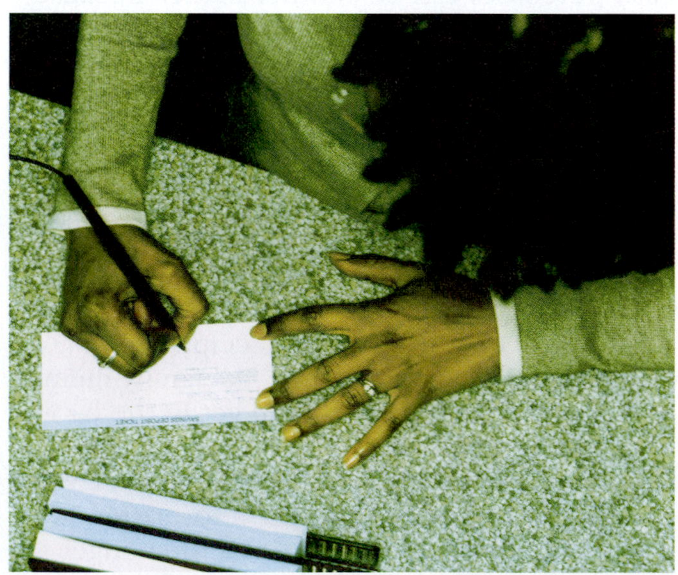

Pay yourself first by putting money into savings.

checking and savings accounts at the same place. Do some comparison shopping. Teresa Romero did.

You may remember from Chapter 23 how Teresa saved money by closing her old checking account and opening a new one at a credit union. So, when it came time to open a savings account, Teresa reviewed the material she had already collected about financial services at various institutions.

After comparing various plans and interest rates, Teresa decided to open a savings account at a mutual savings bank. It is close to her home and does not close until 8 p.m. on Friday evenings. Her money, on which she receives a good interest rate, is insured. She can withdraw funds at any time. Teresa is satisfied to know that she is using her money wisely.

As you learned in Chapter 23, because of changes in banking laws, financial institutions have begun to offer similar services. Shop carefully for the right ones for you. You have many choices. Even within one institution, you may find a variety of savings plans. Your efforts will gain you more interest for your savings dollars.

TYPES OF SAVINGS ACCOUNTS

Financial institutions may advertise many different savings account plans. These plans are generally of two basic types: regular savings accounts and time deposits.

Regular Savings Accounts

Regular savings accounts, also called passbook accounts, are very convenient and flexible. You can make deposits and withdrawals at any time. These accounts get their name from the passbook given to customers for recording deposits, withdrawals, and interest payments. Most institutions, however, now issue computerized statements instead. A statement may be provided at the time a transaction is made. A summary statement may also be mailed monthly or quarterly.

It is easy to open a regular savings account. You simply sign a signature card and make a deposit. An individual account number will be assigned, and the institution will give you a passbook or an identification card for your account.

Regular savings accounts offer safety, convenience, and liquidity. **Liquidity** refers to an asset that can be easily converted into cash. Depositors receive slightly less interest on regular savings accounts than on other types of accounts. This is because passbook accounts are expensive for institutions to service.

Time Deposits

If you can deposit a lump-sum amount for a longer period of time, you may be interested in

SAVINGS DEPOSIT FORM

SAVINGS DEPOSIT

DATE ______

ACCOUNT NUMBER ______

NAME ______

		DOLLARS	CENTS
CASH			
LIST CHECKS SEPARATELY. BE SURE EACH ITEM IS ENDORSED.			
TOTAL DEPOSIT			

TELLER'S STAMP

SUPERVISOR ______

All unpaid items will be charged back to the depositor.

C - 153 500M 2/89-T

SAVINGS WITHDRAWAL FORM

SAVINGS WITHDRAWAL

DATE ______

PAY TO ______ Or Bearer

______ Dollars

I HEREBY CERTIFY ALL PERSONS NAMED IN THIS ACCOUNT ARE STILL LIVING.

ACCOUNT NUMBER ______ ☐ CASH ☐ CHECK AMOUNT WITHDRAWN $

TELLER'S STAMP

CHECK NUMBER ______

______ SIGNATURE

SUPERVISOR ______ ______ SIGNATURE

C - 153 500M 2/89-T

PASSBOOK MUST ACCOMPANY THIS ORDER.

Figure 24-4 There are separate forms for making deposits to and withdrawals from a bank account.

time deposits. A popular type of time deposit is a **certificate of deposit (CD)**.

Most time deposits work in the same way. A depositor puts in money for a fixed period of time. This may be six months, one year, or longer. The saver agrees not to withdraw money during that period. In return, the institution pays a higher rate of interest. The longer the saver agrees to keep the money in the account, the higher the rate of interest will be (Figure 24-5). What if the depositor needs to withdraw the funds? It can be done, but the interest rate will be greatly reduced.

Time deposits are safe and provide a guaranteed rate of return for a fixed time period. On the negative side, they generally do not permit deposits and withdrawals and are not as liquid as regular savings accounts.

Some accounts offer advantages of both regular savings accounts and time deposits. They have names such as "Golden Passbook Account" and "Bonus Savings Account." These accounts have higher rates of interest than regular savings accounts but more flexible terms than time deposits. For example, they allow you to make withdrawals and additional deposits. Such accounts usually require a higher minimum balance than regular savings accounts.

First Trust Bank
Central Avenue Branch
Vero Beach, FL 32969-2347

SUBJECT TO CHANGE

TIME DEPOSIT RATES EFFECTIVE May 3, 20--

THROUGH May 9, 20--

Term	Minimum	Current Rates
32–91 days	$500	6.30
92 days–1 year	$500	6.55
13–18 months	$500	6.65
19–30 months	$500	7.25
31–48 months	$500	7.45
Over 48 months	$500	7.75

Figure 24-5 ***This is an example of how time deposit interest rates vary for different time periods.***

FIGURING INTEREST RATES

Savings account interest rates fluctuate from time to time. In the early 1980s, for example, interest rates were over 10 percent. By the early 1990s, they had dropped below 3 percent. Rates also vary according to the type of savings plan. Determining the best interest rates for different savings plans requires effort on your part. To start, look at this newspaper ad:

Save more at University Bank: 5.25% interest compounded daily, paid quarterly on passbook savings. Yield 5.390%.

From the ad, you learn the annual interest rate (5.25%) and annual percentage yield (5.390%). University Bank also tells you how often interest is compounded (daily) and when it is paid (quarterly). Let's discuss these four points in detail.

Annual Interest Rate

The law requires banks and other financial institutions to clearly state in their ads the true annual interest rate paid on savings. In the preceding ad, 5.25% is the annual interest rate. This means that on each $100 of savings, the institution pays you $5.25 in interest. Interest is figured by multiplying rate × time (in years) × principal (0.0525 × 1 × $100 = $5.25).

PERSONAL DECISIONS

You see an ad in the newspaper for the grand opening of a mutual savings bank. The bank is offering a camera to new customers who deposit a certain amount. You already have a passbook account and a CD at another bank. But you are considering switching banks to get the free camera.

WHAT WOULD YOU DO?

MATH CONNECTION

You just received $2,000 from your aunt. You want to put it into a savings account. If the interest rate is 6%, approximately how long will it take for your money to double?

SOLUTION

You can't do most compound interest problems in your head. But you can do this one, by using the Rule of 72. Simply divide 72 by the rate of interest.

$72 \div 6 = 12$

It will take approximately 12 years for your money to double.

Frequency of Interest Compounding

It is easy to understand the annual interest rate. You want the most interest for your money. But the highest advertised annual rate may not be the best deal. More important than the interest rate is how often the interest is compounded. When an institution adds interest, an account's balance rises. There is then more money to earn interest later. This process is called **compounding**.

A 6 percent interest rate with interest compounded annually means the interest is added every 12 months. So, if $100 is in your account, $106 will be the balance after one year. At the end of the second year, you will have $112.36. The interest for the second year, $6.36, was figured on the new balance of $106. How much, then, would you earn the third year?

If the interest rate is 6 percent but the interest is compounded semiannually, you will have $103 at the end of six months. After a year, you will have $106.09. At the end of two years, you will have $112.55. The more often the interest is compounded, the more money you make. Figure 24-6 shows how the value of a $1,000 deposit varies according to the frequency of compounding.

Interest Pay Periods

How often does the financial institution credit interest to your account? The ad for University Bank says that the bank compounds interest daily and pays it four times a year (quarterly). Should you close the account in mid-quarter, you would lose all the interest for that three-month period. You may want to look instead for an account that pays interest from the day of deposit to the day of withdrawal.

Annual Percentage Yield

When comparing one savings account with another, it is useful to know the annual percentage yield (APY). That figure will tell you the actual yearly interest rate per $100 left on deposit. The number takes into account both the rate for annual interest and compounding. In general, the higher the APY, the better the deal you receive (Figure 24-7 on page 366).

Just as the APR, which you learned about in Chapter 23, provides you with a means for comparing credit costs, the APY gives you a method for comparing the earnings of different savings account plans. Recent federal legislation nicknamed "Truth-in-Savings" requires banks and other savings institutions to provide this information to customers.

Frequency of Compounding	After 1 year	After 5 years	After 10 years	After 20 years
Daily	$1,053.90	$1,300.15	$1,690.40	$2,857.44
Quarterly	1,053.54	1,297.96	1,684.70	2,838.20
Semiannually	1,053.19	1,295.78	1,679.05	2,819.21
Annually	1,052.50	1,291.55	1,668.10	2,782.54

Figure 24-6 ***More frequent interest compounding results in higher returns. The figures are based on a $1,000 deposit at 5.25 percent.***

5.25%, compounded	APY
Daily	5.39%
Quarterly	5.35%
Semiannually	5.32%
Annually	5.25%

Figure 24-7 ***The APY is the best indicator of how much interest you will earn.***

Weekly deposit	After 1 year	After 3 years	After 5 years	After 10 years	After 20 years
$ 5	$ 267.16	$ 845.95	$1,489.54	$ 3,431.69	$ 9,265.67
10	534.32	1,691.89	2,979.08	6,863.37	18,531.35
15	801.48	2,537.84	4,468.62	10,295.06	27,797.02
20	1,068.63	3,383.79	5,958.17	13,726.74	37,062.70
25	1,335.79	4,229.74	7,447.71	17,158.43	46,328.37

Figure 24-8 ***Over the years, a small amount of savings can add up to a large amount (figures based on 5.25 percent interest, compounded daily).***

Other Information

The four factors discussed here are not the only ones that influence savings interest. One bank ad, for instance, contained this statement: "Deposits made by the tenth of the month earn interest from the first. Interest is figured on the low balance per month and there must be a balance at interest-paying days in order to earn interest."

This example illustrates only one of the many different methods that savings institutions use to compute interest. However, if you know the basic principles of figuring interest rates, you should be able to understand and compare the methods used by different institutions.

If you shop around, remember that savings institutions may differ a great deal as to how they figure interest. Try to narrow down your choices to a few institutions offering the highest APY. Speak with bank personnel about requirements. Your best choice will probably be the institution having the highest APY and the fewest restrictions and penalties.

Following this advice will bring you financial rewards. Why settle for just any institution? It is your money. Study Figures 24-8 and 24-9 to see how different amounts of savings can grow according to different interest rates and time periods.

Interest rate	After 1 year	After 3 years	After 5 years	After 10 years	After 20 years
4.5%	$615.13	$1,932.88	$3,376.53	$7,618.34	$19,641.57
5	616.84	1,948.41	3,422.06	7,831.35	20,832.93
5.25	617.70	1,956.25	3,445.16	7,940.88	21,463.05
5.5	618.55	1,964.11	3,468.42	8,052.13	22,115.27
6	620.28	1,979.99	3,515.63	8,281.10	23,496.83
6.5	622.01	1,996.02	3,563.61	8,518.04	24,982.45
7	623.74	2,012.22	3,612.46	8,763.73	26,583.82
7.5	625.48	2,028.60	3,662.20	9,018.48	28,310.47
8	627.23	2,045.16	3,712.83	9,282.67	30,173.06

Figure 24-9 ***This table shows the importance of shopping for the highest interest rates (figures based on a $50 a month deposit, compounded daily).***

LESSON 24.2 REVIEW

1. Explain what is meant by the expression "pay yourself first."
2. There are two reasons to set aside savings. Name them.
3. What are the two basic types of savings accounts? Briefly describe each.
4. What two items does the annual percentage yield (APY) take into account?

HIGH-GROWTH OCCUPATIONS FOR THE 21st CENTURY

Registered Nurses

Registered nurses (R.N.s) work to promote health, prevent disease, and help patients cope with illness. When providing direct patient care, they observe, assess, and record symptoms, reactions, and progress. They assist physicians during treatments and examinations, administer medications, and assist in convalescence and rehabilitation.

R.N.s also develop and manage nursing care plans and instruct patients and their families in proper care. While state laws govern the tasks R.N.s may perform, it is usually the work setting that determines their day-to-day job duties.

Hospital nurses form the largest group of nurses. Most are staff nurses who provide bedside nursing care and carry out medical regimens. Hospital nurses usually are assigned to one area such as surgery, maternity, pediatrics, the emergency room, or intensive care. *Office nurses* care for patients in physicians' offices, clinics, emergency medical centers, and surgicenters (surgical facilities for operations that do not require a hospital stay). *Nursing home nurses* manage nursing care for residents with conditions ranging from a fracture to Alzheimer's disease. *Home health nurses* provide periodic services, prescribed by a physician, to patients at home. *Public health nurses* work in government and private agencies and clinics, schools, retirement communities, and other community settings. *Occupational health* or *industrial nurses* provide nursing care at worksites to employees, customers, and others with minor injuries and illnesses.

R.N.s who work in hospitals may be assigned to pediatrics where they care for injured or ill children.

Head nurses or *nurse supervisors* direct nursing activities. They plan work schedules and assign duties to nurses and aides, provide or arrange for training, and visit patients to observe nurses and to ensure that care is proper. They may also ensure records are maintained and equipment and supplies are ordered.

At the advanced level, *nurse practitioners* provide basic primary health care. They diagnose and treat common acute illnesses and injuries and can prescribe medications. Advanced practice nurses have met higher educational and clinical practice requirements beyond the basic nursing education and licensing required of all R.N.s.

LESSON 24.3
INVESTING MONEY

OBJECTIVES

- DISCUSS ADVANTAGES AND DISADVANTAGES OF INVESTING
- EXPLAIN THE FOLLOWING TYPES OF INVESTMENTS: STOCKS, BONDS, AND MONEY MARKET FUNDS

WHY INVEST?

Investing is the process of using money not required for personal and family needs to increase overall financial worth. Investing is different from saving in that investing is a long-term financial strategy. Money for investing comes from funds left after meeting basic expenditures and short- and medium-range savings goals.

The investor wants to make as much money as possible. In order to make a lot of money, though, there is usually a risk of losing money. For example, buying stock in a new, unproved company is very risky. High-risk investments, however, can sometimes produce big payoffs. Let's take another example. Buying bonds of a large, financially stable corporation involves a relatively low risk. However, lower-risk investments generally produce smaller profits.

When investing, you must learn to balance risks. Probably the best way to balance risks is to **diversify** investments. This means to spread out money over several different types of investment options.

WORKFORCE TRENDS

Workplace stress is an emerging health issue. About one in five Americans works 49 hours or more a week. Studies indicate that three-fourths of workers believe there is more on-the-job stress than a generation ago. A wide range of health effects is attributed to stress, including increased risk of cardiovascular disease, psychological disorders such as depression and burnout, gastrointestinal disorders, and workplace injuries.

TYPES OF INVESTMENTS

Let's now examine four popular types of investments: stocks, mutual funds, bonds, and money market funds.

Stocks

One of the most popular forms of investment is the purchase of shares of **stock**. When you buy stock in a company, you are buying shares of ownership in that company. Stocks vary in price from a few dollars a share to a few hundred dollars. Stock is most often sold in hundred-share lots.

Stocks are usually bought from individuals or companies called **brokers** that specialize in sell-

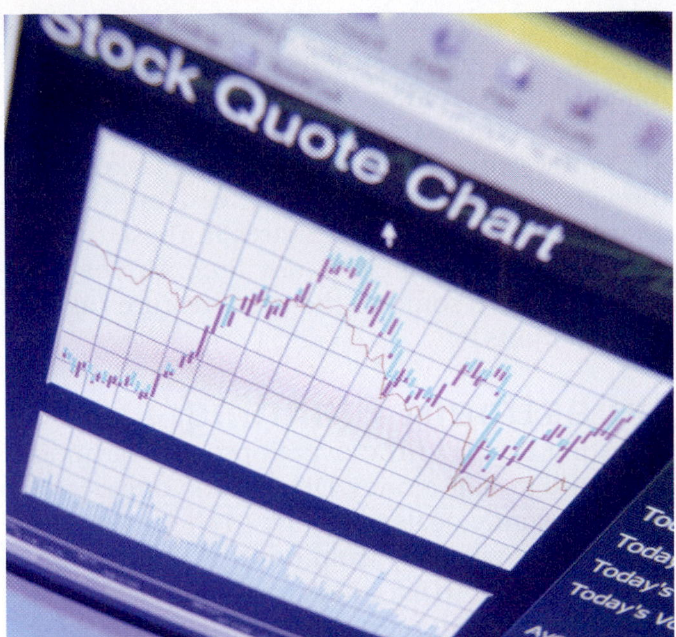

To learn about investing, to research stocks, and to check stock prices, you can visit various web sites.

ing stocks and other financial investments. Stock prices vary from day to day. The purchase price for a stock is the current selling price plus a fee, called a **commission**, charged by the broker.

In recent years, many investors have chosen to buy stocks through the Web. Online investors can use full-service brokers that provide a range of services or discount brokers that provide fewer services but charge less. The Web is also a good resource for learning about investing, researching stocks, and checking stock prices.

You can make money on stocks through dividends, through capital gain, or both. **Dividends** are profits that a company divides among its shareholders. Let's say you bought stock in a company for $24 a share. If the company paid a $.50 per share dividend each quarter, you would make $2 a year on each share of stock that you owned. The return on your investment would be 8.3 percent.

Capital gain refers to an increase in the value of stock or another asset. It is only realized when the asset is sold. For example, suppose the stock you bought at $24 increased in price to $30 a share and you sold it. Your capital gain would be $6 per share. In this case, your return on investment would be 25 percent. The $2 share dividend plus the $6 capital gain would result in a total return of 33.3 percent. Be aware, however, that dividends and stock prices can go down.

Mutual Funds

Instead of buying individual stocks, you can purchase shares in a mutual fund. A **mutual fund** is an investment company that pools the money of thousands of investors and buys a collection of investments that may include stocks, bonds, and other financial assets. This is called a **portfolio**. Mutual funds have two advantages. First, they give you diversified investments less expensively than you could purchase them on your own. Second, your investments are professionally managed for you.

Like profits from stocks, profits from mutual funds can be derived from dividends, capital gains, or both. Any capital gains a fund realizes in selling assets must be distributed to investors. Mutual funds are generally recommended over individual stocks for beginning and small investors.

Bonds

You have learned that stock represents shares of actual ownership in a company. A **bond** represents a loan to a company or government agency. Let's say a large corporation needs $10 million to expand its plant. One way to raise the money is to sell shares of stock in the company. Another way is to issue bonds. A bond is a pledge to repay the borrowed sum plus a certain amount of interest.

To be more specific, suppose Lunar Manufacturing Company issues $1,000 bonds that pay 8.5 percent interest, with a maturity date (date of repayment) of 2015. If you purchase one of these bonds, Lunar Manufacturing Company will pay you $85 in interest per year until 2015, at which time it will return your $1,000. Depending on the type of bond, interest may be paid periodically or be paid at the date of maturity.

Bonds issued by private companies like Lunar Manufacturing Company are called corporate bonds. Government agencies also issue bonds to raise money for roads, schools, sewer systems, and so on. Bonds issued by states, cities, counties, and other units of local government are called municipal bonds. When the federal

Chat rooms are a way to share interests and communicate with others on the Web. You can instantly communicate with family and friends by keying back and forth. This is called chatting. When you are chatting, the text you key appears on the screen of each person participating in the chat.

Chatting is becoming very popular among young people. Before you begin, however, you need to educate yourself about proper behavior, etiquette, and personal safety. Many web portals host chat rooms and provide how-to-do-it information. You can also collect relevant information by searching the Web using the keywords *chat room.*

government issues bonds, they are known as government bonds. The idea behind all bonds is the same. A bond is a certificate that represents a promise to repay a specific borrowed amount in the future and to pay interest.

Bonds can be purchased through the same brokers that sell stocks. Like stocks, bonds are available individually or through mutual funds that specialize in bonds.

Money Market Funds

A **money market fund** is a type of mutual fund that invests in short-term, high-liquidity investments. These might include corporate or U.S. treasury notes (bonds that mature in one to ten years) and certificates of deposit. The objective is usually to earn the highest possible safe interest rate.

The main advantage of money market funds is that they provide a way for small investors to take advantage of the higher interest rates that were once available only to large investors. Most funds require a minimum deposit. However, as little as a few hundred dollars is often sufficient for a beginning investment.

Money market shares can be purchased directly from an investment firm, through a financial institution, or from a broker. The interest rates on these funds go up and down according to the general economy. Money market funds are not insured or guaranteed, but they are regarded as very safe. Shares in these funds can be sold (redeemed) at any time. Money market funds have some of the same features as savings accounts.

Investment Planning

Investing is part of the overall process of budgeting and saving money. Decide on your personal or family goals and stick to them. Do not get greedy. Stay away from hot tips that promise instant wealth. To avoid losing money, educate yourself about investing, be wary, and investigate an investment very carefully before turning over any money. Financial magazines and newspapers are good resources for researching investments. The Internet is another helpful resource for beginning investors.

LESSON 24.3 REVIEW

1. How is investing different from saving money?
2. Explain the two ways in which you can make money on stocks.
3. Name two advantages of investing in a mutual fund.
4. What is the basic difference between a stock and a bond?
5. Name the type of bond issued by a private company. Name the type issued by a local government.
6. What is the main advantage offered by money market funds?

FOCUS ON SKILLS FOR LIVING

CREDIT BILLING BLUES

It is difficult enough to manage a budget without being billed for charges you do not owe. Problems can be taken care of, however, if you know how to use the Fair Credit Billing Act. To be protected under the law, here is what you need to do:

- Write the bank or merchant that issued the credit. A telephone call does not trigger the legal safeguards provided under the act. Your letter must be received within 60 days after the bill containing the error was mailed. Include in the letter your name and account number, the date, the type and dollar amount of the incorrect charge, and why you think there was a mistake.
- Send the letter to the correct place. Do not put your letter in the same envelope as your payment. Your bill will usually explain where you should address inquiries. You may wish to send the letter by certified mail to make sure the creditor receives it.

Billing errors happen occasionally, but they can usually be corrected.

If you follow this procedure, the creditor is required to acknowledge your letter in writing within 30 days after it is received. The alleged error must be investigated. Within 90 days, the mistake must be corrected, or you must be given an explanation and proof of why the bill is accurate.

If you continue to have problems, you should contact your local or state consumer protection agency. Under the law, the creditor cannot close your account just because you disputed a bill.

THINK CRITICALLY

1. Why do you think the Fair Credit Billing Act does not cover complaints made by telephone?
2. A problem that leads to many billing disputes is identity theft—stealing personal information such as bank account, Social Security, and credit card numbers. How can you protect yourself from identity theft?

CHAPTER 24

Chapter in Brief

Lesson 24.1 *Budgeting Money*

A. A good first step in learning how to manage money is to identify sources of income and expenditures. You will do this by maintaining a record of income and expenditures. Keeping a record over a period of time can help you understand your financial condition and spending habits. You can then use the information to set up a budget.

B. A budget is a plan for managing income and expenditures. Such a spending plan will help you get the most benefit from your earnings. The four steps involved in developing a budget are establishing goals, estimating income and expenditures, setting up the budget, and following and revising the budget.

C. Goals should be set before you work out the details of your budget. List short-range, medium-range, and long-range goals. Goals should be realistic. Write them down and use them to plan the budget.

D. Once you have decided on goals, estimate your income and expenditures. Base estimates on actual records. Budgets are usually planned around how often one gets paid.

E. A budget consists of three main parts: savings, regular (fixed) expenses, and variable expenses. Items can be added, subtracted, and arranged in the way that works best for you.

F. Following a budget involves allocation of income to various budgeted items. A good way to do this is to place most of your paycheck in a checking account. Write checks for larger and regular expenses. Keep the remaining cash on hand for smaller purchases. Keeping accurate records is an important part of maintaining a budget.

G. Do not expect to have a perfect budget the first time you set one up. A budget is something you must keep working and reworking.

Lesson 24.2 *Saving Money*

A. Savings refers to cash that has been set aside in a bank account. There are two reasons to set aside cash for savings: (1) to have funds for a financial emergency and (2) to achieve financial goals.

B. There are two basic types of savings accounts. Regular (passbook) savings accounts let you make deposits and withdrawals at any time. Time deposits, such as CDs, require you to deposit a lump sum for a fixed period of time in exchange for a higher rate of return. Some accounts offer advantages of both regular savings accounts and time deposits. All these accounts are safe.

C. Interest earned on savings depends on the annual interest rate, frequency of compounding, and when the interest is paid. In comparing savings options, it is useful to know the annual percentage yield (APY). Generally the higher the APY, the better the deal.

REVIEW

Lesson 24.3 *Investing Money*

A. Investing is the process of using money not required for personal and family needs to increase overall financial worth. Investing involves the risk of losing money. A good way to balance risks is to diversify investments.

B. There are four popular types of investments. Investing in stocks involves buying shares of ownership in a company. Mutual funds give you diversified investments and professional management. For both stocks and mutual funds, money can be made through dividends, capital gains, or both. Bonds represent a loan to a company or government agency in return for interest. A money market fund is a type of mutual fund that invests in short-term, high-liquidity investments.

Activities

1. Write down income and expenditures on a form similar to Figure 24-1. Keep records for a week. Then, study them. List at least three things you noticed about your spending. Discuss your findings in class.
2. Think about your financial goals. Write your financial goal(s) for the next year. Then note your financial goals for the next five years. Discuss your goals in class. How do they compare to your classmates' goals? Discuss how your goals might be different if you and your classmates were five years older.
3. Consider a family consisting of a couple and a young child. Assume the family's net monthly income is $2,200. As a group, in-class activity, prepare an estimated budget for this family. Use or adapt the budget form in Figure 24-3.
4. After completing Activity 3, invite a qualified person to class to examine and discuss the budget you have prepared.
5. In groups of two or three, visit several different financial institutions in person or on the Web and collect information on their regular (passbook) savings accounts. Or individuals or teams could be assigned to visit specific institutions. Compare the alternatives with respect to (a) interest rate, (b) how frequently the interest is compounded, (c) when the interest is paid, (d) annual percentage yield, (e) minimum deposit, (f) service charges, and (g) rules and restrictions. You may wish to prepare some type of chart to help you compare alternatives. Discuss your findings in class.
6. Let's assume that you deposited $500 in a savings account paying 6 percent annual interest. You do not disturb the money for a year. Interest is compounded quarterly. At the end of the year, how much money is in the account? What is the annual percentage yield?
7. Let's assume you bought 100 shares of stock at $25 a share. The stock pays a $.40 dividend each year. How much total dividend do you receive in two years?

CHAPTER 24

8. Locate the listings for the New York Stock Exchange in the financial section of a newspaper, or go to the Exchange web site (http://www.nyse.com). Select a stock and answer the following questions: (a) Does the stock pay a dividend? If so, how much, and what is the yield? (b) How many shares were sold the previous day (newspaper users) or so far today (web site users)? (c) Newspaper users: what were the previous day's high, low, and closing prices, and what was the net change? (d) Web site users: what are today's high, low, and most recent trade prices, and what is the net change over yesterday's close? (e) What does the P/E, or price-earnings, ratio represent?
9. You have inherited $5,000 from your uncle and are trying to decide where to invest it. You would like to have $10,000 nine years from now to open your own business. Approximately what interest rate will your investment need to earn for you to achieve this goal?

Word Power

On a separate sheet of paper, match each definition with the correct term. All definitions will be used, and a definition will be used only once.

10. An increase in the value of a stock or other asset that is only realized when the asset is sold
11. In investing, to spread out money over several different types of investment options
12. The process of using money not required for personal and family needs to increase overall financial worth
13. A type of mutual fund that invests in short-term, high-liquidity investments
14. In budgeting, those essential monthly payments that are usually the same amount each month
15. A single entry in a budget; a budgeted item
16. In budgeting, day-to-day living expenses
17. Individuals or companies that specialize in selling stocks and other financial investments
18. A fee paid to a broker for purchasing stock for you
19. Money that is spent
20. Shares of ownership in a company
21. The distribution or assignment of something; for example, of income to the various items in a budget
22. Money coming in
23. An investment company that pools the money of thousands of investors and buys a collection of investments that may include stocks, bonds, and other financial assets

a. allocation
b. bond
c. brokers
d. budget
e. capital gain
f. certificate of deposit (CD)
g. commission
h. compounding
i. diversify
j. dividends
k. expenditures
l. income
m. investing
n. line item
o. liquidity
p. money market fund
q. mutual fund
r. portfolio
s. regular (fixed) expenditures
t. savings
u. stock
v. variable expenditures

REVIEW

24. Cash set aside in a bank account to be used for financial emergencies and goals
25. The quality of being easily converted into cash; refers to assets
26. A certificate that represents a loan to a company or government agency in exchange for a pledge to repay the borrowed sum plus a certain amount of interest
27. Profits that a company divides among its shareholders
28. A popular type of time deposit in which an amount of savings is deposited for a fixed period of time in return for a specified interest rate
29. A collection of investments that may include stocks, bonds, and other financial assets
30. A process in which interest is earned on both the money put into an account and the interest periodically added to it, causing savings to steadily grow
31. A plan for managing income and expenditures

Think Critically

32. Philanthropy is the act of giving away money. How do you feel about giving money to charity?
33. A big problem for the federal government is staying within a budget. The government routinely spends more than it takes in. (This is called deficit spending.) Why do you think this is the case?
34. It is not unusual to read about the financial difficulties of high-paid professional athletes, entertainers, and other famous people. What are some of the problems created by fame and instant wealth?
35. What is the advantage of using payroll deductions to save and invest money? Are payroll savings and investment options available where you work?
36. Have you ever saved money over a long period of time and then used it to buy something? Describe how it made you feel to accomplish a savings goal.
37. There is an old saying that "you shouldn't invest more in stocks than you can afford to lose." How true do you think this statement is?

CHAPTER 25

INSURING AGAINST LOSS

LESSONS

25.1 *Health Insurance*

25.2 *Life and Home Insurance*

25.3 *Auto Insurance*

PREVIEW

Deciding if you need insurance, evaluating different policies, and comparing costs and coverage can be difficult. This chapter will help answer your questions. The material will deal with the nature of insurance and then discuss the specifics of the four most important kinds of insurance: health, life, home, and auto.

THOUGHTS ON WORK

"Dreams never hurt anybody if you keep working right behind the dreams to make as much of them become real as you can."

Frank W. Woolworth

TAKING ACTION
PROTECTING AGAINST LOSS

The tornado was only on the ground for two minutes as it moved through the town. But in that brief time, it injured 17 people and caused more than $2 million in property damage.

When he heard the warning sirens, Gary raced to an interior room of his apartment. As he passed a window, a tree branch smashed into it. Some of the flying glass injured Gary's arm. When the tornado had passed, a neighbor drove him to the hospital. Gary presented his insurance card. A few hours later, he left the hospital, having paid $15 for his emergency room visit. If he had had to pay himself, just going to the emergency room would have cost $350, and his treatment would have cost an additional $200.

Maria had been at the mall when the tornado hit. She came outside afterwards to discover that her car had been damaged. One fender was badly dented and rubbed on the tire. Maria used her cell phone to call her insurance agent. By the next day, the car had been towed to a repair shop and Maria had gotten a rental car to use while it was being repaired. The bodywork on her car cost $1,800, the tow was $60, and the car rental was $180. After paying the first $250 towards repairs, Maria had no charges.

Manuel had been at work. He returned to his house to find that the tornado had brought down power lines, which had started a fire. Manuel telephoned his insurance agent. Since there was too much damage for him to stay in his house, Manuel went to a motel. The next day, he met his insurance agent at his home. In a few days, he had a check for the damages.

Manuel chose a contractor that his agent had recommended, and repairs were quickly under way. He used the list of personal property that he had made and kept at work to go shopping and replace the possessions that had been too damaged to keep. The repairs to Manuel's home took several weeks. During that time, he continued to stay at the motel and ate at restaurants. Manuel's home insurance paid for everything. The bills amounted to $20,500.

SUCCESS TIP

Make sure to get the insurance coverage you need.

THINK CRITICALLY

1. A tornado is an unlikely event. Should people pay for insurance against things that are not likely to happen? Why or why not?
2. Think of occasions when you or people you know have used insurance. What kind of service did you or they get?

LESSON 25.1
HEALTH INSURANCE

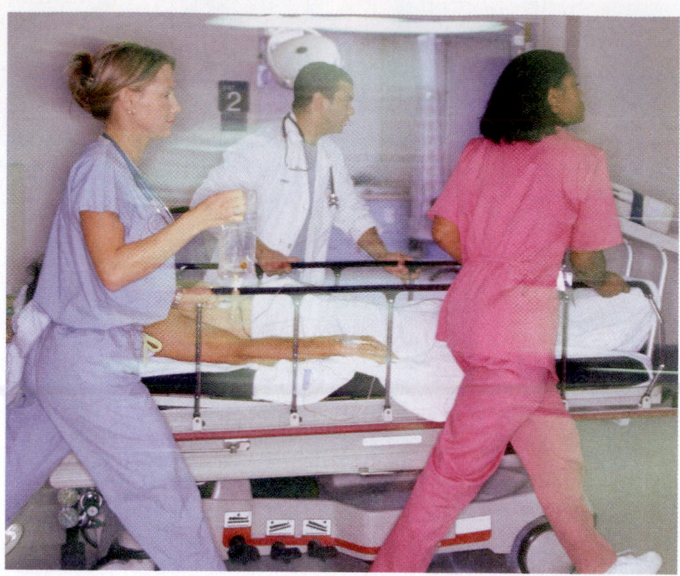

OBJECTIVES

- EXPLAIN THE BASIC IDEA OF INSURANCE
- NAME AND DESCRIBE THE TWO BASIC TYPES OF HEALTH INSURANCE

THE NATURE OF INSURANCE

Major purchases, such as a home or car, can be very costly. Once you have bought such items, you do not want to lose them. Things do happen, though. Suppose you purchase a new car. A week later, you park in the lot of the local library. When you leave the library, the car is gone. The next day, the police call to say your car has been found. Your joy disappears upon learning that the car was wrecked badly.

Throughout history, people have used insurance to protect themselves from **risk**, or the chance of a loss. Losses can result from fires, accidents, or other catastrophes. A **catastrophe** is a disaster or misfortune, often one that occurs suddenly. Few people can bear catastrophes without serious hardship.

Catastrophes can affect society as well. For instance, if a person is injured and does not have medical insurance, treatment costs will ultimately be paid by either charity or the government. When a building burns and a business is forced into bankruptcy, creditors lose money and employees lose their jobs.

The basic idea of insurance is that a large group of individuals pay money into a common fund. When disaster strikes one member of the group, the pooled funds pay for the loss. Insurance shifts the risk of loss from the individual to the group.

When you buy insurance, you are trading a known expenditure (your insurance premium) for protection against the risk of a large, uncertain loss. The kinds of risks against which people seek protection may be grouped in this way:

- ***Personal risks.*** These are catastrophes affecting individuals. Examples include accident, illness, disability, and unemployment.
- ***Property risks.*** There is always a possibility that property will be damaged or destroyed. Property losses can result from automobile accidents, natural disasters, fire, and vandalism.
- ***Liability risks.*** Liability risks are injuries to others or their property that you are responsible for or that occur on your property. Another person may be injured in a car accident you caused. Or a visitor might be hurt in your home.

WORKFORCE TRENDS

The impact of sleep deprivation on the workplace and society is beginning to enter the public consciousness. An astounding 37 percent of adults report being so sleepy during the day that it interferes with their daily activities. Estimates of the costs of sleep deprivation (from lost productivity, absenteeism, illness, and injury) range up to $18 billion annually.

Having the right insurance will help you minimize your risks if an accident occurs.

In addition to providing protection against financial loss, insurance gives people greater peace of mind. Knowing that you have minimized your risks can contribute to your emotional security.

TYPES OF HEALTH INSURANCE

The purpose of health insurance is to pay expenses resulting from illness or accident. This is probably the most necessary form of insurance because the expenses resulting from illness or accident can be enormous. The costs of minor surgery and several days in a hospital are likely to be several thousand dollars. Fees for major surgery and an extended hospital stay can amount to tens of thousands of dollars.

Jim was painting his house. He fell about 20 feet from a ladder. Jim was badly injured. Over the next five years, he was in the hospital 22 times for surgery and other medical care. His total medical expenses were nearly a million dollars. This is a rare case, but it does show why insurance is so important.

Most people obtain health insurance through some type of group plan. This may be through an employer, union, or professional association. The group policy may only cover the individual enrolled, or it may include dependents as well. Persons not eligible for group coverage may buy individual plans. However, group plans usually provide more coverage and are less expensive than individual plans.

For full-time employees, employers often pay much or most of the cost of health insurance. In recent years, however, many businesses have increased the amount that employees must contribute towards health insurance because of rising premiums. There are two basic types of health insurance plans from which to choose.

Traditional Health Insurance Plans

In traditional health insurance plans, sometimes called fee-for-service plans, an insurance company pays a doctor or hospital for services performed in treating a patient who is ill or injured. Routine office visits are not covered. A typical plan might require you to pay the first $100 for a hospital stay (a **deductible**) and 20 percent of the remaining amount. Many policies contain a **stop-loss provision**, which prevents your out-of-pocket expenses from rising above a certain amount.

There are four kinds of fee-for-service coverage. They are usually sold together in various combinations.

- ***Hospital expense.*** This coverage provides for hospital charges such as room and meals, operating room use, laboratory fees, and medications. The policy may specify a certain maximum-per-day room charge or may limit

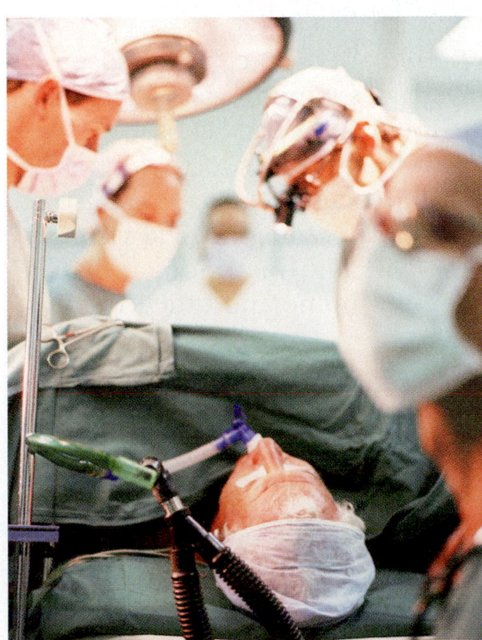

Surgery and a hospital stay can cost thousands of dollars.

COMMUNICATION AT WORK

GETTING INFORMATION

You will sometimes need to get information from others in order to do your job or to make good personal choices. Deciding on a health insurance plan is an example. Suppose you have several plans to choose from. You have carefully read the information about each plan. You have made a checklist to compare the plans. Still, you have questions and need advice.

Find out whom you need to talk to. If you have a brief list of specific questions, you may want to e-mail the person or write a memo. Probably, however, you will want to call or meet. If so, make a list of your questions ahead of time. Organize it and outline important points. For telephone calls, the advice in Chapter 4 on using the telephone as part of a job search will be helpful.

Call ahead to schedule a meeting. If you think you can get the information you need over the telephone, begin by explaining the purpose of your call and asking if this is a convenient time. If it is not, arrange a time that is. Other people are usually glad to give you information if you are considerate of their time.

the number of days a person may stay in the hospital.

- ***Surgical expense.*** This covers a wide variety of medical procedures and operations, ranging from sewing up a cut to replacing a heart valve. Procedures may be performed on an inpatient or outpatient basis, depending on the procedure. A policy may contain a list of covered surgical procedures and the amount that will be paid for each one.
- ***Medical expense.*** Medical expense, also known as physician's expense, is usually combined with hospital and surgical-expense insurance. The three together form what is known as basic coverage. Medical expense coverage pays for a doctor's medical visits while a patient is in a hospital. Some policies provide benefits for home and office visits as well.
- ***Major medical expense.*** This type of insurance protects against huge expenses resulting from a serious illness or accident. Covered expenses generally include the same types as those for basic coverage. Major medical contains a **co-insurance**, or **co-payment**, feature that requires a policyholder to share in the expenses beyond the deductible amount.

One of the most common plans is an "80-20" policy in which the insurance company pays 80 percent and the policyholder takes care of the other 20 percent. In one group plan, for example, the insurance company pays 80 percent of the first $50,000 of covered expenses and 100 percent thereafter, up to a maximum of $500,000.

Health Maintenance Organizations (HMOs)

The **health maintenance organization (HMO)** is an alternative to traditional health insurance. Members in an HMO or their employers pay a regular fee as they would for an insurance policy. However, HMOs cover all health care, including regular office visits and checkups as well as treatment for illness and accidents. Members typically pay a small co-payment for services and prescriptions. An office visit, for example, might cost $5 or $10.

Unlike traditional health insurance plans, HMOs do not require patients to fill out insurance forms for payments to be made. All paperwork is handled through the HMO.

HMOs often require members to choose a primary care physician. This doctor provides most of the person's medical care and makes referrals

WORKPLACE DECISIONS

You are employed as a library assistant at a state university. You have received information about a new health insurance plan to be offered to all state employees. Beginning June 1, you will have the choice of continuing with the regular health insurance or switching to the new HMO option. The premium, which is paid by the state, is the same for both plans. You are not sure which plan to select.

WHAT WOULD YOU DO?

to specialists when needed. Usually, the HMO has a list of doctors from which members must choose.

Which Plan to Choose?

Individual plans can vary widely, so carefully read the information for the plans you are considering. It is a good idea to make a list of items that are important to you. For example, do you have a particular doctor that you like to see? What are your medical needs likely to be? Do you have a spouse and children who will need to be covered on your plan? How much will each plan cost, both in premiums and in out-of-pocket expenses?

Make sure the plan you choose has a stop-loss provision. Both traditional health insurance plans and HMOs may include this coverage.

Both types of plans have advantages and disadvantages. Traditional plans let you choose doctors. With most HMOs, you must choose a doctor that is on the plan. HMOs cover preventative services like checkups and immunizations. Traditional plans usually do not. Fee-for-service plans require a deductible before paying benefits, and you must file your own claim forms.

Disability Coverage

Paying benefits to someone unable to work because of illness or injury is the purpose of disability insurance. This coverage is sometimes called loss-of-income insurance. Disability coverage is not usually part of traditional health insurance or HMOs; you must purchase it separately. A typical policy may pay between 50 and 75 percent of the worker's normal earnings for a specified period.

Helen was in a hurry to get to work and failed to notice that a light rain had fallen and then frozen during the night. As she stepped from her covered porch onto the sidewalk, she slipped and fell. She cried out in pain. A neighbor who was leaving for work at the same time saw her fall. He helped her into the house and called an ambulance.

Helen's injury was diagnosed as a broken hip. Surgery was required, followed by a long period of rest and physical therapy. It was six months before Helen was able to return to work. Fortunately, her disability insurance policy provided her with income while she could not work. Without the disability policy, she would have had to dip into her retirement savings.

Disability insurance is an important type of coverage for workers to consider. It may not be as important for people already covered by such benefits as paid sick leave, workers' compensation, and Social Security.

LESSON 25.1 REVIEW

1. **Explain how insurance shifts the risk of loss from the individual to the group.**
2. **Insurance protects against three kinds of risks. Name them.**
3. **What is meant by basic health insurance coverage? What is major medical coverage?**
4. **Which individuals are most in need of disability coverage?**

LESSON 25.2
LIFE AND HOME INSURANCE

OBJECTIVES

- SUMMARIZE THE ADVANTAGES AND DISADVANTAGES OF TERM AND CASH-VALUE LIFE INSURANCE
- OUTLINE DIFFERENT CHARACTERISTICS OF HOME INSURANCE

LIFE INSURANCE

Life insurance involves a contract written between an insurance company and a policyholder. The document specifies an amount of money (**face value**) to be paid in the event of the policyholder's death. It also states the price of the policy (**premium**) and the name of the person (**beneficiary**) to whom the death benefits are to be paid. The main purpose of life insurance is to provide financial security for dependents after the insured's death.

Individuals differ in terms of their need for life insurance. A young, single person without dependents, for example, has little need for life insurance. All that may be required is a small policy to pay funeral expenses and to cover outstanding debts.

People with children have the greatest need for life insurance. If the wage earner or wage earners should die, the family would need an income to pay day-to-day living expenses. Insurance would help a family member or friend raise surviving children and perhaps provide them with higher education. Even a person not working outside the home should be insured to cover added expenses in the event of death.

As with health insurance, both group and individual life insurance policies are available. Many employers offer some free life insurance to their employees. Most life insurance, though, is in the form of individual policies. The two basic types of life insurance are term and cash value.

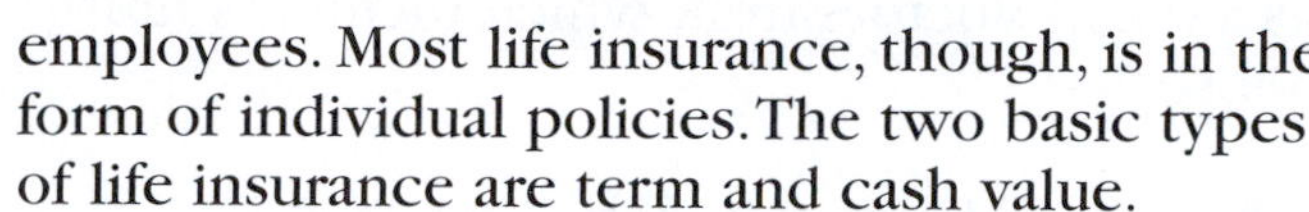

Term Insurance

Term insurance is often called pure insurance because it provides protection only. The policy has no cash value or loan value. People buy term insurance for a specified period of time. Under term insurance, you pay as long as you need the coverage. Then you drop the policy or it terminates automatically. For example, you might purchase a 25-year policy to provide protection while you are making big house payments and your children are growing up.

As you grow older, the likelihood of your dying increases. This is why term insurance premiums go up as you age. Premiums are low at first and then increase steadily throughout the course of your life. By the time you reach age 60, you may be paying 15 times what the same amount of protection cost you at age 18.

In this example, the face value of the policy remains steady and the premium increases yearly. Such insurance is called level term. Another type, called decreasing term insurance, works differently. The premium remains steady, but the face value decreases yearly. In Year 1, for example, your policy might have a face value of \$50,000. In Year 2, it might drop to \$48,000; in Year 3, to \$46,000; and so on.

A home represents a large investment and should be protected by insurance.

Cash-value Insurance

Under cash-value insurance, protection is teamed with the gradual buildup of a savings account. Cash-value insurance is also called permanent insurance because when the policy is paid up after a certain number of years, the policyholder owns the insurance. For example, if you purchase a plan called "Life Paid-up at 65," you pay premiums until you are 65. At that point, you have a permanent policy that will pay the face value upon your death. Other names for cash-value insurance are whole, ordinary, and straight life insurance.

The premium and the face value for cash-value insurance remain the same each year. You pay the same premiums for as long as you live. Or you can purchase plans that are paid up in 20 or 30 years. A portion of the premium is set aside and accumulates in a type of savings account. The interest rate, however, is usually less than for other forms of savings. If the policy is dropped, the cash value is returned to the policyholder.

Which Type to Buy?

There are advantages and disadvantages to both types of insurance. The primary advantage of term insurance is that it is less expensive. But with cash-value insurance, you have protection combined with savings.

Most experts on the subject who do not work for insurance companies seem to agree that term insurance is the better value. They point out that the main purpose of life insurance is protection. About the only way young people can realistically afford the amount of insurance necessary to protect their families is to purchase term insurance. You may want to buy term insurance and save the difference between that and cash-value insurance. Later, you may want to consider cash-value insurance as part of an overall life insurance program. But do not get saddled with a big policy and a big premium at a time when you can least afford it.

How Much Will You Need?

The amount of life insurance coverage you should purchase depends on your personal situation and what you want to protect. The needs of a young, single person are very different from those of someone with a family or a middle-aged couple who have their home paid for and their children raised. Some insurance agents provide the general guideline that you need insurance equal to about four to eight times your annual income.

HOME INSURANCE

For most people, a home is the largest expenditure in their budget. In addition to the home itself, household furnishings and personal belongings represent a sizable investment. For this reason, it is very important to protect a home and the contents against damage or loss. The basis for all home insurance policies is coverage against the various damages or **perils** shown in Figure 25-1 on page 384.

Another important feature of home insurance policies is the provision for living expenses. For example, the Alfanos' home was damaged by a storm and they could not live in it. The insurance company paid for the family's lodgings, meals, and related expenses elsewhere until the house was livable again.

Liability coverage is another important part of home insurance policies. **Liability** refers to legal responsibility for something, such as damages or costs. The most important type of liability coverage is personal liability, which protects you against a claim or lawsuit resulting from an accident or injury occurring on your property. The same coverage will also protect you if someone in your family causes an injury away from home.

1. Fire or lightning
2. Windstorm or hail
3. Explosion
4. Riot or civil commotion
5. Damage caused by aircraft
6. Damage caused by vehicles
7. Smoke
8. Vandalism or malicious mischief
9. Theft
10. Volcanic eruption
11. Falling object
12. Weight of ice, snow or sleet
13. Accidental discharge or overflow of water or steam from within a plumbing, heating, air conditioning, or automatic fire-protective sprinkler system, or from a household appliance
14. Sudden and accidental tearing apart, cracking, burning, or bulging of a steam or hot water heating system, an air conditioning or automatic fire-protective system
15. Freezing of a plumbing, heating, air conditioning or automatic, fire-protective sprinkler system, or of a household appliance
16. Sudden and accidental damage from artificially generated electrical current (does not include loss to a tube, transistor or similar electronic component)

Figure 25-1 ***These are the dangerous situations (perils) against which property is insured. The first ten are typically covered by basic homeowner's insurance.***
Courtesy of Insurance Information Institute.

There are various kinds of homeowner's insurance, depending on the type of coverage desired and whether you live in a house, apartment, condominium, or other dwelling.

Ann and Mark were newlyweds who had just moved into their first apartment. They were awakened one night by a fire alarm. They got up quickly, threw on coats, grabbed the puppy, and fled the apartment. As they raced down the back exit, they heard the siren of a fire truck. The fire was on the floor above theirs.

The fire company put out the blaze in a few minutes. It was not a serious fire, but there was a lot of smoke and water damage. All of Ann's and Mark's clothes and upholstered furniture was ruined.

PERSONAL DECISIONS

You just moved into an apartment with two friends. One of your roommates asks if you have purchased renter's insurance. You laugh and say that you do not have enough possessions to worry about insurance.

"You would be surprised," says your roommate. "It would cost quite a bit of money to replace everything in this room."

"I will think about it," you say. "But I cannot afford insurance for a couple of months."

WHAT WOULD YOU DO?

The next day, the couple went to the apartment manager's office to find out about getting their clothes and furniture replaced. The manager told them that his insurance only covered damage to the building. Apartment tenants should carry insurance on their personal property. Ann and Mark were upset. They had assumed that the building owner carried insurance that also covered their property. They should have had a renter's policy. The fire was a costly lesson for Ann and Mark on the need to understand home insurance.

LESSON 25.2 REVIEW

1. **Describe an advantage and a disadvantage of term and cash-value insurance.**
2. **Which type of term insurance has the same face value throughout the life of the policy?**
3. **What four things are usually covered by homeowner's insurance?**

HIGH-GROWTH OCCUPATIONS FOR THE 21st CENTURY

Respiratory Therapists

Respiratory therapists evaluate, treat, and care for patients with breathing disorders. To measure lung capacity, therapists have patients breathe into an instrument that measures the volume and flow of oxygen during inhalation and exhalation. By comparing the reading with the average for the patient's age, height, weight, and sex, respiratory therapists can determine whether a lung deficiency exists. To analyze oxygen, carbon dioxide, and pH levels, therapists draw a blood sample, place it in a blood gas analyzer, and report results to a physician.

Respiratory therapists treat all types of patients, ranging from premature infants whose lungs are not fully developed to elderly people whose lungs are diseased. They provide temporary relief to patients with asthma or emphysema and emergency care for patients who suffer heart failure or a stroke or are victims of shock. Respiratory therapists most commonly use oxygen or oxygen mixtures, chest physiotherapy (physical therapy), and aerosol medications. To increase a patient's concentration of oxygen, therapists place an oxygen mask on the patient and set the oxygen flow at the prescribed level. Therapists also connect patients who cannot breathe on their own to ventilators that deliver pressurized oxygen into the lungs.

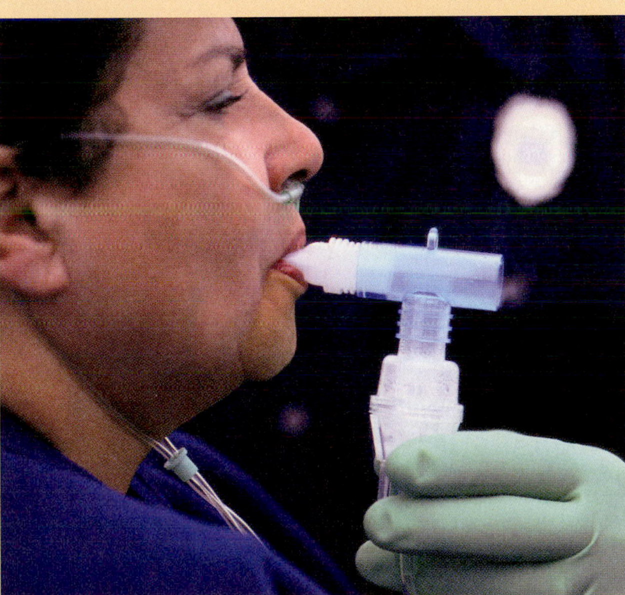

People with breathing disorders are often treated by respiratory therapists.

Respiratory therapists perform chest physiotherapy on patients to remove mucus from their lungs and make it easier for them to breathe. In this procedure, therapists place patients in positions that will help drain mucus, thump and vibrate patients' rib cages, and instruct them to cough. They also administer aerosols and teach patients how to inhale them properly to ensure their effectiveness.

Therapists regularly check on patients and equipment. In home care, therapists teach patients and their families to use ventilators and other life support systems. Additionally, they visit several times a month to inspect and clean equipment and ensure its proper use. They also make emergency visits if equipment problems arise.

LESSON 25.3

AUTO INSURANCE

OBJECTIVES

- NAME AND DESCRIBE THE SIX TYPES OF AUTO INSURANCE COVERAGE
- IDENTIFY FACTORS THAT INFLUENCE THE COST OF AUTO INSURANCE
- EXPLAIN NO-FAULT INSURANCE

TYPES OF COVERAGE

The topic of auto insurance is very important to young people. Unfortunately, they are the ones who most need it. Drivers under age 25 are involved in about 30 percent of all auto accidents.

Everyone who drives a motor vehicle is responsible for operating it safely and paying for any damage the vehicle might cause. All states now have what are called financial responsibility laws that require drivers to pay for damages they cause to people or property. Rather than risk having to come up with thousands of dollars as a result of an accident, most people buy insurance to show proof of financial responsibility. About half of the states have laws specifically requiring registered automobile owners to have liability insurance of some kind.

An auto policy may provide six basic types of coverage:

- ***Bodily injury liability.*** This coverage applies if you kill or injure someone in an accident in which you are at fault. The person may be a pedestrian, a rider in your car, or someone in another car. The policy covers bodily injury expenses and claims, including your legal expenses if you are sued.
- ***Property damage liability.*** What if you damage another person's car or property? This type of insurance won't pay for repairs to your car, but it will cover repairs to the other person's car or property. Property damage liability also pays for legal expenses should you be taken to court.
- ***Protection against uninsured motorists.*** This coverage applies to bodily injuries that you may suffer as a result of a hit-and-run accident. The policy also covers you in the event of an accident in which the other driver does not have insurance.

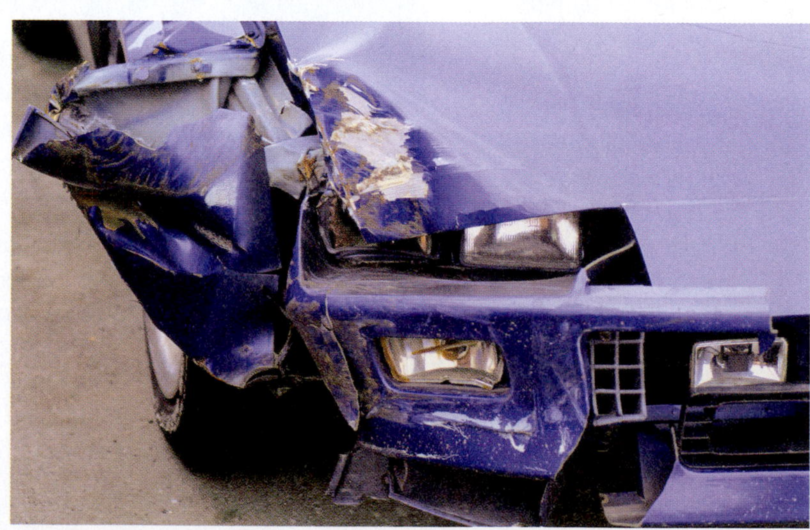

Everyone who drives a motor vehicle is responsible for operating it safely and paying for any damage it causes.

YOU'RE A WHAT? PURSER

If you take a cruise, one of the first individuals you may encounter is the *purser* or a member of the purser's staff. A passenger ship can be thought of as a floating hotel. Pursers serve as the front desk personnel for the ship's passengers. They take care of registration, direct guests to their cabins, establish onboard credit for passengers, and answer a variety of questions.

In addition to serving passengers, pursers have three other functions. They make sure that the ship and passengers conform to all health, safety, and environmental regulations. They perform payroll, passport, and other personnel work for the crew. Finally, pursers manage and account for all revenue generated on the ship. Can you guess why they are called pursers? ■

Keith was sitting in his car at a stoplight waiting for the light to change. Suddenly, a car from behind smashed into him. The other driver was adjusting the radio and not paying attention to the intersection ahead. Keith's car was badly damaged.

The police came and filled out an accident report. They gave Andy, the other driver, a traffic citation for reckless driving. Keith and Andy exchanged information regarding addresses, phone numbers, and so on. Andy said that he could not remember the name of his insurance company but that he would call Keith later with the information. The call never came.

In a recent year, there were more than six million car accidents in the United States.

In the meantime, Keith contacted his insurance company. The representative he spoke to told him to go ahead and have his car fixed. His insurance company would collect from Andy's. As it turned out, Andy did not have auto insurance. However, since Keith was covered by uninsured motorists protection, his insurance company assumed the cost of having the car repaired.

As for Andy, he was found to be in violation of the state financial responsibility law. His driver's license and automobile registration were taken away. In order to get them back, Andy will have to pay Keith's insurance company the $2,200 it cost to repair Keith's car.

- ***Medical payments.*** Under this coverage, your insurance company agrees to pay medical expenses resulting from accidental injury. This insurance covers you and family members whether injured in your car or someone else's. It also applies if you are struck by a car. Payment is made regardless of who is at fault.
- ***Auto collision.*** Your car is covered by this type of insurance. The insurance company will pay to have your car repaired or replaced regardless of who is at fault. Collision insurance does not cover repairs that cost more than the actual cash value of the car. Collision is the most expensive form of coverage. Most collision insurance is sold with a deductible, usually $200 or $250.
- ***Auto comprehensive.*** This coverage protects your car against loss from theft, vandalism,

fire, windstorms, and other perils listed in the policy. If your car is damaged in an accident, collision, not comprehensive, will cover it.

THE COST OF AUTO INSURANCE

Basic rates for automobile insurance vary from area to area. Each state is divided into rating territories that indicate the losses paid in various parts of the state. The price of insurance is then set based on the loss experience of the rating territory. This means that rates in an area having heavy losses will be higher than those in places where losses are not so great.

Many other factors influence the price of insurance. These include the year, make, and model of the car. The sex, age, marital status, and driving record of the operator are also factors. In addition, driving a car a long distance every day will raise premiums.

Even though you cannot do much about influencing basic insurance rates, you do have some control over the final cost.

Many states have set minimum amounts of insurance that you must purchase. It is important to know that these minimums would not come near covering the costs of a serious accident. For liability and uninsured motorists coverage, many experts recommend buying significantly more than the minimum state coverages. Buying more insurance is less expensive than you might think. The more you buy, the less you have to pay for the amount of coverage you get.

Towing and other road services are not covered by most basic auto policies.

In considering medical payments coverage, check carefully to see whether it would duplicate coverage that you already have under your medical insurance.

Whether you purchase collision or comprehensive depends on how much your auto is worth. It would be foolish to have collision on an old car worth only a few hundred dollars. You can also reduce the cost of car insurance by choosing higher deductibles in these categories. For example, raising the deductible on collision or comprehensive coverage from $100 to $250 can save you about 20 percent.

Shop around for insurance coverage and compare rates. Premiums can vary by hundreds of dollars. You can save money by having a parent add you to his or her policy and by not being the principal driver of the car. You may also pay less if you spend part of the year away at school without a car.

What factors influence the cost of insurance for this driver?

Drivers who complete an approved driver's education course may receive a discount on their auto insurance.

Be sure to ask whether the company offers any discounts that might apply to you. Many insurance companies offer discounts to drivers who complete an approved driver's education course. Good grades entitle you to a discount from most insurance companies. Some give discounts for safe driving over a period of years. If your car has automatic seatbelts and airbags, if you carpool, and even if you don't smoke, you may be able to save money on coverage.

More important than price is the quality of service the company provides. You can find reviews of insurance companies at a library or on the Internet. Word of mouth is another good way to find out about insurers.

Motorcycle insurance is similar in coverage to that for cars. If you know the basics of auto insurance, you should have no trouble understanding policies covering motorcycles.

NO-FAULT INSURANCE

A problem for insurance companies is determining who is at fault in an accident. This process often requires the service of lawyers. It may lead to long delays in having bills paid and vehicles repaired, as well as expensive legal fees. Courts award generous compensation to some victims. Others receive little or nothing.

In order to reduce time and costs and provide fair settlements to victims, about half of the states have developed no-fault insurance. Under the no-fault system, each person's losses and expenses are paid for by his or her insurance company regardless of who caused the accident. Lawsuits are permitted only under certain conditions.

No one enjoys paying insurance premiums, especially for something that you do not see or may never use. Do not, however, be tempted to take a chance and go without insurance. You only have to have one big loss to realize why it is so important to have insurance protection.

LESSON 25.3 REVIEW

1. **Name the type of auto insurance coverage that applies to the following situations: (a) You run into someone's parked auto. (b) Your car is damaged when you back into a utility pole. (c) A tree falls on your car during a windstorm.**
2. **Name four factors that influence the cost of auto insurance.**
3. **What factor should you consider in deciding whether to purchase collision or comprehensive auto insurance?**
4. **Explain the idea underlying no-fault auto insurance.**

FOCUS ON HEALTH AND SAFETY

WALK-IN MEDICAL CLINICS

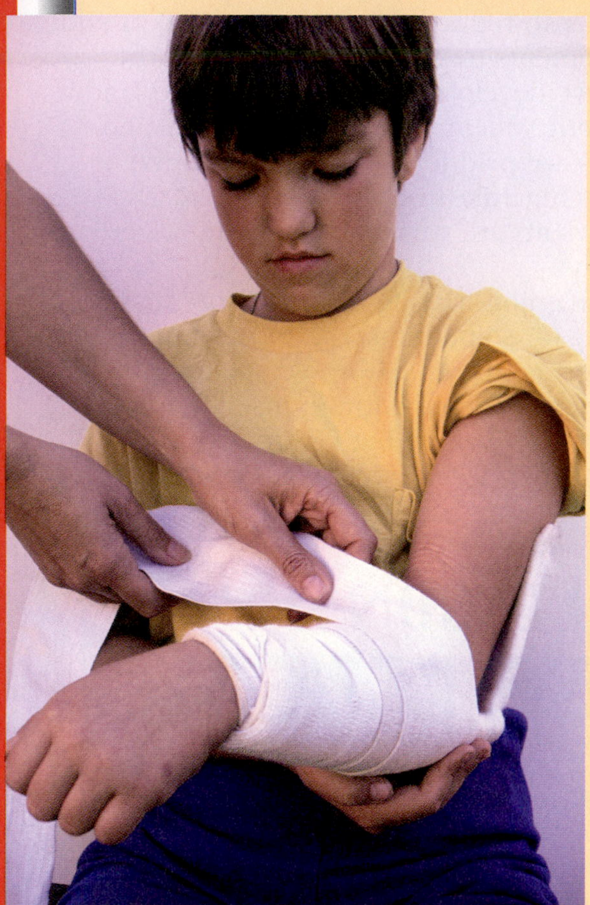

Walk-in medical clinics help hold down costs of many medical services.

What would you do if you severely cut yourself while slicing vegetables or if you woke up on a Sunday morning with a bad earache and high fever? You would probably head for the emergency room of the nearest hospital. Some people now have another option. It is called the walk-in medical clinic.

These new health clinics are one of the hottest trends in medical care. Thousands of them have sprung up across the country in the last several years. Regional and nationwide chains are being created just like fast-food restaurants. They are legitimate medical facilities staffed by licensed doctors and other professional personnel. They provide competition and are changing the way we make decisions about medical treatment.

The clinics take patients without appointments. They are open 12 to 16 (some 24) hours a day, seven days a week. They can treat most typical illnesses or accidents. But they do not do major surgery or handle serious emergencies like auto accidents. Fees for a normal visit are the same as or slightly less than those for a regular doctor. For emergency services, however, clinics can cost substantially less. Treatment of a cut requiring stitches, for example, can be a third to a half of what is charged by a hospital emergency room. Health insurance usually covers such emergency treatment.

Cost and convenience, however, are not the whole story. In our mobile society, many people do not have a regular physician. When they need a doctor, walk-in clinics can provide that service.

THINK CRITICALLY

1. What are some reasons that walk-in clinics have become so popular?
2. List several possible disadvantages of using walk-in clinics for health care.

REVIEW

Chapter in Brief

Lesson 25.1 *Health Insurance*

A. Insurance shifts the risk of loss from the individual to the group. The basic idea of insurance is that a large group of individuals pay a yearly premium that goes into a common fund. When disaster strikes one member of the group, the pooled funds pay for the loss. People buy insurance to protect themselves against three types of risks: personal, property, and liability.

B. The purpose of health insurance is to pay expenses resulting from illness or accident. There are two basic types of health insurance plans: traditional or fee-for-service plans and health maintenance organizations (HMOs). There are four kinds of fee-for-service coverage: hospital, surgical, medical, and major medical. They are usually sold together in various combinations.

C. Disability insurance is usually sold separately. It provides income to people who are unable to work because of illness or injury.

Lesson 25.2 *Life and Home Insurance*

A. The main purpose of life insurance is to provide financial security for dependents after the insured's death. The two basic types of life insurance are term and cash value. Term insurance provides protection at a lower cost. It has no cash or loan value. Cash-value insurance provides protection along with the gradual buildup of a savings account. The amount of life insurance coverage you need depends on your personal situation and what you want to protect.

B. For most people, a home and its contents are their most valuable investment. For this reason, it is very important to protect a home and its contents against damage or loss. An important feature of home insurance is the provision for living expenses. This pays for lodgings, meals, and related expenses while your home is being rebuilt or repaired. Liability coverage is also important. It protects you against a claim or lawsuit resulting from an accident or injury occurring on your property. There are various kinds of homeowner's insurance, depending on the type of coverage desired and whether you live in a house, apartment, condominium, or other dwelling.

Lesson 25.3 *Auto Insurance*

A. All states have financial responsibility laws requiring drivers to pay for damages they cause to people or property. Most people buy insurance to show proof of financial responsibility. An auto policy may provide six basic types of coverage: bodily injury liability, property damage liability, protection against uninsured motorists, medical payments, auto collision, and auto comprehensive.

B. The cost of auto insurance varies from one geographic area to another. Many other factors influence the price of insurance, including the year, make, and model of the car and the sex, age, marital status, and driving record of the operator. You can have some control over the final cost of insurance by purchasing sensible limits for the different types of coverage, comparing rates, and asking about discounts. More important than price is the quality of service the company provides.

C. About half of states have no-fault auto insurance that pays for losses and expenses regardless of who caused the accident.

Activities

1. Mrs. Owen has just recovered from a serious illness. Her hospital stay resulted in a bill of $12,340. She has health insurance that contains the following provisions:
   - A $100 deductible for each hospital visit
   - Co-insurance in which the plan pays 80 percent of the next $5,000 and 100 percent of the costs thereafter

   How much of the bill does Mrs. Owen have to pay?
2. As a class, obtain a policy or descriptive information about disability insurance. What types of illnesses and injury does the insurance cover? How much will the policy provide? What is the cost of the policy?
3. As a class, obtain cost estimates on three different life insurance policies with a $50,000 face value of the following types:

   a. 5-year renewable level-term plan

   b. 30-year decreasing term plan

   c. 30-year cash-value plan

   What is the annual cost for each plan at ages 20, 30, 40, and 50? What is the average yearly cost for insurance over the 30-year period? Is this a fair way to compare the cost of life insurance? What other factors (if any) need to be taken into consideration?
4. Obtain a policy or descriptive information about renter's insurance. What does the policy cover? How much is the annual premium? Does a young person moving into an apartment for the first time need such insurance? Why or why not?
5. Arrange to have an insurance agent or broker visit the class to discuss auto insurance. Ask him or her to discuss how rates are established and how final premiums are computed. Ask for recommendations about liability, medical payments, and uninsured motorists coverage. Ask the agent to discuss the pros and cons of having comprehensive and collision coverage. If you wish, also find out how to decide between different levels of deductibles.

REVIEW

6. Learn your state's requirements for auto insurance coverage. You can call the department of motor vehicles or, in many states, visit its web site. Also find out whether no-fault insurance is available in your state.

Word Power

On a separate sheet of paper, match each definition with the correct term. All definitions will be used, and a definition will be used only once.

7. A provision of health insurance in which the insured person is required to share in the expenses of health care
8. A type of insurance in which all health care is provided for a fixed fee
9. For life insurance, the person to whom the death benefits from a policy are to be paid
10. A condition of health insurance that limits the amount of the bill for which the insured person is responsible
11. For insurance, the cost of a policy
12. Regarding life insurance, the amount of money that is paid in the event of the insured's death
13. The chance of a loss; for example, an accident
14. For home insurance, the possible damages from which one seeks protection through the purchase of insurance
15. In traditional health insurance, a certain initial amount that the insured person is required to pay before the insurance company pays the balance
16. Legal responsibility for something, such as damages or costs
17. A disaster or misfortune, often occurring suddenly

a. beneficiary
b. catastrophe
c. co-insurance (co-payment)
d. deductible
e. face value
f. health maintenance organization (HMO)
g. liability
h. perils
i. premium
j. risk
k. stop-loss provision

Think Critically

18. Hospitals have traditionally been operated as nonprofit community agencies. More and more hospitals and clinics are now being operated as private businesses. Why have these changes come about? What is your opinion of health providers becoming businesses operated for profit?
19. People differ in terms of their need for life insurance. Identify and discuss family situations in which there is a great need for life insurance.
20. Home insurance perils are related to where you live. Identify and discuss different perils that are more common in one part of the country than another.
21. In what ways can you help to control the amount you pay for auto insurance?

CHAPTER 26

TAXES AND TAXATION

LESSONS

THOUGHTS ON WORK

"I find that the harder I work, the more luck I seem to have."
Thomas Jefferson

PREVIEW

As you begin work, you will need to pay income taxes. Perhaps you have already filed an income tax return. This chapter will help you to understand more about the purpose of taxes, the different types of taxes, and what taxes you can expect to pay. It will also show you how to fill out a federal income tax return.

TAKING ACTION
UNDERSTANDING TAXES

John Nye had just completed two weeks on his new job. He could hardly wait to get his first paycheck. His supervisor handed him the check as he was leaving on Friday afternoon. He took the paycheck and put it into his jacket pocket, not wanting to appear too excited.

After he got on the bus headed for home, John unfolded the paycheck and looked at it. He was disappointed. He had known that deductions would be taken from his paycheck. But he had not realized the amount would be so large.

When he got home, John asked his mother why he had to pay taxes. "After all," he said, "I don't make very much money." John's mother explained how every citizen is expected to pay part of the cost of government. Mrs. Nye also explained the types of taxes and John's future need to file an income tax return.

That night, John went to dinner with his older sister, Emily, who worked as a camera operator at a television station downtown. She asked a lot of questions about his new job. John answered her questions. Then he told Emily how he had felt about getting his first paycheck.

"I know," Emily said. "I felt that way, too. But I don't mind the amount of taxes I have to pay, really. I pay more than you do because I earn more. But that doesn't bother me. It seems to me that if you earn more than somebody else, you *should* pay more taxes. And if you think about it, we get a lot of services for the money we pay."

"I'll have to file an income tax return next year," John mused. "Is it as hard as everybody says?"

"I never bother with it," she replied. "I have a tax preparer do it for me. I have dividend and capital gains income from stock I invest in through work. I also deduct interest I pay on my student loan. Every year I kick myself for spending the money on a tax preparer—but you know how bad I am at organizing! Not like you." She smiled. "Maybe when you get yours done next year, you can help me do mine!"

SUCCESS TIP
Learn about how taxes will affect your income.

THINK CRITICALLY

1. What sorts of services do people get for their tax money?
2. What other taxes do we pay besides income taxes?

LESSON 26.1 TAXATION

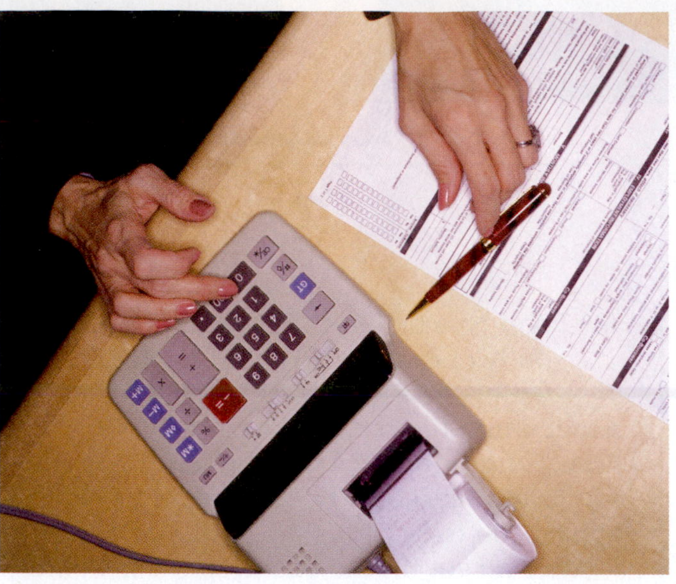

OBJECTIVES

- EXPLAIN THE PURPOSE OF TAXES
- IDENTIFY AND EXPLAIN THE MAJOR TYPES OF TAXES
- ILLUSTRATE THE DIFFERENCE BETWEEN A GRADUATED TAX AND A FLAT TAX

THE PURPOSE OF TAXES

Local, state, and federal are the three levels of U.S. government. These units of government provide a wide variety of services. Supporting schools, building and maintaining roads, and providing for the nation's defense are examples. The process by which the expenses of government are paid is called **taxation**.

A **tax** is a compulsory (required) contribution of money people make to government. Calling a tax compulsory helps to distinguish it from other types of payments. For example, when you buy a postage stamp, you are paying for a government service. The difference between that purchase and taxation is that you are not required to buy a stamp. The main purpose of taxation is to raise **revenue**, or money to pay the cost of government. Most taxes are revenue taxes.

For centuries, governments have used direct and indirect ways of raising money. A direct tax is paid directly to the government. Examples include income taxes and property taxes.

If you buy gasoline, you pay an indirect tax. The oil company pays tax on the gasoline it produces. These increased costs are then passed on to you at the pumps. Passing on taxes to the consumer is known as shifting the tax burden.

Sometimes, a direct tax can become an indirect tax. Karen's landlord told her that the rent was going up by $20 a month. When she asked why, Karen learned that property taxes on the building had risen by about $600 the previous year. What the owner did was to pass the property taxes (a direct tax) on to Karen and other renters in the form of an indirect tax.

The consumer is often aware of indirect taxes. When you buy gas, for example, the price you pay for excise tax is clearly shown on the pump. Or, when you buy tires, the bill will list the amount of federal excise tax. Excise taxes are a type of sales tax placed on specific items. They are one of the most common types of indirect taxes. How much tax is included in the cost of gasoline where you live?

WORKPLACE DECISIONS

You are working about 15 hours a week as part of a work experience program. In looking over your pay statement, you find that money has been withheld for federal and state income taxes. You try to think back to when you filled out Form W-4, the Employee's Withholding Allowance Certificate. You think that you claimed exemption from withholding because you did not expect to owe any taxes this year. Perhaps you made a mistake on Form W-4.

WHAT WOULD YOU DO?

Etiquette refers to rules for good manners and behavior. Network etiquette, or *netiquette*, refers to rules for behaving properly online. If you go to a shopping mall and are loud and behave rudely, you violate the rights of others. The same is true in the world of cyberspace. For example, before e-mailing a large video file to friends, you should ask them when would be a convenient time to receive it, since it might take some time to download and might tie up their computer systems. A good source for more information on netiquette is *The Net: User Guidelines and Netiquette* by Arlene H. Rinaldi, available through the Netiquette Home Page at Florida Atlantic University (http://www.fau.edu/netiquette/).

Some kinds of indirect taxes are hidden. For instance, the price you pay for a stereo receiver includes taxes paid on the labor and raw materials used to produce the product. Taxes were collected on the factory and equipment used in manufacturing. Shipping costs to get the product to market include taxes paid by the transportation company. In fact, hidden taxes may make up as much as 20 percent of the cost of goods you buy.

TYPES OF TAXES

Individuals and businesses pay a variety of direct and indirect taxes for the purpose of raising revenue. The major types of taxes are income; payroll; sales and excise; and estate, inheritance, and gift.

Income Taxes

You pay taxes on the money you earn, and businesses are taxed on their profits. Governments collect most taxes in this manner. The federal government, most state governments, and a few local governments collect income taxes. You pay income taxes not only on salary, wages, and tips but on savings and investment income as well.

Payroll Taxes

Income taxes pay for the overall costs of government. Payroll taxes, however, only go to support Social Security insurance programs. If you work for an employer covered by Social Security, both you and the employer make a contribution. These funds will help to provide you with a retirement income and other benefits. Some workers, such as teachers and government employees, pay into a state retirement program rather than into Social Security. You will learn more about Social Security in the next chapter.

Sales and Excise Taxes

Most state governments and some local ones have a sales tax. When you buy something, a few cents per dollar is added to the amount of the sale. Taxes on large items can be very high. For instance, on a car purchase, the sales tax can amount to several hundred (or thousand) dollars.

Excise taxes are most commonly found on such items as gasoline, tires, and amusements. Why do you suppose the government taxes these things?

Estate, Inheritance, and Gift Taxes

When a person dies, the government may collect two types of taxes. An estate tax is assessed on the value of the dead person's wealth and property *before* it passes on to the heirs of the estate. In addition, an inheritance tax may be taken out of each person's share of the will. The federal government collects only an estate tax. Some state governments levy both inheritance and estate taxes.

You may wonder why people do not just turn over large sums while living so heirs can avoid these taxes. Gifts up to a certain amount are tax-free. Beyond that amount, however, the person giving the money must pay a gift tax.

THE FEDERAL INCOME TAX

In 1913, Congress passed the 16th Amendment to the Constitution, which gave the government the right to tax income. A few months later, an income tax on individuals and corporations was imposed. Since 1913, income tax laws have changed many times, and income tax rates have increased greatly.

In 1911, Wisconsin became the first state to administer an income tax. The success of this tax led many states to pass similar laws. By the mid-1970s, almost all states had passed some form of income tax law. After World War II, many cities also adopted income taxes. Added revenues were needed to catch up with needs neglected during the war.

Who Must Pay?

Unless excused by law, individuals, corporations, trusts, and estates generally must pay income tax. For example, the government does not tax individuals and families who have low incomes. Nonprofit organizations such as churches, charities, and many hospitals are also tax-exempt.

Aliens (citizens of other countries) who live and earn income in the United States must pay income taxes. All corporations are subject to income taxes. Small businesses do not pay corporate taxes unless they have been incorporated. Instead, owners of such businesses pay individual income taxes on their shares of the business income.

The Graduated Income Tax

Most Americans recognize that paying taxes is a necessary part of being a good citizen. The income tax is seen by most of us as being the fairest type of tax. People who earn more money should be able to pay more taxes. A system in which taxes are tied to one's income is called a graduated tax. Figure 26-1 shows the relationship between the federal income tax rate and income.

Single			Married Filing Jointly or Qualifying Widow(er)		
Taxable Income Over	But Not Over	Marginal Tax Rate*	Taxable Income Over	But Not Over	Marginal Tax Rate
$0	$27,050	15%	$0	$45,200	15%
$27,050	$65,550	27.5%	$45,200	$109,250	27.5%
$65,550	$136,750	30.5%	$109,250	$166,500	30.5%
$136,750	$297,350	35.5%	$166,500	$297,350	35.5%
$297,350	—	39.1%	$297,350	—	39.1%
Married Filing Separately			**Head of Household**		
Taxable Income Over	But Not Over	Marginal Tax Rate	Taxable Income Over	But Not Over	Marginal Tax Rate
$0	$22,600	15%	$0	$36,250	15%
$22,600	$54,625	27.5%	$36,250	$93,650	27.5%
$54,625	$83,250	30.5%	$93,650	$151,650	30.5%
$83,250	$148,675	35.5%	$151,650	$297,350	35.5%
$148,675	—	39.1%	$297,350	—	39.1%

*The marginal tax rate is the rate at which the next dollar you earn will be taxed (tax year 2001).

Figure 26-1 ***The rate at which you pay tax is based on the amount of taxable income you earn and your filing status.***

Source: TaxPlanet.com

MATH CONNECTION

Suppose you earned an annual salary of $25,000 and your spouse also earned $25,000. If your state had a flat tax on income of 6%, how much state income tax would your family have to pay?

SOLUTION

To calculate the amount of state income tax you would owe, you must determine your family's total income and multiply that by the flat tax rate.

$$\text{Total income} = \$25{,}000 + \$25{,}000 = \$50{,}000$$

$$\text{Total tax owed} = \$50{,}000 \times 0.06 = \$3{,}000$$

Your family would owe $3,000 in state income tax.

Each taxpayer is allowed a certain level of tax-free income. Two important factors in determining the amount of income that is tax-free are marital status and number of dependents. In a recent year, Ann, a single person without dependents, paid no taxes on her first $7,450 of earned income. Marie and Frank, a married couple with two children, paid no taxes on their first $19,200 of earned income.

The income tax rate, then, requires nothing from people with very low incomes. Large families generally pay less in taxes than small families. A married couple generally pays less than a single person with the same amount of income.

Most state and local income taxes are also graduated. Some state and local governments, however, use a flat tax. This means that all taxpayers have the same tax rate regardless of income. A flat tax is usually 1 to 6 percent. If the flat rate were 5 percent, a person with an income of $20,000 would be assessed $1,000 in taxes. Someone earning $30,000 would have to pay $1,500 in taxes.

Over the years, many provisions have been written into the tax laws that allow people who meet certain requirements to reduce the amount of income on which they are taxed and thereby pay less tax or to avoid paying tax altogether. For example, people who have a home mortgage loan can subtract the interest they pay on the loan. But people paying rent have no similar means of reducing their tax. Such provisions are often criticized because they are regarded by some people as unfair. They are, however, legal tax provisions of which any eligible person can take advantage.

LESSON 26.1 REVIEW

1. Why do all of us need to pay taxes?
2. What is revenue?
3. Is an excise tax on tires a direct or an indirect tax?
4. Name and describe the seven major types of taxes.
5. Do aliens working in the United States have to pay income taxes?
6. How are owners of small businesses taxed?
7. What is a flat tax? How is a graduated tax different?

HIGH-GROWTH OCCUPATIONS FOR THE 21st CENTURY

Securities and Financial Services Sales Representatives

Most investors use *securities and financial services sales representatives* when buying or selling stocks, bonds, shares in mutual funds, insurance annuities, or other financial products. In addition, many clients use them for advice on investments and other financial matters.

Securities sales representatives, also called *brokers* or *stockbrokers*, perform a variety of tasks depending on their specific job duties. When an investor wishes to buy or sell a security, for example, sales representatives may relay the order through their firms' computers to the floor of a securities exchange. There, *floor brokers* negotiate the price with other floor brokers, make the sale, and forward the purchase price to the sales representatives. If a security is not traded on an exchange, as in the case of bonds and over-the-counter stocks, the broker sends the order to the firm's trading department. Here, other sales representatives, known as *dealers*, work directly with other dealers to buy and sell securities for customer accounts.

After interviewing clients to determine their financial status, financial planners develop a plan to fit the clients' needs.

An important part of a sales representative's job is building a customer base. Thus beginning sales representatives spend much of their time searching for customers through telephone solicitations and business and social contacts.

Financial services sales representatives sell banking services. They contact potential customers to explain their services and to determine customers' banking and other financial needs. In doing so, they discuss services such as credit card programs, deposit accounts, lines of credit, sales or inventory financing, or certificates of deposit.

Also included in this occupation are *financial planners*, who use their knowledge of tax and investment strategies, securities, insurance, pension plans, and real estate to develop and implement financial plans for individuals and businesses. Planners interview clients to determine their assets, liabilities, cash flow, insurance coverage, tax status, and financial objectives. They then analyze this information and develop a financial plan tailored to each client's needs.

LESSON 26.2
FILING AN INCOME TAX RETURN

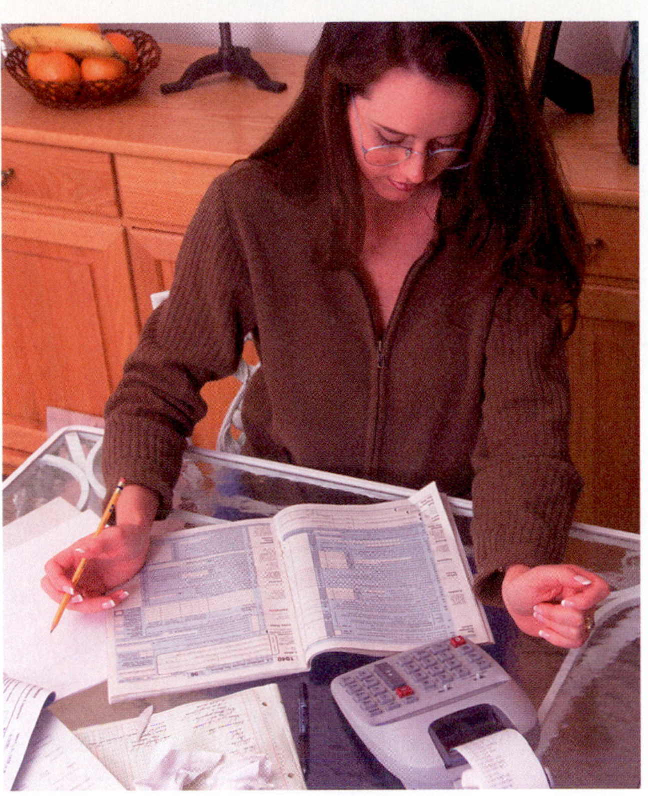

OBJECTIVES

- SUMMARIZE THE GENERAL PROCESS BY WHICH THE AMOUNT OF INCOME TAX IS DETERMINED
- COMPLETE A FORM 1040EZ

DETERMINING YOUR INCOME TAX

Your total income for a given year consists of money you earned from your job plus income from savings, investments, and other sources. But you do not have to pay taxes on your total income. Figure 26-2 on page 402 shows the process you use to determine how much of your income is subject to tax.

First, you may subtract certain nontaxable items called **adjustments to income**. Some examples of adjustments to income are alimony paid and contributions to an individual retirement account (a plan that lets individuals save money for retirement and receive special tax benefits). After you subtract adjustments to income, you are left with an **adjusted gross income**.

Next, you are allowed to subtract various nontaxable items called **deductions**. For example, mortgage interest, property taxes, and contributions to charity or churches can be deducted.

After that, you may subtract a set amount for yourself and each dependent. These are your **exemptions**. A married couple with one child, for example, would have three exemptions. Subtraction of amounts for deductions and exemptions leaves you with your **taxable income**, the amount on which you pay tax.

Determine the amount of tax owed by using the appropriate tax table. A sample tax table is shown in Figure 26-3 on page 402. For example, suppose you are married and filing a joint

PERSONAL DECISIONS

You are in the process of filling out your income tax return. The next line on the form deals with charitable contributions. You go over your canceled checks and discover several that qualify as deductions. You can remember a few other cash contributions, but you do not have the receipts. Also, you had some out-of-pocket expenses for church activities. These are allowable deductions. But you do not have records for them, either. You are not sure how much you should claim for charitable contributions.

WHAT WOULD YOU DO?

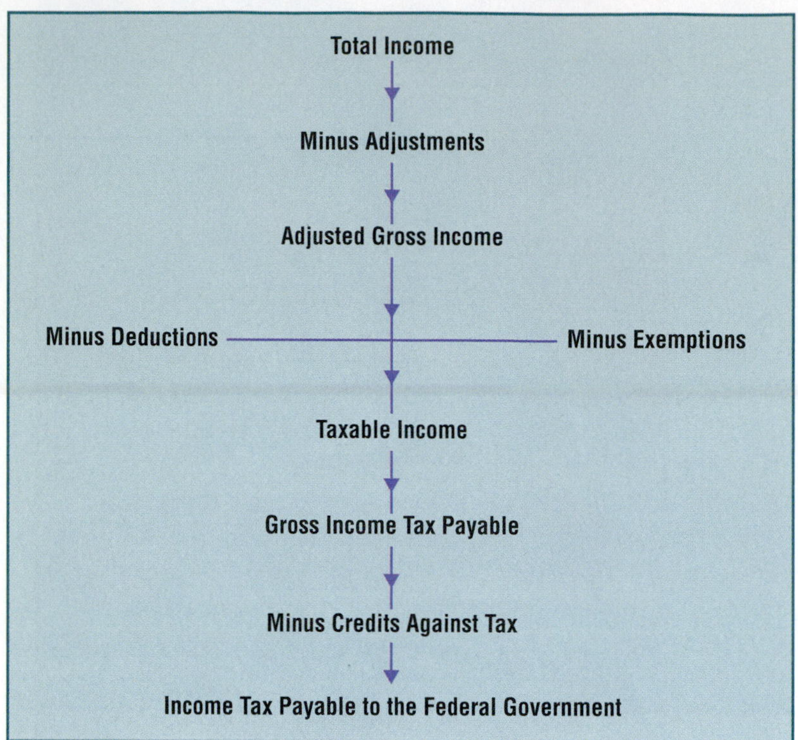

Figure 26-2 ***This is the general process used to determine the amount of federal income tax owed. The actual process varies among individuals.***

If line 39 (taxable income) is—		And you are—			
At least	But less than	Single	Married filing jointly	Married filing sepa-rately	Head of a house-hold
		Your tax is—			
27,000					
27,000	**27,050**	4,155	4,054	4,717	4,054
27,050	**27,100**	4,169	4,061	4,731	4,061
27,100	**27,150**	4,183	4,069	4,745	4,069
27,150	**27,200**	4,197	4,076	4,759	4,076
27,200	**27,250**	4,211	4,084	4,773	4,084
27,250	**27,300**	4,225	4,091	4,787	4,091
27,300	**27,350**	4,239	4,099	4,801	4,099
27,350	**27,400**	4,253	4,106	4,815	4,106
27,400	**27,450**	4,267	4,114	4,829	4,114
27,450	**27,500**	4,281	4,121	4,843	4,121
27,500	**27,550**	4,295	4,129	4,857	4,129
27,550	**27,600**	4,309	4,136	4,871	4,136
27,600	**27,650**	4,323	4,144	4,885	4,144
27,650	**27,700**	4,337	4,151	4,899	4,151
27,700	**27,750**	4,351	4,159	4,913	4,159
27,750	**27,800**	4,365	4,166	4,927	4,166
27,800	**27,850**	4,379	4,174	4,941	4,174
27,850	**27,900**	4,393	4,181	4,955	4,181
27,900	**27,950**	4,407	4,189	4,969	4,189
27,950	**28,000**	4,421	4,196	4,983	4,196

Figure 26-3 ***Sample tax table (tax year 2000)***

Source: Internal Revenue Service

return. If you made $27,430 in taxable income, the tax is $4,114. A single person earning the same amount would owe $4,267.

Your figure from the tax table may be reduced by any **tax credits** for which you are eligible. Tax credits are offered for child care and certain other expenses. The amount left after subtracting credits will be the amount of federal income tax you owe.

A final step in determining your tax is to compare the amount owed with the tax you have already paid. Because your employer withheld taxes from each paycheck, most or all of your tax obligation should be satisfied. If too much tax has been withheld, you can claim a refund. However, if too little has been withheld, you will have to pay an additional amount.

You must sign and mail your return and any attachments by April 15. In signing your name, you signify that everything on the form is accurate and truthful. If you mail the form late, you will have to pay interest and perhaps a penalty. People who do not file their forms at all are practicing tax evasion. **Tax evasion** is illegally avoiding payment of some or all of one's income tax obligation. If they are found guilty of this charge, they will have to pay a heavy fine and perhaps serve a prison sentence.

COMPLETING A FORM 1040EZ

The term **filing** is used to refer to the process of completing and submitting an income tax return. Filing a tax return can be simple or complex, depending on your filing status, source(s) of income, number of deductions, and so on. The easiest form to file is Form 1040EZ. The qualifications for using it change little from year to year. During a recent year, you could use Form 1040EZ if:

- Your filing status was *single* or *married filing jointly*.
- You did not claim any dependents.

WORKFORCE TRENDS

Because healthy employees are more productive, many employers have begun actively to promote personal health in the workplace. Health initiatives such as smoking cessation campaigns and health risk assessments can be found in 81 percent of workplaces. However, employees in small workplaces are less likely to have health promotion programs available to them than are employees in large workplaces.

- You did not claim a student loan interest deduction or an education credit.
- You (and your spouse, if you are married and filing a joint return) were not age 65 or over or blind.
- Your taxable income was less than $50,000.
- You had only wages, salaries, tips, and taxable scholarship or fellowship grants, unemployment compensation, qualified state tuition program earnings, or Alaska Permanent Fund dividends, and your taxable interest income was not more than $400.
- You did not receive any advance earned income credit payments.
- You did not owe any household employment taxes on wages you paid to a household employee.

You can fill out Form 1040EZ on paper. You can also submit it by telephone or computer. You will read more about these two options on page 407 of this chapter.

You may remember John Nye from the Taking Action feature at the beginning of this chapter. Let's see how John fills out his first personal income tax form.

In 2000, John worked afternoons after school and all day Saturdays at Rudden's Ice Cream Parlor. During the summer, he worked a full 40-hour week. In late January 2001, John received a Form W-2 Wage and Tax Statement from his employer (Figure 26-4 on page 404). This is an Internal Revenue Service (IRS) form that your employer prepares and sends to you by January 31 of the following year. The form shows your total earnings for the previous year and the total amount of federal income tax that was withheld from your pay.

When John got his W-2, he went to a nearby IRS office and picked up a copy of Form 1040EZ and the instructions for the form. IRS forms and publications are available in many public buildings, including libraries and post offices. You can also download them from the IRS web site at http://www.irs.gov.

John read through the instructions. He filled out the form, using the information from his W-2. He also used a statement from his bank that reported the interest income he had earned on his savings during 2000. In a short while, he had finished computing his income taxes and had checked his work. John determined that he owed $169 in taxes. A copy of John's completed

Although people usually dislike paying taxes, taxes pay for many things that benefit everyone, including highways, schools, and parks.

a Control number		OMB No. 1545-0008	
b Employer identification number 37-5732196		1 Wages, tips, other compensation 6840.00	2 Federal income tax withheld 208.00
c Employer's name, address, and ZIP code Rudden's Ice Cream Parlor 1640 W. Main Street Carbondale, IL 62901-1409		3 Social security wages 6840.00	4 Social security tax withheld 424.08
		5 Medicare wages and tips 6840.00	6 Medicare tax withheld 99.18
		7 Social security tips .00	8 Allocated tips
d Employee's social security number 315-20-4024		9 Advanced EIC payment	10 Dependent care benefits
e Employee's name, address, and ZIP code John R. Nye 1612 Fredrick St. Carbondale, IL 62901-1482		11 Nonqualified plans	12 Benefits included in box 1
		13 See instrs. for box 13	14 Other
		15 Statutory employee ☐ Deceased ☐ Pension plan ☐ Legal rep. ☐ Deferred compensation ☐	

16 State	Employer's state I.D. no.	17 State wages, tips, etc.	18 State income tax	19 Locality name	20 Local wages, tips, etc.	21 Local income tax
IL	0348-4321	6840.00	205.20		6840.00	.00

Form **W-2** Wage and Tax Statement **2000**

Department of the Treasury—Internal Revenue Service

Copy B To Be Filed With Employee's FEDERAL Tax Return

This information is being furnished to the Internal Revenue Service.

Figure 26-4 ***A Form W-2, Wage and Tax Statement, will be sent to you by your employer in late January following each year that you worked.***

return is shown in Figure 26-5 on pages 405 and 406.

As you can see, it was not difficult for John Nye to file an income tax return. Not all returns, however, are as simple as this. Because John's older sister, Emily, had dividend and capital gains income from stock and deductible student loan interest, she had to use Form 1040A. John's parents used a third common type of form, Form 1040, because they itemize instead of taking the standard deductions and also receive income from a property they rent.

In the process of completing his Form 1040EZ, John discovered that he enjoyed this type of work. When he asked his sister and parents if he might help them with their forms, they quickly accepted his offer. By helping to fill out their forms, John learned a great deal more about income tax returns. Why don't you offer to help a family member or friend with income tax preparation? You will probably learn a lot, too!

LESSON 26.2 REVIEW

1. **Based on Figure 26-3, how much tax does a married couple filing jointly owe on an income of $27,945? How much does a single person owe on the same amount?**
2. **What happens if you have earned income and fail to file an income tax return?**
3. **If you are married, can you use Form 1040EZ to file your federal income tax return?**

Form 1040EZ

Department of the Treasury—Internal Revenue Service

Income Tax Return for Single and Joint Filers With No Dependents (U) **2000**

OMB No. 1545-0675

Use the IRS label here

Your first name and initial: John R. | Last name: Nye

If a joint return, spouse's first name and intital | Last name

Home address (number and street). If you have a P.O. box, see page 7.: 1612 Fredrick St. | Apt. no.

City, town or post office, state, and ZIP code. If you have a foreign address, see page 7.: Carbondale, IL 62901-1482

Your social security number: 315 20 4024

Spouse's social security number:

▲IMPORTANT!▲ You **must** enter your SSN(s) above.

Presidential Campaign (p. 12) **Note:** Checking "Yes" will not change your tax or reduce your refund. Do you, or spouse if a joint return, want $3 to go to this fund? ▶ Yes [X] No [ ]

			Dollars	Cents
Income **Attach Copy B of Form(s) W-2 here.** Enclose, but do not staple, any payment.	1	Total wages, salaries, and tips. This should be shown in box 1 of your W-2 form(s). Attach your W-2 form(s).	6,840	
	2	Taxable interest income. If the total is over $400, you cannot use Form 1040EZ.	63	
	3	Unemployment compensation, qualified state tuition program earnings and Alaska Permanent Fund dividends (see page 14).		
	4	Add lines 1, 2, and 3. This is your **adjusted gross income.**	6,903	
Note: *You* ***must*** *check Yes or No.*	5	Can your parents (or someone else) claim you on their return? **Yes.** Enter amount from worksheet on back. [X] **No.** If **single,** enter 7,200.00 If **married,** enter 12,950.00. See back for explanation. [ ]	4,400	
	6	Subtract line 5 from line 4. If line 5 is larger than line 4, enter 0. This is your **taxable income.** ▶	2,503	
Payments and tax	7	Enter your Federal income tax withheld from box 2 of your W-2 Form(s).	208	
	8a	**Earned income credit** (see page 9).		
	b	Nontaxable earned income: enter type and amount below. Type ___ $ ___		
	9	Add lines 7 and 8a. These are your **total payments.**	208	
	10	**Tax.** Use the amount on **line 6 above** to find your tax in the tax table on pages 20–24 of the booklet. Then, enter the tax from the table on this line.	377	
Refund Have it directly deposited! See page 20 and fill in 11b, 11c, and 11d.	11a	If line 9 is larger than line 10, subtract line 10 from line 9. This is your **refund.**		
	b	Routing number		
	c	Type: Checking [ ] Savings [ ]		
	d	Account number		
Amount you owe	12	If line 10 is larger than line 9, subtract line 9 from line 10. This is the **amount you owe.** See page 21 for details on how to pay.	169	

I have read this return. Under penalties of perjury, I declare that to the best of my knowledge and belief, the return is true, correct, and accurately lists all amounts and sources of income I received during the tax year.

Sign here ▶ Keep copy for your records.

Your signature: John R. Nye | Spouse's signature if joint return. See page 11.

Date: 2/20/2001 | Your occupation: fast food worker | Date | Spouse's occupation

For Official Use Only

May the IRS discuss this return with the preparer shown on back (see page 21)?
For Disclosure, Privacy Act, and Paperwork Reduction Act Notice, see page 18.

Cat. No. 11329W Form 1040EZ

Figure 26-5A ***Most young workers can use Form 1040EZ.***

Form 1040EZ (2000) **page 2**

Use this form if

- Your filing status is single or married filing jointly
- You (and your spouse if married were under 65 on January 1, 2001 and not blind at the end of 2000.
- You do not claim any dependents
- Your taxable income (line 6) is less than $50,000.
- You do not claim a student loan interest deduction or an education credit. See page 3.
- You had **only** wages, salaries, tips, taxable scholarship or fellowship grants, unemployment compensation, qualified state tuition program earnings, or Alaska Permanent Fund dividends, and your taxable interest was not over $400. **But** if you earned tips, including allocated tips, that are not included in box 5 and box 7 of your W-2, you may not be able to use Form 1040EZ. See page 13. If you are planning to use Form 1040EZ for a child who received Alaska Permanent Fund dividends, see page 14.
- You did not receive any advance earned income credit payments.

If you are not sure about your filing status, see page 7. If you have questions about dependents, use TeleTax topic 354 (see page 6). If you **cannot use this form,** use TeleTax topic 352 (see page 6).

Filing in your return

For tips on how to avoid common mistakes, see page 25.

Enter your (and your spouse's if married) social security number on the front. Because this form is read by a machine, please print your numbers inside the boxes like this:

9	8	7	6	5	4	3	2	1	0

Do not type your numbers. Do not use dollar signs.

If you received a scholarship or fellowship grant or tax-exempt interest income, such as on municipal bonds, see the booklet before filling in the form. Also, see the booklet if you received a Form 1099-INT showing Federal income tax withheld or if Federal income tax was withheld from your unemployment compensation or Alaska Permanent Fund dividends.

Remember, you must report all wages, salaries, and tips even if you do not get a W-2 form from your employer. You must also report all your taxable interest, including interest from banks, savings and loans, credit unions, etc., even if you do not get a Form 1099-INT.

Worksheet for dependents who checked "Yes" on line 5

(keep a copy for your records)

Use this worksheet to figure the amount to enter on line 5 if someone can claim you (or your spouse if married) as a dependent, even if that person chooses not to do so. To find out if someone can claim you as a dependent, use TeleTax topic 354 (see page 6).

A. Amount, if any, from line 1 on front 6,840
\+ 250.00 Enter total ▶ **A.** 7,090

B. Minimum standard deduction .... **B.** 700.00

C. Enter the LARGER of line A or line B here .... **C.** 7,090

D. Maximum standard deduction. If **single,** enter 4,400.00; if **married,** enter 7,350.00 .... **D.** 4,400

E. Enter the SMALLER of line C or line D here. This is your standard deduction .... **E.** 4,400

F. Exemption amount.
- If single, enter 0.
- If married and—
—both you and your spouse can be claimed as dependents, enter 0.
—only one of you can be claimed as a dependent, enter 2,800.00.

F. 0

G. Add lines E and F. Enter the total here and on line 5 on the front.... **G.** 4,400

If you checked "No" on line 5 because no one can claim you (or your spouse if married) as a dependent, enter on line 5 the amount shown below that applies to you.

- Single, enter 7,200.00. This is the total of your standard deduction (4,400.00) and your exemption (2,800.00).
- Married, enter 12,950.00. This is the total of your standard deduction (7,350.00), your exemption (2,800.00), and your spouse's exemption (2,800.00).

Mailing return

Mail your return by **April 16, 2001.** Use the envelope that came with your booklet. If you do not have that envelope, see page 32 for the address to use.

Paid preparer's use only

See page 21.

Under penalties of perjury, I declare that I have examined this return, and to the best of my knowledge and belief, it is true, correct, and accurately lists all amounts and sources of income received during the tax year. This declaration is based on all information of which I have any knowledge.

Preparer's signature ▶	Date	Check if self-employed ☐	Preparer's SSN or PTIN
Firm's name (or yours if self-employed), address, and ZIP code ▶			EIN Phone no. ( )

*U.S.GPO:2000-460-555 Printed on recycled paper Form **1040EZ** (2000)

Figure 26-5B *Form 1040EZ (continued)*

FOCUS ON SKILLS FOR LIVING

ELECTRONIC TAX PREPARATION AND FILING

Almost anyone who files a tax return can now file taxes electronically with what the IRS calls *e-file*. The IRS *e-file* program offers quick, easy, and accurate alternatives to paper returns. These options include filing your return (a) through a tax professional, (b) using a personal computer, or (c) using a Touch-Tone telephone. In some states, you can file your federal and state returns electronically in a single step.

When you file electronically, you don't have to worry about your return being lost or delayed in the mail. Upon receipt of an electronic return, the IRS quickly and automatically checks the return for errors or missing information. The error rate for electronic returns is less than 1 percent, compared to about 20 percent for paper returns. Within 48 hours of transmission, the IRS acknowledges acceptance of the return. Best of all, if you are entitled to a refund, it can be sent in half the time that it takes when you file a return on paper. Information about IRS *e-file* is available on the Web at http://www.irs.gov/.

Tax returns can be filed electronically using the IRS e-file program.

Electronic tax filing was begun in 1986 on an experimental basis. The first year, 25,000 returns were filed electronically. Today, millions of returns are transmitted this way. The process is designed to cut down on paperwork. For paper returns, IRS employees must open the envelopes, organize and read the information, and key the data into a computer. When people file electronically, these tasks are eliminated.

The next step, after doing away with paper forms, may be "returnless" systems. In the future, IRS computers may keep wage, interest income, Social Security, and other taxpayer data on file. Then, each year, the IRS would send either a bill or a refund without a return ever being filed.

THINK CRITICALLY

1. Have you used *e-file*, and did you like it? If you have not used *e-file*, would you try it? Give three reasons in support of your answer.
2. Do you think that "returnless" systems are a good idea? Why or why not?

CHAPTER 26

Chapter in Brief

Lesson 26.1 *Taxation*

A. The process by which the expenses of government are paid is called taxation. A tax is a compulsory contribution of money people make to government. Most taxes are revenue taxes.
B. A direct tax is paid directly to the government. An indirect tax is included in the cost of goods and services you buy.
C. Individuals and businesses pay a variety of direct and indirect taxes. The major types are income, payroll, sales, excise, estate, inheritance, and gift.
D. Unless excused by law, individuals and corporations generally pay income taxes. Income from a small, unincorporated business is taxed as individual income rather than as corporate income.
E. A graduated income tax is one in which the amount of tax paid is tied to income. The more you earn, the more you pay. The federal government, and most state and local governments, levy a graduated income tax. Some state and local governments use a flat tax. This means that all taxpayers are taxed at the same rate regardless of income, usually 1 to 6 percent.

Lesson 26.2 *Filing an Income Tax Return*

A. To determine your income tax, subtract from your income any adjustments, deductions, and exemptions for which you are eligible. Figure your tax based on this amount. You may be able to reduce your tax by subtracting tax credits.
B. Most young workers can use Form 1040EZ, the easiest tax form to file.

Activities

1. As a class, obtain a copy of the most recent federal budget. What is the total amount of the budget? What is the primary budget expenditure? What specific items are included in this category? What is the amount of budget deficit or surplus? Discuss your answers in class.
2. Get a copy of and instructions for Form 1040EZ. Fill out the form using the following figures: wages of $15,178, tips of $1,132, and $220 in interest income. Federal income tax in the amount of $1,596 was withheld. What is the amount of tax? Your instructor may assign additional problems.
3. If your state has an income tax, obtain a copy of the income tax form and instructions. Using the amounts shown in Figure 26-4 (except for state income tax), complete the form. Ask your instructor to check the figures.
4. Suppose you make $370 a week. Each year you pay $2,884 in federal income tax, $578 in state income tax, $262 in sales tax, $88 in property tax,

REVIEW

$1,472 in FICA tax, and $158 for other taxes. How much do you pay for taxes during the year? How many weeks must you work just to pay taxes?

5. Visit the IRS web site at http://www.irs.gov/ to become familiar with the variety of information and services offered by the IRS. Locate and read Publication 4, "Student's Guide to Federal Income Tax."
6. Suppose you earned an annual salary of $27,000 and your spouse earned $32,000. If there were a flat tax on income of 5%, how much income tax would your family have to pay?

Word Power

On a separate sheet of paper, match each definition with the correct term. All definitions will be used, and a definition will be used only once.

7. Set amounts for yourself and each dependent that are subtracted from adjusted gross income when filing an income tax form
8. A required contribution of money people make to government
9. The illegal practice of avoiding payment of some or all of one's income tax obligation
10. The amount on an income tax form that results after you subtract adjustments from total income
11. The process by which the expenses of government are paid
12. The process of completing and submitting an income tax return
13. Items that can be subtracted from total income when filing an income tax return to arrive at adjusted gross income
14. Reductions in the amount of income tax owed
15. Various nontaxable items that can be subtracted from adjusted gross income when filing an income tax return
16. Money that is raised through taxes to pay the cost of government
17. The amount of income on which you pay taxes

a. adjusted gross income
b. adjustments to income
c. deductions
d. exemptions
e. filing
f. revenue
g. tax
h. taxable income
i. taxation
j. tax credits
k. tax evasion

Think Critically

18. Why do you think so many people dislike paying income taxes? How do you feel about it?
19. Which do you think is more fair, a graduated tax or a flat tax?
20. In what ways might the federal income tax system be improved? Give specific illustrations.
21. Have you ever heard of the underground economy? To what does it refer? Give examples.

CHAPTER 27

SOCIAL SECURITY AND IRAS

SOCIAL SECURITY ADMINISTRATION
PO BOX 17336
BALTIMORE MD 21235-0001
OFFICIAL BUSINESS
PENALTY FOR PRIVATE USE, $300

LESSONS

PREVIEW

You may have little interest in social security now. After all, it will be a long time before you retire. However, you need to be aware that there is more to social security than just a retirement program. Social security is actually a broad state and federal effort consisting of various types of social programs. These programs will be explained in this chapter.

THOUGHTS ON WORK

"A pessimist sees the difficulty in every opportunity; an optimist sees the opportunity in every difficulty."
Sir Winston Churchill

TAKING ACTION

SECURITY NET

Nina likes her new job. She works on a line assembling computer components. Her best friend at work is Leslie. One Friday afternoon, Nina notices that Leslie has not returned to work after lunch. On Monday, Leslie comes in limping, and Nina can see that she has a brace on her ankle. She will have to wait until morning break to find out what happened.

"I stopped in the women's room after lunch on Friday. The floor was wet, and I slipped. I sprained my ankle," Nina tells her. "My doctor said that if I stayed off my feet over the weekend, I could go back to work today."

"It's lucky we sit at our stations to do our work," said Nina.

"Yes," Leslie replies. "You know Jaime in Shipping, don't you? One day he was lifting a box of components, and he hurt his back. He was off work for a few weeks. And Nancy developed repetitive motion injury from soldering components. She had to have therapy for several months before she could return to work."

"I don't know what I'd do if I couldn't work for a long time," Nina says. "How would I pay my bills?"

"I know what you mean," says Leslie. "But they both got along OK. They got money from workers' compensation and help from other programs here at the company."

"I've heard of workers' compensation, but I don't know exactly what it is," Nina says.

Both women rise to go back to work. Leslie says, "I don't know too much about it, myself. I know it's a state program, and the employees at our company are covered by it. If you're injured, workers' compensation will pay medical bills and will give you some money to replace your income, but not as much as your pay."

That afternoon as she works, Nina thinks about what Leslie has said. She decides to find out more about workers' compensation and the company programs that Leslie mentioned. Nina wants to be sure that she will have enough income to make it if she is ever injured on the job.

SUCCESS TIP

There are government and sometimes company programs to help if you are injured on the job.

THINK CRITICALLY

1. What would you do if you were injured on the job?
2. How could you make your workplace safer?

LESSON 27.1
SOCIAL SECURITY

- *DEFINE* SOCIAL SECURITY
- *DESCRIBE SIX MAJOR FEDERAL AND STATE SOCIAL INSURANCE PROGRAMS*
- *EXPLAIN WHO IS ELIGIBLE FOR SOCIAL SECURITY AND HOW THE PROGRAM IS FINANCED*

WHAT IS SOCIAL SECURITY?

You know that your employer withholds money from your paycheck for federal, and perhaps state and local, income taxes. A sum is probably also withheld for Social Security taxes. Government programs that help people meet social and economic needs are called **social security**. Social Security is also the name of a particular set of programs, the federal system of retirement **benefits**, survivors payments, hospital insurance for the elderly, and other services. The word *benefits* refers to financial help in times of sickness, old age, disability, or the like.

At one time, most Americans lived in rural areas and were farmers. Rural families lived off the land. They built their own homes; raised their own food; and traded or sold surplus food, crops, and livestock. Families and neighbors helped each other during difficult times.

Gradually, the country began to change from an agricultural economy to an industrial one. Increasing numbers of people moved to cities and took jobs in factories. Instead of living off the land, families began to depend on wages paid by an employer. If the income stopped for some reason, such as a worker's illness or old age, the whole family suffered.

The Great Depression of the 1930s showed on a large scale how painful unemployment could be. To help deal with unemployment and the many other social problems brought on by the Depression, Congress, in 1935, passed the Social Security Act. This law provided for a system of old-age (retirement) benefits, unemployment insurance, aid for dependent children, benefits for the blind, and assistance for a few other

The Great Depression caused widespread unemployment and created hardship for many Americans.
California 1935. Courtesy of the Franklin D. Roosevelt Library Digital Archives.

groups and purposes. Over the years, Congress has made several changes in the act. Two examples are the extension of benefits to more groups and an increase in tax rates. Does anyone in your family receive Social Security benefits?

There are two types of social security programs. One type aids the needy regardless of their work record. Public assistance (or welfare) is an example. General taxes finance public assistance.

The second type is social insurance programs. The federal Social Security system is an example. Unlike public assistance, the federal Social Security program pays benefits to people who have earned them by working and paying Social Security payroll taxes. In some cases, a worker's family can receive benefits.

In many ways, social insurance programs are similar to other types of insurance. During your working years, you and your employer pay taxes that go into special funds. The risks and costs are thus spread among many people. When your earnings stop because of retirement or certain other situations, you receive benefits. If you die, payments are made to your survivors.

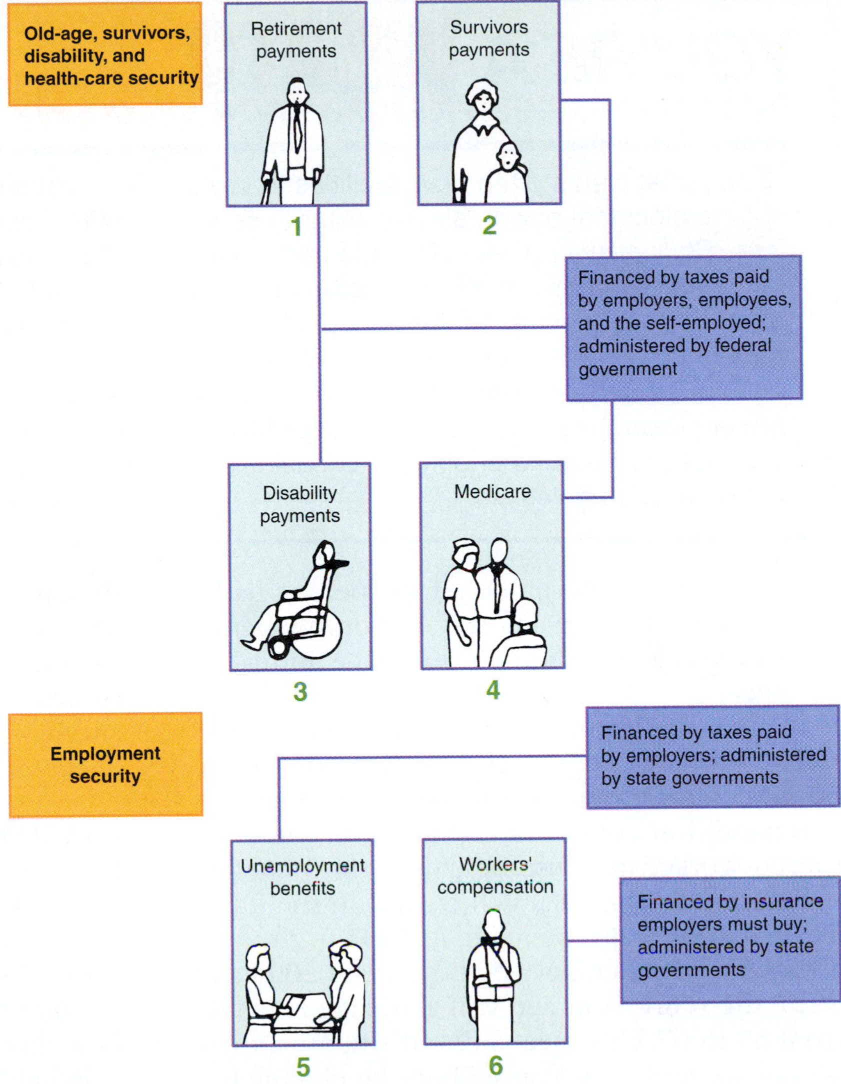

Figure 27-1 ***These are the six major types of social insurance programs in the United States.***

MAJOR SOCIAL INSURANCE PROGRAMS

National and state systems of social security have changed greatly from the way they were in 1935. The six major social insurance programs in the United States are shown in Figure 27-1. The general nature of each of these programs is described in this chapter. As some of the rules are quite technical, no effort is made to explain all details regarding eligibility and payments. For federally administered programs, more specific information can be obtained from your local Social Security Administration (SSA) office or on the Web at http://www.ssa.gov/.

Retirement Payments

This is the best-known program in the federal Social Security system. It provides a monthly pension to retired workers when they reach age 65. A **pension** is a regular payment of money to a person, usually a retired person. Individuals may choose to retire and begin receiving benefits as early as age 62. If they retire early, their monthly payments will be reduced to account for the longer period over which they will be paid. For a person who retires at age 62, for example, monthly payments are 80 percent of

YOU'RE A WHAT? STATIONARY ENGINEER

Industrial plants often have facilities to provide electrical power, steam, or other services. *Stationary engineers* operate and maintain these systems, which can include boilers, air-conditioning equipment, diesel engines, generators, turbines, pumps, and related equipment. The equipment operated by stationary engineers is similar to that operated by locomotive or marine engineers, except it is not on a moving vehicle.

Stationary engineers start up, regulate, and shut down equipment. They ensure that it operates safely, economically, and within established limits. They monitor meters, gauges, and computerized controls and make adjustments as necessary. Keeping records regarding operation, maintenance, and safety is an important part of the work. Increasingly, stationary engineers use computers to operate the mechanical systems of new buildings and plants. ■

what they would have been if the person had retired at age 65. The amount of monthly benefits received is based on your average annual earnings.

Benefits are also payable to the spouse of the retired worker. A spouse's benefits equal about 50 percent of the worker's benefits. Under certain conditions, unmarried children of the retired worker may also be eligible for benefits.

Retirement-age rules will change in the future as a result of revisions made in 1983 to the Social Security Act. Between the years 2003 and 2027, the retirement age will gradually increase from 65 to 67. This means that if you are a high school student now, you will not be eligible to receive full retirement benefits until you reach age 67. Early retirement benefits (ages 62-66) will also be reduced. For example, if you retire at age 62, your monthly payments will be reduced to 75 percent by 2009 and to 70 percent by 2027.

Survivors Payments

If you have worked and paid into Social Security and you die (either before or after retirement), your dependents may be eligible for survivors payments. These are of two types. First, a small **lump-sum payment** is made to your spouse or child. A lump-sum payment is a one-time payment of money. Second, your dependents may be eligible for a monthly survivors benefit.

Monthly payments may be made to a surviving spouse age 60 or older. Under certain conditions, surviving unmarried children and dependent parents may also receive payments. The amount of monthly payments is based on the benefits the worker was getting at the time of death. If the person had not yet retired, the survivor would be entitled to the benefits the deceased worker would have received.

Disability Payments

If you are unable to work because of a severe physical or mental disability, you may be eligible for benefits. The disability must have lasted at least 12 months or be expected to last that long. Payments can start upon the sixth full month of disability.

Benefits may also be paid to a disabled worker's spouse. Unless he or she gets a higher Social Security benefit, a spouse may collect full benefits at age 65 or reduced benefits at ages 62-64. Unmarried children under 18 can receive benefits. If a worker has a disabled child, special benefits may apply.

Medicare

In 1965, Congress added hospital and medical insurance benefits to the Social Security program. This coverage, known since as Medicare, is for people age 65 or older. (This is sometimes confused with Medicaid, which is a health service program for people with low incomes or special needs.) Disabled workers under age 65 who have received disability benefits for two years are also eligible. So are people with certain kidney diseases.

Medicare consists of both hospital insurance and supplementary medical insurance. Hospital coverage (Part A) pays for nursing care as well as for hospital, hospice, and some home health care expenses. (Hospice programs provide care for the terminally ill.) The insured person must pay an initial amount (a deductible) for each hospital stay. Medicare then pays the rest of the hospital expenses for up to 60 days. If a stay lasts more than 60 days, additional limitations apply.

The hospital insurance part of Medicare is automatically provided to eligible workers and spouses. However, the medical coverage (Part B) is an *optional* health insurance plan. It pays the cost of doctors' fees and other medical services not included in hospital insurance. If you want medical coverage, you must pay a monthly premium for the service. Under this plan, you must pay a deductible each year. The program then pays 80 percent of most remaining expenses.

Unemployment Benefits

Unemployment insurance, which was included as part of the original 1935 Social Security Act, is not a federal program. The purpose of the law was to motivate states to pass their own laws. Each state finances and administers its own unemployment insurance program within guidelines established by federal law. In most states, the system is financed by payroll taxes paid by employers.

Unemployment insurance provides weekly payments to workers who have lost their jobs. Paul Miller, for instance, was laid off from his job at the Black Gold Coal Mine. He had to go to the local state employment service office to register for unemployment benefits. Paul has started receiving weekly checks amounting to half of his normal full-time pay. He is eligible to receive payments for up to 26 weeks. However, during the time he is receiving unemployment benefits, Paul is required to accept any suitable job that the employment service has available.

The amount of the weekly payment and the number of weeks of eligibility vary from state to state. Otherwise, state programs of unemployment insurance operate in the same general manner.

Workers' Compensation

Every state in the United States has a workers' compensation law, which helps people who are injured or who develop a disease as a result of their job. The program pays the cost of medical care and helps replace lost income. Workers' compensation also pays death benefits and pensions to spouses and dependent children of workers killed on the job.

Benefits vary among states. How much workers receive depends on the type and duration of the disability and on the worker's weekly earnings. States have minimum and maximum benefit limits and benefit periods. But injured workers typically receive about two-thirds of what they would have earned. In return for compensation, workers give up their right to sue an employer for damages arising from their disability.

In most states, employers are required to participate in a workers' compensation program and to purchase insurance coverage that pays for it. However, many states do not cover farm workers, household workers, and employees of small firms. And some states refuse to extend protection to workers in dangerous jobs.

ELIGIBILITY AND FINANCING

In the previous section, you learned about four federally administered social security

ETHICAL DECISIONS

You injured your leg badly in a warehouse accident. The leg was put into a cast. You have been confined to bed for several weeks. It will probably be months before you can go back to work. You are glad you have workers' compensation benefits.

Your coworkers stop by to see you every few days. During one visit, you remark that you cannot wait to get the cast off and go back to work. Your buddy laughs and says that if he were you, he would lie about the leg hurting and stay home as long as possible. He says that a lot of people do it.

WHAT WOULD YOU DO?

programs and two state-administered ones (review Figure 27-1). This section explains how the federal program is financed, as well as how you become eligible for federal Social Security benefits. You have already learned how the state programs are financed. Eligibility for state programs varies widely among states.

Who Is Eligible

To be eligible for Social Security benefits, you must earn a certain number of **work credits**, points earned in jobs covered by Social Security. Work credits were previously called "quarters of coverage." At the time of this writing, you received one credit for each $830 of covered annual earnings. The amount of earnings needed for a credit increases periodically. You are limited to four credits per year no matter how much money you make.

There are two different eligibility statuses—fully insured and currently insured. A fully insured worker has earned 40 work credits. Fully insured workers are eligible to receive complete retirement, survivors, disability, and health benefits. A currently insured worker has earned at least 6 credits during the 39 months before death or disability. Such a worker is only eligible for limited survivors benefits. For workers who become disabled, other standards apply.

Financing the Program

You and your employer share equally the cost of financing federal Social Security by paying the **Federal Insurance Contributions Act (FICA)** tax. Your employer deducts your share of FICA tax from your paycheck. Your employer then adds an equal contribution and sends the Treasury Department the total amount monthly or quarterly. The department distributes the money among the various funds that will pay benefits.

Up to a certain limit, taxes are figured on your gross annual salary or wages. The salary limit is called the **wage base**. In 1937, when the first FICA taxes were collected, both the worker and the employer paid a 1 percent tax on the first $3,000 (wage base) of earnings. In 2001, the tax rate was 6.2 percent on the first $80,400 of earnings. Earnings in excess of the wage base are not subject to FICA tax. However, you must continue to pay 1.45 percent for Medicare on all earned income. Thus, the total tax rate for most individuals is 7.65 percent (6.20% + 1.45%).

LESSON 27.1 REVIEW

1. There are two types of social security programs. How are they different?
2. List and briefly describe the six major social insurance programs.
3. How long must you have been disabled in order to receive Social Security disability payments?
4. Name the two types of Medicare insurance. Which type is not automatically provided to eligible workers?
5. How are state unemployment benefits and workers' compensation financed?
6. How many work credits are required to be a fully insured worker? A currently insured worker?
7. How is federal Social Security financed?
8. What percentage of a worker's income is currently withheld for FICA tax? What is the wage base?

HIGH-GROWTH OCCUPATIONS FOR THE 21st CENTURY

Social Workers

Social work is a profession for those with a strong desire to help people, to make things better, and to make a difference. *Social workers* help people function the best way they can in their environment, deal with their relationships with others, and solve personal and family problems.

Through direct counseling, social workers help clients identify their concerns, consider effective solutions, and find reliable resources. Social workers typically consult and counsel clients and arrange for services that can help them. Often, social workers refer clients to specialists in areas such as debt counseling, child or elder care, public assistance, or alcohol or drug rehabilitation. Social workers then follow through with clients to ensure that services are helpful and that clients make proper use of the assistance offered. Social workers may review eligibility requirements, help clients fill out forms and applications, visit clients on a regular basis, and provide support during crises.

A social worker provides counseling and support to clients, often visiting them on a regular basis.

Social workers practice in a variety of settings. In mental health and community centers, social workers provide counseling services on marriage, family, and adoption matters, and they help people through personal or community emergencies. In schools, they help children, parents, and teachers cope with problems. In social service agencies, they help people locate basic benefits, such as income assistance, housing, and job training.

Social workers also offer counseling to those receiving therapy for addictive or physical disorders in rehabilitation facilities and to people in nursing homes in need of routine living care. In employment settings, they counsel people with personal, family, professional, or financial problems affecting their work performance. Social workers who work in courts and correction facilities evaluate and counsel individuals in the criminal justice system to help them cope better in society. In private practice, social workers provide clinical or diagnostic testing services covering a wide range of personal disorders.

LESSON 27.2
INDIVIDUAL RETIREMENT ACCOUNTS

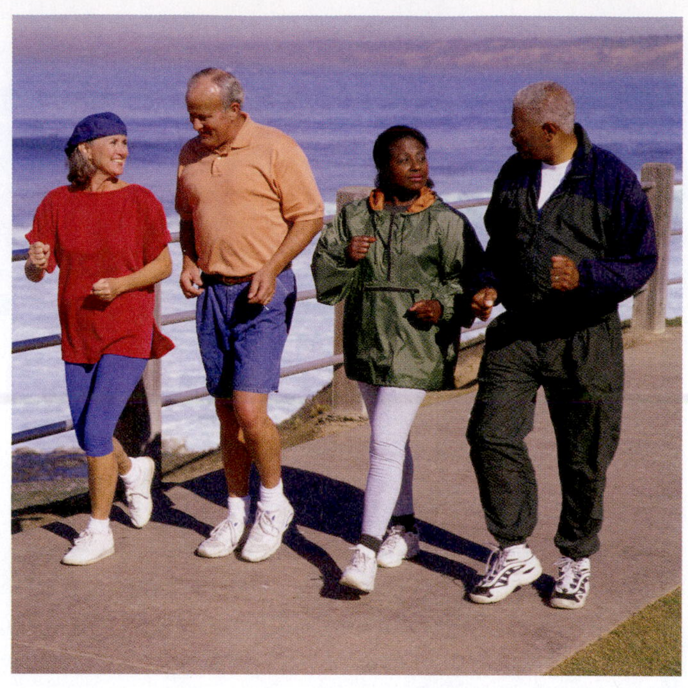

OBJECTIVES

- *EXPLAIN THE PURPOSE OF AN INDIVIDUAL RETIREMENT ACCOUNT (IRA)*
- *NAME AND DESCRIBE THE TWO TYPES OF IRAS*

PURPOSE OF AN IRA

The Social Security retirement program is designed to provide a minimum standard of living for retired workers. Social Security was never designed to meet *all* of a retired person's financial needs. To live reasonably well in retirement, it will be necessary for you to supplement Social Security retirement income with income from other sources. These might include savings, investments, or private pensions.

About 98 percent of all workers are in jobs covered by Social Security. Approximately half of these workers are also covered by a private pension plan. To encourage more people to save for their retirement, Congress passed legislation in 1981 making almost every working person eligible to make contributions to an **individual retirement account (IRA)**. An IRA is a voluntary private pension plan that allows employed individuals to save a certain amount annually toward retirement and receive special tax benefits.

PERSONAL DECISIONS

You work for a large company that employs hundreds of workers. Every several months, the human resources department conducts "brown-bag" lunches for interested employees on such topics as investing and tax planning. An announcement is included in your pay envelope indicating that a program on IRAs will be offered next week. You are supposed to mark and return the form if you are interested. You do not think you will go. You still have about 40 years before retirement.

WHAT WOULD YOU DO?

TWO TYPES OF IRAS

There are two types of IRAs. The first is a traditional IRA. Anyone who earns income from working and is under age $70^1/_2$ can open one of these IRAs. In 2001, depending on your earnings, you could put up to $2,000 a year into it. If you were married, your spouse could also invest up to $2,000 in his or her IRA whether he or she was employed or not.

Yearly Income and Filing Status	If You or Your Spouse is Covered by a Retirement Plan at Work	If You or Your Spouse is not Covered by a Retirement Plan at Work
Married, Filing Jointly Under $53,000 **Single or Head of Household** Under $33,000	Full Deduction	Full Deduction
Married, Filing Jointly $53,000-$62,999 **Single or Head of Household** $33,000-$42,999	Partial Deduction	Full Deduction
Married, Filing Jointly $63,000 and Above **Single or Head of Household** $43,000 and Above	No Deduction	Full Deduction (Limits apply if spouse is covered and income is $150,000 and above)

Note: Yearly income limits change frequently.

Figure 27-2 ***This chart will help you determine whether you can deduct your IRA contribution based on your annual adjusted gross income.***

Source: TaxPlanet.com

Tax Benefits

A traditional IRA has *two* big tax benefits. First, people can deduct IRA contributions from their income tax. This depends, however, on whether you have a retirement plan at work and on how much you earn. In 2001, a person not covered by a retirement plan at work could put up to $2,000 a year into a traditional IRA and deduct the full amount. The limit is $3,000 for 2002–2004, $4,000 for 2005–2007, and $5,000, adjusted for inflation, for 2008 and after (slightly more for older workers). People who have retirement plans at work are able to get the full deduction only if their incomes are below a certain level (Figure 27-2).

Let's say that a married couple, filing jointly, had taxable income of $35,000. By placing $2,000 into an IRA, they would only pay taxes on $33,000. In 2000, this would have resulted in a tax savings of $300. It would have cost this couple, in effect, $1,700 to make a $2,000 investment. For people earning higher incomes, the savings are even greater.

The second tax benefit of a traditional IRA is that interest and other earnings are not taxed until they are withdrawn. This allows an investment to compound at a much greater rate than if taxes were deducted. Examples of how an IRA investment can multiply are shown in Figure 27-3. You can see that it is possible for a young person like you to accumulate several hundred thousand dollars before retirement. The amounts shown would increase dramatically if you put in

Age Open IRA	Age 65	Age 70
18	$288,680	$395,675
19	270,870	371,634
20	254,097	348,994
25	183,793	254,097
30	131,710	183,793
35	93,125	131,710
40	64,540	93,125

Figure 27-3 ***This table shows what an IRA would be worth at retirement, based on a $1,000 annual contribution at 6 percent compounded daily.***

WORKFORCE TRENDS

Advances in the computer industry, coupled with those in telecommunications, have created the new information technology, or IT, industry and inaugurated an information age. By 2006, nearly half of all U.S. workers will be employed in industries that produce or intensively use information technology, products, and services.

the full amount and you earned a higher yield. Remember that inflation will probably increase over the years, too.

Lower-income workers can also benefit from a tax credit for IRA contributions made from 2002 through 2006. The credit may be 10 to 50 percent of the contribution, depending on the worker's income. The maximum credit is $1,000.

Even if you cannot put the full amount into an IRA, try to put in what you can afford. The key to getting the most from an IRA is to start early, put in as much as you can, and make a contribution every year.

Roth IRA

In 1998, another retirement option became available called the Roth IRA (named after the senator who sponsored the legislation). The investment limits for a Roth IRA are the same as those for a traditional IRA. Contributions to a Roth IRA are not tax-deductible, but they grow tax-free. After the account has been in existence for five years and the account holder has attained age 59½, the earnings can be withdrawn tax-free.

In simple terms, a traditional IRA provides a tax deduction and tax-deferred income. A Roth IRA provides no tax deduction but tax-free income. The Roth IRA also has higher income eligibility limits and differs in several other important ways from a traditional IRA. Total Roth and traditional IRA contributions per individual cannot exceed the annual limit ($3,000 in 2002, for example).

Opening an IRA

Deciding whether to open a traditional IRA or a Roth IRA requires a lot of study. Many types of financial institutions can advise you in making a decision and in opening an account. Institutions that offer IRAs include banks, savings and loan associations, insurance companies, brokerage firms, credit unions, and mutual funds. To open an account, you only have to complete a simple application form and make an initial deposit. In most cases, you can make contributions to the account anytime during the year and in any amount.

The type of investment you select can vary widely. You can purchase certificates of deposit, U.S. treasury securities, bonds, stocks, mutual funds, and many other types of investments. You may even choose several different types of investments and build up a diversified account. Also, you can switch from one investment to another as you wish.

In addition to opening an IRA, be sure to learn about and take advantage of retirement plans at work. Benefits may include tax-deferred savings, employer investments, and matching employer contributions. Traditional plans, offered less frequently today, provide a fixed income at retirement, paid for by the employer.

LESSON 27.2 REVIEW

1. **This year, how much can a single worker contribute to an IRA? A married couple in which both people work? A married couple in which only one person works?**
2. **What are the two tax benefits of having a traditional IRA?**
3. **Roth IRA contributions are not tax-deductible, but they are tax-free. Explain what this means.**

FOCUS ON HEALTH AND SAFETY

JOB STRESS AND WORKERS' COMPENSATION

In the early 1900s, several states passed laws to provide benefits for industrial workers injured on the job. Over the years, the idea of workers' compensation expanded to include all states, most occupations, and most job-related accidents and illnesses.

In 1955, workers' compensation took a new turn. Two men had been working on a scaffold when a rope broke. One fell to his death. The other was caught by the rope and dangled in the air until he was rescued. His most serious injury was a rope burn. But the man was too afraid to get on a scaffold ever again. So he filed a claim for workers' compensation. After a lengthy legal battle, Texas courts upheld an award for the man.

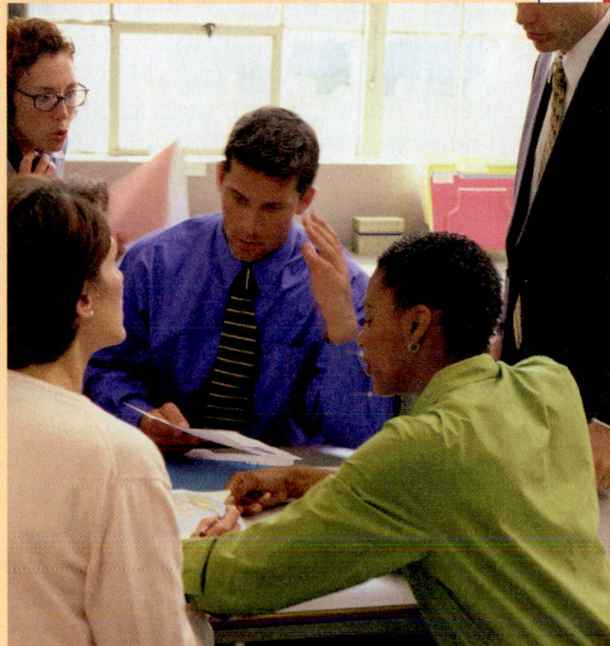

Job stress has become a common workplace problem.

Since then, some state courts have allowed compensation for three new categories of workers: (1) those who suffer a physical injury that leaves a psychological after-effect; (2) those who suffer mental trauma that leads to a physical ailment; and (3) those who suffer mental strain that leads to more serious mental problems. The last type is the most controversial. Here is an example.

The department in which an employee worked was eliminated. The employee transferred to another job. She developed chest pains and suffered an emotional breakdown. She quit working and filed a workers' compensation claim against the company. She argued that the job transfer caused her breakdown. Ultimately, the state supreme court awarded her payment of medical bills and two-thirds of her salary.

Job-stress cases such as this have mushroomed in recent years. Since workers' compensation is governed by state law, states often differ in recognizing everyday mental stress as grounds for covered benefits. This is likely to remain a hot issue for a long time to come.

THINK CRITICALLY

1. It can be difficult for employees to win job-stress cases. Why do you think this is so?
2. Why might job-stress cases have mushroomed in recent years?

CHAPTER 27

Chapter in Brief

Lesson 27.1 *Social Security*

A. Government programs that help people meet social and economic needs are called social security. Social Security is also the name of a particular set of programs, the federal system of retirement benefits, survivors payments, hospital insurance for the elderly, and other services.

B. There are two types of social security programs. One aids the needy regardless of their work record. An example is welfare, which is financed by general taxes. The second is social insurance programs such as Social Security. It is financed by taxes on earnings paid by workers and employers.

C. The four Social Security programs administered by the federal government are retirement payments, survivors payments, disability payments, and Medicare. The two state-administered social insurance programs are unemployment benefits and workers' compensation.

D. To be eligible for federal Social Security benefits, you must earn a certain number of work credits in jobs covered by Social Security. A fully insured worker has earned 40 credits and is eligible to receive complete benefits.

E. Federal Social Security programs are financed by payroll taxes on earnings. In 2001, the tax rate was 7.65 percent on a wage base of $80,400. Your employer contributes the same amount as you. In most states, unemployment benefits are financed by payroll taxes paid by employers, and workers' compensation is financed by insurance that employers must purchase.

Lesson 27.2 *Individual Retirement Accounts*

A. To live comfortably in retirement, most people will find it necessary to supplement Social Security with private retirement savings. An excellent way to provide for retirement is to establish an IRA.

B. In 2001, individuals could contribute up to $2,000 to either a traditional or a Roth IRA. The limit is $3,000 for 2002-2004, $4,000 for 2005-2007, and $5,000 from 2008 on. Each type of IRA has different features and requirements. An IRA started at an early age can grow to a large amount of money by the time you retire.

Activities

1. Have you ever worked at a job in which FICA tax was withheld from your paycheck? If so, prepare a list of all such jobs and the length of time you were employed in each. Then, figure out how many work credits you have accumulated to date. Compare your results with those of your classmates.
2. Go to a Social Security office and pick up several copies of Form SSA-7004, "Request for Social Security Statement" (or download copies from the SSA web site at *http://www.ssa.gov/*). Complete and mail one of the forms to

REVIEW

find out how much you have already contributed to Social Security. You can also complete and submit a version of the form online. If you have not had a job covered by Social Security, fill out a form for a family member.

3. Last year, Shirley James earned $26,700. The FICA tax rate was 7.65 percent. How much money was withheld for Social Security from Ms. James's income? What was the total FICA tax paid by Ms. James and her employer?
4. Three single workers had taxable incomes of $17,000, $21,000, and $25,000, respectively. Each plans to make a full contribution to a traditional IRA this year. Using a current federal tax table, figure how much tax each person will save. Compute how much the contribution costs each person.
5. Invite a banker or stockbroker to class to discuss IRAs and to explain the kinds of investments that can be purchased with an IRA contribution.

Word Power

On a separate sheet of paper, match each definition with the correct term. All definitions will be used, and a definition will be used only once.

6. A one-time payment of money; in the Social Security system, to the surviving spouse or child of a deceased person covered by Social Security
7. Financial help in times of sickness, old age, disability, etc.
8. A voluntary private pension plan that allows employed individuals to save a certain amount annually toward retirement and receive special tax benefits
9. Government programs that help people meet social and economic needs; the federal system of retirement benefits, survivors payments, hospital insurance for the elderly, and other services
10. A regular payment of money to a person, usually retired
11. Points used to determine eligibility for Social Security benefits; linked to amount of earnings
12. The amount of gross annual salary or wages subject to Social Security tax
13. The federal law requiring employers to deduct an amount from workers' paychecks for Social Security and to contribute an equal amount

a. benefits
b. Federal Insurance Contributions Act (FICA)
c. individual retirement account (IRA)
d. lump-sum payment
e. pension
f. social security (Social Security)
g. wage base
h. work credits

Think Critically

14. Assuming they have no house or rent payment, about how much monthly income do you think a retired couple would need to live comfortably?
15. Why is inflation such a major concern for most retired people?
16. Some people would like to make federal Social Security optional. In other words, people could take all or part of the 6.2 percent withheld for FICA and invest it in their own retirement programs. Discuss the positive and negative aspects of such a change.

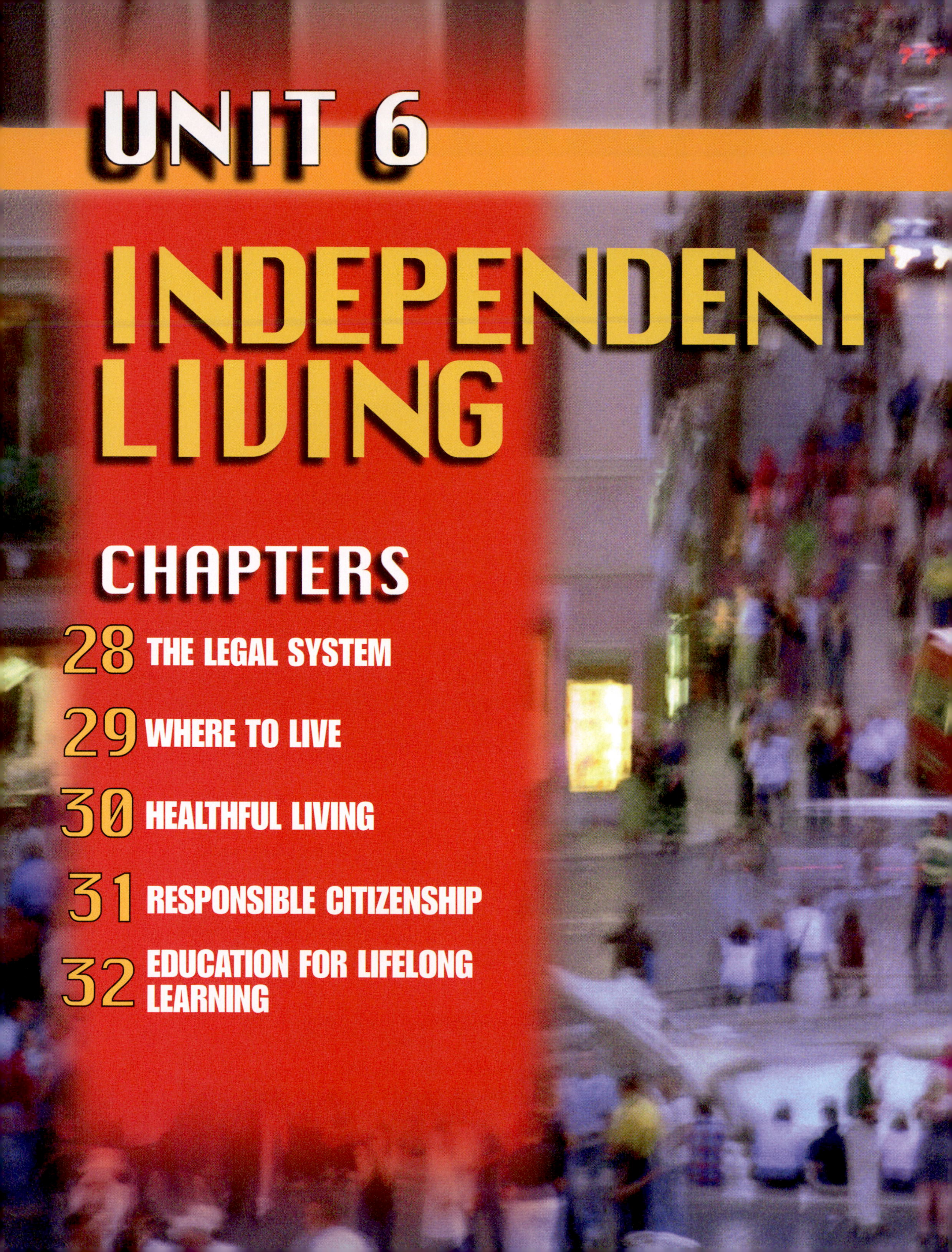

UNIT 6

INDEPENDENT LIVING

CHAPTERS

CO-OP CAREER SPOTLIGHT

April Bartholomew, *Auto Mechanic*

When her 1972 Mustang kept breaking down, April Bartholomew of Olympia, Washington, enrolled in the New Market Vocational Skills Center's Automotive Service Technology program in Tumwater, Washington. By graduation, three years later, 18-year-old April was well on her way to fulfilling her career goal of opening her own automotive business.

The business, which April plans to start in 2007, will be a combination of a used car lot, an automotive repair shop, and an informal school where she will offer classes to the public on how to repair vehicles. Already she has a list of potential students who anxiously await her classes.

In her sophomore year, April began working at NAPA, an auto parts store. She then worked at ADI, another auto parts store. During her first two years, April attended the usual high school classes in the morning and automotive classes in the afternoon. She then worked part-time after school. By her senior year, April was attending regular classes from 8:00 to 10:30 a.m. and then either working or attending automotive classes from 11:30 a.m. to 2:00 p.m. During her senior year, April began an internship at Lincoln-Mercury & Mazda of Olympia, which led to full-time employment as a parts counterman on graduation.

April appreciates the way her school helped her put together a resume and taught her interview skills. Her jobs all came through school postings. The fact that she was from New Market Vocational Skills Center landed her every job she applied for. Employers hiring through the center knew what kind of employees they would get. They also knew the school was working with students to teach them occupational and employability skills.

New Market was also experimenting with a new program called the 4 Ps Project. Teachers assigned to the 4 Ps Project helped students design a 13-year program to map out their career goals. April was one of 40 students who began the program and one of 30 who completed it. Starting with graduation, and for 13 years into the future, April has a plan for her work and career goals. "That's how I know I can open my own business in the future."

Working in the co-op program gave April a lot of hands-on experience, which she found she enjoys. "I can move from little stores to bigger ones," she says. "When people first meet me, they wonder, 'What does she know about automotives?' They're always surprised to learn I know a lot." She even knows how to repair 1972 Mustangs.

CHAPTER 28

THE LEGAL SYSTEM

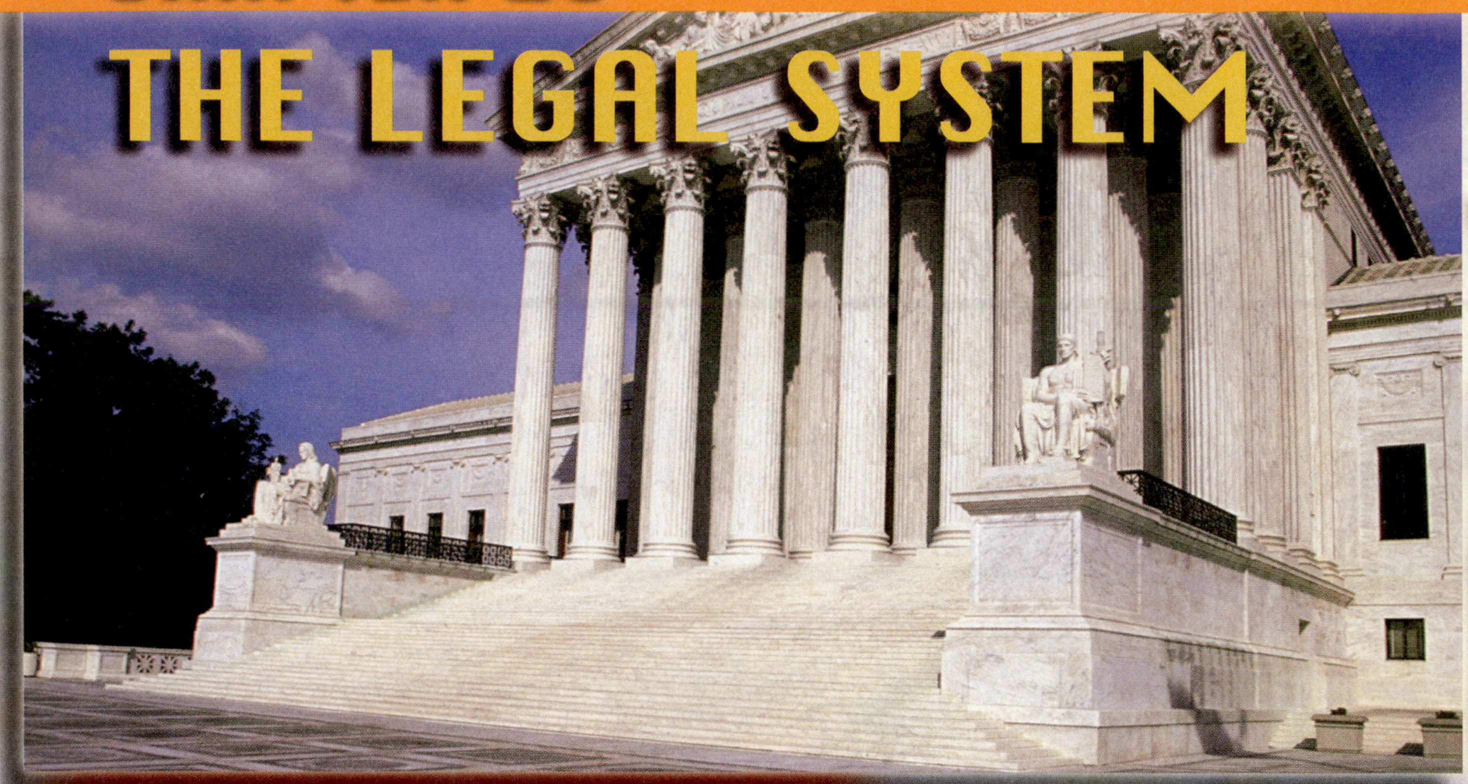

LESSONS

PREVIEW

Law is concerned with many everyday matters. Understanding laws and the court system is an important part of informed citizenship. It is also necessary to know how to find legal help. It is good to learn this before needing such services.

THOUGHTS ON WORK

"The marvelous richness of human experience would lose something of rewarding joy if there were no limitations to overcome. The hilltop hour would not be half so wonderful if there were no dark valleys to traverse."
Helen Keller

TAKING ACTION
EVERYDAY LAW

Janice Lee is very upset. Several months ago, she took her car to a local auto repair shop to have the clutch checked. It had been slipping quite a bit.

The manager, Mr. Jacobs, called her that afternoon and said that the clutch would need to be replaced. The new clutch cost Janice $450. It was the first big expense she had had on her car, which she had bought used and which was now 12 years old. Janice did not mind very much. The car ran well and had never caused her any trouble.

Soon after Janice got her car back, the clutch began slipping again. She called Mr. Jacobs and took the car back to the shop. Mr. Jacobs said that the clutch pedal was out of alignment. When Janice expressed surprise that the pedal had gone out of alignment that quickly, Mr. Jacobs asked if Janice had very much experience driving a car with a manual transmission. He suggested her driving habits might be responsible.

When the clutch began slipping a third time, Janice took her car to another mechanic whom a friend had recommended. The mechanic told her that the new clutch had been improperly installed. He said that it was already showing signs of wear and would probably need to be replaced in a few years. Janice knew that clutches usually last many years.

Janice went home and wrote a letter to Mr. Jacobs. She explained what the other mechanic had said and requested that the shop reimburse her for the new clutch, the adjustment, and the other mechanic's inspection.

Mr. Jacobs did not reply to Janice's letter. She wrote several more letters, which also received no response. Then Janice contacted the Better Business Bureau, but Mr. Jacobs's shop was not a member of the Bureau, and he refused to cooperate in resolving the dispute.

Now a coworker has suggested that Janice get a lawyer. Since Janice does not know any lawyers, she looks in the Yellow Pages. She calls three lawyers. They all recommend that Janice take Mr. Jacobs to small claims court.

Janice has heard of small claims court, but she does not know much about it. She decides that she will find out, though. Janice believes that she is in the right. She wants her money refunded.

SUCCESS TIP

Understanding the law and the legal system can help you in your everyday life.

THINK CRITICALLY

1. What are some ways that Janice might prove that she is in the right?
2. What do you know about small claims court?

LESSON 28.1
THE NATURE OF LAW

OBJECTIVES

- EXPLAIN THE DIFFERENCE BETWEEN CIVIL AND PUBLIC LAW
- DESCRIBE THE GENERAL PROCESS BY WHICH LAWS ARE ENFORCED

CIVIL AND PUBLIC LAW

Hopefully, you will never become involved with the legal system because of lawbreaking. Even if you never break the law, though, you might sometime be accused of a crime that you did not commit. Or you may become an innocent victim of crime.

Not all law deals with crime. For example, Terry and Susan adopted a baby. To finalize the adoption, they had to hire a lawyer and appear before a judge in a court of law.

Law is the body of enforced rules by which people live together. If all people did as they pleased, society could not function. For example, what would happen if everyone drove an auto as fast as they wanted or an employer decided to ignore safety rules? The law defines and makes clear the relationships among individuals and between individuals and society. Law tries to give as much freedom to each person as possible, while protecting the freedom of others.

There are two main sources of law in the United States. In deciding a case, a judge will often look at how similar cases in the past were decided. These decisions made by judges are known as **common law**. The second source of law is **statute law**, or legislation. This refers to laws made by Congress and other government bodies.

The two main branches of law are civil and public.

- ***Civil law.*** Sometimes called private law, civil law determines a person's legal rights and obligations in activities that involve other people. Examples include making credit purchases, renting an apartment, and signing a job contract. Judges and lawyers spend most of their time on civil matters. Most civil law cases are settled out of court. Even so, more than a million lawsuits are tried yearly in U.S. courts.
- ***Public law.*** Public law defines citizens' rights and responsibilities under local, state, federal, and international laws. Criminal law is the most familiar kind of public law. Public law also deals with different divisions of government and their powers. An example of public law is the requirement that all cars have seat belts. Workers' wages and hours and public safety also come under public law.

WORKFORCE TRENDS

Demand for higher-skilled employees is a 50-year trend. Strength and manual dexterity used to ensure employment and a comfortable standard of living. More jobs now and in the future will require verbal, mathematical, organizational, and interpersonal skills. Emerging technologies, globalization, and the information revolution are also increasing demand for high-tech skills.

LAW ENFORCEMENT

Most of us obey laws. But what about people who do not? The police may arrest anyone they see violating the law. They may also arrest someone they reasonably believe has committed a crime. In some cases, a **warrant** is required. A warrant is a court order that authorizes a police officer to make a search, seizure, or arrest.

After the suspect has been arrested, a charge is entered in the arrest book. The criminal evidence is turned over to a government attorney, or prosecutor. An **arraignment** is then held before a judge. This is a hearing in which a prosecutor, police officer, or citizen brings charges against the arrested person. For more serious crimes, the prosecutor usually presents the evidence to a **grand jury** instead. A grand jury is a group of citizens selected to determine if there should be a trial. If the grand jury decides in favor of a trial, it prepares a formal statement charging the person with the offense. This is called an **indictment**.

The person being held can answer the charges. If the individual pleads guilty, the judge gives a sentence or sets a future date for sentencing. If the accused pleads not guilty, a trial must be held. Rather than remain in jail until the trial, an individual is usually released on **bail**. This is money deposited with the court to guarantee that the person will show up for trial. If the person does not, the bail is forfeited. For certain serious crimes, someone may be held without bail. A person without bail remains in jail until the trial. If he or she cannot afford an attorney, the judge ensures that one is provided.

The purpose of a trial is to determine the guilt or innocence of the accused. Attorneys for both sides present their evidence. A decision of guilty or not guilty is then made, usually by a jury. If the defendant is found guilty, the judge imposes a sentence.

Criminal laws generally specify the minimum and maximum prison terms for which a criminal can be sentenced. Not everyone goes to jail, however. In certain cases, the judge may decide to release a person on **probation** instead. In such instances, the person must report regularly to a parole officer. For some crimes, the judge may impose a fine as part of the sentencing.

PERSONAL DECISIONS

You go to answer the door. You open it and are surprised to find a police officer. It seems that a car like yours was seen last night leaving the scene of a gas station holdup. The officer wants you to come to the station to answer some questions.

WHAT WOULD YOU DO?

Any law enforcement officer, such as a police officer, sheriff, state trooper, or game warden, can make an arrest. What if a law enforcement officer wants to arrest you? Do not physically resist. Your guilt or innocence can be determined later. If the arrest is legal and you resist, you may be guilty of the crime of resisting arrest.

Even if you are not arrested, an officer may stop you if he or she has reason to believe that you have committed or are about to commit a crime. The officer may ask for your name and address and for an explanation for your actions. You may be searched for weapons if the officer is fearful for his or her safety.

LESSON 28.1 REVIEW

1. Why do we have laws?
2. Name the two main branches of law. List one area each covers.
3. What happens if a person is arrested and cannot afford to hire an attorney?
4. If you are stopped by a police officer and arrested for a crime you did not commit, how should you act?

LESSON 28.2
THE COURT SYSTEM

OBJECTIVES

- DESCRIBE THE TWO PARTS OF THE COURT SYSTEM
- SUMMARIZE HOW A COURT WORKS

STATE AND FEDERAL COURTS

The court system is the branch of government having the power to settle disputes. Courts are an essential part of government. Without courts to interpret them, laws would be meaningless. Although they differ in some ways, most courts decide civil disputes between individuals or other parties, determine the guilt or innocence of accused persons, and impose punishment on the guilty. The court system has two parts: state and federal.

State courts. Each state has its own court system (Figure 28-1). The lowest or first courts are the police or magistrates' courts in cities and the justices of the peace in villages and rural communities. There may also be various special and municipal courts. Above the magistrates' courts are general trial courts. These courts, also known as county or circuit courts, deal with civil and public law matters.

Many states have an intermediate appellate court, which is between the general trial courts and the state supreme court. Appellate courts hear appeals from the trial courts. The highest appellate court in a state is usually called a supreme court. Several judges (usually five to seven) sit on a state supreme court.

Federal courts. The United States Constitution provides for a federal court system. Federal courts handle cases involving the Constitution, violations of federal laws, suits between citizens of different states, and cases in which the U.S. government is a party.

The lowest courts of the federal system are the U.S. district courts. The trial of both civil and public cases begins in the district courts. The manner of arrest, indictment, trial, and appeal is very similar to that of state courts.

Above the trial level are the circuit courts of appeal. These courts operate about the same way as state appellate courts. Each appeal is heard by a panel of three judges.

The highest federal court is the Supreme Court of the United States. This court is made up of nine justices, or judges. It is presided over by one of them, who is called the Chief Justice of the United States. Most cases the Supreme Court

PERSONAL DECISIONS

In sorting through the day's mail, you find a postcard that says you have been chosen for jury duty. You are instructed to appear at the courthouse next Wednesday at 9 a.m. for possible jury selection. "I cannot go," you think to yourself. "I have to work."

WHAT WOULD YOU DO?

hears are appeals from the circuit courts and appeals from state supreme courts if they present questions of federal or constitutional law.

HOW A COURT WORKS

Disputes may arise between two or more persons over money, personal injury, property, or many other issues. To better understand how a court works, let's outline a typical civil case. One person (the **plaintiff**) files a complaint against the other (the **defendant**) in a court. The court clerk then issues a **summons**, an order that commands the defendant to appear in court on a certain day.

The defendant must then submit a written report that tells his or her side of the story. By comparing the two sides, the court can see where the difference of opinion lies. If grounds for a suit are present, the judge sets a trial date.

When the trial is held, attorneys for the plaintiff and defendant produce evidence to try to show the truth in the case. Part of the evidence may be supplied by other persons (witnesses). The judge, or the jury if there is one, decides factual disputes and then reaches a verdict.

When the case is decided, the judge will make a **judgment**, a decision in favor of either the plaintiff or the defendant. ("Guilty" and "not guilty" are not used in civil cases.) If the case is decided in favor of the plaintiff, the judgment will depend on the nature of the original complaint. One type of judgment is the award of a sum of money to the plaintiff. Another is a solution for the dispute, such as cancellation of a contract. A third type of judgment is for the court to issue a **decree** (an order) requiring the defendant to stop doing whatever he or she was doing that harmed the plaintiff.

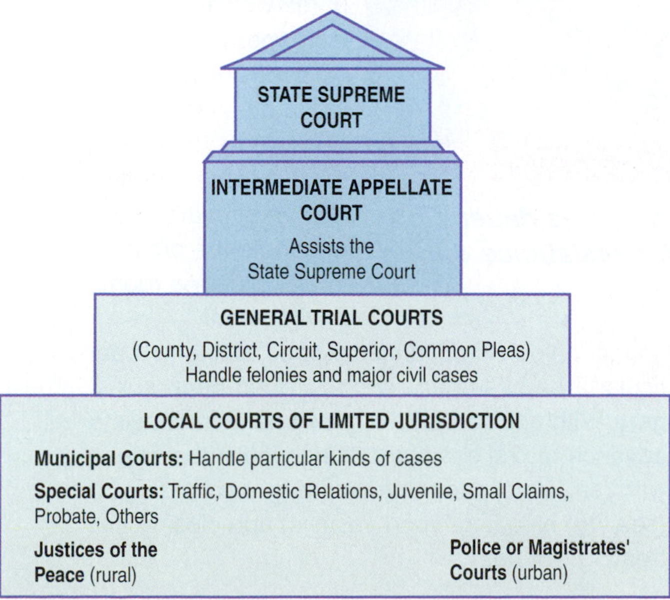

Figure 28-1 ***Although court systems vary from state to state, this pattern is typical.***

NOTHING BUT NET

Using the Internet for e-mail and online chatting has resulted in the evolution of a new type of communication shorthand called emoticons. This involves use of standard punctuation marks to express or emphasize an emotion. The emoticon for happiness, for example, is :-) The "smiley" is made by keying a colon, a hyphen, and a closing parenthesis. Can you guess what :-D or :'-(or :-0 means? To learn more about emoticons, use a search engine.

LESSON 28.2 REVIEW

1. What are the three basic things that most courts do?
2. What is the name of the highest federal court in the United States? Who presides over it?
3. In a court case, whom does the prosecuting attorney represent? Whom does the defense attorney represent?

HIGH-GROWTH OCCUPATIONS
FOR THE 21st CENTURY

Surgical Technologists

Surgical technologists, also called *surgical* or *operating room technicians*, assist in operations under the supervision of surgeons, registered nurses, or other surgical personnel. Before an operation, surgical technologists help set up the operating room with surgical instruments and equipment, sterile (germ-free) linens, and sterile solutions. They assemble, adjust, and check equipment to ensure it is working properly.

Technologists prepare patients for surgery by washing, shaving, and disinfecting incision sites. They transport patients to the operating room, help position them on the operating table, and cover them with sterile surgical cloths, or drapes. Technologists also observe patients' vital signs, check charts, and help the surgical team scrub and put on gloves, gowns, and masks.

During surgery, technologists pass instruments and other sterile supplies to surgeons and surgeon assistants. They may hold retractors (surgical instruments for holding open the edges of a wound); cut sutures (stitches); and help count sponges, needles, supplies, and instruments. Surgical technologists help prepare, care for, and dispose of specimens taken for laboratory analysis and help apply dressings. Some technologists operate sterilizers, lights, or suction machines and help operate diagnostic equipment. They may also maintain supplies of fluids, such as plasma and blood. After an operation, surgical technologists may help transfer patients to the recovery room and clean and restock the operating room.

Surgeons and registered nurses depend on surgical technologists for assistance during an operation.

Most surgical technologists are employed by hospitals, mainly in operating and delivery rooms. Technologists need manual dexterity to handle instruments skillfully. They must respond quickly to needs and know procedures well to have instruments ready for surgeons without having to be asked. Surgical technologists must also be orderly and emotionally stable to handle the pressure of an operating room environment.

Technologists advance by specializing in a particular area of surgery, such as open-heart surgery. With additional training, some technologists advance to first assistant. These individuals help with retracting, sponging, suturing, cauterizing (sealing) bleeding blood vessels, and closing and treating wounds.

LESSON 28.3

LEGAL SERVICES

- IDENTIFY SITUATIONS THAT MAY REQUIRE LEGAL ADVICE
- EXPLAIN HOW TO GO ABOUT CHOOSING A LAWYER
- NAME THE THREE TYPES OF LEGAL FEES

DECIDING IF YOU NEED A LAWYER

During your lifetime, you will probably face many legal problems. You may be able to resolve some of them yourself. If you cannot, you will need an attorney.

Whether or not you need a lawyer depends on your situation. The following are some types of situations that may require legal advice:

- Being charged with a crime
- Buying a house
- Starting a business
- Suffering an accident or injury
- Buying a faulty consumer product or service
- Being discriminated against in employment
- Preparing a will
- Declaring bankruptcy
- Getting a divorce

A lawyer is not absolutely necessary in all these cases. The more you learn about the law and legal services, the better able you will be to decide whether you need a lawyer.

Small claims courts, sometimes called people's courts, have been around since 1913. They allow you to sue someone without using an attorney. For example, let's say that you worked two days for Ms. Adams, a local businessperson, and she refuses to pay you. To get your money, you could file a claim in small claims court.

The amount of money that can be recovered in small claims court varies among states. Usually, though, the amount is limited to several thousand dollars. You cannot generally sue for lost time, nor can you sue for hurt pride, and you cannot collect damages beyond your loss.

A small claims court is usually part of the general trial court system in a county or city. To learn more about the court in your area, call the office of the county or city government.

CHOOSING A LAWYER

Lawyers, like doctors, are in either a general or a specialized practice. Most lawyers are general practitioners who handle a variety of legal work. For most situations, a general attorney will be adequate. General lawyers who cannot handle a particular problem will usually refer clients to a specialist.

Choosing a lawyer is similar to selecting a doctor, banker, or other professional. Ask enough people and the same name may come up repeatedly. This is a good sign that you are on the right track.

The Lawyer Referral Service (LRS) was established in 1937 to help people obtain legal assistance at moderate costs. In more than 250 U.S. cities, the LRS is administered through the state or local bar association. You can contact the LRS by looking in the Yellow Pages under "Lawyer (or Attorney) Referral Service" or on the Web at http://www.abanet.org/referral/home.html.

Another way to choose a lawyer is through advertising. In recent years, lawyers have been able to advertise their services, although few do so. If you read or hear an ad that you like, give the attorney a try. Many attorneys provide a free initial consultation. Before deciding on an attorney, it may be wise to meet with several different ones.

If you cannot afford a lawyer, you have several options. In a criminal case, the court will ensure that a lawyer is provided for you. For civil cases, there are more than 800 free legal services and defender programs in the United States. You can find such agencies by looking up "Legal Aid" or "Legal Assistance" in the phone book. Another source is the *Directory of Legal Aid and Defender Offices*, which is available in many libraries.

LEGAL FEES

The fees lawyers charge vary depending on the type of situation you have. Do not be afraid to ask about fees at your first meeting. You are entitled to know in advance the approximate cost of legal services.

Lawyers may charge a flat fee, an hourly fee, or a contingency fee. A flat fee often covers routine services that take about the same amount of time in all instances. Examples might be a real estate closing or an uncontested divorce. An hourly fee is a specific amount paid for each hour the lawyer spends on your case. Rates may range from about $100 to several hundred dollars per hour.

The contingency fee is used for certain kinds of cases, such as personal injury or medical malpractice. It is called a contingency fee because whether you pay is contingent, or depends, upon whether the case is won. If the attorney does win, you must pay a certain percentage of the amount awarded. A one-third contingency fee is common. For example, if you receive $15,000 in a legal judgment, the attorney will receive $5,000.

ON-THE-JOB ACCIDENTS
CONSTRUCTION ACCIDENTS
CRAIG G. BOWAN
NO CHARGE FOR CONSULTATION
555-0106
723 MULTRIE AVE., ALBANY

MOTORCYCLE INJURIES
FREE CONSULTATION
555-0199
SANDRA J. MELENDEZ
723 MULTRIE AVE.
ALBANY, NY

Figure 28-2 ***More and more lawyers now advertise their services.***

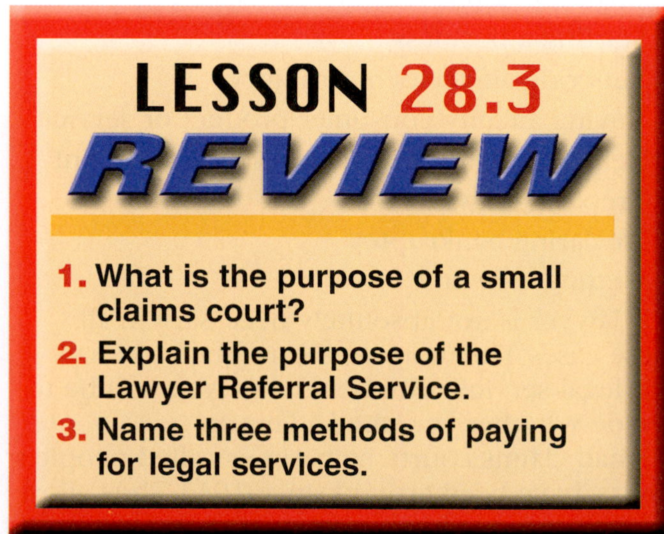

LESSON 28.3
REVIEW
1. What is the purpose of a small claims court?
2. Explain the purpose of the Lawyer Referral Service.
3. Name three methods of paying for legal services.

FOCUS ON SKILLS FOR LIVING

COMMON LAW

The system of law used in the United States is called common law, except in Louisiana where the Code Napoleon is followed. Common law originated in England as a way of settling disputes.

The law at first was based on customs. That changed in the twelfth century, when the king's courts began to take over the settlement of disputes from the local customary courts. The decisions of the king's justices were supposed to be based on customs. On occasion, there were no customs. The courts then had to reach a decision based upon logic and reason. As a result, a body of common law grew up from the judges' decisions.

Common law originated in England.

The early colonists who settled in America brought with them the practices of common law. After the American Revolution, the tradition of English common law continued. Over the years, American judges gradually changed the common law to make it more suitable for our society.

As new conditions arose, common law often did not apply. A new source for law emerged. This was statute law, or legislation. Statute law is that type of law made by Congress and state legislatures. In present-day society, legislation and judge-made law are equally important.

THINK CRITICALLY

1. In Chapter 27, you read about workers' compensation. As the United States became more industrialized, an increasing number of workers sued employers for work-related injuries or diseases. This was their right under common law. Soon lawsuits bogged down the court system. Partly to address this problem, workers' compensation laws were written. Why was legislation rather than common law the solution to this problem?
2. Some people believe that there are too many laws in the United States, that they harm business and interfere in people's private lives. Do you agree? Why or why not?

CHAPTER 28

Chapter in Brief

Lesson 28.1 *The Nature of Law*

A. Law is the body of enforced rules by which people live together. The law defines and makes clear the relationships among individuals and between individuals and society. The two main branches of law are civil and public.

B. The police may arrest anyone they see violating the law or reasonably believe has committed a crime. At an arraignment or before a grand jury, charges are brought against the person. If the accused pleads not guilty, a trial is held. If he or she is found guilty, the judge imposes a sentence.

C. If a law enforcement officer wants to arrest or search you, do not physically resist. Your guilt or innocence can be determined later.

Lesson 28.2 *The Court System*

A. The court system is the branch of government having the power to settle disputes. Most courts decide civil disputes between individuals or other parties, determine the guilt or innocence of accused persons, and impose punishment on the guilty. The court system has two parts: state and federal.

B. In a typical civil case, the plantiff files a complaint and a summons is issued for the defendant to appear in court. The defendant submits a written report of his or her side of the story. If there are grounds for a suit, the judge sets a trial date. Attorneys present evidence, the judge or jury reaches a verdict, and the judge makes a judgment for one party.

Lesson 28.3 *Legal Services*

A. During your lifetime, you will probably face many legal problems. If you cannot resolve a legal problem yourself, you will need a lawyer.

B. Small claims courts allow you to sue someone without using an attorney.

C. Choosing a lawyer is similar to selecting other professionals. The Lawyer Referral Service helps people get legal assistance at moderate costs.

D. Lawyers may charge a flat, hourly, or contingency fee, depending on the type of situation. Ask about fees at your first meeting.

Activities

1. The United States Supreme Court has a very important role in our society. With the help of your teacher, identify a recent Supreme Court decision. Investigate this decision and give a short oral report to the class.
2. As a class, invite a department store manager to talk about the problem of shoplifting and how a shoplifter is dealt with.
3. Invite a member of SADD (Students Against Drunk Driving) to class. Talk with him or her about the legal issues surrounding drunk driving.

REVIEW

4. Contact the clerk's office of the nearest small claims court and get a copy of any written guidelines and forms on how to file a complaint. Discuss in class the types of situations that may be taken to small claims court.

Word Power

On a separate sheet of paper, match each definition with the correct term. All definitions will be used, and a definition will be used only once.

5. A main source of law in the United States; judge-made law
6. A court order authorizing a police officer to make a search, seizure, or arrest
7. Releasing a convicted person under supervision and upon specified conditions
8. A hearing before a judge during which formal charges are brought against an arrested person
9. The complaining party in a lawsuit
10. The formal statement of a grand jury charging a person with an offense
11. The judge's decision in a civil suit in favor of either the plaintiff or the defendant
12. Money deposited with a court to guarantee that an accused person will show up for trial
13. The body of enforced rules by which people live together
14. An order commanding a party or a witness to a lawsuit to appear in court on a certain day
15. A person required to answer charges in a lawsuit
16. An order issued by a court; for example, requiring a defendant to stop doing whatever is harming the plaintiff
17. Legislation; laws made by Congress and other government bodies
18. A group of citizens to which a prosecutor presents evidence of a serious crime who must determine if there should be a trial

a. arraignment
b. bail
c. common law
d. decree
e. defendant
f. grand jury
g. indictment
h. judgment
i. law
j. plaintiff
k. probation
l. statute law
m. summons
n. warrant

Think Critically

19. How might you be influenced in the future by having a criminal record?
20. What is white-collar crime? Should white-collar criminals be treated differently than other criminals? Why or why not?
21. In what types of legal situations would you probably need a specialized lawyer, as opposed to a general lawyer?
22. The United States is said to be a "litigious-intensive society," meaning we have a tendency as a people to file too many lawsuits. Do you agree? Why or why not?

CHAPTER 29

WHERE TO LIVE

LESSONS

29.1 *Planning for Housing*

29.2 *Apartment Living*

PREVIEW

At some point in your life, you will probably leave your parents' home. When that time comes, deciding where to live will become important to you. The choice is a difficult one that involves both personal and financial considerations. Young people who have never before lived away from home may not know what is involved in renting or buying their own place. They may also underestimate the total cost of a house or an apartment.

THOUGHTS ON WORK

"You gain strength, experience, and confidence by every experience where you really stop to look fear in the face. . . . You must do the thing you cannot do."

Eleanor Roosevelt

TAKING ACTION

A FIRST APARTMENT

Jack's life is changing very rapidly. In a few weeks, he will graduate from high school. He has accepted a job as a mechanic at Porter Tire and Auto. Although he does not mind living at home, he would like a place of his own.

Jack and his brother have shared a room since Jack was five years old. So when Jack thinks about an apartment, he thinks it would be great to have it all to himself. He knows, though, that apartment living is less expensive if you have a roommate.

Jack has noticed an apartment complex near his job. He calls to find out how much it would cost to rent a one-bedroom and a two-bedroom apartment. The one-bedroom apartment would be too expensive, but he could afford the two-bedroom apartment with a roommate.

Jack talks to his best friend, Mike, about renting an apartment together. Jack and Mike have been friends for years. Mike does not have a job yet, though, so he is not planning to look for an apartment for some time.

Then Jack thinks about furnishing an apartment. His parents would let him take his bed, dresser, and desk, but he does not have any other furniture. Maybe his Aunt Lorraine has some pieces he could borrow. He calls her.

"I have a kitchen table and chairs, an armchair, and an old sofa that you can take and keep," his aunt tells him.

Then she describes some of her experiences in renting apartments. One apartment manager had told her that an air conditioner would be installed in an apartment she was planning to rent. When his aunt moved in, there was no air conditioner. She asked the manager about it. The manager replied that air conditioners were not in the rental agreement and refused to install one.

Jack thinks some more about renting an apartment. He is not so sure it is a good idea. He might continue to live with his parents and save his money for a while.

SUCCESS TIP

Think carefully about your housing options.

THINK CRITICALLY

1. What are some things to consider when deciding whether to rent an apartment?
2. What steps should you take to find and rent an apartment?

LESSON 29.1
PLANNING FOR HOUSING

- IDENTIFY HOUSING ALTERNATIVES
- DISCUSS ADVANTAGES AND DISADVANTAGES OF RENTING AND BUYING

CHOOSING A TYPE OF HOUSING

If you decide to get a place of your own, housing will probably be the largest single expense in your budget. In many areas, rents and home prices are high and costs continue to increase. But cost is not the only problem. Many desirable communities have housing shortages.

Since housing is such a major expense, plan carefully. Begin by analyzing your needs and wants. Based on what you learn, you can then decide whether buying or renting is best for you.

Housing Needs and Wants

The perfect place to live may not be available or affordable. So it may be necessary to make some compromises that suit you and your budget. Nonetheless, it will be important to consider needs and wants in a place to live. Identify your needs and wants *before* you start looking. (Review the difference between needs and wants on page 316.)

It is a good idea to make a list of the features you think are essential or important in a place to live. That way you will not be attracted by some eye-catching feature that you do not really need or want. Know the difference between *essential* and *important*.

Rosanna is looking for an apartment. She does not want a long commute to work. For Rosanna, being near her office is essential. She also thinks having a garage is important. But if she found a place near the office that did not have a garage, Rosanna would probably rent it anyway.

Individuals and families differ greatly in how they feel about housing. For some people, a house or apartment is simply a place to stay. For others, their lifestyles, hobbies, and goals revolve around their home.

INTERPERSONAL DECISIONS

You want to get an apartment closer to work but have not located anything you can afford. You get a call one evening from a person who works at an office near yours. She heard from a mutual acquaintance that you were looking for an apartment. The caller's roommate has left and she is looking for someone to move in and share expenses. You write down the information and indicate that you will think it over. You are uneasy about the idea of sharing an apartment with someone you do not know.

WHAT WOULD YOU DO?

YOU'RE A WHAT? TECHNOLOGY RECYCLER

Many people have an old computer, VCR, television, or other piece of electronic equipment stored in the garage or attic because they don't know where to get rid of it. Individuals and companies called *technology recyclers* are stepping in to help dispose of technology trash. In addition to representing a huge volume of trash, millions of pieces of electronic equipment contain dangerous pollutants such as lead, mercury, and CFCs.

Equipment is disassembled and disposed of in several ways. Some parts such as computer hard drives are erased and recycled. Valuable metals like silver and copper are salvaged and sold. Toxic chemicals have to be carefully extracted and disposed of in accordance with state and federal laws. Finally, plastic cases and similar parts are ground into pellets and used in road construction or in the manufacture of new consumer products. ■

Housing Alternatives

Different types of housing are available. One alternative is the single-family detached house. This kind of house usually offers more space, a larger yard, and more privacy than other types of housing. Also, many people consider a house the most convenient and desirable place to raise children. A detached house is often the most expensive type of housing. Attached houses, also called **townhouses**, are common in some communities. This kind of housing often includes a small yard. The houses may share common properties such as a pool, tennis courts, and other extras.

Housing is also available in apartments. These may range in size from one room to many rooms. An apartment usually does not include a yard. A townhouse or apartment may be a **cooperative** (part of a property jointly owned by residents) or a **condominium** (an individually owned unit with shared ownership of common facilities, like the grounds).

Still another housing alternative is a mobile home. Mobile homes may have several rooms. They are usually located on small lots in mobile home parks in or near a city or a town.

RENT OR BUY?

To get the type of housing that you or your family needs and wants, should you rent or buy? Now that you have analyzed your needs and wants and considered the types of housing available, give some serious thought to this question.

Buying and renting have advantages and disadvantages. In deciding which is best for you, you will want to consider various factors. These include the number and ages of the people in

Townhouses are common in some communities.

Renting has many advantages.

your family, your financial situation, your lifestyle, and the housing alternatives available in your community. Remember that buying generally means making a down payment and then a mortgage payment every month for 15 to 30 years. A **mortgage** is a loan, typically for 30 years, obtained from a financial institution to buy housing.

Renting

Some advantages of renting are as follows:

- Rent is usually a fixed amount for the term of the **lease** (the rental agreement between a **tenant**, or renter, and a **landlord**, the owner or manager of the property). Renters face fewer unexpected costs.
- Renting only obligates you for the length of the lease. If you want to move, you can make other arrangements when the lease expires.
- Renters have limited responsibility. You are not responsible for taxes and repairs.
- Overall expenditures for renters are usually lower than those for buyers.
- If a job opportunity in another city comes along, it is easier to move if you are renting.
- When you are new to an area, renting gives you an opportunity to learn about the community. After you have been there a while, you may decide to move somewhere else.
- When future housing needs are uncertain, you can postpone a decision by renting.

Renting may involve different costs and responsibilities depending on what you rent. If you rent a detached house, you will probably have to pay not only the rent but also all the normal expenses for running a home. You are also likely to be responsible for maintenance and repairs. Likewise, if you rent a townhouse, you will probably have some maintenance and repair responsibilities.

If you rent an apartment, you will generally not be responsible for maintenance or repairs. They will be taken care of by the landlord. Also, if you do not want to buy furniture, you can find apartments where the major pieces are provided. Renting an apartment is often more economical than renting other types of housing or buying. For all these reasons, renting an apartment is probably the most common choice of young people who are living away from home for the first time.

Buying

Some of the advantages of buying a home are as follows:

- Spending money to buy a home is a fairly safe form of investment. Unlike most investments, a home can be used.
- During inflationary times, property values rise. If you have a mortgage, you will be paying it off with cheaper dollars.
- Owning your home saves money on income taxes through deductions for mortgage interest and real estate taxes.

WORKFORCE TRENDS

A recent American Management Association survey of midsized and larger businesses found that almost 36 percent of job applicants taking employer-administered tests lacked the math and reading skills necessary in the jobs for which they were applying. According to the report, the deficiency rate is due not to a "dumbing down" of the incoming workforce but to the higher literacy and math skills required in today's workplace.

COMMUNICATION AT WORK

DOING RESEARCH

The need to do research does not end when you finish school. You may need to shop for the best price for a computer part or compare printers to see which one your company should buy. A customer may ask you what kind of cap you recommend for his chimney. You may be looking for an apartment, deciding where to open a savings account, or choosing an IRA. You can do some of these things without research, but research will almost certainly result in a better recommendation or decision.

Like research for school, research for work might mean going to a library or using the Internet. But it might mean other things as well. Suppose you work for a landscaping company. Your boss might ask you to plant several different kinds of grasses and observe them over time to see how well each grows. Or suppose someone at the company knows a lot about different kinds of chimney caps. The best way to get the information you need would be to talk to this person.

Take notes as you do your research. Once you have finished, organize your information. Then examine it carefully. What conclusions can you draw?

- The **equity**, or money invested in a home above the amount owed on a mortgage, can be used as security for a loan.
- Home ownership can improve your credit rating.
- When you own your own home, you can decorate the way you wish. You may also make structural or landscaping alterations. These alterations sometimes increase the value of the property.

Buying involves different costs and levels of responsibility depending on what you buy. When you buy a house, you pay not only the mortgage but also all expenses for home operation, upkeep, and repairs. Maintenance and repair work are also your responsibility.

When you buy a cooperative or a condominium, you are sharing with others the responsibilities, obligations, and maintenance costs. Very often, cooperative and condominium owners form a homeowners' or maintenance association. Owners pay monthly fees to the association. The money is used to provide for maintenance and improvements to common properties such as grounds and tennis courts. A maintenance fee may add considerably to the cost of owning a cooperative or condominium.

Mobile homes are much less expensive to buy than houses. Mobile homes allow more people to enjoy the benefits of home ownership. However, mobile homes do not increase in value as much over time as houses, cooperatives, and condominiums generally do. Mobile homes may also be unsafe in storms and high winds.

LESSON 29.1 REVIEW

1. **What is the first step in deciding where to live? Why is this important?**
2. **What are the four major types of housing alternatives?**
3. **There are reasons for renting and buying housing. Name three of each.**

HIGH-GROWTH OCCUPATIONS FOR THE 21st CENTURY

Secondary School and Special Education Teachers

Teachers use interactive discussions and hands-on learning to help students learn and apply concepts in various subjects. *Secondary school teachers* help students delve more deeply into subjects introduced in elementary school. Secondary school teachers specialize in a specific subject, such as English, Spanish, mathematics, history, or biology.

Teachers design classroom presentations to meet student needs and abilities. They also work with students individually. Teachers plan, evaluate, and assign lessons; prepare, administer, and grade tests; listen to oral presentations; and maintain classroom discipline. They observe and evaluate a student's performance and potential. Teachers also grade papers, prepare report cards, and meet with parents and school staff to discuss a student's academic progress or personal problems.

Teachers may use films, slides, overhead projectors, and the latest technology in teaching, including computers, telecommunication systems, and video discs. Use of computer resources, such as educational software and the Internet, exposes students to a vast range of experiences and promotes interactive learning.

In addition to classroom activities, teachers oversee study halls and homerooms and supervise extracurricular activities. They identify physical or mental problems and refer students to the proper resource or agency for diagnosis and treatment. Teachers also participate in education conferences and workshops.

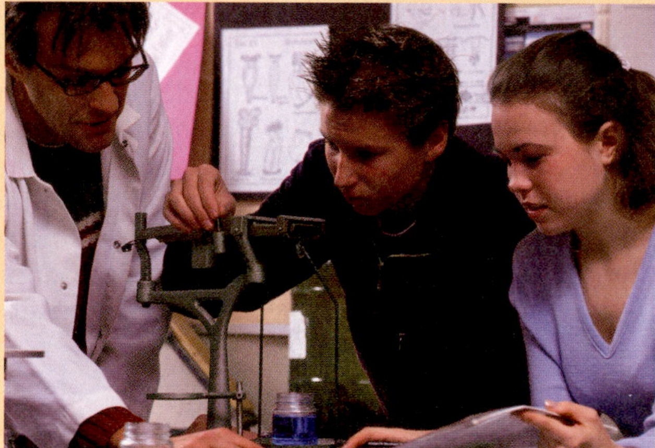

In secondary school, students have classes with teachers who specialize in one subject area, such as English or chemistry.

Special education teachers work with children and youths who have a variety of disabilities, including speech or language impairments; mental retardation; emotional disturbances; hearing, visual, or orthopedic impairments; autism; deafness and blindness; traumatic brain injury; multiple disabilities; and other health impairments. Special education teachers are prepared to work with specific groups.

Most special education teachers instruct students at the elementary, middle, and secondary school levels. Special education teachers design and modify instruction to meet a student's special needs. Teachers also work with students who have other special instructional needs, including the gifted and talented.

LESSON 29.2

APARTMENT LIVING

OBJECTIVES

- NAME AND DESCRIBE FACTORS TO CONSIDER IN APARTMENT HUNTING
- SUMMARIZE ITEMS INCLUDED IN AN APARTMENT LEASE
- EXPLAIN RIGHTS AND RESPONSIBILITIES OF A TENANT

APARTMENT HUNTING

Let's assume you have decided to rent an apartment. Available rental housing is often listed with a real estate agency or an apartment-finding business that charges fees for its services. More often, people find an apartment by checking the newspaper classified ads, searching the Web, following through on tips from friends or coworkers, or just walking or driving through a particular neighborhood. College students can often find an apartment through the school's housing office.

Things to Consider

Suppose you and a friend are looking for separate places at the same time. What you consider important in a rental may not be important to your friend. But both of you will need to be concerned about certain things.

Location. The neighborhood in which an apartment is located is important. However, the location is usually not as critical to a renter as it is to a homebuyer. Renters have no financial investment in the property. So their interest is limited more to convenience factors. Depending on the person, finding an apartment that is close to work or school, has nearby shopping, and is accessible to public transportation may be important.

Safety. Because of the nature of apartment living, you should pay careful attention to several things. The first one is safety. Well-lighted and uncluttered entrances, hallways, and stairways contribute to security. A locked outside entrance is another good feature. Apartment doors should be securely constructed and

> **PERSONAL DECISIONS**
>
> You come home from work to discover the landlord leaving your apartment. He seems surprised and says that he was checking on the furnace. Several times over the next month, you notice little things that suggest someone has been in the apartment. You are aware that the landlord has the right to enter your apartment for emergencies, maintenance, and the like. But you are upset by the thought that he may be in the apartment for other reasons.
>
> **WHAT WOULD YOU DO?**

should have deadbolts or other types of strong locks. Basement or first-floor apartments should have special window grilles or locking features in addition to regular window latches.

Another aspect of safety is fire protection. Each apartment should have one or more smoke detectors in good working order. The kitchen area ought to have a fire extinguisher available. (*Buy one yourself if it doesn't.*) Check to see if the apartment has an external fire-escape exit. If not, is there an evacuation plan to follow in case of fire?

Privacy and noise. Find out about the people who currently live in the building. If possible, meet and talk with some of the tenants. Remember that you may be sharing a relatively small area with dozens or even hundreds of other people.

Since apartment residents live closely together, noise can be a real problem. Noise can come either from outside streets and parking lots or from within other apartments. Buildings should be soundproofed to dampen the sounds of talking, plumbing, and music between apartments and between hallways and apartments. Noises from apartments above are usually more noticeable than sounds from apartments below.

Scott and Sandy Foster, for instance, have an upstairs neighbor who works from 3:30 to midnight. He usually wakes them up about 12:20 a.m. when he gets home and opens the apartment door. A few minutes later, he is heard taking a shower. Off and on throughout the night, Scott and Sandy are awakened by sounds of footsteps, closing doors, music, and so on. Their neighbor is not unusually loud or inconsiderate. He just happens to have a different lifestyle than they do. This is not an uncommon situation for apartment dwellers.

Ventilation. Can air enter easily? Most apartments that have air-conditioning are well ventilated. In places without this feature, cooking odors and stagnant air may be problems. Does the stove have an exhaust fan for ventilating the kitchen? Is the number of windows adequate, and do they all open easily? Besides permitting good air circulation, windows provide natural light that adds to the cheerfulness of a place.

For apartment residents, noise can be a problem.

Other considerations. Check appliances such as refrigerators, stoves, and dishwashers. Do they work well? Be sure you know who pays for utilities. Is the electricity your responsibility? How about heat? Can you give other examples? Ask for an estimate of typical costs for utilities and other services for which you will be responsible. Also notice how well the landlord keeps up the property. Does he or she keep the lawn cut, the hedges trimmed, and the hallways clean?

As you look through the apartment before renting, take notes on its condition. Include items such as chipped paint, marked-up walls, and worn or stained carpeting or other flooring. Check the bathroom and kitchen for water leaks and make sure all the drains work properly. Also, look inside all the closets and cabinets to see if there is any damage. If you are renting a furnished apartment, list each piece of furniture and write down a description of its condition. If possible, take pictures of anything that is not in good repair.

Write up an inventory from your notes. Go over it with your landlord, and make sure it is part of the rental agreement.

You probably have friends or relatives who live in apartments. If so, ask them to describe how they found their living quarters. Also, find out if they have any advice to share about what to look for.

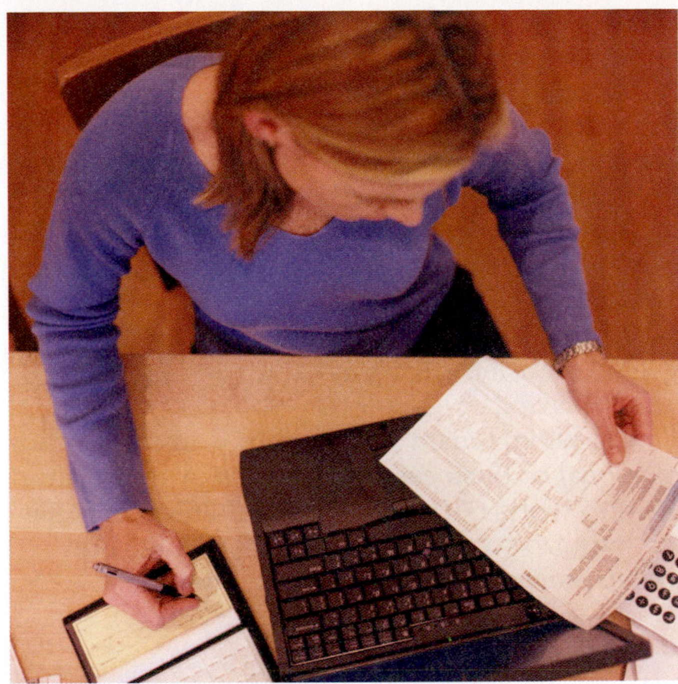

Be sure to consider all the expenses you will have in renting an apartment.

How to Approach a Landlord

Looking for a place to live is a great deal like getting a job. As with a potential employer, it is important to make a good impression on the landlord or apartment manager. Apply for an apartment in person. Be courteous and friendly.

Most landlords will ask you to fill out an application. The landlord is interested in checking your past rental record and credit references. Fill out the application form honestly and completely. Do not leave any blank spaces.

Some landlords will charge an application fee. Before you pay such a fee, ask if you will get it back. Also find out if you must rent the unit if your application is accepted. Be sure you know when you will be notified of the landlord's decision.

Find out whether you will be required to pay a security deposit. A **security deposit** is a sum of money, usually equal to one month's rent, which the landlord holds during the time you rent the apartment. It is intended to be used for any damage you cause. If the apartment is clean and in good condition at the time you leave it, your security deposit should be refunded.

THE RENTAL AGREEMENT

Most apartments are rented according to an agreement called a lease. This is a written legal contract between you and the landlord. For agreeing to pay rent and following the lease's rules, you are allowed to rent the apartment. The lease is often a preprinted form that contains most or all of the following parts and rules:

- The names of the landlord and tenant
- The address of the property
- The beginning and ending dates of occupancy
- The amount of rent and when and where it is to be paid for the term of the lease
- The amount of any security deposit
- Limits on the number of renters
- Any rules regarding pets
- Who is responsible for normal maintenance and repairs. The renter must pay for any damage caused by carelessness.
- Who is responsible for electricity, trash pick-up, and the like
- An attached inventory that describes the condition of the apartment and lists and describes the condition of any furnishings
- Sublease permission. Suppose you need to move before the lease is up. Can you rent out the apartment, or **sublet** it?

If you have a pet, make sure any rules regarding pets are listed in your lease.

- When the landlord can enter the apartment. The lease should explain such conditions.
- The procedures to be followed when the tenant wishes to end the lease. An automatic renewal clause may also be a part of the lease.

Any special arrangements between you and the landlord should be written into the lease. An example would be any repairs that the landlord agrees to make and a date when they will be completed.

Read the lease very carefully before signing it. When you put your name on a lease, you say that you understand and accept all conditions contained in it. Make sure you are provided with a signed copy of the agreement.

LANDLORD-TENANT RELATIONSHIPS

The relationship between you and a landlord is a legal one. Both of you have certain rights and responsibilities.

Rights and Responsibilities of Landlords

The landlord has the right to set reasonable rules and regulations for the management of the rental units. Unless you have agreed to repair or maintain the property, the landlord must keep it in reasonable repair. This means the landlord must keep the premises in a clean, safe condition.

Rights and Responsibilities of Tenants

Your rights as a tenant are essentially the reverse of the landlord's responsibilities. You pay rent for housing, and you expect to receive a safe and livable apartment. If something goes wrong, it should be repaired in a reasonable amount of time. You are entitled to peace, quiet, and privacy. You should not be cheated or overcharged.

On the other hand, you have the responsibility to follow the rules in the lease. These basically deal with paying the rent on time, keeping your area clean and safe, and not abusing the landlord's property or the rights of other tenants.

Beyond your responsibilities as a tenant, try to maintain a proper business relationship with the landlord. Report all problems as they occur. The landlord will appreciate knowing this information as soon as possible. In addition, have in writing all communication with the landlord, and make copies of everything. This will protect your rights. The landlord is used to dealing with people on a businesslike basis and will appreciate this behavior.

A landlord-tenant relationship is like any other personal or business association. For the relationship to work, both parties must fulfill their obligations. Do your part by understanding your obligations and then carrying them out.

LESSON 29.2 REVIEW

1. In what four ways do most people locate an apartment?
2. What two types of fire protection devices should you look for in an apartment?
3. Explain how renting an apartment is similar to getting a job.
4. What is the purpose of a security deposit? Do you think it is fair to require one?
5. What should be attached to a lease?
6. What is the landlord's basic responsibility? The tenant's basic responsibility?
7. In what way is the landlord-tenant relationship like any other personal or business association?

FOCUS ON SKILLS FOR LIVING

DEALING WITH A ROOMMATE

Most people have a roommate at one or more times in their lives. Living with a roommate is a business relationship because money is exchanged. But it is also an emotional relationship.

Before choosing or becoming a roommate, you should have a serious discussion with the other person. Items you will need to agree on in advance include housework and laundry, food and beverage supplies, overnight guests, the security deposit and how it will be refunded, pets (and who takes care of them), boyfriends or girlfriends, and stereos and musical instruments. Particularly important are the terms for moving out. It is a good idea to have a written agreement to give each other a 30- or 60-day notice.

Sharing an apartment can work if roommates communicate well.

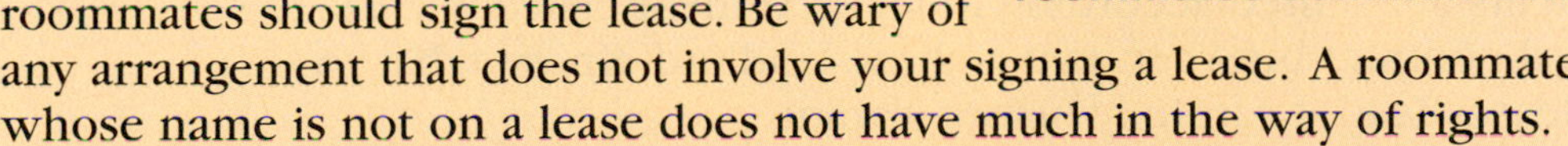

Unless the tenant is allowed to sublet, all roommates should sign the lease. Be wary of any arrangement that does not involve your signing a lease. A roommate whose name is not on a lease does not have much in the way of rights.

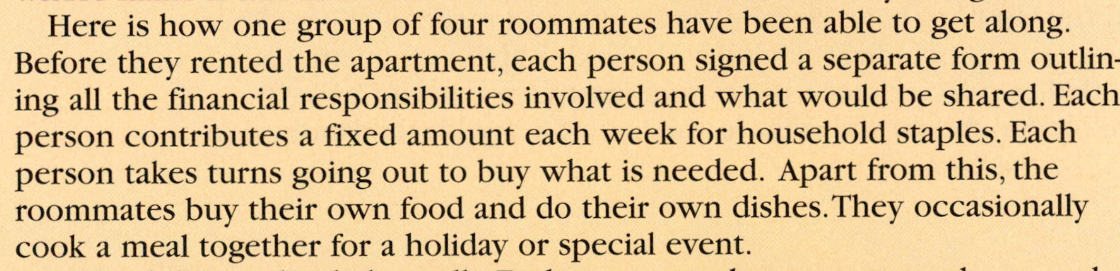

Here is how one group of four roommates have been able to get along. Before they rented the apartment, each person signed a separate form outlining all the financial responsibilities involved and what would be shared. Each person contributes a fixed amount each week for household staples. Each person takes turns going out to buy what is needed. Apart from this, the roommates buy their own food and do their own dishes. They occasionally cook a meal together for a holiday or special event.

Utility bills are divided equally. Each roommate has a separate phone, and no one answers anyone else's phone. Every two weeks, the group meets to discuss any problems.

Sharing living space can be difficult. But many roommate crises can be easily prevented or resolved. Set ground rules from the start. Discuss your feelings and expectations with your roommate. And always be willing to negotiate and compromise.

THINK CRITICALLY

1. What are some things that roommates should discuss before signing a lease?
2. What are some keys to living successfully with a roommate?

CHAPTER 29

Chapter in Brief

Lesson 29.1 *Planning for Housing*

A. At some point in your life, you will probably move from your parents' home. When that time comes, deciding where to live will become important to you. The choice is a difficult one that involves both personal and financial considerations.

B. Since housing is such a major expense, plan carefully. Begin by analyzing your needs and wants. It may be necessary to make compromises that suit you and your budget. Your housing alternatives may include a detached house, townhouse, apartment, or mobile home.

C. Buying and renting have advantages and disadvantages. Become familiar with these. Renting an apartment is probably the most common choice of young people who are living away from home for the first time.

Lesson 29.2 *Apartment Living*

A. When hunting for an apartment, you need to be concerned with certain things such as location (neighborhood and convenience factors), personal safety and fire protection, privacy and noise, ventilation, and furnishings. Looking for a place to live is a great deal like getting a job. It is important to make a good impression on the landlord or apartment manager.

B. Most apartments are rented according to an agreement called a lease. It is a written legal contract between you and the landlord. Know what to expect in a lease. Read it carefully before signing.

C. You and the landlord have certain legal rights and responsibilities. Your rights as a tenant include receiving a safe and livable apartment. You are also entitled to peace, quiet, privacy, and fair treatment. You have the responsibility to follow the rules in the lease. Deal with the landlord in a businesslike manner.

Activities

1. Assume you are going to move to a nearby town in a few months to begin a new job. A friend who works for the same company is also moving. The two of you decide to share a place to live. Prepare a list of what you need and want in housing. Turn the list in to your instructor. Then discuss this subject in class.
2. As a class, invite a landlord or apartment manager to visit and discuss landlord-tenant relationships. Prepare well. You may want to begin by asking the person what he or she looks for in someone who comes to rent an apartment.

REVIEW

3. Check local classified ads to find out the cost of renting in your area.
4. Find out if your state or city has a tenancy law, tenant ordinance, or housing code (not building code). What is the warranty of habitability? Can a tenant be evicted from an apartment? How may a tenant resolve complaints with a landlord?

Word Power

On a separate sheet of paper, match each definition with the correct term. All definitions will be used, and a definition will be used only once.

5. A townhouse or apartment that is part of a property jointly owned by residents
6. The owner or manager of a rental property
7. An individually owned townhouse or apartment with shared ownership of common facilities, like the grounds
8. Renter; the person who rents an apartment
9. A rental agreement between a tenant and a landlord
10. Individually owned houses that are attached to other houses on one or both sides
11. To lease a property as a tenant to another person
12. The value of (money invested in) a home above the amount owed on a mortgage
13. A loan, typically for 30 years, obtained from a financial institution to buy housing
14. A sum of money, usually equal to one month's rent, which a landlord holds while you rent an apartment

a. condominium
b. cooperative
c. equity
d. landlord
e. lease
f. mortgage
g. security deposit
h. sublet
i. tenant
j. townhouses

Think Critically

15. Sharing an apartment with others is a good way to economize on housing. However, living with roommates can be difficult at times. What do you think might be the most common problems with roommates? How can they be avoided?
16. Does your community have a neighborhood watch, neighborhood patrol, or other type of citizen-oriented crime prevention program? Discuss how such programs operate.
17. The price and availability of housing are often important factors in the decision to accept a first job or to relocate in another job. Discuss and provide illustrations of this.

CHAPTER 30
HEALTHFUL LIVING

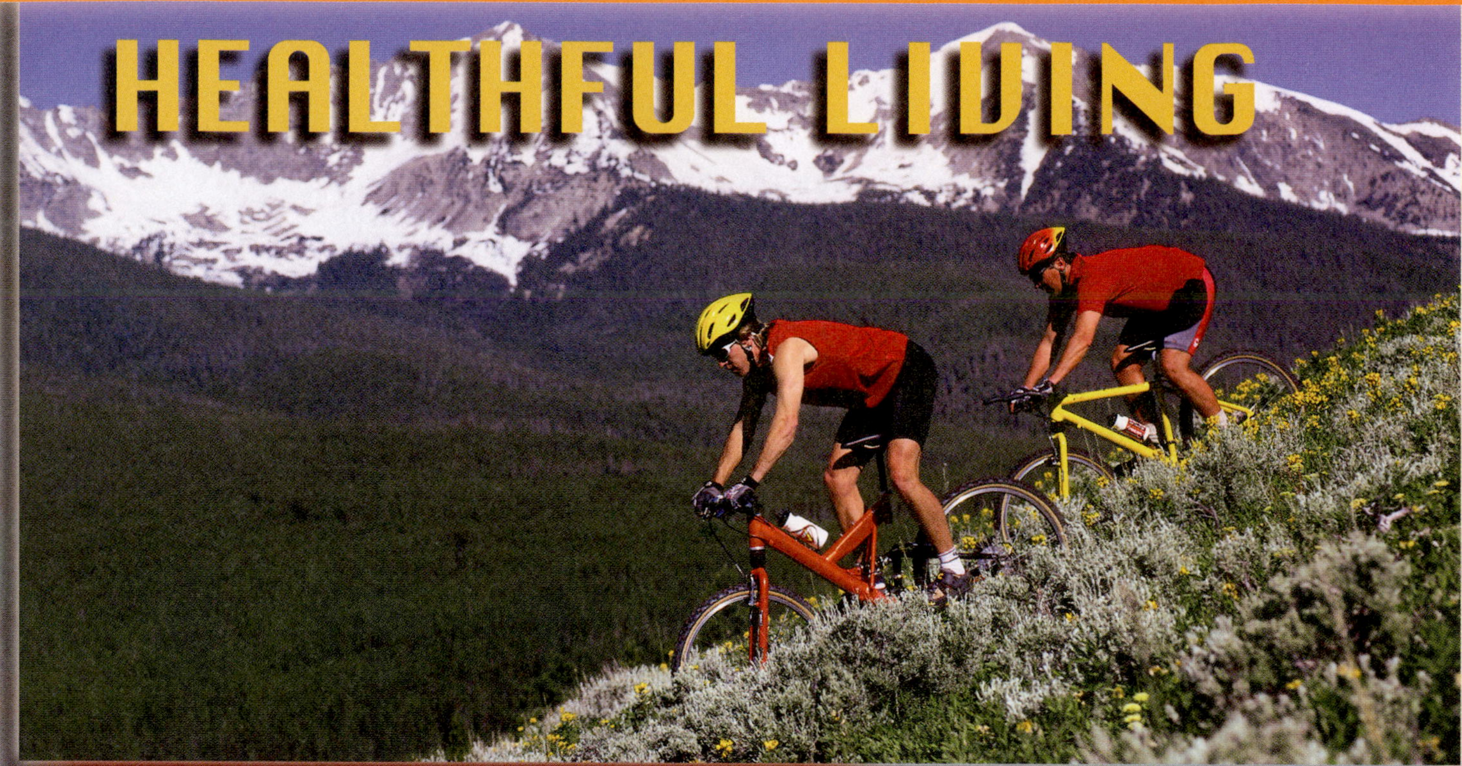

LESSONS

30.1 *Nutrition and Diet*

30.2 *Stress and Physical Fitness*

PREVIEW

Good health is essential for success as a student and worker. Eating right, exercising, and finding ways to manage stress will improve your health, appearance, and attitude. When life gets hectic, stress levels can rise. Taking good care of yourself can become a low priority. In this chapter, you will learn about the benefits of paying attention to your body and its health.

THOUGHTS ON WORK

"You learn to speak by speaking, to study by studying, to run by running, to work by working. . . . All those who think to learn in any other way deceive themselves."

Saint Francis de Sales

TAKING ACTION
EATING RIGHT

Janine and Manuela were roommates in their first apartment. As soon as they had unpacked all of their belongings, they realized they were hungry and there was no food in the kitchen.

The young women went to the local grocery store. They had never lived away from their parents before, so they decided to get all the junk food and snacks that they liked. The cart was soon filled with candy, chips, soft drinks, and other junk food.

Janine and Manuela enjoyed being able to eat whatever they wanted. They ate ice cream for dinner. They ate chips and salsa for lunch. They ate cookies for breakfast.

After about a week of eating this way, Janine sat down with Manuela one morning. She said, "You know, I do not feel very good. I think it's the food we're eating. I hate to say this, but I think I want a home-cooked meal with a big salad."

"You're right," Manuela replied. "Let's make a list."

The two young women got out a cookbook that Janine's mother had given them. They made a list of basic items that their kitchen should have. Janine and Manuela decided that they would each prepare a good dinner three times a week that they would share. They would eat out or cook for themselves the other night.

Manuela called her father and wrote down recipes for several of her favorite meals. Janine found some recipes in the cookbook that sounded great.

SUCCESS TIP

Tasty, healthy meals can be inexpensive and easy to prepare.

Janine and Manuela went to the grocery store again. On the way, they saw a lot of people in the community center parking lot. The center was hosting a tailgate market where local farmers could sell their produce. Janine and Manuela bought homegrown lettuce, carrots, sweet corn, and peppers. They bought tomatoes, Swiss chard, cantaloupe, and strawberries. Janine and Manuela found out that the tailgate market was held once a week. They decided to buy fresh vegetables and fruit there.

"It's my turn to cook tonight," said Janine on the way home. "How about stir-fried chicken and peppers with rice and a salad?"

THINK CRITICALLY

1. What would you buy at the grocery store if you could buy anything you wanted?
2. How does what you eat affect how you feel?

LESSON 30.1

NUTRITION AND DIET

OBJECTIVES

- DESCRIBE HOW THE FOOD GUIDE PYRAMID IS USED IN CHOOSING A HEALTHFUL DIET
- IDENTIFY YOUR OWN RECOMMENDED WEIGHT AND DAILY CALORIE NEEDS

EATING RIGHT

Sherri had not been feeling well for a long time. Her appetite was poor and she always seemed tired. She was spending a great deal of time in her room and had little interest in going out with her friends. She had frequent headaches. Sherri's parents became very concerned and took her to the doctor for a checkup.

After a complete exam and several tests, Dr. Williams sat down with Sherri to explain the results. "Well, Sherri," said the doctor, "I don't find any major problems. But I don't think you're in very good health."

The doctor's statement confused Sherri. Dr. Williams then explained to Sherri that being healthy means more than just being free from illness or disease. Good health involves a person's overall physical and mental well-being.

Dr. Williams told Sherri that achieving and maintaining good health depends on nutrition and diet, stress control, and exercise. In this chapter, you will read about what Sherri learned from her doctor. Good health is related to your success and productivity at school and on the job.

Nutrition is the process by which plants and animals take in and use food. What we eat provides certain chemical substances needed for good health. These substances, called **nutrients**, serve as fuel to provide energy, help regulate body processes, and furnish basic materials for building, repairing, and maintaining body tissues.

Nutrients are supplied by foods that people eat. Foods vary in the kinds and amount of nutrients they contain. Nutrition scientists have developed the easy-to-use daily food guide shown in Figure 30-1. The Food Guide Pyramid emphasizes foods from the five major food groups shown in the three lower levels. Each of these food groups provides some, but not all, of the nutrients you need. Foods in one group cannot replace those in another. No one food group is more important than another. You need them all for good health.

PERSONAL DECISIONS

It seems like you are always on a diet. You do not eat much, but still, you cannot lose weight. For instance, all that you have had today is a couple of donuts for breakfast and an order of french fries and a soft drink for lunch. You guess that you will just have to get used to dieting continually.

WHAT WOULD YOU DO?

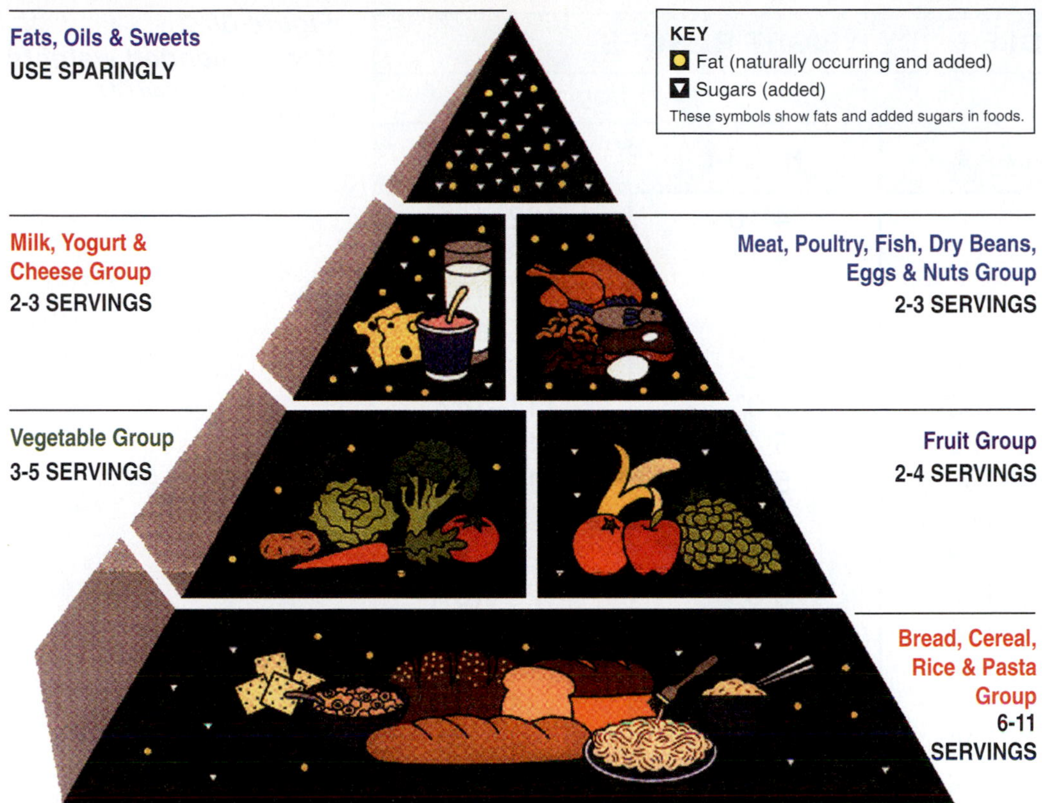

Figure 30-1 ***How closely does the food you eat daily follow this food guide?***
Source: U.S. Department of Agriculture and U.S. Department of Health and Human Services

At the base of the Pyramid are foods from grain. You need the most servings of these foods each day. The second level includes fruit and vegetables. Most people need to eat more of these foods for the vitamins, minerals, and fiber they supply. On the third level are two groups of foods that come mostly from animals. These foods are important because they provide protein, calcium, iron, and zinc.

The small tip of the Food Guide Pyramid shows fats, oils, and sweets. These are foods such as salad dressings and oils, cream, butter, margarine, sugars, soft drinks, candies, and sweet desserts. These foods provide calories and little else nutritionally. Most people should use them sparingly.

CALORIES AND WEIGHT

Calories are units of energy produced by food when it is used by the body. We need calories for continuous body functions such as breathing and heart rate and for work and leisure activities. How many calories you need depends on your age, your sex, your size, and how active you are. The National Academy of Sciences has suggested the following approximate calorie levels: 1,600 calories for many **sedentary** (inactive) women and some older adults; 2,200 calories for most children, teenage girls, active women, and many sedentary men; and 2,800 calories for teenage boys, many active men, and some very active women.

Now, let's look at the Food Guide Pyramid again. Note that a range of servings is shown for all food groups except Fats, Oils, & Sweets. For most food groups, the number of servings that is right for you depends on which of the above categories you belong to. For example, a child needs three servings from the vegetable group; a teenage girl, four servings; and a teenage boy, five servings.

When the foods you eat provide more energy than you need to meet the demands of the body, your body stores the extra energy as fat. If you regularly eat too much food, you gain weight. On the other hand, if your energy level requires more calories than you take in, your body uses stored fat. You then lose weight.

DESIRABLE BODY WEIGHT RANGES			
Men		Women	
Height	Weight	Height	Weight
		4′10″	102–131
		4′11″	103–134
		5′0″	104–137
		5′1″	106–140
5′2″	128–150	5′2″	108–143
5′3″	130–153	5′3″	111–147
5′4″	132–156	5′4″	114–151
5′5″	134–160	5′5″	117–155
5′6″	136–164	5′6″	120–159
5′7″	138–168	5′7″	123–163
5′8″	140–172	5′8″	126–167
5′9″	142–176	5′9″	129–170
5′10″	144–180	5′10″	132–173
5′11″	146–184	5′11″	135–176
6′0″	149–188	6′0″	138–179
6′1″	152–192		
6′2″	155–197		
6′3″	158–202		
6′4″	162–207		
Ages 25–59, with indoor clothing weighing 5 lb (men) or 3 lb (women) and shoes with 1″ heels			

Figure 30-2
Recommended weights
Source: Metropolitan Life Insurance Company

Ideal weight varies among individuals. You can get an idea of your desirable weight from the table shown in Figure 30-2. For example, if you are a 6-foot male, your ideal weight should be between 149 and 188 pounds. The range takes into account that there are small, average, and large body frames.

The number of calories used by the body each day to maintain weight is called the daily calorie need. Part of this is the minimum necessary for continuous body functioning and is called the **basal metabolism**. The remainder is used by the body as it carries out various work and leisure activities.

For good health, it is wise to maintain your recommended weight. Do this by controlling the amount and kinds of foods you eat (calories), your level of activity, or both. For you to maintain the same body weight, the amount of calories in the food you eat must balance the amount of calories you use. To lose weight, you need to take in fewer calories than your body needs (or use up calories through exercise). To gain weight, you must consume extra calories.

Labels provide calorie and nutrient information.

MATH CONNECTION

Suppose you are overweight and want to lose 10 pounds. For each pound you want to lose, you must take in about 3,500 fewer calories than your body needs (or use them up through exercise). With a sensible diet and moderate exercise, you plan to consume 1,750 fewer calories per week than your body uses. How many weeks will it take to lose the 10 pounds?

SOLUTION

Multiply the number of pounds you want to lose by the number of calories it takes to lose a pound.

$$\text{Total calories to cut or use up} = 10 \times 3{,}500 = 35{,}000$$

Divide this total by the number of calories you will cut or use up each week.

$$\text{Number of weeks to lose} = 35{,}000 \div 1{,}750 = 20$$

It will take 20 weeks to lose the 10 pounds.

For each pound you want to gain or lose, you must take in about 3,500 more or fewer calories than the body uses.

If you are interested in gaining or losing weight, the first step is to learn about the number of calories that various foods contain. Charts showing the calorie values of common foods appear in most cookbooks and can be found on the Internet. If you cannot locate a calorie chart on your own, a librarian can help you.

If you are trying to gain or lose weight, remember that you still need proper nutrients. Even though the number of calories may vary, you need the appropriate number of servings from each level of the Food Guide Pyramid. It is a good idea never to go below 1,200 calories a day. If you take in fewer calories than that, you probably will not get the vitamins and minerals you need.

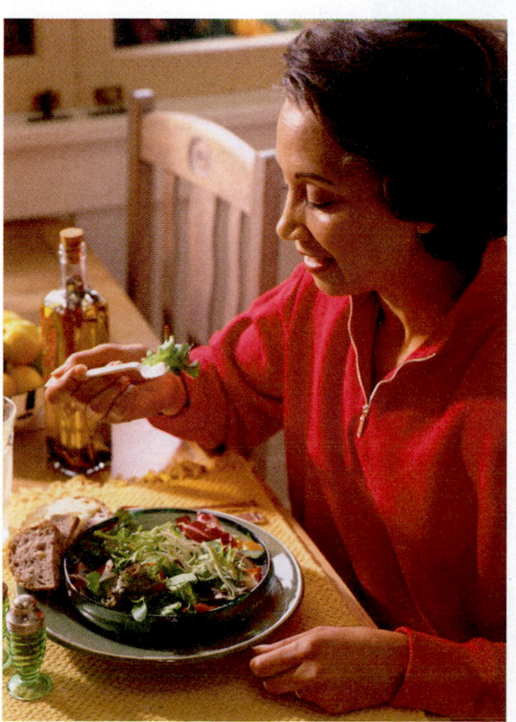

A salad offers many nutrients for few calories.

LESSON 30.1 REVIEW

1. Name the three functions that nutrients perform.
2. Name the five major food groups in the Food Guide Pyramid.
3. Based on the table shown in Figure 30-2, what is your ideal weight? About how many calories should you eat each day?
4. Why is it important not to go below 1,200 calories a day?

HIGH-GROWTH OCCUPATIONS FOR THE 21st CENTURY

Teacher Assistants

Teacher assistants, also called *teacher aides* or *instructional aides*, provide instructional and clerical support for classroom teachers, allowing teachers more time for lesson planning and teaching. Teacher assistants tutor and assist children in learning class material using the teacher's lesson plans, providing students with individualized attention. Teacher assistants also supervise students in the cafeteria, schoolyard, or school discipline center or on field trips. They record grades, set up equipment, and help prepare materials for instruction.

Large school districts hire some teacher assistants to perform exclusively noninstructional or clerical tasks, such as playground and lunchroom supervision. Most teacher assistants, however, perform a combination of instructional, supervisory, and clerical duties. They generally instruct children, under the direction and guidance of teachers. They work with students individually or in small groups—listening while students read, reviewing or reinforcing class work, or helping them find information for reports. At the secondary school level, teacher assistants often specialize in a certain subject, such as math or science. Teacher assistants often take charge of special projects and prepare equipment or exhibits, such as for a science demonstration. Some assistants work in computer laboratories, helping students using computers and educational software programs.

By working with small groups of children, teacher assistants provide individualized attention.

In addition to instructing, assisting, and supervising students, teacher assistants grade tests and papers; check homework; keep health and attendance records; and key, file, and duplicate materials. They also stock supplies, operate audiovisual equipment, and keep classroom equipment in order.

Many teacher assistants work extensively with special education students. They attend to the physical needs of students with disabilities, including feeding, teaching good grooming habits, or assisting in riding the school bus. They also provide personal attention to students with other special needs, such as students whose families live in poverty, who speak English as a second language, or who need to correct or improve their skills in a particular subject. Teacher assistants help assess a student's progress by observing performance and recording relevant data.

LESSON 30.2

STRESS AND PHYSICAL FITNESS

OBJECTIVES

- ***NAME AND ILLUSTRATE THE THREE MAJOR WAYS TO REDUCE OR ELIMINATE STRESS***
- ***DISCUSS BENEFITS OF PHYSICAL EXERCISE***
- ***NAME AND DESCRIBE THE THREE TYPES OF EXERCISES THAT SHOULD BE INCLUDED IN A WORKOUT***

STRESS AND ITS CONTROL

Stress, an unavoidable part of life, is mental, physical, or emotional strain. Causes of stress, called **stressors**, may be events, activities, experiences, or situations; they may be good or bad; and they may range from mild to severe. The following are the most common causes of stress:

- Daily activities, events, frustrations, and challenges cause stress. Examples include missing a bus to school, giving a speech, taking a test, overcooking dinner, or going on a blind date.
- Illness adds to stress because it forces the body to use its defenses. Stress also results when the body must heal an injury or adjust to conditions such as extreme heat, noise, or air pollution.
- A life change is often stressful. Examples might include moving into a new house, getting married, or changing schools. Such changes require many adaptations to new surroundings and situations.
- Life crises produce the greatest stress. These events might include the death of a parent, the loss of a job, or a divorce. The more serious the crisis, the greater the stress.

An event that causes great stress for one person may only be a minor problem for another. Your physical or mental condition influences your ability to handle a new stress. Your response may also depend on whether you feel in control of the situation. A difficulty may cause little stress if you can predict it, overcome it, or at least understand it.

Most people are able to cope with life's everyday stresses. However, when stressors build up faster than you can deal with them,

PERSONAL DECISIONS

You have been studying all weekend for a test on Monday. You feel tense, and your neck and shoulders ache from leaning over a desk. One of your friends calls asking you to go to the recreation center for a workout. You would like to go, but you do not feel that you can take time away from studying.

WHAT WOULD YOU DO?

your capacity may be overloaded. Continual stress exhausts the body's resources that maintain energy and resist disease. The result may be anxiety, depression, or serious illness.

A well-balanced life can help you prevent or reduce stress. Ways of managing stress may include alternating mental activity with physical activity, sharing feelings with others, reading inspirational books, and having interests outside of school or work. In addition, cultivating positive emotions such as hope, confidence, faith, and love can enable you to develop a lifestyle that will help you resist daily life stresses. Worrying less and having a sense of humor also help a great deal. Three major ways to reduce or eliminate stress are to plan how to deal with stress, learn how to relax, and change your life.

Plan How to Deal with Stress

Some crises and other types of stressors cannot be predicted. For instance, a loved one may die suddenly. Other stressors, though, such as taking a test, leaving home to go to school, or giving a speech, are known in advance. For those kinds of stressors, you can plan and prepare. For example, you can reduce stress associated with test taking by thoroughly studying the test material until you are confident that you know it well.

If possible, do not schedule several stressful activities during the same time period. When you know a stressful activity or event is coming up, learn to pace yourself. During stressful times, eat well, get plenty of rest, and exercise at an enjoyable pace.

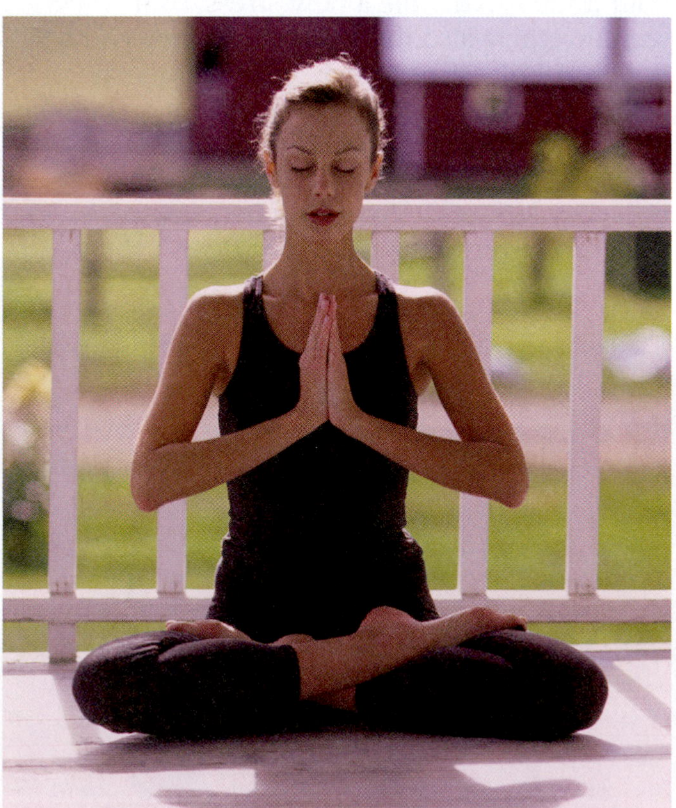

Yoga is a proven mothod of reducing stress.

WORKFORCE TRENDS

Many employers are trying to improve productivity by reforming the way they organize work and motivate workers. To increase quality and lower costs, some firms are experimenting with greater worker involvement and interaction. These innovative work practices include worker teams, total quality management, quality circles, peer review of employee performance, worker involvement in purchase decisions, and job rotation.

Learn How to Relax

Because stress is unavoidable, it is very useful to learn a method that reduces or eliminates stress. One doctor suggests this very simple relaxation method. Sit or lie in a comfortable position in a quiet place where you will not be disturbed. Close your eyes, and silently repeat the word *one* over and over for 10 to 20 minutes. This activity seems to produce bodily changes that are the reverse of the ones stress cause. Muscle tension is reduced, and a variety of other changes occur in the heart and the circulatory and respiratory systems. In order to learn and use a meditation technique like this, you should practice it once or twice a day.

If meditation does not appeal to you, learn some other method that will help you relax and will have a calming effect. The activity may be jogging, listening to music, walking in a park, riding a horse, or sitting in a sauna. Use whatever works for you. Bear in mind that the bodily changes associated with stress can be reversed if you take steps to do so.

Change Your Life

The methods previously mentioned are some important ways of managing stress. However, if the same stressor is always present, stress-release techniques may not be very beneficial. You may have a situation in your life that simply makes you miserable. This may be a class at school, a job, a conflict with a roommate, or some other ongoing problem. If the situation cannot be relieved through other means, your last resort may be to drop the class, quit the job, or find a new roommate.

Of course, turning away from all stressful situations would be bad. But some situations and relationships are so stress-producing that it is often better to change them than to continue.

PHYSICAL FITNESS

No matter how good your diet or how well you control stress, you cannot be healthy without physical fitness. People have different ideas of what fitness means. For some, it is not being ill. For others, it is having a trim body.

Physical fitness refers to how well your heart and other organs function. Your physical fitness is determined by such factors as age, heredity, and behavior. Although you cannot control your age or heredity, your behavior can help you become physically fit. People vary greatly in their capacity for physical fitness, but almost anyone can improve by exercising regularly.

All of us need physical exercise. The years between adolescence and middle age are generally the peak period for physical fitness. However, people of all ages can stay fit if they maintain good health habits and get regular exercise. According to the American Medical Association, exercise:

- Improves strength, endurance, and coordination, thus increasing the ease with which daily tasks are accomplished.
- Aids in weight control, thus helping to ward off heart disease, arthritis, diabetes, and other ailments often associated with being overweight.
- Helps ensure the proper growth and development of young bones and muscles.
- Improves the ability to avoid and recover from illnesses and accidents.
- Strengthens muscles that support the body, improving posture and appearance.
- Increases poise by developing grace and ease of movement.
- Reduces stress, thus acting as a natural tranquilizer.

You have probably heard or read news reports about computer viruses. A virus is a program or piece of code in a program that can damage or erase files on your computer. Viruses can be spread by any method used to share files between computers. The most common way to get a virus is to open an infected file—from a floppy disk, the Web, or e-mail (an attached file, not an e-mail message). Avoid opening e-mail attachments from people you do not know. The best way to prevent viruses is to install anti-virus software on your computer.

TYPES OF EXERCISES

Your level of physical fitness depends largely on how often and how hard you exercise. Some experts say that you should exercise at least three times weekly for at least 30 minutes at a stretch. Improvement in fitness may occur faster with even more frequent workouts.

The President's Council on Physical Fitness and Sports recommends a 30-minute workout of moderate, continuous exercise each day. To be beneficial, the exercise does not have to be difficult or strenuous. But, as your condition improves, you should increase the number of times that you do each activity. Every workout should include exercises for flexibility, endurance, and strength.

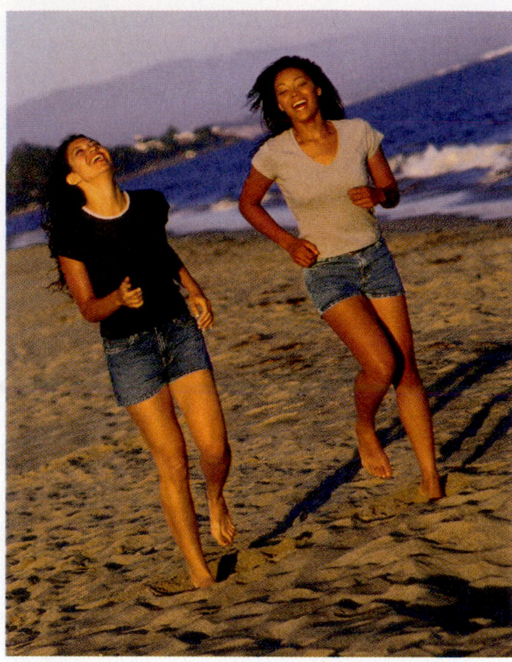

Enjoy yourself. Exercise can be fun.

Flexibility Exercises

These exercises stretch the connective tissues and move the joints through a wide range of motions. Such exercises include touching the toes, swinging the arms in circles, rotating the upper body from the waist, and jogging slowly. Flexibility exercises should be performed before and after each workout.

Endurance Exercises

Running, cycling, skipping rope, swimming, and brisk walking strengthen and speed up the action of the heart and lungs by increasing the body's ability to take in oxygen. They also strengthen the blood vessels. These are called **aerobic exercises**.

Strength Exercises

Pull-ups, push-ups, sit-ups, weight lifting, and other exercises increase the strength and endurance of the body's major muscle groups. For example, lifting weights increases the strength of arms, shoulders, and back muscles.

Guidelines for Physical Fitness

Exercise is basic to healthful living. When beginning or maintaining an exercise program, keep the following guidelines in mind:

- Do not keep finding excuses not to exercise.
- Do not think of fitness as a crash program. To avoid injury and fatigue, start slowly and build yourself up.
- Enjoy yourself. Exercise can be fun.
- Do not set unrealistic expectations. Remember, you are not training for the Olympics.
- To avoid boredom, vary your exercise routine.
- Once you get in shape, keep up your exercise program. If you get lazy and quit, your fitness level can deteriorate rather rapidly. The longer you allow yourself to be inactive, the harder it is to get back in shape.
- Harmful health habits such as taking drugs, smoking, drinking alcohol, and not getting enough sleep can undo the benefits of regular exercise.

As a young person, you have most of your life ahead of you. The quality of that life will depend a great deal on your physical and mental health. Begin now to follow the guidelines in this chapter regarding nutrition and diet, reducing stress, and physical fitness. This will better allow you to live and enjoy your life to its fullest.

LESSON 30.2 REVIEW

1. **Stress sometimes comes from a positive event. Give an example.**
2. **Do people respond in the same way to stress? Explain your answer.**
3. **Name three major ways to reduce or eliminate stress.**
4. **Name four benefits of exercise.**
5. **Briefly explain the three basic types of exercises.**
6. **Harmful health habits can undo the benefits of exercise. Name four unhealthy habits.**

FOCUS ON HEALTH AND SAFETY

CORPORATE FITNESS PROGRAMS

Faced with spiraling medical costs and insurance premiums, more companies are promoting preventive health care. This may include health screening for employees, educational seminars and workshops, and opportunities for physical activity.

Here is how preventive health care is being encouraged at one large corporation. Its program, called "Live for Life," offers classes on stress management and how to quit smoking. It teaches employees the importance of blood pressure testing, weight control, and exercise.

The company has a fitness center onsite. In the center, an aerobics instructor leads exercise classes before and after work and at lunchtime. The company distributes a monthly newsletter on fitness and sponsors regular seminars on good nutrition and other topics.

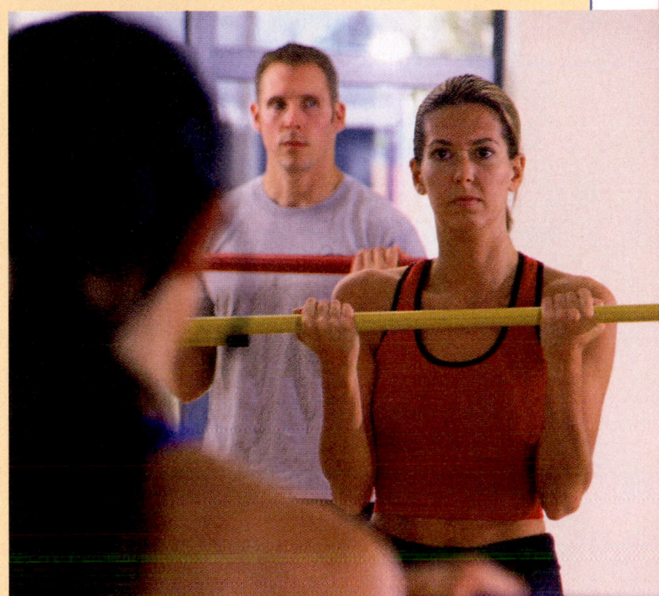

Seventy-five percent of U.S. employers offer some type of workplace health program.

The program is voluntary, but incentives to participate are provided. For every 20 minutes of exercise, employees get a certain amount of "play money." They can use it to purchase jogging suits, ankle weights, and other health-related items. About 60 percent of the company's 30,000 employees participate.

Research has shown that fitness programs such as this pay off. There are fewer illnesses and accidents, reduced absenteeism, and a more vigorous, creative, positive workforce. In one company, it was found that the average yearly medical cost for exercisers was less than 50 percent of that for nonexercisers. Some companies even share the reduced medical costs with employees.

THINK CRITICALLY

1. Fitness programs result in "a more vigorous, creative, positive workforce." What does this suggest about the relationship between mind and body?
2. What are some other preventive health care programs that a company might adopt?

CHAPTER 30

Chapter in Brief

Lesson 30.1 *Nutrition and Diet*

A. What we eat provides nutrients needed for good health. To make sure you get the required nutrients, you need to eat a variety of foods each day. The Food Guide Pyramid is an easy-to-use daily food guide.

B. Calories are units of food energy needed for continuous body functions and for work and leisure activities.

C. For good health, it is wise to maintain your recommended weight. Do this by controlling the amount and kind of foods you eat (calories), your level of activity, or both.

Lesson 30.2 *Stress and Physical Fitness*

A. Stress is mental, physical, or emotional strain. The most common causes are daily activities, events, frustrations, and challenges; illness, injury, or adjustment to environmental conditions; life changes; and life crises. Continual stress exhausts the body's resources that maintain energy and resist disease. The result may be anxiety, depression, or serious illness.

B. A well-balanced life can help you prevent or reduce stress. Three major ways to reduce or eliminate stress are to plan how to deal with stress, learn how to relax, and change your life.

C. You cannot be healthy without physical fitness. This refers to how well your heart and other organs function. Physical fitness is determined by such factors as age, heredity, and behavior.

D. Your level of physical fitness depends largely on how often and how hard you exercise. Some experts recommend exercising at least three times weekly for at least 30 minutes; others, a 30-minute workout daily. Every workout should include exercises for flexibility, endurance, and strength.

E. Harmful health habits such as taking drugs, drinking alcohol, smoking, and not getting enough sleep can undo the benefits of regular exercise. You have most of your life ahead of you. The quality of that life will depend a great deal on your physical and mental health.

Activities

1. For one full day, keep track of everything you eat and the approximate amount of each food. Then compare what you have eaten with the Food Guide Pyramid shown in Figure 30-1. How well does your diet compare with the recommendations? What foods, if any, are missing from your diet?

2. Using the Food Guide Pyramid and a calorie chart as references, plan a sample menu for one day. Be sure to include snacks. The total calories for all menu items should be enough to maintain your weight. Turn the menu in to your teacher.

REVIEW

3. Learning a relaxation method can be very helpful. For several days, practice the method described under "Learn How to Relax" on page 460. In class, discuss whether you notice any difference in how you feel as a result.
4. As a class, survey various businesses and industries in your area (or search for information at a library or on the Web) to find out what employers do to encourage workers to be more physically fit. How do employers benefit from exercise breaks, exercise rooms, and related activities and facilities?
5. Federal rules require food companies to put nutrition labels on their packaged food products. Labels must list calories, total fat, cholesterol, sodium, carbohydrates, and similar data. For many nutrients, the percentage of the recommended daily amount that the food contains is also provided. Bring a label from one of your favorite foods to class. Compare its nutritional value with the recommended daily intake shown on the label. Discuss how such nutritional information can help you make better food choices.

Word Power

On a separate sheet of paper, match each definition with the correct term. All definitions will be used, and a definition will be used only once.

6. Mental, physical, or emotional strain
7. The process by which plants and animals take in and use food
8. Events, activities, experiences, or situations that cause stress
9. Inactive
10. Chemical substances in food that are needed for good health
11. Exercises that condition the heart and lungs by increasing the body's ability to take in oxygen
12. The minimum amount of energy (calories) necessary for continuous body functioning
13. How well your heart and other organs function
14. Units of energy produced by food when it is used by the body

a. aerobic exercises
b. basal metabolism
c. calories
d. nutrients
e. nutrition
f. physical fitness
g. sedentary
h. stress
i. stressors

Think Critically

15. It has been said that Americans are the most "overfed and undernourished" people in the world. Why might this be true?
16. Eating disorders such as anorexia and bulimia have become serious health problems. What are some of the possible causes of these disorders?
17. In what ways may short-term stress be beneficial?
18. How does physical fitness differ from bodybuilding?
19. A good diet, control of stress, and physical exercise are all interrelated. Discuss how one may benefit the others.

CHAPTER 31

RESPONSIBLE CITIZENSHIP

LESSONS

PREVIEW

One of your most important roles in life is that of citizen. Citizenship is a part of daily living. It involves participation in home, school, community, and work life. In this chapter, you will learn about citizenship and how to be a more effective citizen.

THOUGHTS ON WORK

"Careers, like rockets, don't always take off on schedule. The key is to keep working the engines."
Gary Sinise

TAKING ACTION

POLITICS MATTER

Jerry lives in a community that has a mayor and a city council. Often the mayor and the council are portrayed on the news as never getting anything done. It seems as though they cannot agree on programs that Jerry thinks are vital to his community.

Last week, the local newspaper ran a story about a proposal before the council to increase fines for parking violations. Since these fines had not risen in ten years, proponents argued that it was time for at least a 10 percent increase. The extra revenue would be used to pay for road repairs, which were badly needed.

This proposal was expected to pass the city council easily. However, the mayor opposed it. The funds for road repairs could be found elsewhere, he said. The mayor had the power to veto this proposal if it passed the city council. He announced publicly his plans to do just that.

Jerry agrees with the city council that road repairs are badly needed. Springtime flooding and frigid winter temperatures make continual repairs a necessity. And the city is growing, putting increased strain on a road system designed 60 years ago for far fewer vehicles.

While Jerry agrees with the council, he knows that there are many others who agree with the mayor. People who work downtown are frustrated by the lack of parking. Often, parking at a meter is the only option. When people forget to keep the meter fed, they get a ticket. The city has a lot of commuters, and they are not happy about the proposed increase. The city council plans to hold a public hearing on the issue on Tuesday.

In the past few days, the newspaper has printed many letters to the editor arguing for or against the fine increase. Jerry has read the letters to get different people's points of view. He wonders how much the road repairs will cost. How much could be raised from the fine increase? If the funds for repairs could be found elsewhere as the mayor said, where would they come from? Are there any other solutions to the problem?

SUCCESS TIP

Be aware of the issues and decisions that you can influence through your vote.

THINK CRITICALLY

1. How can Jerry get answers to his questions?
2. What are some ways that Jerry can express his point of view?

LESSON 31.1

BEING A CITIZEN

OBJECTIVES

- EXPLAIN THE FOUR RESPONSIBILITIES OF CITIZENSHIP
- SUMMARIZE THE PROCESS OF REGISTERING TO VOTE AND CASTING A BALLOT
- DISCUSS THE IMPORTANCE OF VOTING IN LOCAL, STATE, AND NATIONAL ELECTIONS

RESPONSIBILITIES OF CITIZENSHIP

Citizenship is membership in a community, state, county, or nation. It also means carrying out the duties and responsibilities of a citizen. The responsibilities of citizenship involve personal, economic, political, and national-defense activities.

On the personal level, good citizens are considerate of the needs of others. They help develop and preserve basic institutions such as community. They adhere to the customs and laws of society. Good citizens stand up for what they believe is right and take action against what they know is wrong.

Economically, being a good citizen means producing efficiently and consuming wisely. It also means helping to protect the rights of others to work. Good citizens use their talents and abilities to further the economic welfare of the society.

In the political area, every citizen of age should be a registered voter and should participate in all elections. A good citizen keeps up with local, national, and international issues and informs elected representatives of his or her opinions. People can serve the government directly in such ways as performing jury duty when asked. They also can contribute to the national defense.

Some full-time workers belong to the military reserve. Dan Hartley, for instance, is a member of the Air National Guard. His regular job is working as a cabinetmaker at Blue Ridge Woodworks. Dan attends monthly reserve meetings and spends two weeks at reserve summer camp. In a national emergency, Dan could be called into active duty.

PERSONAL DECISIONS

The school board has voted to make drastic cuts in the district's career and vocational education program. The board says that it is too expensive to operate. Many students are very upset. A group of them is meeting after school to discuss what they might do. You have been asked to come to the meeting. You are concerned about the cuts, but you are not sure you want to get involved.

WHAT WOULD YOU DO?

COMMUNICATION AT WORK

PERSUASIVE WRITING

Thomas Jefferson said that his intention in writing the Declaration of Independence was "to place before mankind the common sense of the subject, in terms so plain and firm as to command their assent." That is the purpose of good persuasive writing. You have a cause that requires the support of others. It may be ending the night shift or getting a company to clean up pollution. You may need to write a proposal (persuasive report), letter to the editor, or other persuasive document.

Persuasive writing begins with research. Find out the best way to accomplish the change. Pay special attention to costs involved and how your plan will affect others. Gather facts and statistics. Find respected authorities that support your position. Learn about the arguments against your cause and determine ways to address them.

Here is one way to organize your writing:

1. Introduce the topic. Say what you think needs to be done.
2. Explain why it should be done. State your strongest reasons in order starting with the best. Support each with facts, examples, and other information.
3. Address objections. List major objections and respond to them.
4. Conclude by summarizing the issue and restating your position.

VOTING AND SELF-GOVERNMENT

Voting is both a privilege and a right. In many countries, people have no say in how they are governed or in the laws that are passed. You have the responsibility to vote in local, state, and national elections. If everyone refused to vote, self-government would come to a standstill. "What difference will my vote make?" you ask. Election outcomes often hinge on a few votes. Yours might make the difference!

Voting Qualifications and Procedures

In all states, voters must be U.S. citizens and at least 18 years old. They must also meet the residency requirements of their state. As soon as you meet these three conditions, you should register to vote. Every state except North Dakota has some form of voter registration.

In the registration process, a person's name is added to the list of eligible voters. In many areas, voters may register in person or by mail. Registration forms can be obtained at election offices; in most states, at department of motor vehicles or driver's licensing offices; in many public buildings, including libraries, high schools, and universities; and on the Internet. To be eligible to vote in an election, it is usually necessary to register 10 to 30 days beforehand.

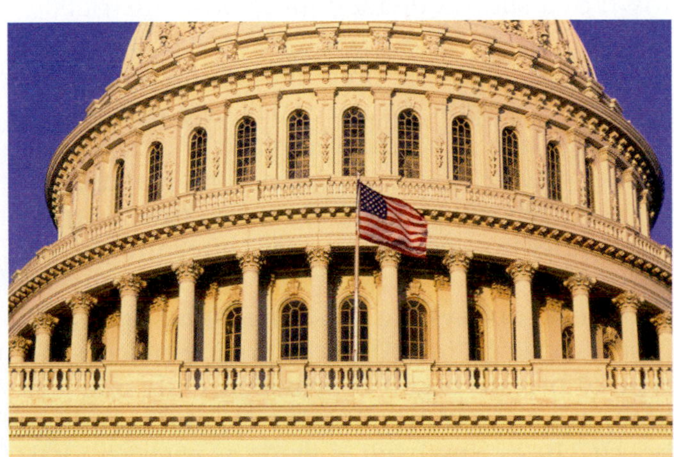

An elected representative acts as your voice in government.

A person's vote is private.

In most states, registration is permanent unless the voter moves to another town. Many states may cancel registration if a voter fails to vote for several years. If you move to a different place in the same county, notify the appropriate county office. It will need to update its records.

Casting a Ballot

In the United States, each county, ward, city, or town of a state is divided into voting districts called **precincts**. A person must vote at the polling place for the precinct in which he or she lives. The polling place may be a public building such as a school, a place of business, or even a private home. At the polling place, election officials check eligibility for voting, distribute ballots, and count the votes after the polls close.

Basic to our system of voting is the right to cast a secret ballot. At every polling place, some type of private booth is provided. Only one voter at a time is permitted to be in the voting booth. The voting itself is made as easy as possible. Voters either mark a printed ballot or use some type of voting machine.

When voting for various offices, people may vote a "straight ticket" or "split" their ballots. Voting a straight ticket is when someone simply votes for all candidates of a particular party. Splitting a ticket is voting for some candidates of one party and some of another. For example, someone might vote for a Democratic candidate for President and a Republican candidate for Governor. In most states, people may also write in the name of someone whose name is not on the ballot. Any issues and questions on the ballot require only a yes or no vote.

The Election of Candidates

In most elections, the candidate with the most votes is the winner. Suppose that in a class election Leroy Johnson receives 98 votes; Tiffany Anderson, 95 votes; and Eric Washington, 80 votes. Leroy Johnson would be the winner.

In some elections, though, a candidate must have a majority of the votes cast. If that were the case in the class election, Leroy Johnson would not be the winner. He failed to receive at least half of the 273 votes. When no candidate receives a majority, a "runoff" election is usually held between the top two candidates. Johnson would run against Anderson. The person with the most votes is the winner.

VOTING BEHAVIOR

Our ancestors struggled to earn the right to vote. Unfortunately, too many people now take this privilege for granted. Middle-aged and older citizens are much more likely to vote than are young adults. Only a minority of the people under age 25 vote. In the 1988, 1992, and 1996 Presidential elections, an average of about 34 percent of 18- to 20-year-olds voted. (Results were not available for the 2000 election at the time of this writing.) In the last three off-year Congressional elections (elections in years when there is no Presidential election), only about 16 percent of 18- to 20-year-olds voted.

Too many people are like Roger's friend, Ted. On election day, Roger awoke before the alarm sounded. He got up and dressed quickly. This was the first election in which he was old enough to vote. After breakfast, he headed off to the polling place. On the way, Roger saw Ted jogging on the sidewalk.

"Hey Ted," said Roger, "Do you want to go with me to vote?"

"Are you nuts, man?" exclaimed Ted. "It doesn't do any good to vote. Those politicians don't care about anyone except themselves."

Roger was very disappointed in Ted's reaction. He went on to the polling place. There was a short line in front of the building, but no one seemed to mind. People quietly chatted among themselves until their turns came. Roger signed the register and got in line.

Several minutes later, a booth became available. Roger entered and marked his ballot. After he finished, Roger gave the ballot to a clerk and watched her put it into a box. He left the polling place with a feeling of satisfaction. He was glad he had voted, but he could not help but think about Ted. "I wonder what I could do to change Ted's mind," he thought. Do you have any suggestions about what Roger might do?

Because of the publicity of a national campaign, more people vote in a Presidential election than in any other. On the average, fewer voters participate in elections for state and local officials. This is interesting because our lives are influenced directly by the actions of our state and local officials. What reasons might people give for not voting in these elections?

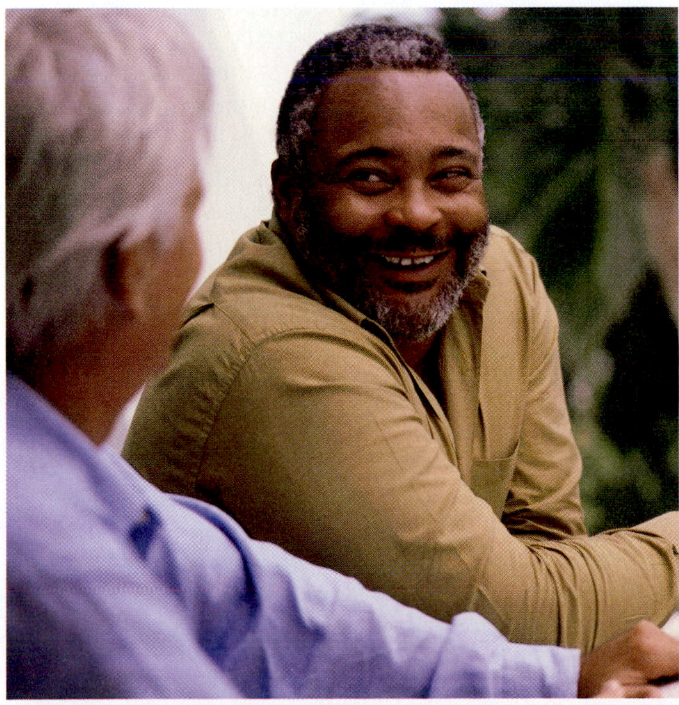

Why do you think middle-aged and older citizens are more likely to vote than are young adults?

WORKFORCE TRENDS

Many firms are experimenting with linking worker pay and company performance more directly through profit sharing. Gain sharing is another type of compensation system in which pay corresponds more directly to worker performance. Some companies also allow workers to buy company stock through payroll deductions at rates discounted from the market share price. These practices increase the economic stake that workers have in company performance.

LESSON 31.1 REVIEW

1. Name the four types of citizenship responsibilities.
2. Give three examples of how citizens might exercise economic responsibilities.
3. What would happen if all but a very few people failed to vote?
4. In order to vote in an election, what must you do beforehand?
5. What is it called when a person votes for candidates of different political parties?
6. Why do more people tend to vote in a national than in a local election?

HIGH-GROWTH OCCUPATIONS FOR THE 21st CENTURY

Visual Artists

Visual artists create art to communicate ideas, thoughts, or feelings. *Illustrators* paint or draw pictures for books, magazines, and other publications; films; and paper products, including wrapping paper, stationery, greeting cards, and calendars. Some work may be done using computers, which allows art to be mailed electronically between clients or presented on the Internet. Many of these artists do a variety of illustrations, whereas others specialize in a particular style, such as medical illustration, fashion illustration, cartoons, or animation.

Some illustrators draw storyboards for television commercials, movies, and animated features. Storyboards present a story in a series of scenes similar to a comic strip. They allow an advertising agency to evaluate proposed commercials with the company doing the advertising. They also serve as guides to producers, actors, directors, and writers.

Some visual artists use computer software to create images.

Graphic designers use a variety of print, electronic, and film media to create designs that meet client needs. Most graphic designers use computer software to create images. They design promotional displays and marketing brochures for products and services, develop distinctive company logos for products and businesses, and create visual designs of annual reports and other corporate literature. Additionally, graphic designers develop the overall layout and design of magazines, newspapers, journals, corporate reports, and other publications. Many graphic designers develop the graphics and layout of web sites. Graphic designers also produce the credits that appear before and after television programs and movies.

Art directors develop design concepts and review material that is to appear in periodicals, newspapers, and other printed or visual media. They decide how best to present the information visually, so it is appealing and organized. They make decisions about which photographs or artwork to use and oversee the layout, design, and production of the printed material. Art directors also may review graphics that appear on the Internet.

LESSON 31.2

THINKING CLEARLY

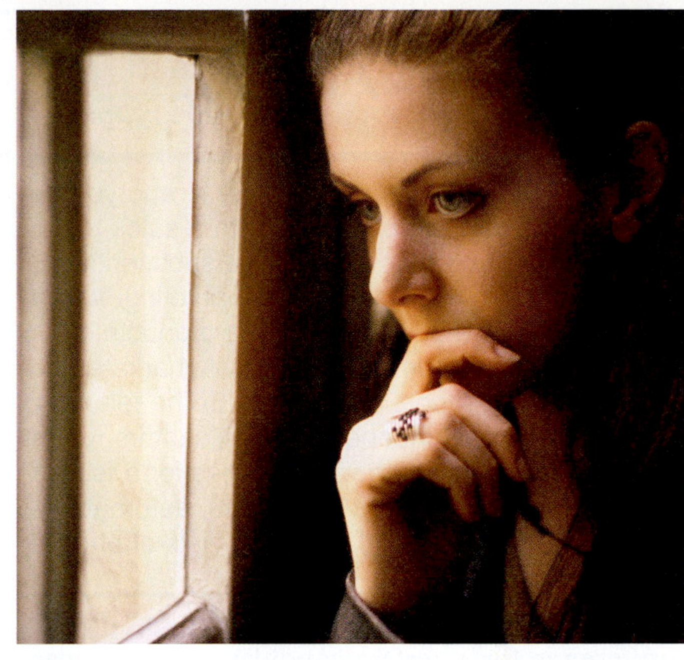

OBJECTIVES

- LIST SOURCES OF FACTS ON CANDIDATES AND ISSUES
- IDENTIFY AND DESCRIBE THOSE THINGS THAT GET IN THE WAY OF CLEAR THINKING

GATHER THE FACTS

It is not always easy to choose between two political candidates or to decide which position on an issue is the correct one for you. Many issues such as nuclear power, federal spending, and the role of labor unions are not clear-cut. To clarify your thinking about a candidate or an issue, gather all the facts you can.

Newspapers, magazines, and television and radio news programs are good sources. The League of Women Voters is a national organization that works to encourage the informed and active participation of citizens in government. Its state and local chapters issue printed newsletters before an election describing the candidates and issues. The League has a web site at http://www.lwv.org.

Many people use the Internet to prepare for an election. A growing number of web sites provide candidate biographies, information on issues, voting records, campaign finance data, and the like.

ETHICAL DECISIONS

An election will be held in a couple of weeks for class officers. Small groups of students have organized to push for certain candidates. Campaign workers are putting up posters and passing out literature. The campaign is starting to get dirty. A representative of one group has come to you asking that you not vote for Christine because "we do not want a girl for president."

WHAT WOULD YOU DO?

RECOGNIZE THE FACTS

Facts can be proven. It is fact, for example, that the earth is round and not flat. The following are a number of things that are frequently confused with facts.

Rumor

A **rumor** is a popular report or story that has not been proven. Most rumors are spread by word of mouth. People often treat rumors as if they are fact.

Opinion

An **opinion** is one person's views about something. We reveal our opinions when we show a

YOU'RE A WHAT? TELEMARKETER

The phone rings, you answer it, and you are immediately confronted with a sales pitch for a credit card or a magazine subscription. Welcome to the world of telemarketing! A *telemarketer* is a person who sells products by phone. Many companies hire telemarketers to sell their products or services. Some telemarketers work at independent call centers, which sell on behalf of other companies for a fee.

Telemarketers use computers, automated dialing systems, and electronic lists of phone numbers to reach prospective customers. When someone answers a call, the telemarketer has only seconds to make an introduction and explain the purpose of the call. A professional, upbeat tone and an ability to engage customers in conversation are often keys to a successful call. Telemarketers also need to be motivated, persistent, and mature, because only a small percentage of calls translate into sales. ■

preference for a certain candidate or take a particular side in an issue. Although opinions may be based on fact, they are not fact in themselves.

Prejudice

A **prejudice** is an opinion that is based on insufficient information (a prejudgment). People might express prejudice about a person's sex, race, or religion or about some other quality. Prejudice frequently causes great harm to people and is the opposite of clear thinking.

Allegation

An **allegation** is an unproven statement about someone or something. For example, you might state that Elliot Chemical Company dumps hazardous waste into the river. Making an allegation is a very serious thing to do. You should never make an allegation unless you have the supporting facts. You could be hurting an innocent party. You could also be sued.

Bias

When you have a tendency to favor something because of familiarity or preference, you have a **bias**. You might then make exaggerated claims. For example, even though running is good exercise, some joggers overstate its benefits. Biases are not necessarily harmful. We all have them. But, when making choices and decisions, carefully keep in mind who is saying what.

Propaganda

Propaganda involves any organized effort or movement to spread certain information. The information may be true or false. Like biases, propaganda is not always negative. For example, the American Heart Association uses propaganda to convince people of the hazards of smoking.

LESSON 31.2 REVIEW

1. List six sources of facts on candidates and issues.
2. A prejudice can be thought of as a prejudgment. Give an example.
3. Why should you be careful in making an allegation?

FOCUS ON SKILLS FOR LIVING

CITIZEN LAWMAKERS

Most laws are passed by national, state, and local legislative bodies. However, through a method called an initiative, citizens can introduce a law. The initiative is used primarily at the state and local levels. Twenty-four states provide for initiatives.

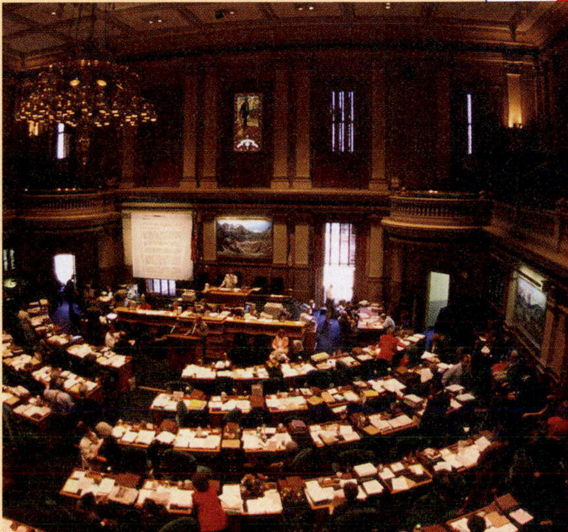

Lawmaking is not limited to elected officials.

In states or cities that use initiatives, anyone can draw up a proposed law. The next step is to collect a specific number of signatures on a petition favoring it. Once the initiative petition has qualified, it is voted on.

An initiative may be direct or indirect. In the first case, the proposed law is placed on a ballot and goes directly to the voters. In an indirect initiative, the proposed law goes first to the legislature. Should the legislative body approve the initiative, it goes into law. In some states, the question is ended if the legislature votes the bill down. In other states, a rejected bill is submitted to the people. If they vote for it, the bill becomes law. In most states, the governor cannot veto a bill passed in this way.

In recent years, the following initiatives have appeared on ballots in various states:

- Create overnight shelters for the homeless.
- Remove sales tax from food products.
- Roll back tax hikes.
- Establish a state lottery.
- Regulate adult content on cable TV.
- Limit medical malpractice damages.

Initiatives work in much the same way in a city as they do in a state. Whether at the state or local level, an initiative enables people to take direct political action if their elected representatives ignore their wishes.

THINK CRITICALLY

1. Citizen initiatives have been described as "direct democracy." What do you think this means?
2. Opponents say that citizen initiatives are not democratic because they infringe on the power of legislatures to make laws and do not protect minority rights. Do you agree or disagree? Give reasons for your answer.

CHAPTER 31

Chapter in Brief

Lesson 31.1 *Being a Citizen*

A. Citizenship is a part of daily living. The responsibilities of citizenship involve personal, economic, political, and national-defense activities.

B. You have the responsibility to vote in local, state, and national elections. In all states, voters must be U.S. citizens and at least 18 years old. They must also meet state residency requirements. To be eligible to vote, you must register beforehand.

C. A person must vote at the polling place for the precinct in which he or she lives. At every polling place, some type of private booth is provided. People may vote a straight ticket or split their ballots.

D. Too many people take the privilege of voting for granted. Only a minority of the people under age 25 vote. On the average, fewer voters participate in elections for state and local officials than in Presidential elections.

Lesson 31.2 *Thinking Clearly*

A. It is not always easy to choose between two political candidates or to decide which position on an issue is the correct one for you. Many issues are not clear-cut. To clarify your thinking, gather all the facts you can. Six sources of facts are newspapers, magazines, television news programs, radio news programs, the League of Women Voters, and the Internet.

B. Facts can be proven. A number of things are confused with facts. These include rumor, opinion, prejudice, allegation, bias, and propaganda.

Activities

1. Identify someone (perhaps a friend or relative) in your community who is a naturalized citizen. Invite the person to class to talk about why he or she chose to become a U.S. citizen. Make a list of questions to ask.
2. Find out the residency requirements for voting in your community or city. Also, find out how you go about registering to vote where you live. Discuss your findings in class.
3. Newspaper and magazine editorials are a special type of opinion. Bring editorials of interest to class. Discuss them. Are there any about which the class disagrees? If so, compose a class opinion and send it to the proper source. Follow the persuasive writing guidelines on page 469.
4. Bring to class a brochure or other statement that can be considered propaganda. Identify the main idea that the propaganda is attempting to communicate. Then, discuss the following questions: (a) Who wants you to believe this? (b) Why does the person or group want you to believe it? (c) Are there arguments on the other side?

REVIEW

5. The United States government has developed a web site called FirstGov to provide a single location for information produced by the federal government. Visit FirstGov at *http://firstgov.gov/* and explore the various topics and subjects available. Identify one web site of interest and explain its contents to your classmates.

Word Power

On a separate sheet of paper, match each definition with the correct term. All definitions will be used, and a definition will be used only once.

6. A tendency to favor something because of familiarity or preference
7. One person's views about something
8. An unproven statement about someone or something
9. Any organized effort or movement to spread certain information
10. Divisions of a county, ward, city, or town for election purposes; voting districts
11. A popular report or story that has not been proven
12. A prejudgment; an opinion that is based on insufficient information
13. Membership in a community, state, county, or nation; carrying out the duties and responsibilities of a citizen

a. allegation
b. bias
c. citizenship
d. opinion
e. precincts
f. prejudice
g. propaganda
h. rumor

Think Critically

14. If you were an employer, how might you feel if several of your employees were called away for emergency military reserve duty?
15. Citizens may be of three types. One type is like a stone that stays where it is, neither hearing nor responding. A second type is like a sponge that absorbs and retains but does not respond. The third type is like a generator that converts energy into power. Generators are the people who get things done.

    What percentages of students in your school, do you think, fall into each of these three groups? In which group do you belong? Discuss your answers in class.
16. Why do you think so few young adults vote? What can be done to increase the number of young voters?
17. On federal income tax forms, there is a place to mark if you want $3 of your tax to go to the Presidential Election Campaign Fund. How is this money used? Do you support this effort?

CHAPTER 32

EDUCATION FOR LIFELONG LEARNING

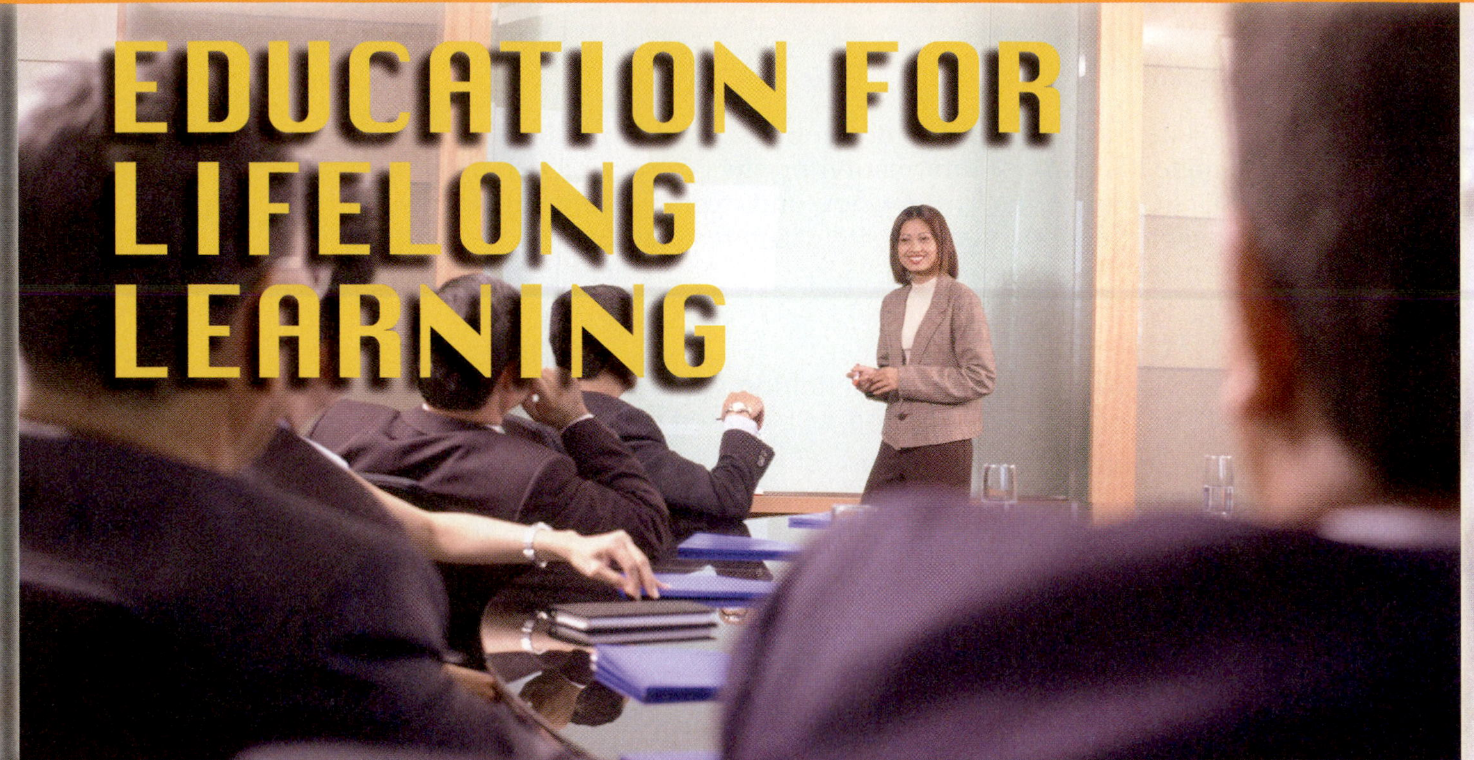

LESSONS

32.1 *Education and Training*

32.2 *Educational Information*

PREVIEW

Education and training beyond high school can make you a more valuable employee and can open many career opportunities to you. In this chapter, you will learn about the importance of lifelong learning, types of education and training, and how to get information about education and training.

THOUGHTS ON WORK

"By working faithfully eight hours a day you may eventually get to be boss and work twelve hours a day."

Robert Frost

TAKING ACTION

LEARNING TO EARN

Jaime is interested in becoming a bookkeeper or an accountant. He is having a difficult time deciding which occupation is right for him. He will be graduating next year, so he needs to make a decision soon.

Jaime decides to ask his Uncle Roberto, who is a bookkeeper, for advice. He visits him at work one day. Uncle Roberto shows Jaime around and demonstrates the accounting software that he uses. Then the two go out to lunch together.

"How long does it take to learn to become a bookkeeper?" Jaime asks. "What kinds of courses do you have to take?"

"That depends," Uncle Roberto replies. "You should call some potential employers and find out what their job requirements are and what kind of accounting software they use. Then, check with your business department at school or the local community college for courses.

"Actually, if I were you," he continues, "I would seriously consider becoming an accountant instead. You could make more money. You could continue your education by becoming a certified public accountant or certified financial planner, which might increase your earning potential even more. Also, you might be able to become your own boss one day."

"That sounds great," says Jaime, "but I need to get a job as soon as possible. I don't have much money for college, and I do not want to go into debt."

"You can start by taking accounting classes now at your high school. Then you could work and go to school part-time. But think carefully about applying for a student loan or other assistance and going to college full-time. Federal student loans have long repayment periods and low interest rates. There are some things that are worth going into debt for. You should talk to your school career counselor and get more information before you make this decision."

Jaime thanks Uncle Roberto for his advice. Jaime knows what he needs to do next.

SUCCESS TIP

Find out the educational and training requirements for occupations that interest you.

THINK CRITICALLY

1. What does Jaime need to do next?
2. Think of an occupation that interests you. What education and training does it require?

LESSON 32.1 EDUCATION AND TRAINING

OBJECTIVES

- *DISCUSS WHY EDUCATION OR TRAINING BEYOND HIGH SCHOOL MAY BE NEEDED*
- *ILLUSTRATE HOW THE AMOUNT OF REQUIRED PREPARATION VARIES AMONG OCCUPATIONS*
- *NAME AND DESCRIBE SIX COMMON TYPES OF EDUCATION AND TRAINING*

INVESTING IN YOUR FUTURE

One day Lionel and several of his friends were discussing what they were going to do after high school. "I can't wait to get my diploma," said Lionel. "I'm sick of school."

"I'm going to get a job in a factory," remarked Marty. "That way, I don't have to go on with school."

"Yeah," said Henry, "who wants to get more education? I have a cousin who graduated from college and she can't get a job."

"I think you people are wrong," said Samantha. "*Most jobs require some type of education or training*. And there is a lot of competition for jobs, even among people who have degrees or training."

The conversation among these students shows some truths and some misunderstandings about the relationship between education and employment. It is true that some jobs do not require additional schooling. But such jobs tend to be low-paying and have little job security.

It is also true that getting a college degree will not automatically guarantee you a job. Some types of degrees do not lead directly to employment. For instance, to get a job in psychology, most students will need at least one graduate degree. And, with some programs, there are more graduates with degrees than there are available jobs. So people take jobs requiring less education. These are often jobs that high school graduates usually fill. So competition for those jobs increases.

On the other hand, it is a mistake to think that you will not need more education or training after high school. Most entry-level jobs in factories, businesses, mines, and other workplaces require on-the-job training. If you want to advance in a company, you will probably have to continue learning throughout your lifetime. Your

CAREER DECISIONS

After several years in your present job, you have reached a dead end. You cannot advance without additional training. But you never were a very good student. You are a poor reader, have difficulty memorizing, and nearly panic whenever you have to take a test. You do not want to admit it, but you are scared by the thought of taking a course.

WHAT WOULD YOU DO?

In 1999, half of all people over age 17 participated in some form of adult learning.

attitude toward future schooling is one of the things your employer will probably consider in judging you for a promotion or raise.

Linda and Vicki were in the same high school graduation class. After graduating, they were both hired as assemblers at General Electronics. Their work involved putting together electrical components for motherboards.

General Electronics has an agreement with Northwest Community College to offer courses at the plant. Classes start at 4 p.m. after employees get off work. The company pays the tuition. Linda enrolled in the program because she wanted a more challenging, better-paying job. Vicki ignored the program, saying that the courses were a waste of time.

New jobs at General Electronics frequently open up at all levels from assemblers to supervisors. Employees with two years of experience may apply for higher-level jobs. As soon as they were eligible, both Linda and Vicki applied for the first available job in the records department. Linda got the job. The personnel manager was impressed by the fact that she had the initiative to continue her education. Vicki has since been passed over for several other jobs. Could it be due to her feelings about further training?

Career ladders exist in most industries. A **career ladder** is a group of related occupations with different skill requirements organized into ranks like steps on a ladder. Two examples of career ladders in the food service industry are shown in Figure 32-1. It is possible to start at the bottom of a career ladder and climb to the top. To do so, however, a person will need on-the-job experience and additional training.

Even though you are looking forward now to completing high school, do not turn your back on education at a later time. Some type of education or training program will probably be suited to your interests and abilities. Think it over carefully. Additional education and training will be one of the best investments you can make in your future.

PREPARING FOR AN OCCUPATION

Do you have any idea of how you might go about becoming a hotel manager? A toolmaker? A computer programmer? A pilot? The first thing you would have to do for each of these occupations is learn a set of skills. To work as a hotel manager, you would have to learn about accounting, hiring, employee relations, and food service management. Toolmakers need to know machining operations and math. They also need

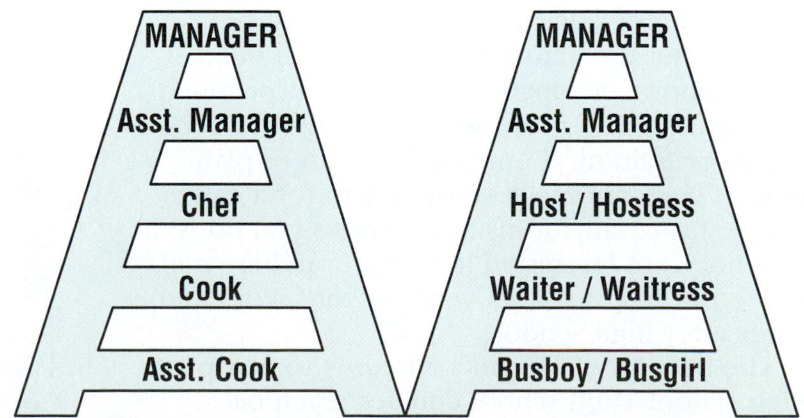

Figure 32-1 ***These career ladders show how workers can progress in the food service industry. They master one job and then move up to the next.***

Courtesy of Educational Foundation of the National Restaurant Association.

Onboard Internet access is making automobiles smarter and more fun. "E-cars" allow you to retrieve e-mail, check stocks, keep up with sports scores, and request mechanical help if needed. The new wireless technology that transmits information to and from a vehicle is called *telematics*. In 2001, auto manufacturers began to offer telematics on many new-model cars. It is estimated that the number of telematics users will reach 16 million by 2004. An important feature of this technology is voice recognition that allows you to communicate without taking your hands off the wheel.

to be able to read blueprints and use machine tools and special measuring instruments. To work as a computer programmer, you would have to learn how to translate ideas into language the computer could understand and write instructions it could follow. To become a pilot, of course, you would have to learn how to fly a plane.

Like a hobby or a sport, every occupation involves knowledge and skills that must be learned. But the amount of preparation needed varies among occupations. Deciding how much time and effort you are willing to put into education or training is important to career planning. It does not make sense to aim for a career as a veterinarian, for instance, unless you do well in school, are interested in science, and are willing to put in at least six years of hard work and study after high school.

The best way to begin a career is to complete high school. High school courses teach basic skills that will help you be a better worker, consumer, and citizen. A high school diploma is necessary if you want to go to college, too. And you will usually need one to get into trade schools, technical institutes, apprenticeship programs, or the military. Moreover, most employers prefer to hire people who are at least high school graduates.

The choices that are open to you after high school are shown in Figure 32-2. As you can see, many options are available to get necessary education and training. The path you choose depends on the kind of occupation you have in mind—and the time and effort you are willing to put into your education and training.

TYPES OF EDUCATION AND TRAINING

From hearing people talk, you may sometimes get the feeling that almost everyone gets a college education. That is not so. About three-fourths of all high school graduates do continue their schooling, though not necessarily in college. Six common types of education and training are described below.

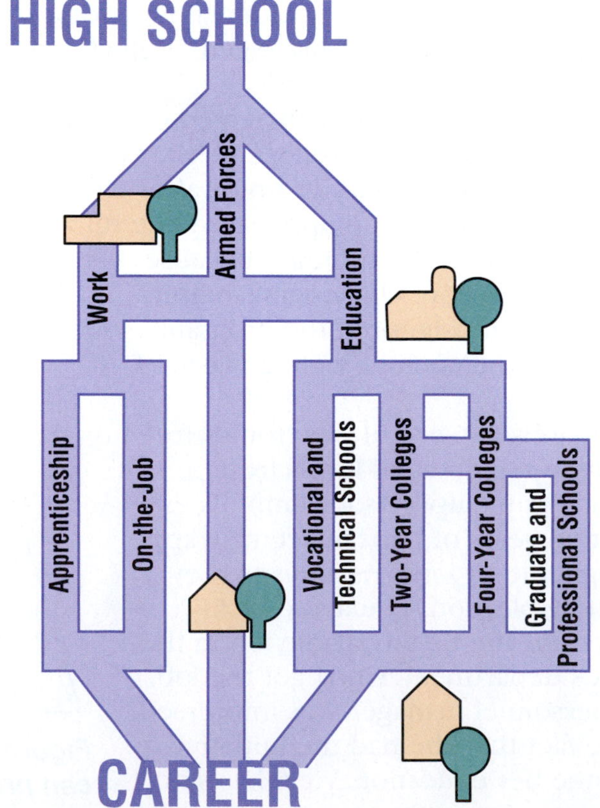

Figure 32-2 ***Several different paths may lead to your career goal.***

Apprenticeship programs are common in building trades.

On-the-Job Training

Almost all occupations involve some sort of learning by doing, also known as on-the-job training (OJT). A skilled worker teaches you as you watch. You then do the task under that worker's supervision. An advantage of OJT is that you are paid while you learn. Some jobs are almost always learned through OJT. Examples include postal clerk, machine-tool setter, shoe repairer, and furniture upholsterer. Generally, OJT is given for jobs that take more than a few days to learn, but less than formal apprenticeship would require.

Very often, OJT is combined with short-term classroom training. A power truck operator, for example, may take a safe driving course lasting several days. In some cases, OJT takes a few years. Air traffic controllers, for example, need two or three years of training and work experience before they are considered fully qualified.

Apprenticeship

An **apprenticeship** is a formal on-the-job program during which a worker (called an **apprentice**) learns a trade. Extensive OJT and related instruction are involved. Apprenticeships usually last about four years, but they may range from one to six years. During this time, the apprentice works under a skilled, experienced worker called a **journey worker**. Upon completion of the apprenticeship program, the apprentice becomes a journey worker.

Under the journey worker's guidance, the apprentice gradually learns the trade and performs

Electrician
Carpenter
Plumber
Pipe fitter (any industry)
Sheet metal worker
Electrician, maintenance
Machinist
Tool-and-die maker
Roofer
Firefighter
Bricklayer (construction)
Cook (hotel and restaurant)
Structural steel worker
Painter
Operating engineer
Correction officer
Maintenance mechanic (any industry)
Electronics mechanic
Automobile mechanic
Millwright
Construction equipment mechanic
Police officer I
Airframe and power plant mechanic
Diesel mechanic
Electrician, airplane
Insulation worker
Welder, combination
Line maintainer
Refrigeration mechanic (any industry)
Cement mason
Boilermaker I
Environmental control system installer-servicer
Fire medic
Line erector
Cook (any industry)
Toolmaker
Radio station operator
Car repairer (railroad)
Stationary engineer
Telegraphic-typewriter operator

***Figure 32-3* A majority of apprentices work in these occupations.**
Source: Occupational Outlook Quarterly

MATH CONNECTION

You are considering two occupations: office assistant and dental hygienist. You would not require any further training to become an office assistant, and you would earn $10 an hour. To become a dental hygienist, you would have to go to school for two years, but you could make $20 an hour to start. You have a relative who will pay your tuition. Five years from now, assuming you work 40 hours per week for 50 weeks of the year, in which job will you have earned more income before taxes?

SOLUTION

To calculate the amount of income, you must multiply the hourly wage, the number of hours worked per week, the number of weeks worked per year, and the number of years worked.

Total income for office assistant position $= \$10 \times 40 \times 50 \times 5$

$= \$100{,}000$

Total income for dental hygienist position $= \$20 \times 40 \times 50 \times 3$ (two years spent in school)

$= \$120{,}000$

You would earn $20,000 more working for three years as a beginning dental hygienist than you would working for five years as an office assistant.

the work under less and less supervision. Apprentices are full-time employees. An apprentice's pay generally starts out at about half that of an experienced worker and gradually increases throughout the apprenticeship. Many programs are cosponsored by trade unions that offer apprentices union membership.

The main drawback to apprenticeship is the stiff competition to get into a program. Generally, program sponsors seek people who seem to have the greatest chances of completing the program. To get your name placed on an **apprenticeship register** (waiting list), you usually have to take an aptitude test, have an interview, and meet the necessary physical requirements. Once you are on the register, the wait can last months or even years.

Vocational and Technical Schools

Many types of schools offer vocational training to teach skills used on the job. Vocational programs are offered by high schools, vocational high schools, and area vocational centers. Common areas of study include business, office, and distributive education; family and consumer sciences; technical and technology education; health occupations; and agriculture/agribusiness.

Other sources of training include trade schools, technical institutes, business schools, and correspondence or home-study schools. Privately run schools such as these are often called **proprietary schools**. In classes lasting from several weeks to several years, these schools will teach you cosmetology, barbering, flying, office procedures, computer operations, fashion design, locksmithing, and many other skills. A proprietary school is often more expensive than a public institution such as a community college.

In a vocational or technical school, you will practice in the classroom those skills you will need on the job. In business school, you might do word processing, file, use copy machines, or keep financial records. In programs for health occupations, you might operate medical equipment. People learning to be mechanics and repairers would take classes in blueprint reading and shop math.

When you complete your program, you will receive a certificate. You will then be ready to begin work, though your employer may also want to give you some on-the-job training.

Community and Junior Colleges

These two-year colleges provide two types of programs. One is the college transfer program, a two-year general education program for students who plan to transfer to a four-year college. General education courses include English, history, science, art, and music. The other is the occupational or career program, which offers specialized skill training leading directly to employment. Though a typical occupational program lasts two years, some, such as licensed practical nurse, can be learned in one year.

A community or junior college offers training in many occupational areas. Examples include computer service technician, dental hygienist, forestry technician, emergency medical technician, recreation leader, auto mechanic, and welder.

Community and junior colleges offer two main advantages. First, they have close ties with local business and industry and try to tailor their training programs to the needs of the local area. This makes it easier for students to find jobs after training. Another advantage is that these colleges are usually less expensive to attend. Since they are supported by local property taxes, many colleges charge low tuition.

Colleges and Universities

Colleges and universities are four-year institutions that vary widely in terms of whether they or their different programs of study are intended to prepare students for specific occupations. Some are primarily liberal arts schools that offer a broad, general education. Others are very specialized and are oriented toward engineering and technology. Still others, such as large state universities, offer a combination of general and specialized education.

A typical state college or university offers 100 or more areas of study called **majors**. Common majors include business and administration, journalism, education, engineering, political science, chemistry, economics, plant and soil science, art, theater, and psychology.

By and large, college does not prepare you for one particular occupation. Instead, most undergraduate programs give you a foundation upon which many careers can be built. In four years of college, you can expect to gain a basic education in your chosen field of study. In addition, you will be expected to broaden your knowledge of literature, mathematics, science, history, the fine arts, and many other areas. One advantage of college is that you usually have a lot of freedom in choosing courses that interest you.

Kurt is attending a state university. His major is Administration of Justice. Within his major, he takes courses in law enforcement, correctional management, juvenile justice, and delinquency prevention. Administration of Justice graduates get jobs as police officers, corrections counselors, parole officers, and so on. Kurt plans to get additional training and hopes to become an FBI agent.

Military Training

Another way to get education and training is to join a branch of the Armed Forces—Army, Navy, Air Force, Marines, or Coast Guard. The military prepares people for a variety of occupations in which civilians also work. These include cook, nurse, computer operator, mechanic, firefighter, and hundreds of others. While in the service, you can learn occupational skills and gain work experience. Then, when you get out, you can use your skills to get a civilian job. Or you may decide to make a career of military service.

LESSON 32.1 REVIEW

1. Give three reasons why you should consider getting additional education or training beyond high school.
2. What is the best way to begin a career?
3. Identify six common types of education and training.
4. What is the difference between OJT and apprenticeship?
5. Which is more expensive to attend, a community college or a proprietary school? Why?
6. Community and junior colleges provide two main types of programs. Name them.

HIGH-GROWTH OCCUPATIONS FOR THE 21st CENTURY

Writers and Editors

Writers and editors communicate through the written word. *Writers* develop original fiction and nonfiction for books, magazines, trade journals, newspapers, technical reports, web sites, company newsletters, radio and television broadcasts, movies, and advertisements. *Editors* select and prepare material for publication or broadcast and review and edit a writer's work.

Newswriters prepare news items for newspapers or news broadcasts, based on information supplied by reporters or wire services. *Columnists* analyze and interpret the news and write commentaries, based on reliable sources, personal knowledge, and experience. *Editorial writers* express opinions, often in accordance with their publication's viewpoint, to stimulate public debate on current affairs.

Technical writers put scientific and technical information into easily understandable language. They prepare operating and maintenance manuals, catalogs, parts lists, assembly instructions, sales promotion materials, and project proposals. They also write and edit technical reports and oversee preparation of photographs, diagrams, charts, and other illustrations.

Writers develop various types of original materials, including fictional books, newspaper columns, and technical reports.

Copywriters prepare advertising copy for use by publication or broadcast media, to promote the sale of goods and services.

Editors frequently write and almost always review, rewrite, and edit the work of writers. An editor's responsibilities vary depending on the employer and editorial position held. In the publishing industry, an editor's primary duties are to plan and edit the contents of books, technical journals, trade magazines, and general-interest publications.

Major newspapers and news magazines usually employ several types of editors. The *executive editor* oversees assistant editors who have responsibility for particular subjects, such as local news, international news, feature stories, or sports. Executive editors generally have the final say about what stories get published and how they should be covered. The *managing editor* usually is responsible for the daily operation of the news department. *Assignment editors* determine which reporters will cover a given story. *Copy editors* review and edit a reporter's copy for accuracy, grammar, punctuation, and style.

LESSON 32.2 EDUCATIONAL INFORMATION

OBJECTIVES

- KNOW SOURCES OF INFORMATION REGARDING EDUCATION AND TRAINING
- KNOW SOURCES OF INFORMATION REGARDING FINANCIAL AID

EDUCATION AND TRAINING

To make a good educational decision, you will need information on various schools—their courses of study, admissions requirements, costs, and so on.

In Chapter 14, you learned how to use the *Occupational Outlook Handbook (OOH)* in an occupational search. At the end of every occupational description in the *OOH*, a section titled "Sources of Additional Information" appears. For each occupation in which you are interested, write to the sources listed. The information you receive will frequently list places where education and training are available.

Both private and government publishers put out guides to education and training programs. Your school guidance office or career center should have a collection of such guides. So, too, should your local public library. And, of course, such material is available on the Web. Many of these guides are updated annually, so be sure to use the most recent edition.

Most colleges and universities have web sites. To find the web site for a school that interests you, visit a web portal such as Yahoo! and choose the "College" or "Education" link.

If you want to learn more about apprenticeship, your local Job Service is probably the best source of information. In some cities, Apprenticeship Information Centers (AICs) furnish information, counseling, and aptitude testing. They also direct people needing more specific help to union hiring halls, Joint Apprenticeship Committees, and employer sponsors. Ask a Job Service counselor if there is an AIC in your community.

For information about education and training in the Armed Forces, contact the local recruiting office of the branch in which you are interested. Each service has information available describing its specific program.

CAREER DECISIONS

You notice an advertisement in the paper for Whitney Business College. The ad states, "Flexible hours, credit for life experiences, tuition financing arranged, guaranteed job upon graduation." The school is not too far from your home.

"This could be just what I am looking for," you say to yourself. "I think I will give them a call."

WHAT WOULD YOU DO?

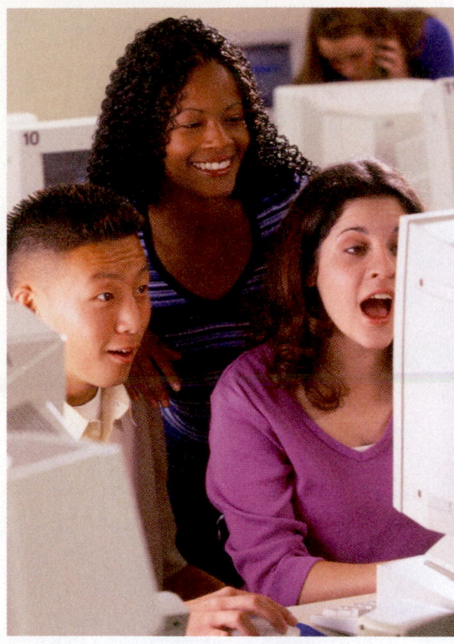

You can find information about education, training, and financial aid on the Internet.

WORKFORCE TRENDS

Educational levels are rising, as is the demand for highly educated workers. Yet for workers who do not attend college, skills will still play an important role. The majority of jobs being created today, while requiring less than an associate's degree, will call for specific cognitive and communication skills. Continued technological change will increase the number of occupations that require at least some technical skills. Lifelong learning will grow in importance.

FINANCIAL AID

The cost of education or training is an important consideration in making educational decisions. You will have to think about how much training you and your family can afford as well as how much you would like to get.

In some cases, the training requirements for a specific occupation will vary greatly. For example, to become a registered nurse, you could attend one of three different types of programs:

- A two-year associate degree program at a junior or community college
- A two- to three-year diploma program operated in connection with a hospital
- A four- or five-year degree program at a college or university

The costs per year of training will also be quite different.

Do not be discouraged if you want to pursue education beyond high school, but you or your family cannot afford the cost. Begin by talking to your school guidance counselor. **Financial aid** may be available. Financial aid can include **scholarships** (money awarded on the basis of outstanding academic achievement), loans, **grants** (funds given to qualified persons), and the like. It is offered to individuals pursuing postsecondary education by schools, educational foundations, business firms, religious groups, community organizations, and the government. A good discussion, "Financial Aid Information," is in the *OOH* and available on the Web at http://stats.bls.gov/oco/oco20023.htm. Make sure you use the most recent edition if you use the printed *OOH*.

Take advantage of educational opportunities. Education is never wasted. Whether you take formal course work, learn on the job, or study on your own, you benefit as a worker and human being by continuing to learn and grow.

LESSON 32.2 REVIEW

1. **List three types of information that you will need to make a good educational decision.**
2. **Give two sources of information about apprenticeships.**
3. **Provide an example to illustrate how education or training requirements may vary for a given occupation.**
4. **Name a publication with information about types of financial aid.**

FOCUS ON THE WORKER

TRAINING AND MORE TRAINING

In the last decade or so, the automobile industry has undergone dramatic change. Competition has forced companies to modernize plants and alter manufacturing methods to improve quality and productivity. A different kind of worker is being recruited and trained. The following is a description of a typical hiring and training process.

Some employees may receive weeks or months of OJT before beginning work.

Job applicants must take general aptitude tests, drug tests, and written exams. Counseling and in-depth interviews are conducted to determine each person's company loyalty, team spirit, and versatility. Assembly-line simulations are also performed. The application and screening process takes about a day and a half per person. Employees are hired 13 or 14 weeks before they are placed on the assembly line.

New hires receive three weeks of "soft training" in which they learn the basics of teamwork and company philosophy. Then they are assigned to an area such as the body shop where they get seven weeks of classroom and hands-on training. During this time, they are screened according to job capabilities. Individuals are assigned to the job for which they are best suited. Next, they are sent to a unit leader (similar to a foreman). The unit leader further screens the workers and decides at which point on the assembly line they will work best. Then three or four more weeks of off-line training is given.

Recruiting and training a single employee costs thousands of dollars. Companies invest such sums because they believe that the key to success is picking the best employees and training them well. Similar recruitment and training efforts are becoming standard throughout the automobile manufacturing industry. The emphasis on quality employees and training is shared by hundreds of other businesses and industries.

THINK CRITICALLY

1. Do you think more businesses and industries will adopt this kind of approach to recruiting and training employees? Why or why not?
2. Suppose you wanted to apply for a job at this company. How would you prepare?

CHAPTER 32

Chapter in Brief

Lesson 32.1 *Education and Training*

A. Some jobs do not require additional schooling. Such jobs, however, tend to be low-paying and have little job security. Getting a college degree will not guarantee you a job. Yet, it is a mistake to think that you will not need more education or training after high school. Additional education and training will be one of the best investments you can make in your future.

B. Every occupation involves knowledge and skills that must be learned. But the amount of preparation needed varies among occupations. Deciding how much time and effort you are willing to put into education or training is important to career planning.

C. Six common education and training options are on-the-job training, apprenticeship, vocational and technical schools, community and junior colleges, colleges and universities, and military training.

Lesson 32.2 *Educational Information*

A. To make a good educational decision, you will need information on various schools. Private and government publishers produce guides to education and training programs. Such material is also available on the Web.

B. The cost of education or training is an important consideration in making educational decisions. There are many sources of financial aid.

C. Education is never wasted. You will benefit as a worker and human being by continuing to learn and grow.

Activities

1. Select an entry-level occupation of interest. Develop a career ladder for the occupation similar to those in Figure 32-1. You will probably need to ask people in related occupations for assistance.
2. Go to your school or public library or browse the Web. What sources of education and training information do you find? Is there information about financial aid? Your instructor may assign you a specific task. List the information your teacher requests and make a copy for each class member.
3. Ask your local Job Service what types of information it has about apprenticeship and where the nearest Apprenticeship Information Center is.
4. Identify a school or college that interests you. Use one of the resources in this chapter to find the following information: (a) What are the entrance requirements? (b) How long does it take to complete the program you are interested in? (c) How much does it cost to attend? (d) Is financial aid available? (e) Does the institution provide job-placement services? Prepare a written report summarizing your findings and submit it to your instructor.

REVIEW

5. Invite a recruiter from one of the military services to class to discuss types of training programs and educational benefits provided by the military.

Word Power

On a separate sheet of paper, match each definition with the correct term. All definitions will be used, and a definition will be used only once.

6. Primary areas of study chosen by students for a college or other degree
7. Financial aid awarded to a student on the basis of outstanding academic achievement
8. A trainee engaged in learning an occupation under the guidance and direction of a skilled worker
9. A group of related occupations with different skill requirements that can be arranged in a ladder-type fashion from low to high
10. A waiting list for individuals who have met the preliminary requirements for entrance into an apprenticeship program
11. A broad term that includes all forms of financial assistance (scholarships, loans, grants, and so on) to individuals pursuing postsecondary education
12. A skilled, experienced worker; the status achieved by an apprentice upon completion of an apprenticeship program
13. Funds provided to qualified persons to assist them in attending college or in other postsecondary education
14. A formal program of on-the-job training and related instruction by which a worker learns an occupation under the direction of a journey worker
15. Privately operated postsecondary vocational, technical, or business schools

a. apprentice
b. apprenticeship
c. apprenticeship register
d. career ladder
e. financial aid
f. grants
g. journey worker
h. majors
i. proprietary schools
j. scholarships

Think Critically

16. Most of you are probably employed as part of a work experience education program. Discuss how learning on the job is different from learning at school.
17. Has working made you more aware of the need for education or training? If so, how?
18. Many companies encourage their employees to pursue additional education (beyond that received on the job). How does this benefit the employer?
19. More and more adults are returning to college and other types of education. What is behind this trend?
20. If you are working now, find out what type of education or training you would need to move ahead in your job. Discuss this in class.

GLOSSARY

accident An unplanned event often resulting in personal injury, property damage, or both (p. 240)

adjusted gross income In preparing an income tax return, the amount of income left after certain expenses have been subtracted (p. 401)

adjustments to income Certain nontaxable expenses, such as alimony and IRA contributions, subtracted from income in preparing an income tax return (p. 401)

advertising Any type of public notice or message intended to aid in the sale of a product or service (p. 319)

aerobic exercises Exercises that speed up the action of the heart and lungs by increasing the body's ability to take in oxygen (p. 462)

affirmative action Set of policies and programs designed to correct past discrimination (p. 109)

agenda The list of items to be discussed in a meeting of an organization (p. 261)

allegation Unproven statement about someone or something (p. 474)

allocation Distribution of income to various items in a budget (p. 361)

allowances Tax exemptions to which a person is entitled (p. 88)

alternatives Options to choose from in making a decision (p. 158)

annual percentage rate (APR) Percentage cost of credit on a yearly basis (p. 349)

anxiety State of feeling worried or uneasy, usually about something that may happen in the future (p. 80)

appraise To evaluate someone or something for specific qualifications or qualities (p. 64)

apprentice Person who learns a trade in a formal on-the-job program (p. 483)

apprenticeship Formal on-the-job program during which a worker learns a trade (p. 483)

apprenticeship register A waiting list for entry into an apprenticeship program (p. 484)

aptitudes Things that one is good at doing; natural talents or developed abilities (p. 172)

area The number of square units of space on the surface of a figure enclosed by the perimeter (p. 230)

arraignment Hearing in which a prosecutor, police officer, or citizen brings charges against the arrested person (p. 429)

assertive To be firm and positive in stating one's position or point of view (p. 325)

authority Power or rank to give orders and make assignments to others (p. 82)

automated teller machines (ATMs) Electronic banking terminals that allow customers to withdraw cash, make deposits, or transfer funds to another account (p. 334)

automatic raise Regular pay raise received by all employees (p. 136)

bail Money deposited with a court to guarantee that an accused person will show up for trial (p. 429)

basal metabolism The minimum amount of energy (calories) necessary for continuous body functioning (p. 456)

beneficiary Person to whom an insurance company pays benefits (p. 382)

benefits Financial help in times of sickness, old age, or disability (p. 412)

bias A person's tendency to favor something because of familiarity or preference (p. 474)

board of directors Elected by the stockholders of a corporation to make major business decisions about the company (p. 287)

body language Unspoken communication through physical movements, expressions, and gestures (p. 68)

bond A loan to a company or government agency on which interest is paid periodically or when the bond is due (p. 369)

brand-name products Goods that have a unique name given to them by the manufacturer that affiliates the product with the manufacturer (p. 317)

brokers Individuals who specialize in selling stocks and other financial investments (p. 368)

browser Type of software used to locate and display information on the Web (p. 278)

budget Plan for managing income and expenditures (p. 356)

bylaws Rules that define the basic characteristics of an organization and describe how it will operate (p. 260)

calories Units of energy produced by food when it is used by the body (p. 455)

capital gain An increase in the value of stock or another asset that is only realized when the asset is sold (p. 369)

career and technical student organizations (CTSOs) Nonprofit nationwide organizations with state and local chapters that are supported primarily by student-paid dues; each organization is linked with an occupational area, such as business, family and consumer sciences, or health occupations (p. 256)

career guidance Assisting students in career planning and decision making (p. 9)

career ladder Group of related occupations with different skill requirements that are organized into ranks like steps on a ladder (p. 481)

cash discount A reduction in price, often of several percent, offered to a buyer to encourage early payment on an account (p. 226)

catastrophe Disaster or misfortune that often occurs suddenly (p. 378)

certificate of deposit (CD) Money that is deposited into an interest-bearing account for a predetermined length of time and rate of return (p. 364)

charter Legal document that gives a corporation permission to conduct certain business activities (p. 287)

check register Booklet or forms for recording checking account transactions (p. 340)

circumference The perimeter of a circle (p. 230)

citizenship Membership in a community, state, county, or nation; carrying out the duties of a citizen (p. 468)

civil service test Test administered to a job applicant seeking a government position. (p. 57)

clients The business customers of a professional worker (p. 122)

code of ethics Rules for professional practice and behavior (p. 256)

co-insurance (co-payment) A provision of health insurance that requires a policyholder to share in the expenses beyond the deductible amount (p. 380)

commission The fee charged by a broker for purchasing or selling stocks for customers (p. 369)

common law Laws arising from decisions made by judges (p. 428)

communication Sending information, ideas, or feelings from one person to another through language (p. 206)

comparison shopping Finding the cost of a product or service at several different places before making a decision to buy (p. 318)

compatible Pleasant or agreeable (p. 67)

compensation Total amount of income and benefits a person receives for his or her job (p. 132)

competition The efforts of sellers to win potential customers (p. 304)

complaint An expression of dissatisfaction with a product or service (p. 325)

compounding A process in which an institution adds interest to an account, the balance rises, and the account continues to earn more interest based on the higher balance (p. 365)

computer An electronic tool that helps people do various kinds of work (p. 270)

computer literacy General knowledge of what computers are, how they work, and for what they can be used (p. 270)

conditions of employment Specific details of a job offer, such as working hours, salary or wages, and fringe benefits (p. 72)

condominium Individually owned townhouse or apartment with shared ownership of common facilities, like the gounds (p. 441)

confirm To verify or make firm, such as calling to check on an appointment (p. 66)

consumer Someone who buys or uses goods and services (p. 316)

consumption The process of using goods and services that have been produced (p. 303)

cooperation Getting along with and working well with others (p. 96)

cooperative A townhouse or apartment that is part of a property jointly owned by residents (p. 441)

corporation A business that is owned by stockholders (p. 287)

cover letter Letter of application accompanied by a resume that is sent to a potential employer (p. 54)

credit The receipt of goods, money, or services in exchange for a promise to pay (p. 348)

creditors Persons or companies to which one owes money (p. 288)

debit card Plastic card that is used to immediately transfer funds for a purchase from a bank account to a seller. Funds are taken directly from the user's checking account. (p. 336)

decision making The process of choosing between two or more alternatives or options (p. 158)

decision-making styles Typical ways in which people make decisions (p. 163)

decree Order requiring the defendant to stop doing whatever he or she was doing that was bringing harm to the plaintiff (p. 431)

deductible In traditional health insurance, amount the insured must pay on medical expenses before the insurer begins to pay (p. 379)

deductions Certain amounts that are withheld from the paycheck of an employee (p. 133); various nontaxable items such as donations to charity or churches and mortgage interest (p. 401)

defendant Person required to answer charges in a lawsuit (p. 431)

deficit The amount spent over budget or over what has been taken in (p. 310)

delegates Assigns tasks to lower-ranking employees (p. 83)

demand The willingness of consumers to spend money for goods and services (p. 303)

deposit ticket A preprinted form used to deposit any combination of currency, coins, and checks into a checking account (p. 343)

depression Severe recession marked by stagnant business activity (p. 309)

direct-mail advertising Advertising received through the mail (p. 319)

disabling injury An injury causing death, permanent disability, or any degree of temporary total disability beyond the day of the accident (p. 240)

discrimination Favoring one person over another (p. 108)

diversify To spread out money over several different types of investment options (p. 368)

dividends Profits that a company divides among its shareholders (p. 369)

due process The legal right to be notified of a complaint against you and to state your case or point of view before a decision is made (p. 85)

economics The study of how goods and services are produced, distributed, and used (p. 302)

electrocute To cause death by electric shock (p. 242)

electronic banking Term used to describe various types of electronic fund transfers (EFTs) (p. 336)

employability skills General work habits and attitudes required in all jobs (p. 9)

employment practices The manners and methods by which employers deal with their employees (p. 107)

endorsement Signature, sometimes with a brief message, on a check needed to cash, deposit, or transfer ownership of it (p. 342)

enthusiasm Eagerness; a strong interest in something (p. 97)

entrepreneur Person who runs his or her own business (p. 286)

entry-level job Job that requires little or no experience (p. 33)

enunciation How distinctly or clearly one speaks (p. 209)

environment One's surroundings; including neighborhood, family, friends, and school (p. 166)

equal employment opportunity The ideas, supported by law, that employers, unions, and employment agencies cannot discriminate against people because of race, religion, sex, or national origin (p. 108)

Equal Employment Opportunity Commission (EEOC) Federal agency that administers the Civil Rights Act and related employment laws (p. 109)

equity Money invested in a home above the amount owed on a mortgage (p. 443)

exempt To be free from something, such as taxes (p. 88)

exemptions In preparing an income tax return, set amounts deducted from income for oneself and dependents such as children and a spouse (p. 401)

expenditures Money that is spent (p. 356)

experiences What people do and what happens to them in their environment (p. 166)

face value For life insurance, the amount paid in the event of the policyholder's death (p. 382)

Federal Insurance Contributions Act (FICA) The federal law requiring employers to deduct an amount from workers' paychecks for Social Security and to contribute an equal amount (p. 416)

fee Sum of money charged by a private employment agency for helping someone find a job; it is paid by either the employer or the employee (p. 35)

filing The process of completing and submitting an income tax return (p. 402)

finance charge The total dollar amount one pays for using credit (p. 349)

financial aid All forms of financial assistance, including scholarships, grants, and loans, to individuals pursuing postsecondary education (p. 488)

follow-up letter A thank-you letter a job applicant sends to an interviewer following a job interview (p. 71)

franchise Contract with a company to sell its goods and services within a certain area (p. 292)

full-service banks Banks that offer customers a wide range of services, including loans, checking and savings accounts, credit cards, safety deposit boxes, and traveler's checks (p. 334)

generic products Products that state only the name of the product on the label without affiliation with a specific manufacturer (p. 317)

goods Articles that are produced or manufactured (p. 316)

goods-producing industries Companies and businesses, such as manufacturing, construction, mining, and agriculture, which produce some type of product (p. 189)

goodwill Acts of kindness, consideration, or assistance (p. 123)

grammar Set of rules about the correct speaking and writing of a language (p. 209)

grand jury For serious crimes, a group of citizens selected to determine if there should be a trial based on the evidence presented to them (p. 429)

grants Funds provided to qualified persons to assist them in attending college or in other postsecondary education (p. 488)

graphical user interface (GUI) A feature of the operating system of a computer that provides icons and menus from which the user can select commands, typically with a mouse (p. 274)

grooming Maintaining a neat, attractive appearance (p. 146)

gross pay Amount of salary or wages that a person earns during a certain period of time (p. 133)

guarantee Pledge that something is exactly as stated or advertised (p. 322)

hardware The physical equipment that makes up a computer (p. 273)

health maintenance organization (HMO) Alternative to traditional insurance in which all health care is provided for a fixed fee (p. 380)

honesty A refusal to lie, steal, or mislead in any way (p. 97)

human relations Interactions among people (p. 120)

hypothetical Imagined or pretended situations or ideas (p. 65)

icons Small pictures that are used by a GUI instead of keyed commands (p. 274)

incentive Potential reward to work toward (p. 135)

income Money coming in (p. 356)

indictment Formal statement charging a person with an offense (p. 429)

individual retirement account (IRA) A voluntary private pension plan that allows employed individuals to save a certain amount annually toward retirement and receive special tax benefits (p. 418)

industries In the SIC system, all places of employment, such as factories and hospitals (p. 186)

inflation When prices of goods and services rise sharply (p. 309)

interest A feeling of excitement and involvement (p. 97)

interests Things that one likes to do (p. 172)

Internet An "*inter*connected *net*work of networks" that links millions of small computer networks worldwide (p. 277)

interpersonal attraction The tendency to be drawn to another person, often because of similar characteristics and preferences (p. 121)

intuition A feeling or a hunch (p. 163)

investing Process of using money not required for personal and family needs to increase overall financial worth (p. 368)

invoice A bill for goods (p. 225)

job Paid position at a specific place or setting (p. 6)

job application form Form used by employers to collect personal, educational, and occupational information from a job applicant (p. 47)

job interview Face-to-face meeting between a job seeker and potential employer (p. 64)

job-lead card Card on which to record information and notes about a job lead (p. 36)

Job Service A state system of public employment offices that help unemployed people find jobs (p. 35)

journey worker Skilled, experienced worker under whom an apprentice trains (p. 483)

judgment Thinking about a problem and making the right decision (p. 95); decision by the judge in a civil suit in favor of either the plaintiff or the defendant (p. 431)

keyboarding skills The ability to type and give commands to a computer using a keyboard (p. 270)

landlord The owner or manager of a rental property (p. 442)

law The body of enforced rules by which people live together (p. 428)

leadership Process of influencing people in order to accomplish the goals of the organization (p.254)

lease The rental agreement between a tenant and a landlord (p. 442)

letter of resignation Letter written by an employee notifying an employer of the intent to quit a job (p. 140)

liability Legal responsibility for something, such as damages or costs (p. 383)

life roles The various parts of a person's life, such as parent, citizen, spouse, or worker (p. 180)

lifestyle Way in which a person lives (p. 180)

line item Single budgeted item (p. 361)

liquidity The quality of being easily converted into cash; refers to assets (p. 363)

loyalty Faithfulness; believing in and being devoted to something (p. 97)

lump-sum payment A one-time payment of money to the surviving spouse or child of a deceased person who is covered by Social Security (p. 414)

majority A vote of at least one more than half of the people who vote (p. 261)

majors Primary areas of study chosen by a student for a college or other degree (p. 485)

markdown A reduction in the selling price of a product (p. 227)

market An area of economic activity created whenever goods and services are bought and sold (p. 303)

markup Amount added by a retailer to the cost price of goods that allows it to cover expenses and make a fair profit (p. 226)

measurement The act of determining the dimensions, quantity, or degree of something (p. 229)

merit raise Raise based on the amount and quality of an employee's work (p. 136)

microprocessor A CPU contained on a single tiny silicon chip (p. 273)

minimum wage The lowest hourly wage the law permits employers to pay workers (p. 107)

minors Persons who have not reached the full legal age (p. 32)

modem Electronic device for transmitting computer data over standard telephone lines or fiberoptic cable (p. 271)

money market fund Type of mutual fund that invests in short-term, high-liquidity investments (p. 370)

monopoly Exclusive control over the supply of a product or service (p. 307)

morale Mood or spirit, such as the attitude and emotion of employees (p. 84)

mortgage A loan, typically for 30 years, obtained from a financial institution to buy housing (p. 442)

motion Brief statement of a proposed action by a participant in a meeting (p. 261)

mutual fund An investment company that pools the money of thousands of investors and buys a collection of investments that may include stocks, bonds, and other financial assets (p. 369)

natural disaster An uncontrollable event in nature that destroys life or property (p. 244)

negotiable order of withdrawal (NOW) account Interest-bearing checking account often offered by a savings and loan institution.The funds are drawn against a savings account and the money earns interest until the day it is withdrawn. (p. 338)

net pay Pay that a person has left to take home after all deductions have been made (p. 134)

network Two or more computers linked together by cable or wireless means (p. 277)

nutrients Chemical substances in food that provide energy, help regulate body processes, and furnish basic materials for building, repairing, and maintaining body tissues (p. 454)

nutrition Process by which plants and animals take in and use food (p. 454)

obsolete No longer used (p. 21)

occupation The name given to a group of similar tasks that a person performs for pay (p. 6)

occupational description Describes what the work in an occupation is like—the tasks involved, the working environment, the earnings, and so on (p. 195)

Occupational Outlook Handbook (OOH) A reference source produced by the federal government that provides occupational information and data (p. 186)

Occupational Safety and Health Administration (OSHA) Federal agency that sets and enforces standards for safe and healthful working conditions (p. 111)

occupational search Search in which a person collects information about an occupation of interest using one or more printed resources or databases (p. 195)

occupational skills Skills needed to perform the tasks or duties of a specific occupation (p. 8)

opinion One person's views about something (p. 473)

order of business Standard series of steps followed in a meeting (p. 261)

overdraft A check written for more than is in an account (p. 338)

overtime Time worked beyond the standard 40-hour workweek (p. 107)

overtime pay Wage received for working more than 40 hours a week, usually $1\frac{1}{2}$ times the normal hourly wage (p. 132)

parliamentarian A group member who advises the chair on matters of procedure (p. 264)

parliamentary procedure Formal rules used to conduct a meeting in a fair and orderly manner (p. 260)

partnership A business that is owned by two or more persons who share in the company's management and profits (p. 287)

patients Persons under treatment or care by a medical practitioner (p. 122)

patronize To trade with or give business to a certain individual or company (p. 123)

patrons Customers of certain service-producing businesses or institutions (p. 122)

payee Person or institution to which a check is written (p. 339)

pension A regular payment of money to a person, usually a retired person (p. 413)

performance evaluation Process of judging how well an employee is doing on the job (p. 99)

perils For home insurance, the possible damages against which a home is insured (p. 383)

perimeter The distance around an object (p. 229)

peripherals Input and output devices of a computer that are located outside the CPU (p. 273)

personal data sheet Summary of personal, educational, and occupational information (p. 44)

personal hygiene The act of keeping one's body clean and healthy (p. 146)

physical fitness How well a person's heart and other organs function (p. 461)

plaintiff The complaining party in a lawsuit (p. 431)

policy manual Booklet given to new employees that explains a company's policies and rules (p. 84)

portfolio Collection of diverse investments (p. 369)

postdating Putting a date on a check that is later than the current date (p. 339)

posture The position of a person's body while standing, walking, or sitting (p. 147)

precedence In parliamentary procedure, the order of priority among the four types of motions used in a meeting (p. 261)

precincts Divisions of a county, ward, city, or town for election purposes; voting districts (p. 470)

pre-employment test Paper-and-pencil test or performance test administered by an employer as part of the job application process (p. 57)

prejudice Opinion that is based on insufficient information (p. 474)

premium For insurance, the price of a policy (p. 382)

pride A feeling of satisfaction with what you or someone you know has accomplished or possesses (p. 95)

probation Trial period during which one's performance is being observed and evaluated (p. 85)

problem Question in need of a solution or an answer (p. 158)

production The making of goods available for human needs and wants (p. 302)

productivity The output of a worker; how much a worker produces on the job (p. 94)

program Instructions to a computer on how to solve a certain problem or do a certain task; the instructions that tell a computer what to do (p. 271)

promotion Advancement to a higher-level job or position within a company (pp. 20, 138)

pronunciation The way in which words are spoken (p. 208)

propaganda Any organized effort or movement to spread certain information (p. 474)

proprietary schools Privately operated postsecondary vocational, technical, or business schools (p. 484)

proprietorship A business that is owned by one person who receives all the profits (p. 287)

prosperity Period of expanding economic growth (p. 309)

public safety All efforts by federal, state, and local governments to protect persons and property (p. 247)

punctuality Being on time (p. 96)

qualify Meet the preliminary requirements for a job or position (p. 18)

quorum Majority of the total membership of an organization (p. 261)

reality factors Persons, events, or situations over which we have little control that often influence decisions (p. 166)

recall Public request by a manufacturer for the return of a product that may be defective or contaminated (p. 324)

recession Downturn in the economy (p. 309)

reconciling Process of comparing a bank statement with one's personal check register to verify accuracy (p. 344)

references Names of individuals who are qualified to provide information about a job applicant to a potential employer (p. 44)

referrals Given to a student or worker by a job or career counselor in order to direct them to employers who are hiring (p. 34)

regular (fixed) expenditures Essential monthly payments that are usually the same amount each month, such as rent and car payments (p. 359)

reimburse To pay back money that has already been spent (p. 85)

responsibility At work, the duty to follow an order or carry out a work assignment (p. 82)

resume A one-page description of a job seeker's history and qualifications for employment (p. 49)

retailers Businesses that sell directly to consumers (p. 288)

revenue Money raised through taxes to pay the cost of government (p. 396)

risk Chance of loss (p. 378)

rumor Popular report or story that has not been proven and is mostly spread by word of mouth (p. 473)

safety Freedom from harm or the danger of harm (p. 241)

savings Cash that is set aside in a bank account to be used for financial emergencies and goals (p. 359)

scholarships Money awarded on the basis of outstanding academic achievement (p. 488)

security deposit A sum of money, usually equal to one month's rent, which a landlord holds while one rents an apartment (p. 447)

sedentary Inactive (p. 455)

self The sum of everything one is, including physical characteristics, behavior, and how one thinks (p. 172)

self-direction Personal act of setting goals and taking steps towards meeting them (p. 20)

self-employed Owning and operating one's own business (p. 286)

self-information Knowledge about one's self, particularly in relation to career decision making (p. 172)

seniority The length of time someone has worked for a company (p. 121)

service-producing industries Companies and businesses that produce or provide some type of personal or business service, such as transportation, finance, insurance, and trade (p. 189)

services Work performed by individuals or businesses for others (p. 316)

share draft account An interest-bearing checking account offered by credit unions in which a draft (check) is written against a savings account (p. 338)

signature card Form one fills out in order to open a checking account that holds information such as name, address, Social Security number, and phone number. The card is signed with the account owner's legal name. (p. 339)

social security Government programs that help people meet social and economic needs (p. 412)

Social Security The federal system of retirement benefits, survivors payments, hospital insurance for the elderly, and other services (p. 412)

software See *program*.

stable job Job that is considered to be permanent and that may last several years (p. 20)

Standard English The usual form of language used by the majority of Americans (p. 209)

Standard Industrial Classification (SIC) A system of grouping industries according to the type of product produced or service performed (p. 186)

Standard Occupational Classification (SOC) A system of grouping occupations based on the type of work performed (p. 186)

standard workweek By law, the completion of 40 hours of work within a seven-day period (p. 107)

statement of account Statement a bank sends monthly to its customers that shows a record of all transactions for the stated time period (p. 344)

statement of earnings Pay statement; the attachment to a paycheck that shows gross pay, deductions, and net pay (p. 134)

statute law Laws made by Congress and other government bodies (p. 428)

stock Shares of ownership in a company (p. 368)

stockholders The owners of a corporation who have stock or shares of ownershp in the company (p. 287)

stop-loss provision A condition of health insurance that prevents a person's out-of-pocket expenses from rising above a certain amount (p. 379)

stress Mental, emotional, or physical strain (p. 459)

stressors Good or bad events, activities, experiences, or situations, ranging from mild to severe, that cause stress (p. 459)

sublet To lease a property as a tenant to another person (p. 447)

summons Order issued by the clerk of courts commanding a party or witness to a lawsuit to appear in court on a certain day (p. 431)

sunscreens Special lotions or creams used to protect the skin from the sun's ultraviolet rays (p. 151)

supervisor Person with the power or rank to give orders and oversee the work of others (p. 87)

supplier Person or agency that distributes goods to retailers (p. 288)

supply The amount of goods or services available for sale (p. 303)

task group Work group that is formed to accomplish a particular objective (p. 125)

tax Required contribution of money people make to government (p. 396)

taxable income The amount of income on which you pay taxes (p. 401)

taxation Process by which the expenses of government are paid (p. 396)

tax credits Reductions in the amount of income tax owed (p. 402)

tax evasion Illegally avoiding the payment of some or all of one's income tax (p. 402)

technology Application of scientific knowledge to practical uses (p. 21)

tenant Person who rents a property (p. 442)

terms Stated time limit within which the buyer must pay for merchandise (p. 225)

territorial rights Unwritten rules concerning respect for the property and territory of others (p. 122)

townhouses Attached houses that may share common properties such as a pool or tennis courts (p. 441)

trade discount Deduction from the catalog price (or list price) of an item usually given to retailers to enable them to sell merchandise at a greater profit (p. 225)

training agreement A signed agreement outlining the relationships and responsibilities of the parties involved in a work experience education program (p. 9)

training plan A description of the knowledge, attitudes, and skills to be developed by the student participating in a work experience education program (p. 9)

training station Work experience student's place of employment (p. 9)

training wage Wage that may be paid to employees under the age of 20 for the first 90 days of employment. The training wage is set at 85 percent of the minimum wage. (p. 107)

variable expenditures Day-to-day living expenses that may change depending on the time of year, spending habits, and so on (p. 360)

vocabulary The total of all the words a person knows (p. 212)

wage base The amount of gross annual salary or wages subject to Social Security tax (p. 416)

wardrobe Wearing apparel; one's clothing (p. 150)

warrant A court order that authorizes a police officer to make a search, seizure, or arrest (p. 429)

warranty Guarantee or promise given by the manufacturer that a product is free from defects (p. 318)

wholesale houses Businesses that sell to retailers rather than to consumers (p. 289)

work Activity directed toward a purpose or a goal that produces something of value to oneself and/or to society (p. 5)

work credits Points used to determine eligibility for Social Security benefits that are linked to the amount of earnings (p. 416)

work experience education Education programs designed to provide opportunities for students to explore or participate in work as an extension of the regular school environment (p. 8)

work history All of the jobs that one holds during the course of a working lifetime (p. 18)

work permit Form issued by a student's school that gives a student legal permission to work during school hours as part of a work experience education program. This permit restricts the number of hours worked and the types of jobs a student can perform. (p. 32)

work values Attitudes and beliefs about the importance of various work activities (p. 172)

world of work Network of occupations and industries in the American economic system (p. 186)

World Wide Web A network within the Internet that provides sounds, pictures, and moving images in addition to text (p. 278)

INDEX

D

E

F

S

T

PHOTO CREDITS

Unit 1 Opener. xvi–1: Copyright 1997–1999 PhotoDisc, Inc. 1: Kelli Spurgeon. Photo used with permission.
Chapter 1. 2, 4, 5, 7, 8, 9, 11, and 13: Copyright 1997–1999 PhotoDisc, Inc.
Chapter 2. 16, 18, 19, 20, 22, 23, 24, and 25: Copyright 1997–1999 PhotoDisc, Inc.
Chapter 3. 28, 30, 31, 33, 38, and 39: Copyright 1997–1999 PhotoDisc, Inc.
Chapter 4. 42, 44, 49, 52, 53, 54, 58, and 59: Copyright 1997–1999 PhotoDisc, Inc.
Chapter 5. 62, 64, 67, 68, 70, 71, and 73: Copyright 1997–1999 PhotoDisc, Inc.

Unit 2 Opener. 76–77: Copyright 1997–1999 PhotoDisc, Inc. 77: Marcos Lopez. Photo used with permission.
Chapter 6. 78, 80, 81, 82, 86, 87, and 89: Copyright 1997–1999 PhotoDisc, Inc.
Chapter 7. 92, 94, 98, 99, and 101: Copyright 1997–1999 PhotoDisc, Inc.
Chapter 8. 104, 106, 107, 108, 110, 111, and 112: Copyright 1997–1999 PhotoDisc, Inc. 113: © CORBIS. 115: Copyright 1997–1999 PhotoDisc, Inc.
Chapter 9. 118, 120, 122, 124, 125, 126, and 127: Copyright 1997–1999 PhotoDisc, Inc.
Chapter 10. 130, 132, 133, 136, 137, 138, and 141: Copyright 1997–1999 PhotoDisc, Inc.
Chapter 11. 144, 146, 148, 149, and 151: Copyright 1997–1999 PhotoDisc, Inc.

Unit 3 Opener. 154–155: Copyright 1997–1999 PhotoDisc, Inc. 155: Pearlena Warren. Photo used with permission.
Chapter 12. 142, 156, 158, 162, 163, 166, and 167: Copyright 1997–1999 PhotoDisc, Inc.
Chapter 13. 170, 172, 173, 177, 178, 179, 180, and 181: Copyright 1997–1999 PhotoDisc, Inc.
Chapter 14. 184, 186, 191, 194, 195, and 199: Copyright 1997–1999 PhotoDisc, Inc.

Unit 4 Opener. 202–203: Copyright 1997–1999 PhotoDisc, Inc. Josh Trochelman. Photo used with permission.
Chapter 15. 202: Copyright 1997–1999 PhotoDisc, Inc. 204: © CORBIS. 206, 208, 209, 211, 212, 214, and 219: Copyright 1997–1999 PhotoDisc, Inc.
Chapter 16. 222: Copyright 1997–1999 PhotoDisc, Inc. 224: © CORBIS. 226, 227, 228, 229, 231, and 235: Copyright 1997–1999 PhotoDisc, Inc.
Chapter 17. 238, 240, 242, 243, 244, 246, 247, and 249: Copyright 1997–1999 PhotoDisc, Inc.
Chapter 18. 252: © CORBIS. 254, 255, 259, 260, and 265: Copyright 1997–1999 PhotoDisc, Inc.
Chapter 19. 268, 270, 273, 274, 276, and 277: Copyright 1997–1999 PhotoDisc, Inc. 281: © 2001 Thomson Learning.
Chapter 20. 284: © CORBIS. 286, 288, 290, 291, and 295: Copyright 1997–1999 PhotoDisc, Inc.

Unit 5 Opener. 298–299: Copyright 1997–1999 PhotoDisc, Inc. Andrea Gusty. Photo used with permission.
Chapter 21. 298, 300, 302, 305, 306, 307, 309, and 310: Copyright 1997–1999 PhotoDisc, Inc. 311: U.S. Customs/Photo by James Tourtellote.
Chapter 22. 314, 316, 318, 319, 323, 324, 325, and 328: Copyright 1997–1999 PhotoDisc, Inc.
Chapter 23. 332, 334, 336, and 337: Copyright 1997–1999 PhotoDisc, Inc. 339: (213902) Tomas del Amo. 341, 347, 348, 349, 350, and 351: Copyright 1997–1999 PhotoDisc, Inc.
Chapter 24. 354, 356, 360, 362, 367, 368, 369, and 371: Copyright 1997–1999 PhotoDisc, Inc.
Chapter 25. 376, 378, 379, 379, and 382: Copyright 1997–1999 PhotoDisc, Inc. 383: © CORBIS. 385, 386, 387, 388, 389, and 390: Copyright 1997–1999 PhotoDisc, Inc.
Chapter 26. 394, 396, and 400: Copyright 1997–1999 PhotoDisc, Inc. 401: (291804) Myrleen Cate. 403: Copyright 1997–1999 PhotoDisc, Inc.
Chapter 27. 410, 412: Copyright 1997–1999 PhotoDisc, Inc. 412 (bottom): *California 1935.* Courtesy of the Franklin D. Roosevelt Library Digital Archives. 417, 418, and 421: Copyright 1997–1999 PhotoDisc, Inc.

Unit 6 Opener. 424–425: Copyright 1997–1999 PhotoDisc, Inc. 425: April Bartholomew. Photo used with permission.
Chapter 28. 424, 426, 428, 430, 432, 433, and 435: Copyright 1997–1999 PhotoDisc, Inc.
Chapter 29. 438, 440, 441, 442, 444, 445, 446, 447, and 449: Copyright 1997–1999 PhotoDisc, Inc.
Chapter 30. 452: © CORBIS. 454, 456, 457, 458, 459, 460, 462, and 463: Copyright 1997–1999 PhotoDisc, Inc.
Chapter 31. 466, 468, 469, 470, and 471: Copyright 1997–1999 PhotoDisc, Inc. 472: © CORBIS. 473 and 475: Copyright 1997–1999 PhotoDisc, Inc.
Chapter 32. 478: © CORBIS. 480, 481, 483, 486, 487, and 488: Copyright 1997–1999 PhotoDisc, Inc. 489: (369891) Ed Lallo.